THE ESSENTIAL KIERKEGAARD

THE ESSENTIAL KIERKEGAARD

Edited by

Howard V. Hong and
Edna H. Hong

PRINCETON UNIVERSITY PRESS
PRINCETON, NEW JERSEY

Copyright © 1995,1997,1998, 2000 by Postscript, Inc.
Copyright © 1978,1980 by Princeton University Press
Copyright © 1990 by Julia Watkin
Copyright © 1997 by Todd W. Nichol
Published by Princeton University Press,
41 William Street, Princeton, New Jersey 08540
In the United Kingdom: Princeton University Press, 3 Market Place,
Woodstock, Oxfordshire OX20 1SY

Library of Congress Cataloging-in-Publication Data

Kierkegaard, Søren, 1813–1855.
[Selections. English. 2000]
The essential Kierkegaard / edited by Howard V. Hong and Edna H. Hong.
p.   cm.
Includes bibliographical references (p.) and index.
ISBN 0-691-03309-9 (cloth : alk. paper)—ISBN 0-691-01940-1 (pbk. : alk. paper)
1. Philosophy.   I. Hong, Howard Vincent, 1912–
II. Hong, Edna Hatlestad, 1913–   III. Title
B4372 .E5 2000
198'.9—dc21   99-039031

Production of this volume has been made possible in part by grants
from the Division of Research Programs of the National Endowment
for the Humanities, an independent federal agency, and the General Mills Foundation

Princeton University Press books are printed on acid-free paper
and meet the guidelines for permanence and durability of the Committee
on Production Guidelines for Book Longevity of the Council on Library Resources

www.pup.princeton.edu

Printed in the United States of America
13   15   17   19   20   18   16   14
20
(PBK.)

ISBN-13: 978-0-691-01940-6

ISBN-10: 0-691-01940-1

CONTENTS

INTRODUCTION

Kierkegaard's principal pseudonymous author, Johannes Climacus, declared that his task was "to make difficulties everywhere,"[1] and in commenting on the structure of *Stages on Life's Way* he said, "Thus it is left to the reader to put it all together by himself, if he so pleases, but nothing is done for a reader's comfort."[2]

The difficulties for a reader of Kierkegaard's writings are due in part to the multiplicity of pseudonymous writers who present their own views in a complex dialogue. Avoiding a conclusive system, Kierkegaard lets each pseudonymous writer have his voice. "My role is the joint role of being the secretary and, quite ironically, the dialectically reduplicated author of the author or the authors."[3] The reader is thereby in the position of entering, if he so pleases, into the complex dialogue and putting it all together. The pseudonymity also discourages the diversionary tendency to commit the genetic fallacy of psychologizing and historicizing the works as autobiography and thereby supposedly "explaining" them. There is also a pedagogical aim in the complexity: "The task must be made difficult, for only the difficult inspires the noble-hearted."[4]

Even though, especially in the writing up to and including *Concluding Unscientific Postscript*, Kierkegaard gave the "whole enterprise the appearance of choice and caprice," it is still possible "to show how everything hangs together, what exceedingly rigorous ordering formed the basis."[5] There is in the varied complex of thirty-eight works, in two parallel series of pseudonymous works and signed works, a dialectical structure, a "coherence," a "comprehensive plan [*total Anlæg*]."[6]

This comprehensive plan is made less apparent also by the developmental character of the authorship. "The movement the authorship describes is *from* 'the poet,' from the esthetic—*from* 'the philosopher,' from the speculative—*to* the indication of the most inward qualification of the essentially Christian; **from** the pseudonymous *Either/Or*, **through** *Concluding Postscript*, with *my name as editor*, **to** *Discourses at the Communion on Fridays*. . . . Later, however, there appeared a new pseudonym: Anti-Climacus. But the very fact that it is a pseudonym signifies that he is, inversely, coming to a halt, as the name

---

[1] *Concluding Unscientific Postscript*, p. 187, *KW* XII.1 (*SV* VII 155).

[2] Ibid., p. 298 (255–56).

[3] Ibid., p. [627] ([547]).

[4] *JP* I 656 (*Pap.* VIII² B 88).

[5] *JP* V 5891 (*Pap.* VII¹ A 104).

[6] *JP* VI 6346 (*Pap.* X¹ A 116).

(*Anti*-Climacus) indeed suggests. All the previous pseudonymity is lower than 'the upbuilding author'; the new pseudonymity is a higher pseudonymity."[7]

"If one is truly to succeed in leading a person to a specific place, one must first and foremost take care to find him where **he** is and begin there."[8] Accordingly, the published writings begin with the esthetic (the immediate, the life of inclination, what comes naturally, the life of desire and aversion, of satisfaction and despair) and move to the ethical (the life of commitment, task, of existential striving to actualize the vision of the good) and to the religious (the life of receptivity, of gift and the expression of gratitude).

The simplest, yet radically profound, crystallization of the developing comprehensive plan of the authorship is the easily overlooked simple issue: "What it means to exist; . . . what it means to be a human being,"[9] what it means to become a self, a person, an authentic individual. As a proponent of Socrates, Kierkegaard penetratingly applies the dictum "the unreflected life is not worth living." As a Christian humanist, Kierkegaard avoids and transcends the possible addition, "but the reflected life may be unlivable," and in a philosophy of possibility and hope he movingly addresses both of the perennial pitfalls: thoughtless superficiality and thoughtful dissolution.

Kierkegaard's works, written over a century ago in a minor language, have been rediscovered throughout the world because they speak to the human condition, especially in a period that is an exacerbated continuation of what Kierkegaard called "an age of disintegration, an esthetic, enervating disintegration,"[10] "an age of moral disintegration."[11] For example, now in this present time of growing despair and an increasing number of suicides among both the young and old, Kierkegaard's original and penetrating treatment of anxiety and despair is decidedly pertinent. Now when "ethics" has come into the common vocabulary in political and professional contexts, his robust and evocative characterization of the deepening ethical consciousness is addressed to the concrete locus of initiative: the existing person. In this era of assertive romantic individualism and growing disdain for law and the common good, his consideration of the relation of the universal and the individual is insightful and constructive. In a time of decay of the family, his portrayal of the meaning of marriage is refreshing and invigorating. In a time when love is frequently regarded as "making love," his incisive defining of

---

[7] *On My Work as an Author,* in *The Point of View,* pp. 5–6, *KW* XXII (*SV* XIII 494).

[8] *The Point of View for My Work as an Author,* in *The Point of View,* p. 45, *KW* XXII (*SV* XIII 533).

[9] *Postscript,* pp. 301–02, *KW* XII.1 (*SV* VII 258).

[10] *JP* VI 6255 (*Pap.* IX B 63:7).

[11] *JP* VI 6581 (*Pap.* X² A 415).

erotic love and intrinsic love (*Elskov* and *Kjerlighed*) is acute and ennobling. In a time when universal suffrage and freedom are live political categories and even elements in foreign policy, his views on the universally human and the essential nature of every human being are ammunition against political-social totalitarianism and coercive special-interest groups. These are among the universally human issues, especially urgent in our time, that are at the heart of the unique writings of this nineteenth-century poet-philosopher, and this accounts for their being discovered throughout the world in the twentieth century.

The combination of variety and development in this complex multiple authorship places special requirements upon the composing of an adequately representative volume of selections. Despite the comprehensive plan, the authorship is not one uniform set that can be represented by a few samples that adequately stand for the whole. The widely ranging spectrum of the works is like a family with many children, each of whom is related in some way to all the others and yet is so decidedly distinctive that no single one or no partial group can adequately represent all the offspring, the family as a whole. Furthermore, the developing authorship requires a series of many samples in order to mirror the sequential movement in the dialectical totality.

Faced with these difficulties arising from the nature of the authorship (and compounded by the great range of "must-be-included" selections nominated by scores of advisers), the editors have chosen a plan that is chronological in order and pluralistic in substance. Although this plan has for a reader the disadvantage of a stricter quantitative limitation of the selection from a given volume, it has also the advantage of an introduction to some works that would otherwise have remained *terra incognita* and whose omission would constitute a hole in the totality of the dialectical mosaic. A sample is certainly not the whole, and a plurality of samples is still not the totality of the comprehensive plan. Each sample, however, is an invitation, an invitation to appropriate the part and then to move on to the source, the work itself, which in turn invites the reader to seek out its neighbor volumes. Although alone in the reading, a reader of the writings is in good company. In *On My Work as an Author*, Kierkegaard says, "I regard myself as a reader of the books, not as the author."[12]

All the passages in *The Essential Kierkegaard* are from *Kierkegaard's Writings*, I–XXVI (Princeton: Princeton University Press, 1978–2000). See the Bibliography at the end of this volume. In *Kierkegaard's Writings* the marginal volume and page numbers refer to the first collected Danish edition, *Søren Kierkegaards samlede Værker*, I–XIV (Copenhagen: Gyldendal, 1901–06). The same marginal notations in the present volume indicate also the location of the selected passages in the various volumes of *Kierkegaard's Writings*. Omis-

---

[12] *On My Work as an Author*, in *The Point of View*, p. 12, *KW* XXII.

sions are indicated by additional space between selected passages and also by the marginal pagination. References to the journals and papers in English are to *Søren Kierkegaard's Journals and Papers* [*JP*], I–VII (Bloomington: Indiana University Press, 1967–78), and in Danish to *Søren Kierkegaards Papirer* [*Pap.*], I–XVI (Copenhagen: Gyldendal, 1968–78).

THE ESSENTIAL KIERKEGAARD

SELECTED EARLY ENTRIES
FROM KIERKEGAARD'S JOURNALS
AND PAPERS

The first two entries are ostensibly addressed to Peter Wilhelm Lund (1801–1880), brother of Johan Christian Lund and Henrik Ferdinand Lund (married to Kierkegaard's sisters Nicoline Christine and Petrea Severine). In 1833 he returned to Brazil to continue his work as a paleontologist. Emanuel Hirsch has made a case for regarding the two letters and many other entries from the same period as parts of Kierkegaard's first, but not completed, writing plan, a series of letters by a Faustian doubter. The two entries were written at the end of Kierkegaard's fifth year as a student at the University of Copenhagen. The third entry (see p.12 and note 2) is the most frequently and variously quoted line by Kierkegaard, and it does crystalize many elements of his outlook.

Copenhagen, June 1, 1835

YOU KNOW how inspiring I once found it to listen to you and how enthusiastic I was about your description of your stay in Brazil, although not so much on account of the mass of detailed observations with which you have enriched yourself and your scholarly field as on account of the impression your first journey into that wondrous nature made upon you: your paradisiacal happiness and joy. Something like this is bound to find a sympathetic response in any person who has the least feeling and warmth, even though he seeks his satisfaction, his occupation, in an entirely different sphere, but especially so in a young person who as yet only dreams of his destiny. Our early youth is like a flower at dawn with a lovely dewdrop in its cup, harmoniously and pensively reflecting everything that surrounds it. But soon the sun rises over the horizon, and the dewdrop evaporates; with it vanish the fantasies of life, and now it becomes a question (to use a flower metaphor once more) whether or not a person is able to produce—by his own efforts as does the *oleander*—a drop that may represent the fruit of his life. This requires, above all, that one be allowed to grow in the soil where one really belongs, but that is not always so easy to find. In this respect there exist fortunate creatures who have such a decided inclination in a particular direction that they faithfully follow the path once it is laid out for them without ever falling prey to the thought that perhaps they ought to have followed an entirely different path. There are others who let themselves be influenced so completely by their surroundings that it never becomes clear to them in what direction they are really striving. Just as the former group has its own implicit categorical imperative, so the latter recognizes an explicit categorical imperative. But how few there are in the former group, and to the latter I do not wish to belong. Those who get to experience the real meaning of Hegelian dialectics in their lives are greater in number. Incidentally, it is altogether natural for wine to ferment before it becomes clear; nevertheless this process is often disagreeable in its several stages, although regarded in its totality it is of course agreeable, provided it does in the end yield its relative results in the context of the usual doubt. This is of major significance for anybody who has come to terms with his destiny by means of it, not only because of the calm that follows in contrast to the preceding storm, but because one then *has life* in a quite different sense than before. For many, it is this Faustian element that makes itself more or less applicable to every intellectual development, which is why it has always seemed to me that we should concede cosmic significance to the *Faust* concept. Just as our ancestors worshiped a goddess of yearning, so I think that Faust represents doubt personified. He need be no more than that, and Goethe probably sins against the concept when he permits Faust to convert, as does Mérimée when he permits Don Juan to convert. One cannot use the argument against me that Faust is taking a positive step at the instant he applies to the Devil, for right here, it seems to me, is one of the most significant elements in the Faust legend. He surrendered himself to the Devil for the express purpose of attaining enlightenment, and it follows that he was not in possession of it prior to this; and precisely because he surrendered himself to the Devil, his doubt increased (just as a sick person who falls into the hands of a medical quack usually gets sicker). For although Mephistopheles permitted him to look through his spectacles into humankind and into the secret hiding places of the earth, Faust must forever doubt him because of his inability to provide enlightenment about the most profound intellectual matters. In accordance with his own idea he could never turn to God because in the very instant he did so he would have to admit to himself that here in truth lay enlightenment; but in that same instant he would, in fact, have denied his character as one who doubts.

But such a doubt can also manifest itself in other spheres. Even though a person may have come to terms with a few of these main issues, life offers other significant questions. Naturally every person desires to work according to his abilities in this world, but it follows from this that he wishes to develop his abilities in a particular direction, namely, in that which is best suited to him as an individual. But which is that? Here I am confronted with a big question mark. Here I stand like Hercules—not at a crossroads—no, but at a multitude of roads, and therefore it is all the harder to choose the right one. Perhaps it is my misfortune in life that I am interested in far too many things rather than definitely in any one thing. My interests are not all subordinated to one but are all coordinate.

I shall attempt to show how matters look to me.

1. *The natural sciences.* (In this category I include all those who seek to explain and interpret the runic script of nature, ranging from him who calculates the speed of the stars and, so to speak, arrests them in order to study them more closely, to him who describes the physiology of a particular animal, from him who surveys the surface of the earth from the mountain peaks to him who descends to the depths of the abyss, from him who follows the development of the human body through its countless nuances to him who examines intestinal worms.) First, when I consider this whole scholarly field, I realize that on this path as well as on every other (but indeed primarily here) I have of course seen examples of men who have made names for themselves in the annals of scholarship by means of enormous diligence in collecting. They master a great wealth of details and have discovered many new ones, but no more than that. They have merely provided the substratum for the thought and elaboration of others. These men are content with tbeir details, and yet to me they are like the rich farmer in the gospel; they have gathered great stores in their barn, yet science may declare to them: "Tomorrow I demand your life," inasmuch as it is that which determines the significance of each particular finding for the whole. To the extent that there is a sort of unconscious life in such a man's knowledge, the sciences may be said to demand his life, but to the extent that there is not, his activity is comparable to that of the man who nourishes the earth by the decay of his dead body. The case differs of course with respect to other phenomena, with respect to those scholars in the natural sciences who have found or have sought to find by their speculation that Archimedean point that does not exist in the world and who from this point have considered the totality and seen the component parts in their proper light. As far as they are concerned, I cannot deny that they have had a very salutary effect on me. The tranquillity, the harmony, the joy one finds in them is rarely found elsewhere. We have three worthy representatives here in town: an Ørsted, whose face has always seemed to me like a chord that nature has sounded in just the right way; a Schouw, who provides a study for the painter who wanted to paint Adam naming the animals; and finally, a Hornemann, who, conversant with every plant, stands like a patriarch in nature. In this connection, I also remember with pleasure the impression you made upon me as the representative of a great nature which also ought to be represented in the National Assembly. I have been and am still inspired by the natural sciences; and yet I do not think that I shall make them my principal field of study. By virtue of reason and freedom, life has always interested me most, and it has always been my desire to clarify and solve the riddle of life. The forty years in the desert before I could reach the promised land of the sciences seem too costly to me, and the more so as I believe that nature may also be observed from another side, which does not require insight into the

secrets of science. It matters not whether I contemplate the whole world in a single flower or listen to the many hints that nature offers about human life; whether I admire those daring designs in the firmament; or whether, upon hearing the sounds of nature in Ceylon, for example, I am reminded of the sounds of the spiritual world; or whether the departure of the migratory birds reminds me of the more profound yearnings of the human heart.

2. *Theology.* This seems to be what I have most clearly chosen for my own, yet there are great difficulties here as well. In Christianity itself there are contradictions so great that they prevent an unobstructed view, to a considerable extent, at any rate. As you know, I grew up in orthodoxy, so to speak. But from the moment I began to think for myself, the gigantic colossus began to totter. I call it a gigantic colossus advisedly, for taken as a whole it does have a good deal of consistency, and in the course of many centuries past, the component parts have become so tightly fused that it is difficult to come to terms with them. I might now agree with some of its specific points, but then these could only be considered like the seedlings one often finds growing in rock fissures. On the other hand, I might also see the inconsistencies in many specific points, but I would still have to let the main basis stand *in dubito* for some time. The instant *that* changed, the whole would of course assume an entirely different cast, and thus my attention is drawn to another phenomenon: rationalism, which by and large cuts a pretty poor figure. There is really nothing to object to in rationalism as long as reason consistently pursues its own end and—in rendering an explanation of the relation between God and the world—again comes to see humankind in its most profound and spiritual relation to God. In this respect, rationalism from its own point of view considers Christianity that which for many centuries has satisfied humankind's deepest need. But then it is in fact no longer rationalism, for rationalism is given its real coloring by Christianity. Hence it occupies a completely different sphere and does not constitute a system but a Noah's Ark (to adopt an expression Professor Heiberg used on another occasion), in which the clean and the unclean animals lie down side by side. It makes roughly the same impression as our Citizens' Volunteer Company of old would have made alongside the Royal Potsdam Guards. Therefore it attempts essentially to ally itself with Christianity, bases its arguments upon Scripture, and in advance of every single point dispatches a legion of Biblical quotations that in no way penetrate the argument. The rationalists behave like Cambyses, who in his campaign against Egypt dispatched the sacred chickens and cats in advance of his army, but they are prepared, like the Roman Consul, to throw the sacred chickens overboard when they refuse to eat. The fallacy is that when they are in agreement with Scripture they use it as a basis, but otherwise not. Thus they adopt mutually exclusive points of view.

Nonnulla desunt [something missing].

As to minor discomforts I will merely say that I am now studying for my theological qualifying examinations, an occupation that holds no interest for me at all and that accordingly does not proceed with the greatest efficiency. I have always preferred the free and thus perhaps somewhat indefinite course of study to that service offered at a pre-set table where one knows in advance the guests one will meet and the food one will be served every single day of the week. Nevertheless, it is a necessity, and one is scarcely permitted out onto the scholarly commons without having been branded. In my present state of mind, I also consider it useful for me to do so and furthermore, I also know that in this way I can make Father very happy (for he thinks that the true land of Canaan lies beyond the theological qualifying examinations, but at the same time, as Moses once did, he climbs Mount Tabor and reports that I will never get in—but I do hope that his prophecy will not come true this time), so I suppose I must get to work. How fortunate you are to have found in Brazil a vast field of investigation where every step offers strange new objects and where the cries of the rest of the learned republic cannot disturb your peace. To me the learned theological world seems like Strandvej on a Sunday afternoon in the season when everybody goes to Bakken in Dyrehaven: they tear past each other, yell and scream, laugh and make fun of each other, drive their horses to death, overturn and are run over. Finally, when they reach Bakken covered with dust and out of breath—well, they look at each other—and go home.

As far as your returning is concerned, it would be childish of me to hasten it, as childish as when the mother of Achilles attempted to hide him in order that he might avoid a speedy honorable death.—Take care of yourself!—*JP* V 5092 (*Pap.* I A 72) June 1, 1835; *Letters*, Letter 3, *KW* XXV.

Gilleleie, August 1, 1835

A S I HAVE TRIED to show in the preceding pages, this is how things actually looked to me. But when I try to get clear about my life, everything looks different. Just as it takes a long time for a child to learn to distinguish itself from objects and thus for a long time disengages itself so little from its surroundings that it stresses the objective side and says, for example, "me hit the horse," so the same phenomenon is repeated in a higher spiritual sphere. I therefore believed that I would possibly achieve more tranquillity by taking another line of study, by directing my energies toward another goal. I might have succeeded for a time in banishing a certain restlessness, but it probably would have come back more intense, like a fever after drinking cold water.

What I really need is to get clear about *what I am to do*,* not what I must know, except insofar as knowledge must precede every act. What matters is to find my purpose, to see what it really is that God wills that I shall do; the crucial thing is to find a truth that is truth *for me*,** to find *the idea for which I am willing to live and die.* Of what use would it be to me to discover a so-called objective truth, to work through the philosophical systems so that I could, if asked, make critical judgments about them, could point out the fallacies in each system; of what use would it be to me to be able to develop a theory of the state, getting details from various sources and combining them into a whole, and constructing a world I did not live in but merely held up for others to see; of what use would it be to me to be able to formulate the meaning of Christianity, to be able to explain many specific points—if it had no deeper meaning *for me and for my life?* And the better I was at it, the more I saw others appropriate the creations of my mind, the more tragic my situation would be, not unlike that of parents who in their poverty are forced to send their children out into the world and turn them over to the care of others. Of what use would it be to me for truth to stand before me, cold and naked, not caring whether or not I acknowledged it, making me uneasy rather than trustingly receptive. I certainly do not deny that I still accept an *imperative of knowledge* and that through it men may be influenced, but *then it must come alive in me*, and *this* is what I now recognize as the most important of all. This is what my soul thirsts for as the African deserts thirst for water. This is what is lacking, and this is why I am like a man who has collected furniture, rented an apartment, but as yet has not found the beloved to share life's ups and downs with him. But in order to find that idea—or, to put it more correctly—to find myself, it does no good to plunge still further into the world. That was just what I did before. The reason I thought it would be good to throw myself into *law* was that I believed I could develop my keenness of mind in the many muddles and messes of life. Here, too, was offered a whole mass of details in which I could lose myself; here, perhaps, with the given facts, I could construct a totality, an organic view of criminal life, pursue it in all its dark aspects (here, too, a certain fraternity of spirit is very evident). I also wanted to become an *acteur* [actor] so that by putting myself in another's role I could, so to speak, find a substitute for my own life and by means of this external change find some diversion. This was what I needed to lead a *completely human life* and not merely one of *knowledge*, so that I could base the development of my thought not on—yes, not on something called objective—something that in any case is not my own, but upon something

* How often, when a person believes that he has the best grip on himself, it turns out that he has embraced a cloud instead of Juno.

** Only then does one have an inner experience, but how many there are who experience life's different impressions the way the sea sketches figures in the sand and then promptly erases them without a trace.

that is bound up with the deepest roots* of my existence [*Existents*], through which I am, so to speak, grafted into the divine, to which I cling fast even though the whole world may collapse. *This is what I need, and this is what I strive for.* I find joy and refreshment in contemplating the great men who have found that precious stone for which they sell all, even their lives,** whether I see them becoming vigorously engaged in life, confidently proceeding on their chosen course without vacillating, or discover them off the beaten path, absorbed in themselves and in working toward their high goal. I even honor and respect the bypath that lies so close by. It is this inward action of a person, this God-side of a person, that is decisive, not a mass of data, for the latter will no doubt follow and will not then appear as accidental aggregates or as a succession of details, one after the other, without a system, without a focal point where all the radii come together. I, too, have certainly looked for this focal point. I have vainly sought an anchor in the boundless sea of pleasure as well as in the depths of knowledge. I have felt the almost irresistible power with which one pleasure reaches a hand to the next; I have felt the counterfeit enthusiasm it is capable of producing. I have also felt the boredom, the shattering, which follows on its heels. I have tasted the fruits of the tree of knowledge and time and again have delighted in their savoriness. But this joy was only in the moment of cognition and did not leave a deeper mark on me. It seems to me that I have not drunk from the cup of wisdom but have fallen into it. I have sought to find the principle for my life through resignation [*Resignation*], by supposing that since everything proceeds according to inscrutable laws it could not be otherwise, by blunting my ambitions and the antennae of my vanity. Because I could not get everything to suit me, I abdicated with a consciousness of my own competence, somewhat the way decrepit clergymen resign with pension. What did I find? Not my self [*Jeg*], which is what I did seek to find in that way (I imagined my soul, if I may say so, as shut up in a box with a spring-lock, which external surroundings would release by pressing the spring).—Consequently the seeking and finding of the kingdom of heaven was the first thing to be resolved. But it is just as useless for a person to want first of all to decide the externals and after that the fundamentals as it is for a cosmic body, thinking to form itself, first of all to decide the nature of its surface, to what bodies it should turn its light, to which its dark side, without first letting the harmony of cen-

---

* How close does man, despite all his knowledge, usually live to madness? What is truth but to live for an idea? When all is said and done, everything is based on a postulate; but not until it no longer stands outside him, not until he lives in it, does it cease to be a postulate for him. (Dialectic—Dispute)

** Thus it will be easy for us once we receive that ball of yarn from Ariadne (love) and then go through all the mazes of the labyrinth (life) and kill the monster. But how many are there who plunge into life (the labyrinth) without taking that precaution (the *young* girls and the little boys who are sacrificed every year to Minotaurus)—?

trifugal and centripetal forces realize its existence [*Existents*] and letting the rest come of itself. One must first learn to know oneself before knowing anything else (γνῶθι σεαυτόν). Not until a person has inwardly understood *himself* and then sees the course he is to take does his life gain peace and meaning; only then is he free of that irksome, sinister traveling companion— that irony of life* that manifests itself in the sphere of knowledge and invites true knowing to begin with a not-knowing (Socrates),** just as God created the world from nothing. But in the waters of morality it is especially at home to those who still have not entered the tradewinds of virtue. Here it tumbles a person about in a horrible way, for a time lets him feel happy and content in his resolve to go ahead along the right path, then hurls him into the abyss of despair. Often it lulls a person to sleep with the thought, "After all, things cannot be otherwise," only to awaken him suddenly to a rigorous interrogation. Frequently it seems to let a veil of forgetfulness fall over the past, only to make every single trifle appear in a strong light again. When he struggles along the right path, rejoicing in having overcome temptation's power, there may come at almost the same time, right on the heels of perfect victory, an apparently insignificant external circumstance that pushes him down, like Sisyphus, from the height of the crag. Often when a person has concentrated on something, a minor external circumstance arises that destroys everything. (As in the case of a man who, weary of life, is about to throw himself into the Thames and at the crucial moment is halted by the sting of a mosquito.) Frequently a person feels his very best when the illness is the worst, as in tuberculosis. In vain he tries to resist it, but he has not sufficient strength, and it is no help to him that he has gone through the same thing many times; the kind of practice acquired in this way does not apply here. Just as no one who has been taught a great deal about swimming is able to keep afloat in a storm, but only the person who is intensely convinced and has experienced that he is actually lighter than water, so a person who lacks this inward point of poise is unable to keep afloat in life's storms.—Only when a person has understood himself in this way is he able to maintain an independent existence and thus avoid surrendering his own I. How often we see (in a period when we extol that Greek historian because he knows how to appropriate an unfamiliar style so delusively like the original author's, instead of censuring him,

---

* It may very well in a certain sense remain, but he is able to bear the squalls of this life, for the more a man lives for an idea, the more easily he comes to sit on the "wonder stool" before the whole world.—Frequently, when a person is most convinced that he has understood himself, he is assaulted by the uneasy feeling that he has really only learned someone else's life by rote.

** There is also a proverb that says: "One hears the truth from children and the insane." Here it is certainly not a question of having truth according to premises and conclusions, but how often have not the words of a child or an insane person thundered at the man with whom penetrating discernment could accomplish nothing—?

since the first praise always goes to an author for having his own style—that is, a mode of expression and presentation qualified by his own individuality)—how often we see people who either out of mental-spiritual laziness live on the crumbs that fall from another's table or for more egotistical reasons seek to identify themselves with others, until eventually they believe it all, just like the liar through frequent repetition of his stories. Although I am still far from this kind of interior understanding of myself, with profound respect for its significance I have sought to preserve my individuality—worshiped the unknown God. With a premature anxiety I have tried to avoid coming in close contact with the phenomena whose force of attraction might be too powerful for me. I have sought to appropriate much from them, studied their distinctive characteristics and meaning in human life, but at the same time guarded against coming, like the moth, too close to the flame. I have had little to win or to lose in association with the ordinary run of men, partly because what they did—so-called practical life*—does not interest me much, partly because their coldness and indifference to the spiritual and deeper currents in man alienate me even more from them. With few exceptions my companions have had no special influence upon me. A life that has not arrived at clarity about itself must necessarily exhibit an uneven side-surface; confronted by certain facts [*facta*] and their apparent disharmony, they simply halted there, for they did not have sufficient interest in me to seek a resolution in a higher harmony or to recognize the necessity of it. Their opinion of me was always one-sided, and I have vacillated between putting too much or too little weight on what they said. I have now withdrawn from their influence and the potential variations of my life's compass resulting from it. Thus I am again standing at the point where I must begin again in another way. I shall now calmly attempt to look at myself and begin to initiate inner action; for only thus will I be able, like a child calling itself "I" in its first consciously undertaken act, be able to call myself "I" in a profounder sense.

But that takes stamina, and it is not possible to harvest immediately what one has sown. I will remember that philosopher's method of having his disciples keep silent for three years; then I dare say it will come. Just as one does not begin a feast at sunrise but at sundown, just so in the spiritual world one must first work forward for some time before the sun really shines for us and rises in all its glory; for although it is true as it says that God lets his sun shine upon the good and the evil and lets the rain fall on the just and the unjust, it is not so in the spiritual world. So let the die be cast—I am crossing the Rubicon! No doubt this road takes me *into battle*, but I will not renounce it.

* This life, which is fairly prevalent in the whole era, is manifest also in big things; whereas the past ages built works before which the observer must stand in silence, now they build a tunnel under the Thames (utility and advantage). Yes, almost before a child gets time to admire the beauty of a plant or some animal, it asks: Of what use is it?

I will not lament the past—why lament? I will work energetically and not waste time in regrets, like the person stuck in a bog and first calculating how far he has sunk without recognizing that during the time he spends on that he is sinking still deeper. I will hurry along the path I have found and shout to everyone I meet: Do not look back as Lot's wife did, but remember that we are struggling up a hill.—*JP* V 5100 (*Pap.* I A 75) August 1, 1835

Philosophy is perfectly right in saying that life must be understood backward. But then one forgets the other clause—that it must be lived forward. The more one thinks through this clause, the more one concludes that life in temporality never becomes properly understandable, simply because never at any time does one get perfect repose to take a stance—backward. —*JP* I 1030 (*Pap.* IV A 164) *n.d.*, 1843

FROM THE PAPERS OF ONE STILL LIVING
PUBLISHED AGAINST HIS WILL (SEPTEMBER 7, 1838)
BY S. KJERKEGAARD

The title may have been prompted inversely by Pückler-Muskau's *Tutti Frutti aus den Papieren des Verstorbenen* [. . . from the Papers of One Deceased] (1834), mentioned by Kierkegaard in *Pap.* I A 41, 1835 (*JP* V 5071). "Against His Will" refers to Kierkegaard's hesitancy about publishing the piece. The family name is a rare variant of *Kierkegaard* [church-farm], a place-name derived from the farm owned by the parish in Sæding, Jylland, Denmark. *From the Papers* was intended for Johan Ludvig Heiberg's *Perseus*, which, however, ceased publication in August 1838. Kierkegaard did not regard *From the Papers* as part of his authorship but rather as an early piece of experimental writing. As a review of another writer's work (Hans Christian Andersen's *Kun en Spillemand*), the piece did not qualify as part of the authorship proper. It did, however, introduce the emphasis on authentic individual existence that is continued in all the later works. Kierkegaard's criticism is of a view of life that regards even a genius not as a shaping subject but as a passive object who is molded by circumstances. Andersen in his autobiography, *Mit Livs Eventyr*, wrote that perhaps only he and Kierkegaard had read *From the Papers*. Meanwhile, however, Andersen caricatured Kierkegaard as the parrot ("Let us be men.") in "Galoshes of Fortune" (1838) and as the hairdresser in *A Comedy in the Open Air. Vaudeville in One Act Based on the Old Comedy An Actor against His Will* (1840). In 1848 and 1849 Andersen and Kierkegaard exchanged gift volumes (*Nye Eventyr* and *Enten/Eller*, 2 ed.) with friendly greetings (see *Letters*, Letter 206, *KW* XXV).

WHEN we now say that Andersen totally lacks a life-view, this statement is as much substantiated by the preceding as this latter is substantiated by the statement itself verified in its truth. For a life-view is more than a quintessence or a sum of propositions maintained in its abstract neutrality; it is more than experience [*Erfaring*], which as such is always fragmentary. It is, namely, the transubstantiation of experience; it is an unshakable certainty in oneself won from all experience [*Empirie*], whether this has oriented itself only in all worldly relationships (a purely human standpoint, Stoicism, for example), by which means it keeps itself from contact with a deeper experience—or whether in its heavenward direction (the religious) it has found therein the center as much for its heavenly as its earthly existence, has won the true Christian conviction "that neither death, nor life, nor angels, nor principalities, nor powers, nor the present, nor the future, nor height, nor depth, nor any other creation will be able to separate us from the love of God in Christ Jesus our Lord."[1] If we now look and see how things are with Andersen in this respect, we find the relationship to be just as we had expected. On the one hand, single propositions stick out like hieroglyphs* that at times are the object of a pious veneration. On the other, he dwells on the individual phenomena coming from his own experience, which at times are further elevated to propositions and are then to be subsumed under the previous class, and at times are brought out more as something experienced, without one's therefore being rightly able, as long as these remain in their bachelor state, to draw any further conclusions from them.

If one will now perhaps say that the life-view we have depicted is a standpoint one can approach only gradually and that it is unjust to make such great demands on so young a man as Andersen, then we shall, as far as the last point is concerned, although willingly admitting that Andersen is a young man, nevertheless remind readers that we are dealing with Andersen only as a novelist and, *anticipando* [anticipating], add that such a life-view is, for a novelist of the class to which Andersen belongs, *conditio sine qua non* [a necessary condition]. With regard to the first point, we readily admit a certain approximation in the full sense of the word but also say stop in time, before we are saddled with the consequence, annulling our whole view, that the life-view proper commences first (*demum*) [at last]) at the hour of one's death or perhaps even on one of the planets. If we now ask how such a life-view is brought about, then we answer that for the one who does not allow his life to fizzle out too much but seeks as far as possible to lead its single expressions back to himself again, there must necessarily come a moment in which a strange light spreads over life without one's therefore even remotely needing to have understood all possible particulars, to the progressive understanding of which, however, one now has the key. There must come a moment, I say, when, as Daub observes, life is understood backward through the idea.[2] If one has not yet come this far, yes, even totally lacks understanding of what all this means, then one comes to set oneself a life-task parodically, either by its already having been solved, if one can call it that, though in another sense it has never been posed, or by its never being able to be solved. In further corroboration of this, we find both situations described in Andersen, since both views are presented in borrowed maxims and also to a certain extent are illustrated in individual poetic personalities. On the one hand, it is taught that on every person there is written a *mene mene*[3] etc. In analogy to this, individuals appear whose actual task lies behind them, but this does not help them to come into the right "backward" position for viewing life, since this task is placed rather like a hump on their own backs,** and there-

---

* This standpoint is very prevalent, and one can usually identify the species belonging to it by a tendency, even when the conversation is about the most insignificant subject, to begin with a "maxim."

** For example, O. T.[4]

Was ich nicht weisz, macht mich nicht heisz, so denkt der Ochse, wenn er vor dem Kopf ein Brett hat

fore they never actually come to see it or could never possibly become conscious of it in a spiritual sense, unless for a change Andersen puts into them a consciousness that disturbs the whole conception—individuals appear who, like other heavenly bodies, go their once-allotted way with an undeviating precision. Or, on the other hand, Andersen loses himself not so much in high-flown [*høitravende*] as in long-winded [*langtravende*] observations, in which the hero is a superb peripatetic who, because he has no essential reason for stopping anywhere and because existence [*Tilværelse*] on the contrary is always a circle, ends up going in a circle, even though Andersen and others who have lived for many years on the hill believe he is walking straight ahead because the earth is as flat as a pancake. In between, that is to say in the unity of these standpoints, lies the happy medium, but from this it by no means follows that through a new inconsistency, which, please note, does not annul the preceding (for that would be the most fortunate), new phenomena cannot appear, for example, that Andersen suddenly breaks off their undaunted wandering, sentences them to an arbitrary punishment, cuts off their noses and ears, and sends them to Siberia, and then our Lord, or whoever else wants to, must take care of them.—

But is it, then, absolutely necessary for a novelist to have such a life-view, or is there not a certain poetic mood that as such, in union with an animated portrayal, can achieve the same? Our reply to this lies for the most part in what we developed earlier with regard to Blicher, in which we have specifically sought to point out the significance of such a unity born of mood and, through a succession of modifications, understood by the readers as a whole picture. And furthermore, insofar as one wants to make a similar view valid for a countless number of given standpoints arrived at through reflection—and here one must remember that, where productivity is concerned, all these standpoints as such have a diminishing effect and increasingly allow the original mood to evaporate—we shall merely add that productivity is certainly possible from all these standpoints, but that when one is a little fastidious about one's designations, what is produced should be called studies for short novels etc. rather than short novels, since also at the level of studies productivity will be unsuccessful to the same extent as one really sets oneself the task of a short novel or novel.

XIII
71

Perhaps one wants to go further and—pleading that there is nevertheless one idea that continually appears in Andersen's novels (something I admit myself)—thereby salvage a life-view for Andersen and reproach me for my inconsistency. To this I must reply that I have never maintained that an idea as such (least of all a fixed idea) is to be regarded as a life-view, and furthermore, in order to embark upon this examination, I must have a little more

---

[What I do not know, I do not get heated about, thus thinks the ox when it wears a blinder]. See Grabbe.[5]

detailed information about the content of this idea. If the idea is that life is not a process of development but a process of the downfall of the great and distinguished that would sprout up, then I think I can indeed justly protest against the application of the designation "life-view"* to this, insofar as one will agree with me at all that skepticism as such is not a theory of knowledge or, to keep to my theme, that such a mistrust of life certainly contains a truth insofar as it leads to finding a trust (for example, when Solomon says that all is vanity[6]), but, on the other hand, at the same moment as it ends up as a final decision on life's questions it contains an untruth.

But to proceed. We shall for a moment assume that one could be right in calling such a view, arbitrarily brought to a standstill in reflection and now elevated to ultimate truth, a life-view. We shall imagine an individual who, greatly tossed about by an intensely agitated age, finally decides upon such a standpoint. We shall let him produce short novels. They will all receive a birthmark, but to the extent that he had experienced much, to the extent that he had really participated in life's vicissitudes, to the same extent he would also be able to develop in his short novels a great sequence of appalling consequences, all pointing to his hero's final downfall,** and to the same extent one would for a long time feel tempted to believe in the truth of his conception of life. But is this the case with Andersen? Surely no one will maintain this. On the contrary, Andersen skips over the actual development,

XIII
72

sets an appropriate interval of time between, first shows as well as he can the great forces and natural capacities, and then shows their loss.† Here, however, one will surely agree with us that it is no life-view. To clarify our opinion further, we shall merely add that such a loss-theory can emanate partly from a seriously undertaken but nevertheless abortive attempt to understand the world, in that the individual, depressed by the world, although long working against it, at last succumbs. Or it can be brought about by this, that at the very first awakening of reflection one does not then look outward but instantaneously into oneself and in one's so-called contemplation of the world merely carries through accurately one's own suffering. The first is an abortive activity, the second an original passivity.†† The first is a broken manliness, the second a consistent womanliness.

* In order to keep the question as clear as possible, I must remind readers that I do not seek
XIII   to make one life-view valid, and Andersen another, but, uninterested in advancing any partic-
71   ular life-view, I seek only to combat this negative standpoint and its right to try to pass itself off as a life-view.

** How far this final downfall is poetically true, such an individual as a rule cannot judge,
XIII   because he lacks the proper vantage point.
72   † One could almost be tempted to encourage him to demonstrate the identity of the character.

†† Andersen actually seems to regard such an original passivity as belonging to genius. See
Kun en Spillemand, I, p. 161: "Genius is an egg that needs warmth for the fertilization of good fortune; otherwise it becomes a wind-egg." I, p. 160: "He had intimations of the pearl in his

We return to our theme: to explain, through a brief suggestion of the necessity of a life-view for the novel and short-novel writer, how things stand with Andersen in this respect. A life-view is really providence in the novel; it is its deeper unity, which makes the novel have the center of gravity in itself. A life-view frees it from being arbitrary or purposeless, since the purpose is immanently present everywhere in the work of art. But when such a life-view is lacking, the novel either seeks to insinuate some theory (dogmatic, doctrinaire short novels) at the expense of poetry or it makes a finite and incidental contact with the author's flesh and blood. This latter, however, can take place through a great multiplicity of modifications, from an involuntary overflow of cleverness in the personality to the point where the author paints himself in, as landscape painters sometimes like to do; yes, they even forget that this could have significance only insofar as it is understood as situation, and therefore, totally forgetting the landscape, go on to paint themselves elaborately in their own vain Solomonic pomp and glory, which suits flowers but not people. (When I contrast doctrinaire and subjective novels in this respect, I can very well see that it is indeed only through a subdivision that these become coordinated with each other, for the doctrinaire novels also stand in an incidental relation to the personality, because their authors, through an incidental resolution of will, rest satisfied with propositions that they have not yet sufficiently experienced.) Yet, although both classes of novels stand in a finite and wrong relation to the personality, I by no means think that the novel in a certain prosaic* sense should abstract from the personality or that one could from another standpoint justly exact as much from the novel as from rigorous speculation. Instead, the poet himself must first and foremost win a competent personality, and it is only this dead and transfigured personality that ought to and is able to produce, not the many-angled, worldly, palpable one. How difficult it is to win oneself such a personality can also be seen from the fact that in many otherwise fine novels there is to be found a residue, as it were, of the author's finite character, which, like an impudent third person, like a badly brought-up child, often joins in the conversation at unseemly places. If we now apply this to Andersen, not so much arguing from as appealing to the rather prevalent judgment arising in conversation, "That is just like Andersen, he is always himself, etc.,"

XIII
73

XIII
74

---

soul, the glorious pearl of art; he did not know that like the pearl in the sea it must await the diver who brings it up to the light or cling fast to mussels and oysters, the high fellowship of patrons, in order to come to view in this way." This is a quite special kind of genius. Even in the classicism of the ancient world, they sprang in full armor from the head of Jupiter. So genius needs warmth! Genius must use petticoat influence! Let us not be ungrateful to the geniuses we have, and let us not trouble the heads of the younger ones!

* As has happened with the word "impartiality," which in our lukewarm time more or less indicates what a man already long ago has expressed as his standpoint: to be neither partial nor impartial.

XIII
73

we justly believe we might include him in the class of novelists who give an unpoetic surplus of their own merely phenomenological personality, without therefore wanting to attribute to him such a strong determination of will in this respect that it would prevent him from straying into the territory of doctrinaire short novels also, yet not as if he had some major theory he wanted to advance, but rather, as shown above, through a partiality for and an over-estimation of certain particular propositions, which, in so strict a celibacy as the author keeps them, have nothing much to say.

One will best convince oneself of how markedly Andersen's novels stand in a wrong relation to his person by reproducing the total impression his novels leave behind them. We by no means think that it is wrong that an individual succumbs in the novel, but then it must be a poetic truth, not, as in some poets, a *pia fraus* [pious fraud] of upbringing or, as in Andersen, his final will. We by no means require, in any stricter understanding of the words, good sense and clarity about life in every single one of his poetically created individuals. On the contrary, if the worst comes to the worst, we shall grant him full authority to let them go out of their minds, only it must not happen in such a way that a madness in the third person is replaced by one in the first, that the author himself takes the mad person's role. In a novel there must be an immortal spirit that survives the whole. In Andersen, however, there is absolutely no grip on things: when the hero dies, Andersen dies, too, and at most forces from the reader a sigh over them both as the final impression.

Having thus referred several times here to Andersen's person and personality, I shall—in answer to an objection, although one possible only through misunderstanding and misinterpretation, as if by mentioning Andersen as a person I here overstepped the limit of my esthetic jurisdiction and the competence admitted within this—I shall, without appealing to the circumstance that I as good as do not know Andersen personally, merely state that the poetic production proper, especially in the domain of the short novel and novel, is nothing but a copious second power, shaping itself in a freer world and moving about in it, reproducing from what has already in various ways been poetically experienced to the first power. Moreover, in Andersen's novels, on the one hand one misses the consolidating total survey (a life-view), and on the other one encounters again and again situations, comments, etc. that are indeed undeniably poetic but in Andersen remain undigested and poetically (not commercially) unused, unappropriated, unfiltered.

XIII
75

XIII
91

With regard to what I have to say in conclusion—prompted by the misrelation, certainly on the whole conceded to be factual, between a reading and a criticizing world's judgment of Andersen, insofar as this misrelation has also repeated itself in my consciousness—I could wish that I might succeed in speaking about this just as personally as I have tried to keep the fore-

XIII
92

going free of any oblique relation to my personality. That is, as I reproduce the first stage [reading the book], the recollection of a variety of poetical moods is brought to life, moods with which every poetic life, even the most obscure (and this, in a certain sense, perhaps most of all), must be interwoven. And as I once again seek to retain every single one, the one displaces the other so rapidly that the totality of them assembles as if for departure in one single concentration, assembles in a present that nevertheless at the same moment feels in itself the necessity of becoming a past and thereby evokes from me a certain nostalgic smile as I consider them, a feeling of thankfulness as I recollect the man to whom I owe it all, a feeling that I would prefer to whisper in Andersen's ear rather than confide to paper. Not that at any moment it has been anything but a joy for me to be able to give him what is his due and what, especially in our time, anyone who still has a little feeling for poetry in the *ecclesia pressa* in which we live must almost be tempted to give more warmly than the truth perhaps could demand. Nor that such an utterance could not be brought into harmony with my whole earlier expressed view of Andersen, because in spite of all his tossing about, all his bending before every poetic breeze, it still always gives me joy that as yet he has not come under the all-embracing devil-may-care trade wind of politics.—I wished to say this to Andersen rather than write it because such an utterance is on the whole very exposed to misunderstanding, something, however, I hope that I shall be able to put up with if only Andersen, in order to avoid it, will hold what I have written with sympathetic ink up to that light which alone makes the writing readable and the meaning clear.

THE CONCEPT OF IRONY,
WITH CONTINUAL REFERENCE TO SOCRATES
(SEPTEMBER 16, 1841)
BY S. A. KIERKEGAARD

On September 29, 1841, Kierkegaard defended his dissertation on irony in a seven-and-one-half hour public colloquium. By special permission the dissertation was written in Danish, not in Latin. Adolph Peter Adler and two others had been granted similar permission. In his petition Kierkegaard stated that Latin would be inappropriate for a discussion of irony in the modern period. He also pointed out that he had taught Latin and that the public defense would be in Latin. One member of the audience at the colloquium wrote that Kierkegaard "played toss-in-a-blanket" with the official faculty opponents. Kierkegaard himself was particularly critical of a passage in which Socrates' view of the state and the individual was regarded as a defect. "What a Hegelian fool I was! It is precisely this that powerfully demonstrates what a great ethicist Socrates was" (*JP* IV 4281; *Pap.* X³ A 477). Because *Irony* was a university dissertation, Kierkegaard did not regard it as part of the authorship proper. But many of the important themes in *Irony*—immediacy, reflection, selfhood, subjectivity, objectivity, the esthetic, the ethical, the religious, and anthropological contemplation—are later developed in various ways in the pseudonymous and the signed works. Not least is the development in *Philosophical Fragments* of the first thesis (on the relation of Socrates and Christ).

PART ONE
THE POSITION OF SOCRATES
VIEWED AS IRONY

Xenophon and Plato

If Plato's view of Socrates were to be expressed in a few words, it could be said that he provides him with the idea. Where the empirical ends, Socrates begins; his function is to lead speculation out of finite qualifications, to lose sight of finitude and steer out upon the Oceanus where ideal striving and ideal infinity recognize no alien considerations but are themselves their infinite goal. Thus, just as the lower sense perception turns pale before this higher knowledge—indeed, becomes a delusion, a deception by comparison—just so every consideration of a finite goal becomes a disparagement, a profanation of the holy. In short, Socrates has gained ideality, has conquered those vast regions that hitherto were a *terra incognita* [unknown land]. For this reason, he disdains the useful, is indifferent to the established [*Bestaaende*], is an out-and-out enemy of the mediocrity that in empiricism is the highest, an object of pious worship, but for speculation a troll changeling.

But if we remember the conclusion we arrived at through Xenophon, namely, that here we found Socrates busily functioning as an apostle of finitude, as an officious bagman for mediocrity, tirelessly recommending his one and only saving secular gospel, that here we found the useful rather than the good, the useful rather than the beautiful, the established rather than the true, the lucrative rather than the sympathetic, pedestrianism rather than harmonious unity, then one will surely admit that these two conceptions cannot very well be joined.

Either Xenophon must be charged with sheer arbitrariness, with an incomprehensible hatred of Socrates that sought satisfaction in such slander, or an equally incomprehensible idiosyncrasy must be attributed to Plato because of his opposition, which just as puzzlingly resulted in changing Socrates into conformity with himself. If we momentarily let the actuality of Socrates be an unknown quantity, one may say of these two interpretations that Xenophon, like a huckster, has deflated his Socrates and that Plato, like an artist, has created his Socrates in supranatural dimensions.

But what was Socrates actually like? What was the point of departure for his activity? The answer to this must, of course, also help us out of the dilemma in which we have been situated until now. The answer is: Socrates' existence is irony. Just as this answer, in my opinion, removes the problem, so the fact that it removes the problem makes it the right answer as well— thus it simultaneously appears as a hypothesis and as the truth. In other words, the point, the line that makes the irony into irony, is very difficult to grasp. Along with Xenophon, therefore, one can certainly assume that Socrates was fond of walking around and talking with all sorts of people because every external thing or event is an occasion for the ever quick-witted ironist; along with Plato, one can certainly let Socrates touch on the idea, except that the idea does not open up to him but is rather a boundary. Each of these two interpretations has, of course, sought to give a complete characterization of Socrates—Xenophon by pulling him down into the lower regions of the useful, Plato by elevating him into the supramundane regions of the idea. But the point, one that lies between, invisible and so very difficult to grasp securely, is irony. On the one hand, the manifold variety of actuality is the very element of the ironist. On the other hand, his passage across actuality is floating and ethereal; he is continually just touching the ground, but since the real kingdom of ideality is still foreign to him, he has not as yet emigrated to it but seems always to be on the point of departure. Irony oscillates between the ideal *I* and the empirical *I;* the one would make Socrates a philosopher, the other a Sophist; but what makes him more than a Sophist is that his empirical *I* has universal validity.

XIII
213

Aristophanes

Aristophanes' view of Socrates will provide just the necessary contrast to Plato's and precisely by means of this contrast will open the possibility of a new approach for our evaluation. Indeed, it would be a great lack if we did not have the Aristophanic appraisal of Socrates; for just as every process usually ends with a parodying of itself, and such a parody is an assurance that this process has outlived its day, so the comic view is an element, in many ways a perpetually corrective element, in making a personality or an enterprise completely intelligible. Therefore, even though we lack direct evidence about Socrates, even though we lack an altogether reliable view of him, we do have in recompense all the various nuances of misunderstanding, and in my opinion this is our best asset with a personality such as Socrates.

Plato and Aristophanes do have in common an ideality of depiction, but at opposite poles; Plato has the tragic ideality, Aristophanes the comic. What motivated Aristophanes to view Socrates this way, whether he was bribed to do it by Socrates' accusers, whether he was embittered by Socrates' friendly relations with Euripides, whether through him he opposed Anaxagoras's speculations about nature, whether he identified him with the Sophists, in short, whether any finite and mundane motivation determined him in his view is totally irrelevant to this study, and insofar as it should provide an answer on this point, it would, of course, have to be negative, since it acknowledges the conviction that Aristophanes' conception is ideal and thereby already freed from any such concerns, does not cringingly creep along the ground but, free and light, takes flight above it. Simply to apprehend the empirical actuality of Socrates, to bring him on stage as he walked and stood in life, would have been beneath the dignity of Aristophanes and would have changed his comedy into a satirical poem; on the other hand, to idealize him on a scale whereby he became completely unrecognizable would lie entirely outside the interest of Greek comedy. That the latter was not the case is attested by antiquity, which recounts that the performance of *The Clouds* was honored in this respect by the presence of its severest critic, Socrates himself, who to the public's delight stood up during the performance so that the theater crowd could see for themselves the fitting likeness. We certainly must agree with the perspicacious Rötscher* that such a purely eccentric ideal view would not lie within the interest of Greek comedy either. He has so excellently explained how the essence of comedy consisted expressly in viewing actuality ideally, in bringing an actual personality on stage, yet in such a way that this one is indeed seen as a representative of the idea, which is why we find also in Aristophanes the

---

* Heinrich Theodor Rötscher, *Aristophanes und sein Zeitalter, eine philologisch-philosophische Abhandlung zur Alterthumsforschung.* Berlin: 1827.

three great comic paradigms: Cleon, Euripides, and Socrates, whose roles comically represent the aspiration of the age in its three trends. Just as the scrupulously detailed view of actuality filled the distance between the audience and the stage, so also the ideal view in turn separated these two forces to the extent to which art must always do this. That Socrates in actual life presented many comic sides, that he, to put it bluntly once and for all, was to a certain degree a *Sonderling* [eccentric]* cannot be denied; neither can it be denied that this is enough justification for a comic poet; but there is no denying, either, that this would not have been enough for an Aristophanes.

XIII
216

PART TWO

THE CONCEPT OF IRONY

Introduction

XIII
317

The object of investigation in this part has already been given to a certain extent in the first part, insofar as this permitted one aspect of the concept to appear in the form of contemplation. Therefore, in the first part I have not so much assumed the concept as I have let it come into existence while I

---

* Cf. Johann Georg Sulzer, *Nachträge zu Sulzers allgemeiner Theorie der schönen Künste,* VII, 1, p. 162: "Leider kennen wir den Socrates nur aus den verschönernden Gemählden eines Plato und Xenophon, indesz geht aus diesen so manches hervor, was Befremden erregt und auf einen seltsamen Mann hindeutet. Die Leitung eines unsichtbaren Genius, deren der Weise sich zu erfreuen glaubte, seine Zurückgezogenheit und Versenkung in sich selbst, die sogar im Lager tagelang dauerte und allen seinen Zeltgenossen auffiel, seine Unterhaltungen, deren Gegenstand, Zweck und Wendungen sich durch so viel Eigenthümlichkeiten auszeichneten, sein vernachlässigtes Aeuszere und sein in vielen Hinsichten ungewöhnliches Betragen—alles diesz muszte ihm nothwendig in den Augen der Menge den Anstrich eines Sonderlings geben [Unfortunately, we know Socrates only from Plato's and Xenophon's embellished portraits, from which a great deal follows that seems strange and suggests a peculiar person. The guidance of an invisible daimon in which the philosopher was pleased to believe, his withdrawal and absorption into himself lasting for days even while at camp and quite to the astonishment of fellow campers, his conversation, whose object, aim, and manner were distinguished by so much that was odd, his neglected exterior and in many respects unusual behavior—all this must inevitably have given him the appearance of an eccentric in the eyes of the crowd]."—Also p. 140, where the author observes that if we knew Socrates more accurately, Aristophanes would no doubt be given even more credence: "wir würden und dann unfehlbar überzeugen, dasz er, bei allen seinen groszen Tugenden und herrlichen Eigenschaften, doch die Fehler und Gebrechen der Menschheit im reichen Maasze an sich trug, dasz er, wie so gar mehrere unverdächtige Winke vermuthen lassen, in noch mancher Rücksicht zu der Classe der Sonderlinge gehörte, seine Lehrart von dem Vorwurfe der Weitschweifigkeit und Pedanterei nicht frei war [we would then be unmistakably convinced that in spite of his many virtues and splendid qualities he still had the faults and defects of humanity in great measure, that, as several reliable indications suggest, he belonged in many respects to the class of eccentrics, and that his mode of teaching was not exempt from the reproach of verbosity and pedantry]."

XIII
215

XIII
216

sought to orient myself in the phenomenon. In so doing, I have found an unknown quantity, a position that appeared to have been characteristic of Socrates. I have called this position irony, but in the first part of the dissertation the term for it is of minor importance; the main thing is that no factor or feature has been slighted, also that all the factors and features have grouped themselves into a totality. Whether or not this position is irony will first be decided now as I come to that point in developing the concept in which Socrates must fit if his position was really irony at all. But just as I dealt in the first part of the dissertation solely with Socrates, so in the development of the concept it will become apparent in what sense he is a factor in the development of the concept—in other words, it will become apparent whether the concept of irony is absolutely exhausted in him or whether there are other modes to be inspected before we can say that the concept has been adequately interpreted.

Therefore, just as in the first part of the dissertation the concept always hovered in the background with a continual craving to take shape in the phenomenon, just so in this part of the dissertation the phenomenal manifestation of the concept, as a continual possibility to take up residence among us, will accompany the progress of the discussion. These two factors are inseparable, because if the concept were not in the phenomenon or, more correctly, if the phenomenon were not understandable, actual, only in and with the concept, and if the phenomenon were not in the concept or, more correctly, if from the outset the concept were not understandable, actual, in and with the phenomenon, then all knowledge would be impossible, inasmuch as I in the first case would be lacking the truth and in the second case the actuality.

Now, if irony is a qualification of subjectivity, we shall promptly see the necessity of two manifestations of this concept, and actuality has indeed attached the name to them. The first one, of course, is the one in which subjectivity asserts its rights in world history for the first time. Here we have Socrates, that is, we are hereby shown where we should look for the concept in its historical manifestation. But once having made its appearance in the world, subjectivity did not vanish again without a trace, the world did not sink back again into the earlier form of development; on the contrary, the old vanished and everything became new. For a new mode of irony to be able to appear now, it must result from the assertion of subjectivity in a still higher form. It must be subjectivity raised to the second power, a subjectivity's subjectivity, which corresponds to reflection's reflection. With this we are once again world-historically oriented—that is, we are referred to the development that modern philosophy attained in Kant and that is completed in Fichte, and more specifically again to the positions that after Fichte sought to affirm subjectivity in its second potency. Actuality bears out that this hangs together properly, for here again we meet irony. But since this position is an intensified subjective consciousness, it quite naturally is clearly and definitely conscious of irony and declares irony as its position. This was indeed the case with Friedrich Schlegel, who sought to bring it to bear in relation to actuality; with Tieck, who sought to bring it to bear in poetry; and with Solger, who became esthetically and philosophically conscious of it. Finally, here irony also met its master in Hegel. Whereas the first form of irony was not combated but was pacified by subjectivity as it obtained its rights, the second form of irony was combated and destroyed, for inasmuch as subjectivity was unauthorized it could obtain its rights only by being annulled.

If these observations are adequate for orientation in the history of the concept of irony, this by no means implies that an interpretation of this concept, insofar as it seeks a stronghold and support in what was developed earlier, is not fraught with difficulty. Insofar as we seek a thorough and coherent development of this concept, we shall soon be convinced that it has a strange history or, more correctly, no history. In the period after Fichte, when it was especially current, we find it mentioned again and again, suggested again and again, presupposed again and again. However, if we are looking for a clear exposition, we look in vain.* Solger laments that A. W. v. Schlegel in his *Vorlesungen über dramatische Kunst und Litteratur,* where, if anywhere, we would expect to find adequate information, cursorily mentions it but once. Hegel** laments that with Solger it was the same and no better with Tieck.

XIII
319

* *Solgers nachgelassene Schriften und Briefwechsel,* ed. Ludwig Tieck and Friedrich v. Raumer, II, p. 514 (in a critique of A. W. v. Schlegel's lectures): "Es war dem Rec. höchst auffallend, der Ironie, in welcher er den wahren Mittelpunct der ganzen dramatischen Kunst erkennt, so dasz sie auch beim philosophischen Dialog, wenn er einigermaszen dramatisch seyn soll, nicht zu entbehren ist, in dem ganzen Werke nur Einmal erwähnt zu finden, Th. II. Abth. 2, S. 72, und noch dazu um ihr alle Einmischung in das eigentliche Tragische zu untersagen; und doch erinnert er sich an frühere Aeuszerungen des Verfassers, welche sich an diese Ideen wenigstens sehr anzunähern schienen. Die Ironie ist aber auch das gerade Gegentheil jener Ansicht des Lebens, in welcher Ernst und Scherz, wie sie der Verfasser annimmt, wurzeln [As reviewer I was stunned by finding irony (which I regard as the true focus of all dramatic art and also as indispensable to philosophical dialogue if it is to be properly dramatic) mentioned only once in the entire work (pt. II, sec. 2, p. 72) and then for the sake of prohibiting irony from any and all intermingling in the genuinely tragic. And yet the reviewer can recall previous statements of this author that at least appear to approximate this idea. But irony is the very opposite of that view of life in which, as the author supposes, seriousness and jest are rooted]."

** Hegel, *Werke,* XVI, p. 492 (in a review of Solger's posthumous writings): "Dasselbe ist Solger'n begegnet; in den speculativen Expositionen der höchsten Idee, die er in der oben angeführten Abhandlung mit dem innersten Geistesernste giebt, *erwähnt* er der Ironie *gar nicht,* sie, welche mit der Begeisterung auf's Innigste vereint, und in deren Tiefe Kunst, Religion und Philosophie identisch seyen. Gerade dort, hätte man geglaubt, müsse der Ort seyn, wo man in's Klare gesetzt finden werde, was es denn mit dem vornehmen Geheimnisse, dem groszen Unbekannten—der Ironie—für eine philosophische Bewandtnisz habe [The same happened with Solger; in the speculative exposition of the highest Idea, which in the above-mentioned work

Since they all lament, why should I not also lament? My lament is that it is just the reverse with Hegel. At the point in all his systems where we could expect to find a development of irony, we find it referred to. Although, if it all were copied, we would have to concede that what is said about irony is in one sense not so inconsiderable, in another sense it is not much, since he says just about the same thing on every point. Add to this the fact that he directs his attack against the particular and often disparate ideas we have attached to the word "irony," and as a result, since usage is not constant, his polemic is not always entirely clear. Yet I am far from being able to lament justifiably over Hegel in the same sense as Hegel laments over his predecessors. There are excellent observations especially in his review of Solger's posthumous writings (in vol. XVI of his collected works). And even if the presentation and characterization of negative positions (since *loquere ut videam te* [speak, so that I may see you] is particularly pertinent to the characterization of these positions) are not always as exhaustive, as rich in content, as we could wish, Hegel knows all the better how to deal with them, and thus the positivity he asserts contributes indirectly to his characterization. While the Schlegels and Tieck had their major importance in the polemic with which they destroyed a previous development, and while precisely for this reason their position became somewhat scattered, because it was not a principal battle they won but a multitude of skirmishes, Hegel, on the other hand, has absolute importance by defeating with his positive total view the polemic prudery, the subjugation of which, just as Queen Brynhild's virginity required more than an ordinary husband, required a Sigurd. Jean Paul also mentions irony frequently, and some things are found in his *Aesthetik,* but without any philosophic or genuinely esthetic authority. He speaks mainly as an esthetician, from a rich esthetic experience, instead of actually giving grounds for his esthetic position. Irony, humor, moods seem for him to be different languages, and his characterization is limited to expressing the same thought ironically, humorously, in the language of moods—somewhat as Franz Baader at times, after having described some mystical theses, then translates them into mystical language.

But since the concept of irony has often acquired a different meaning in this way, the point is that one is not to use it altogether arbitrarily either knowingly or unknowingly; the point is that, having embraced the ordinary use of language, one comes to see that the various meanings the word has acquired in the course of time can still all be included here.

XIII
320

XIII
321

---

is presented with the most intense intellectual earnestness, he *does not even mention* irony, that very irony that is in intimate union with enthusiasm and in whose depth art, religion, and philosophy are identical. Here, if anywhere, one would have expected to find a lucid presentation of what might philosophically be the case with that exclusive secret, that great unknown—irony]." See the same place for Hegel's comments concerning Tieck.

The World-Historical Validity
of Irony,
the Irony of Socrates

If we turn back to the foregoing general description of irony as infinite absolute negativity, it is adequately suggested therein that irony is no longer directed against this or that particular phenomenon, against a particular existing thing, but that the whole of existence has become alien to the ironic subject and the ironic subject in turn alien to existence, that as actuality has lost its validity for the ironic subject, he himself has to a certain degree become unactual. The word "actuality," however, must here primarily be understood as historical actuality—that is, the given actuality at a certain time and in a certain situation. This word can be understood metaphysically—for example, as it is used when one treats the metaphysical issue of the relation of the idea to actuality, where there is no question of this or that actuality but of the idea's concretion, that is, its actuality—and the word "actuality" can also be used for the historically actualized idea. The latter actuality is different at different times. By this it is in no way meant that in the sum total of its existence the historical actuality is not supposed to have an eternal and intrinsic coherence, but for different generations separated by time and space the given actuality is different. Even though the world spirit in any process is continually in itself, this is not the case with the generation at a certain time and the given individuals at a certain time in the same generation. For them, a given actuality does not present itself as something that they are able to reject, because the world process leads the person who is willing to go along and sweeps the unwilling one along with it. But insofar as the idea is concrete in itself, it is necessary for it to become continually what it is—that is, become concrete. But this can occur only through generations and individuals.

In this way, a contradiction appears, by means of which the world process takes place. The given actuality at a certain time is the actuality valid for the generation and the individuals in that generation, and yet, if there is a reluctance to say that the process is over, this actuality must be displaced by another actuality, and this must occur through and by individuals and the generation. Catholicism was the given actuality for the generation living at the time of the Reformation, and yet it was also the actuality that no longer had validity as such. Consequently, one actuality collides here with another actuality. Herein lies the profoundly tragic aspect of world history. At one and the same time, an individual may be world-historically justified and yet unauthorized. Insofar as he is the latter, he must become a sacrifice; insofar as he is the former, he must prevail—that is, he must prevail by becoming a sacrifice. Here we see how intrinsically consistent the world process is, for as the more true actuality presses onward, it nevertheless itself esteems the past; it is not a revolution but an evolution. The past actuality shows itself to be still justified by demanding a sacrifice, the new actuality by providing a sacrifice. But a sacrifice there must be, because a new element must actually emerge, since the new actuality is not just a conclusion to the past but contains something more in itself; it is not a mere corrective of the past but is also a new beginning.

At any such turning point in history, two movements must be noted. On the one hand, the new must forge ahead; on the other, the old must be displaced. Inasmuch as the new must forge ahead, here we meet the prophetic individual who spies the new in the distance, in dim and undefined contours. The prophetic individual does not possess the future—he has only a presentiment of it. He cannot claim it, but he is also lost to the actuality to which he belongs. His relation to it, however, is peaceful, because the given actuality senses no clash. Then comes the tragic hero in the strict sense. He battles for the new and strives to destroy what for him is a vanishing actuality, but his task is still not so much to destroy as to advance the new and thereby destroy the past indirectly. But the old must be superseded; the old must be perceived in all its imperfection. Here we meet the ironic subject. For the ironic subject, the given actuality has lost its validity entirely; it has become for him an imperfect form that is a hindrance everywhere. But on the other hand, he does not possess the new. He knows only that the present does not match the idea. He is the one who must pass judgment. In one sense the ironist is certainly prophetic, because he is continually pointing to something impending, but what it is he does not know. He is prophetic, but his position and situation are the reverse of the prophet's. The prophet walks arm in arm with his age, and from this position he glimpses what is coming. The prophet, as was noted above, is lost to his generation, but essentially that is the case only because he is preoccupied with his visions. The ironist, however, has stepped out of line with his age, has turned around and faced it. That which is coming is hidden from him, lies behind his back, but the actuality he so antagonistically confronts is what he must destroy; upon this he focuses his burning gaze. The words of Scripture, "The feet of those who will carry you out are at the door,"[7] apply to his relation to his age. The ironist is also a sacrifice that the world process demands, not as if the ironist always needed in the strictest sense to fall as a sacrifice, but his fervor in the service of the world spirit consumes him.

XIII
335

Here, then, we have irony as the infinite absolute negativity. It is negativity, because it only negates; it is infinite, because it does not negate this or that phenomenon; it is absolute, because that by virtue of which it negates is a higher something that still is not. The irony establishes nothing, because that which is to be established lies behind it. It is a divine madness that rages like a Tamerlane and does not leave one stone upon another. Here, then, we have irony. To a certain degree, every world-historical turning point must have this formation also, and it certainly would not be without historical interest to track this formation through world history. Without engaging in this, I shall merely cite as examples taken from the period closest to the Reformation, Cardanus, Campanella, and Bruno. To some extent, Erasmus of Rotterdam was also an example of irony. In my opinion, the significance of this formation has not received sufficient attention hitherto—all the more strange, since Hegel has treated the negative with such decided partiality. But the negative in the system corresponds to irony in the historical actuality. In the historical actuality, the negative exists, which is never the case in the system.

Irony is a qualification of subjectivity. In irony, the subject is negatively free, since the actuality that is supposed to give the subject content is not there. He is free from the constraint in which the given actuality holds the subject, but he is negatively free and as such is suspended, because there is nothing that holds him. But this very freedom, this suspension, gives the ironist a certain enthusiasm, because he becomes intoxicated, so to speak, in the infinity of possibilities, and if he needs any consolation for everything that is destroyed, he can have recourse to the enormous reserve fund of possibility. He does not, however, abandon himself to this enthusiasm; it simply inspires and feeds his enthusiasm for destroying. XIII
336

But since the ironist does not have the new in his power, we might ask how, then, does he destroy the old, and the answer to that must be: he destroys the given actuality by the given actuality itself; but it should be remembered nevertheless that the new principle is present within him χατὰ δύναμιν [potentially], as possibility.* But by destroying actuality by means of actuality itself, he enlists in the service of world irony. In his *Geschichte der Philosophie* (II, p. 62), Hegel says: "Alle Dialectik läszt das gelten, was gelten soll, als ob es gelte, läszt die innere Zerstörung selbst sich daran entwickeln—allgemeine Ironie der Welt [All dialectic allows as valid that which is to be valid as if it were valid, allows the inner destruction to develop in it—the universal irony of the world]," and in this the world irony is very accurately interpreted.

Precisely because every particular historical actuality is continually but an element in the actualization of the idea, it carries within itself the seeds of its own downfall. This appears very clearly particularly in Judaism, whose significance as a transitional element is especially remarkable. It was already a profound irony over the world when the law, after having declared the commandments, added the promise: If you obey these, you will be saved, since it turned out that people could not fulfill the law, and thus a salvation linked

---

* Like water in relation to what it reflects, the negative has the quality of showing as high above itself that which it supports as it shows beneath itself that which it is battling; but the negative, like the water, does not know this.

to this condition certainly became more than hypothetical. That Judaism destroyed itself by itself is expressly shown in its historical relation to Christianity. If, without entering into a study of the significance of Christ's coming, we merely keep this as a turning point in world history, then one cannot miss the ironic formation there as well. This time it is provided by John the Baptizer. He was not the one who was supposed to come; he did not know what was to come—and yet he destroyed Judaism. Thus he destroyed it not by means of the new but by means of Judaism itself. He required of Judaism what Judaism wanted to give—justice, but this it was unable to give, and thereby it foundered. Consequently, he let Judaism continue to exist and at the same time developed the seeds of its own downfall within it. Nevertheless, the personality of John the Baptizer recedes completely into the background; in him we see the irony of the world in its objective shape, so to speak, so that he becomes but an instrument in its hand.

XIII
337

But in order for the ironic formation to be perfectly developed, it is required that the subject also become conscious of his irony, feel negatively free as he passes judgment on the given actuality, and enjoy this negative freedom. So that this might take place, the subjectivity must be in an advanced stage or, more correctly, as the subjectivity asserts itself, irony emerges. Face-to-face with the given actuality, the subjectivity feels its power, its validity and meaning. But as it feels this, it rescues itself, as it were, from the relativity in which the given actuality wants to keep it. Insofar as this irony is world-historically justified, the subjectivity's emancipation is carried out in the service of the idea, even if the ironic subject is not clearly conscious of this. This is the genius of justified irony. It holds true of unjustified irony that whoever wants to save his soul must lose it.[8] But only history can judge whether the irony is justified or not.

But just because the subject views actuality ironically, it in no way means that he conducts himself ironically as he asserts his view of actuality. For example, there has been sufficient talk in modern times about irony and about the ironic view of actuality, but this view has rarely taken ironic form. But the more this happens, so much the more certain and inevitable is the downfall of the actuality, so much greater is the superiority of the ironic subject over the actuality he wishes to destroy, and so much more free is he also. Here he quietly carries out the same operation as world irony. He permits the established to remain, but for him it has no validity; meanwhile, he pretends as if it did have validity for him, and under this mask he leads it to its certain downfall. To the extent that the ironic subject is world-historically justified, there is here a unity of genius and artistic presence of mind.

But if irony is a qualification of subjectivity, then it must manifest itself the first time subjectivity makes its appearance in world history. Irony is, namely, the first and most abstract qualification of subjectivity. This points to the historical turning point where subjectivity made its appearance for the first time, and with this we have come to Socrates.

The nature of Socrates' irony has been sufficiently covered in the first part of this investigation. For him, the whole given actuality had entirely lost its validity; he had become alien to the actuality of the whole substantial world. This is one side of irony, but on the other hand he used irony as he destroyed Greek culture. His conduct toward it was at all times ironic; he was ignorant and knew nothing but was continually seeking information from others; yet as he let the existing go on existing, it foundered. He kept on using this tactic until the very last, as was especially evident when he was accused. But his fervor in this service consumed him, and in the end irony overwhelmed him; he became dizzy, and everything lost its reality. To me, this view of Socrates and of the significance of his position in world history seems to be so well balanced that I hope it finds acceptance with some readers. But since Hegel declares himself against viewing Socrates' position as irony, it becomes necessary to look at the objections found here and there in his books.

Before proceeding to this, however, I shall try as well as I can to explain a weakness from which Hegel's whole understanding of the concept of irony seems to suffer. Hegel always discusses irony in a very unsympathetic manner; in his eyes, irony is anathema. Hegel's appearance coincides with Schlegel's most brilliant period. But just as the irony of the Schlegels had passed judgment in esthetics on an encompassing sentimentality, so Hegel was the one to correct what was misleading in the irony. On the whole, it is one of Hegel's great merits that he halted or at least wanted to halt the prodigal sons of speculation on their way to perdition. But he did not always use the mildest means for this, and when he called out to them his voice was not always gentle and fatherly but at times was harsh and schoolmasterly. The partisans of irony gave him the most trouble; he soon gave up hope of their salvation and now treats them as irreclaimable and obdurate sinners. He takes every opportunity to talk about these ironists and always in the most unsympathetic manner. Indeed, Hegel looks down with immense scorn and superiority on those whom he often calls "superior people." But the fact that Hegel became irritated with the form of irony closest to him naturally impaired his interpretation of the concept. Explanation is often lacking—but Schlegel is always reprimanded. In no way does this mean that Hegel was not right about the Schlegels and that the Schlegelian irony was not on a very dubious wrong road. All it says is that Hegel has surely conferred a great benefit through the earnestness with which he takes a stand against any isolation, an earnestness that makes it possible to read much that he has written with much invigoration and considerable edification. But on the other hand, it must be said that by his one-sided attack on the post-Fichtean irony he has overlooked the truth of irony, and by his identifying all irony with this, he has done irony an injustice. As soon as Hegel mentions the word "irony," he

promptly thinks of Schlegel and Tieck, and his style is immediately marked
by a certain resentment. What was wrong and unwarranted with Schlegel's
irony as well as Hegel's good services in this respect will be discussed in the
appropriate place. We turn now to his view of Socrates' irony.

We called attention earlier to the fact that Hegel, in his description of
Socrates' method, stresses two forms: his irony and his midwifery. His discussion of this is found in *Geschichte der Philosophie,* II, pp. 59–67. Although
the discussion of Socratic irony is very brief, Hegel nevertheless uses the occasion to rant against irony as a general principle and on page 62 adds:
"Friedrich von Schlegel ist es, der diese Gedanken zuerst aufgebracht, Ast
hat es nachgesprochen [It was Friedrich von Schlegel who first brought forward this idea, and Ast repeated it]"; and then follow the earnest words that
Hegel customarily delivers on such an occasion. Socrates pretends to be ignorant, and in the role of being taught he teaches others. P. 60: "Dieses ist
dann die Seite der berühmten *socratischen Ironie.* Sie hat bei ihm die subjective Gestalt der Dialectik, sie ist Benehmungsweise im Umgang; die Dialectik ist Gründe der Sache, die Ironie ist besondere Benehmungsweise von
Person zu Person [This, then, is the aspect of the celebrated Socratic irony.
In him it has the subjective form of dialectic, it is a way of dealing with
people; the dialectic is the reasons of things, the irony is a special way of dealing person to person]." But inasmuch as just before that Hegel noted that
Socrates uses the same irony "wenn er die Manier der Sophisten zu Schan-
den machen will [when he wishes to bring the manner of the Sophists into
disrepute]," we promptly encounter a difficulty here, because in the one instance he does indeed want to teach, but in the other merely to disgrace.
Hegel then points out that this Socratic irony seems to contain something
false but thereupon shows the correctness of his conduct. Finally he shows
the real meaning of Socratic irony, the greatness in it—namely, that it seeks
to make abstract conceptions concrete and developed. He goes on to add
(p. 62): "Wenn ich sage, ich weisz, was Vernunft, was Glaube ist, so sind diesz
nur ganz abstracte Vorstellungen; dasz sie nun concret werden, dazu gehört,
dasz die explicirt werden, dasz vorausgesetzt werde, es sey nicht bekannt, was
es eigentlich sey. Diese Explication solcher Vorstellungen bewirkt nun
Socrates; und diesz ist das wahrhafte der socratischen Ironie [In saying that I
know what reason is, what belief is, these remain but quite abstract conceptions; in order to become concrete, they must indeed be explicated and presupposed to be unknown in terms of what they really are. Socrates effected
the explications of such conceptions, and this is the truth of Socratic irony]."

But this confuses everything; the description of Socratic irony completely
loses its historical weight, and the passage quoted is so modern that it hardly
reminds us of Socrates. To be specific, Socrates' undertaking was by no means
one of making the abstract concrete, and the examples cited are certainly
very poorly chosen, because I do not think that Hegel would be able to cite

analogies to this unless he were to take the whole of Plato and plead the continual use of Socrates' name in Plato, whereby he would come into conflict with both himself and everyone else. Socrates' undertaking was not to make the abstract concrete, but to let the abstract become visible through the immediately concrete. In a refutation of these Hegelian observations, it is sufficient to remember two things: first, the double nature of the irony we found in Plato (for it is obviously the irony we have called Platonic irony that Hegel meant and that on page 64 he identifies with Socratic irony); second, the principle of movement in Socrates' whole life—that it proceeded not from the abstract to the concrete but from the concrete to the abstract and continually arrived at this. Thus, when Hegel's whole examination of Socratic irony ends in such a way that Socratic irony becomes identified with Platonic irony and both ironies become (p. 64) "mehr Manier der Conversation, die gesellige Heiterkeit, als dasz jene reine Negation, jenes negative Verhalten darunter verstanden wäre [more a manner of conversation, sociable pleasantry, and not that pure negation, not the negative attitude]," this comment has indeed already been answered.

Hegel's description of Socrates' art of midwifery does not fare much better. Here he develops the significance of Socrates' asking questions, and this discussion is both beautiful and true, but the distinction we made earlier between asking in order to get an answer and asking in order to disgrace is overlooked here. At the end, the example of the concept "to become" that he chooses is once again totally un-Socratic, unless he intends to find a Socratic development in the *Parmenides*. XIII
341

As for Hegel's ever really discussing Socrates' tragic irony, one must bear in mind that it is not the irony of Socrates but the world's irony with Socrates. Therefore, it cannot shed any light on the question of Socratic irony.

In his review of the works of Solger, Hegel again points out on page 488 the difference between Schlegelian irony and Socratic irony. That there is a difference we have fully conceded and shall point out in more detail in the appropriate place, but it is by no means to be concluded from this that Socrates' position was not irony. Hegel upbraids Friedrich Schlegel because, with his lack of judgment with regard to the speculative and his neglect of it, he has wrenched the Fichtean thesis on the constitutive validity of the ego out of its metaphysical context, wrenched it out of the domain of thought, and applied it directly to actuality, "zum Verneinen der Lebendigkeit der Vernunft und Wahrheit, und zur Herabsetzung derselben zum Schein im Subject und zum Scheinen für Andere [in order to deny the vitality of reason and truth and to relegate these to an illusory status in the subject and to illusion for others]." He then points out that in order to designate this vitiation of truth into appearance, the name of innocent Socratic irony has been allowed to be vitiated. If the similarity is based particularly on the circumstance that Socrates always introduced his inquiry with the declaration that he knew nothing, in order to disgrace the Sophists, then the outcome of this conduct is always something negative and without any scientific-scholarly conclusion. In that case, Socrates' protesting that he knew nothing is given in dead earnest and consequently is not ironic. I shall not at this point become further involved in the issue that arises here from Hegel's showing that Socrates' teaching ended without a conclusion, if we compare this with what he advanced earlier about Socrates' making the abstract concrete through his ironic teaching, but on the other hand I shall in a little detail investigate how earnest Socrates really was about his ignorance.

As pointed out earlier, when Socrates declared that he was ignorant, he nevertheless did know something, for he knew about his ignorance; on the other hand, however, this knowledge was not a knowledge of something, that is, did not have any positive content, and to that extent his ignorance was ironic, and since Hegel has tried in vain, in my opinion, to reclaim a positive content for him, I believe that the reader must agree with me. If his knowledge had been a knowledge of something, his ignorance would merely have been a conversational technique. His irony, however, was complete in itself. Inasmuch, then, as his ignorance was simultaneously earnest and yet again not earnest, it is on this prong Socrates must be held. To know that one is ignorant is the beginning of coming to know, but if one does not know more, it is merely a beginning. This knowledge was what kept Socrates ironically afloat.

When Hegel next hopes to show that Socrates' ignorance was not irony by pointing out that Socrates was in earnest about his ignorance, it seems to me that here again Hegel is not consistent. To be specific, if irony is going to advance a supreme thesis, it does as every negative position does—it declares something positive and is earnest about what it says. For irony, nothing is an established order; it plays helter-skelter *ad libitum* [at will] with everything; but when it wants to declare this, it says something positive, and to that extent its sovereignty is thereby at an end. Therefore, when Schlegel or Solger says: Actuality is only appearance, only semblance, only vanity, a nothing, he obviously is saying this in earnest, and yet Hegel assumes it to be irony. The difficulty here is that, strictly speaking, irony actually is never able to advance a thesis, because irony is a qualification of the being-for-itself subject, who in incessant agility allows nothing to remain established and on account of this agility cannot focus on the total point of view that it allows nothing to remain established. Schlegel's and Solger's consciousness that finitude is a nothing is obviously just as earnestly intended as Socrates' ignorance. Ultimately the ironist always has to posit something, but what he posits in this way is nothing. But then it is impossible to be earnest about nothing without either arriving at something (this happens if one becomes speculatively earnest about it) or despairing (if one takes it personally in earnest). But the ironist does neither, and thus we can also say that he is not in earnest about it.

XIII
342

Irony is the infinitely light playing with nothing that is not terrified by it but even rises to the surface on occasion. But if one does not speculatively or personally take nothing in earnest, then one obviously is taking it lightly and thus does not take it in earnest. If Hegel thinks that Schlegel was not in earnest in holding that existence is a nothing devoid of reality [*Realitet*], then there certainly must have been something that did have validity for him, but in that case his irony was merely a form. Therefore we can say of irony that it is earnestness about nothing—insofar as it is not earnestness about something. It continually conceives of nothing in contrast to something, and in order to free itself of earnestness about anything, it grasps the nothing. But it does not become earnestness about nothing, either, except insofar as it is not earnestness about anything.

So it is also with Socrates' ignorance; his ignorance is the nothing with which he destroys any knowledge. This is best seen in his view of death. He is ignorant of what death is and of what there is after death, whether there is anything or nothing at all; consequently, he is ignorant. But he does not take this ignorance greatly to heart; on the contrary, he genuinely feels quite liberated in this ignorance. Consequently, he is not in earnest about this ignorance, and yet he is altogether earnest about being ignorant.—I believe, therefore, that everyone will agree with me that there is nothing in these Hegelian observations to preclude the assumption that Socrates' position was irony.

We shall now summarize what was stressed in the first part of this dissertation as characteristic of Socrates' position, namely: that the whole substantial life of Greek culture had lost its validity for him, which means that to him the established actuality was unactual, not in this or that particular aspect but in its totality as such; that with regard to this invalid actuality he let the established order of things appear to remain established and thereby brought about its downfall; that in the process Socrates became lighter and lighter, more and more negatively free; consequently, that we do indeed perceive that according to what is set forth here Socrates' position was, as infinite absolute negativity, irony. But it was not actuality in general that he negated; it was the given actuality at a particular time, the substantial actuality as it was in Greece, and what his irony was demanding was the actuality of subjectivity, of ideality.

On this issue, history has judged Socrates to be world-historically justified. He became a sacrifice. This is certainly a tragic fate, but nevertheless Socrates' death is not basically tragic; and the Greek state really comes too late with its death sentence. On the other hand, the execution of the death sentence has little upbuilding effect, because death has no reality for Socrates. For the tragic hero, death has validity; for him, death is truly the final battle and the final suffering. Therefore the age he wanted to destroy can in that way satisfy its fury for revenge. But obviously the Greek state could not find this satisfaction in Socrates' death, since by his ignorance Socrates had frustrated any more meaningful connection with the thought of death. Admittedly the tragic hero does not fear death, but still he knows it as a pain, as a hard and harsh course, and to that extent it has validity if he is condemned to die; but Socrates knows nothing at all, and thus it is an irony over the state that it condemns him to death and believes that it has inflicted punishment upon him.

The anonymous manuscripts found in the secret desk-compartment by the editor, Victor Eremita, were the papers of a witty, ironical, disillusioned young esthete the editor called A, who had seen through everything in life and found it wanting. Therefore, according to the opening section, "Diapsalmata," "Rotation of Crops," and "The Seducer's Diary," the best approach is to play shuttlecock with life by maintaining esthetic distance from relationships and circumstances and arbitrarily controlling one's experiences on the basis of "the interesting." The aim, then, is always to have "the laughter on my side" and continually to change "the eye with which one sees actuality." This stance is presented in the final section, "The Seducer's Diary," a case study of "living poetically," the story of esthetically distanced enjoyment of the process of seduction without the fulfillment and its consequences. In the interpretation by A (an anonym who presents the diary as the writing of another anonym), "the poetic was the plus he himself brought along. This plus was the poetic he enjoyed in the poetic situation of actuality; this he recaptured in the form of poetic reflection. This was the second enjoyment, and his whole life was intended for enjoyment." Other modes of the esthetic view of life and its underside are represented by "The Immediate Erotic Stages or the Musical-Erotic" (a rhapsodic penetrating analysis of Mozart's *Don Giovanni*, with insightful discussions of immediacy and reflection, of the momentary and the historical) and "The Tragic in Ancient Drama Reflected in the Tragic in Modern Drama" (on cultural disintegration and numerical association, isolation and responsibility, esthetic guilt and ethical guilt, doubt and despair, sorrow and repentance). The underside of the esthetic is the theme of "Silhouettes" (unhappy love and reflective sorrow epitomized by Marie Beaumarchais, Donna Elvira, and Margarete). The personal absence of hoping individualities and of recollecting individualities underlies the pessimism of "The Unhappiest One." "The First Love" is a review of a play by a reviewer who had lost "faith in the first love" and for whom the dramatic performance of the actors overshadowed the ironical witty substance.

Grandeur, savoir, renommée,
  Amitié, plaisir et bien,
    Tout n'est que vent, que fumée:
Pour mieux dire, tout n'est rien
  [Greatness, knowledge, renown,
    Friendship, pleasure and possessions,
      All is only wind, only smoke:
To say it better, all is nothing].

I
1

ΔΙΑΨΑΛΜΑΤΑ

AD SE IPSUM

[TO HIMSELF]

I
3

What is a poet? An unhappy person who conceals profound anguish in his heart but whose lips are so formed that as sighs and cries pass over them they sound like beautiful music. It is with him as with the poor wretches in Phalaris's bronze bull, who were slowly tortured over a slow fire; their screams could not reach the tyrant's ears to terrify him; to him they sounded like sweet music. And people crowd around the poet and say to him, "Sing again soon"—in other words, may new sufferings torture your soul, and may your lips continue to be formed as before, because your screams would only alarm us, but the music is charming. And the reviewers step up and say, "That is right; so it must be according to the rules of esthetics." Now of course a reviewer resembles a poet to a hair, except that he does not have the anguish in his heart, or the music on his lips. Therefore, I would rather be a swineherd out on Amager and be understood by swine than be a poet and be misunderstood by people.

I
4

How unreasonable people are! They never use the freedoms they have but demand those they do not have; they have freedom of thought—they demand freedom of speech.

I don't feel like doing anything. I don't feel like riding—the motion is too powerful; I don't feel like walking—it is too tiring; I don't feel like lying down, for either I would have to stay down, and I don't feel like doing that, or I would have to get up again, and I don't feel like doing that, either. *Summa Summarum:* I don't feel like doing anything.

Tested Advice for Authors

One carelessly writes down one's personal observations, has them printed, and in the various proofs one will eventually acquire a number of good ideas. Therefore, take courage, you who have not yet dared to have something printed. Do not despise typographical errors, and to become witty by means of typographical errors may be considered a legitimate way to become witty.

I
5

Old age fulfills the dreams of youth. One sees this in Swift: in his youth he built an insane asylum; in his old age he himself entered it.

I
6

I say of my sorrow what the Englishman says of his house: My sorrow is *my castle.* Many people look upon having sorrow as one of life's conveniences.

I feel as a chessman must feel when the opponent says of it: That piece cannot be moved.

The tremendous poetical power of folk literature is manifest, among other ways, in its power to desire. In comparison, desire in our age is simultaneously sinful and boring, because it desires what belongs to the neighbor. Desire in folk literature is fully aware that the neighbor does not possess what it seeks any more than it does itself. And if it is going to desire sinfully, then it is so flagrant that people must be shocked. It is not going to let itself be beaten down by the cold probability calculations of a pedestrian understanding. Don Juan still strides across the stage with his 1,003 ladyloves. Out of reverence for the venerableness of tradition, no one dares to smile. If a poet had dared to do this in our age, he would be laughed to scorn.

I have, I believe, the courage to doubt everything; I have, I believe, the courage to fight against everything; but I do not have the courage to acknowledge anything, the courage to possess, to own, anything. Most people complain that the world is so prosaic that things do not go in life as in the novel, where opportunity is always so favorable. I complain that in life it is not as in the novel, where one has hardhearted fathers and nisses and trolls to battle, and enchanted princesses to free. What are all such adversaries together compared with the pale, bloodless, tenacious-of-life nocturnal forms with which I battle and to which I myself give life and existence.

How sterile my soul and my mind are, and yet constantly tormented by empty voluptuous and excruciating labor pains! Will the tongue ligament of my spirit never be loosened; will I always jabber? What I need is a voice as piercing as the glance of Lynceus, as terrifying as the groan of the giants, as sustained as a sound of nature, as mocking as an icy gust of wind, as malicious as echo's heartless taunting, extending in range from the deepest bass to the most melting high notes, and modulated from a solemn-silent whisper to the energy of rage. That is what I need in order to breathe, to give voice to what is on my mind, to have the viscera of both anger and sympathy shaken.—But my voice is only hoarse like the scream of a gull or moribund like the blessing on the lips of the mute.

What is going to happen? What will the future bring? I do not know, I have no presentiment. When a spider flings itself from a fixed point down into its consequences, it continually sees before it an empty space in which it can find no foothold, however much it stretches. So it is with me; before me is continually an empty space, and I am propelled by a consequence that lies behind me. This life is turned around and dreadful, not to be endured.

The most ludicrous of all ludicrous things, it seems to me, is to be busy in the world, to be a man who is brisk at his meals and brisk at his work. Therefore, when I see a fly settle on the nose of one of those men of business in a decisive moment, or if he is splashed by a carriage that passes him in even greater haste, or Knippelsbro⁹ tilts up, or a roof tile falls and kills him, I laugh from the bottom of my heart. And who could keep from laughing? What, after all, do these busy bustlers achieve? Are they not just like that woman who, in a flurry because the house was on fire, rescued the fire tongs? What more, after all, do they salvage from life's huge conflagration?

I
10   No one comes back from the dead; no one has come into the world without weeping. No one asks when one wants to come in; no one asks when one wants to go out.

I
11   Virgilius [*sic*] the sorcerer had himself hacked to pieces and put in a caldron to be cooked for eight days in order by this process to be rejuvenated. He arranged for someone to watch so that no interloper would peer into the caldron. But the watchman could not resist the temptation; it was too soon, and Virgilius, as an infant, disappeared with a scream. I dare say that I also peered too soon into the caldron, into the caldron of life and the historical process, and most likely will never manage to become more than a child.

I
12   Let others complain that the times are evil. I complain that they are wretched, for they are without passion. People's thoughts are as thin and fragile as lace, and they themselves as pitiable as lace-making girls. The thoughts of their hearts are too wretched to be sinful. It is perhaps possible to regard it as sin for a worm to nourish such thoughts, but not for a human being, who is created in the image of God. Their desires are staid and dull, their passions drowsy. They perform their duties, these mercenary souls, but just like the Jews, they indulge in trimming the coins a little; they think that, even though our Lord keeps ever so orderly an account book, they can still manage to trick him a little. Fie on them! That is why my soul always turns back to the Old Testament and to Shakespeare. There one still feels that those who speak are human beings; there they hate, there they love, there they murder the enemy, curse his descendants through all generations— there they sin.

My life achievement amounts to nothing at all, a mood, a single color. My achievement resembles the painting by that artist who was supposed to paint the Israelites' crossing of the Red Sea and to that end painted the entire wall red and explained that the Israelites had walked across and that the Egyptians were drowned.

I
13   Human dignity is still acknowledged even in nature, for when we want to keep birds away from the trees we set up something that is supposed to resemble a human being, and even the remote resemblance a scarecrow has to a human being is sufficient to inspire respect.

Most people rush after pleasure so fast that they rush right past it. They are like that dwarf who guarded a kidnapped princess in his castle. One day he took a noon nap. When he woke up an hour later, she was gone. Hastily he pulls on his seven-league boots; with one step he is far past her.

How empty and meaningless life is.—We bury a man; we accompany him to the grave, throw three spadefuls of earth on him; we ride out in a carriage, ride home in a carriage; we find consolation in the thought that we have a long life ahead of us. But how long is seven times ten years? Why not settle it all at once, why not stay out there and go along down into the grave and draw lots to see to whom will befall the misfortune of being the last of the living who throws the last three spadefuls of earth on the last of the dead?

Those two familiar violin strains! Those two familiar violin strains here this very moment out in the street. Have I lost my mind; out of love for Mozart's music, have my ears ceased to hear? Is this a reward of the gods, to give unhappy me, who sits like a beggar at the door of the temple, ears that themselves perform what they hear? Only those two violin strains, for now I hear nothing more. Just as in that immortal overture they burst forth out of the deep chorale tones, so here they disentangle themselves from the noise and tumult of the street with the total surprise of a revelation.—It must be close by, for now I hear the light dance tunes.—So it is to you that I owe this joy, you two unfortunate artists.—One of them was probably seventeen years old, wearing a green Kalmuk coat with large bone buttons. The coat was much too large for him. He held the violin tightly under his chin; his cap was pulled down over his eyes. His hand was concealed in a fingerless glove; his fingers were red and blue with cold. The other one was older and wore a chenille coat. Both were blind. A little girl, who presumably guided them, stood in front of them, thrust her hands under her scarf. We gathered one by one, a few admirers of those melodies—a postman with his mailbag, a little boy, a maidservant, a couple of dock workers. The elegant carriages rolled noisily by; the carts and wagons drowned out the melodies, which emerged fragmentarily for a moment. You two unfortunate artists, do you know that those strains hide in themselves the glories of the whole world?—Was it not like a rendezvous?—

In a theater, it happened that a fire started offstage. The clown came out to tell the audience. They thought it was a joke and applauded. He told them again, and they become still more hilarious. This is the way, I suppose, that the world will be destroyed—amid the universal hilarity of wits and wags who think it is all a joke.

What, if anything, is the meaning of this life? If people are divided into two great classes, it may be said that one class works for a living and the other does not have that need. But to work for a living certainly cannot be the meaning of life, since it is indeed a contradiction that the continual production of the conditions is supposed to be the answer to the question of the meaning of that which is conditional upon their production. The lives of the rest of them generally have no meaning except to consume the conditions. To say that the meaning of life is to die seems to be a contradiction also.

Real enjoyment consists not in what one enjoys but in the idea. If I had in my service a submissive jinni who, when I asked for a glass of water, would bring me the world's most expensive wines, deliciously blended, in a goblet, I would dismiss him until he learned that the enjoyment consists not in what I enjoy but in getting my own way.

I
16

What philosophers say about actuality [*Virkelighed*] is often just as disappointing as it is when one reads on a sign in a secondhand shop: Pressing Done Here. If a person were to bring his clothes to be pressed, he would be duped, for the sign is merely for sale.

For me nothing is more dangerous than to recollect [*erindre*]. As soon as I have recollected a life relationship, that relationship has ceased to exist. It is said that absence makes the heart grow fonder. That is very true, but it becomes fonder in a purely poetic way. To live in recollection is the most perfect life imaginable; recollection is more richly satisfying than all actuality, and it has a security that no actuality possesses. A recollected life relationship has already passed into eternity and has no temporal interest anymore.

I
17

It takes a lot of naïveté to believe that it helps to shout and scream in the world, as if one's fate would thereby be altered. Take what comes and avoid all complications. In my early years, when I went to a restaurant, I would say to the waiter: A good cut, a very good cut, from the loin, and not too fat. Perhaps the waiter would scarcely hear what I said. Perhaps it was even less likely that he would heed it, and still less that my voice would penetrate into the kitchen, influence the chef—and even if all this happened, there perhaps was not a good cut in the whole roast. Now I never shout anymore.

I
18

The same thing happened to me that, according to legend, happened to Parmeniscus, who in the Trophonean cave lost the ability to laugh but acquired it again on the island of Delos upon seeing a shapeless block that was said to be the image of the goddess Leto. When I was very young, I forgot in the Trophonean cave how to laugh; when I became an adult, when I opened my eyes and saw actuality, then I started to laugh and have never stopped laughing since that time. I saw that the meaning of life was to make a living, its goal to become a councilor, that the rich delight of love was to acquire a well-to-do girl, that the blessedness of friendship was to help each other in financial difficulties, that wisdom was whatever the majority assumed it to be, that enthusiasm was to give a speech, that courage was to risk being fined ten dollars, that cordiality was to say "May it do you good" after a meal, that piety was to go to communion once a year. This I saw, and I laughed.

What is it that binds me? From what was the chain formed that bound the Fenris wolf?[10] It was made of the noise of cats' paws walking on the ground, of the beards of women, of the roots of cliffs, of the grass of bears, of the breath of fish, and of the spittle of birds. I, too, am bound in the same way by a chain formed of gloomy fancies, of alarming dreams, of troubled thoughts, of fearful presentiments, of inexplicable anxieties. This chain is "very flexible, soft as silk, yields to the most powerful strain, and cannot be torn apart."

I
19

My life is utterly meaningless. When I consider its various epochs, my life is like the word *Schnur* in the dictionary, which first of all means a string, and second a daughter-in-law. All that is lacking is that in the third place the word *Schnur* means a camel, in the fourth a whisk broom.

I
20

How dreadful boredom is—how dreadfully boring; I know no stronger expression, no truer one, for like is recognized only by like. Would that there were a loftier, stronger expression, for then there would still be one movement. I lie prostrate, inert; the only thing I see is emptiness, the only thing I live on is emptiness, the only thing I move in is emptiness. I do not even suffer pain. The vulture pecked continually at Prometheus's liver; the poison dripped down continually on Loki; it was at least an interruption, even though monotonous. Pain itself has lost its refreshment for me. If I were offered all the glories of the world or all the torments of the world, one would move me no more than the other; I would not turn over to the other side either to attain or to avoid. I am dying death. And what could divert me? Well, if I managed to see a faithfulness that withstood every ordeal [*Prøvelse*], an enthusiasm that endured everything, a faith that moved mountains; if I were to become aware of an idea that joined the finite and the infinite. But my soul's poisonous doubt consumes everything. My soul is like the Dead Sea, over which no bird is able to fly; when it has come midway, it sinks down, exhausted, to death and destruction.

I
21

Either / Or
An Ecstatic Discourse

I
22

Marry, and you will regret it. Do not marry, and you will also regret it. Marry or do not marry, you will regret it either way.[11] Whether you marry or you do not marry, you will regret it either way. Laugh at the stupidities of the world, and you will regret it; weep over them, and you will also regret it. Laugh at the stupidities of the world or weep over them, you will regret it

I
23

either way. Whether you laugh at the stupidities of the world or you weep over them, you will regret it either way. Trust a girl, and you will regret it. Do not trust her, and you will also regret it. Trust a girl or do not trust her, you will regret it either way. Whether you trust a girl or do not trust her, you will regret it either way. Hang yourself, and you will regret it. Do not hang yourself, and you will also regret it. Hang yourself or do not hang yourself, you will regret it either way. Whether you hang yourself or do not hang yourself, you will regret it either way. This, gentlemen, is the quintessence of all the wisdom of life. It is not merely in isolated moments that I, as Spinoza says, view everything *aeterno modo* [in the mode of eternity], but I am continually *aeterno modo*. Many believe they, too, are this when after doing one thing or another they unite or mediate these opposites. But this is a misunderstanding, for the true eternity does not lie behind either/or but before it. Their eternity will therefore also be a painful temporal sequence, since they will have a double regret on which to live. My wisdom is easy to grasp, for I have only one maxim, and even that is not a point of departure for me. One must differentiate between the subsequent dialectic in either/or and the eternal one suggested here. So when I say that my maxim is not a point of departure for me, this does not have the opposite of being a point of departure but is merely the negative expression of my maxim, that by which it comprehends itself in contrast to being a point of departure or not being a point of departure. My maxim is not a point of departure for me, because if I made it a point of departure, I would regret it, and if I did not make it a point of departure, I would also regret it. If one or another of my esteemed listeners thinks there is anything to what I have said, he merely demonstrates that he has no head for philosophy. If he thinks there is any movement in what has been said, this demonstrates the same thing. But for those listeners who are able to follow me, although I do not move, I shall now elucidate the eternal truth by which this philosophy is self-contained and does not concede anything higher. That is, if I made my maxim a point of departure, then I would be unable to stop, for if I did not stop, I would regret it, and if I did stop, I would also regret it, etc. But if I never start, then I can always stop, for my eternal starting is my eternal stopping. Experience shows that it is not at all difficult for philosophy to begin. Far from it. It begins, in fact, with nothing and therefore can always begin. But it is always difficult for philosophy and philosophers to stop. This difficulty, too, I have avoided, for if anyone thinks that I, in stopping now, actually stop, he demonstrates that he does not have speculative comprehension. The point is that I do not stop now, but I stopped when I began. My philosophy, therefore, has the advantageous characteristic of being brief and of being irrefutable, for if anyone disputes me, I daresay I have the right to declare him mad. The philosopher, then, is continually *aeterno modo* and does not have, as did the blessed Sintenis, only specific hours that are lived for eternity.

Wine no longer cheers my heart; a little of it makes me sad—much, depressed. My soul is dull and slack; in vain do I jab the spur of desire into its side; it is exhausted, it can no longer raise itself up in its royal jump. I have lost all my illusions. In vain do I seek to abandon myself in joy's infinitude; it cannot lift me, or, rather, I cannot lift myself. Previously, when it merely beckoned, I mounted, light, hearty, and cheerful. When I rode slowly through the forest, it seemed as if I were flying. Now, when the horse is covered with lather and is almost ready to drop, it seems to me that I do not move from the spot. I am alone, as I have always been—forsaken not by men, that would not pain me, but by the happy jinn of joy, who trooped around me in great numbers, who met acquaintances everywhere, showed me an opportunity everywhere. Just as an intoxicated man collects a wanton throng of young people around him, so they flocked about me, the elves of joy, and my smile was meant for them. My soul has lost possibility. If I were to wish for something, I would wish not for wealth or power but for the passion of possibility, for the eye, eternally young, eternally ardent, that sees possibility everywhere. Pleasure disappoints; possibility does not. And what wine is so sparkling, so fragrant, so intoxicating!

Where the rays of the sun do not reach, the tones still manage to come. My apartment is dark and gloomy; a high wall practically keeps out the light of day. It must be in the next courtyard, very likely a wandering musician. What instrument is it? A reed pipe? . . . . . What do I hear—the minuet from *Don Giovanni.* Carry me away, then, you rich, strong tones, to the ring of girls, to the delight of the dance.—The pharmacist pounds his mortar, the maid scrubs her kettle, the groom curries his horse and knocks the currycomb on the cobblestones. These tones are only for me; only to me do they beckon. Oh, thank you, whoever you are! Thank you! My soul is so rich, so hearty, so intoxicated with joy!

The sun is shining brilliantly and beautifully into my room; the window in the next room is open. Everything is quiet out on the street. It is Sunday afternoon. I distinctly hear a lark warbling outside a window in one of the neighboring courtyards, outside the window where the pretty girl lives. Far away in a distant street, I hear a man crying "Shrimp for sale." The air is so warm, and yet the whole city is as if deserted.—Then I call to mind my youth and my first love—when I was filled with longing; now I long only for my first longing. What is youth? A dream. What is love? The content of the dream.

Something marvelous has happened to me. I was transported to the seventh heaven. There sat all the gods assembled. As a special dispensation, I was granted the favor of making a wish. "What do you want," asked Mercury. "Do you want youth, or beauty, or power, or a long life, or the most beautiful girl, or any one of the other glorious things we have in the treasure chest? Choose—but only one thing." For a moment I was bewildered; then I addressed the gods, saying: My esteemed contemporaries, I choose one thing—that I may always have the laughter on my side. Not one of the gods said a word; instead, all of them began to laugh. From that I concluded that my wish was granted and decided that the gods knew how to express themselves with good taste, for it would indeed have been inappropriate to reply solemnly: It is granted to you.

THE IMMEDIATE EROTIC STAGES

OR

THE MUSICAL-EROTIC

I
48

If I imagined two kingdoms bordering each other, one of which I knew rather well and the other not at all, and if however much I desired it I was not allowed to enter the unknown kingdom, I would still be able to form some idea of it. I would go to the border of the kingdom known to me and follow it all the way, and in doing so I would by my movements describe the outline of that unknown land and thus have a general idea of it, although I had never set foot in it. And if this was a labor that occupied me very much, if I was unflaggingly scrupulous, it presumably would sometimes happen that as I stood with sadness at the border of my kingdom and gazed longingly into that unknown country that was so near and yet so far, I would be granted an occasional little disclosure. And even though I feel that music is an art that requires considerable experience if one is really to have an opinion on it, I comfort myself again as so often before with the paradox that also in presentiment and ignorance one can have a kind of experience. It is a comfort to me that Diana, who had not given birth herself, came to the aid of women in labor—indeed, that she had this ability from infancy as an inborn gift, so that when she was born she herself helped Latona in her labor pains.[12]

I
49

The kingdom that I know, to whose outermost boundary I shall go to discover music, is language. If the various media are ordered according to a specific process of development, language and music must be placed closest to each other, and that is also why it has been said that music is a language, which is more than a clever observation. If one is inclined to indulge in cleverness, one could say that sculpture and painting, too, are each a kind of language, inasmuch as every expression of an idea is always a language, since the essence of the idea is language. Clever folk therefore speak of the language of nature, and soft-headed clergy occasionally open the book of nature for us and read something that neither they nor their listeners understand. If the observation that music is a language did not amount to anything more than that, I would not bother with it but would let it go unchallenged and pass for what it is. But that is not the case. Not until spirit is posited is language installed in its rights, but when spirit is posited, everything that is not spirit is excluded. Yet this exclusion is a qualification of spirit, and consequently, insofar as that which is excluded is to affirm itself, it requires a medium that is qualified in relation to spirit, and this medium is music. But a medium that is qualified in relation to spirit is essentially language; now, since music is qualified in relation to spirit, it is legitimately called a language.

Language, regarded as medium, is the medium absolutely qualified by spirit, and it is therefore the authentic medium of the idea. To elaborate this more thoroughly is neither within my competence nor in the interest of this little inquiry. Just one specific comment, which again leads me into music, should find a place here. In language, the sensuous as medium is reduced to a mere instrument and is continually negated. That is not the case with the other media. Neither in sculpture nor in painting is the sensuous a mere instrument; it is rather a component. It is not to be negated continually, either, for it is continually to be seen conjointly. It would be a strangely backward consideration of a piece of sculpture or of a painting if I were to behold it in such a way that I took pains to see it independently of the sensuous, whereby I would completely cancel its beauty. In sculpture, architecture, and painting, the idea is integral to the medium, but the fact that the idea does not reduce the medium to a mere instrument, does not continually negate it, expresses, as it were, that this medium cannot speak. It is the same with nature. Therefore, it is properly said that nature is dumb, and architecture and sculpture and painting; it is properly said despite all the fine, sensitive ears that can hear them speak. Therefore, it is foolish to say that nature is a language, certainly as foolish as to say that the mute speaks, since it is not even a language in the way sign language is. But that is not the case with language. The sensuous is reduced to a mere instrument and is thus annulled. If a person spoke in such a way that we heard the flapping of his tongue etc., he would be speaking poorly; if he heard in such a way that he heard the vibrations of the air instead of words, he would be hearing poorly; if he read a book in such a way that he continually saw each individual letter, he would be reading poorly. Language is the perfect medium precisely when everything sensuous in it is negated. That is also the case with music; that which is really supposed to be heard is continually disengaging itself from the sensuous. It has already been pointed out that music as a medium does not rank as high as language, and that is why I said that music, understood in a certain way, is a language.

Language addresses itself to the ear. No other medium does this. The ear, in turn, is the most spiritually qualified sense. Most people, I believe, will agree with me on this point. If anyone wishes more information about this, I refer him to the preface to Steffens's *Karrikaturen des Heiligsten.*[13] Apart from language, music is the only medium that is addressed to the ear. Here again is an analogy and a testimony to the sense in which music is a language. There is much in nature that is addressed to the ear, but what affects the ear is the purely sensate; therefore nature is mute, and it is a ludicrous fancy that one hears something because one hears a cow bellow or, what is perhaps more pretentious, a nightingale warble; it is a fancy that one hears something, a fancy that the one is worth more than the other, since it is all six of one and a half dozen of the other.

Language has its element in time; all other media have space as their element. Only music also occurs in time. But its occurrence in time is in turn a negation of the feelings dependent upon the senses [*det Sandselige*]. That which the other arts produce suggests their sensuousness precisely by having its continuance in space. There is, of course, much in nature that occurs in time. For example, when a brook ripples and keeps on rippling, there seems to be a qualification of time involved therein. But this is not so, and if anyone absolutely insists that the qualification of time must be present here, then one must say that it certainly is so but that it is spatially qualified. Music does not exist except in the moment it is performed, for even if a person can read notes ever so well and has an ever so vivid imagination, he still cannot deny that only in a figurative sense does music exist when it is being read. It actually exists only when it is being performed. That might seem an imperfection in this art in comparison with the other arts whose works continually exist because they have their continuance in the sensuous. But this is not so. It is indeed a demonstration that it is a higher, a more spiritual art.

Now, if I start with language in order, by a movement through it to sound out music, as it were, the matter looks something like this. If I assume that prose is the language form that is most remote from music, I already detect in the oration, in the sonorous construction of its periods, an echo of the musical, which emerges ever more strongly at various stages in the poetic declamation, in the metrical construction, in the rhyme, until finally the musical element has developed so strongly that language leaves off and everything becomes music. Indeed, this is a pet phrase poets use to indicate that they, as it were, abandon the idea; it disappears for them, and everything ends in music. This might seem to imply that music is even closer to perfection as a medium than language. But this is one of those sentimental misconceptions that sprout only in empty heads. That it is a misconception will be pointed out later. Here I wish only to draw attention to the remarkable circumstance that by a movement in the opposite direction I once again encounter music, namely, when I descend from prose permeated by the concept until I end up with interjections, which in turn are musical, just as a child's first babbling is musical. Here the point certainly cannot be that music is closer to perfection as a medium than language, or that music is a richer medium than language, unless it is assumed that saying "Uh" is more valuable than a complete thought. But what does this mean—that where language leaves off I find the musical? This indeed expresses perfectly that language is bounded by music on all sides.

I
51

From this we also see the connection with that misconception that music
is supposed to be a richer medium that language. In other words, when language leaves off, music begins; when, as is said, everything is musical, one is
not progressing but retrogressing. This is why—and perhaps the experts will
agree with me on this—I have never had any sympathy for the sublimated
music that thinks it does not need words. Ordinarily, it thinks itself superior
to words, although it is inferior. The objection presumably could be made
that if it is true that language is a richer medium than music, then it is incomprehensible that an esthetic analysis of the musical involves such great
difficulty, incomprehensible that here language continually shows itself to be
a poorer medium than music. But this is neither incomprehensible nor unexplainable. Music always expresses the immediate in its immediacy. This is
also the reason that in relation to language music appears first and last, but
this also shows that it is a mistake to say that music is closer to perfection as
a medium. Reflection is implicit in language, and therefore language cannot
express the immediate. Reflection is fatal to the immediate, and therefore it
is impossible for language to express the musical, but this apparent poverty
in language is precisely its wealth. In other words, the immediate is the in-
determinate, and therefore language cannot grasp it; but its indeterminacy is
not its perfection but rather a defect in it. We indirectly acknowledge this in
many ways. For example, we say: I cannot really explain why I do this or that
in such a way—I play it by ear. For something that has no connection with
the musical, we often use a phrase taken from music but denote thereby the
vague, the unexplained, the immediate.

Now, if it is the immediate, qualified by spirit, that receives its proper expression in the musical, the question may be raised again more pointedly:
What kind of immediacy is it that is essentially the theme of music? The immediate, qualified by spirit, can be qualified in such a way that it either comes
within the realm of spirit or is outside the realm of spirit. When the immediate, qualified by spirit, is qualified in such a way that it falls within the realm
of spirit, it can certainly find its expression in the musical, but this immediacy still cannot be music's absolute theme, for when it is qualified in such a
way that it will fall within the realm of spirit, this suggests that music is in
alien territory; it forms a prelude that is continually being annulled. But if
the immediate, qualified by spirit, is qualified in such a way that it is outside
the realm of spirit, then music has in this its absolute theme. For the former
immediacy, it is unessential for it to be expressed in music, whereas it is essential for it to become spirit and consequently to be expressed in language.
For the latter, however, it is essential that it be expressed in music; it can be
expressed only therein and cannot be expressed in language, since it is qualified by spirit in such a way that it does not come within the realm of spirit
and thus is outside the realm of language. But the immediacy that is thus excluded by spirit is sensuous immediacy. This is linked to Christianity. Sensu-

ous immediacy has its absolute medium in music, and this also explains why music in the ancient world did not become properly developed but is linked to the Christian world. So it is the medium for the immediacy that, quali-fied by spirit, is qualified in such a way that it is outside the realm of spirit. Of course, music can express many other things, but this is its absolute theme. It is also easy to discern that music is a more sensuous medium than language, inasmuch as considerably more emphasis is placed on the sensuous sound in music than in language.

Consequently, sensuousness in its elemental originality is the absolute theme of music. The sensuous in its essential nature is absolutely lyrical, and in music it erupts in all its lyrical impatience. That is, it is qualified by spirit and therefore is power, life, movement, continual unrest, continual succes-sion. But this unrest, this succession, does not enrich it; it continually remains the same; it does not unfold but incessantly rushes forward as if in a single breath. If I were to describe this lyricism with a single predicate, I would have to say: It sounds—and with this I come back again to the elemental originality of the sensuous as that which in its immediacy manifests itself musically.

I
56
    The difficulties that always arise when music is made the object of esthetic consideration will of course not be absent here either. The chief difficulty in the foregoing was that, whereas I wanted to demonstrate by way of thought that the elemental originality of the sensuous is music's essential theme, this still can be demonstrated properly only by music, just as I myself also came to a knowledge of it through music. The difficulty with which the subsequent discussion must struggle is more particularly this: since that which music expresses, the theme under discussion here, is essentially the proper theme of music, music expresses it much better than language is capable of doing, which shows up very poorly alongside it. Indeed, if I were dealing with the different levels of consciousness, the advantage naturally would be on my side and on the side of language, but that is not the case here. Con-sequently, what will be developed here can have meaning only for the per-son who has heard and continually keeps on listening. For him it perhaps may contain a particular hint that can prompt him to listen again.

ROTATION OF CROPS
A VENTURE IN A THEORY
OF SOCIAL PRUDENCE

I
257
People with experience maintain that proceeding from a basic principle is supposed to be very reasonable; I yield to them and proceed from the basic principle that all people are boring. Or is there anyone who would be bor-ing enough to contradict me in this regard? This basic principle has to the highest degree the repelling force always required in the negative, which is

actually the principle of motion. It is not merely repelling but infinitely repulsive, and whoever has the basic principle behind him must necessarily have infinite momentum for making discoveries. If, then, my thesis is true, a person needs only to ponder how corrupting boredom is for people, tempering his reflections more or less according to his desire to diminish or increase his *impetus,* and if he wants to press the speed of the motion to the highest point, almost with danger to the locomotive, he needs only to say to himself: Boredom is the root of all evil. It is very curious that boredom, which itself has such a calm and sedate nature, can have such a capacity to initiate motion. The effect that boredom brings about is absolutely magical, but this effect is one not of attraction but of repulsion.

How corrupting boredom is, everyone recognizes also with regard to children. As long as children are having a good time, they are always good. This can be said in the strictest sense, for if they at times become unmanageable even while playing, it is really because they are beginning to be bored; boredom is already coming on, but in a different way. Therefore, when selecting a nursemaid, one always considers essentially not only that she is sober, trustworthy, and good-natured but also takes into esthetic consideration whether she knows how to entertain children. Even if she had all the other excellent virtues, one would not hesitate to give her the sack if she lacked this qualification. Here, indeed, the principle is clearly acknowledged, but things go on so curiously in the world, habit and boredom have gained the upper hand to such a degree, that justice is done to esthetics only in the conduct of the nursemaid. It would be quite impossible to prevail if one wanted to demand a divorce because one's wife is boring, or demand that a king be dethroned because he is boring to behold, or that a clergyman be exiled because he is boring to listen to, or that a cabinet minister be dismissed or a journalist be executed because he is frightfully boring.

I
258

Since boredom advances and boredom is the root of all evil, no wonder, then, that the world goes backwards, that evil spreads. This can be traced back to the very beginning of the world. The gods were bored; therefore they created human beings. Adam was bored because he was alone; therefore Eve was created. Since that moment, boredom entered the world and grew in quantity in exact proportion to the growth of population. Adam was bored alone; then Adam and Eve were bored together; then Adam and Eve and Cain and Abel were bored *en famille.* After that, the population of the world increased and the nations were bored *en masse.* To amuse themselves, they hit upon the notion of building a tower so high that it would reach the sky. This notion is just as boring as the tower was high and is a terrible demonstration of how boredom had gained the upper hand. Then they were dispersed around the world, just as people now travel abroad, but they continued to be bored. And what consequences this boredom had: humankind stood tall and fell far, first through Eve, then from the Babylonian tower.

On the other hand, what was it that delayed the fall of Rome? It was *panis* [bread] and *circenses* [games]. What is being done in our day? Is consideration being given to any means of amusement? On the contrary, our doom is being expedited. There is the idea of convening a consultative assembly. Can anything more boring be imagined, both for the honorable delegates as well as for one who will read and hear about them? The country's financial situation is to be improved by economizing. Can anything more boring be imagined? Instead of increasing the debt, they want to pay it off in installments. From what I know about the political situation, it would be easy for Denmark to borrow fifteen million rix-dollars. Why does no one think of this? Now and then we hear that someone is a genius and does not pay his debts; why should a nation not do the same, provided there is agreement? Borrow fifteen million; use it not to pay off our debts but for public entertainment. Let us celebrate the millennium with fun and games. Just as there currently are boxes everywhere for contributions of money, there should be bowls everywhere filled with money. Everything would be free: the theater would be free, prostitutes would be free, rides to Deer Park would be free, funerals would be free, one's funeral eulogy would be free. I say "free," for if money is always available, everything is free in a way.

No one would be allowed to own any property. An exception should be made only for me. I shall set aside for myself one hundred rix-dollars a day deposited in a London bank, partly because I cannot manage on less, partly because I am the one who provided the idea, and finally because no one knows if I will not be able to think up a new idea when the fifteen million is exhausted.

What would be the result of this prosperity? All the great would stream to Copenhagen: the greatest artists, actors, and dancers. Copenhagen would become another Athens. What would be the result? All the wealthy would settle in this city. Among others, the emperor of Persia and the king of England would undoubtedly also come here. Here is my second idea: kidnap the emperor. Someone may say that then there would be a revolution in Persia, a new emperor placed on the throne—it has frequently happened before— and the price of the old emperor would slump. In that case, my idea is that we should sell him to the Turks. They will undoubtedly know how to make money out of him.

In addition, there is yet another circumstance that our politicians seem to ignore entirely. Denmark holds the balance of power in Europe. A more propitious position is inconceivable. This I know from my own experience. I once held the balance of power in a family. I could do as I wished. I never suffered, but the others always did.

O may my words penetrate your ears, you who are in high places to counsel and control, you king's men and men of the people, you wise and sensible citizens of all classes! You just watch out! Old Denmark is foundering—

it is a matter of life and death; it is foundering on boredom, which is the most fatal of all. In olden days, whoever eulogized the deceased most handsomely became the king. In our age, the king ought to be the one who delivers the best witticism and the crown prince the one who provides the occasion for the best witticism.

But how you do carry me away, beautiful stirring enthusiasm! Should I raise my voice this way in order to address my contemporaries, to initiate them into my wisdom? Not at all, for my wisdom is really not *zum Gebrauch für Jedermann* [for use by everyone], and it is always most prudent to be silent about rules of prudence. Therefore, I want no followers, but if someone were standing beside my deathbed and if I were sure it was all over for me, then in a fit of philanthropic delirium I might whisper my doctrine into his ear, not quite sure whether I would have done him a favor or not. There is so much talk about man's being a social animal, but basically he is a beast of prey, something that can be ascertained not only by looking at his teeth. Therefore, all this chatter about sociality and community is partly inherited hypocrisy and partly studied perfidy.

All human beings, then, are boring. The very word indicates the possibility of a classification. The word "boring" can designate just as well a person who bores others as someone who bores himself. Those who bore others are the plebians, the crowd, the endless train of humanity in general; those who bore themselves are the chosen ones, the nobility. How remarkable it is that those who do not bore themselves generally bore others; those, however, who bore themselves entertain others. Generally, those who do not bore themselves are busy in the world in one way or another, but for that very reason they are, of all people, the most boring of all, the most unbearable. Certainly this class of animals is not the fruit of man's appetite and woman's desire. Like all lower classes of animals, it is distinguished by a high level of fecundity and propagates beyond belief. It is incomprehensible, too, that nature should need nine months to produce such creatures, which presumably could rather be produced by the score. The other class of human beings, the superior ones, are those who bore themselves. As noted above, they generally amuse others—at times in a certain external way the masses, in a deeper sense their co-initiates. The more thoroughly they bore themselves, the more potent the medium of diversion they offer others, also when the boredom reaches its maximum, since they either die of boredom (the passive category) or shoot themselves out of curiosity (the active category).

Idleness, we are accustomed to say, is the root of all evil. To prevent this evil, work is recommended. But it is just as easy to see from the dreaded occasion as from the recommended remedy that this whole view is of very plebian extraction. Idleness as such is by no means a root of evil; on the contrary, it is a truly divine life, if one is not bored. To be sure, idleness may be the occasion of losing one's property etc., but the noble nature does not fear such things but does indeed fear being bored. The Olympian gods were not bored; happy they lived in happy idleness. A female beauty who neither sews nor spins nor irons nor reads nor plays an instrument is happy in idleness, for she is not bored. Idleness, then, is so far from being the root of evil that it is rather the true good. Boredom is the root of evil; it is that which must be held off. Idleness is not the evil; indeed, it may be said that everyone who lacks a sense for it thereby shows that he has not raised himself to the human level. There is an indefatigable activity that shuts a person out of the world of spirit and places him in a class with the animals, which instinctively must always be in motion. There are people who have an extraordinary talent for transforming everything into a business operation, whose whole life is a business operation, who fall in love and are married, hear a joke, and admire a work of art with the same businesslike zeal with which they work at the office. The Latin proverb *otium est pulvinar diaboli* [idleness is the devil's pillow] is quite correct, but the devil does not find time to lay his head on this pillow if one is not bored. But since people believe that it is man's destiny to work, the antithesis idleness/work is correct. I assume that it is man's destiny to amuse himself, and therefore my antithesis is no less correct.

Boredom is the demonic pantheism. It becomes evil itself if one continues in it as such; as soon as it is annulled, however, it is the true pantheism. But it is annulled only by amusing oneself—*ergo,* one ought to amuse oneself. To say that it is annulled by working betrays a lack of clarity, for idleness can certainly be canceled by work, since this is its opposite, but boredom cannot, as is seen in the fact that the busiest workers of all, those whirring insects with their bustling buzzing, are the most boring of all, and if they are not bored, it is because they do not know what boredom is—but then the boredom is not annulled.

Boredom is partly an immediate genius, partly an acquired immediacy. On the whole, the English nation is the model nation. The true genius of indolence is seldom encountered; it is not found in nature; it belongs to the world of spirit. At times one meets an English tourist who is an incarnation of this genius, a heavy, inert woodchuck whose total resource of language consists of a single monosyllable, an interjection with which he indicates his highest admiration and his deepest indifference, for admiration and indifference have become undifferentiated in the unity of boredom. No nation other than the English produces such oddities of nature; every individual belonging to another nation will always be a bit more lively, not so altogether stillborn. The only analogy I know is the apostle of empty enthusiasm, who likewise travels through life on an interjection, people who make a profession of being enthusiastic everywhere, who are present everywhere and, no matter whether what happens is something significant or insignificant, shout: Oh! or Ah! because the difference between what is important and unimportant is undifferentiated in the emptiness of blind, clamorous enthusiasm.

The boredom that comes later is usually a fruit of a misguided diversion. It seems doubtful that a remedy against boredom can give rise to boredom, but it can give rise to boredom only insofar as it is used incorrectly. A mistaken, generally eccentric diversion has boredom within itself, and thus it works its way up and manifests itself as immediacy. Just as a distinction is made between blind staggers and mad staggers in horses, but both kinds are called staggers, so also a distinction can be made between two kinds of boredom that nevertheless are both joined in the category of boredom.

Pantheism ordinarily implies the qualification of fullness; with boredom it is the reverse: it is built upon emptiness, but for this very reason it is a pantheistic qualification. Boredom rests upon the nothing that interlaces existence [*Tilværelsen*]; its dizziness is infinite, like that which comes from looking down into a bottomless abyss. That the eccentric diversion is based upon boredom is seen also in the fact that the diversion sounds without resonance, simply because in nothing there is not even enough to make an echo possible.

Now, if boredom, as discussed above, is the root of all evil, what then is more natural than to seek to conquer it? But here, as everywhere, it is primarily a matter of calm deliberation, lest, demonically possessed by boredom in an attempt to escape it, one works one's way into it. All who are bored cry out for change. In this, I totally agree with them, except that it is a question of acting according to principle.

My deviation from popular opinion is adequately expressed by the phrase "rotation of crops." There might seem to be an ambiguity in this phrase, and if I were to find room in this phrase for a designation of the ordinary method I would have to say that rotation of crops consists in continually changing the soil. But the farmer does not use the expression in this way. For a moment, however, I will use it in this way to discuss the rotation of crops that depends upon the boundless infinity of change, its extensive dimension.

This rotation of crops is the vulgar, inartistic rotation and is based on an illusion. One is weary of living in the country and moves to the city; one is weary of one's native land and goes abroad; one is *europamüde* [weary of Europe] and goes to America etc.; one indulges in the fanatical hope of an endless journey from star to star. Or there is another direction, but still extensive. One is weary of eating on porcelain and eats on silver; wearying of that, one eats on gold; one burns down half of Rome in order to visualize the Trojan conflagration. This method cancels itself and is the spurious infinity. What, after all, did Nero achieve? No, then the emperor Antoninus was wiser; he says: ἀναβιῶναί σοι ἔξεστιν ἴδε πάλιν τὰ πράγματα, ὡς ἑώρας· ἐν τούτῳ γὰρ τὸ ἀναβιῶναι (Βιβλιον Ζ., 6.) [You can begin a new life. Only see things afresh as you used to see them. In this consists the new life (Book VII, 2)].[14]

The method I propose does not consist in changing the soil but, like proper crop rotation, consists in changing the method of cultivation and the kinds of crops. Here at once is the principle of limitation, the sole saving principle in the world. The more a person limits himself, the more resourceful he becomes. A solitary prisoner for life is extremely resourceful; to him a spider can be a source of great amusement. Think of our school days; we were at an age when there was no esthetic consideration in the choosing of our teachers, and therefore they were often very boring—how resourceful we were then! What fun we had catching a fly, keeping it prisoner under a nutshell, and watching it run around with it! What delight in cutting a hole in the desk, confining a fly in it, and peeking at it through a piece of paper! How entertaining it can be to listen to the monotonous dripping from the roof! What a meticulous observer one becomes, detecting every little sound or movement. Here is the extreme boundary of that principle that seeks relief not through extensity but through intensity.

The more resourceful one can be in changing the method of cultivation, the better, but every particular change still falls under the universal rule of the relation between *recollecting* and *forgetting.* It is in these two currents that all life moves, and therefore it is a matter of having them properly under one's control. Not until hope has been thrown overboard does one begin to live artistically; as long as a person hopes, he cannot limit himself. It is indeed beautiful to see a person put out to sea with the fair wind of hope; one may utilize the chance to let oneself be towed along, but one ought never have it on board one's craft, least of all as pilot, for it is an untrustworthy shipmaster. For this reason, too, hope was one of Prometheus's dubious gifts; instead of giving human beings the foreknowledge of the immortals, he gave them hope.

To forget—this is the desire of all people, and when they encounter something unpleasant, they always say: If only I could forget! But to forget is an art that must be practiced in advance. To be able to forget always depends upon how one remembers, but how one remembers depends upon how one experiences actuality. The person who runs aground with the speed of hope will recollect in such a way that he will be unable to forget. Thus *nil admirari* [marvel at nothing] is the proper wisdom of life. No part of life ought to have so much meaning for a person that he cannot forget it any moment he wants to; on the other hand, every single part of life ought to have so much meaning for a person that he can remember it at any moment. The age that remembers best is also the most forgetful: namely, childhood. The more poetically one remembers, the more easily one forgets, for to remember poetically is actually only an expression for forgetting. When I remember poetically, my experience has already undergone the change of having lost everything painful. In order to be able to recollect in this way, one must be very much aware of how one lives, especially of how one enjoys. If one enjoys indiscriminately to the very end, if one continually takes the utmost that enjoyment can give, one will be unable either to recollect or to forget. That is, one has nothing else to recollect than a satiation that one only wishes to forget but that now torments with an involuntary recollection. Therefore, if a person notices that enjoyment or a part of life is carrying him away too forcefully, he stops for a moment and recollects. There is no better way to give a distaste for going on too long. From the beginning, one curbs the enjoyment and does not hoist full sail for any decision; one indulges with a certain mistrust. Only then is it possible to give the lie to the proverb that says that one cannot eat one's cake and have it, too. It is true that the police forbid carrying secret weapons, and yet there is no weapon as dangerous as the art of being able to recollect. It is a singular feeling when in the midst of enjoyment one looks at it in order to recollect it.

When an individual has perfected himself in the art of forgetting and the art of recollecting in this way, he is then able to play shuttlecock with all existence.

A person's resiliency can actually be measured by his power to forget. He who cannot forget will never amount to much. Whether or not a Lethe[15] wells up anywhere, I do not know, but this I do know—that this art can be developed. But it by no means consists in the traceless disappearance of the particular impression, because forgetfulness is not identical with the art of being able to forget. What little understanding people generally have of this art is readily seen, for they usually want to forget only the unpleasant, not the pleasant. This betrays a total one-sidedness. Indeed, forgetting is the right expression for the proper assimilation that reduces experience to a sounding board. The reason nature is so great is that it has forgotten that it was chaos, but this thought can appear at any time. Since forgetting is usually thought of in relation to the unpleasant, it is generally conceived of as a wild force that stifles. But forgetting, on the contrary, is a quiet pursuit, and it ought to be related to the pleasant just as much as to the unpleasant. Furthermore, the pleasant as a bygone, specifically as a bygone, has an intrinsic unpleasantness with which it can awaken a sense of loss; this unpleasantness is canceled by forgetting. The unpleasant has a sting—everyone admits that. This, too, is removed by forgetting. But if one behaves as many do who dabble in the art of forgetting, who brush the unpleasant away entirely, one will soon see what good that is. In an unguarded moment, it often surprises a person with the full force of the sudden. This is completely at odds with the well-ordered pattern in an intelligent head. No misfortune, no adversity is so unfriendly, so deaf that it cannot be flattered a little; even Cerberus[16] accepted honey cakes, and it is not only young maidens one beguiles. One talks around it and thereby deprives it of its sharpness and by no means wishes to forget it—but forgets it in order to recollect it. Indeed, even with reminiscences of such a kind that one would think eternal forgetfulness would be the only means against them, one allows oneself such cunning, and the fakery is successful for the adept. Forgetting is the scissors with which one snips away what cannot be used, but, please note, under the maximal supervision of recollection.

I
266

In this way, forgetting and recollecting are identical, and the artistically achieved identity is the Archimedean point with which one lifts the whole world.[17] When we speak of writing something in the book of oblivion, we are indeed suggesting that it is forgotten and yet at the same time is preserved.

I
267

The art of recollecting and forgetting will also prevent a person from foundering in any particular relationship in life—and assures him complete suspension.

Guard, then, against *friendship.* How is a *friend* defined? A friend is not what philosophy calls the necessary other but the superfluous third. What are the rituals of friendship? One drinks *dus;*[18] one opens an artery, mingles one's blood with the friend's. Just when this moment arrives is difficult to determine, but it proclaims itself in a mysterious way; one feels it and can no longer say *De* to the other. Once this feeling is present, it can never turn out that one has made a mistake such as Gert Westphaler made when he drank *dus* with the executioner.—What are the sure signs of friendship? Antiquity answers: *idem velle, idem nolle, ea demum firma amicitia* [agreement in likes and dislikes, this and this only is what constitutes true friendship]—and is also extremely boring. What is the meaning of friendship? Mutual assistance with counsel and action. Two friends form a close alliance in order to be everything to each other, even though no human being can be anything for another human being except to be in his way. Well, we can help each other with money, help each other into and out of our coats, be each other's humble servants, gather for a sincere New Year's congratulation, also for weddings, births, and funerals.

But just because one stays clear of friendship, one will not for that reason live without contact with people. On the contrary, these relationships can take a deeper turn now and then, provided that one always—even though keeping the same pace for a time—has enough reserve speed to run away from them. It may be thought that such conduct leaves unpleasant recollections, that the unpleasantness consists in the diminishing of a relationship from having been something to being nothing. This, however, is a misunderstanding. The unpleasantness is indeed a piquant ingredient in the perverseness of life. Moreover, the same relationship can regain significance in another way. One should be careful never to run aground and to that end always to have forgetting in mind. The experienced farmer lets his land lie fallow now and then; the theory of social prudence recommends the same thing. Everything will surely come again but in a different way; what has once been taken into the rotation process remains there but is varied by the method of cultivation.

I
268

Therefore, one quite consistently hopes to meet one's old friends and acquaintances in a better world but does not share the crowd's fear that they may have changed so much that one could not recognize them again. One fears, instead, that they may be altogether unchanged. It is unbelievable what even the most insignificant person can gain by such sensible cultivation.

Never become involved in *marriage*. Married people pledge love for each other throughout eternity. Well, now, that is easy enough but does not mean very much, for if one is finished with time one is probably finished with eternity. If, instead of saying "throughout eternity," the couple would say "until Easter, until next May Day," then what they say would make some sense, for then they would be saying something and also something they perhaps could carry out. What happens in marriage? First, one of them detects after a short time that something is wrong, and then the other one complains and screams: Faithlessness! Faithlessness! After a while, the other one comes to the same conclusion and a state of neutrality is inaugurated through a balancing of accounts by mutual faithlessness, to their common satisfaction and gratification. But it is too late now, anyway, because a divorce involves all kinds of huge problems.

Since marriage is like that, it is not strange that attempts are made in many ways to shore it up with moral props. If a man wants to be separated from his wife, the cry goes up: He is a mean fellow, a scoundrel, etc. How ridiculous, and what an indirect assault upon marriage! Either marriage has intrinsic reality [*Realitet*], and then he is adequately punished by losing it, or it has no reality, and then it is unreasonable to vilify him because he is wiser than others. If someone became weary of his money and threw it out the window, no one would say he is a mean fellow, for either money has reality, and then he is adequately punished by not having it anymore, or it has no reality, and then, of course, he is indeed wise.

One must always guard against contracting a life relationship by which one can become many. That is why even friendship is dangerous, marriage even more so. They do say that marriage partners become one, but this is very obscure and mysterious talk. If an individual is many, he has lost his freedom and cannot order his riding boots when he wishes, cannot knock about according to whim. If he has a wife, it is difficult; if he has a wife and perhaps children, it is formidable; if he has a wife and children, it is impossible. Admittedly, there is the example of a gypsy woman who carried her husband on her back throughout life, but for one thing this is a great rarity and, for another, it is very tiring in the long run—for the husband. Moreover, through marriage one falls into a very deadly continuity with custom, and custom is like the wind and weather, something completely indeterminable. To the best of my knowledge, it is the custom in Japan for the husbands also to be confined during childbirth. Perhaps the time is coming when Europe will import the customs of foreign lands.

Even friendship is dangerous; marriage is still more dangerous, for the woman is and will be the man's ruination as soon as he contracts a continuing relationship with her. Take a young man, spirited as an Arabian horse; let him marry and he is lost. At the outset, the woman is proud, then she is weak, then she swoons, then he swoons, then the whole family swoons. A woman's love is only pretense and weakness.

I
269

Just because one does not become involved in marriage, one's life need not for that reason be devoid of the erotic. The erotic, too, ought to have infinity—but a poetic infinity that can just as well be limited to one hour as to a month. When two people fall in love with each other and sense that they are destined for each other, it is a question of having the courage to break it off, for by continuing there is only everything to lose, nothing to gain. It seems to be a paradox, and indeed it is, for the feelings, not for the understanding. In this domain it is primarily a matter of being able to use moods; if a person can do that, an inexhaustible variation of combinations can be achieved.

Never take any *official post*. If one does that, one becomes just a plain John Anyman, a tiny little cog in the machine of the body politic. The individual ceases to be himself the manager of the operation, and the theories can be of little help. One acquires a title, and implicit in that are all the consequences of sin and evil. The law under which one slaves is equally boring no matter whether advancement is swift or slow. A title can never be disposed of; it would take a criminal act for that, which would incur a public whipping, and even then one cannot be sure of not being pardoned by royal decree and acquiring the title again.

Even though one stays clear of official posts, one should nevertheless not be inactive but attach great importance to all the pursuits that are compatible with aimlessness; all kinds of unprofitable pursuits may be carried on. Yet in this regard one ought to develop not so much extensively as intensively and, although mature in years, demonstrate the validity of the old saying: It doesn't take much to amuse a child.

Just as one varies the soil somewhat, in accordance with the theory of social prudence (for if one were to live in relation to only one person, rotation of crops would turn out badly, as would be the case if a farmer had only one acre of land and therefore could never let it lie fallow, something that is extremely important), so also must one continually vary oneself, and this is the real secret. To that end, it is essential to have control over one's moods. To have them under control in the sense that one can produce them at will is an impossibility, but prudence teaches us to utilize the moment. Just as an experienced sailor always scans the sea and detects a squall far in advance, so one should always detect a mood a little in advance. Before entering into a mood, one should know its effect on oneself and its probable effect on others. The first strokes are for the purpose of evoking pure tones and seeing what is inside a person; later come the intermediate tones. The more practice one has, the more one is convinced that there is often much in a person that was never imagined. When sentimental people, who as such are very boring, become peevish, they are often amusing. Teasing in particular is an excellent means of exploration.

Arbitrariness is the whole secret. It is popularly believed that there is no

I
270

art to being arbitrary, and yet it takes profound study to be arbitrary in such a way that a person does not himself run wild in it but himself has pleasure from it. One does not enjoy the immediate object but something else that one arbitrarily introduces. One sees the middle of a play; one reads the third section of a book. One thereby has enjoyment quite different from what the author so kindly intended. One enjoys something totally accidental; one considers the whole of existence [*Tilværelse*] from this standpoint; one lets its reality run aground on this. I shall give an example. There was a man whose chatter I was obliged to listen to because of the circumstances. On every occasion, he was ready with a little philosophical lecture that was extremely boring. On the verge of despair, I suddenly discovered that the man perspired exceptionally much when he spoke. This perspiration now absorbed my attention. I watched how the pearls of perspiration collected on his forehead, then united in a rivulet, slid down his nose, and ended in a quivering glob- ule that remained suspended at the end of his nose. From that moment on, everything was changed; I could even have the delight of encouraging him to commence his philosophical instruction just in order to watch the perspiration on his brow and on his nose.

I
271

Baggesen tells somewhere that a certain man is no doubt a very honest fellow but that he has one thing against him: nothing rhymes with his name. It is very advantageous to let the realities of life be undifferentiated in an arbitrary interest like that. Something accidental is made into the absolute and as such into an object of absolute admiration. This is especially effective when the feelings are in motion. For many people, this method is an excellent means of stimulation. Everything in life is regarded as a wager etc. The more consistently a person knows how to sustain his arbitrariness, the more amusing the combinations become. The degree of consistency always makes manifest whether a person is an artist or a bungler, for up to a point everyone does the same. The eye with which one sees actuality must be changed continually. The Neoplatonists assumed that people who fell short of perfection on earth became after death more or less perfect animals according to their merits; those who, for example, had practiced social virtues on a minor scale (punctilious people) turned into social creatures—for example, bees. Such a view of life, which here in this world sees all human beings transformed into animals or plants (Plotinus also believed this—that some were changed into plants) offers a rich multiplicity of variation. The artist Tischbein[19] has attempted to idealize every human being as an animal. His method has the defect that it is too serious and tries to discover an actual resemblance.

The accidental outside a person corresponds to the arbitrariness within him. Therefore he always ought to have his eyes open for the accidental, always ought to be *expeditus* [ready] if something should come up. The so- called social pleasures for which we prepare ourselves a week or a fortnight in advance are of little significance, whereas even the most insignificant thing

I
272

can accidentally become a rich material for amusement. To go into detail here is not feasible—no theory can reach that far. Even the most elaborate theory is merely poverty compared with what genius in its ubiquity easily discovers.

THE SEDUCER'S DIARY

I
276

In itself, the title of the book did not startle me. I took it to be a collection of excerpts, which to me seemed quite natural, since I knew that he had always taken to his studies with zeal. But it contained something altogether different. It was neither more nor less than a diary, painstakingly kept. On the basis of my former acquaintance with him, I did not consider that his life was in great need of a commentary, but according to the insight I now had, I do not deny that the title was chosen with great discernment and much understanding, with truly esthetic, objective mastery of himself and of the situation. The title is in perfect harmony with the entire contents. His life has been an attempt to accomplish the task of living poetically. With a sharply developed organ for discovering the interesting in life, he has known how to find it and after having found it has continually reproduced his experiences

I
277

half poetically. Therefore, his diary is not historically accurate or strictly narrative; it is not indicative but subjunctive. Although his experiences were of course recorded after they were experienced, sometimes perhaps even a long time afterward, they nevertheless are frequently described as if they were taking place right now and with such dramatic vividness that it sometimes seems as if everything were taking place before one's eyes. It is highly improbable that he did this because he had some other purpose with this diary; it is obvious that in the strictest sense it had only personal importance for him, and to assume that I have before me a poetic work, perhaps even intended for publication, is excluded by the whole as well as by its parts. It is true that he would not need to fear anything personally in publishing it, for most of the names are so odd that it is altogether improbable that they are historical. My only suspicion has been that the first name is historically accurate, and in this way he has always been sure of identifying the actual person, whereas every interloper would be misled by the family name. At least this is the case with the girl I knew, Cordelia, on whom the main interest centers; she was very correctly named Cordelia but not, however, Wahl.

How then can it be explained that the diary nevertheless has taken on such a poetic tinge? The answer to this is not difficult; it is easily explained by his poetic nature, which is not abundant enough or, if you please, not deficient enough to separate poetry and actuality from each other. The poetic was the plus he himself brought along. This plus was the poetic he enjoyed in the poetic situation of actuality; this he recaptured in the form of poetic reflection. This was the second enjoyment, and his whole life was intended for enjoyment. In the first case, he personally enjoyed the esthetic; in the second case, he esthetically enjoyed his personality. The point in the first case was that he egotistically enjoyed personally that which in part actuality has given to him and which in part he himself had used to fertilize actuality; in the second case, his personality was volatilized, and he then enjoyed the situation and himself in the situation. In the first case, he continually needed actuality as the occasion, as an element; in the second case, actuality was drowned in the poetic. Thus, the fruit of the first stage was the mood from which the diary emerged as the fruit of the second stage, with these words taken in a somewhat different sense in the second case than in the first. In this way he has continually possessed the poetic through the ambiguity in which his life elapsed.

My Cordelia,   I
      I am in love with myself, people say of me. That does not surprise me, for   371
how would it be possible for them to see that I can love, since I love only
you? How could anyone else suspect it, since I love only you? I am in love   I
with myself. And why? Because I am in love with you; for you I love and   372
you alone and everything that truly belongs to you, and thus I love myself
because this self of mine belongs to you, so that if I stopped loving you, I
would stop loving myself. Therefore, what is an expression of the utmost
egotism in the world's profane eyes is in your initiated eyes an expression of
the purest sympathy; what is an expression of the most prosaic self-preserva-
tion in the world's profane eyes is in your sanctified sight an expression of
most inspired self-annihilation.

YOUR JOHANNES

      An ancient philosopher has said that if a person carefully chronicles all his   I
experiences, he is, before he knows where he is, a philosopher.[20] For a long   383
time now, I have lived in association with the fellowship of the engaged. Such
a connection certainly ought to yield some harvest. I have thought of gathering material for a book titled: *A Contribution to a Theory of the Kiss,* dedicated to all doting lovers. Incidentally, it is curious that there is no book on
this topic. If I manage to finish it, I shall also fill a long-felt need. Can the
reason for this deficiency in the literature be that philosophers do not think
about such things or that they do not understand them?—I am already in a
position to offer some hints. A perfect kiss requires that the agents be a girl
and a man. A man-to-man kiss is in bad taste, or, worse yet, it tastes bad.—
In the next place, it is my opinion that a kiss comes closer to the idea when
a man kisses a girl than when a girl kisses a man. When over the years the
distinction has been lost in this relationship, the kiss has lost its meaning. That
is the case with the conjugal domestic kiss, by which husband and wife, for

want of a napkin, wipe each other's mouth while saying "May it do us good [*Velbekom's*]."

If the age gap is very great, the kiss lies outside the idea. I recall a special expression used by the senior class of an outlying girls' school—"to kiss the councilor"—an expression with anything but agreeable connotations. It began this way. The teacher had a brother-in-law living in the house. He was an elderly man, formerly a councilor, and because of his age he took the liberty of kissing the young girls.

The kiss must be the expression of a particular passion. When a brother and sister who are twins kiss each other, it is not an authentic kiss. The same holds for a kiss paid in Christmas games, also for a stolen kiss. A kiss is a symbolic act that is meaningless if devoid of the feeling it is supposed to signify, and this feeling can be present only under specific conditions.

If one wants to try to classify kisses, numerous possible principles of classification come to mind. The kiss can be classified according to sound. Unfortunately, language does not have an adequate range for my observations. I do not believe all the languages of the world have the stock of onomatopoeia necessary to designate the variations I have come across just in my uncle's house. Sometimes it is a smacking sound, sometimes whistling, sometimes slushy, sometimes explosive, sometimes booming, sometimes full, sometimes hollow, sometimes like calico, etc. etc.

The kiss can be classified according to touch—the tangential kiss, the kiss *en passant,* and the clinging kiss.

The kiss can be classified according to time as short or long. In the category of time, there is another classification, really the only one I like. A distinction is made between the first kiss and all the others. What is under consideration here cannot be used as the measure of what appears in the other classification—it has nothing to do with sound, touch, time in general. The first kiss is qualitatively different from all others. Very few people think about this. It would be a shame if there were not even one who thinks about it.

My Cordelia,

A good answer is like a sweet kiss, says Solomon.[21] As you know, I have a weakness for asking questions; I may almost be censured for it. This happens because people do not understand what I am asking about, for you and you alone understand what I am asking about, and you and you alone know how to answer, and you and you alone know how to give a good answer, for, as Solomon says, a good answer is like a sweet kiss.

YOUR JOHANNES

In my relation to Cordelia, have I been continually faithful to my pact? That is, my pact with the esthetic, for it is that which makes me strong—that

I continually have the idea on my side. It is a secret like Samson's hair, one that no Delilah can wrest from me.[22] Plainly and simply to deceive a girl, for that I certainly would not have the stamina; but the fact that the idea is present in motion, that I am acting in its service, that I dedicate myself to its service—this gives me rigorousness toward myself, abstinence from every forbidden pleasure. Has the interesting been preserved at all times? Yes—I dare to say that freely and openly in this secret conversation. The engagement itself was the interesting precisely because it did not yield that which is commonly understood as the interesting. It preserved the interesting precisely through the contradiction between the outward appearance and the inner life. If I had had a secret connection with her, it would have been interesting only to the first power. But this is the interesting raised to the second power, and therefore only then is it the interesting for her. The engagement is broken, but she herself breaks it in order to soar into a higher sphere. So it should be; this is precisely the form of the interesting that will occupy her the most.

September 25   I
412

Why cannot such a night last longer? If Alectryon[23] could forget himself, why cannot the sun be sympathetic enough to do so? But now it is finished, and I never want to see her again. When a girl has given away everything, she is weak, she has lost everything, for in a man innocence is a negative element, but in woman it is the substance of her being. Now all resistance is impossible, and to love is beautiful only as long as resistance is present; as soon as it ceases, to love is weakness and habit. I do not want to be reminded of my relationship with her; she has lost her fragrance, and the times are past when a girl agonizing over her faithless lover is changed into a heliotrope. I shall not bid her farewell; nothing is more revolting than the feminine tears and pleas that alter everything and yet are essentially meaningless. I did love her, but from now on she can no longer occupy my soul. If I were a god, I would do for her what Neptune did for a nymph: transform her into a man.

Yet it would really be worth knowing whether or not one could poetize oneself out of a girl in such a way as to make her so proud that she imagined it was she who was bored with the relationship. It could be a very interesting epilogue, which in and by itself could have psychological interest and besides that furnish one with many erotic observations.

EITHER/OR, A FRAGMENT OF LIFE

(FEBRUARY 20, 1843)

EDITED BY VICTOR EREMITA

PART II CONTAINING THE PAPERS OF B,

LETTERS TO A

The second volume of *Either/Or* consists of two long letters by B, Judge William, to his young friend, whose papers constitute the contents of the first volume. The two letters, titled "The Esthetic Validity of Marriage" and "The Balance between the Esthetic and the Ethical in the Development of the Personality," are a critical analysis of the esthetic life-view of the ironical, witty, disillusioned young man. In contrast to the episodic, momentary, ultimately desperate esthetic life, Judge William advocates the integrated life of ethical reflection, normative judgment, and qualitative resolution, whereby the discontinuous life of immediacy, inclination, and desire is caught up in life as a task oriented to the actualization of the highest good, personal and social. In radically choosing the categories of good and evil, one chooses oneself in one's eternal validity. In despair, to choose to despair, one thereby chooses oneself and the categories of good and evil. The esthetic is that by which one immediately and inclinationally is what one is; the ethical is that whereby one becomes what one becomes. Social morality is temporarily normative but itself is subject to the critique based on the universally human and ultimately a transcendent norm, which is intimated in "*Ultimatum* [A Final Word]" in the form of a sermon sent to Judge William by a rural pastor friend: "The Upbuilding That Lies in the Thought That in Relation to God We Are Always in the Wrong."

THE ESTHETIC VALIDITY OF MARRIAGE

My Friend,

The lines on which your eye falls first were written last. My intention with them is to attempt once again to compress into the form of a letter the extended exploration that is hereby transmitted to you. These lines correspond to the last lines and together form an envelope, and thus in an external way they evince what the internal evidence will in many ways convince you of— that it is a letter you are reading. This thought—that it was a letter I wrote to you—I have been unwilling to give up, partly because my time has not permitted the more painstaking elaboration that a treatise requires, and partly because I am reluctant to miss the opportunity of addressing you in the more admonishing and urgent tone appropriate to the epistolary form. You are all too skilled in the art of talking in generalities about everything without letting yourself be personally involved for me to tempt you by setting your dialectical powers in motion. You know how the prophet Nathan dealt with

King David when he presumed to understand the parable the prophet had told him but was unwilling to understand that it applied to him. Then to make sure, Nathan added: Thou art the man, O King.[24] In the same way I also have continually tried to remind you that you are the one who is being discussed and you are the one who is spoken to.

With respect to individual life, there are two kinds of history—the outer and the inner. It has two currents that flow in opposite directions. The first, in turn, has two sides. The individual does not have that for which he strives, and history is the struggle in which he acquires it. Or the individual has it but nevertheless cannot take possession of it, because there is continually something external that prevents him. History, then, is the struggle in which he overcomes these obstacles. The other kind of history begins with possession, and history is the process by which he acquires it. Since in the first case the history is external and what it strives for lies outside, history does not have true reality [*Realitet*], and the poetic and artistic representation consists altogether properly in foreshortening it and hastening on to the intensive moment.

II 121

To hold to the subject we are most concerned with, let us imagine a romantic love. Imagine, then, a knight who has slain five wild boars, four dwarfs, has freed three princes from a spell, brothers of the princess he adores. To the romantic mentality, this has its perfect reality. But to the artist and poet it is of no importance whatever whether there are five or only four. On the whole, the artist is more limited than the poet, but even the latter has no interest in punctiliously describing what happened in the slaying of each particular wild boar. He hastens on to the moment. Perhaps he curtails the number, focuses the hardships and dangers in poetic intensity, and speeds on to the moment, the moment of possession. To him the entire historical sequence is of minor importance.

II 122

But when it is a matter of inner history, every single little moment is of utmost importance. Inner history is the only true history, but the true history struggles with that which is the life principle in history—with time—but when one struggles with time, the temporal and every single little moment thereby has its great reality. Wherever the individuality's inner blossoming has not yet begun, wherever the individuality is still closed up, it is a matter of outer history. As soon, however, as this bursts into leaf, so to speak, inner history begins.

Think now of our point of departure, the difference between the conquering and the possessing natures. The conquering nature is continually outside itself, the possessing nature is within itself; therefore the first gains an outer history, and the second an inner history. But since outer history can be concentrated without any damage, it is natural for art and poetry to choose it and thus in turn choose for representation the unopened individ-

uality and what pertains to him. To be sure, it is said that love opens the individuality, but not if love is understood as it is in romanticism, since it is
brought only to a point where he is supposed to open, and there it ends, or
he is about to open but is interrupted. But just as outer history and the closed
individuality, if anything, will be the most immediate subject of artistic and
poetic portrayal, so everything that constitutes the content of such an individuality will also be their subject. But all this is basically what belongs to
the natural man.

A few examples. Pride can be portrayed very well, because what is essential in pride is not sequence but intensity in the moment. Humility is
hard to portray precisely because it is sequence, and whereas the observer
needs to see pride only at its climax, in the second case he really needs to
see something that poetry and art cannot provide, to see its continuous coming into existence, for it is essential to humility to come into existence con-
tinuously, and if this is shown to him in its ideal moment, he misses something, for he senses that its true ideality consists not in its being ideal at the
moment but in its being continuous. Romantic love can be portrayed very
well in the moment; marital love cannot, for an ideal husband is not one
who is ideal once in his life but one who is that every day. If I wish to portray a hero who conquers kingdoms and countries, this can be done very
well in the moment, but a cross-bearer who takes up his cross every day can
never be portrayed in either poetry or art, for the point is that he does it
every day. If I imagine a hero who loses his life, this can be concentrated
very well in the moment, but the daily dying cannot, because the point is
that it goes on every day. Courage can be concentrated very well in the moment; patience cannot, precisely because patience contends against time.
You will say that art nevertheless has portrayed Christ as the image of patience, as bearing all the sin of the world, that religious poems have concentrated all the bitterness of life in one cup and had one individual empty
it at one moment. That is true, but that is because they have concentrated
it almost spatially. But anyone who knows anything about patience knows
very well that its real opposite is not intensity of suffering (for then it more
approximates courage) but time, and that true patience [*Taalmod*] is that
which contends against time or is essentially long-suffering [*Langmod*]; but
long-suffering cannot be portrayed artistically, for the point of it is incommensurable with art; neither can it be poetized, for it requires the protrac-
tion of time.

What more I want to say here you may regard as a poor married man's
trivial offering on the altar of esthetics, and if you and all the priests of esthetics disdain it, I certainly know how to console myself, and so much more
so because what I bring is not shew-bread, which only the priests can eat,
but homemade bread, which like all homemade food is plain and unspiced
but healthful and nourishing.

II
123

If one traces dialectically and just as much historically the development of the esthetically beautiful, one will find that the direction of this movement is from spatial categories to temporal categories, and that the perfecting of art is contingent upon the possibility of gradually detaching itself more and more from space and aiming toward time. This constitutes the transition and the significance of the transition from sculpture to painting, as Schelling early pointed out. Music has time as its element but has no continuance in time; its significance is the continual vanishing in time; it sounds in time, but it also fades and has no continuance. Ultimately poetry is the highest of all the arts and therefore also the art that best knows how to affirm the meaning of time. It does not need to limit itself to the moment in the sense that painting does; neither does it disappear without a trace in the sense that music does. But despite all this, it, too, is compelled, as we have seen, to concentrate in the moment. It has, therefore, its limitation and cannot, as shown above, portray that of which the truth is precisely the temporal sequence. And yet this, that time is affirmed, is not a disparagement of the esthetic; on the contrary, the more this occurs, the richer and fuller the esthetic ideal becomes.

II
124

How, then, can the esthetic that is incommensurable even for portrayal in poetry be represented? Answer: by being lived. It thereby has a similarity to music, which is only because it is continually repeated, is only in the moment of being performed. That is why in the foregoing I called attention to the ruinous confusing of the esthetic and that which can be esthetically portrayed in poetic reproduction. Everything I am talking about here certainly can be portrayed esthetically, but not in poetic reproduction, but only by living it, by realizing it in the life of actuality. In this way the esthetic elevates itself and reconciles itself with life, for just as poetry and art in one sense are precisely a reconciliation with life, yet in another sense they are enmity to life, because they reconcile only one side of the soul.

Here I am at the summit of the esthetic. And in truth, he who has humility and courage enough to let himself be esthetically transformed, he who feels himself present as a character in a drama the deity is writing, in which the poet and the prompter are not different persons, in which the individual, as the experienced actor who has lived into his character and his lines is not disturbed by the prompter but feels that he himself wants to say what is being whispered to him, so that it almost becomes a question whether he is putting the words in the prompter's mouth or the prompter in his, he who in the most profound sense feels himself creating and created, who in the moment he feels himself creating has the original pathos of the lines, and in the moment he feels himself created has the erotic ear that picks up every sound—he and he alone has brought into actual existence the highest in esthetics.

II
125

But this history that proves to be incommensurable even for poetry is the

inner history. This has the idea within itself and precisely therefore is the esthetic. Therefore it begins, as I expressed it, with the possession, and its
progress is the acquiring of this possession. It is an eternity in which the temporal has not disappeared as an ideal element, but in which it is continually
present as a real element. Thus, when patience acquires itself in patience, it
is inner history.

Let us now consider the relation between romantic and marital love, for
the relation between the conquering and the possessing natures presents no
difficulties at all. Romantic love continually remains abstract in itself, and if
it can find no outer history, death is already lying in wait for it, because its
eternity is illusory. Marital love begins with possession and gains an inner history. It is faithful—and so also is romantic love, but now mark the difference.

The faithful romantic lover waits, let us say for fifteen years; then comes
the moment [*Øieblikke*] that rewards him. Here poetry very properly perceives that the fifteen years can easily be concentrated; now it hastens to the
moment [*Moment*]. A married man is faithful for fifteen years, and yet during these fifteen years he has had possession; therefore in this long succession he has continually acquired the faithfulness he possessed, since marital
love has in itself the first love and thereby the faithfulness of the first love.
But an ideal married man of this sort cannot be portrayed, for the point is
time in its extension. At the end of the fifteen years, he seems to have come
no further than he was in the beginning, and yet to a high degree he has
been living esthetically. For him his possession has not been inert property,
but he has been continually acquiring its possession. He has not fought with
lions and trolls but with the most dangerous enemy, which is time. But now
eternity does not come afterward, as for the knight, but he has had eternity
in time, has preserved eternity in time. Therefore only he has been victorious over time, for it may be said of the knight that he has killed time, just
as one to whom time has no reality always wishes to kill time, but this is
never the right victory. Like a true victor, the married man has not killed

time but has rescued and preserved it in eternity. The married man who
does this is truly living poetically; he solves the great riddle, to live in eternity and yet to hear the cabinet clock strike in such a way that its striking
does not shorten but lengthens his eternity, a contradiction that is just as
profound as, but far more glorious than, the one in the familiar situation described in a story from the Middle Ages about a poor wretch who woke up
in hell and shouted, "What time is it?"—whereupon the devil answered,
"Eternity!" And although this cannot be portrayed artistically, then let your
consolation be, as it is mine, that we are not to read about or listen to or
look at what is the highest and the most beautiful in life, but are, if you
please, to live it.

Therefore, when I readily admit that romantic love lends itself much better to artistic portrayal than marital love, this does not at all mean that it is

less esthetic than the other—on the contrary, it is more esthetic. In one of the most brilliant stories from the romantic school, there is a character[25] who, unlike the others with whom he is living, has no desire to write poetry, because it is a waste of time and deprives him of genuine pleasure; he, on the contrary, wants to live. Now, if he had had a more valid idea of what it is to live, he would have been my man.

Marital love, then, has its enemy in time, its victory in time, its eternity in time—therefore, even if I were to imagine away all its so-called outer and inner trials, it would always have its task. Ordinarily it does have them, but if one is to view them properly one must pay attention to two things: that they are always inner qualifications and that they always have in them the qualification of time. For this reason, too, it is obvious that this love cannot be portrayed. It always moves inward and spends itself (in the good sense) in time, but that which is to be portrayed by reproduction must be lured forth, and its time must be foreshortened. You will be further persuaded of this by pondering the adjectives used to describe marital love. It is faithful, constant, humble, patient, long-suffering, tolerant, honest, content with little, alert, persevering, willing, happy. All these virtues have the characteristic that they are qualifications within the individual. The individual is not fighting against external enemies but is struggling with himself, struggling to bring his love out of himself. And these virtues have the qualification of time, for their veracity consists not in this, that they are once and for all, but that they are continually. And by means of these virtues nothing else is acquired; only they themselves are acquired. Therefore, marital love is simultaneously commonplace—as you have often mockingly called it—and also divine (in the Greek sense), and it is divine by virtue of being commonplace. Marital love does not come with external signs, not like that bird of fortune with rustling and bustling, but is the incorruptible essence of a quiet spirit.[26]

II
127

THE BALANCE BETWEEN THE ESTHETIC AND THE ETHICAL IN THE DEVELOPMENT OF THE PERSONALITY

II
141

My Friend,

What I have said so often to you I say once again, or, more exactly, I shout it to you: Either/Or, *aut/aut,* for the introduction of a single corrective *aut* does not clarify the matter, inasmuch as the subject under discussion is too insignificant for anyone to be satisfied with just a part of it and in itself too coherent to be capable of being possessed in part. There are conditions of life in which it would be ludicrous or a kind of derangement to apply an Either/Or, but there are also people whose souls are too dissolute to comprehend the implications of such a dilemma, whose personalities lack the energy to be able to say with pathos: Either/Or.

II
143

II
144

And now you, you certainly do use these words often enough—indeed, they have almost become a byword to you. What meaning do they have for you? None whatsoever. For you, to remind you of your own expression, they are a wink, a turn of the hand, a *coup de mains* [sudden attack], an abracadabra. You know how to apply them on any occasion, and they are not without effect either. On you they work like strong drink on a high-strung person; you become completely intoxicated in what you call the higher madness.

"Therein is contained the whole wisdom of life, but no one has ever rendered them as impressively—as if he were a god in the shape of a scarecrow who spoke to suffering humanity—as that great thinker and genuine philosopher of life who said to a man who had hurled his hat to the floor: Pick it up, and you will get a beating; leave it there, and you will also get a beating; now you may choose." You have your great joy "comforting" people when they turn to you in crucial situations; you listen to their expositions and then say: Yes, now I see it all perfectly; there are two possible situations—one can do either this or that. My honest opinion and my friendly advice is this: Do it or do not do it—you will regret both. But the person

II
145

who mocks others mocks himself, and it is not meaningless but is rather a profound mockery of yourself, a tragic proof of how flabby your soul is, that your view of life is concentrated in one single sentence: "I say simply Either/Or."

II
148

Now, if a person could continually keep himself on the spear tip of the moment of choice, if he could stop being a human being, if in his innermost being he could be nothing more than an ethereal thought, if personality meant nothing more than being a nisse who admittedly goes through the motions but nevertheless always remains the same—if that were the situation, it would be foolish to speak of its being too late for a person to choose, since in a deeper sense there could be no question of a choice at all. The choice itself is crucial for the content of the personality: through the choice the personality submerges itself in that which is being chosen, and when it does not choose, it withers away in atrophy. For a moment that between which the choice is to be made lies—for a moment it seems to lie—outside the person who is choosing; he stands in no relation to it, can maintain himself in a state of indifference toward it. This is the moment of deliberation, but, like the Platonic [moment], it actually is not at all, and least of all in the abstract sense in which you wish to hold onto it; and the longer one stares at it, the smaller it is. That which is to be chosen has the deepest relation to the one who is choosing, and when the choice is about an issue of elemental importance to life, the individual must at the same time continue to live, and this is why the longer he puts off the choice, the more easily he comes

II
149

to alter it, although he goes on pondering and pondering and thereby believes that he is really keeping separate the two alternatives of the choice.

No wonder that these words have become an offense and a foolishness to you, "that they appear to you to be like the arms of the virgin whose embrace was death." You look down on people, make them objects of ridicule, and you have become what you most abominate—a critic, a universal critic in all the branches of learning. At times I cannot help smiling at you, and yet it is sad that your truly remarkable intellectual capacities have been dispersed in this way. But here again is the same contradiction in your nature, for you discern the ludicrous very well, and God help the person who falls into your hands if he is in the same situation. And yet the entire difference is that he perhaps becomes bowed down and crushed, whereas you become erect and more jocular than ever and make yourself and others happy with the gospel *vanitas vanitatum vanitas* [vanity of vanities all is vanity],[27] hurrah! But this is no choice; it is what we say in Danish: *Lad gaae* [Let it pass]! Or it is a compromise like making five an even number. Now you feel yourself to be free; tell the world "Farewell."

> *So zieh' ich hin in alle Ferne,*
> *Ueber meiner Mütze nur die Sterne*
> [So I move on to places afar,
> Above my cap only the stars].[28]

With that you have chosen—not, of course, as you yourself will probably acknowledge, the better part; but you have not actually chosen at all, or you have chosen in a figurative sense. Your choice is an esthetic choice, but an esthetic choice is no choice. On the whole, to choose is an intrinsic and stringent term for the ethical. Wherever in the stricter sense there is a question of an Either/Or, one can always be sure that the ethical has something to do with it. The only absolute Either/Or is the choice between good and evil, but this is also absolutely ethical.

The esthetic choice is either altogether immediate, and thus no choice, or it loses itself in a great multiplicity. For example, when a young girl follows her heart's choice, this choice, however beautiful it is otherwise, is no choice in the stricter sense, because it is altogether immediate. If a man esthetically ponders a host of life tasks, then he, as is the case with you in the preceding portion, does not readily have one Either/Or but a great multiplicity, because the self-determining aspect of the choice has not been ethically stressed and because, if one does not choose absolutely, one chooses only for the moment and for that reason can choose something else the next moment.

Therefore, the ethical choice is in a certain sense much easier, much simpler, but in another sense it is infinitely more difficult. The person who wants to decide his life task ethically does not ordinarily have such a wide range; the act of choosing, however, is much more meaningful to him. Now, if you are to understand me properly, I may very well say that what is important in choosing is not so much to choose the right thing as the energy, the earnest-

II
150

II
151

II
152

ness, and the pathos with which one chooses. In the choosing the personality declares itself in its inner infinity and in turn the personality is thereby consolidated. Therefore, even though a person chose the wrong thing, he nevertheless, by virtue of the energy with which he chose, will discover that he chose the wrong thing. In other words, since the choice has been made with all the inwardness of his personality, his inner being is purified and he himself is brought into an immediate relationship with the eternal power that omnipresently pervades all existence [*Tilværelse*]. The person who chooses only esthetically never reaches this transfiguration, this higher dedication. Despite all its passion, the rhythm in his soul is only a *spiritus lenis* [weak aspiration].

Like a Cato,[29] then, I shout my Either/Or to you, and yet not like a Cato, for my soul has not yet attained the resigned coldness that he had. But I know that this adjuration alone, if I have sufficient strength, will be able to arouse you, not to the activity of thinking, for in that you are not deficient, but to earnestness of spirit. Without it, you may succeed in accomplishing a great deal, even in astounding the world (for I am not stingy), and yet you will miss out on the highest, on the only thing that truly gives life meaning; you may win the whole world and lose yourself.

What, then, is it that I separate in my Either/Or? Is it good and evil? No, I only want to bring you to the point where this choice truly has meaning for you. It is on this that everything turns. As soon as a person can be brought to stand at the crossroads in such a way that there is no way out for him except to choose, he will choose the right thing. Therefore, if it should so happen that before you finish reading this somewhat lengthy exploration, which again is being sent to you in the form of a letter, you feel that the moment of choice has arrived, then throw away the remainder—do not bother with it; you have lost nothing. But choose, and you will see the validity inherent in so doing; indeed, no young girl can be as happy with her heart's choice as a man who has known how to choose. Consequently, either a person has to live esthetically or he has to live ethically. Here, as stated, it is still not a matter of a choice in the stricter sense, for the person who lives esthetically does not choose, and the person who chooses the esthetic after the ethical has become manifest to him is not living esthetically, for he is sinning and is subject to ethical qualifications, even if his life must be termed unethical. You see, this is, so to speak, the *character indelebilis*[30] of the ethical, that the ethical, although it modestly places itself on the same level as the esthetic, nevertheless is essentially that which makes the choice a choice.

And this is what is sad when one contemplates human life, that so many live out their lives in quiet lostness; they outlive themselves, not in the sense that life's content successively unfolds and is now possessed in this unfolding, but they live, as it were, away from themselves and vanish like shadows. Their immortal souls are blown away, and they are not disquieted by the question of its immortality, because they are already disintegrated before they die. They do not live esthetically, but neither has the ethical become manifest to them in its wholeness; nor have they actually rejected it, and therefore they are not sinning either, except insofar as it is a sin to be neither one thing nor the other. Nor do they doubt their immortality, for the person who deeply and fervently doubts it on his own behalf is sure to find what is right. I say "on his own behalf," and it certainly is high time that someone warns against the magnanimous, gallant objectivity with which many thinkers think on behalf of all others and not on their own. If anyone calls what I am claiming here self-love, then I shall answer: That comes from having no idea of what this "self" is and from the futility of a person's gaining the whole world but losing himself, and also it is bound to be a poor argument that does not first and foremost convince the person who presents it.

Rather than designating the choice between good and evil, my Either/Or designates the choice by which one chooses good and evil or rules them out. Here the question is under what qualifications one will view all existence and personally live. That the person who chooses good and evil chooses the good is indeed true, but only later does this become manifest, for the esthetic is not evil but the indifferent. And that is why I said that the ethical constitutes the choice. Therefore, it is not so much a matter of choosing between willing good or willing evil as of choosing to will, but that in turn posits good and evil. The person who chooses the ethical chooses the good, but here the good is altogether abstract; its being is thereby merely posited, and this by no means precludes that the one choosing cannot in turn choose evil even though he chose the good. Here you see again how important it is that a choice is made and that it does not depend so much upon deliberation as on the baptism of the will, which assimilates this into the ethical. The more time that passes by, the more difficult it becomes to choose, for the soul is continually in one part of the dilemma, and hence it becomes more and more difficult to work itself free. And yet this is necessary if a choice is to be made, and consequently extremely important if a choice means anything, and that this is the case I shall point out later.

II
154

What takes precedence in my Either/Or is, then, the ethical. Therefore, the point is still not that of choosing something; the point is not the reality of that which is chosen but the reality of choosing. This, however, is what is crucial, and it is to this that I shall strive to awaken you. Up to that point, one person can help another; when he has reached that point, the significance the one person can have for the other becomes more subordinate. In my previous letter, I noted that to have loved gives a person's being a harmony that is never entirely lost. Now I will say that to choose gives a person's being a solemnity, a quiet dignity, that is never entirely lost.

II
160

There are many who attach great importance to having seen some extraordinary world-historical individuality face to face. They never forget this impression; it has given their souls an ideal image that ennobles their natures, and yet, however significant this very moment can be, it is nothing compared with the moment of choice. When around one everything has become silent, solemn as a clear, starlit night, when the soul comes to be alone in the whole world, then before one there appears, not an extraordinary human being, but the eternal power itself, then the heavens seem to open, and the *I* chooses itself or, more correctly, receives itself. Then the soul has seen the highest, which no mortal eye can see and which can never be forgotten; then the personality receives the accolade of knighthood that ennobles it for an eternity. He does not become someone other than he was before, but he becomes himself. The consciousness integrates, and he is himself. Just as an heir, even if he were heir to the treasures of the whole world, does not possess them before he has come of age, so the richest personality is nothing before he has chosen himself; and on the other hand even what might be called the poorest personality is everything when he has chosen himself, for the greatness is not to be this or that but to be oneself, and every human being can be this if he so wills it.

II
161

That in a certain sense the point is not a choice of something, you will perceive from this—that what appears on the other side is the esthetic, which is the indifferent. And yet the point here is a choice, indeed, an absolute choice, for only by choosing absolutely can one choose the ethical. Consequently, the ethical is posited by the absolute choice, but it by no means follows that the esthetic is excluded. In the ethical, the personality is brought into a focus in itself; consequently, the esthetic is absolutely excluded or it is excluded as the absolute, but relatively it is continually present. In choosing itself, the personality chooses itself ethically and absolutely excludes the esthetic; but since he nevertheless chooses himself and does not become another being by choosing himself but becomes himself, all the esthetic returns in its relativity.

The Either/Or I have advanced is, therefore, in a certain sense absolute, for it is between choosing and not choosing. But since the choice is an absolute, choice, the Either/Or is absolute. In another sense, the absolute Either/Or does not make its appearance until the choice, because now the choice between good and evil appears. I shall not concern myself here with this choice posited in and with the first choice; I wish only to force you to the point where the necessity of making a choice manifests itself and thereafter to consider existence under ethical qualifications. I am no ethical rigorist, enthusiastic about a formal, abstract freedom. If only the choice is posited, all the esthetic returns, and you will see that only thereby does existence become beautiful, and that this is the only way a person can save his soul and win the whole world, can use the world without misusing it.

But what does it mean to live esthetically, and what does it mean to live ethically? What is the esthetic in a person, and what is the ethical? To that I would respond: the esthetic in a person is that by which he spontaneously and immediately is what he is; the ethical is that by which he becomes what he becomes. The person who lives in and by and from and for the esthetic that is in him, that person lives esthetically.

You have various good ideas, many droll fancies, many foolish ones. Keep them all; I do not ask for them. But you do have one idea I beg you to hold onto firmly, an idea that convinces me that my mind has kinship with yours. You have often said that you would prefer to be anything in the world to being a poet, since as a rule a poet-existence is a human sacrifice. As far as I am concerned, it must in no way be denied that there have been poets who had found themselves before they began to write or who found themselves through writing, but on the other hand it is also certain that the poet-existence as such lies in the darkness that is the result of a despair that was not carried through, the result of the soul's continuing to quake in despair and of the spirit's inability to achieve its true transfiguration. The poetic ideal is always an untrue ideal, for the true ideal is always the actual. So when the spirit is not allowed to rise into the eternal world of spirit, it remains in transit and delights in the pictures reflected in the clouds and weeps over their transitoriness. Therefore, a poet-existence as such is an unhappy existence; it is higher than the finite and yet is not the infinite. The poet sees the ideals, but he must run away from the world in order to delight in them. He cannot carry these idols within him in the midst of life's confusion, cannot calmly go his way unmoved by the caricature that appears around him, to say nothing of his having the strength to put on the ideals. For this reason the poet's life is often the object of a shabby pity on the part of people who think they have their own lives safe and sound because they have remained in the finite. Once, in a discouraged moment, you said that no doubt there were even some people who had secretly settled their accounts with you and were willing to give a receipt on the following conditions: you would be acknowledged to be a brilliant fellow and in return you would drop out of sight and not be an officious member of society. Yes, beyond a doubt there is such a shabbiness in the world that in this way wants to gain the upper hand over anything that so much as sticks a finger ahead. But do not let it bother you; do not defy them, do not disdain them—here I shall say as you are in the habit of saying: It is not worth the trouble. But if you do not want to be a poet, then there is no other way for you than the one I have pointed out to you: Despair!

Choose despair, then, because despair itself is a choice, because one can doubt [*tvivle*] without choosing it, but one cannot despair [*fortvivle*] without choosing it. And in despairing a person chooses again, and what then does

II
188

II
189

he choose? He chooses himself, not in his immediacy, not as this accidental individual, but he chooses himself in his eternal validity.

II
190
This point I shall attempt to explain in a little more detail with reference to you. There has been more than sufficient talk in modern philosophy about all speculation beginning with doubt [*Tvivl*], but insofar as I have been able on occasion to be occupied by such deliberations, I sought in vain for some enlightenment on how doubt is different from despair [*Fortvivlesle*]. At this point I will try to explain this difference, in the hope that it will help orient and situate you properly. Far be it from me to credit myself with any real philosophic competence. I do not have your virtuosity in playing with categories, but what in the most profound sense is the meaning of life must be capable of being grasped even by a more simple person.

Doubt is thought's despair; despair is personality's doubt. That is why I cling so firmly to the defining characteristic "to choose"; it is my watchword, the nerve in my life-view, and that I do have, even if I can in no way presume to have a system. Doubt is the inner movement in thought itself, and in my doubt I conduct myself as impersonally as possible. I assume that thought, when doubt is carried through, finds the absolute and rests therein; therefore, it rests therein not pursuant to a choice but pursuant to the same necessity pursuant to which it doubted, for doubt itself is a qualification of necessity, and likewise rest.

This is the grandeur of doubt; this is why it so often has been recommended and promoted by people who hardly understood what they were saying. But its being a qualification of necessity indicates that the whole personality is not involved in the movement. That is why there is much truth in a person's saying "I would like to believe, but I cannot—I must doubt." Therefore, we often also see that a doubter can nevertheless have in himself a positive substance that has no communication at all with his thinking, that he can be an extremely conscientious person who by no means doubts the validity of duty and the precepts for his conduct, by no means doubts a host of sympathetic feelings and moods. On the other hand, especially in our day, we see people who have despair in their hearts and yet have conquered doubt. This was especially striking to me when I looked at some of the German philosophers. Their minds are at ease; objective, logical thinking has been brought to rest in its corresponding objectivity, and yet, even though they divert themselves by objective thinking, they are in despair, for a person can divert himself in many ways, and there is scarcely any means as dulling and deadening as abstract thinking, for it is a matter of conducting oneself as impersonally as possible.

II
191
Doubt and despair, therefore, belong to completely different spheres; different sides of the soul are set in motion. But I am not at all satisfied with this, because then doubt and despair would become coordinate, and that is not the case. Despair is precisely a much deeper and more complete expres-

sion; its movement is much more encompassing than that of doubt. Despair is an expression of the total personality, doubt only of thought. The supposed objectivity that doubt has, and because of which it is so exalted, is a manifestation precisely of its imperfection. Thus doubt is based on differences among people, despair on the absolute. It takes a natural aptitude to doubt, but it does not at all take a natural aptitude to despair; but a natural aptitude as such is a difference, and whatever requires a difference to validate itself can never be the absolute, because the absolute can be as the absolute only for the absolute. The lowliest, least endowed person can despair; a young girl who is anything but a thinker can despair—whereas everyone readily senses the foolishness of saying that such people are doubters. The reason a person's doubt can be set at ease and he can still be in despair and go on being in despair is that in a deeper sense he does not will despair. Generally speaking, a person cannot despair at all without willing it, but in order truly to despair, a person must truly will it; but when he truly wills it, he is truly beyond despair. When a person has truly chosen despair, he has truly chosen what despair chooses: himself in his eternal validity. The personality is first set at ease in despair, not by way of necessity, for I never despair necessarily, but in freedom, and only therein is the absolute attained. In this respect, I think that our age will advance, provided I may have any opinion at all about our age, inasmuch as I know it only from reading the papers and a book or two or from talking with you. The time is not far off when we shall experience—quite likely at a high price—that the true point of departure for finding the absolute is not doubt but despair.

But I go back to my category—I am not a logician, and I have only one category, but I assure you that it is the choice of both my heart and my thought, my soul's delight and my salvation—I go back to the significance of choosing. When I choose absolutely, I choose despair, and in despair I choose the absolute, for I myself am the absolute; I posit the absolute, and I myself am the absolute. But in other words with exactly the same meaning I may say: I choose the absolute that chooses me; I posit the absolute that posits me—for if I do not keep in mind that this second expression is just as absolute, then my category of choosing is untrue, because it is precisely the identity of both. What I choose, I do not posit, for if it were not posited I could not choose it, and yet if I did not posit it by choosing it then I would not choose it. It is, for if it were not I could not choose it; it is not, for it first comes into existence through my choosing it, and otherwise my choice would be an illusion.

But what is it, then, that I choose—is it this or that? No, for I choose absolutely, and I choose absolutely precisely by having chosen not to choose this or that. I choose the absolute, and what is the absolute? It is myself in my eternal validity. Something other than myself I can never choose as the absolute, for if I choose something else, I choose it as something finite and consequently do not choose absolutely. Even the Jew who chose God did not choose absolutely, for he did indeed choose the absolute, but he did not choose it absolutely, and thereby it ceased to be the absolute and became something finite.

But what is this self of mine? If I were to speak of a first moment, a first expression for it, then my answer is this: It is the most abstract of all, and yet in itself it is also the most concrete of all—it is freedom.

II
196 Despair's choice, then, is "myself," for it certainly is true that when I despair, I despair over myself just as over everything else. But the self over which I despair is something finite like everything else finite, whereas the self I choose is the absolute self or my self according to its absolute validity. This being so, you will perceive again here why I said previously and go on saying that the Either/Or I erected between living esthetically and living ethically is not an unqualified dilemma, because it actually is a matter of only one choice. Through this choice, I actually do not choose between good and evil, but I choose the good, but when I choose the good, I choose *eo ipso* the choice between good and evil. The original choice is forever present in every succeeding choice.

Despair, then, and your light-mindedness will never more make you wander like a fitful phantom, like a ghost, among the ruins of a world that is lost to you anyway; despair, and your spirit will never sigh in despondency, for the world will once again become beautiful and happy for you, even if you look at it with other eyes than before, and your liberated spirit will vault up into the world of freedom.

II
224 A human being's eternal dignity lies precisely in this, that he can gain a history. The divine in him lies in this, that he himself, if he so chooses, can give this history continuity, because it gains that, not when it is a summary of what has taken place or has happened to me, but only when it is my personal deed in such a way that even that which has happened to me is transformed and transferred from necessity to freedom. What is enviable about human life II
225 is that one can assist God, can understand him, and in turn the only worthy way for a human being to understand God is to appropriate in freedom everything that comes to him, both the happy and the sad. Or do you not think so? This is the way it appears to me—indeed, I think that to say this aloud to a person is all one needs to do to make him envy himself.

II
227 Here I now want to call to mind the definition of the ethical I gave before—that it is that by which a person becomes what he becomes. It does not want to make the individual into someone else but into the individual himself; it does not want to destroy the esthetic but to transfigure it. For a person to live ethically it is necessary that he become conscious of himself, so thoroughly that no accidental element escapes him. The ethical does not

want to wipe out this concretion but sees in it its task, sees the material with which it is to build and that which it is to build. Ordinarily we view the ethical altogether abstractly and therefore have a secret horror of it. In that case the ethical is viewed as something alien to the personality, and we shrink from devoting ourselves to it, since we cannot be really sure what it will lead to in the course of time. In the same way, many people fear death, because they harbor obscure and confused notions that the soul in death has to cross over into another order of things where the established laws and conventions are completely different from the ones they have learned to know in this world. The reason for such a fear of death is the individual's aversion to becoming transparent to himself, for if he is willing to do this, he readily perceives the unreasonableness of this fear. So it is with the ethical also; if a person fears transparency, he always avoids the ethical, because the ethical really does not want anything else.

II
228

The person who chooses himself ethically has himself as his task, not as a possibility, not as a plaything for the play of his arbitrariness. Ethically he can choose himself only if he chooses himself in continuity, and then he has himself as a multiply defined task. He does not try to blot out or evaporate this multiplicity; on the contrary, he repents himself firmly in it, because this multiplicity is himself, and only by penitently immersing himself in it can he come to himself, since he does not assume that the world begins with him or that he creates [skabe] himself. The latter has been branded with contempt by language itself, for we always speak contemptuously of a man when we say: He is putting on airs [skabe sig]. But in choosing himself penitently he is acting—not in the direction of isolation but in the direction of continuity.

II
231

Let us now compare an ethical and an esthetic individual. The primary difference, the crux of the matter, is that the ethical individual is transparent to himself and does not live *ins Blaue hinein* [in the wild blue yonder], as does the esthetic individual. This difference encompasses everything. The person who lives ethically has seen himself, knows himself, penetrates his whole concretion with his consciousness, does not allow vague thoughts to rustle around inside him or let tempting possibilities distract him with their juggling; he is not like a "magic" picture that shifts from one thing to another, all depending on how one shifts and turns it. He knows himself. The phrase γνῶθι σεαυτόν [know yourself][31] is a stock phrase, and in it has been perceived the goal of all a person's striving. And this is entirely proper, but yet it is just as certain that it cannot be the goal if it is not also the beginning. The ethical individual knows himself, but this knowing is not simply contemplation, for then the individual comes to be defined according to his necessity. It is a collecting of oneself, which itself is an action, and this is why I have with aforethought used the expression "to choose oneself" instead of "to know oneself."

II
232

II
235
By now you have easily seen that in his life the ethical individual goes through the stages we previously set forth as separate stages. He is going to develop in his life the personal, the civic, the religious virtues, and his life advances through his continually translating himself from one stage to another. As soon as a person thinks that one of these stages is adequate and that he dares to concentrate on it one-sidedly, he has not chosen himself ethically but has failed to see the significance of either isolation or continuity and above all has not grasped that the truth lies in the identity of these two.

The person who has ethically chosen and found himself possesses himself defined in his entire concretion. He then possesses himself as an individual who has these capacities, these passions, these inclinations, these habits, who is subject to these external influences, who is influenced in one direction thus and in another thus. Here he then possesses himself as a task in such a way that it is chiefly to order, shape, temper, inflame, control—in short, to produce an evenness in the soul, a harmony, which is the fruit of the personal virtues. Here the objective for his activity is himself, but nevertheless not arbitrarily determined, for he possesses himself as a task that has been assigned him, even though it became his by his own choosing. But although he himself is his objective, this objective is nevertheless something else also, for the self that is the objective is not an abstract self that fits everywhere and therefore nowhere but is a concrete self in living interaction with these specific surroundings, these life conditions, this order of things.

The self that is the objective is not only a personal self but a social, a civic self. He then possesses himself as a task in an activity whereby he engages in the affairs of life as this specific personality. Here his task is not to form himself but to act, and yet he forms himself at the same time, because, as I noted

II
236
above, the ethical individual lives in such a way that he is continually transferring himself from one stage to another. If the individual has not originally conceived of himself as a concrete personality in continuity, he will not gain this next continuity either. If he thinks that the art is to begin like a Robinson Crusoe, he remains an adventurer all his life. If, however, he realizes that if he does not begin concretely he will never make a beginning, and that if he never makes a beginning he will never finish, he will then be simultaneously in continuity with the past and the future. He transfers himself from personal life to civic life, from this to personal life. Personal life as such was an isolation and therefore imperfect, but when he turns back into his personality through the civic life, the personal life appears in a higher form. The personality appears as the absolute that has its teleology in itself. When living for the fulfillment of duty is made a person's task in life, what is often pointed out is the skepticism that duty itself is unstable, that laws can be changed. You easily see that this last remark concerns the fluctuations to which civic virtues are always exposed.

He is well aware that every human being develops in freedom, but he is also aware that a person does not create himself out of nothing, that he has himself in its concretion as his task; he will once again be reconciled with existence in perceiving that in a certain sense every person is an exception, and that it is equally true that every human being is the universally human and also an exception.

Here you have my view of what it is to be an extraordinary person. I love life and being a human being too much to believe that the way to become an extraordinary person is easy or without spiritual trials. But even if a person is an extraordinary human being in the nobler sense, he nevertheless will continually admit that it would be even more perfect to incorporate the entire universal in himself.

So accept my greeting, take my friendship, for although, strictly speaking, I dare not describe our relationship this way, I nevertheless hope that my young friend may some day be so much older that I shall dare to use this word legitimately. Be assured of my fellow-feeling. Accept a greeting from her whom I love, whose thoughts are hidden in my thoughts; accept a greeting that is inseparable from mine, but accept also a special greeting from her, friendly and honest as always.

When you were here with us a few days ago, you perhaps had no idea that I once again had finished writing so voluminous a letter. I know that you do not take kindly to having anyone speak to you about your inner history; I have, therefore, chosen to write and will never speak to you of such matters. It will remain a secret that you are receiving a letter like this, and I would not want it to have any influence in changing your relationship with me and my family. I know that you have virtuosity enough to do that if you so desire, and this is why I ask it for your sake and for my own. I have never wanted to thrust myself upon you and am well able to love you at a distance, although we see each other frequently. You are too inclosed by nature for me to believe it would do any good to speak to you, but I do hope that my letters will not be without meaning. So when you work on yourself in the sealed-off machinery of your personality, I put in my contributions and am sure that they will be incorporated into the movement.

Since our relationship by letter remains a secret, I observe all the formalities, bid you farewell as if we lived a long way from each other, although I hope to see you at my house just as often as before.

II
298

II
298

FOUR UPBUILDING DISCOURSES
(AUGUST 31, 1844)
BY S. KIERKEGAARD

The first pseudonymous line of writings (from *Either/Or* to *Stages on Life's Way*[32]) was accompanied by a parallel line of signed writings (from *Two Upbuilding*[33] *Discourses* to *Three Discourses on Imagined Occasions*). Eighteen signed discourses were published serially in six volumes (two, three, and four discourses in 1843 and two, three, and four in 1844) in conjunction with six pseudonymous works: *Either/Or, Fear and Trembling, Repetition, Philosophical Fragments, The Concept of Anxiety,* and *Prefaces.* The volume of *Three Upbuilding Discourses* (1843) was published on the very same day as *Fear and Trembling* and *Repetition; Four Upbuilding Discourses* (1844) was paired with *Prefaces* (June 17, 1844); and *Three Discourses on Imagined Occasions* was published the day before *Stages* appeared (April 30, 1845). Therefore the pseudonymous esthetic-ethical writings had explicitly ethical-religious counterparts.

The focus of the eighteen discourses is on what in *Postscript* is called religiousness *A*, a universal immanental ethical-religiousness. In their own way they shared in the aim of the total authorship: "to **make aware** of the religious, the essentially Christian."[34] The selected discourse on the human being's highest perfection is a good representative of the tone and substance of the other seventeen, which center more specifically on the expectancy of faith, good and perfect gifts from above, patience, cowardliness, struggling in prayer, self-knowledge, and self-denial. All eighteen discourses are addressed to "that single individual whom I with joy and gratitude call *my* reader,"[35] and all six volumes have similar prefaces, and an explanatory disclaimer: ". . . this little book (which is called 'discourses,' not sermons, because its author does not have authority to *preach*, 'upbuilding discourses,' not discourses for upbuilding, because the speaker by no means claims to be a *teacher*) wishes to be only what it is, a superfluity, and desires only to remain in hiding just as it came into existence in concealment." The purpose of the discourses and the invitation to the single individual, "*my* reader," are given in the title of a later work, *For Self-Examination,* and in its preface: "My dear reader, read aloud, if possible! . . . By reading aloud you will gain the strongest impression that you have only yourself to consider, not me, who, after all, am 'without authority,' nor others, which would be a distraction."[36]

PREFACE

Although this little book (which is called "discourses," not sermons, because its author does not have authority to *preach*, "upbuilding" discourses, not discourses for upbuilding, because the speaker by no means claims to be a *teacher*) is once again going out into the world, it is even less fearful of drawing any impeding attention to itself than it was the first time it started on the journey; it hopes rather that because of the repetition the passersby will scarcely notice it, or if at all only to let it shift for itself. Just as a messenger now and then goes his routine way at set times and soon is a familiar sight, so familiar that the passerby scarcely sees him, does not turn to look after him—in the same way this little book goes out like a messenger, but not like a messenger who comes back again. It seeks that single individual whom I with joy and gratitude call *my* reader, in order to pay him a visit, indeed, to stay with him, because one goes to the person one loves, makes one's home with him, and remains with him if this is allowed. That is, as soon as he has received it, then it has ceased to be; it is nothing for itself and by itself, but all that it is, it is only for him and by him. And although the trail always leads ahead to *my* reader, not back, and although the previous messenger never returns home, and although the one who sends him never discovers anything about his fate, the next messenger nevertheless goes intrepidly through death to life, cheerfully goes its way in order to disappear, happy never to return home again—and this is precisely the joy of him who sends it, who continually comes to his reader only to bid him farewell, and now bids him farewell for the last time.

Copenhagen, August 9, 1844

S. K.

TO NEED GOD IS A HUMAN BEING'S HIGHEST PERFECTION

V
81

"A person needs only a little in order to live and needs that little only a little while"—this is a high-minded proverb that is worthy of being received and understood as it wants to be understood; it is too earnest to want to be admired as a beautiful expression or an elegant locution. As such it is thoughtlessly used at times: one calls it out to the needy person, perhaps in order to console him in passing, perhaps also just to have something to say; one says it to oneself, even on a lucky day, since the human heart is very deceitful, is all too eager to take high-mindedness in vain and is proud of needing only a little—while using much. One says it to oneself on a day of need, and hurries ahead to welcome oneself admiringly at the goal—when one has accomplished something glorious—but one is as little served thereby as the proverb is.

"Needs only a little," the proverb said, but to know that a person needs only a little without knowing for sure at any moment that he can obtain the little he needs—anyone who can bear this needs only a little; he does not even need (this does, after all, amount to something) to know that this little is secure. If, then, it is true that a person needs only a little—in order to live—then he needs no more, since he will indeed find a grave, and in the grave every human being needs equally little. Whether the dead man owns (alas, what a strange contradiction), perhaps for a hundred years, the grave

V
83

in which he lies or he has had to elbow his way in among others, has had
to fight his way ahead even in death in order to have a little place, they own
equally much and need equally little and need that for only a little while.
But the first little while that the proverb speaks about may become long,
because even if the way to the grave was not long, if you perhaps not in-
frequently saw him wend his weary way out there in order to conquer with
his eyes the little land he intended to occupy as a dead man, could not the
way become very long in another sense? If he sometimes became despondent, if he did not always understand that a person needs only a little, did
you have nothing else to say to him than a repetition of that proverb? Or
did you probably say to him something that came quite naturally, so naturally that in your heart even you yourself perhaps did not have confidence
in the comfort you were offering to another: Then be contented with the
grace of God.[37]

V
85   If a destitute person dared to enjoy the friendship of a powerful personage, but this powerful man could do nothing for him (that the grace of God
allows the absence of earthly evidence corresponds to this), nevertheless, the
fact that he had such a friendship was nevertheless already very much. But
perhaps the difficulty lies here, because the destitute person could indeed be
V
86   convinced that the powerful man actually was not able to do anything for
him, but how could he be definitively convinced that God cannot—he is,
after all, almighty! This presumably accounts for the fact that the thought of
impatience continually insists, as it were, that God can surely do it, and therefore, because people are so impatient, therefore the language says: to be contented with the grace of God. In the beginning, when impatience is most
strident and vociferous, it can scarcely understand that this is a laudable contentment; as it is cooled and calmed down in the quiet incorruptibility of the
inner being, it comprehends this better and better until the heart is stirred
and sometimes, at least, sees the divine glory that had taken on a lowly form.
And if this glory again vanishes for a person so that he is again destitute, as
he still was also while he saw the glory, if it again seems to him that contentment still belongs to being contented with the grace of God, then he
still at times shamefully admits that the grace of God is in itself worth being
contented with—indeed, it alone is worth being desired; indeed, to possess
it is the only blessedness.

    Then in a beautiful sense the human heart will gradually (the grace of
God is never taken by force) become more and more discontented—that is,
it will desire more and more ardently, will long more and more intensely, to
be assured of grace. See, now everything has become new,[38] everything has
been changed. With respect to the earthly, one needs little, and to the degree that one needs less, the more perfect one is. A pagan who knew how
to speak only of the earthly has said that the deity is blessed because he needs

nothing, and next to him the wise man,[39] because he needs little. In a human being's relationship with God, it is inverted: the more he needs God, the more deeply he comprehends that he is in need of God, and then the more he in his need presses forward to God, the more perfect he is. Therefore, the words "to be contented with the grace of God" will not only comfort a person, and then comfort him again every time earthly want and distress make him, to speak mundanely, needful of comfort, but when he really has become attentive to the words they will call him aside, where he no longer hears the secular mentality's earthly mother tongue, the speech of human beings, the noise of the shopkeepers, but where the words explain themselves to him, confide to him the secret of perfection: that to need God is nothing to be ashamed of but is perfection itself, and that it is the saddest thing of all if a human being goes through life without discovering that he needs God.

Let us, then, clarify for ourselves this upbuilding thought:

V
87

To Need God Is a Human Being's Highest Perfection.

But what is a human being? Is he just one more ornament in the series of creation; or has he no power, is he himself capable of nothing? And what is his power, then; what is the utmost he is able to will? What kind of answer should be given to this question when the brashness of youth combines with the strength of adulthood to ask it, when this glorious combination is willing to sacrifice everything to accomplish great things, when burning with zeal it says, "Even if no one in the world has ever achieved it, I will nevertheless achieve it; even if millions degenerated and forgot the task, I will nevertheless keep on striving—but what is the highest?" Well, we do not want to defraud the highest of its price; we do not conceal the fact that it is rarely achieved in this world, because the highest is this: that a person is fully convinced that he himself is capable of nothing, nothing at all.

V
90

But in heaven, my listener, there lives the God who is capable of all things, or, more correctly, he lives everywhere, even if people do not perceive it. "Indeed, O Lord, if you were a weak, lifeless body like a flower that withers, if you were like a brook that flows by, if you were like a building that collapses in due time—then people would pay attention to you, then you would be an appropriate object for our low and brutish thoughts." But this is not the way it is, and your very greatness makes you invisible, since in your wisdom you are much too far away from man's thoughts for him to be able to see you, and in your omnipresence you are too close to him for him to see you; in your goodness you conceal yourself from him, and your omnipotence makes it impossible for him to see you, since in that case he himself would become nothing. But God in heaven is capable of all things, and man of nothing at all.

V
92

Is it not so, my listener, that these two correspond to each other: God and man? But if they correspond to each other, then, of course, there is only the question of whether you are going to be happy about this wonderful good fortune—that you two correspond to each other—or whether you prefer to be such a one who does not correspond to God at all, such a one who is capable of something himself and consequently does not correspond completely to God, for indeed you cannot change God, and indeed you do not want to change God so that he would not be capable of all things. To become nothing seems hard—oh, but we speak differently even about human matters. If misfortune taught two human beings that they corresponded to each other in friendship or in love, how negligible the distress caused by the misfortune would seem compared with the joy the misfortune also brought—that these two corresponded to each other! And if two human beings did not understand until the day of death that they corresponded to each other for all eternity—oh, how brief, though bitter, that moment of separation that is death would be compared with an eternal understanding!

V
94
   If, however, this view, that to need God is man's highest perfection, makes life more difficult, it does this only because it wants to view man according to his perfection and bring him to view himself in this way, because in and through this view *man learns to know himself.* And for the person who does not know himself, his life is, in the deeper sense, indeed a delusion.

V
95
   When a person turns and faces himself in order to understand himself, he steps, as it were, in the way of that first self, halts that which was turned outward in hankering for and seeking after the surrounding world that is its object, and summons it back from the external. In order to prompt the first self to this withdrawal, the deeper self lets the surrounding world remain what it is—remain dubious. This is indeed the way it is; the world around us is inconstant and can be changed into the opposite at any moment, and there is not one person who can force this change by his own might or by the conjuration of his wish. The deeper self now shapes the deceitful flexibility of the surrounding world in such a way that it is no longer attractive to that first self. Then the first self either must proceed to kill the deeper self, to render it forgotten, whereby the whole matter is given up; or it must admit that the deeper self is right, because to want to predicate constancy of something that continually changes is indeed a contradiction, and as soon as one confesses that it changes, it can, of course, change in that same moment. However much that first self shrinks from this, there is no wordsmith so ingenious or no thought-twister so wily that he can invalidate the deeper self's eternal claim. There is only one way out, and that is to silence the deeper self by letting the roar of inconstancy drown it out.

V
96
   What has happened? The first self is halted; it cannot move at all. Alas, the surrounding world can actually be so favorable, so tangibly trustworthy, so

apparently undeviating, that everyone will vouch for splendid progress if one just begins—it does not help. The person who witnesses that struggle in his inner being must concede that the deeper self is right: in that minute everything can be changed, and one who does not discover this continually runs aimlessly.[40] Never in the world has there been so quick a tongue that it could beguile the deeper self if only it gains a chance to speak. Ah, it is a painful situation. The first self sits and looks at all the beckoning fruits, and it is indeed so clear that if one just makes a move everything will succeed, as everyone will admit—but the deeper self sits there as earnest and thoughtful as the physician at the bedside of the sick, yet also with transfigured gentleness, because it knows that this sickness is not unto death but unto life.

Now the first self has a specific craving; it is conscious of possessing the conditions; the surrounding world, as it understands it, is as favorable as possible; they are just waiting for each other, as it were: the happy self and the favors of fortune—oh, what a pleasant life! But the deeper self does not give ground, does not haggle, does not give its consent, does not compromise; it merely says: Even in this moment everything can be changed. Yet people come to the aid of that first self with the explanation. They call to him; they explain that this is the way it goes in life, that there are some people who are fortunate and are supposed to enjoy life and that he is one of them. Then the heart beats fast; he wants to be off . . . . .

That a child who has a strict father must stay at home is something one must submit to, because the father is indeed the stronger. But the first self is certainly no child, and that deeper self, after all, is himself, and yet it seems stricter than the strictest father, tolerating no wheedling, speaking candidly or not speaking at all. Then there is danger afoot—both of them, both the first self and the deeper self, notice it, and the latter sits there as concerned as the experienced pilot, while a secret council is held on whether it is best to throw the pilot overboard since he is creating a contrary wind. That, however, does not happen, but what is the outcome? The first self cannot move from the spot, and yet, yet it is clear that the moment of joy is in a hurry, that fortune is already in flight. Therefore people do indeed say that if one does not make use of the moment at once, it is soon too late. And who is to blame? Who else but that deeper self? But even this scream does not help.

V
97

What kind of unnatural condition is this? What does it all mean? When such a thing occurs in a person's soul, does it not mean that he is beginning to lose his mind? No, it means something altogether different; it means that the child must be weaned. One can be thirty years old and more, forty years old, and still be just a child—yes, one can die as an aged child. But to be a child is so delightful! So one snuggles at the breast of temporality in the cradle of finitude, and probability sits by the cradle and sings to the child. If the wish is not fulfilled and the child becomes restless, then probability calms him and says: Just lie still and sleep, and I shall go out and buy something for you, and next time it will be your turn. So the child goes to sleep again and the pain is forgotten, and the child glows again in the dream of new wishes, although he thought it would be impossible to forget the pain. Of course, if he had not been a child, he surely would not have forgotten the pain so easily, and it would have become apparent that it was not probability that had sat beside the cradle, but it was the deeper self that had sat beside him at the deathbed in self-denial's hour of death, when it itself rose from the dead to an eternity.

When the first self submits to the deeper self, they are reconciled and walk on together. Then the deeper self probably says, "It is true that I had almost forgotten it in our great struggle—what was it now that you so fervently wished; at this moment I do not think there is anything to hinder the fulfillment of your wish if you will only not forget that little secret we two have between us. Now, you see, now you can be gratified." The first self may answer, "Yes, but now I do not care as much about it; no, I shall never be as happy as before, as I was then when my soul craved it, and you do not really understand me." "I do not think so, either, nor would it be desirable for me to understand you in such a way that I craved just as much as you. But have you lost anything by not caring about it in that way? Consider the other side. Suppose, on the other hand, that the surrounding world had deceived you— and you do realize that it could have done that. More I did not say; I merely said that it is possible, and by that I also said that what you regarded as certainty was actually only a possibility. What then? Then you would have despaired, and you would not have had me to rely on. You do recollect, do you not, that the ship's council was almost of a mind to throw me overboard. Would you not be better off now by having lost some of that burning desire and having won the understanding that life cannot deceive you; is not that kind of losing a winning?"

That little secret we two have between us, as the deeper self said. What, presumably, is this secret, my listener? What else but this, that with regard to the external a person is capable of nothing at all. If he wants to seize the external immediately, it can be changed in the same instant, and he can be deceived; on the other hand, he can take it with the consciousness that it could also be changed, and he is not deceived even though it is changed, because he has the deeper self's consent. If he wants to act immediately in the external, to accomplish something, everything can come to nothing in that same moment; on the other hand, he can act with this consciousness, and even if it came to nothing, he is not deceived, because he has the deeper self's consent.

But even if the first self and the deeper self have been reconciled in this way and the shared mind has been diverted away from the external, this is still only the condition for coming to know himself. But if he is actually to know himself, there are new struggles and new dangers. Let not the struggling one himself simply be terrified and frightened by the thought, as if being in need were an imperfection when the discourse is about needing God, as if being in need were a humiliating secret one would rather conceal when the discourse is about needing God, as if being in need were a dismal necessity one would seek to mitigate by enunciating it oneself when the discourse is about needing God. Through more profound self-knowledge, one learns precisely that one needs God, but at first glance the discouraging aspect of this would frighten a person away from beginning if in due time he were not aware of and inspired by the thought that precisely this is the perfection, inasmuch as not to need God is far more imperfect and only a misunderstanding. Even though someone had accomplished the most glorious exploits, if he still thought that it was all by his own power, if by overcoming his mind he became greater than someone who captured a city, if he still thought it had happened through his own power, then his perfection would be essentially just a misunderstanding; but a perfection such as that would indeed be scarcely commendable. But the person who perceived that he was not capable of the least thing without God, unable even to be happy about the most happy event—he is closer to perfection. And the person who understood this and found no pain whatsoever in it but only the overabundance of bliss, who hid no secret desire that still preferred to be happy on its own account, felt no shame that people noticed that he himself was capable of nothing at all, laid down no conditions to God, not even that his weakness be kept concealed from others, but in whose heart joy constantly prevailed by his, so to speak, jubilantly throwing himself into God's arms in unspeakable amazement at God, who is capable of all things—indeed, he would be the perfect one whom the Apostle Paul describes better and more briefly: he "boasts of his weakness" and has not even had experiences so numerous and ambiguous that he knows how to express himself more profusely.—People do say that not to know oneself is a deception and an imperfection, but often they are unwilling to understand that someone who actually knows himself perceives precisely that he is not capable of anything at all.

In the external world, he was capable of nothing; but in the internal world, is he not capable of anything there, either? If a capability is actually to be a capability, it must have opposition, because if it has no opposition, then it is either all-powerful or something imaginary. But if he is supposed to have opposition, from whence is it supposed to come? In the internal world, the opposition can come only from himself. Then he struggles with himself in the internal world, not as previously, where the deeper self struggled with the first self to prevent it from being occupied with the external. If a person does not discover this conflict, his understanding is faulty and consequently his life is imperfect; but if he does discover it, then he will once again understand that he himself is capable of nothing at all.

It seems odd that this is what a person is supposed to learn from himself.

V
99

Then why praise self-knowledge? And yet this is the way it is, and from the whole world a person cannot learn that he is capable of nothing at all. Even if the whole world united to crush and annihilate the weakest, he nevertheless could still continually preserve a very faint idea that he himself was capable of something under other circumstances when the superior power was not as great. That he is capable of nothing at all, he can discover only by himself, and whether he is victorious over the whole world or trips over a straw, it is still the case that by himself he knows or can know that he himself is capable of nothing at all. If someone wants to explain it some other way, then he has indeed nothing to do with others but only with himself, and then every subterfuge is seen through. It is so hard, people think, to know oneself, especially if one is very talented and has a multitude of aptitudes and capabilities and then is supposed to become informed about all these. Oh, the self-knowledge of which we are speaking is really not complicated, and every time a person properly comprehends this brief and pithy truth, that he himself is capable of nothing at all, then he knows himself.

FEAR AND TREMBLING,

DIALECTICAL LYRIC

(OCTOBER 16, 1843)

BY JOHANNES DE SILENTIO

Of all the pseudonymous writings, *Fear and Trembling* and *Repetition* are closest to being, yet obliquely, autobiographical. Surrounded by the Climacus works and the eighteen discourses, they are an island among the works published after the breaking of the engagement to Regine Olsen. They represent, however, excellent examples, of the "law manifest in poetic production. . . . As soon as the productive artist must give over his own actuality, its facticity, he is no longer essentially productive; his beginning will be his end."[41] The autobiography is the vanishing occasion, irrelevant to the reading of the works, and the universalized refiguration is a kind of literary alchemy, a transmutation of leaden personal particulars into the gold of the imaginatively and reflectively shaped pseudonymous work. The theme of *Fear and Trembling* is faith, with Abraham as a prototype of this highest human passion, and the presumptuousness of wanting to go further beyond faith. In the memorable figures of the Knight of Resignation and the Knight of Faith, the movement to faith is illustrated. The vexatious issues involved are considered as Problema I, "Is there a Teleological Suspension of the Ethical?" Problema II, "Is there an Absolute Duty to God?" and Problema III, "Was It Ethically Defensible for Abraham to Conceal His Undertaking?" The work ends with a parting shot at the presumptuous who claim to surpass faith: the disciple of Heraclitus who in trying to improve upon the master's dictum of flux transformed it into the Eleatic thesis of permanence by affirming the impossibility, not only of going through the same river twice, but of doing it even once.

PREFACE

Not only in the business world but also in the world of ideas, our age stages *ein wirklicher Ausverkauf* [a real sale]. Everything can be had at such a bargain price that it becomes a question whether there is finally anyone who will make a bid. Every speculative monitor who conscientiously signals the important trends in modern philosophy, every assistant professor, tutor, and student, every rural outsider and tenant incumbent in philosophy is unwilling to stop with doubting everything but goes further. Perhaps it would be premature and untimely to ask them where they really are going, but in all politeness and modesty it can probably be taken for granted that they have doubted everything, since otherwise it certainly would be odd to speak of their having gone further. They have all made this preliminary movement and presumably so easily that they find it unnecessary to say a word about how, for not even the person who in apprehension and concern sought a little enlightenment found any, not one suggestive hint or one little dietetic prescription with respect to how a person is to act in carrying out this enormous task.

What those ancient Greeks, who after all did know a little about philosophy, assumed to be a task for a whole lifetime, because proficiency in doubting is not acquired in days and weeks, what the old veteran disputant attained, he who had maintained the equilibrium of doubt throughout all the specious arguments, who had intrepidly denied the certainty of the senses and the certainty of thought, who, uncompromising, had defied the anxiety of self-love and the insinuations of fellow feeling—with that everyone begins in our age.

In our age, everyone is unwilling to stop with faith but goes further. It perhaps would be rash to ask where they are going, whereas it is a sign of urbanity and culture for me to assume that everyone has faith, since otherwise it certainly would be odd to speak of going further. It was different in those ancient days. Faith was then a task for a whole lifetime, because it was assumed that proficiency in believing is not acquired either in days or in weeks. When the tried and tested oldster approached his end, had fought the good fight and kept the faith, his heart was still young enough not to have forgotten the anxiety and trembling that disciplined the youth, that the adult learned to control, but that no man outgrows—except to the extent that he succeeds in going further as early as possible. The point attained by those venerable personages is in our age the point where everyone begins in order to go further.

It is commonly supposed that what faith produces is no work of art, that it is a coarse and boorish piece of work, only for the more uncouth natures, but it is far from being that. The dialectic of faith is the finest and the most extraordinary of all; it has an elevation of which I can certainly form a conception, but no more than that. I can make the mighty trampoline leap whereby I cross over into infinity; my back is like a tightrope dancer's, twisted in my childhood, and therefore it is easy for me. One, two, three—I can walk upside down in existence, but I cannot make the next movement, for the marvelous I cannot do—I can only be amazed at it. Indeed, if Abraham,[42] the moment he swung his leg over the ass's back, had said to himself: Now Isaac is lost, I could just as well sacrifice him here at home as ride the long way to Moriah—then I do not need Abraham, whereas now I bow seven

times to his name and seventy times to his deed. This he did not do, as I can prove by his really fervent joy on receiving Isaac and by his needing no preparation and no time to rally to finitude and its joy. If it had been otherwise with Abraham, he perhaps would have loved God but would not have had faith, for he who loves God without faith reflects upon himself; he who loves God in faith reflects upon God.

This is the peak on which Abraham stands. The last stage to pass from his view is the stage of infinite resignation. He actually goes further and comes to faith. All those travesties of faith—the wretched, lukewarm lethargy that thinks: There's no urgency, there's no use in grieving beforehand; the despicable hope that says: One just can't know what will happen, it could just possibly be—those travesties are native to the paltriness of life, and infinite resignation has already infinitely disdained them.

Abraham I cannot understand; in a certain sense I can learn nothing from him except to be amazed. If someone deludes himself into thinking he may be moved to have faith by pondering the outcome of that story, he cheats himself and cheats God out of the first movement of faith—he wants to suck worldly wisdom out of the paradox. Someone might succeed, for our generation does not stop with faith, does not stop with the miracle of faith, turning water into wine[43]—it goes further and turns wine into water.

Would it not be best to stop with faith, and is it not shocking that everyone wants to go further? Where will it all end when in our age, as declared in so many ways, one does not want to stop with love? In worldly shrewdness, in petty calculation, in paltriness and meanness, in everything that can make man's divine origin doubtful. Would it not be best to remain standing at faith and for him who stands to see to it that he does not fall, for the movement of faith must continually be made by virtue of the absurd, but yet in such a way, please note, that one does not lose the finite but gains it whole and intact. For my part, I presumably can describe the movements of faith, but I cannot make them. In learning to go through the motions of swimming, one can be suspended from the ceiling in a harness and then presumably describe the movements, but one is not swimming. In the same way I can describe the movements of faith. If I am thrown out into the water, I presumably do swim (for I do not belong to the waders), but I make different movements, the movements of infinity, whereas faith makes the opposite movements: after having made the movements of infinity, it makes the movements of finitude. Fortunate is the person who can make these movements! He does the marvelous, and I shall never weary of admiring him; it makes no difference to me whether it is Abraham or a slave in Abraham's house, whether it is a professor of philosophy or a poor servant girl—I pay attention only to the movements. But I do pay attention to them, and I do not let myself be fooled, either by myself or by anyone else. The knights of the infinite resignation are easily recognizable—their walk is light and bold. But they who carry the treasure of faith are likely to disappoint, for externally they have a striking resemblance to bourgeois philistinism, which infinite resignation, like faith, deeply disdains.

I honestly confess that in my experience I have not found a single authentic instance, although I do not therefore deny that every second person may be such an instance. Meanwhile, I have been looking for it for many years, but in vain. Generally, people travel around the world to see rivers and

III
89

mountains, new stars, colorful birds, freakish fish, preposterous races of mankind; they indulge in the brutish stupor that gawks at life and thinks it has seen something. That does not occupy me. But if I knew where a knight of faith lived, I would travel on foot to him, for this marvel occupies me absolutely. I would not leave him for a second, I would watch him every minute to see how he made the movements; I would consider myself taken care of for life and would divide my time between watching him and practicing myself, and thus spend all my time in admiring him. As I said before, I have not found anyone like that; meanwhile, I may very well imagine him. Here he is. The acquaintance is made, I am introduced to him. The instant I first lay eyes on him, I set him apart at once; I jump back, clap my hands, and say half aloud, "Good Lord, is this the man, is this really the one—he looks just like a tax collector!" But this is indeed the one. I move a little closer to him, watch his slightest movement to see if it reveals a bit of heterogeneous optical telegraphy from the infinite, a glance, a facial expression, a gesture, a sadness, a smile that would betray the infinite in its heterogeneity with the finite. No! I examine his figure from top to toe to see if there may not be a crack through which the infinite would peek. No! He is solid all the way through. His stance? It is vigorous, belongs entirely to finitude; no spruced-up burgher walking out to Fresberg on a Sunday afternoon treads the earth more solidly. He belongs entirely to the world; no bourgeois philistine could belong to it more. Nothing is detectable of that distant and aristocratic nature by which the knight of the infinite is recognized. He finds pleasure in everything, takes part in everything, and every time one sees him participating in something particular, he does it with an assiduousness that marks the worldly man who is attached to such things. He attends to his job. To see him makes one think of him as a pen-pusher who has lost his soul to Italian bookkeeping, so punctilious is he. Sunday is for him a holiday. He goes to church. No heavenly gaze or any sign of the incommensurable betrays him; if one did not know him, it would be impossible to distinguish him from the rest of the crowd, for at most his hearty and powerful singing of the hymns proves that he has good lungs. In the afternoon, he takes a walk to the woods. He enjoys everything he sees, the swarms of people, the new omnibuses, the Sound. Encountering him on Strandveien, one would take him for a mercantile soul enjoying himself. He finds pleasure in this way, for he is not a poet, and I have tried in vain to lure the poetic incommensurability out of him. Toward evening, he goes home, and his gait is as steady as a postman's. On the way, he thinks that his wife surely will have a special hot meal for him when he comes home—for example, roast lamb's head with vegetables. If he meets a kindred soul, he would go on talking all the way to Østerport about this delicacy with a passion befitting a restaurant operator. It so happens that he does not have four shillings to his name, and yet he firmly believes that his wife has this delectable meal waiting for him. If she has, to see him eat would be the envy of the elite and an inspiration to the common man, for his appetite is keener than Esau's. His wife does not have it—curiously enough, he is just the same. On the way he passes a building site and meets another man. They converse for a moment; in an instant he erects a building, and he himself has at his disposition everything required. The stranger leaves him thinking that he surely is a capitalist, while my admired knight thinks: Well, if it came right down to it, I could easily get it. He sits at an open window and surveys the neighborhood where he lives: everything that happens—a rat scurrying under a plank across the gutter, children playing—engages him with an equanimity akin to that of a sixteen-year-old girl. And yet he is no genius, for I have sought in vain to spy out the incommensurability of genius in him. In the evening, he smokes his pipe; seeing him, one would swear it was the butcher across the way vegetating in the gloaming. With the freedom from care of a reckless good-for-nothing, he lets things take care of themselves, and yet every moment of his life he buys the opportune time at the highest price, for he does not do even the slightest thing except by virtue of the absurd. And yet, yet—yes, I could be infuriated over it if for no other reason than envy—and yet this man has made and at every moment is making the movement of infinity. He drains the deep sadness of life in infinite resignation, he knows the blessedness of infinity, he has felt the pain of renouncing everything, the most precious thing in the world, and yet the finite tastes just as good to him as to one who never knew anything higher, because his remaining in finitude would have no trace of a timorous, anxious routine, and yet he has this security that makes him delight in it as if finitude were the surest thing of all. And yet, yet the whole earthly figure he presents is a new creation by virtue of the absurd. He resigned everything infinitely, and then he grasped everything again by virtue of the absurd. He is continually making the movement of infinity, but he does it with such precision and assurance that he continually gets finitude out of it, and no one ever suspects anything else. It is supposed to be the most difficult feat for a ballet dancer to leap into a specific posture in such a way that he never once strains for the posture but in the very leap assumes the posture. Perhaps there is no ballet dancer who can do it—but this knight does it. Most people live completely absorbed in worldly joys and sorrows; they are benchwarmers who do not take part in the dance. The knights of infinity are ballet dancers and have elevation. They make the upward movement and come down again, and this, too, is not an unhappy diversion and is not unlovely to see. But every time they come down, they are unable to assume the posture immediately, they waver for a moment, and this wavering shows that they are aliens in the world. It is more or less conspicuous according to their skill, but even the most skillful of these knights cannot hide this wavering. One does not need to see them in the air; one needs only to see them the instant they touch and have touched the earth—and then one recognizes them. But to be able to come down in such a way that instantaneously one seems to stand and to walk, to change the leap into life into walking, absolutely to express the sublime in the pedestrian—only that knight can do it, and this is the one and only marvel.

    The act of resignation does not require faith, for what I gain in resignation is my eternal consciousness. This is a purely philosophical movement that I venture to make when it is demanded and can discipline myself to make, because every time some finitude will take power over me, I starve myself into submission until I make the movement, for my eternal consciousness is my love for God, and for me that is the highest of all. The act of resignation does not require faith, but to get the least little bit more than my eternal consciousness requires faith, for this is the paradox. The movements are often confused. It is said that faith is needed in order to renounce everything. Indeed, one hears what is even more curious: a person laments that he has lost his faith, and when a check is made to see where he is on the scale, curiously enough, he has only reached the point where he is to make the infinite movement of resignation. Through resignation I renounce everything. I make this movement all by myself, and if I do not make it, it is because I am too cowardly and soft and devoid of enthusiasm and do not feel the significance of the high dignity assigned to every human being, to be his own censor, which is far more exalted than to be the censor general of the whole Roman republic. This movement I make all by myself, and what I gain thereby is my eternal consciousness in blessed harmony with my love for the eternal being. By faith I do not renounce anything; on the contrary, by faith I receive everything exactly in the sense in which it is said that one who has faith like a mustard seed can move mountains. It takes a purely human courage to renounce the whole temporal realm in order to gain eternity, but this I do gain and in all eternity can never renounce—it is a self-contradic-

tion. But it takes a paradoxical and humble courage to grasp the whole temporal realm now by virtue of the absurd, and this is the courage of faith. By faith Abraham did not renounce Isaac, but by faith Abraham received Isaac. By virtue of resignation, that rich young man[44] should have given away everything, but if he had done so, then the knight of faith would have said to him: By virtue of the absurd, you will get every penny back again—believe it! And the formerly rich young man should by no means treat these words lightly, for if he were to give away his possessions because he is bored with them, then his resignation would not amount to much.

    Be it a duty or whatever, I cannot make the final movement, the paradoxical movement of faith, although there is nothing I wish more. Whether a person has the right to say this must be his own decision; whether he can come to an amicable agreement in this respect is a matter between himself and the eternal being, who is the object of faith. Every person can make the movement of infinite resignation, and for my part I would not hesitate to call a coward anyone who imagines that he cannot do it. Faith is another matter, but no one has the right to lead others to believe that faith is something inferior or that it is an easy matter, since on the contrary it is the greatest and most difficult of all.

The story of Abraham is understood in another way. We praise God's mercy, that he gave him Isaac again and that the whole thing was only an ordeal [*Prøvelse*].

PROBLEMA I

Is There a Teleological Suspension of the Ethical?

The ethical as such is the universal, and as the universal it applies to everyone, which from another angle means that it applies at all times. It rests immanent in itself, has nothing outside itself that is its τέλος [end, purpose] but is itself the τέλος for everything outside itself, and when the ethical has assimilated this, it does not go any further. The single individual, sensately and psychically qualified in immediacy, is the individual who has his τέλος in the universal, and it is his ethical task continually to express himself in this, to annul his singularity in order to become the universal. As soon as the single individual asserts himself in his singularity before the universal, he sins; and only by acknowledging this can he be reconciled again with the universal. Every time the single individual, after having entered the universal, feels an impulse to assert himself as the single individual, he is in a spiritual trial [*Anfægtelse*], from which he can work himself only by repentantly surrendering as the single individual in the universal. If this is the highest that can be said of man and his existence, then the ethical is of the same nature as a person's eternal salvation, which is his τέλος forevermore and at all times, since it would be a contradiction for this to be capable of being surrendered (that is, teleologically suspended), because as soon as this is suspended it is relinquished, whereas that which is suspended is not relinquished but is preserved in the higher, which is its τέλος.

Faith is namely this paradox that the single individual is higher than the universal—yet, please note, in such a way that the movement repeats itself, so that after having been in the universal he as the single individual isolates himself as higher than the universal. If this is not faith, then Abraham is lost, then faith has never existed in the world precisely because it has always existed. For if the ethical—that is, social morality—is the highest and if there is in a person no residual incommensurability in some way such that this incommensurability is not evil (i.e., the single individual, who is to be expressed in the universal), then no categories are needed other than what Greek philosophy had or what can be deduced from them by consistent

III
104

III
105

thought. Hegel should not have concealed this, for, after all, he had studied Greek philosophy.

   The difference between the tragic hero and Abraham is very obvious. The tragic hero is still within the ethical. He allows an expression of the ethical to have its τέλος in a higher expression of the ethical; he scales down the ethical relation between father and son or daughter and father to a feeling that has its dialectic in its relation to the idea of moral conduct. Here there can be no question of a teleological suspension of the ethical itself.

   Abraham's situation is different. By his act he transgressed the ethical altogether and had a higher τέλος outside it, in relation to which he suspended it. For I certainly would like to know how Abraham's act can be related to the universal, whether any point of contact between what Abraham did and the universal can be found other than that Abraham transgressed it. It is not to save a nation, not to uphold the idea of the state that Abraham does it; it is not to appease the angry gods. If it were a matter of the deity's being angry, then he was, after all, angry only with Abraham, and Abraham's act is totally unrelated to the universal, is a purely private endeavor. Therefore, while the tragic hero is great because of his moral virtue, Abraham is great because of a purely personal virtue. There is no higher expression for the ethical in Abraham's life than that the father shall love the son. The ethical in the sense of the moral is entirely beside the point. Insofar as the universal was present, it was cryptically in Isaac, hidden, so to speak, in Isaac's loins, and must cry out with Isaac's mouth: Do not do this, you are destroying everything.

   Why, then, does Abraham do it? For God's sake and—the two are wholly identical—for his own sake. He does it for God's sake because God demands this proof of his faith; he does it for his own sake so that he can prove it. The unity of the two is altogether correctly expressed in the word already used to describe this relationship. It is an ordeal, a temptation. A temptation—but what does that mean? As a rule, what tempts a person is something that will hold him back from doing his duty, but here the temptation is the ethical itself, which would hold him back from doing God's will. But what is duty? Duty is simply the expression for God's will.

   Here the necessity of a new category for the understanding of Abraham becomes apparent. Paganism does not know such a relationship to the divine. The tragic hero does not enter into any private relationship to the divine, but the ethical is the divine, and thus the paradox therein can be mediated in the universal.

   Abraham cannot be mediated; in other words, he cannot speak. As soon as I speak, I express the universal, and if I do not do so, no one can understand me. As soon as Abraham wants to express himself in the universal, he must declare that his situation is a spiritual trial [*Anfægtelse*], for he has no higher expression of the universal that ranks above the universal he violates.

It is great when the poet in presenting his tragic hero for public admiration dares to say: Weep for him, for he deserves it. It is great to deserve the tears of those who deserve to shed tears. It is great that the poet dares to keep the crowd under restraint, dares to discipline men to examine themselves individually to see if they are worthy to weep for the hero, for the slop water of the snivellers is a debasement of the sacred.—But even greater than all this is the knight of faith's daring to say to the noble one who wants to weep for him: Do not weep for me, but weep for yourself.

We are touched, we look back to those beautiful times. Sweet sentimental longing leads us to the goal of our desire, to see Christ walking about in the promised land. We forget the anxiety, the distress, the paradox. Was it such a simple matter not to make a mistake? Was it not terrifying that this man walking around among the others was God? Was it not terrifying to sit down to eat with him? Was it such an easy matter to become an apostle? But the result, the eighteen centuries—that helps, that contributes to this mean deception whereby we deceive ourselves and others. I do not feel brave enough to wish to be contemporary with events like that, but I do not for that reason severely condemn those who made a mistake, nor do I depreciate those who saw what was right.

But I come back to Abraham. During the time before the result, either Abraham was a murderer every minute or we stand before a paradox that is higher than all mediations.

The story of Abraham contains, then, a teleological suspension of the ethical. As the single individual he became higher than the universal. This is the paradox, which cannot be mediated. How he entered into it is just as inexplicable as how he remains in it. If this is not Abraham's situation, then Abraham is not even a tragic hero but a murderer. It is thoughtless to want to go on calling him the father of faith, to speak of it to men who have an interest only in words. A person can become a tragic hero through his own strength—but not the knight of faith. When a person walks what is in one sense the hard road of the tragic hero, there are many who can give him advice, but he who walks the narrow road of faith has no one to advise him— no one understands him. Faith is a marvel, and yet no human being is excluded from it; for that which unites all human life is passion, and faith is a passion.

III
115

III
115

REPETITION, A VENTURE
IN EXPERIMENTING PSYCHOLOGY
(OCTOBER 16, 1843)
BY CONSTANTIN CONSTANTIUS

Repetition is a small work, but in it repetition is defined and illustrated in numerous ways. For the author it means the recurrence of an experience. For the Young Man it means the recovery of his split self after the experienced breach caused by the ethical dilemma of his breaking an engagement. They both fail and become parodies of repetition. Constantin despairs of esthetic repetition because of the accidental, contingent aspects of life, and ends in a life of monotonous routine. The Young Man, despairing of personal repetition because of guilt, obtains esthetic repetition through the accidental intervention of his former fiancée's marriage and is transported into the poet's world of imagination. Constantin Constantius also points to another conception of repetition: "If he had had a deeper religious background, he would not have become a poet." Vigilius Haufniensis, author of *The Concept of Anxiety*, picks out from *Repetition* three lines that are left undeveloped in the earlier work: "'Recollection is the ethnical [*ethniske*] view of life, repetition the modern; repetition is the interest [*Interesse*] of metaphysics and also the interest upon which metaphysics comes to grief; repetition is the watchword [*Løsnet*] in every ethical view; repetition is *conditio sine qua non* [the indispensable condition] for every issue of dogmatics'"—and adds: "eternity is the true repetition"; "repetition begins in faith."[45]

[REPORT BY CONSTANTIN CONSTANTIUS]

When the Eleatics denied motion, Diogenes, as everyone knows, came forward as an opponent. He literally did come forward, because he did not say a word but merely paced back and forth a few times, thereby assuming that he had sufficiently refuted them. When I was occupied for some time, at least on occasion, with the question of repetition—whether or not it is possible, what importance it has, whether something gains or loses in being repeated—I suddenly had the thought: You can, after all, take a trip to Berlin; you have been there once before, and now you can prove to yourself whether a repetition is possible and what importance it has. At home I had been practically immobilized by this question. Say what you will, this question will play a very important role in modern philosophy, for *repetition* is a crucial expression for what "recollection" was to the Greeks. Just as they taught that all knowing is a recollecting, modern philosophy will teach that all life is a repetition. The only modern philosopher who has had an intimation of this is Leibniz. Repetition and recollection are the same movement, except in opposite directions, for what is recollected has been, is repeated backward, whereas genuine repetition is recollected forward. Repetition, therefore, if it is possible, makes a person happy, whereas recollection makes him unhappy—assuming, of course, that he gives himself time to live and does not promptly at birth find an excuse to sneak out of life again, for example, that he has forgotten something.

III
174

Repetition is the new category that will be discovered. If one knows anything of modern philosophy and is not entirely ignorant of Greek philosophy, one will readily see that this category precisely explains the relation between the Eleatics and Heraclitus, and that repetition proper is what has mistakenly been called mediation. It is incredible how much flurry has been made in Hegelian philosophy over mediation and how much foolish talk has enjoyed honor and glory under this rubric. One should rather seek to think through mediation and then give a little credit to the Greeks. The Greek explanation of the theory of being and nothing, the explanation of "the moment," "nonbeing," etc. trumps Hegel. "Mediation" is a foreign word; "repetition" is a good Danish word, and I congratulate the Danish language on a philosophical term. There is no explanation in our age as to how mediation takes place, whether it results from the motion of the two factors and in what sense it is already contained in them, or whether it is something new that is added, and, if so, how. In this connection, the Greek view of the concept of κίνησις [motion, change] corresponds to the modern category "transition" and should be given close attention. The dialectic of repetition is easy, for that which is repeated has been—otherwise it could not be repeated—but the very fact that it has been makes the repetition into something new. When the Greeks said that all knowing is recollecting, they said that all existence, which is, has been; when one says that life is a repetition, one says: actuality, which has been, now comes into existence. If one does not have the category of recollection or of repetition, all life dissolves into an empty, meaningless noise. Recollection is the ethnical [*ethniske*] view of life, repetition the modern; repetition is the *interest* [*Interesse*] of metaphysics, and also the interest upon which metaphysics comes to grief; repetition is the watchword [*Løsnet*] in every ethical view; repetition is *conditio sine qua non* [the indispensable condition] for every issue of dogmatics.

III
189

With regard to the meaning that repetition has for something, much can be said without making oneself guilty of a repetition. When Professor Ussing once gave a speech at the May 28 Society and a statement in the speech did not meet with approval, what did he do, this professor who at that time was always resolute and forceful—he pounded the table and said: I repeat. What he meant at the time was that what he said gained by repetition. Some years ago I heard a pastor give the very same talk on two festive occasions.

III
190

If he had been of the same mind as the professor, the second time he ascended the pulpit he would have pounded the pulpit and said: I repeat what
I said last Sunday. He did not do so and made no allusion whatsoever. He
was not of the same mind as Professor Ussing, and who knows, perhaps the
professor himself no longer thinks that his speech would be of benefit if it
were repeated again. When the queen had finished telling a story at a court
function and all the court officials, including a deaf minister, laughed at it,
the latter stood up, asked to be granted the favor of also being allowed to
tell a story, and then told the same story. Question: What was his view of
the meaning of repetition? When a schoolteacher says: For the second time
I repeat that Jespersen is to sit quietly—and the same Jespersen gets a mark
for repeated disturbance, then the meaning of repetition is the very opposite.

III
191

I shall not dwell any longer on such examples but shall proceed to speak
a little of the investigative journey I made to test the possibility and meaning of repetition. Without anyone's knowing about it (lest any gossip render me incapable of the experiment and in another way weary of repetition), I went by steamship to Stralsund and took a seat in the *Schnellpost*
[express coach] to Berlin. The learned disagree on which seat is the most
comfortable in a stagecoach; in my *Ansicht* [opinion], they are all wretched,
the whole lot. Last time I had an end seat forward inside the carriage (some
regard this as the big prize) and after thirty-six hours was so jounced together with those sitting next to me that when I arrived in Hamburg I had
lost not only my mind but my legs as well. During those thirty-six hours,
we six people sitting inside the carriage were so worked together into one
body that I got a notion of what happened to the Wise Men of Gotham,
who after having sat together a long time could not recognize their own
legs. Hoping at least to remain a limb on a lesser body, I chose a seat in the
forward compartment. That was a change. Everything, however, repeated
itself. The postilion blew his horn. I shut my eyes, surrendered to despair,
and thought the thoughts I usually think on such occasions: God knows if
you can endure it, if you actually will get to Berlin, and in that case if you
will ever be human again, able to disengage yourself in the singleness of
isolation, or if you will carry a memory of your being a limb on a larger
body.

So I arrived in Berlin. I hurried at once to my old lodgings to ascertain
whether a repetition is possible. May I assure any commiserating reader that
the previous time I managed to get one of the most pleasant apartments in
Berlin; may I now give even more emphatic assurance, inasmuch as I have
seen many. Gensd'arme Square is certainly the most beautiful in Berlin; *das
Schauspielhaus* [the theater] and the two churches are superb, especially when
viewed from a window by moonlight. The recollection of these things was
an important factor in my taking the journey. One climbs the stairs to the

first floor in a gas-illuminated building, opens a little door, and stands in the entry. To the left is a glass door leading to a room. Straight ahead is an anteroom. Beyond are two entirely identical rooms, identically furnished, so that one sees the room double in the mirror. The inner room is tastefully illuminated. A candelabra stands on a writing table; a gracefully designed armchair upholstered in red velvet stands before the desk. The first room is not illuminated. Here the pale light of the moon blends with the strong light from the inner room. Sitting in a chair by the window, one looks out on the great square, sees the shadows of passersby hurrying along the walls; everything is transformed into a stage setting. A dream world glimmers in the background of the soul. One feels a desire to toss on a cape, to steal softly along the wall with a searching gaze, aware of every sound. One does not do this but merely sees a rejuvenated self doing it. Having smoked a cigar, one goes back to the inner room and begins to work. It is past midnight. One extinguishes the candles and lights a little night candle. Unmingled, the light of the moon is victorious. A single shadow appears even blacker; a single footstep takes a long time to disappear. The cloudless arch of heaven has a sad and pensive look as if the end of the world had already come and heaven, unperturbed, were occupied with itself. Once again one goes out into the hallway, into the entry, into that little room, and—if one is among the fortunate who are able to sleep—goes to sleep.

But here, alas, again no repetition was possible. My landlord, the druggist, *er hatte sich verändert,* in the pointed sense in which the German understands this phrase, and as far as I know "to change oneself" is similarly used in some of Copenhagen's streets—that is, he had married. I wanted to congratulate him, but since I am not such a master of the German language that I know how to improvise in a pinch and did not have suitable idioms at hand for such an occasion, I limited myself to a gesture. I laid my hand on my heart and looked at him with tender sympathy legible on my face. He pressed my hand. After this show of mutual understanding, he went on to prove the esthetic validity of marriage. He succeeded marvelously, just as well as he had the last time in proving the perfection of bachelorhood. When I speak German, I am the most accommodating man in the world.

My former landlord was only too glad to be of service to me and I only too glad to live with him; consequently, I took one room and the entry. When I came home the first evening and had lit the candles, I thought: Alas! Alas! Alas! Is this the repetition? I became completely out of tune, or, if you please, precisely in tune with the day, for fate had strangely contrived it so that I arrived in Berlin on the *allgemeine Busz- und Bettag* [Universal Day of Penance and Prayer]. Berlin was prostrate. To be sure, they did not throw ashes into one another's eyes with the words: *Memento o homo! quod cinis es et in cinerem revertaris* [Remember, O man! that you are dust and to dust you will return].[46] But all the same, the whole city lay in

III
192

III
193

one cloud of dust. At first I thought it was a government measure, but later I was convinced that the wind was responsible for this nuisance and without respect of persons followed its whim or its bad habit, for in Berlin at least every other day is Ash Wednesday. But this is of little concern to my project. This discovery had no connection with "repetition," for the last time I was in Berlin I had not noticed this phenomenon, presumably because it was winter.

When a fellow has settled himself cosily and comfortably in his quarters, when he has a fixed point like this from which he can rush out, a safe hiding place to which he can retreat and devour his booty in solitude—something I especially appreciate, since, like certain beasts of prey, I cannot eat when anyone is looking on—then he familiarizes himself with whatever notable sights there may be in the city. If he is a traveler *ex professo* [by trade], a courier who travels to smell what everybody has smelled or to write the names of notable sights in his journal, and in return gets his in the great autograph book of travelers, then he engages a *Lohndiener* [a temporary servant] and buys *das ganze Berlin* for four *Groschen*. This way he becomes an impartial observer whose utterances ought to have the credibility of any police record. But if on his journey he has no particular purpose, he lets matters take their course, occasionally sees things others do not see, disregards the most important, receives a random impression that is meaningful only to him. A careless wanderer like this usually does not have much to communicate to others, and if he does, he very easily runs the risk of weakening the good opinion good people might have regarding his morality and virtue. If a person has traveled abroad for some time and has never been on a train, would he not be thrown out of all the better circles! What if a man had been in London and had never driven in the tunnel! What if a man went to Rome, fell in love with a little part of the city that was an inexhaustible source of joy to him, and left Rome without having seen one single notable sight!

Berlin has three theaters. The opera and ballet performances in the opera house are supposed to be *groszartig* [magnificent]; performances in the theater are supposed to be instructive and refining, not only for entertainment. I do not know. But I do know that Berlin has a theater called the Königstädter Theater. Professional travelers visit this theater seldom, though more frequently—which also has its own significance—than they visit the congenial, more out-of-the-way places of entertainment, where a Dane has the opportunity to refresh his memory of Lars Mathiesen and Kehlet. When I came to Stralsund and read in the newspaper that *Der Talisman*[47] would be performed at that theater, I was in a good mood at once. The recollection of it awakened in my soul; the first time I was there, it seemed as if the first impression evoked in my soul only a recollection that pointed far back in time.

III
194

I hurried to the theater. No box was available for me alone, not even a seat in number five or six on the left. I had to take the right. There I encountered a group that was not sure whether it should be amused or be blasé, and one can be sure that such company is boring. There was scarcely a single empty box. The young girl was not to be found, or, if she was present, I was unable to recognize her because she was together with others. Beckmann could not make me laugh. I endured it for half an hour and then left the theater, thinking: There is no repetition at all. This made a deep impression on me. I am not so very young, am not altogether ignorant of life, and long before my previous trip to Berlin I had cured myself of calculating on the basis of uncertainties. I did believe, however, that the enjoyment I had known in that theater would be of a more durable nature, precisely because a person must have learned to let himself be trimmed by existence in many ways and yet learned to manage somehow until he actually got a sense of life—but then life also ought to be all the more secure. Should life [*Tilværelsen*] be even more deceitful than a bankrupt! He still gives 50 percent or 30 percent, at least something. After all, the least one can ask for is the comic—should not even that be capable of repetition!

With these thoughts in my mind, I went home. My desk was in place. The velvet armchair was still there, but when I saw it, I became so furious I almost smashed it to pieces, all the more so because everyone in the house had gone to bed and no one could take it away. Of what good is an armchair of velvet when the rest of the environment does not match; it is like a man going around naked and wearing a three-cornered hat. When I went to bed without having had one single rational thought, it was so light in the room that, half-awake, half-dreaming, I kept on seeing the armchair, until in the morning I got up and carried out my resolve to have it thrown into an out-of-the-way nook.

My home had become dismal to me simply because it was a repetition of the wrong kind. My mind was sterile, my troubled imagination constantly conjured up tantalizing attractive recollections of how the ideas had presented themselves the last time, and the tares of these recollections choked out every thought at birth. I went out to the café where I had gone every day the previous time to enjoy the beverage that, according to the poet's precept, when it is "pure and hot and strong and not misused," can always stand alongside that to which the poet compares it, namely, friendship. At any rate, I prize coffee. Perhaps the coffee was just as good as last time; one would almost expect it to be, but it was not to my liking. The sun through the café windows was hot and glaring; the room was just about as humid as the air in a saucepan, practically cooking. A draft, which like a small trade wind cut through everything, prohibited thoughts of any repetition, even if the opportunity had otherwise offered itself.

In the evening, I went to the restaurant I had frequented the previous time

III
207

III
208

and, no doubt by force of habit, had even found satisfactory. Coming there every evening as I did, I was thoroughly familiar with everything: I knew when the early guests would leave, how they would greet the brotherhood whom they left, whether they put on their hats in the inner room or the outer or not until they opened the door or until they stepped outside. No one escaped my attention. Like Proserpine, I plucked a hair from every head, even the bald ones.——It was just the same, the same witticisms, the same civilities, the same patronage; the place was absolutely the same—in short, the same sameness. Solomon says that a woman's nagging is like rain dripping from the roof; I wonder what he would say about this still life. What an appalling thought—here a repetition was possible!

The next evening I went to the Königstädter Theater. The only repetition was the impossibility of a repetition. Unter den Linden was unbearably dusty; every attempt to mingle with people and thus take a human bath was extremely disappointing. No matter how I turned and shifted, all was futile. The little dancer who last time had enchanted me with her gracefulness, who, so to speak, was on the verge of a leap, had already made the leap. The blind man at the Brandenburger Tor, my harpist—for I probably was the only one who cared about him—had acquired a coat of mixed gray in place of the light green one for which I was pensively nostalgic and in which he looked like a weeping willow—he was lost to me and won for the universally human. The beadle's admired nose had become pallid; Professor A. A. had gotten a pair of new trousers with an almost military fit.——

When this had repeated itself several days, I became so furious, so weary of the repetition, that I decided to return home. My discovery was not significant, and yet it was curious, for I had discovered that there simply is no repetition and had verified it by having it repeated in ever possible way.

My hope lay in my home. Justinus Kerner tells somewhere of a man who became bored with his home; he had his horse saddled so he could ride out into the wide, wide world. When he had ridden a little way, the horse threw him off. This turn of events became crucial for him, because as he turned to mount his horse, his eyes fell once again on the home he wanted to forsake. He gazed at it, and behold, it was so beautiful that he promptly turned back. I could be fairly certain of finding everything in my home prepared for repetition. I have always strongly mistrusted all upheavals, yes, to the extent that for this reason I even hate any sort of housecleaning, especially floor scrubbing with soap. I had left the strictest instructions that my conservative principles should be maintained also in my absence. But what happens. My faithful servant thought otherwise. When he began a shakeup very shortly after I left, he counted on its being finished well before my return, and he certainly was the man to get everything back in order very punctually. I arrive. I ring my doorbell. My servant opens the door. It was a moment eloquent with meaning. My servant turned as pale as a corpse. Through the door half-

III
209

opened to the rooms beyond I saw the horror: everything was turned upside down. I was dumbfounded. In his perplexity, he did not know what to do; his bad conscience smote him—and he slammed the door in my face. That was too much. My desolation had reached its extremity, my principles had collapsed; I was obliged to fear the worst, to be treated like a ghost as was Grønmeyer, the business manager. I perceived that there is no repetition, and my earlier conception of life was victorious.

The older a person grows, the more he understands life and the more he relishes the amenities and is able to appreciate them—in short, the more competent one becomes, the less satisfied one is. Satisfied, completely, absolutely satisfied in every way, this one never is, and to be more or less satisfied is not worth the trouble, so it is better to be completely dissatisfied. Anyone who has painstakingly pondered the matter will certainly agree with me that it has never been granted to a human being in his whole life, not even for as much as a half hour, to be absolutely satisfied in every conceivable way. Certainly it is unnecessary for me to say that for this it takes something more than having food and clothes. III 210

At one time I was very close to complete satisfaction. I got up feeling unusually well one morning. My sense of well-being increased incomparably until noon; at precisely one o'clock, I was at the peak and had a presentiment of the dizzy maximum found on no gauge of well-being, not even on a poetic thermometer. My body had lost its terrestrial gravity; it was as if I had no body simply because every function enjoyed total satisfaction, every nerve delighted in itself and in the whole, while every heartbeat, the restlessness of the living being, only memorialized and declared the pleasure of the moment. My walk was a floating, not like the flight of the bird that cuts through the air and leaves the earth behind, but like the undulating of the wind over a field of grain, like the longing rocking of the sea, like the dreaming drifting of clouds. My being was transparent, like the depths of the sea, like the self-satisfied silence of the night, like the soliloquizing stillness of midday. Every mood rested in my soul with melodic resonance. Every thought volunteered itself, and every thought volunteered itself jubilantly, the most foolish whim as well as the richest idea. I had a presentiment of every impression before it arrived and awakened within me. All existence seemed to have fallen in love with me, and everything quivered in fateful rapport with my being. Everything was prescient in me, and everything was enigmatically transfigured in my microcosmic bliss, which transfigured everything in itself, even the most disagreeable: the most boring remark, the most disgusting sight, the most calamitous conflict. As stated, it was one o'clock on the dot when I was at the peak and had presentiments of the highest of all; then suddenly something began to irritate one of my eyes, whether it was an eyelash, a speck of something, a bit of dust, I do not know, III 211 but this I do know—that in the same instant I was plunged down almost into the abyss of despair, something everyone will readily understand who has been as high up as I was and while at that point has also pondered the theoretical question of whether absolute satisfaction is attainable at all. Since that time, I have abandoned every hope of ever feeling satisfied absolutely and in every way, abandoned the hope I had once nourished, perhaps not to be absolutely satisfied at all times but nevertheless at certain moments, even though all those instances of the moment were no more, as Shakespeare says, than "an alehouse keeper's arithmetic would be adequate to add up."

That was how far I had come before I learned to know that young man.

III
214

Some time went by. My servant, like a housewifely Eve, had remedied his earlier wrongdoing. A monotonous and unvarying order was established in my whole economy. Everything unable to move stood in its appointed place, and everything that moved went its calculated course: my clock, my servant, and I, myself, who with measured pace walked up and down the floor. Although I had convinced myself that there is no repetition, it nevertheless is always certain and true that by being inflexible and also by dulling one's powers of observation a person can achieve a sameness that has a far more anesthetic power than the most whimsical amusements and that, like a magical formulary, in the course of time also becomes more and more powerful. In the excavation of Herculaneum and Pompeii, everything was found in its place just as the respective owners left it. If I had lived at that time, the archeologists, perhaps to their amazement, would have come upon a man who walked with measured pace up and down the floor. To maintain this established and enduring order, I made use of every possible expedient. At certain times, like Emperor Domitian, I even walked around the room armed with a flyswatter, pursuing every revolutionary fly. Three flies, however, were preserved to fly buzzing through the room at specified times. Thus did I live, forgetting the world and, as I thought, forgotten, when one day a letter ar-

III
215

rived from my young friend. More followed, always spaced about a month apart, but from this I dared not draw any conclusion as to the distance of his place of residence. He himself divulges nothing, and he could very well be trying to perplex me by deliberately and carefully varying the intervals between five weeks and just a day over three weeks. He does not wish to trouble me with a correspondence, and even if I were willing to reciprocate or at least to answer his letters, he does not care to receive anything like that— he simply wishes to pour himself out.

III
216

But if in the meantime he believes that I have completely forgotten him, then he wrongs me once again. His sudden disappearance actually made me fear that in his despair he had done away with himself. As a rule, such an event does not remain hidden very long; therefore, since I neither heard nor read anything, I decided that he presumably must be alive, wherever he was lurking. The girl he left in the lurch knew nothing whatsoever. One day he did not show up and sent no word at all. Her transition to pain was not sudden, for at first the uneasy suspicion awakened little by little and at first the pain consolidated itself little by little, so that she slumbered sweetly in a dreamlike ambiguity about what had happened and what it could mean. For me the girl was new material for observation. My friend was not one of those who know how to squeeze everything out of the beloved and then throw her away; on the contrary, his disappearance left her in the most desirable state: healthy, in full bloom, enriched by all his poetic yield, powerfully nourished by the priceless cordial of poetic illusion. Rarely does one meet a jilted girl in this state. When I saw her a few days later, she was still as lively as a freshly caught fish; usually a girl like that is likely to be as famished as a fish that has lived in a tank. I was in all conscience convinced that he must be alive and rejoiced that he had not seized the desperate means of passing himself off as dead. It is unbelievable how confusing an erotic relationship can be if one party wants to die of grief or wants to die to get away from it all.

The issue that brings him to a halt is nothing more nor less than repetition. He is right not to seek clarification in philosophy, either Greek or modern, for the Greeks make the opposite movement, and here a Greek would choose to recollect without tormenting his conscience. Modern philosophy makes no movement; as a rule it makes only a commotion, and if it makes any movement at all, it is always within immanence, whereas repetition is and remains a transcendence. It is fortunate that he does not seek any explanation from me, for I have abandoned my theory, I am adrift. Then, too, repetition is too transcendent for me. I can circumnavigate myself, but I cannot rise above myself. I cannot find the Archimedean point. Fortunately, my friend is not looking for clarification from any world-famous philosopher or any *professor publicus ordinarius* [regularly appointed state professor]; he turns to an unprofessional thinker who once possessed the world's glories but later withdrew from life—in other words, he falls back on Job, who does not posture on a rostrum and make reassuring gestures to vouch for the truth of his propositions but sits on the hearth and scrapes himself with a potsherd and without interrupting this activity casually drops clues and comments. He believes that here he has found what he sought, and in his view truth sounds more glorious and gratifying and true in this little circle of Job and his wife and three friends than in a Greek symposium.

Even if he were still to seek my guidance, it would be futile. I am unable to make a religious movement; it is contrary to my nature. Yet I do not therefore deny the reality [*Realiteten*] of such a thing or that one can learn very much from a young man. If he succeeds, he will have no admirer more ardent than I. If he succeeds, he will be free of all the irritation in his rela-

III
216

III
222

tionship with me. But I cannot deny that the more I ponder the matter the more I have new misgivings about the girl, that in one way or another she has allowed herself to want to trap him in his melancholy. If so, I would rather not be in her shoes. It will end in disaster. Life always wreaks the severest revenge upon such conduct.

III
234
                                                                October 11
My Silent Confidant:

I am at the end of my rope. I am nauseated by life; it is insipid—without salt and meaning. If I were hungrier than Pierrot, I would not choose to eat the explanation people offer. One sticks a finger into the ground to smell what country one is in; I stick my finger into the world—it has no smell. Where am I? What does it mean to say: the world? What is the meaning of that word? Who tricked me into this whole thing and leaves me standing here? Who am I? How did I get into the world? Why was I not asked about it, why was I not informed of the rules and regulations but just thrust into the ranks as if I had been bought from a peddling shanghaier of human beings? How did I get involved in this big enterprise called actuality? Why should I be involved? Isn't it a matter of choice? And if I am compelled to be involved, where is the manager—I have something to say about this. Is there no manager? To whom shall I make my complaint? After all, life is a debate—may I ask that my observations be considered? If one has to take life as it is, would it not be best to find out how things go? What does it mean: a deceiver? Does not Cicero say that such a person can be exposed by asking: *cui bono* [to whose benefit]? Anyone may ask me and I ask everyone whether I have benefited in any way by making myself and a girl unhappy.

III
235
Guilt—what does it mean? Is it hexing? Is it not positively known how it comes about that a person is guilty? Will no one answer me? Is it not, then, of the utmost importance to all the gentlemen involved?

III
238
                                                              November 15
My Silent Confidant:

If I did not have Job! It is impossible to describe all the shades of meaning and how manifold the meaning is that he has for me. I do not read him as one reads another book, with the eyes, but I lay the book, as it were, on my heart and read it with the eyes of the heart, in a *clairvoyance* interpreting the specific points in the most diverse ways. Just as the child puts his schoolbook under his pillow to make sure he has not forgotten his lesson when he wakes up in the morning, so I take the book to bed with me at night. Every word by him is food and clothing and healing for my wretched soul. Now a word by him arouses me from my lethargy and awakens new restlessness; now it calms the sterile raging within me, stops the dreadfulness in the mute nausea of my passion. Have you really read Job? Read him, read him again and again. I do not even have the heart to write one single outcry from him in a letter to you, even though I find my joy in transcribing over and over everything he has said, sometimes in Danish script and sometimes in Latin script, sometimes in one format and sometimes in another. Every transcription of this kind is laid upon my sick heart as a God's-hand-plaster. Indeed, on whom did God lay his hand as on Job! But quote him—that I cannot do. That would be wanting to put in my own pittance, wanting to make his words my own in the presence of another. When I am alone, I do it, appropriate everything, but as soon as anyone comes, I know very well what a young man is supposed to do when the elderly are speaking.

February 17   III
247

My Silent Confidant:

I am inside. With clean hands—as the thieves usually say—or at the king's pleasure? I do not know. All I know is that I am inside here and that I do not stir from the spot. Here I stand. On my head or on my feet? I do not know. All I know is that I am standing and have been standing *suspenso gradu* [immobilized] for a whole month now, without moving a foot or making one single movement.

I am waiting for a thunderstorm—and for repetition. And yet I would be happy and indescribably blessed if the thunderstorm would only come, even if my sentence were that no repetition is possible.

What will be the effect of this thunderstorm? It will make me fit to be a husband. It will shatter my whole personality—I am prepared. It will render me almost unrecognizable to myself—I am unwavering even though I am standing on one foot. My honor will be saved, my pride will be redeemed, and no matter how it transforms me, I nevertheless hope that the recollection of it will remain with me as an unfailing consolation, will remain when I have experienced what I in a certain sense dread more than suicide, because it will play havoc with me on quite another scale. If the thunderstorm does not come, then I will become crafty. I will not die, not at all, but I will pretend to be dead so that my relatives and friends may bury me. When they lay me in my coffin, I will in all secrecy hide my expectancy. No one will get to   III
know it, for people would take care not to bury someone in whom there is   248
still some life.

In other respects, I am doing my best to make myself into a husband. I sit and clip myself, take away everything that is incommensurable in order to become commensurable.

May 31   III
253

My Silent Confidant:

She is married—to whom I do not know, for when I read it in the newspaper I was so stunned that I dropped the paper and have not had the patience since then to check in detail. I am myself again. Here I have repetition; I understand everything, and life seems more beautiful to me than ever. It did indeed come like a thunderstorm, although I am indebted to her generosity for its coming. Whoever it is she has chosen—I will not even say preferred, because in the capacity of a husband any one is preferable to me—she has certainly shown generosity toward me. Even if he were the handsomest man in the world, the epitome of charm, capable of enchanting any woman, even if she drove her whole sex to despair by giving him her "yes," she still acted generously, if in no other way than by completely forgetting me. Indeed, what is as beautiful as feminine generosity. Let the earthly beauty fade, let her eyes grow dull, let her erect form bend with the years, let her curly locks lose their alluring power when they are concealed by the modest hood, let her regal glance that ruled the world simply embrace and watch with motherly love over the little circle she safeguards—a girl who has been so generous never grows old. Let existence [*Tilværelsen*] reward her as it has, let it give her what she loved more; it also gave me what I loved more—myself, and gave it to me through her generosity.

I am myself again. This "self" that someone else would not pick up off the street I have once again. The split that was in my being is healed; I am unified again. The anxieties of sympathy that were sustained and nourished by my pride are no longer there to disintegrate and disrupt.

III
254 Is there not, then, a repetition? Did I not get everything double? Did I not get myself again and precisely in such a way that I might have a double sense of its meaning? Compared with such a repetition, what is a repetition of worldly possessions, which is indifferent toward the qualification of the spirit? Only his children did Job not receive double again, for a human life cannot be redoubled that way. Here only repetition of the spirit is possible, even though it is never so perfect in time as in eternity, which is the true repetition.

I am myself again; the machinery has been set in motion. The inveiglements in which I was entrapped have been rent asunder; the magic formula that hexed me so that I could not come back to myself has been broken. There is no longer anyone who raises his hand against me. My emancipation is assured; I am born to myself, for as long as Ilithyia folds her hands, the one who is in labor cannot give birth.

It is over, my skiff is afloat. In a minute I shall be there where my soul longs to be, there where ideas spume with elemental fury, where thoughts arise uproariously like nations in migration, there where at other times there is a stillness like the deep silence of the Pacific Ocean, a stillness in which one hears oneself speak even though the movement takes place only in one's interior being, there where each moment one is staking one's life, each moment losing it and finding it again.

I belong to the idea. When it beckons to me, I follow; when it makes an appointment, I wait for it day and night; no one calls me to dinner, no one expects me for supper. When the idea calls, I abandon everything, or, more correctly, I have nothing to abandon. I defraud no one, I sadden no one by being loyal to it; my spirit is not saddened by my having to make another sad. When I come home, no one reads my face, no one questions my demeanor. No one coaxes out of my being an explanation that not even I myself can give to another, whether I am beatific in joy or dejected in desolation, whether I have won life or lost it.

The beaker of inebriation is again offered to me, and already I am inhaling its fragrance, already I am aware of its bubbling music—but first a libation to her who saved a soul who sat in the solitude of despair: Praised be feminine generosity! Three cheers for the flight of thought, three cheers for the perils of life in service to the idea, three cheers for the hardships of battle, three cheers for the festive jubilation of victory, three cheers for the dance in the vortex of the infinite, three cheers for the cresting waves that hide me in the abyss, three cheers for the cresting waves that fling me above the stars!

III
255

PHILOSOPHICAL FRAGMENTS,
OR A FRAGMENT OF PHILOSOPHY (JUNE 13, 1844)
BY JOHANNES CLIMACUS
EDITED BY S. KIERKEGAARD

Fragments is the first of three works by Johannes Climacus, but in form it is different from the other two. Whereas *Johannes Climacus, or De omnibus dubitandum est* is a "Narrative" and *Concluding Unscientific Postscript to* Philosophical Fragments is a "Mimetetical-Pathetical-Dialectical Composition, an Existential Contribution" on the subject of *Fragments* in "its historical costume," the form of *Fragments* is what Kierkegaard calls "speaking . . . algebraically."[48] The particular structure in *Fragments* is: If . . . , then . . .—a hypothesis, an imaginary construction. Cast in a Platonic mode, the "Thought-Project" raises the question of the possible relation of an eternal consciousness and happiness to a historical point of departure. If one is to go beyond Socrates, then the learner must not possess the truth (subjectivity is untruth) and the moment in time must be of decisive importance, not a vanishing occasion, as Socrates was. The discussion of a qualitatively new relation of the teacher and the learner is interrupted by the "Interlude": Is the Past More Necessary than the Future? Or Has the Possible, by Having Become Actual, Become More Necessary than It Was?—the issues of change, coming into existence, the nature of the historical, and freedom/necessity. The concluding chapter continues the theme of contemporaneity and the learner who is a contemporary follower of the paradoxical teacher and points out the essential contemporaneity of the later follower. The "If . . . , then . . ." Thought-Project goes beyond the Platonic-Socratic in positing what the hypothesis requires: a new organ, "faith; and a new presupposition: the consciousness of sin; and a new decision: the moment; and a new teacher: the god in time."[49]

Can a historical point of departure be given for an eternal consciousness; how can such a point of departure be of more than historical interest; can an eternal happiness be built on historical knowledge?

The question is asked by one who in his ignorance does not even know what provided the occasion for his questioning in this way.

THOUGHT-PROJECT

A.

Can the truth be learned? With this question we shall begin. It was a Socratic question or became that by way of the Socratic question whether virtue can be taught—for virtue in turn was defined as insight (see *Protagoras, Gorgias, Meno, Euthydemus*). Insofar as the truth is to be learned, it of course must be assumed not to be—consequently, because it is to be learned, it is sought. Here we encounter the difficulty that Socrates calls attention to in the *Meno* (80, near the end) as a "pugnacious proposition": a person cannot possibly seek what he knows, and, just as impossibly, he cannot seek what he does not know, for what he knows he cannot seek, since he knows it, and what he does not know he cannot seek, because, after all, he does not even know what he is supposed to seek. Socrates thinks through the difficulty by means [of the principle] that all learning and seeking are but recollecting. Thus the ignorant person merely needs to be reminded in order, by himself, to call to mind what he knows. The truth is not introduced into him but was in him. Socrates elaborates on this idea, and in it the Greek pathos is in fact concentrated, since it becomes a demonstration for the immorality of the soul—retrogressively, please note—or a demonstration for the pre-existence of the soul.*

In view of this, it is manifest with what wonderful consistency Socrates remained true to himself and artistically exemplified what he had understood. He was and continued to be a midwife, not because he "did not have the positive,"** but because he perceived that this relation is the highest relation a human being can have to another. And in that he is indeed forever right, for even if a divine point of departure is ever given, this remains the true relation between one human being and another, if one reflects upon the absolute and does not dally with the accidental but with all one's heart re-

IV
180

---

* If the thought is thought absolutely—that is, so that the various states of pre-existence are not considered—this Greek idea is repeated in ancient and modern speculation: an eternal creating, an eternal emanating from the Father, an eternal becoming of the deity, an eternal self-sacrifice, a past resurrection, a judgment over and done with. All these ideas are that Greek idea of recollection, although this is not always noticed, because they have been arrived at by going further. If the idea is analyzed in a tallying of the various states of pre-existence, then the eternal "pre's" of that approximating thinking are similar to the eternal "post's" of the corresponding approximation. The contradiction of existence [*Tilværelse*] is explained by positing a "pre" as needed (by virtue of a prior state, the individual has arrived at his present, otherwise unexplainable state) or by positing a "post" as needed (on another planet the individual will be better situated, and in consideration of that, his present state is not unexplainable).

** As it is said in our age, in which one has "the positive" more or less in the way a polytheist would make light of monotheism's negativity, because polytheism, of course, has many gods, the monotheist but one. The philosophers have many ideas—all valid up to a point. Socrates has but one, which is absolute.

nounces understanding the half-measures that seem to be the inclination of
men and the secret of the system. Socrates, however, was a midwife examined by the god himself. The work he carried out was a divine commission
(see Plato's *Apology*), even though he struck people as an eccentric (ἀτοπώ
τατος, *Theaetetus,* 149), and the divine intention, as Socrates also understood
it, was that the god forbade him to give birth (μαιεύεσθαι με ὁ θέος ἀναγκάζει,
γεννᾶν δὲ ἀπεκώλυσεν [the god constrains me to serve as a midwife, but has
debarred me from giving birth], *Theaetetus,* 150 c), because between one
human being and another μαιεύεσθαι [to serve as a midwife] is the highest;
giving birth indeed belongs to the god.

Viewed Socratically, any point of departure in time is *eo ipso* something
accidental, a vanishing point, an occasion. Nor is the teacher anything more,
and if he gives of himself and his erudition in any other way, he does not
give but takes away. Then he is not even the other's friend, much less his
teacher. This is the profundity of Socratic thinking, this his noble, thoroughgoing humanity, which does not exclusively and conceitedly cultivate
the company of brilliant minds but feels just as kin to a tanner, and for that
reason he soon "became convinced that the study of nature is not man's concern and therefore began to philosophize about the ethical in workshops and
in the market-place" (Diogenes Laertius, II, V, 21) but philosophized just as
absolutely with whomever he spoke. With half-thoughts, with higgling and
haggling, with claiming and disclaiming, as if the individual to a certain degree owed something to another person but then again to a certain degree
did not, with vague words that explain everything except what is meant by
this "to a certain degree"—with all such things one does not go beyond
Socrates or reach the concept of revelation, either, but simply remains in
empty talk. In the Socratic view, every human being is himself the midpoint,
and the whole world focuses only on him because his self-knowledge is God-
knowledge. Moreover, this is how Socrates understood himself, and in his
view this is how every human being must understand himself, and by virtue
of that understanding he must understand his relation to the single individual, always with equal humility and with equal pride. For that purpose,
Socrates had the courage and self-collectedness to be sufficient unto himself,
but in his relations to others he also had the courage and self-collectedness
to be merely an occasion even for the most stupid person. What rare magnanimity—rare in our day, when the pastor is little more than the deacon,
when every second person is an authority, while all these distinctions and all
this considerable authority are mediated in a common lunacy and in a *commune naufragium* [common shipwreck], because since no human being has
ever truly been an authority or has benefited anyone else by being that or
has ever really managed successfully to carry his dependent along, there is
better success in another way, for it never fails that one fool going his way
takes several others along with him.

If this is the case with regard to learning the truth, then the fact that I have learned from Socrates or from Prodicus or from a maidservant can concern me only historically or—to the extent that I am a Plato in my enthusiasm—poetically. But this enthusiasm, even though it is beautiful, even though I wish for myself and for everyone else this εὐχαταφορία εἰς πάθος [disposition to passion], which only the Stoic could warn against, although I do not have the Socratic magnanimity and the Socratic self-denial to think its nothingness—this enthusiasm, Socrates would say, is still but an illusion, indeed, a muddiness of mind in which earthly distinction ferments almost grossly. Neither can the fact that the teaching of Socrates or of Prodicus was this or that have anything but historical interest for me, because the truth in which I rest was in me and emerged from me. Not even Socrates would have been capable of giving it to me, no more than the coachman is capable of pulling the horse's load, even though he may help the horse do it by means of the whip.* My relation to Socrates and Prodicus cannot concern me with regard to my eternal happiness, for this is given retrogressively in the possession of the truth that I had from the beginning without knowing it. If I were to imagine myself meeting Socrates, Prodicus, or the maidservant in another life, there again none of them would be more than an occasion, as Socrates intrepidly expresses it by saying that even in the underworld he would only ask questions, for the ultimate idea in all questioning is that the person asked must himself possess the truth and acquire it by himself. The temporal point of departure is a nothing, because in the same moment I discover that I have known the truth from eternity without knowing it, in the same instant that moment is hidden in the eternal, assimilated into it in such a way that I, so to speak, still cannot find it even if I were to look for it, because there is no Here and no There, but only an *ubique et nusquam* [everywhere and nowhere].

IV
183

B.

If the situation is to be different, then the moment in time must have such decisive significance that for no moment will I be able to forget it, neither in time nor in eternity, because the eternal, previously nonexistent, came into existence [*blev til*]⁵⁰ in that moment. With this presupposition, let us now examine the relations involved in the question: Can the truth be learned?

---

* I cite one passage in *Clitophon* merely as a remark by a third party, since this dialogue is considered to be spurious. Clitophon laments that, with respect to virtue, Socrates is only encouraging (προτετραμένος), so that from the moment he has adequately recommended virtue in general, he leaves everyone on his own. Clitophon believes that this conduct must have its basis either in Socrates' not knowing more or in his not wanting to communicate more. (See para. 410.)

a. The Preceding State

We begin with the Socratic difficulty: How is one able to seek the truth, since it is indeed equally impossible whether one has it or one does not. The Socratic line of thought in effect annulled the disjunction, since it appeared that basically every human being possesses the truth. That was his explanation. We have seen what resulted with regard to the moment. Now if the moment is to acquire decisive significance, then the seeker up until that moment must not have possessed the truth, not even in the form of ignorance, for in that case the moment becomes merely the moment of occasion; indeed, he must not even be a seeker. This is the way we have to state the difficulty if we do not want to explain it Socratically. Consequently, he has to be defined as being outside the truth (not coming toward it like a proselyte, but going away from it) or as untruth. He is, then, untruth. But how, then, is he to be reminded, or what would be the use of reminding him of what he has not known and consequently cannot call to mind?

IV
184

b. The Teacher

If the teacher is to be the occasion that reminds the learner, he cannot assist him to recollect that he actually does know the truth, for the learner is indeed untruth. That for which the teacher can become the occasion of his recollecting is that he is untruth. But by this calling to mind, the learner is definitely excluded from the truth, even more than when he was ignorant of being untruth. Consequently, in this way, precisely by reminding him, the teacher thrusts the learner away, except that by being turned in upon himself in this manner the learner does not discover that he previously knew the truth but discovers his untruth. To this act of consciousness, the Socratic principle applies: the teacher is only an occasion, whoever he may be, even if he is a god, because I can discover my own untruth only by myself, because only when *I* discover it is it discovered, not before, even though the whole world knew it. (Under the assumed presupposition about the moment, this becomes the one and only analogy to the Socratic.)

Now, if the learner is to obtain the truth, the teacher must bring it to him, but not only that. Along with it, he must provide him with the condition for understanding it, for if the learner were himself the condition for understanding the truth, then he merely needs to recollect, because the condition for understanding the truth is like being able to ask about it—the condition and the question contain the conditioned and the answer. (If this is not the case, then the moment is to be understood only Socratically.)

But the one who not only gives the learner the truth but provides the condition is not a teacher. Ultimately, all instruction depends upon the presence of the condition; if it is lacking, then a teacher is capable of nothing, because in the second case, the teacher, before beginning to teach, must transform, not reform, the learner. But no human being is capable of doing this; if it is to take place, it must be done by the god himself.

Now, inasmuch as the learner exists [*er til*], he is indeed created, and, accordingly, God must have given him the condition for understanding the truth (for otherwise he previously would have been merely animal, and that teacher who gave him the condition along with the truth would make him a human being for the first time). But insofar as the moment is to have decisive significance (and if this is not assumed, then we do in fact remain with the Socratic), he must lack the condition, consequently be deprived of it. This cannot have been due to an act of the god (for this is a contradiction) or to an accident (for it is a contradiction that something inferior would be able to vanquish something superior); it must therefore have been due to himself. If he could have lost the condition in such a way that it was not due to himself, and if he could be in this state of loss without its being due to himself, then he would have possessed the condition only accidentally, which is a contradiction, since the condition for the truth is an essential condition. The untruth, then, is not merely outside the truth but is polemical against the truth, which is expressed by saying that he himself has forfeited and is forfeiting the condition.

The teacher, then, is the god himself, who, acting as the occasion, prompts the learner to be reminded that he is untruth and is that through his own fault. But this state—to be untruth and to be that through one's own fault— what can we call it? Let us call it *sin*.

The teacher, then, is the god, who gives the condition and gives the truth. Now, what should we call such a teacher, for we surely do agree that we have gone far beyond the definition of a teacher. Inasmuch as the learner is in untruth but is that by his own act (and, according to what has already been said, there is no other way he can be that), he might seem to be free, for to be on one's own certainly is freedom. And yet he is indeed unfree and bound and excluded, because to be free from the truth is indeed to be excluded, and to be excluded by oneself is indeed to be bound. But since he is bound by himself, can he not work himself loose or free himself, for that which binds me should also be able to set me free at will, and since that is himself, he should certainly be able to do it. But first of all he must will it. But just suppose that he was very profoundly reminded of that for which that teacher became the occasion (and this must never be forgotten) of his recollecting—just suppose that he willed it. In that case (if by willing it he could do it by himself), his having been bound would become a bygone state, one that in the moment of liberation would vanish without a trace—and the moment would not gain

IV
185

IV
186

decisive significance. He would be unaware that he had bound himself and now set himself free.*

Considered in this way, the moment acquires no decisive significance, and yet this was what we wanted to assume as the hypothesis. According to the hypothesis, then, he will not be able to set himself free. (And this is truly just the way it is, for he uses the power of freedom in the service of unfreedom, since he is indeed freely in it, and in this way the combined power of unfreedom grows and makes him the slave of sin.)

IV
187

What, then, should we call such a teacher who gives him the condition again and along with it the truth? Let us call him a *savior,* for he does indeed save the learner from unfreedom, saves him from himself. Let us call him a *deliverer,* for he does indeed deliver the person who had imprisoned himself, and no one is so dreadfully imprisoned, and no captivity is so impossible to break out of as that in which the individual holds himself captive! And yet, even this does not say enough, for by his unfreedom he had indeed become

---

* We shall take our time—after all, there is no need to hurry. By going slowly, one sometimes does indeed fail to reach the goal, but by going too fast, one sometimes passes it. We shall discuss this somewhat in Greek fashion. If a child who has received the gift of a little money— enough to be able to buy either a good book, for example, or one toy, for both cost the same— buys the toy, can he use the same money to buy the book? By no means, for now the money has been spent. But he may go to the bookseller and ask him if he will exchange the book for the toy. Suppose the bookseller answers: My dear child, your toy is worthless; it is certainly true that when you still had the money you could have bought the book just as well as the toy, but the awkward thing about a toy is that once it is purchased it has lost all value. Would not the child think: This is very strange indeed. And so it was also once, when man could buy freedom and unfreedom for the same price, and this price was the free choice of the soul and the surrender of the choice. He chose unfreedom, but if he then were to approach the god and ask whether he could make an exchange, the answer presumably would be: Undeniably there was a time when you could have bought what you wanted, but the curious thing about unfreedom is that once it is purchased it has no value whatsoever, even though one pays the same price for it. I wonder if such a person would not say: This is very strange indeed. Or if two hostile armies faced each other, and there came a knight whom both sides invited to join; but he chose the one side, was defeated and taken prisoner. As prisoner he was brought before the conqueror and was foolish enough to offer him his services on the conditions originally offered. I wonder if the conqueror would not say to him: My dear fellow, you are my prisoner now; true enough, at one time you could have chosen differently, but now everything is changed. Would this not be strange indeed! If it were otherwise, if the moment did not have decisive significance, then the child, after all, must indeed have bought the book and merely have been ignorant of it, mistakenly thinking that he had bought the toy; the prisoner, after all, must have fought on the other side, but had not been seen because of the fog, and had really sided with the one whose prisoner he now imagined himself to be.—"The depraved person and the virtuous person presumably do not have power over their moral condition, but in the beginning they did have the power to become the one or the other, just as the person who

IV
187

throws a stone has power over it before he throws it but not when he has thrown it" (Aristotle). Otherwise the throwing would become an illusion, and the person throwing, despite all his throwing, would keep the stone in his hand, since the stone, like the skeptics' "flying arrow," did not fly.

guilty of something, and if that teacher gives him the condition and the truth, then he is, of course, a *reconciler* who takes away the wrath that lay over the incurred guilt.

A teacher such as that, the learner will never be able to forget, because in that very moment he would sink down into himself again, just as the person did who once possessed the condition and then, by forgetting that God is, sank into unfreedom. If they were to meet in another life, that teacher would again be able to give the condition to the person who had not received it, but he would be quite different for the person who had once received it. After all, the condition was something entrusted, and therefore the receiver was always responsible for an accounting. But a teacher such as that—what should we call him? A teacher certainly can evaluate the learner with respect to whether or not he is making progress, but he cannot pass judgment on him, for he must be Socratic enough to perceive that he cannot give the learner what is essential. That teacher, then, is actually not a teacher but is a *judge.* Even when the learner has most fully put on the condition and then, by doing so, has become immersed in the truth, he still can never forget that teacher or allow him to disappear Socratically, which still is far more profound than all unseasonable punctiliousness and deluded fanaticism— indeed, it is the highest if that other is not truth.

And, now, the moment. A moment such as this is unique. To be sure, it is short and temporal, as the moment is; it is passing, as the moment is, past, as the moment is in the next moment, and yet it is decisive, and yet it is filled with the eternal. A moment such as this must have a special name. Let us call it: *the fullness of time.* IV
188

c. The Follower

When the learner is untruth (and otherwise we go back to the Socratic) but is nevertheless a human being, and he now receives the condition and the truth, he does not, of course, become a human being for the first time, for he already was that; but he becomes a different person, not in the jesting sense—as if he became someone else of the same quality as before—but he becomes a person of a different quality or, as we can also call it, a *new* person.

Inasmuch as he was untruth, he was continually in the process of departing from the truth; as a result of receiving the condition in the moment, his course took the opposite direction, or he was turned around. Let us call this change *conversion,* even though this is a word hitherto unused; but we choose it precisely in order to avoid confusion, for it seems to be created for the very change of which we speak.

Inasmuch as he was in untruth through his own fault, this conversion cannot take place without its being assimilated into his consciousness or without his becoming aware that it was through his own fault, and with this consciousness he takes leave of his former state. But how does one take leave without feeling sorrowful? Yet this sorrow is, of course, over his having been so long in the former state. Let us call such sorrow *repentance,* for what else is repentance, which does indeed look back, but nevertheless in such a way that precisely thereby it quickens its pace toward what lies ahead!

Inasmuch as he was in untruth and now along with the condition receives the truth, a change takes place in him like the change from "not to be" to "to be." But this transition from "not to be" to "to be" is indeed the transition of birth. But the person who already *is* cannot be born, and yet he is born. Let us call this transition *rebirth,* by which he enters the world a second time just as at birth—an individual human being who as yet knows nothing about the world into which he is born, whether it is inhabited, whether there are other human beings in it, for presumably we can be baptized *en masse* but can never be reborn *en masse.* Just as the person who by Socratic midwifery gave birth to himself and in so doing forgot everything else in the world and in a more profound sense owed no human being anything, so also the one who is born again owes no human being anything, but owes that divine teacher everything. And just as the other one, because of himself, forgot the whole world, so he in turn, because of this teacher, must forget himself.

If, then, *the moment* is to have decisive significance—and if not, we speak only Socratically, no matter what we say, even though we use many and strange words, even though in our failure to understand ourselves we suppose we have gone beyond that simple wise man who uncompromisingly distinguished between the god, man, and himself, more uncompromisingly than Minos, Aeacus, and Rhadamanthus—then the break has occurred, and the person can no longer come back and will find no pleasure in recollecting what remembrance wants to bring him in recollection, and even less will he by his own power be capable of drawing the god over to his side again.

But is what has been elaborated here thinkable? We shall not be in a hurry with the answer, for someone who because of prolonged pondering never comes up with an answer is not the only one who fails to answer—so too the one who admittedly manifests a marvelous quickness in answering but not the desirable slowness in considering the difficulty before explaining it. Before we answer, we shall ask who ought to answer the question. This matter of being born—is it thinkable? Well, why not? But who is supposed to think it—one who is born or one who is not born? The latter, of course, is unreasonable and cannot occur to anyone, for this notion certainly cannot occur to one who is born. When one who is born thinks of himself as born, he of course is thinking of this transition from "not to be" to "to be." The situation must be the same with rebirth. Or is the matter made more difficult by this—that the non-being preceding the rebirth has more being than the non-being that precedes birth? But who, then, is supposed to think this? It must, of course, be one who is reborn, for it would be unreasonable to think that one who is not reborn should do it, and would it not be ludicrous if this were to occur to one who is not reborn?

IV
190

If a person originally possesses the condition to understand the truth, he thinks that, since he himself is, God is. If he is in untruth, then he must of course think this about himself, and recollection will be unable to help him to think anything but this. Whether or not he is to go any further, *the moment* must decide (although it already was active in making him perceive that he is untruth). If he does not understand this, then he is to be referred to Socrates, even though his opinion that he has gone much further will cause that wise man a great deal of trouble, as did those who became so exasperated with him when he took away some foolish notion from them (ἐπειδάν τινα λῆρον αὐτῶν ἀφαιρῶμαι) that they positively wanted to bite him (see *Theaetetus,* 151).—In *the moment,* a person becomes aware that he was born, for his previous state, to which he is not to appeal, was indeed one of "not to be." In *the moment,* he becomes aware of the rebirth, for his previous state was indeed one of "not to be." If his previous state had been one of "to be," then under no circumstances would the moment have acquired decisive significance for him, as explained above. Whereas the Greek pathos focuses on recollection, the pathos of our project focuses on the moment, and no wonder, for is it not an exceedingly pathos-filled matter to come into existence from the state of "not to be"?

THE MORAL

IV
272

This project indisputably goes beyond the Socratic, as is apparent at every point. Whether it is therefore more true than the Socratic is an altogether different question, one that cannot be decided in the same breath, inasmuch as a new organ has been assumed here: faith; and a new presupposition: the consciousness of sin; and a new decision: the moment; and a new teacher: the god in time. Without these, I really would not have dared to present myself for inspection before that ironist who has been admired for millennia, whom I approach with as much ardent enthusiasm as anyone. But to go beyond Socrates when one nevertheless says essentially the same as he, only not nearly so well—that, at least, is not Socratic.

JOHANNES CLIMACUS,
OR *DE OMNIBUS DUBITANDUM EST*
(*PAPIRER* IV B 1, 1842–43)

After the writing of *Either/Or,* Kierkegaard became preoccupied with Greek philosophy and modern philosophy. The metaphysical and epistemological aspects of that interest are reflected in *Fragments* and in *Johannes Climacus.* The central issue in *Johannes Climacus,* although written in the form of a narrative, is Descartes' philosophical maxim that all is to be doubted down to the bedrock of indisputable clear and distinct ideas. This was one of the subjects envisioned in young Kierkegaard's writing plans, which included also the master thief, the wandering Jew, Don Juan, and Faust. The question of doubt in *Johannes Climacus* is the only one of the early contemplated themes that Kierkegaard developed in a specific work, but this was not completed and was not published until it appeared in the *Papier.* The theme, however, is found in relevant contexts in other works, as are also Don Juan and Faust, but the other two scarcely ever appear. The Introduction, the story of the young Johannes Climacus, is followed by *Pars Prima,* "Johannes Climacus Begins to Philosophize with the Aid of Traditional Ideas," an analysis of modern philosophy and doubt and the relation of the doubter to the skeptical thesis. *Pars Secunda* centers on Johannes's own venture in trying to get clear on what it means to doubt. Although the piece is incomplete, Hannah Arendt considered it to be "perhaps still the deepest interpretation of Descartes' doubt."[51]

IV
B 1
104

INTRODUCTION

Some years ago in the city of H . . . . . there lived a young student by the name of Johannes Climacus, who had no desire whatsoever to become prominent in the world, inasmuch as, on the contrary, he enjoyed living a quiet, secluded life. Those who knew him somewhat intimately tried to explain his inclosed nature, which shunned all close contacts with people, by supposing that he was either melancholy or in love. In a certain sense, those who supposed the latter were not incorrect, although they erred if they assumed that a girl was the object of his dreams. Such sentiments were totally foreign to his heart, and just as his external appearance was delicate and ethereal, almost transparent, his soul was likewise far too intellectual and spiritual to be captivated by a woman's beauty. In love he was, ardently in love— with thought, or, more accurately, with thinking. No young lover can be more intensely moved by the incomprehensible transition that comes when erotic love [*Elskov*] awakens in his breast, by the stroke of lightning with which reciprocated love bursts forth in the beloved's breast, than he was moved by the comprehensible transition in which one thought connects with another, a transition that for him was the happy moment when, in the

IV
B 1
105

stillness of his soul, his presentiments and expectations were fulfilled. Thus, when in thought his head was bowed down like a ripe spike of wheat, it was not because he was listening to his beloved's voice but because he was listening to the secret whispering of thoughts; when he had a dreamy look, it was not because he had intimations of her picture but because the movement of thought was becoming visible to him. It was his delight to begin with a single thought and then, by way of coherent thinking, to climb step by step to a higher one, because to him coherent thinking was a *scala paradisi* [ladder of paradise], and his blessedness seemed to him even more glorious than the angels'. Therefore, when he arrived at the higher thought, it was an indescribable joy, a passionate pleasure, for him to plunge headfirst down into the same coherent thoughts until he reached the point from which he had proceeded. Yet this did not always turn out according to his desire. If he did not get just as many pushes as there were links in the coherent thinking, he became despondent, for then the movement was imperfect. Then he would begin all over again. If he was successful, he would be thrilled, could not sleep for joy, and for hours would continue making the same movement, for this up-and-down and down-and-up of thought was an unparalleled joy. In those happy times, his step was light, almost floating; at other times, it was troubled and unsteady. As long as he labored to climb up, as long as coherent thinking had as yet not managed to make its way, he was oppressed, because he feared losing all those coherent thoughts he had finished but which as yet were not perfectly clear and necessary. When we see someone carrying a number of fragile and brittle things stacked one upon the other, we are not surprised that he walks unsteadily and continually tries to maintain balance. If we do not see the stack, we smile, just as many smiled at Johannes Climacus, not suspecting that his soul was carrying a stack far taller than is usually enough to cause astonishment, that his soul was anxious lest one single coherent thought slip out, for then the whole thing would collapse. He did not notice that people smiled at him, no more than at other times he would notice an individual turn around in delight and look at him when he hurried down the street as lightly as in a dance. He did not pay any attention to people and did not imagine that they could pay any attention to him; he was and remained a stranger in the world.

IV
B 1
106

If Climacus's conduct must have seemed somewhat remarkable to someone who did not know him very well, it was by no means unexplainable to someone who knew a little about his earlier life, for now in his twenty-first year he was to a certain extent the same as he had always been. His natural disposition had not been disturbed in childhood but had been developed by favorable circumstances. His home did not offer many diversions, and, since he practically never went out, he very early became accustomed to being occupied with himself and with his own thoughts. His father was a very strict man, seemingly dry and prosaic, but underneath this rough homespun cloak he concealed a glowing imagination that not even his advanced age managed to dim. When at times Johannes asked permission to go out, his request was usually refused; but occasionally his father, by way of compensation, offered to take his hand and go for a walk up and down the floor. At first glance, this was a poor substitute, and yet, like the rough homespun coat, it concealed something altogether different. The offer was accepted, and it was left entirely up to Johannes to decide where they should go for a walk. They walked through the city gate to the country palace nearby or to the seashore or about the streets—according to Johannes's wish, for his father was capable of everything. While they walked up and down the floor, his father would tell about everything they saw.

IV
B 1
107
They greeted the passers-by; the carriages rumbled past, drowning out his father's voice; the pastry woman's fruits were more tempting than ever. Whatever was familiar to Johannes, his father delineated so exactly, so vividly, so directly and on the spot, down to the most trifling detail, and so minutely and graphically whatever was unfamiliar to him, that after a half-hour's walk with his father he was as overwhelmed and weary as if he had been out a whole day. Johannes quickly learned his father's magic art. What formerly took place as epic narrative now became a drama; they carried on a dialogue on their tour. If they walked along familiar paths, they watched each other lest something be overlooked. If the path was unfamiliar to Johannes, he made associations, while his father's omnipotent imagination was able to fashion everything, to use every childish wish as an ingredient in the drama that was taking place. For Johannes, it was as if the world came into existence during the conversation, as if his father were our Lord and he himself his favored one who had permission to insert his own foolish whims as hilariously as he wished, for he was never rebuffed, his father was never disturbed—everything was included and always to Johannes's satisfaction.

While life in his paternal home was contributing in this way to the development of his imagination, teaching him to relish ambrosia, the education he received in school was in harmony with this. The sublime authority of Latin grammar and the divine dignity of rules developed a new enthusiasm. Greek grammar in particular appealed to him. Because of it, he forgot to read Homer aloud to himself as he usually did in order to enjoy the rhythms of the poem. The Greek teacher presented grammar in a more philosophical way. When it was explained to Johannes that the accusative case, for example, is an extension in time and space, that the preposition does not govern the case but that the relation does, everything expanded before him. The preposition vanished; the extension in time and space became like an enormous empty picture for intuition. Once again his imagi-

IV
B 1
108
nation was engaged, but in a way different from before. What had enter-

tained him on the walking tours was the filled space into which he could not fit snugly enough. His imagination was so creative that a little went a long way. Outside the one window in the living room grew approximately ten blades of grass. Here he sometimes discovered a little creature running among the stems. These stems became an enormous forest that still had the compactness and darkness the grass had. Instead of the filled space, he now had empty space; he stared again but saw nothing except the enormous expanse.

While an almost vegetative dozing in imagination—at times more esthetic, at times more intellectual—was being developed, another side of his soul was also being acutely fashioned—namely, his sense for the sudden, the surprising. This came about not through the magic means customarily used to keep children spellbound but by means of something far superior. His father combined an irresistible dialectic with an omnipotent imagination. Whenever his father on occasion engaged in an argument with someone else, Johannes was all ears, all the more so because everything proceeded with an almost festive formality. His father always let his opponent say everything he had to say and, as a precaution, always asked him if he had anything more to say before he began his response. Johannes, having followed the opponent's case with keen attention, had in his own way a co-interest in the outcome. Then came the pause; his father's response followed, and—look!—in a twinkling everything was changed. How it happened remained a riddle to Johannes, but his soul delighted in this drama. The opponent spoke again, and Johannes listened even more attentively, lest he lose the thread of thought. The opponent summed up his argument, and Johannes could almost hear his heart beating, so impatiently did he wait to see what would happen. —It did happen. In an instant, everything was turned upside down; the explicable was made inexplicable, the certain doubtful, the opposite was made obvious. When a shark wants to snatch its prey, it has to turn over on its back, since its mouth is on the belly side; its back is dark, its belly silvery white. It is said to be a glorious sight to see this shift in color. It is supposed to gleam so brightly at times that it almost hurts the eyes, and yet they take pleasure in seeing it. Johannes witnessed a similar shift when he listened to his father argue. He forgot what was said by both his father and the opponent, but he never forgot this thrill in his soul. In his life at school, he had similar experiences. He saw how one word could change a whole sentence, how a subjunctive in the middle of an indicative sentence could throw a different light on the whole. The older he grew, the more his father involved himself with him and the more he became aware of that inexplicable quality. It was as if his father had a secret understanding of what Johannes wanted to say and, therefore, with a single word could confuse everything for him. When his father was not acting just as critic but was himself discoursing on something, Johannes perceived how he went about it, how he step by step arrived at what he wanted. He began to suspect that the reason his father could turn everything upside down with a single word had to be that he, Johannes, must have forgotten something in the step-by-step process of thought.

What other children have in the enchantment of poetry and the surprise of fairy tales, Johannes Climacus had in the repose of intuition and the interchange of dialectic. These delighted the child, became the boy's play, the young man's desire. In this way, his life had a rare continuity, not marked by the various transitions that generally denote the separate periods. As Johannes grew older, he had no toys to lay aside, for he had learned to play with what would be his life's earnest occupation, and yet it did not thereby lose its appeal. A little girl plays so long with her doll that at last it is transformed into her beloved, for woman's whole life is love. His life had a similar continuity, for his whole life was thinking.

Climacus became a university student, took the qualifying examination, reached the age of twenty, and yet no change took place in him—he was and remained a stranger to the world. He did not, however, avoid people; on the contrary, he tried to find like-minded people. But he did not express his views, never betrayed what was going on inside him—the erotic in him was too deep for that. He felt that he might blush if he talked about it; he was afraid of learning too much or learning too little. He was always attentive, however, when others were speaking. Just as a young girl deeply in love prefers not to speak about her love but with almost painful tension listens when other girls talk about theirs, in order to test in silence whether or not she is just as happy or even happier, to snatch every important clue—just so did Johannes silently pay attention to everything. Then, when he came home, he reflected on what the philosophizers had said, for it was their company, of course, that he sought.

To want to be a philosopher, to want to devote himself exclusively to speculation, had not occurred to him. He was still not profound enough for that. It is true that he did not dart from one thing to another—thinking was and remained his passion—but he still lacked the reflective composure required for grasping a deeper coherence. The least significant and the most significant things tempted him alike as points of departure for his pursuits; for him the result was not important—only the processes interested him. At times, he did become aware of how he would arrive at one and the same result from quite different points, but this did not attract his attention in a deeper sense. His desire at all times was only to press his way through. Wherever he suspected a labyrinth, he had to find the way. Once he began, nothing could influence him to stop. If he ran into difficulty, if he tired of it too early, he usually resorted to a very simple remedy. He would lock himself in his room, make everything as festive as possible, and

IV
B 1
110

loudly and clearly say: I *will* do it. From his father he had learned that one can do what one wills, and his father's life had not disproved the theory. This experience had given Johannes's soul an indescribable pride. That there might be something one could not do even though one willed it was intolerable to him. But his pride was not a matter of a weak will, because once he had spoken these dynamic words, he was ready for everything; he then had an even higher goal: with his will to press his way through the windings of the difficulty. This again was an adventure that inspired him. In this way his life was always adventurous. He did not require forests and travels for his adventures but merely what he had: a little room with one window.

Although he was led into ideality at an early age, this by no means weakened his belief and trust in actuality [*Virkelighed*]. The ideality by which he was nourished was so close to him, everything took place so naturally, that this ideality became his actuality, and in turn he was bound to expect to find ideality in the actuality all around him. His father's depression contributed to this. That his father was an extraordinary man was the last thing Johannes came to know about him. That his father amazed him more than any other person did, he already knew; yet he knew so few people that he had no standard of measurement. That his father, humanly speaking, was rather extraordinary, he did not learn in his paternal home. Once in a while, when an older, trusted friend visited the family and engaged in a more confidential conversation with his father, Johannes frequently heard him say, "I am good for nothing; I cannot do a thing; my one and only wish would be to find a place in a charitable institution." This was no jest. There was not a trace of irony in his father's words; on the contrary, there was a gloomy earnestness about them that troubled Johannes. Nor was it a casual comment, for his father could demonstrate that a person of the least importance was a genius compared with him. No counter-demonstration achieved anything, for his irresistible dialectic could make one forget what was most obvious, could compel one to stare fixedly at the observation he made as if there were nothing else in the world. Johannes, whose whole view of life was, so to speak, hidden in his father, since he himself did not get to see very much, became entangled in a contradiction, because it was a long time before it dawned on him that his father contradicted himself—if by nothing else, then by the skill with which he could vanquish any opponent and reduce him to silence. Johannes's trust in actuality was not weakened; he had not imbibed ideality from books that do not leave those they bring up ignorant of the fact that the glory they describe is nevertheless not found in this world. His formative influence was not a man who knew how to propound his knowledge as valuable but was instead one who knew how to render it as unimportant and valueless as possible.

IV
B 1
111

IV
B 1
112

PARS PRIMA

JOHANNES CLIMACUS BEGINS TO PHILOSOPHIZE
WITH THE AID OF TRADITIONAL IDEAS

In listening to others talk, he also observed that he had not encountered the writings of the great thinkers among the recent philosophers. Again and again he heard these names mentioned with enthusiasm, almost with adoration. It gave him unspeakable joy to hear their names, even though he did not dare to read them, because he had heard that they were so difficult that the study of them would require ages. It was not cowardice or indolence that deterred him but a painful feeling inherent in him from early childhood: he was not like other people. He was far from feeling happy about this difference but instead he felt it as a pressure he probably would have to endure all his life. He felt like a child who was delivered into the world with much pain and who could not forget this pain even if his mother had forgotten it in her joy over his birth.

As for reading, Johannes now experienced a strange contradiction. The familiar books did not satisfy him, but still he did not dare to lay the blame on the books. The outstanding books he did not dare to read. So he read less and less, followed his inclination to ponder in silence, became increasingly shy, fearful that the major thinkers would smile at him if they heard that he, too, wanted to think, just as fine ladies smile at the lowly maiden if she has the audacity of also wanting to know the bliss of erotic love. He was silent, but listened all the more attentively.

When he listened to the others speak, he noted that a particular main idea came up again and again, whereupon he snatched it and made it the object of his own thinking. Thus fate came to his aid by providing him with subject matter in exactly the way he needed it. The purer, the more virginal, so to speak, the task, the more precious it was to him; the less others had assisted his thinking, the happier he was and the better everything went for him. He seemed to consider it an imperfection that he could do his best thinking about an idea if it came to him as new-fallen snow without having passed through the hands of others. He truly considered it a great thing to be able, as were the others, to toss about in the multiple thoughts of multiple thinkers. Yet he soon forgot this pain in the joy of thinking.

By listening to the conversation of others, he became particularly aware of one thesis that came up again and again, was passed from mouth to mouth, was always praised, always venerated.* He now encountered the thesis that would come to play a decisive role in his life. This thesis became for his life

In margin: * Many were the times he heard it repeated: *De omnibus dubitandum est* [Everything must be doubted].

what in other respects a name frequently is in a person's history—everything can be said in all brevity by mentioning this name.

This thesis became a task for his thinking. Whether it would take a long or a short time to think it through, he did not know. But this he did know: until that time came, he would not let go of it, even though it were to cost him his life.

What made him even more enthusiastic was the connection usually made between this thesis and becoming a philosopher. Whether he would be able to become a philosopher, he did not know, but he would do his best. With quiet solemnity, it was decreed that he should begin. He encouraged himself by recalling the enthusiasm of Dion, who, upon going aboard ship with a handful of men to begin the war with Dionysius, said: It is enough for me just to have participated. If I were to die the moment I set foot on land without having achieved a thing, I would still regard this death as happy and honorable.

He now sought to clarify for himself the connection between that thesis and philosophy. Preoccupation with it would become for him an encouraging prelude; the clearer the connection became, the more enthusiastically he would proceed to the main concern. So he closed himself up in himself with that philosophical thesis, and at the same time he paid careful attention to every clue he could glean. If he perceived that his own thought process was different from that of others, he memorized theirs, went home, and began all over from the beginning. That their thought process was generally very brief did indeed strike him, but he saw that only as a new point to their advantage.

Now he began his operations and immediately juxtaposed the three principal statements he had heard regarding the relation of this thesis to philosophy. These three theses were as follows: (1) *philosophy begins with doubt;* (2) *in order to philosophize, one must have doubted;* (3) *modern philosophy begins with doubt.*

PARS SECUNDA

What Is It to Doubt?

1. What Must the Nature of Existence be in Order for Doubt to be Possible?

As Johannes began his deliberation on this question, he of course perceived that if he demanded an empirical answer to it, life would offer a multifariousness that would only hide a perplexing diffusion over the whole range of extremes. In other words, not only could that which evokes doubt in the single individual be extremely different, but it could also be the opposite, for if someone were to discourse on doubt in order to arouse doubt in another, he could precisely thereby evoke faith, just as faith, conversely, could evoke doubt. Because of this paradoxical dialectic, which, as he had realized ear-

IV
B 1
115

IV
B 1
116

IV
B 1
141

IV
B 1
144

IV
B 1
145
lier, had no analogy in any sphere of knowledge since all knowledge stands
in a direct and immanent relation to its object and the knower, not in an inverse and transcendent relation to a third, he easily perceived that at this point
any empirical observation would lead to nothing. He had to take another
route if he sought to find an answer to that question. He had to search out
doubt's ideal possibility in consciousness. This, of course, had to remain the same,
however different the occasioning phenomenon was, since it, without itself
being explained by the phenomenon, explained the effect of the phenomenon. Then whatever produced doubt in the individual could be as different
as it pleased; if this possibility were not in the individual, nothing would be
able to evoke it. Moreover, since the difference of the occasioning phenomenon could be one of contrariety, the possibility would have to be total, essential for human consciousness.

He then sought to orient himself in consciousness as it is in itself, as that
which explains every specific consciousness, yet without being itself a specific consciousness. He asked what the nature of consciousness would be
when it had doubt outside itself. There is consciousness in the child, but this
has doubt outside itself. How, then, is the child's consciousness qualified? It
actually is not qualified at all, which can also be expressed by saying that it is
immediate. *Immediacy* is precisely *indeterminateness.* In immediacy there is no
relation, for as soon as there is a relation, immediacy is canceled. *Immediately,*
IV
B 1
146
therefore, everything is true,* but this truth is untruth the very next moment, *for
in immediacy everything is untrue.* If consciousness can remain in immediacy,
then the question of truth is canceled.

How does the question of truth arise? By way of untruth, because the moment I ask about truth, I have already asked about untruth. In the question
of truth, consciousness is brought into relation with something else, and what
makes this relation possible is untruth.

Which is first, immediacy or mediacy? That is a captious question. It reminded him of the response Thales is supposed to have given someone who
asked whether night or day came into existence first: Night is one day earlier. Ἡ νύξ, ἔφη, μιᾷ ἡμέρα πρότερον [Night, he said, is older by one day] (see
Diogenes Laertius, I, 36).

Cannot the consciousness, then, remain in immediacy? This is a foolish
question, because if it could, there would be no consciousness at all. But
how, then, is immediacy canceled? By mediacy, which cancels immediacy
by *pre*-supposing it. What, then, is immediacy? It is reality itself [*Realitet*].

---

* *Note.* The Greek Sophists' thesis that everything is true. Plato's attempts to disprove them,
especially by showing that the negative exists (cf. *Sophist*).—Schleiermacher's teaching with respect to feelings, that everything is true (see the beginning of his *Dogmatics;* some rejoinders
by Erdmann in Bruno Baur's journal, III, Part 1, p. 11). Heraclitus's thesis that everything is
and everything is not, which Aristotle interprets to mean that everything is true. See Tenne-
mann's *Geschichte der Philosophie,* 1, p. 237, note.

What is mediacy? It is the word. How does the one cancel the other? By giving expression to it, for that which is given expression is always *presupposed*.

Immediacy is reality; language is ideality; consciousness is contradiction [*Modsigelse*]. The moment I make a statement about reality, contradiction is present, for what I say is ideality.

The possibility of doubt, then, lies in consciousness, whose nature is a contradiction that is produced by a duplexity [*Dupplicitet*] and that itself produces a duplexity.

A duplexity of this sort inevitably has two manifestations. The duplexity is reality and ideality; consciousness is the relation. I can either bring reality into relation with ideality or bring ideality into relation with reality. In reality by itself there is no possibility of doubt; when I express it in language, contradiction is present, since I do not express it but produce something else. Insofar as what was said is supposed to be an expression of reality, I have brought this into relation with ideality; insofar as what was said is something produced by me, I have brought ideality into relation with reality.

So long as this exchange takes place without mutual contact, consciousness exists only according to its possibility. In ideality, everything is just as perfectly true as in reality. Therefore, just as I can say that immediately everything is true, so I can also say that immediately everything is actual [*virkelig*], for not until the moment that ideality is brought into relation with reality does *possibility* appear. In immediacy, the most false and the most true are equally true; in immediacy, the most possible and the most impossible are equally actual. So long as this exchange takes place without collision, consciousness does not actually exist, and this colossal fallacy causes no annulments. Reality is not consciousness, ideality no more so. Yet consciousness does not exist without both, and this contradiction is the coming into existence [*Tilbliven*] of consciousness and is its nature.

Before proceeding any further, he considered whether or not what he at this point called consciousness was what usually was called *reflection*.* He formulated the relevant definition as follows: Reflection is the *possibility of the relation;* consciousness is *the relation, the first form of which is contradiction.* As a result, he also noted, reflection's categories are always *dichotomous.* For example, ideality and reality, soul and body, to know the true, to will the good, to love the beautiful, God and the world, etc. are categories of reflection. In

IV
B 1
147

* *Note.* What Johannes is explaining here is not without significance. The terminology of modern philosophy is often confusing. For example, it speaks of *sinnliches Bewusstsein, wahrnehmendes B., Verstand* [sense-consciousness, perceiving-consciousness, understanding], etc., although it would be far preferable to call it "sense perception," "experience," for in consciousness there is more. It would really be interesting to see how Hegel would formulate the transition from consciousness to self-consciousness, from self-consciousness to reason [*Fornuft*]. When the transition consists merely of a heading, it is easy enough.

IV
B 1
148

reflection, they touch each other in such a way that a relation becomes possible. The categories of consciousness, however, are *trichotomous,* as language
also demonstrates, for when I say, *I* am conscious of *this sensory impression,* I
am expressing a triad. Consciousness is mind [*Aand*], and it is remarkable that
when one is divided in the world of mind, there are three, never two. Consciousness, therefore, presupposes reflection. If this were not the case, then it
would be impossible to explain doubt. Admittedly, language seems to conflict with this, for in most languages, as far as he knew, the term "to doubt"
is etymologically related to the word "two." Yet he surmised that this merely
suggested the presupposition of doubt, all the more so since it was clear to
him that as soon as I as mind become two, I am *eo ipso* three. If there were
nothing but dichotomies, doubt would not exist, for the possibility of doubt
resides precisely in the third, which places the two in relation to each other.
We could not therefore say that reflection produces doubt, unless we would
express ourselves in reverse; we must say that doubt *pre*-supposes reflection,
without, however, this *prius* being temporary. Doubt arises by way of a relation between two, but for this to happen the two must be. Yet doubt, which
is a higher expression, precedes and does not come afterward.

Reflection is the possibility of the relation. This can also be stated as follows: Reflection is *disinterested.* Consciousness, however, is the relation and
thereby is interest, a duality that is perfectly and with pregnant double meaning expressed in the word "interest" (*interesse* [being between]). Therefore, all
disinterested knowledge (mathematics, esthetics, metaphysics) is only the
presupposition of doubt. As soon as the interest is canceled, doubt is not conquered but is neutralized, and all such knowledge is simply a retrogression.
Thus it would be a misunderstanding for someone to think that doubt can
be overcome by so-called objective thinking. Doubt is a higher form than
any objective thinking, for it presupposes the latter but has something more,
a third, which is interest or consciousness.

In this respect, he considered the conduct of the Greek skeptics far more
consistent than the modern overcoming of doubt. They were well aware that
doubt is based on interest, and therefore with perfect consistency they thought
they could cancel doubt by transforming interest into apathy. In this method
there was a consistency, whereas it was an inconsistency, seemingly based on
ignorance of what doubt is, that motivated modern philosophy to want to
conquer doubt systematically. Even if the system were absolutely perfect, even
if the actuality [*Virkelighed*] exceeded the advance reports, doubt would still
not be overcome—it only begins—for doubt is based on interest, and all systematic knowledge is disinterested. From this it is apparent that doubt is the
beginning of the highest form of existence [*Tilværelse*], because it can have
everything else as its presupposition. The Greek skeptics perceived so exceptionally well that it is unreasonable to speak of doubt when interest is canceled, but presumably they would also have perceived that it is a play on words

IV
B 1
149

to speak about an objective doubt. Let ideality and reality [*Realitet*] be in conflict forever and a day—as long as there is no consciousness, no interest, no consciousness that has an interest in this struggle, there is no doubt—but let them be reconciled, and doubt can continue just as actively.

Consciousness, then, is the relation, a relation whose form is contradiction. But how does consciousness discover the contradiction? If that fallacy discussed above could remain, that ideality and reality in all naiveté communicated with one another, consciousness would never emerge, for consciousness emerges precisely through the collision, just as it presupposes the collision. Immediately there is no collision, but mediately it is present. As soon as the question of a *repetition* arises, the collision is present, for only a repetition of what has been before is conceivable.

In reality as such, there is no repetition. This is not because everything is different, not at all. If everything in the world were completely identical, in reality there would be no repetition, because reality is only in the moment. If the world, instead of being beauty, were nothing but equally large unvariegated boulders, there would still be no repetition. Throughout all eternity, in every moment, I would see a boulder, but there would be no question as to whether it was the same one I had seen before. In ideality alone there is no repetition, for the idea is and remains the same, and as such it cannot be repeated. When ideality and reality touch each other, then repetition occurs. When, for example, I see something in the moment, ideality enters in and will explain that it is a repetition. Here is the contradiction, for that which is, is also in another mode. That the external is, that I see, but in the same instant I bring it into relation with something that also is, something that is the same and that also will explain that the other is the same. Here is a redoubling [*Fordobling*]; here it is a matter of repetition. Ideality and reality therefore collide—in what medium? In time? That is indeed an impossibility. In eternity? That is indeed an impossibility. In what, then? In consciousness—there is the contradiction. The question is not disinterested, as if one asked whether all existence is not an image of the idea and to that extent whether visible existence is not, in a certain volatilized sense, a repetition. Here the question is more specifically one of a repetition in consciousness, consequently of recollection. Recollection involves the same contradiction. Recollection is not ideality; it is ideality that has been. It is not reality; it is reality that has been—which again is a double contradiction, for ideality, according to its concept, has been, and the same holds true of reality according to its concept.

IV
B 1
150

THE CONCEPT OF ANXIETY
A SIMPLE PSYCHOLOGICAL ORIENTING
DELIBERATION ON THE DOGMATIC ISSUE OF
HEREDITARY SIN (JUNE 17, 1844)
BY VIGILIUS HAUFNIENSIS

The elemental themes involved in the analysis of anxiety are freedom/necessity, continuity/discontinuity, good/evil, innocence/guilt, and the becoming of the self. *Fragments* (published four days earlier) deals with the ontology of freedom, and *Anxiety* and *The Sickness unto Death* deal with the anthropological aspects of freedom. Anxiety is the "dizziness of freedom," the awareness of the "possibility of *being* able." The term "psychological" is therefore used in the earlier sense of philosophical anthropology, the conception of human nature. Anxiety in this view, like despair in *The Sickness unto Death,* is therefore not simply a defect but a mark of the human being's possibility of becoming spirit, an authentic self, qualitatively beyond the given duality of the psychical-physical. The actualization of this possibility entails reflection and a decisive qualitative leap, whereby the individual enters the ethical sphere of good/evil, of guilt and sin. The development of the elemental themes involves discussions of various forms of anxiety, the consequence of guilt and sin in the history of the human race, and the possibility of the loss of freedom. The final chapter is "Anxiety as Saving through Faith." "Therefore he who in relation to guilt is educated by anxiety will rest only in the Atonement,"[52] a conclusion that in a reformulation is echoed in the final lines of *The Sickness unto Death.*[53]

IV
276

The age of making distinctions is past. It has been vanquished by the system. In our day, whoever loves to make distinctions is regarded as an eccentric whose soul clings to something that has long since vanished. Be that as it may, yet Socrates still is what he was, the simple wise man, because of the peculiar distinction that he expressed both in words and in life, something that the eccentric Hamann first reiterated with great admiration two thousand years later: "For Socrates was great in 'that he distinguished between what he understood and what he did not understand.'"

THE CONCEPT OF ANXIETY

IV
313

Innocence is ignorance. In innocence, man is not qualified as spirit but is psychically qualified in immediate unity with his natural condition. The spirit in man is dreaming. This view is in full accord with that of the Bible, which by denying that man in his innocence has knowledge of the difference between good and evil denounces all the phantasmagoria of Catholic meritoriousness.

In this state there is peace and repose, but there is simultaneously something else that is not contention and strife, for there is indeed nothing against which to strive. What, then, is it? Nothing. But what effect does nothing have? It begets anxiety. This is the profound secret of innocence, that it is at the same time anxiety. Dreamily the spirit projects its own actuality, but this actuality is nothing, and innocence always sees this nothing outside itself.

Anxiety is a qualification of the dreaming spirit, and as such it has its place in psychology. Awake, the difference between myself and my other is posited; sleeping, it is suspended; dreaming, it is an intimated nothing. The actuality of the spirit constantly shows itself as a form that tempts its possibility but disappears as soon as it seeks to grasp for it, and it is a nothing that can only bring anxiety. More it cannot do as long as it merely shows itself. The concept of anxiety is almost never treated in psychology. Therefore, I must point out that it is altogether different from fear and similar concepts that refer to something definite, whereas anxiety is freedom's actuality as the possibility of possibility. For this reason, anxiety is not found in the beast, precisely because by nature the beast is not qualified as spirit.

When we consider the dialectical determinations of anxiety, it appears that exactly these have psychological ambivalence. Anxiety is *a sympathetic antipathy* and *an antipathetic sympathy*. One easily sees, I think, that this is a psychological determination in a sense entirely different from the *concupiscentia* [inordinate desire] of which we spoke. Linguistic usage confirms this perfectly. One speaks of a pleasing anxiety, a pleasing anxiousness [*Beængstelse*], and of a strange anxiety, a bashful anxiety, etc.

The anxiety that is posited in innocence is in the first place no guilt, and in the second place it is no troublesome burden, no suffering that cannot be brought into harmony with the blessedness of innocence. In observing children, one will discover this anxiety intimated more particularly as a seeking for the adventurous, the monstrous, and the enigmatic. That there are children in whom this anxiety is not found proves nothing at all, for neither is it found in the beast, and the less spirit, the less anxiety. This anxiety belongs so essentially to the child that he cannot do without it. Though it causes him anxiety, it captivates him by its pleasing anxiousness [*Beængstelse*]. In all cul-

IV
314

tures where the childlike is preserved as the dreaming of the spirit, this anxiety is found. The more profound the anxiety, the more profound the culture. Only a prosaic stupidity maintains that this is a disorganization. Anxiety has here the same meaning as melancholy at a much later point, when freedom, having passed through the imperfect forms of its history, in the profoundest sense will come to itself.*

Just as the relation of anxiety to its object, to something that is nothing (linguistic usage also says pregnantly: to be anxious about nothing), is altogether ambivalent, so also the transition that is to be made from innocence to guilt will be so dialectical that it can be seen that the explanation is what it must be, psychological. The qualitative leap stands outside of all ambivalence. But he who becomes guilty through anxiety is indeed innocent, for it was not he himself but anxiety, a foreign power, that laid hold of him, a power that he did not love but about which he was anxious. And yet he is guilty, for he sank in anxiety, which he nevertheless loved even as he feared it. There is nothing in the world more ambivalent; therefore this is the only psychological explanation. But, to repeat once more, it could never occur to the explanation that it should explain the qualitative leap. Every notion that suggests that the prohibition tempted him, or that the seducer deceived him, has sufficient ambivalence only for a superficial observation, but it perverts ethics, introduces a quantitative determination, and will by the help of psychology pay man a compliment at the sacrifice of the ethical, a compliment that everyone who is ethically developed must reject as a new and more profound seduction.

That anxiety makes its appearance is the pivot upon which everything turns. Man is a synthesis of the psychical and the physical; however, a synthesis is unthinkable if the two are not united in a third. This third is spirit.[54] In innocence, man is not merely animal, for if he were at any moment of his life merely animal, he would never become man. So spirit is present, but as immediate, as dreaming. Inasmuch as it is now present, it is in a sense a hostile power, for it constantly disturbs the relation between soul and body, a relation that indeed has persistence and yet does not have endurance, inasmuch as it first receives the latter by the spirit. On the other hand, spirit is a friendly power, since it is precisely that which constitutes the relation. What, then, is man's relation to this ambiguous power? How does spirit relate itself to itself and to its conditionality? It relates itself as anxiety. Do away with itself, the spirit cannot; lay hold of itself, it cannot, as long as it has itself outside of itself. Nor can man sink down into the vegetative, for he is qualified as spirit; flee away from anxiety, he cannot, for he loves it; really love it, he cannot, for

* Concerning this, one should consult *Either/Or* (Copenhagen: 1843), especially if one is aware that the first part expresses the melancholy in its anguished [*angestfulde*] sympathy and egotism, which is explained in the second part.

he flees from it. Innocence has now reached its uttermost point. It is ignorance; however, it is not an animal brutality but an ignorance qualified by
spirit, and as such innocence is precisely anxiety, because its ignorance is
about nothing. Here there is no knowledge of good and evil etc., but the
whole actuality of knowledge projects itself in anxiety as the enormous
nothing of ignorance.

Innocence still is, but only a word is required and then ignorance is concentrated. Innocence naturally cannot understand this word, but at that moment anxiety has, as it were, caught its first prey. Instead of nothing, it now
has an enigmatic word. When it is stated in Genesis that God said to Adam,
"Only from the tree of the knowledge of good and evil you must not eat,"
it follows as a matter of course that Adam really has not understood this
word, for how could he understand the difference between good and evil
when this distinction would follow as a consequence of the enjoyment of
the fruit?

When it is assumed that the prohibition awakens the desire, one acquires
knowledge instead of ignorance, and in that case Adam must have had a
knowledge of freedom, because the desire was to use it. The explanation
is therefore subsequent. The prohibition induces in him anxiety, for the
prohibition awakens in him freedom's possibility. What passed by innocence as the nothing of anxiety has now entered into Adam, and here again
it is a nothing—the anxious possibility of *being able*. He has no conception   IV
of what he is able to do; otherwise—and this is what usually happens—   316
that which comes later, the difference between good and evil, would have
to be presupposed. Only the possibility of being able is present as a higher
form of ignorance, as a higher expression of anxiety, because in a higher
sense it both is and is not, because in a higher sense he both loves it and
flees from it.

After the word of prohibition follows the word of judgment: "You shall
certainly die."[55] Naturally, Adam does not know what it means to die. On
the other hand, there is nothing to prevent him from having acquired a notion of the terrifying, for even animals can understand the mimic expression
and movement in the voice of a speaker without understanding the word. If
the prohibition is regarded as awakening the desire, the punishment must also
be regarded as awakening the notion of the deterrent. This, however, will
only confuse things. In this case, the terror is simply anxiety. Because Adam
has not understood what was spoken, there is nothing but the ambivalence
of anxiety. The infinite possibility of being able that was awakened by the
prohibition now draws closer, because this possibility points to a possibility
as its sequence.

In this way, innocence is brought to its uttermost. In anxiety it is related
to the forbidden and to the punishment. Innocence is not guilty, yet there is
anxiety as though it were lost.

Further than this, psychology cannot go, but so far it can go, and above all, in its observation of human life, it can point to this again and again.

Here, in the conclusion, I have adhered to the biblical narrative. I have assumed the prohibition and the voice of punishment as coming from without. Of course, this is something that has troubled many thinkers. But the difficulty is merely one to smile at. Innocence can indeed speak, inasmuch as in language it possesses the expression for everything spiritual. Accordingly, one need merely assume that Adam talked to himself. The imperfection in the story, namely, that another spoke to Adam about what he did not understand, is thus eliminated. From the fact that Adam was able to talk, it does not follow in a deeper sense that he was able to understand what was said. This applies above all to the difference between good and evil, which indeed can be expressed in language but nevertheless *is* only for freedom, because for innocence it can have only the meaning we have indicated in the preceding account. Innocence can indeed express this difference, but the difference is not for innocence, and for innocence it can only have the meaning that was indicated in the preceding account.

IV
317

Anxiety as the Presupposition of Hereditary Sin
and as Explaining Hereditary Sin Retrogressively
in Terms of Its Origin

Let us now examine the narrative in Genesis more carefully as we attempt to dismiss the fixed idea that it is a myth, and as we remind ourselves that no age has been more skillful than our own in producing myths of the understanding, an age that produces myths and at the same time wants to eradicate all myths.

Adam was created; he had given names to the animals (here there is language, though in an imperfect way similar to that of children who learn by identifying animals on an A B C board) but had not found company for himself. Eve was created, formed from his rib. She stood in as intimate a relation to him as possible, yet it was still an external relation. Adam and Eve are merely a numerical repetition. In this respect, a thousand Adams signify no more than one. So much with regard to the descent of the race from one pair. Nature does not favor a meaningless superfluity. Therefore, if we assume that the race descended from several pairs, there would be a moment when nature had a meaningless superfluity. As soon as the relationship of generation is posited, no man is superfluous, because every individual is himself and the race.

Now follows the prohibition and the judgment. But the serpent was more cunning than all the animals of the field. He seduced the woman. Even though one may call this a myth, it neither disturbs thought nor confuses the concept, as does a myth of the understanding. The myth allows something that is inward to take place outwardly.

First we must note that the woman was the first to be seduced, and that therefore she in turn seduced the man. In what sense woman is the weaker sex, as it is commonly said of her, and also that anxiety belongs to her more than to man,* I shall try to develop in another chapter.

In the foregoing, it has been said several times that the view presented in this work does not deny the propagation of sinfulness through generation, or, in other words, that sinfulness has its history through generation. Yet it is said only that sinfulness moves in quantitative categories, whereas sin constantly enters by the qualitative leap of the individual. Here already one can see one significant aspect of the quantitation that takes place in generation. Eve is a derived creature. To be sure, she is created like Adam, but she is created out of a previous creature. To be sure, she is innocent like Adam, but there is, as it were, a presentiment of a disposition that indeed is not sinfulness but may seem like a hint of the sinfulness that is posited by propagation. It is the fact of being derived that predisposes the particular individual, yet without making him guilty.

Here we must remember what was said about the prohibition and the word of judgment in §5. The imperfection in the narrative—how it could have occurred to anyone to say to Adam what he essentially could not understand—is eliminated if we bear in mind that the speaker is language, and also that it is Adam himself who speaks.**

There remains the serpent. I am no friend of cleverness and shall, *volente deo* [God willing], resist the temptations of the serpent, who, as at the dawn of time when he tempted Adam and Eve, has in the course of time tempted writers to be clever. Instead, I freely admit my inability to connect any definite thought with the serpent. Furthermore, the difficulty with the serpent is something quite different, namely, that of regarding the temptation as coming from without. This is simply contrary to the teaching of the Bible, contrary to the well-known classical passage in James,[56] which says that God tempts no one and is not tempted by anyone, but each person is tempted by

---

* Nothing is hereby determined about woman's imperfection in relation to man. Although anxiety belongs to her more than to man, anxiety is by no means a sign of imperfection. If one is to speak of imperfection, this must be found in something else, namely, that in anxiety she moves beyond herself to another human being, to man.

** If one were to say further that it then becomes a question of how the first man learned to speak, I would answer that this is very true, but also that the question lies beyond the scope of the present investigation. However, this must not be understood in the manner of modern philosophy as though my reply were evasive, suggesting that I *could* answer the question in another place. But this much is certain, that it will not do to represent man himself as the inventor of language.

himself. If one indeed believes that he has rescued God by regarding man as tempted by the serpent and believes that in this way one is in accord with James, "that God tempts no one," he is confronted with the second statement, that God is not tempted by anyone. For the serpent's assault upon man is also an indirect temptation of God, since it interferes in the relation between God and man, and one is confronted by the third statement, that every man is tempted by himself.

Now follows the fall. This is something that psychology is unable to explain, because the fall is the qualitative leap. However, let us for a moment consider the consequence as it is presented in the narrative in order to fix our attention once more on anxiety as the presupposition for hereditary sin.

The consequence is a double one, that sin came into the world and that sexuality was posited; the one is to be inseparable from the other. This is of utmost importance in order to show man's original state. If he were not a synthesis that reposed in a third, one thing could not have two consequences. If he were not a synthesis of psyche and body that is sustained by spirit, the sexual could never have come into the world with sinfulness.

We shall leave project makers out of consideration and simply assume the presence of the sexual difference before the fall, except that as yet it was not, because in ignorance it is not. In this respect we have support in the Scriptures.

In innocence, Adam as spirit was a dreaming spirit. Thus the synthesis is not actual, for the combining factor is precisely the spirit, and as yet this is not posited as spirit. In animals the sexual difference can be developed instinctively, but this cannot be the case with a human being precisely because he is a synthesis. In the moment the spirit posits itself, it posits the synthesis, but in order to posit the synthesis it must first pervade it differentiatingly, and the ultimate point of the sensuous is precisely the sexual. Man can attain this ultimate point only in the moment the spirit becomes actual. Before that time he is not animal, but neither is he really man. The moment he becomes man, he becomes so by being animal as well.

So sinfulness is by no means sensuousness, but without sin there is no sexuality, and without sexuality, no history. A perfect spirit has neither the one nor the other, and therefore the sexual difference is canceled in the resurrection, and therefore an angel has no history. Even if Michael had made a record of all the errands he had been sent on and performed, this is nevertheless not his history. First in sexuality is the synthesis posited as a contradiction, but like every contradiction it is also a task, the history of which begins at that same moment. This is the actuality that is preceded by freedom's possibility. However, freedom's possibility is not the ability to choose the good or the evil. Such thoughtlessness is no more in the interest of Scriptures than in the interest of thought. The possibility is to *be able*. In a logical system, it is convenient to say that possibility passes over into actuality. However, in actuality it is not so convenient, and an intermediate term is required.

The intermediate term is anxiety, but it no more explains the qualitative leap than it can justify it ethically. Anxiety is neither a category of necessity nor a category of freedom; it is entangled freedom, where freedom is not free in itself but entangled, not by necessity, but in itself. If sin has come into the world by necessity (which is a contradiction), there can be no anxiety. Nor can there by any anxiety if sin came into the world by an act of an abstract *liberum arbitrium*[57] (which no more existed in the world in the beginning than in a late period, because it is a nuisance for thought). To want to give a logical explanation of the coming of sin into the world is a stupidity that can occur only to people who are comically worried about finding an explanation.

Were I allowed to make a wish, then I would wish that no reader would be so profound as to ask: What if Adam had not sinned? In the moment actuality is posited, possibility walks by its side as a nothing that entices every thoughtless man. If only science could make up its mind to keep men under discipline and to bridle itself! When someone asks a stupid question, care should be taken not to answer him, lest he who answers becomes just as stupid as the questioner. The foolishness of the above question consists not so much in the question itself as in the fact that it is directed to science. If one stays at home with it, and, like Clever Elsie with her projects, calls together like-minded friends, then one has tolerably understood one's own stupidity. Science, on the contrary, cannot explain such things. Every science lies either in a logical immanence or in an immanence within a transcendence that it is unable to explain. Now sin is precisely that transcendence, that *discrimen rerum* [crisis] in which sin enters into the single individual as the single individual. Sin never enters into the world differently and has never entered differently. So when the single individual is stupid enough to inquire about sin as if it were something foreign to him, he only asks as a fool, for either he does not know at all what the question is about, and thus cannot come to know it, or he knows it and understands it, and also knows that no science can explain it to him. However, science at times has been adequately accommodating in responding to wishes with weighty hypotheses that it at last admits are inadequate as explanations. This, of course, is entirely true, yet the confusion is that science did not energetically dismiss foolish questions but instead confirmed superstitious men in their notion that one day there would come a project maker who is smart enough to come up with the right answer. That sin came into the world six thousand years ago is said in the same way that one would say about Nebuchadnezzar that it was four thousand years ago that he became an ox. When the case is understood in this way, it is no wonder that the explanation accords with it. What in one respect is the simplest thing in the world has been made the most difficult. What the most ordinary man understands in his own way, and quite correctly so—because he understands

IV
321

that it is not just six thousand years since sin came into the world—science
with the art of speculators has announced as a prize subject that as yet has
not been answered satisfactorily. How sin came into the world, each man
understands solely by himself. If he would learn it from another, he would
eo ipso misunderstand it. The only science that can help a little is psychology, yet it admits that it explains nothing, and also that it *cannot* and *will not*
explain more. If any science could explain it, everything would be confused. That the man of science ought to forget himself is entirely true; nevertheless, it is therefore also very fortunate that sin is no scientific problem,
and thus no man of science has an obligation (and the project maker just
as little) to forget how sin came into the world. If this is what he wants to
do, if he magnanimously wants to forget himself in the zeal to explain all
of humanity, he will become as comical as that privy councilor who was so
IV
322   conscientious about leaving his calling card with every Tom, Dick, and
Harry that in so doing he at last forgot his own name. Or his philosophical enthusiasm will make him so absent-minded that he needs a good-natured, level-headed wife whom he can ask, as Soldin asked Rebecca when
in enthusiastic absent-mindedness he also lost himself in the objectivity of
the chatter: "Rebecca, is it I who is speaking?"

That the admired men of science in my most honored contemporary age,
men whose concern in their search after the system is known to the whole
congregation and who are concerned also to find a place for sin within it,
may find the above position highly unscientific is entirely in order. But let
the congregation join in the search, or at least include these profound seek-
ers in their pious intercessions; they will find the place as surely as he who
hunts for the burning tow finds it when he is unaware that it is burning in
his own hand.

IV
350   In the two previous chapters, it was maintained continually that man is a
synthesis of psyche and body that is constituted and sustained by spirit. In
the individual life, anxiety is the moment—to use a new expression that says
the same as was said in the previous discussion, but that also points toward
that which follows.

In recent philosophy there is a category that is continually used in logical
no less than in historical philosophical inquiries. It is the category of transition. However, no further explanation is given. The term is freely used without any ado, and while Hegel and the Hegelian school startled the world
with the great insight of the presuppositionless beginning of philosophy, or
the thought that before philosophy there must be nothing but the most complete absence of presuppositions, there is no embarrassment at all over the
use in Hegelian thought of the terms "transition," "negation," "mediation,"
i.e., the principles of motion, in such a way that they do not find their place
in the systematic progression. If this is not a presupposition, I do not know

what a presupposition is. For to use something that is nowhere explained is indeed to presuppose it. The system is supposed to have such marvelous transparency and inner vision that in the manner of the *omphalopsychoi* [navel souls] it would gaze immovably at the central nothing until at last everything would explain itself and its whole content would come into being by itself. Such introverted openness to the public was to characterize the system. Nevertheless, this is not the case, because systematic thought seems to pay homage to secretiveness with respect to its innermost movements. Negation, transition, mediation are three disguised, suspicious, and secret agents (*agentia* [main springs]) that bring about all movements. Hegel would hardly call them presumptuous, because it is with his gracious permission that they carry on their ploy so unembarrassedly that even logic uses terms and phrases borrowed from transition in time: "thereupon," "when," "as being it is this," "as becoming it is this," etc.

Let this be as it may. Let logic take care to help itself. The term "transition" is and remains a clever turn in logic. Transition belongs in the sphere of historical freedom, for transition is a *state* and it is actual.* Plato fully recognized the difficulty of placing transition in the realm of the purely metaphysical, and for that reason the category of *the moment*** cost him so much effort. To ignore the difficulty certainly is not to "go further" than Plato. To ignore it, and thus piously to deceive thought in order to get speculation afloat and the movement in logic going, is to treat speculation as a rather fi-

IV
351

IV
352

IV
353

---

* Therefore, when Aristotle says that the transition from possibility to actuality is a κίνησις [movement], it is not to be understood logically but with reference to historical freedom.

** Plato conceives of the moment as purely abstract. In order to become acquainted with its dialectic, one should keep in mind that the moment is non-being under the category of time. Non-being (τὸ μὴ ὄν; τὸ κενόν [that which is not; the empty] of the Pythagoreans) occupied the interest of ancient philosophers more than it does modern philosophers. Among the Eleatics, non-being was conceived ontologically in such a way that what was affirmed about it could be stated only in the contradictory proposition that only being is. If one pursues this further, he will see that it reappears in all the spheres. In metaphysical propaedeutics, the proposition was expressed thus: He who expresses non-being says nothing at all (this misunderstanding is refuted in *The Sophist,* and in a more mimical way it was refuted in an earlier dialogue, *Gorgias*). Finally, in the practical spheres the Sophists used non-being as a means to do away with all moral concepts; non-being is not, *ergo* everything is true, *ergo* everything is good, *ergo* deceit etc. are not. This position is refuted by Socrates in several dialogues. Plato dealt with it especially in *The Sophist,* which like all of his dialogues at the same time artistically illustrates what it also teaches, for the Sophist, whose concept and definition the dialogue seeks while it deals principally with non-being, is himself a non-being. Thus the concept and the example come into being at the same time in the warfare in which the Sophist is attacked, and which ends not with his annihilation but with his coming into being [bliver til], which is the worst thing that can happen to him, for despite his sophistry, which like the armor of Mars enables him to become invisible, he must come forth into the light. Recent philosophy has not essentially come any further in its conception of non-being, even though it presumes to be Christian. Greek philosophy and the modern alike maintain that everything turns on bringing non-being into being, for to do away with it or to make it vanish seems extremely easy. The Christian

IV
351

IV
352

nite affair. However, I remember once having heard a speculator say that
one must not give undue thought to the difficulties beforehand, because
then one never arrives at the point where one can speculate. If the important thing is to get to the point where one can begin to speculate, and not
that one's speculation in fact becomes true speculation, it is indeed res-

---

view takes the position that non-being is present everywhere as the nothing from which things
were created, as semblance and vanity, as sin, as sensuousness removed from spirit, as the temporal forgotten by the eternal; consequently, the task is to do away with it in order to bring
forth being. Only with this orientation in mind can the concept of Atonement be correctly
understood historically, that is, in the sense in which Christianity brought it into the world. If
the term is understood in the opposite sense (the movement proceeding from the assumption
that non-being is not), the Atonement is volatilized and turned inside out.

It is in *Parmenides* that Plato sets forth "the moment." This dialogue is engaged in pointing
out contradictions within the concepts themselves, something that Socrates expressed in so decisive a way, that while it does not serve to put to shame the beautiful old Greek philosophy,
it may well put to shame a more recent boastful philosophy, which unlike the Greek does not
make great demands upon itself but upon men and their admiration. Socrates points out that
there is nothing wonderful about being able to demonstrate contrariety (τὸ ἐναντίον) of a particular thing participating in diversity, but if anyone were able to show contradictions in the
concepts themselves, that would be something to admire (ἀλλ᾽ εἰ ὅ ἐστιν ἕν, αὐτὸ τοῦτο πολλὰ
ἀποδείξει καὶ αὖ τὰ πολλὰ δὴ ἕν, τοῦτο ἤδη θαυμάσομαι. καὶ περὶ τῶν ἄλλων ἁπάντων ὡσαύτως
[But if anyone can prove that what is simply unity itself is many or that plurality itself is one,
then I shall begin to be surprised] 129 B C).

The procedure is that of an imaginatively constructing dialectic. It is assumed both that the
one (τὸ ἕν) is and that it is not, and then the consequences for it and for the rest are pointed
out. As a result, the moment appears to be this strange entity (ἄτοπον [that which has no place],
the Greek word is especially appropriate) that lies between motion and rest without occupy-
ing any time, and into this and out from this that which is in motion changes into rest, and
that which is at rest changes into motion. Thus the moment becomes the category of transition (μεταβολή), for Plato shows in the same way that the moment is related to the transition
of the one to the many, of the many to the one, of likeness to unlikeness, etc., and that it is the
moment in which there is neither ἕν [one] nor πολλά [many], neither a being determined nor
a being combined (οὔτε διακρίνεται οὔτε ξυγκρίνεται, §157 A). Plato deserves credit for having clarified the difficulty; yet the moment remains a silent atomistic abstraction, which, however, is not explained by ignoring it. Now if logic would be willing to state that it does not
have the category of transition (and if it does have this category, it must find a place for it within
the system itself, although in fact it also operates in the system), it will become clearer that the
historical spheres and all the knowledge that rests on a historical presupposition have the moment. This category is of utmost importance in maintaining the distinction between Christianity and pagan philosophy, as well as the equally pagan speculation in Christianity. Another
passage in the dialogue *Parmenides* points out the consequence of treating the moment as such
an abstraction. It shows how, if the one is assumed to have the determination of time, the contradiction appears that the one (τὸ ἕν) becomes older and younger than itself and the many (τὰ
πολλά), and then again neither younger nor older than itself or the many (§151 E). The one
must nevertheless be, so it is said, and then "to be" is defined as follows: Participation in an
essence or a nature in the present time (τὸ δὲ εἶναι ἄλλο τί ἐστι ἢ μέθεξις οὐσίας μετὰ χρό-
νου τοῦ παρόντος, §151 E). In the further development of the contradictions [§152 B C], it
appears that the present (τὸ νῦν) vacillates between meaning the present, the eternal, and the
moment. This "now" (τὸ νῦν) lies between "was" and "will become," and naturally "the one"

olutely said that the important thing is to get to the point of speculating, just as it is praiseworthy for a man who has no means of riding to Deer Park in his own carriage to say: One must not trouble oneself about such things, because one can just as well ride a coffee grinder. This, of course, is the case. Both riders hope to arrive at Deer Park. On the other hand, the man who firmly resolves not to trouble himself about the means of conveyance, just as long as he can get to the point where he can speculate, will hardly reach speculation.

In the sphere of historical freedom, transition is a state. However, in order to understand this correctly, one must not forget that the new is brought about through the leap. If this is not maintained, the transition will have a quantitative preponderance over the elasticity of the leap.

Man, then, is a synthesis of psyche and body, but he is also a *synthesis of the temporal and the eternal.* That this often has been stated, I do not object to at all, for it is not my wish to discover something new, but rather it is my joy and dearest occupation to ponder over that which is quite simple. IV 355

As for the latter synthesis, it is immediately striking that it is formed differently from the former. In the former, the two factors are psyche and body, and spirit is the third, yet in such a way that one can speak of a synthesis only when spirit is posited. The latter synthesis has only two factors, the temporal and the eternal. Where is the third factor? And if there is no third factor, there really is no synthesis, for a synthesis that is a contradiction cannot be completed as a synthesis without a third factor, because the fact that the synthesis is a contradiction asserts that it is not. What, then, is the temporal?

If time is correctly defined as an infinite succession, it most likely is also defined as the present, the past, and the future. This distinction, however, is incorrect if it is considered to be implicit in time itself, because the distinction appears only through the relation of time to eternity and through the reflection of eternity in time. If in the infinite succession of time a foothold could be found, i.e., a present, which was the dividing point, the division would be quite correct. However, precisely because every moment, as well as the sum of the moments, is a process (a passing by), no moment is a present, and accordingly there is in time neither present, nor past, nor future. If it is claimed that this division can be maintained, it is because the moment

---

cannot, in passing from the past to the future, bypass this "now." It comes to a halt in the now, does not become older but is older. In the most recent philosophy, abstraction culminates in pure being, but pure being is the most abstract expression for eternity, and again as "nothing" it is precisely the moment. Here again the importance of the moment becomes apparent, because only with this category is it possible to give eternity its proper significance, for eternity and the moment become the extreme opposites, whereas dialectical sorcery, on the other hand, makes eternity and the moment signify the same thing. It is only with Christianity that sensuousness, temporality, and the moment can be properly understood, because only with Christianity does eternity become essential.

is *spatialized,* but thereby the infinite succession comes to a halt, it is because representation is introduced that allows time to be represented instead of being thought. Even so, this is not correct procedure, for even as representation, the infinite succession of time is an infinitely contentless present (this is the parody of the eternal). The Hindus speak of a line of kings that has ruled for 70,000 years. Nothing is known about the kings, not even their names (this I assume). If we take this as an example of time, the 70,000 years are for thought an infinite vanishing; in representation it is expanded and is spatialized into an illusionary view of an infinite, contentless nothing.* As soon as the one is regarded as succeeding the other, the present is posited.

IV
356

The present, however, is not a concept of time, except precisely as something infinitely contentless, which again is the infinite vanishing. If this is not kept in mind, no matter how quickly it may disappear, the present is posited, and being posited it again appears in the categories: the past and the future.

The eternal, on the contrary, is the present. For thought, the eternal is the present in terms of an annulled succession (time is the succession that passes by). For representation, it is a going forth that nevertheless does not get off the spot, because the eternal is for representation the infinitely contentful present. So also in the eternal there is no division into the past and the future, because the present is posited as the annulled succession.

Time is, then, infinite succession; the life that is in time and is only of time has no present. In order to define the sensuous life, it is usually said that it is in the moment and only in the moment. By the moment, then, is understood that abstraction from the eternal that, if it is to be the present, is a parody of it. The present is the eternal, or rather, the eternal is the present, and the present is full. In this sense the Latin said of the deity that he is *praesens* (*praesentes dii* [the presence of the gods]), by which expression, when used about the deity, he also signified the powerful assistance of the deity.

The moment signifies the present as that which has no past and no future, and precisely in this lies the imperfection of the sensuous life. The eternal also signifies the present as that which has no past and no future, and this is the perfection of the eternal.

IV
357

If at this point one wants to use the moment to define time and let the moment signify the purely abstract exclusion of the past and the future and as such the present, then the moment is precisely not the present, because the intermediary between the past and the future, purely abstractly conceived, is not at all. Thus it is seen that the moment is not a determination of time, because the determination of time is that it "passes by." For this rea-

---

* Incidentally, this is space. The skillful reader will no doubt see herein the proof of the correctness of my presentation, because for abstract thought, time and space are entirely identical (*nacheinander, nebeneinander*), and become so for representation, and are truly so in the definition of God as *omnipresent.*

son time, if it is to be defined by any of the determinations revealed in time itself, is time past. If, on the contrary, time and eternity touch each other, then it must be in time, and now we have come to the moment.

"The moment" is a figurative expression, and therefore it is not easy to deal with. However, it is a beautiful word to consider. Nothing is as swift as a blink of the eye, and yet it is commensurable with the content of the eternal. Thus when Ingeborg looks out over the sea after Frithiof, this is a picture of what is expressed in the figurative word. An outburst of her emotion, a sigh or a word, already has as a sound more of the determination of time and is more present as something that is vanishing and does not have in it so much of the presence of the eternal. For this reason a sigh, a word, etc. have power to relieve the soul of the burdensome weight, precisely because the burden, when merely expressed, already begins to become something of the past. A blink is therefore a designation of time, but mark well, of time in the fateful conflict when it is touched by eternity.* What we call the moment, Plato calls τὸ ἐξαίφνης [the sudden]. Whatever its etymological explanation, it is related to the category of the invisible, because time and eternity were conceived equally abstractly, because the concept of temporality was lacking, and this again was due to the lack of the concept of spirit. The Latin term is *momentum* (from *movere* [to move]), which by derivation expresses the merely vanishing.**

IV
358

Thus understood, the moment is not properly an atom of time but an atom of eternity. It is the first reflection of eternity in time, its first attempt, as it were, at stopping time. For this reason, Greek culture did not comprehend the moment, and even if it had comprehended the atom of eternity, it did not comprehend that it was the moment, did not define it with a for-

---

* It is remarkable that Greek art culminates in the plastic, which precisely lacks the glance. This, however, has its deep source in the fact that the Greeks did not in the profoundest sense grasp the concept of spirit and therefore did not in the deepest sense comprehend sensuousness and temporality. What a striking contrast to Christianity, in which God is pictorially represented as an eye.

** In the New Testament there is a poetic paraphrase of the moment.[58] Paul says the world will pass away ἐν ἀτόμῳ καὶ ἐν ῥιπῇ ὀφθαλμοῦ [in a moment and in the twinkling of an eye]. By this he also expresses that the moment is commensurable with eternity, precisely because the moment of destruction expresses eternity at the same moment. Permit me to illustrate what I mean, and forgive me if anyone should find the analogy offensive. Once here in Copenhagen there were two actors who probably never thought that their performance could have a deeper significance. They stepped forth onto the stage, placed themselves opposite each other, and then began the mimical representation of one or another passionate conflict. When the mimical act was in full swing and the spectators' eyes followed the story with expectation of what was to follow, they suddenly stopped and remained motionless as though petrified in the mimical expression of the moment. The effect of this can be exceedingly comical, for the moment in an accidental way becomes commensurable with the eternal. The plastic effect is due to the fact that the eternal expression is expressed eternally; the comic effect, on the other hand, consists in the eternalization of the accidental expression.

ward direction but with a backward direction. Because for Greek culture the atom of eternity was essentially eternity, neither time nor eternity received what was properly its due.

The synthesis of the temporal and the eternal is not another synthesis but is the expression for the first synthesis, according to which man is a synthesis of psyche and body that is sustained by spirit. As soon as the spirit is posited, the moment is present. Therefore one may rightly say reproachfully of man that he lives only in the moment, because that comes to pass by an arbitrary abstraction. Nature does not lie in the moment.

It is with temporality as it is with sensuousness, for temporality seems still more imperfect and the moment still more insignificant than nature's apparently secure endurance in time. However, the contrary is the case. Nature's security has its source in the fact that time has no significance at all for nature. Only with the moment does history begin. By sin, man's sensuousness is posited as sinfulness and is therefore lower than that of the beast, and yet this is because it is here that the higher begins, for at this point spirit begins.

The moment is that ambiguity in which time and eternity touch each other, and with this the concept of *temporality* is posited, whereby time constantly intersects eternity and eternity constantly pervades time. As a result, the above-mentioned division acquires its significance: the present time, the past time, the future time.

By this division, attention is immediately drawn to the fact that the future in a certain sense signifies more than the present and the past, because in a certain sense the future is the whole of which the past is a part, and the future can in a certain sense signify the whole. This is because the eternal first signifies the future or because the future is the incognito in which the eternal, even though it is incommensurable with time, nevertheless preserves its association with time. Linguistic usage at times also takes the future as identical with the eternal (the future life—the eternal life). In a deeper sense, the Greeks did not have the concept of the eternal; so neither did they have the concept of the future. Therefore Greek life cannot be reproached for being lost in the moment, or more correctly, it cannot even be said that it was lost, for temporality was conceived by the Greeks just as naively as sensuousness, because they lacked the category of spirit.

The moment and the future in turn posit the past. If Greek life in any way denotes any qualification of time, it is past time. However, past time is not defined in its relation to the present and the future but as a qualification of time in general, as a passing by. Here the significance of the Platonic "recollection" is obvious. For the Greeks, the eternal lies behind as the past that can only be entered backwards.* However, the eternal thought of as the past

IV
359

IV
360

---

* Here the category that I maintain should be kept in mind, namely, repetition, by which eternity is entered forwards.

is an altogether abstract concept, whether the eternal is further defined philosophically (a philosophical dying away), or historically.

On the whole, in defining the concepts of the past, the future, and the eternal, it can be seen how the moment is defined. If there is no moment, the eternal appears behind as the past. It is as when I imagine a man walking along a road but do not posit the step, and so the road appears behind him as the distance covered. If the moment is posited but merely as a *discrimen* [boundary], the future is the eternal. If the moment is posited, so is the eternal, but also the future, which reappears as the past. This is clearly seen in the Greek, the Jewish, and the Christian views. The pivotal concept in Christianity, that which made all things new, is the fullness of time, but the fullness of time is the moment as the eternal, and yet this eternal is also the future and the past. If attention is not paid to this, not a single concept can be saved from a heretical and treasonable admixture that annihilates the concept. One does not get the past by itself but in a simple continuity with the future (with this the concepts of conversion, atonement, and redemption are lost in the world-historical significance and lost in the individual historical development). One does not get the future by itself but in a simple continuity with the present (thereby the concepts of resurrection and judgment are destroyed).

In one of Grimm's fairy tales[59] there is a story of a young man who goes in search of adventure in order to learn what it is to be in anxiety. We will let the adventurer pursue his journey without concerning ourselves about whether he encountered the terrible on his way. However, I will say that this is an adventure that every human being must go through—to learn to be anxious in order that he may not perish either by never having been in anxiety or by succumbing in anxiety. Whoever has learned to be anxious in the right way has learned the ultimate.   IV
421

If a human being were a beast or an angel, he could not be in anxiety. Because he is a synthesis, he can be in anxiety; and the more profoundly he is in anxiety, the greater is the man—yet not in the sense usually understood, in which anxiety is about something external, about something outside a person, but in the sense that he himself produces the anxiety. Only in this sense can the words be understood when it is said of Christ that he was anxious unto death, as well as the words spoken by Christ to Judas: What you are going to do, do quickly. Not even the terrifying verse that made even Luther anxious when preaching on it—"My God, my God, why have you abandoned me"—not even these words express suffering so profoundly. For the latter signify a condition in which Christ finds himself. And the former signify the relation to a condition that is not.   IV
422

Anxiety is freedom's possibility, and only such anxiety is through faith absolutely educative, because it consumes all finite ends and discovers all their deceptiveness. And no Grand Inquisitor has such dreadful torments in readiness as anxiety has, and no secret agent knows as cunningly as anxiety how to attack his suspect in his weakest moment or to make alluring the trap in which he will be caught, and no discerning judge understands how to interrogate and examine the accused as does anxiety, which never lets the accused escape, neither through amusement, nor by noise, nor during work, neither by day nor by night.

Whoever is educated by anxiety is educated by possibility, and only he who is educated by possibility is educated according to his infinitude. Therefore possibility is the weightiest of all categories. It is true that we often hear the opposite stated, that possibility is so light, whereas actuality is so heavy. But from whom does one hear such words? From wretched men who never knew what possibility is, and who, when actuality had shown that they were not good for anything and never would be, mendaciously revived a possibility that was very beautiful and very enchanting, while the foundation of this possibility was at the most a little youthful giddiness, of which they ought rather to be ashamed. Therefore this possibility that is said to be so light is commonly regarded as the possibility of happiness, fortune, etc. But this is not possibility. It is rather a mendacious invention that human depravity has dressed up so as to have a reason for complaining of life and Governance and a pretext for becoming self-important. No, in possibility all things are equally possible, and whoever has truly been brought up by possibility has grasped the terrible as well as the joyful. So when such a person graduates from the school of possibility, and he knows better than a child knows his ABC's that he can demand absolutely nothing of life and that the terrible, perdition, and annihilation live next door to every man, and when he has thoroughly learned that every anxiety about which he was anxious came upon him in the next moment—he will give actuality another explanation, he will praise actuality, and even when it rests heavily upon him, he will remember that it nevertheless is far, far lighter than possibility was. Only in this way can possibility be educative, because finiteness and the finite relations in which every individual is assigned a place, whether they be small, or everyday, or world-historical, educate only finitely, and a person can always persuade them, always coax something else out of them, always bargain, always escape from them tolerably well, always keep himself a little on the outside, always prevent himself from absolutely learning something from them; and if he does this, the individual must again have possibility in himself and himself develop that from which he is to learn, even though in the next moment that from which he is to learn does not at all acknowledge that it is formed by him but absolutely deprives him of the power.

However, in order that an individual may thus be educated absolutely and infinitely by the possibility, he must be honest toward possibility and have faith. By faith I understand here what Hegel somewhere in his way cor-

IV
423

rectly calls the inner certainty that anticipates infinity. When the discoveries of possibility are honestly administered, possibility will discover all the finitudes, but it will idealize them in the form of infinity and in anxiety overwhelm the individual until he again overcomes them in the anticipation of faith.

PREFACES. LIGHT READING FOR PEOPLE
IN VARIOUS ESTATES ACCORDING TO TIME AND
OPPORTUNITY (JUNE 17, 1844)
BY NICOLAUS NOTABENE

During two weeks in 1844, a number of quite different books appeared from two publishers: *Three Upbuilding Discourses* (June 8), *Philosophical Fragments* (June 13), *The Concept of Anxiety* (June 17), and *Prefaces* (June 17). The first two were in the pattern of a pair of works in the two parallel series of pseudonymous and signed publications. The third and fourth volumes were both in the pseudonymous series and were followed in a few weeks by the signed *Four Upbuilding Discourses* (August 31).

Prefaces is a literary spoof of the tradition of lavish New Year's books intended primarily as Christmas gifts, a nineteenth-century anticipation of twentieth-century coffee-table books and highly promoted cinema productions scheduled for initial showing in December. *Prefaces* is unmistakably a Copenhagen book, full of allusions, for example, to J. L. Heiberg, dramatist, poet, and critic as well as the chief representative of Hegel's philosophy in Denmark, to Bishop Jakob Mynster, and to H. L. Martensen, who eventually became Mynster's successor. The satire in *Prefaces* is directed against the leadership in a collective, socializing culture that, misconstrued and abused, could lead individuals to abandon proper responsibility for themselves. The selected passage, from the preface to a volume of prefaces, represents the whimsical humor and irony (here, self-irony) that run through the entire work. The unpublished *Writing Sampler*, like *Prefaces*, to which it was intended as a sequel, is also a Copenhagen book, a polemical miscellany marked by humor, satire, and irony.

V
6
THE PREFACE has received its deathblow in recent scholarship. Looked at from its point of view, an older author easily becomes a pitiful figure over whom one does not know whether to laugh or to cry, because his halting manner in getting to the point makes him comic, and his naïveté, as if there were anyone who cared about him, makes him pathetic. Nowadays a situation like this cannot be repeated, because when one begins the book with the subject and the system with nothing there apparently is nothing left over to say in a prologue. This state of affairs has given me occasion to become aware that the preface is an altogether unique kind of literary production, and since it is elbowed aside it is high time for it to liberate itself like everything else. In this way it can still come to be something good. The incommensurable, which in an earlier period was placed in the preface to a book, can now find its place in a preface that is not the preface to any book. I believe that in this way the conflict will be settled to mutual satisfaction and benefit; if the preface and the book cannot be hitched up together, then let the one give the other a decree of divorce.

The most recent scholarly method has made me aware that it would have to come to a break. My merit will be this, to make the break in earnest; now there is only a phenomenon that points to the deeper reason. Every esthetically cultivated author surely has had moments when he did not care to write a book but when he really wanted to write a preface to a book, no matter whether it was by himself or by someone else. This indicates that a preface is essentially different from a book and that to write a preface is something entirely different from writing a book; if not, this need would express itself only when one had written a book, or when one imagined that one would write it just as one superficially imagines it, and thus raises the question of whether one should write the preface first or last. Nonetheless, as soon as a person is in one of these situations, he either has had a subject or imagines having it. But now when lacking also this he desires to write a preface, it is easy to perceive that this must not deal with a subject, because in that case the preface itself would become a book, and the question of the preface and the book would be pushed aside. The preface as such, the liberated preface, must then have no subject to treat but must deal with nothing, and insofar as it seems to discuss something and deal with something, this must nevertheless be an illusion and a fictitious motion.

The preface is thereby defined purely lyrically and defined according to its concept, while in the popular and traditional sense the preface is a ceremony according to period and custom. A preface is a mood. Writing a preface is like sharpening a scythe, like tuning a guitar, like talking with a child, like spitting out of the window. One does not know how it comes about; the desire comes upon one, the desire to throb fancifully in a productive mood, the desire to write a preface, the desire to do these things *leves sub noctem susurri* [in a low whisper as night falls]. Writing a preface is like ringing someone's doorbell to trick him, like walking by a young lady's window and gazing at the paving stones; it is like swinging one's cane in the air to hit the wind, like doffing one's hat although one is greeting nobody. Writing a preface is like having done something that justifies claiming a certain attention, like having something on one's conscience that tempts confidentiality, like bowing invitingly in the dance although one does not move, like pressing hard with the left leg, pulling the reins to the right, hearing the steed say "Pst," and oneself not caring a straw for the whole world; it is like being along without having the slightest inconvenience of being along, like standing on Valdby Hill and gazing at the wild geese. Writing a preface is like arriving by stagecoach at the first station, stopping in the dark shed, having a presentiment of what will appear, seeing the gate and then the open sky, gazing at the continually receding road beyond, catching a glimmer of the pregnant mystery of the forest, the alluring fading away of the footpath; it is like hearing the sound of the posthorn and the beckoning invitation of the echo, like hearing the powerful crack of the coachman's whip and the forest's perplexed

V
7

V
8

repetition and the jovial conversation of the travelers. Writing a preface is like having arrived, standing in a comfortable parlor, greeting longing's desired object, sitting in an easy chair, filling a pipe, lighting it—and then having endlessly much to converse about. Writing a preface is like being aware that one is beginning to fall in love—the soul sweetly restless, the riddle abandoned, every event an intimation of the transfiguration. Writing a preface is like bending aside a branch in a bower of jasmine and seeing her who sits there in secret: my beloved. Oh, this is how it is, this is how it is to write a preface; and the one who writes it, what is he like? He moves in and out among people like a dupe in winter and a fool in summer; he is hello and good-bye in one person, always joyful and nonchalant, contented with himself, really a light-minded ne'er-do-well, indeed an immoral person, since he does not go to the stock exchange to feather his nest but only strolls through it; he does not speak at public meetings, because the atmosphere is too confined; he does not propose toasts in any society, because this requires notice several days in advance; he does not run errands on behalf of the system; he does not pay installments on the national debt and in fact does not even take it seriously; he goes through life the way a shoemaker's apprentice walks whistling down the street, even though the one who is to use the boots stands and waits—then he must wait so long as there remains a single place left for sliding or the slightest object of interest to see. This, yes this is what one who writes prefaces is like.

See, everyone can ponder all this as he wishes, just as it crosses his mind and when it crosses his mind. With me it is different because a promise and an obligation bind me to busy myself only and solely with this kind of writing. I will without delay tell the reader how all this hangs together, since it is in exactly the right place here, and just as defamation belongs at a coffee party, this is something that very properly belongs in a preface.

Although happily married as only few are and also thankful for my happiness as perhaps only few are, I have nevertheless run up against difficulties in my marriage, the discovery of which is due to my wife, because I suspected nothing. Several months had passed by since the wedding. I had gradually become somewhat practiced in the pattern of marital life; then little by little there awakened again in me a desire that I had always nourished and in which I in all innocence thought I might indulge myself: engagement in some literary task. The subject was chosen, books along this line that I myself owned were set out, particular works were borrowed from the Royal Library, my notes were arranged synoptically, and my pen was, so to speak, dipped. Meanwhile, my wife had scarcely conceived a suspicion that some such thing was in the wind before she began watching my movements very carefully. Occasionally she dropped an enigmatic word, vaguely suggested that all my busyness in the study, my longer sojourns there, and my literary ruminations were not altogether to her liking. I did, however, keep all my wits about me and pretended not to understand her, which I actually did not at first. Then one day she catches me off guard and extracts from me the formal confession that I was on the way to wanting to be an author. If until now her conduct had been more a reconnoitering, she now zeroed in more and more definitely, until she finally declared open war, *et quidem* [and this] so openly that she intended to confiscate everything I wrote, in order to use it in a better way as the underlayment of her embroidery, for curlers, etc. An author's situation can hardly be more desperate than mine; even a person under special censorship can still hope to get his work to the point where it "may be printed," but my writing is always suffocated at birth. How desperate my position was became clearer and clearer to me in another way. I had scarcely discovered that I had become the object of persecution of the press before, as is natural, something became clear to me that previously had not entered my mind at all: that it would be an irretrievable loss to humanity if my writing did not see the light of day. What is now to be done about it? Unlike a censored author, I do not have recourse to the chancery, the provincial estates, the esteemed public, or posterity's memory. I live and die, stand and fall, with my wife. Now, I certainly am considered by my contemporaries to be a good and very experienced debater who can adequately plead my case, but here this proficiency will be of only slight benefit to me, because even if I can debate with the devil himself, I cannot debate with my wife. She has, namely, only one syllogism, or rather none at all. What learned people call sophistry, she, who wants nothing to do with being learned, calls teasing. Now, the procedure is very simple, that is, for the one who knows how to proceed properly. Whenever I say something that she does not like, whether it is in the form of a syllogism or not, whether a long speech or a short remark— the form does not matter—but when she does not like what has been said, she looks at me with a countenance that is lovable, charming, good-natured, and captivating, yet at the same time is triumphant, devastating, and she says: It is only teasing. The consequence of this is that all my skill in debating becomes a luxury item for which there is no demand at all in my domestic life. If I, the experienced dialectician, fairly well exemplify the course of justice, which according to the poet's dictum is so very long, my wife is like the royal Danish chancery, *kurz und bündig* [short and to the point], except that she is very different from that august body in being very lovable. It is precisely this lovableness that gives her an authority that she knows how to maintain in a charming way at every moment.

That is how things stand. I have never gone further than an introductory paragraph. Since this was of a general nature and in my view so successfully composed that it would be enjoyable to her if I were not the author, it crossed my mind whether I might not be able to win her to the enterprise by reading it to her. I was prepared for her to reject my offer and for her to utilize

the advantage to say, "Now it has even gone so far that not only did you occupy yourself with writing but I am obliged to listen to lectures." Not at all.
She received my proposal as kindly as possible; she listened, she laughed, she
admired. I thought that all was won. She came over to the table where I was
sitting, put her arm intimately around my neck, and asked me to read a passage again. I begin to read, holding the manuscript high enough so that she
can see to follow me. Superb! I am beside myself but am not quite through
that passage when the manuscript suddenly bursts into flames. Without my
noticing it, she had pushed the single candle under the manuscript. The fire
won out; there was nothing to save; my introductory paragraph went up in
flames—amid general rejoicing, since my wife rejoiced for both of us. Like
an elated child she clapped her hands and then threw herself about my neck
with a passion as if I had been separated from her, yes, lost to her. I could not
get in a word. She begged my forgiveness for having fought in this way for
her love, begged with an emotion that almost made me believe that I had
been on the way to becoming the prodigal husband. She explained that she
could not endure my being changed in this way. "Your thought belongs to
me," she said, "it must belong to me. Your attentiveness is my daily bread.
Your approval, your smile, your jests are my life, my inspiration. Grant me
that—oh, do not deny me what is justly due me—for my sake, for the sake
of my joy, so that with joy I may be able to do what is my only joy: to think
of you and to find all my satisfaction in being able, day in and day out, to
continue wooing you as once you wooed me."

V
11

Now, what justifies a wife in such conduct, a wife who is lovable not only
in the eyes of all who know her but above all is lovable in my eyes, is as delightful as the day is long? Her view is *in contento* [in substance] as follows: a
married man who is an author is not much better than a married man who
goes to his club every evening, yes, even worse, because the one who goes
to his club must himself still admit that it is an infraction, but to be an author is a distinguished unfaithfulness that cannot evoke regret even though
the consequences are worse. The one who goes to his club is away only as
long as he is away, but an author—"Well, you probably do not know it yourself, but a total change has taken place in you. You are in a cocoon of thoughtfulness from morning til night, and it is especially obvious at the dinner table.
There you sit and stare off into space like a ghost or like King Nebuchadnezzar who is reading the invisible writing.[60] Then when I myself have prepared coffee for you, have set it out on the tray, come joyfully to you, stand
before you, and curtsy to you—then, then out of fright I almost drop the
tray, and above all I have then lost my cheerfulness and my joy and cannot
curtsy to you."

Just as my wife on each occasion knows how to get in her Catonian *preterea
censeo* [furthermore I am of the opinion] even though she does not do it as
tiresomely as Cato,[61] so must everything also serve her for argument. Her

argumentation is like an invocation of nature. If in a doctoral dissertation defense I was in the position that an opponent offered similar arguments, I would probably turn my back on him and say about him what the *Magister* [Master of Arts] says in Holberg: An ignoramus who does not know how to distinguish between *ubi praedicamentale* [the where predicative] and *ubi transcendentale* [the where transcendental].[62] With my wife it is something else. Her argumentation comes straight from the shoulder—and to the heart, from which it actually comes. In this regard she has taught me to understand how a Roman Catholic can be built up by a service in Latin, because her argumentation, viewed as such, is what Latin is for the one who does not understand it, and yet she always builds me up, moves and affects me.

"To be an author when one is a married man," she says, "is downright unfaithfulness, directly contrary to what the pastor said, since the validity of marriage is in this, that a man is to hold fast to his wife and to no other." She is by no means at a loss for an answer if I reply that one might almost think that she was so neglected that she needs to go to confirmation instruction again, that she perhaps was not really listening to what the pastor said, that marriage is a special duty, a *specific* duty, and that all duties can be divided into the general and the specific and are duties to God, to ourselves, and to the neighbor. Then she will get into no difficulty at all. The whole thing is declared to be teasing, and "moreover, she has not forgotten what is said about marriage in the catechism, that it is the husband's duty in particular." I futilely seek to explain to her that she is in linguistic error, that she is construing these words illogically, ungrammatically, against all principles of exegesis, because this passage is only about the husband's particular duties with regard to marriage, just as the very next paragraph is about the wife's particular duties. It is futile. She takes her stand on the preceding, "that to be an author when one is a married man is the worst kind of unfaithfulness." Now it has even become the "worst" unfaithfulness. If I then remind her that according to all divine and human laws the husband is the ruler, that otherwise my position in life becomes exceedingly low, since I become only an *encliticon*[63] to her, which still is claiming too much, she reproaches me for my unfairness, "since I know very well that she demands nothing, that in relation to me she desires only to be nothing at all." If, however, I protest because, if ultimately I am to be only an *encliticon*, it becomes important to me that she become as much as possible so that I will not become even less by being an *encliticon* to nothing, then she looks at me and says: Just teasing.

My wife is consistent, fixed in her idea. I have tried to flatter her: that it would indeed be pleasant to see my, our, name praised, that she is the muse who inspires me. She will hear nothing of it. She regards the former as the greatest disaster and my complete perdition, because she wishes with her whole heart that emphatic criticism would send me home again. She does

V
12

V
13

not believe the latter, wishes it even less, and from the depths of her soul prays God to forbid that she should in this way deserve the loss of her wedded bliss. She is inaccessible, and the *summa summarum* [sum of sums], "when everything has been said," comes down to this, "Either," she says, "a proper married man—or else . . . . . well, the rest is unimportant."

Now, although the reader will no doubt find, as I do, that her argumentation is rather weak and that she entirely disregards all the issues actually in question, namely, the boundary disputes involving the marital and the individual, which could give a profound and also acute mind enough to work on, she still has an argument *in subsidio* [in reserve], to which the reader will perhaps give more weight. One day after we had threshed through our differences and the conflict as usual had resolved itself in a *redintegratio amoris* [re-establishment of love], she finally took me intimately by the arm, looked as winsomely as possible at me, and said, "My dear, I have not wanted to say this to you so bluntly, because I hoped in another way to get you to give up this project and hoped to be able to save you from humiliation, but since that will not succeed, I will say it to you with all the frankness you can require of your wife: I do not think you are cut out to be an author—but on the other hand, yes, now laugh at me just a little, but on the other hand, you have the genius and talent and extraordinary gift to be my husband in such a way that I would ceaselessly admire you while I myself would happily feel my own lowliness and make my love apparent to you with thanksgiving." She did not, however, embark upon a development of the argument in detail. As soon as I wanted to embark upon a whether, to what extent, and how, she would have another explanation, "that someday I would regret having been unfaithful to her by becoming an author, and then I would not be able to disregard this regret but would suffer its bitterness."

And what, then, was the end of this conflict? Who was victorious, my *hostis domesticus* [domestic enemy] or the author? It certainly is not difficult to guess, even though it is momentarily difficult for the reader when he reads this and thus sees that I became an author. The end was that I promised not to insist on being an author. But just as at academic disputations, when the author has disarmed all of one's objections, one comes forward with some linguistic triviality in order nevertheless to turn out to be right about something, and the author politely agrees that one is right in order nevertheless to admit that one is right about something, I thus reserved for myself permission to venture to write "Prefaces." In this connection I appealed to analogies, that husbands who had promised their wives never to use snuff any more had as recompense obtained permission to have as many snuffboxes as they wished. She accepted the proposal, perhaps with the idea that one could not write a preface without writing a book, which I indeed do not dare to do, unless one is a famous author who writes such a thing on request, which, to be sure, could not possibly be the case with me.

So it is with regard to my promise and my obligation. The little or the trifles that I hereby publish I was able to write *salva conscientia* [with good conscience]. Yet I have done so without my wife's knowledge by using a sojourn in the country for this. My request to criticism is that it will go easy on me, because, suppose it found that it was as my wife said, that I was not cut out to be an author, suppose that it unmercifully raked me over the coals, suppose my wife learned of it—then very likely I would in vain seek encouragement and consolation from my companion in life. She would probably exult with joy over carrying her point and over my having been taught a lesson in this way, and she would find her faith in a righteous Governance confirmed and her idea strengthened that to be an author when one is a married man is the worst unfaithfulness.

V
15

THREE DISCOURSES ON
IMAGINED OCCASIONS (APRIL 29, 1845)
BY S. KIERKEGAARD

Published one day before *Stages on Life's Way*, *Three Discourses* constitutes another element in the series of signed works that parallel the pseudonymous publications. The Preface addresses the reader with an invitation to the "appropriation" of what one reads, an intimation of the thesis "subjectivity is truth" in *Postscript*. The theme of the first discourse, "On the Occasion of a Confession," affirms that to seek God begins in silent wonder and holy fear and culminates in the awareness that "God is near enough, but no one *without purity* can *see God*, and sin is impurity and *therefore no one can become aware of God without becoming a sinner.*"[64] The final clause is a repetition of the subject of the final section of *Either/Or, II*, "...That in Relation to God We Are Always in the Wrong," and the preceding italicized line anticipates the theme in Part One of *Upbuilding Discourses in Various Spirits*: "Purity of heart is to will one thing." The second discourse, "On the Occasion of a Wedding," points ahead to *Works of Love* in reaffirming Judge William's distinction (in *Either/Or, II*, and *Stages*) between *Elskov* (erotic love) and *Kjerlighed* (*agapē* love) and emphasizes the resolution that is the heart of marriage. The third discourse is on the educational value of the contemplation of death, particularly one's own, echoed in many of the later works.

Discourses on Imagined Occasions and *Stages* are not only publication companion pieces but are also inversely related in content. "On the Occasion of a Confession," with an emphasis on stillness, wonder, and seeking God, is Kierkegaard's counterpoise to *"In Vino Veritas"* in *Stages*, with its banquet and speechmaking on erotic love. "On the Occasion of a Wedding" deepens and rectifies Judge William's panegyric on marriage in *Either/Or, II*, and in the second part of *Stages*. And "At a Graveside," on the earnestness in life evoked by the earnest thought of death, constitutes an unambiguous sharpening of the implicit ethical and religious earnestness in Quidam's "'Guilty?'/'Not Guilty?'" in Part Three of *Stages*. Some readers see the relationship in reverse order (the first discourse and the last as balancing the last part and the first in *Stages*). In both views the two works are related in content, and one is perhaps justified in imagining that Kierkegaard alternated between his ordinary desk, spread with the ongoing manuscript of *Stages*, and his high desk, at which he intermittently worked on *Three Discourses on Imagined Occasions*.

AT A GRAVESIDE

Then all is over!—And when the person stepped up to the grave first because he was the next of kin, and when after the brief moment of the speech he was the last one at the grave, alas, because he was the next of kin—then all is over. If he remained out there, he still would not learn what the deceased is doing, because the deceased is a quiet man; if in his trouble he called out his name, if in his grief he sat listening, he still would learn nothing, because in the grave there is quiet, and the deceased is a silent man; and if recollecting he visited the grave every day, the one dead would not recollect him—.

In the grave there is no recollection, not even of God. See, the man did know this, the one of whom it must now be said that he no longer recollects anything, to whom it would now be too late to say this. But because he knew this, he acted accordingly, and therefore *he recollected God* while he was living. His life was passed in honorable obscurity; not many were aware of his existence; among those few only one or two knew him. He was a citizen of the town here; a hard worker in his modest occupation, he disturbed no one by disregarding his civic obligations, disturbed no one by misplaced concern about the whole. So it went year after year, uniformly but not emptily. He grew up, he grew old, he became aged—his work was and remained the same, the same occupation in the different periods of his life. He leaves behind a wife, happy to have been united with him in the past, now an old woman who grieves for the lost one, a true widow who, forsaken, has her hope in God. He leaves behind a son who learned to love him and to find contentment in his situation and his father's work. At one time as a child joyful in his father's house, as a youth he never found it too cramped; now it is a house of mourning for him.

V
227

Not many inquiries are made about the death of such an obscure man, and if anyone shortly thereafter walks past the house where he lived in lowliness and reads his name over the door, because the little business is continued under his name, it will indeed seem as if he were not dead. Just as he slept gently and peacefully away, so in the surrounding world his death is a departure in silence. Respectable as a citizen, honest in his business, thrifty in his household, charitable according to his means, sincerely sympathetic, faithful to his wife, a father to his son—all this and all the truth with which this can be said do not raise expectations for a momentous ending; here it is a life's activity to which a quiet death became a beautiful ending.

Yet he still had one more work; in simplicity of heart it was performed with the same faithfulness: he recollected God. He was a man, old, he became aged, and then he died, but the recollection of God remained the same, a guide in all his activity, a quiet joy in his devout contemplation. Indeed, if there were no one at all who missed him in death, yes, if he were not with God now, God would miss him in life and know his dwelling and seek him there, because the deceased walked before him and was better known by him than by anyone else. He recollected God and became proficient in his work; he recollected God and became joyful in his work and joyful in his life; he recollected God and became happy in his modest home with his dear ones; he disturbed no one by indifference to public worship, disturbed no one by untimely zeal, but God's house was to him a second home—and now he has gone home.

But in the grave there is no recollection—therefore it remains behind, remains with the two who were dear to him in life: they will recollect him. And now when the person who stepped up to the grave first because he was the next of kin and after the brief moment of the speech was the last one at the grave because he was the next of kin, when he, recollecting, departs, he goes home to the sorrowing widow—and the name over the door becomes a recollection. Now and then for a time there will come a customer who casually or more solicitously asks about the man, and when he hears of his death the customer will say, "Well, so he is dead." When all the old customers have done that once, the life of the locality has no longer any means of preserving the recollection of him. But the old widow will need no reminder in order to recollect, and the busy son will not find it a hindrance to recollect. When no one asks about him anymore, then the name over the door—when the house is no longer visibly a house of sorrow, when also the grief in the house has abated and the daily loss has with consolation practiced recollection—then the name over the door will signify to the two that they also have one additional work: to recollect the one who is dead.

Now the speech is over. Just one act remains—with the three spadefuls of earth to commit the deceased, like everything that has come from the earth, to earth again—and then all is over.

If it is certain that death exists, which it is; if it is certain that with death's decision all is over; if it is certain that death itself never becomes involved in giving any explanation—well, then it is a matter of understanding oneself, and the earnest understanding is that if death is night then life is day, that if no work can be done at night then work can be done during the day; and the terse but impelling cry of earnestness, like death's terse cry, is: This very day.

Death in earnest gives life force as nothing else does; it makes one alert as nothing else does. Death induces the sensual person to say: Let us eat and drink, because tomorrow we shall die—but this is sensuality's cowardly lust for life, that contemptible order of things where one lives in order to eat and drink instead of eating and drinking in order to live. The idea of death may induce weakness in the more profound person so that he sinks relaxed in mood, but the thought of death gives the earnest person the right momentum in life and the right goal toward which he directs his momentum. No bowstring can be tightened in such a way and is able to give the arrow such momentum the way the thought of death is able to accelerate the living when earnestness stretches the thought. Then earnestness grasps the present this very day, disdains no task as too insignificant, rejects no time as too short, works with all its might even though it is willing to smile at itself if this effort is said to be merit before God, in weakness is willing to understand that a human being is nothing at all and that one who works with all one's might gains only the proper opportunity to wonder at God.

V
228

V
236

V
237

So, then, let death keep its power, "that all is over," but let life also keep   v
the right to work while it is day; and let the earnest person seek the thought   238
of death as an aid in that work. The vacillating person is only a witness to
the continual boundary struggle between life and death, his life only doubt's
statement of the situation, the ending of his life an illusion, but the earnest
person has made friends with the contenders and in the earnest thought of
death he has the most faithful ally. Even though the equality of all the dead
is that now all is over, there is still one difference, my listener, a difference
that cries aloud to heaven—the difference of what that life was that now in
death is over. So all is not over, and despite all death's terror—no, supported
by the earnest thought of death, the earnest person says, "All is not over."
But if this bright prospect is tempting, if he once again merely glimpses it in
the half-light of contemplation, if it puts distance between him and the task,
if time does not become a scarcity, if the possession of it is secure for him—
then again he is not earnest. If death says, "Perhaps this very day," then
earnestness says, "Let it perhaps be today or not," but I say, "This very day."

The earnest person looks at himself. If he is young, the thought of death   v
teaches him that a young person will become its booty here if it comes today,   245
but he does not dally in ordinary talk about youth as death's booty. The
earnest person looks at himself; so he knows the nature of the one who would
become death's booty here if it were to come today; he looks at his own work
and so he knows what work it is that would be interrupted here if death were
to come today. Thus the game ends, the enigma is solved. The ordinary view
of death only confuses thought, just as wanting to experience in general does.
The certainty of death is the earnestness; its uncertainty is the instruction,   v
the practice of earnestness. The earnest person is the one who through un-   246
certainty is brought up to earnestness by virtue of certainty.

How does a person learn earnestness? Is it by having an earnest person
dictate something to him so that he can learn it? Not at all. If you have not
yourself learned in this way from an earnest man, then imagine how it goes.
See, the learner concerns himself (without concern there is no learner) about
some object with his whole soul, and in this way the certainty of death becomes an object of concern. Now the concerned person turns to the teacher
of earnestness, and thus death is indeed not a monster except for the imagination. The learner now wants this or that; he wants to do it thus and so and
under these assumptions—"And it is bound to succeed, is it not so?" But the
earnest person answers nothing at all, and finally he says, yet without mockery but with the calmness of earnestness, "Yes, it is possible!" The learner already becomes a little impatient; he suggests a new plan, changes the assumptions, and concludes his speech in a still more urgent way. But the
earnest person is silent, looks calmly at him, and finally says, "Yes, it is pos-

sible!" Now the learner becomes passionate; he resorts to pleas or, if he is so equipped, to clever locutions—indeed, he perhaps even insults the earnest person and becomes totally confused himself and everything around him seems to be confusion. But when with these weapons and in this condition he charges at the earnest person, he has to endure his unaltered calm gaze and put up with his silence, because the earnest person merely looks at him and finally says, "Yes, it is possible."

This is the way it is with death. The certainty is the unchanging, and the uncertainty is the brief statement: It is possible. Every condition that wants to make the certainty of death into a conditional certainty for the wisher, every agreement that wants to make the certainty of death into a conditional certainty for the person making up his mind, every arrangement that wants to condition the certainty of death as to time and hour for the one who is acting, every condition, every agreement, every arrangement runs aground on this statement; and all passionateness and all cleverness and all defiance are rendered powerless by this statement—until the learner sees the error of his ways. But the earnestness lies in just this, and it was to this that certainty and uncertainty wanted to help the learner. If certainty is allowed to leave open the question of what it can be, like a universal caption over life, instead of being like the endorsement of the particular and the daily by usage, as happens with the help of uncertainty—then earnestness is not learned. Uncertainty lends a hand and, like the teacher, points steadily to the object of learning and says to the learner, "Pay close attention to the certainty"—then earnestness comes into existence. No teacher is able to teach the pupil to pay attention to what is said the way the uncertainty of death does when it points to the certainty of death; and no teacher is able to keep the pupil's thoughts concentrated on the one object of instruction the way the thought of the uncertainty of death does when it practices the thought of the certainty of death.

The person who has spoken here is young, still at the age of a learner; he comprehends only the difficulty and the rigorousness of the instruction— oh, would that he might succeed in doing it in such a way that he would become worthy of daring at some time to rejoice in the teacher's friendship! The person who has spoken here is, of course, not your teacher, my listener; he is merely letting you witness, just as he himself is doing, how a person seeks to learn something from the thought of death, that teacher of earnestness who at birth is appointed to everyone for a whole lifetime and who in the uncertainty is always ready to begin the instruction when it is requested. Death does not come because someone calls it (for the weaker one to order the stronger one in that way would be only a jest), but as soon as someone opens the door to uncertainty, the teacher is there, the teacher who will at some time come to give a test and examine the pupil: whether he has wanted to use his instruction or not. And this testing by death—or with a more commonly used foreign word to designate the same thing—this final examination [*Examen*] of life, is equally difficult for all. It is not as it usually is— namely, that the fortunately gifted person passes easily and the poorly gifted person has a hard time—no, death adapts the test to the ability—oh, so very accurately, and the test becomes equally difficult because it is the test of earnestness.

V
253

STAGES ON LIFE'S WAY.
STUDIES BY VARIOUS PERSONS (APRIL 30, 1845)
COMPILED, FORWARDED TO THE PRESS, AND PUBLISHED
BY HILARIUS BOOKBINDER

Three Discourses on Imagined Occasions and *Stages on Life's Way* were not only published at the same time (one day apart) as another pair of works in the two parallel series of signed and pseudonymous writings, but the three parts of each are related as balances in substance. Part One, "*In Vino Veritas*," which has been judged qualitatively comparable to Plato's *Symposium*, gathers Johannes the Seducer, the editor of *Either/Or*, the author of *Repetition*, a Young Man, a Fashion Designer, and the Narrator at a banquet devoted to speeches on erotic love and women. Part Two is Judge William's eulogy on marital love (see *Either/Or*, II), and Part Three is an "imaginary construction [*Experiment*]" by Frater Taciturnus on the torments occasioned by the breaking of an engagement (cf. "The Seducer's Diary," *Either/Or*, I), with a concluding interpretive letter by the pseudonymous author. "This imaginary construction ("'Guilty?'/'Not Guilty?'") is the first attempt in all the pseudonymous writings at an existential dialectic in double-reflection. It is not the communication that is in the form of double reflection (for all the pseudonymous works are that), but the existing person himself exists in this. Thus he does not give up immediacy, but he keeps it and yet gives it up, keeps erotic love's desire and yet gives it up."[65] The view of the potential stages of life is scarcely discussed (only briefly in the concluding letter) but rather is represented by characters and their thought: Part One, the esthetic as immediacy of desire and the underside of disillusion and despair; Part Two, the ethical as basic with intimations of the religious; and Part Three, the ethical and its underside, guilt, and its deepest expression, repentance, pointing to the religious as the sphere of fulfillment. "But the issue itself," the pseudonymous author writes, "the idea of forgiveness of sins, is extraneous to the task the imaginary construction has assigned itself, for Quidam is only a demonic figure oriented to the religious, and the issue is beyond both my understanding and my capacities."[66] Thus, as with *Either/Or*, the reader is again left with the dialogue of contrasting positions and attitudes and the task of coming to a conclusion.

"IN VINO VERITAS":
A RECOLLECTION RELATED BY WILLIAM AFHAM

Solche Werke sind Spiegel: wenn ein Affe hinein guckt,
kann kein Apostel heraus sehen
[Such works are mirrors: when an ape looks in,
no apostle can look out].

LICHTENBERG[67]

Preface

What a splendid occupation to prepare a secret for oneself, how seductive to   VI
enjoy it, and yet at times how precarious to have enjoyed it, how easy for it   15
to miscarry for one. In other words, if someone believes that a secret is trans-
ferable as a matter of course, that it can belong to the bearer, he is mistaken,
for the [riddle] "Out of the eater comes something to eat"[68] is valid here;
but if anyone thinks that the only difficulty entailed in enjoying it is not to
betray it, he is also mistaken, for one also takes on the responsibility of not
forgetting it. Yet it is even more disgusting to recollect incompletely and to
turn one's soul into a transit warehouse for damaged goods. In relation to
others, then, let forgetting be the silken curtain that is drawn, recollection
[*Erindring*] the vestal virgin who goes behind the curtain; behind the curtain
is the forgetting again—if it is not a true recollection, for in that case the
forgetting is excluded.

The recollection must be not only accurate; it must also be happy. The
bottling of the recollection must have preserved the fragrance of the experience before it is sealed. Just as grapes cannot be pressed at any time whatsoever, just as the weather at the time of pressing has great influence on the
wine, so also what is experienced can neither be recollected nor be inwardly
recollected at any time whatsoever or under any and all circumstances.

To recollect [*erindre*] is by no means the same as to remember [*huske*]. For
example, one can remember very well every single detail of an event without thereby recollecting it. Remembering is only a vanishing condition.
Through memory, the experience presents itself to receive the consecration   VI
of recollection. The distinction is already discernible in the difference be-   16
tween generations. The old person loses memory, which as a rule is the first
faculty to be lost. Yet the old person has something poetic about him; in the
popular mind he is prophetic, inspired. But recollection is indeed his best
power, his consolation, which consoles him with its poetic farsightedness.
Childhood, on the other hand, has memory and quickness of apprehension
to a high degree but does not have recollection at all. Instead of saying, "Old
age does not forget what youth apprehends," one could perhaps say, "What
the child remembers the old person recollects." The old person's glasses are
ground for seeing close at hand. When youth wears glasses, the lens is for seeing at a distance, for it lacks the power of recollection, which is the power
to distance, to place at a distance. But the happy recollection of old age, just
like the happy apprehension of the child, is nature's gracious gift, which pref-
erentially embraces the two most helpless and yet in a certain sense happiest
periods of life. But for this very reason recollection, as well as memory, is
sometimes only the holder of accidental happenings.

Although the difference between memory and recollection is great, they
are frequently confused. In human life, this confusion lends itself to study-

ing the depth of the individual. That is, recollection is ideality, but as such it is strenuous and conscientious in a way completely different from indiscriminate memory. Recollection wants to maintain for a person the eternal continuity in life and assure him that his earthly existence remains *uno tenore* [uninterrupted], one breath, and expressible in one breath. Therefore it declines to have the tongue be constrained to chatter on and on in order to ape the chattering nature of life's content. The condition for man's immortality is that life is *uno tenore*. Strangely enough, Jacobi is the only one who, as far as I know, has commented on the terror in thinking oneself immortal. At times it seemed to him as if the thought of immortality, if he held on to it a little longer in the single moment, would confuse his mind. Is the reason for this that Jacobi had bad nerves? A robust man who has acquired callouses on his hand simply by pounding the pulpit or the lectern every time he proved immortality feels no such terror, and yet he surely knows all about immortality, for in Latin to have callouses means to understand something completely. However, as soon as one confuses memory and recollection, the thought is not so terrible—in the first place because one is bold, manly, and robust, and in the second place because one is not thinking the thought at all. No doubt many a man has written memoirs of his life in which there was not a trace of recollection, and yet the recollections were indeed his proceeds for eternity. In recollection, a person draws on the eternal. The eternal is sufficiently humane to honor every claim and to regard everyone as solvent. But it is not the fault of the eternal that a person makes a fool of himself—and remembers instead of recollects and as a result forgets instead of recollects, for what is remembered is also forgotten. But in turn, memory makes life free and easy. One cavalierly goes through the most ludicrous metamorphoses; even at an advanced age one still plays blindman's buff, still plays the lottery of life, and still can become almost anything, although one has been an incredible number of things. Then one dies—and thereupon becomes immortal. And precisely by having lived in such a way, should one not have richly provided oneself with enough to recollect for a whole eternity? Yes, if recollection's ledger were nothing more than a notebook in which one scribbles anything that comes to mind. But recollection's bookkeeping is a curious thing. One could assign oneself a few such problems—but not in fellowship. One person talks day in and day out to general assemblies and always about what the times demand, yet not repetitiously in a Cato-like, tedious way,[69] but always interestingly and intriguingly he follows the moment and never says the same thing; at parties, too, he imposes himself and doles out his fund of eloquence, at times with full even measure, at times heaped up, and always to applause; at least once a week there is something about him in the newspaper; also at night he bestows his favors, on his wife, that is, by talking even in his sleep about the demands of the times as if he were at a general assembly. Another person is silent before he speaks and goes so far that he does not speak at all; they live the same length of time—and here the question of the result is raised: Who has more to recollect? One person pursues one idea, one single idea, is preoccupied only with it; another is an author in seven branches of scholarship and "is interrupted in this significant work" (it is a journalist who is speaking) "just as he was about to transform veterinary science"; they live the same length of time—and here the question of the result is raised: Who has more to recollect?

Actually, only the essential can be recollected, for the old man's recollecting, as stated, is basically of an accidental character; the same holds true of analogies to his recollecting. The essential is conditioned not only by itself but also by its relation to the person concerned. The person who has broken with the idea cannot act essentially, can undertake nothing that is essential; the essential would then be to repent, which is the only new ideality. Despite external indications, anything else he does is unessential. To take a wife is indeed something essential, but anyone who has ever dallied with erotic love [*Elskov*] may very well strike his brow and his heart and his r—— in sheer seriousness and solemnity; it is still frivolity. Even if his marriage involved a whole nation and the bells were rung and the pope married them, it nevertheless is not anything essential to him but essentially is frivolity. The external noise makes no difference, just as the fanfare and presentation of arms do not make the lottery-drawing an essential act for the boy who draws the numbers. Acting essentially does not depend essentially on the blowing of trumpets. But what is recollected cannot be forgotten either. What is recollected is not inconsequential to recollecting in the way that what is remembered is inconsequential to remembering. What is recollected can be thrown away, but just like Thor's hammer, it returns, and not only that, like a dove it has a longing for the recollection, yes, like a dove, however often it is sold, that can never belong to anyone else because it always flies home. But no wonder, for it was recollection itself that hatched out what was recollected, and this hatching is hidden and secret, solitary, and thus immune to any profane knowledge—in just the same way the bird will not sit on its egg if some stranger has touched it.

Memory is immediate and is assigned immediately, recollection only reflectively. This is why it is an art to recollect. Rather than remember, I, along with Themistocles, wish only to be able to forget,[70] but to recollect and to forget are not opposites. The art of recollecting is not easy, because in the moment of preparation it can become something different, whereas memory merely fluctuates between remembering correctly and remembering incorrectly. For example, what is homesickness? It is something remembered that is recollected. Homesickness is prompted simply by one's being absent. The art would be to be able to feel homesickness even though one is at home. This takes proficiency in illusion. To go on living in an illusion in which there is continual dawning, never daybreak, or to reflect oneself out of all illusion

VI
18

VI
19

is not as difficult as to reflect oneself into an illusion, plus being able to let it work on oneself with the full force of illusion even though one is fully aware. To conjure up the past for oneself is not as difficult as to conjure away the present for the sake of recollection. This is the essential art of recollection and its reflection to the second power.

To bring about a recollection for oneself takes an acquaintance with contrasting moods, situations, and surroundings. An erotic situation in which the salient feature was the cozy remoteness of rural life can at times be best recollected and inwardly recollected in a theater, where the surroundings and the noise evoke the contrast. Yet the direct contrast is not always the happy one. If it were not unbecoming to use a human being as a means, the happy contrast for recollecting an erotic relationship might be to arrange a new love affair merely in order to recollect.

The contrast can be extremely reflective. The ultimate in the reflective relationship between memory and recollection is to use memory against recollection. For opposite reasons, two people could wish not to see again a place that reminds them of an event. The one has no inkling at all that there is something called recollection but merely fears the memory. Out of sight, out of mind, he thinks; if only he does not see, then he has forgotten. Precisely because the other wants to recollect, he does not want to see. He uses memory only against unpleasant recollections. One who understands recollection but does not understand this indeed has ideality but lacks experience in using *consilia evangelica adversus casus conscientiae* [the evangelical counsels against a matter of conscience]. Indeed, he will probably even regard the advice as a paradox and shy away from enduring the first pain, which, nevertheless, just like the first loss, is always to be preferred. When memory is refreshed again and again, it enriches the soul with a mass of details that distract recollection. Thus repentance is a recollection of guilt. From a purely psychological point of view, I really believe that the police aid the criminal in not coming to repent. By continually recounting and repeating his life experiences, the criminal becomes such a memory expert at rattling off his life that the ideality of recollection is driven away. Really to repent, and especially to repent at once, takes enormous ideality; therefore nature also can help a person, and delayed repentance, which in regard to remembering is negligible, is often the hardest and the deepest. The ability to recollect is the condition for all productivity. If a person no longer wishes to be productive, he needs merely to remember the same thing that recollecting he wanted to produce, and production is rendered impossible, or it will become so repulsive to him that the sooner he abandons it the better.

VI
20

Strictly speaking, a fellowship of recollection does not exist. A kind of *quasi*-fellowship is a contrast-form that the one recollecting uses on his own behalf. Sometimes recollection is prompted best by seeming to confide in someone else only in order to conceal behind this confidence a new reflection in which the recollection comes into existence for oneself. As far as memory is concerned, people can certainly join together for mutual assistance. In this respect, banquets, birthday celebrations, love tokens, and expensive mementos serve the same purpose as turning a dog-ear in a book in order to remember where one left off reading and by the dog-ear to be sure of having read the whole book through. The wine press of recollection, however, everyone must tread alone. In itself, this is far from being a curse. Inasmuch as one is always alone with recollection, every recollection is a secret. Even if several persons are interested in what is the object of recollecting to the one recollecting, he is nevertheless alone with his recollection—the seeming public character is merely illusory.

What has been propounded here is for my own personal recollection of thoughts and intellectual preoccupations that have engrossed my soul many times and in many ways. The occasion for jotting them down is that I now feel inclined to redeem for recollection something I once experienced, to record something that has laid completely remembered for some time now and also partially recollected. What I have to remember is small in scope, and thus the work of memory is easy; but I have had difficulty getting it out properly for recollection simply because for me it has become something entirely different than for the honorable participants, who probably would smile to see any importance whatsoever attributed to such a trifle—a playful whim, a preposterous idea, as they themselves would call it. Indeed, how meaningless the memory is to me I see in the fact that at times it seems as if I never experienced it at all but invented it myself.

VI
21

I know very well that I shall not soon forget that banquet in which I participated without being a participant; but just the same I cannot now decide to release it without having provided myself with a scrupulous written ἀπομνημόνευμα [memoir] of what for me was actually *memorabile* [worthy of memory].

It was on one of the last days in July, about ten o'clock in the evening, that the participants gathered for that banquet. The date and the year I have forgotten; such matters, after all, are of interest only to memory, not to recollection. The only subject matter for recollection is mood and whatever is classified under mood. And just as noble wine is improved by crossing the line[71] because the particles of water vaporize, so recollection also is improved by losing the water particles of memory; yet recollection no more becomes a figment of the imagination thereby then does the noble wine.

VI
25

The participants were five in number: Johannes, called the Seducer, Victor Eremita, Constantin Constantius, and two more whose names I have not exactly forgotten, which would not have been important, but whose names I did not learn. It seemed as if these two had no *proprium* [proper name], for they were always named only by an epithet. The one was called: the Young Man. He presumably was in his early twenties, of slender and delicate build, and of rather dark complexion. He had a thoughtful expression, but even more pleasing was his charming, engaging demeanor, which betokened a purity of soul that completely harmonized with the almost femininely luxuriant softness and transparency of his whole figure. But in turn one forgot this external beauty with the next impression or kept it only *in mente* [in mind] while contemplating a young man who, cultivated—or, to use an even more delicate expression, fostered—by intellect alone, nourished by the content of his own soul, had had nothing to do with the world, had been neither awakened and inflamed nor disquieted and disturbed. Like a sleepwalker, he carried the law for his behavior within himself, and his loving sympathetic demeanor involved no one but reflected only the fundamental mood of his soul.

VI
26

The other one they called the Fashion Designer, which was his occupation in civil life. It was impossible to get a genuine impression of this man. He was dressed in the very latest fashion, was curled and perfumed and smelled of *eau de Cologne*. One moment his behavior was not without aplomb, but the next moment his walk assumed a certain dancelike festiveness, a certain floating motion, to which his corpulence nevertheless set limits at some point. Even when he was talking most maliciously, his voice always had an element of boutique-pleasantness and polite sweetness, which certainly must have been extremely nauseating to him personally and only satisfied his defiance. When I think about him now, I certainly understand him better than when I saw him step out of the carriage and could not help but laugh. But a contradiction still remains. He has charmed or bewitched himself, by the wizardry of his will has conjured himself into an almost silly character, but has not quite satisfied himself with it, which is why now and then reflection peeks out.

VI
30

The place chosen was in a wooded area a few miles from Copenhagen. The salon in which they were to dine had been redecorated and altered recently beyond all recognition; a small room separated from the salon by a corridor was prepared for an orchestra. Shutters and curtains were placed before all the windows, and behind these the windows stood open. Constantin's wish was that, as a preliminary, they arrive by carriage in the evening. Even though one knows that one is driving to a banquet and consequently indulges momentarily in imagining the sumptuousness of it, yet the impact of the natural environment is so powerful that it must prevail. The only fear Constantin had was that this would not happen, for just as there is no force so proficient as the imagination in embellishing everything, so, too, there is no other force able to play havoc with everything when things go wrong for one in the moment of encounter with actuality. Driving on a summer evening does not, however, turn the imagination toward the sumptuous but does the very opposite. Even if one does not see and hear it, the imagination nevertheless involuntarily creates an image of the evening's cozy, comfortable longing; thus one sees girls and farmhands on their way home from their field work, hears the hurried clattering of the harvest wagon, interprets even the bellowing far off in the meadow as a longing. In this way the summer evening lures forth the idyllic, refreshes even a craving mind with its tranquillity, prompts even the fleeting fantasy to remain with autochthonic homesickness on the earth as the place of one's origin, teaches the insatiable mind to be satisfied with little, makes one content, for in the evening hours time stands still and eternity lingers.

So they arrived in the evening, the invited guests, for Constantin had come out somewhat earlier. Victor E., who was staying out in the country nearby, came on horseback; the others came by carriage, and just as their carriage drove in, a wagonette swung through the gate—a lively crew of four workmen, who were entertained and thereupon kept in readiness for the crucial moment as a dismantling crew, just as firemen for the opposite reason are present in the theater to extinguish a fire at once.

As long as one is a child one has enough imagination, even if the waiting in a dark room lasts an hour, to be able to keep one's soul at a high level, at the peak of anticipation; when we are adults, imagination tends to make us bored with the Christmas tree before we get to see it.

The double doors were opened; the effect of the brilliant lighting, the coolness that flowed toward them, the spicy fascination of the scent, and the tasteful table setting overwhelmed the entering guests for a moment, and when at the same time the orchestra began playing the dance music from *Don Giovanni,* the forms of those entering were transfigured, and as if in deference to an invisible spirit encompassing them, they stood still a moment, like someone whom admiration has awakened and who has risen in order to admire.
VI
31

As for the content of the speeches, Constantin proposed that the subject should be erotic love [*Elskov*] or the relation between man and woman; love affairs, however, should not be related, but indeed they might very well be the basis of the point of view.
VI
34

The conditions were accepted.—All of a host's just and reasonable demands upon guests were fulfilled: they ate, drank and drank, and became drunk,[72] as it says in Hebrew—that is, they drank mightily.

The dessert was served. If Victor had not yet had his request fulfilled to hear the splashing of a fountain, something that fortunately for him he had forgotten about since that conversation, now the champagne effervesced to overflowing. The clock struck twelve; then Constantin asked for silence and toasted the Young Man with a glass and these words: *Quod felix sit faustumque* [May it be to good fortune and success] and asked him to speak first.

VI
65

Scarcely had Victor finished before the Fashion Designer leaped to his feet, upset a bottle of wine standing in front of him, and then began as follows.

Well spoken, dear drinking companions, well spoken! The more I hear you talk, the more I am convinced that you are fellow conspirators. I greet you as such, I understand you as such, for one understands conspirators even at a distance. And yet what do you know, what is your bit of theory that you pass off as experience, what is your bit of experience that you remake into a theory, and finally you even on occasion believe it for a moment and are inveigled for a moment. No, I know woman from her weak side; that means, I know her. In my study, I shun no terror and shun no means to make sure of what I have understood, for I am a madman, and a madman one must be in order to understand her, and if one was not that before, one becomes that once one has understood her. Just as the robber has his hideout beside the

VI
66

noisy highway and the anteater its funnel in the loose sand and the pirate ship its hiding place by the roaring sea, so I have my fashion boutique right in the middle of the human swarm, as seductive and irresistible to a woman as Venusberg to the man. Here in a fashion boutique one learns to know her practically and from the ground up without all that theoretical fuss. Indeed, if fashion meant nothing more than that a woman in the concupiscence of desire puts everything aside, that would still be something. But that is not the way it is; fashion is not open sensuality, is not tolerated dissipation, but is a sneaky trafficking in impropriety that is authorized as propriety. And just as in pagan Prussia the marriageable girl carried a bell whose ringing was a signal to the men, so a woman's existence in fashion is a perpetual carillon—not to the profligate but to sweet-toothed sensualists. Fortune is thought to be a woman—oh, to be sure, it is indeed fickle, but nevertheless it is fickle in something, for it can give much, provided it is not a woman. No, fashion is a woman, for fashion is fickle in nonsense, which knows but one consequence: that it inevitably becomes more and more extravagantly mad. If one wishes to learn to know women, one hour in my boutique is worth more than years and days on the outside; in my fashion boutique there is no thought of competition, for it is the only one in the royal city. Who would dare to compete with someone who has completely dedicated himself and dedicates himself as high priest in this idol worship? No, there is no distinguished social gathering where my name is not first and last, and there is no middle-class social gathering where the mention of my name does not inspire holy awe as does the king's, and there is no costume so crazy that, if it is from my boutique, it is not accompanied by whispering as it walks through the salon. And there is no aristocratic lady who dares to walk past my boutique, and no middle-class maiden walks past without sighing and thinking: If only I could afford it. But then she was not deceived, either. I deceive no one; I supply the finest and the most expensive things at the cheapest prices—indeed, I sell below cost. Hence I am not out to gain—no, every year I lose huge sums. And yet I want to gain; I do want it; I spend my last farthing in order to suborn, in order to bribe, the organs of fashion so that my game may be won. To me it is a sensual pleasure without rival to take out the costliest fabrics, to cut them, to clip genuine Brussels lace in order to create a fool's costume; I sell genuine and fashionable material at the lowest prices.

You may think that it is only in odd moments that she wishes to be in fashion. Far from it, she wants to be that at all times, and it is her one and only thought. Woman does have spirit, but it is invested just about as well as the prodigal son's resources; and woman is reflective to an incomprehensibly high degree, for there is nothing so sacred that she does not immediately find it suitable for adornment, and the most exclusive manifestation of adornment is fashion. No wonder she finds it suitable, for fashion, after all, is the sacred. And there is nothing so insignificant that she does not in turn know how to relate it to adornment, and the manifestation of adornment most devoid of ideas is fashion. And there is nothing, not one thing in her whole attire, not the smallest ribbon, without her having a notion of its relevance to fashion, and without her detecting at once whether the lady passing by has noticed it—because for whom does she adorn herself if it is not for other ladies! Even in my boutique, where she comes, of course, to be fitted out in fashion, even there she is in fashion. Just as there are a special bathing costume and a riding costume, so there is also a special attire that is in vogue to wear for going to the boutique. This costume is not as casual as the negligee in which a lady likes to be surprised earlier in the forenoon. The whole point then is her femininity and coquetry in letting herself be surprised. Her boutique attire, on the other hand, is calculated to be casual, a bit frivolous without thereby causing embarrassment, because a fashion designer has a relation to her quite different from a cavalier's. The coquetry consists in appearing this way before a man, who, because of his position, does not dare claim the lady's feminine recognition but must be satisfied with the uncertain profits that richly pay off but without her thinking about it or without her dreaming of wanting to be the lady in relation to a fashion designer. Thus the whole point is that femininity is in a way left out and coquetry is invalidated in the exclusive superiority of the distinguished lady, who would smile if anyone were to allude to such a relationship. In her negligee on the occasion of a [surprise] call, she covers herself and thereby gives herself away; in the boutique she uncovers herself with utmost nonchalance, for it is only a fashion designer—and she is a woman. Now the shawl slips down a bit and shows a little white skin—if I do not know what that means and what she wants, then my reputation is lost. Now she puckers her lips apriorally, then gesticulates aposteriorally; now she wriggles her hips, then looks in the mirror and sees my admiring face; now she lisps, walks with a mincing gait, then hardly seems to touch the floor; now she trails her foot daringly, sinks weakly into an armchair, while I obsequiously hand her a scent-flacon and cool her with

VI
67

my adoration; now she roguishly hits at me with her hand, then drops her handkerchief and lets her hand remain in a loose, drooping position, while I bow low and pick it up, offer it to her, and receive a little patronizing nod.

This is how a woman of fashion deports herself in a boutique. Whether Diogenes disturbed the woman praying in a somewhat immodest position by asking her whether she did not believe that the gods could see her from behind, I do not know, but this I do know—if I were to say to her kneeling ladyship: The folds of your gown do not fall in a fashionable way, she would dread this more than offending the gods. Woe to the outcast, the Cinderella who does not understand this. *Pro dii immortales* [By the immortal gods], what is a woman really when she is not in fashion; *per deos obsecro* [I swear by the gods], what is she when she is in fashion!

Is this true? Well, test it: just when the beloved sinks ecstatic upon the lover's breast and whispers incomprehensibly "yours forever," hiding her head in his bosom, have him say to her: Sweet Katy, your hairdo is not at all in style. Perhaps men do not give this any thought, but the one who knows this and has a reputation for knowing it is the most dangerous man in the kingdom. What blissful hours the lover spends with the beloved before the wedding, I do not know, but the blissful hours she spends in my boutique pass him by. Without my special license and my sanction, a wedding is still an invalid act or else a very plebian affair. Suppose the time has already come when they are to meet at the altar, suppose she comes forward with the clearest conscience in the world since everything has been bought in my boutique and in every way put to the test before me—if I were to rush up and say: But good heavens, my lady, the myrtle wreath is fastened entirely wrong— the ceremony would very likely be postponed. But men are ignorant of all such things; to know that, one must be a fashion designer. It takes such prodigious reflection to supervise a woman's reflection that only a man who devotes himself to it is able to do it, and then only if he is originally so endowed. Lucky, then, is the man who does not become involved with any woman; even if she belongs to no other man, she does not belong to him, for she belongs to that phantom produced by feminine reflection's unnatural intercourse with feminine reflection: fashion. This, you see, is why a woman should always swear by fashion; then there would be substance to her oath, for fashion, after all, is the only thing she is always thinking about, the only thing she is able to think together with and in the midst of everything else.

From my boutique has gone out to the elite world the glad gospel for all ladies of distinction that fashion decrees that a certain kind of headgear be worn when one goes to church, and that in turn this headgear must be different for the morning service and for vespers. So when the bells ring, the carriage stops at my door. Her ladyship steps out (for it has also been proclaimed that no one but me, the fashion designer, can adjust the headgear properly); I rush to greet her with a deep bow, lead her into my dressing room; while she softly vegetates, I put everything in order. She is ready, has looked at herself in the mirror. Swiftly as an emissary of the gods, I hurry ahead, open the door of the dressing room and bow, hurry to the boutique door, place my arm across my chest like an oriental slave, but then, encouraged by a gracious nod, even dare to throw her an adoring and admiring kiss. She sits down in the carriage—but look! she has forgotten her hymnbook; I hurry out and hand it to her through the window, allowing myself once again to remind her to hold her head just a trifle to the right and to adjust her headgear herself if in stepping out she should disarrange it a bit. She drives off and is edified.

You may think that it is only high-society ladies who pay homage to fashion—far from it. Behold my seamstresses, on whose grooming I spare no pains in order that the dogmas of fashion may be proclaimed emphatically from my boutique. They form a chorus of the half-mad, and I myself as high priest set a shining example and squander away everything just in order to make every woman ludicrous by means of fashion. For when a seducer boasts that every woman's virtue is salable to the right purchaser, I do not believe him, but I do believe that in a short time every woman is going to be made a fanatic by the demented and defiling mirrored image of fashion, which corrupts her in quite another way than if she were seduced. I have tested this out more than once. If I am unable to do it myself, then I set a couple of fashion's slave-women of her own class on her, for just as one trains rats to bite rats, so the bite of the fanatic woman is just like the tarantula's. And it is most dangerous of all when a man enters into it in a supportive role. Whether I am serving the devil or the god, I do not know, but I am right and I am determined to be right. I will be right as long as I have a single farthing; I am determined to be right until the blood spurts from my fingers. The physiologist draws a woman's shape in order to show the terrible results of corsets; alongside he draws the normal shape. This is correct, but only the one has the validity of actuality; they all wear corsets. Describe, then, the wretched, stunted affectation of the fashion-addicted woman, describe this insidious reflection that devours her and depict the feminine modesty that least of all knows something about itself, do a good job of it and you will also have condemned woman and in reality condemned her terribly. If I ever find a girl who is humble and content and uncorrupted by indecent association with women, she will fall nevertheless. I bring her into my snare; now she stands at the place of sacrifice, that is, in my boutique. With the most contemptuous glance that snobbish nonchalance can exercise, I measure her. She is perishing with dread; a laugh from the next room where my trained minions are sitting demolishes her. Then when I have her dolled up in fashion, when she looks crazier than a mad hatter, as crazy as someone who would not even be admitted to a loony bin, she blissfully sallies forth from me. No one, not even a god, could dismay her, for she is indeed in fashion.

VI
70

Do you understand me now, do you understand why I call you fellow conspirators, even though at a distance? Do you understand my view of woman?
Everything in life is a matter of fashion; the fear of God is a matter of fashion, and love and hoopskirts and a ring in the nose. So, then, I will do my
utmost to aid and abet that sublime genius[73] who likes to laugh at the most
ludicrous of all animals. If woman has reduced everything to fashion, then I
will use fashion to prostitute her as she deserves. I never rest [*raste*], I, the
Fashion Designer; my soul rages [*rase*] when I think about my task; eventually she is going to wear a ring in her nose. So do not go looking for a love
affair, stay clear of erotic love as you would the most dangerous neighborhood, for your beloved, too, might eventually wear a ring in her nose.

VI
78   The signal was given to rise from the table. It took but a sign from Constantin; with military timing the participants understood one another when
it was a matter of right-about-face.

VI
443   *Letter to the Reader*

There are three existence-spheres: the esthetic, the ethical, the religious. The
metaphysical is abstraction, and there is no human being who exists metaphysically. The metaphysical, the ontological, is [*er*], but it does not exist [*er
ikke til*], for when it exists it does so in the esthetic, in the ethical, in the religious, and when it is, it is the abstraction from or a *prius* [something prior]
to the esthetic, the ethical, the religious. The ethical sphere is only a transition sphere, and therefore its highest expression is repentance as a negative
action. The esthetic sphere is the sphere of immediacy, the ethical the sphere
of requirement (and this requirement is so infinite that the individual always
goes bankrupt), the religious the sphere of fulfillment, but, please note, not
a fulfillment such as when one fills an alms box or a sack with gold, for repentance has specifically created a boundless space, and as a consequence the
religious contradiction: simultaneously to be out on 70,000 fathoms of water
and yet be joyful.

    Just as the ethical sphere is a passageway—which one nevertheless does
not pass through once and for all—just as repentance is its expression, so repentance is the most dialectical. No wonder, then, that one fears it, for if one
gives it a finger it takes the whole hand. Just as Jehovah in the Old Testament
visits the iniquities of the fathers upon the children unto the latest generations,[74] so repentance goes backward, continually presupposing the object
of its investigation. In repentance there is the impulse of the motion, and
therefore everything is reversed. This impulse signifies precisely the difference between the esthetic and the religious as the difference between the external and the internal.

A Concluding Word

VI
450

My dear reader—but to whom am I speaking? Perhaps no one at all is left. Probably the same thing has happened to me in reverse as happened to that noble king whom a sorrowful message taught to hurry, whose precipitous ride to his dying beloved has been made unforgettable by the unforgettable ballad in its celebration of the hundred young men who accompanied him from Skanderborg, the fifteen who rode with him over Randbøl Heath, but when he crossed the bridge at Ribe the noble lord was alone. The same, in reverse, to be sure, and for opposite reasons, happened to me, who, captivated by one idea, did not move from the spot—all have ridden away from me. In the beginning, no doubt, the favorably disposed reader reined in his swift steed and thought I was riding a pacer, but when I did not move from the spot, the horse (that is, the reader) or, if you please, the rider, became impatient, and I was left behind alone: a nonequestrian or a Sunday rider whom everybody outrides.

VI
451

Inasmuch as there is nothing at all to hasten after, I have forever and a day for myself and can talk with myself about myself undisturbed and without inconveniencing anyone. In my view, the religious person is the wise. But the person who fancies himself to be that without being that is a fool, but the person who sees one side of the religious is a sophist. Of these sophists I am one, and even if I were capable of devouring the others I would still not become fatter—which is not inexplicable as in the case of the lean cows in Egypt, for with respect to the religious the sophists are not fat cows but skinny herring. I look at the religious position from all sides, and to that extent I continually have one more side than the sophist, who sees only one side, but what makes me a sophist is that I do not become a religious person. The very least one in the sphere of religiousness is infinitely greater than the greatest sophist. The gods have alleviated my pain over this by granting me many a beautiful observation and by equipping me with a certain amount of wittiness, which will be taken away from me if I use it against the religious.

Sophists can be grouped in three classes. (1) Those who from the esthetic reach an immediate relation to the religious. Here religion becomes poetry, history; the sophist himself is enthusiastic about the religious, but poetically enthusiastic; in his enthusiasm he is willing to make any sacrifice, even lose his life for it, but does not for that reason become a religious person. At the peak of his prestige, he becomes confused and lets himself be confused with a prophet and an apostle. (2) Those who from the immediate ethical enter into an immediate relation to the religious. For them religion becomes a positive doctrine of obligation, instead of repentance being the supreme task of the ethical and expressly negative. The sophist remains untested in infinite reflection, a paragon of positive epitomization. Here is the sphere of his enthusi-

VI
452

asm, and without guile he has joy in inspiring others to the same. (3) Those who place the metaphysical in an immediate relation to the religious. Here religion becomes history, which is finished; the sophist is finished with religion and at most becomes an inventor of the system. —The masses admire the sophists because—in comparison with the poetic intuition in which the first category loses itself, in comparison with the positive striving toward a goal outside oneself that beckons the second category, in comparison with the enormous result that the third category acquires by putting together what is finished—they are magnanimously unconcerned about themselves. But the religious consists precisely in being religiously, infinitely concerned about oneself and not about visions, in being infinitely concerned about oneself and not about a positive goal, which is negative and finite because the infinitely negative is the only adequate form for the infinite, in being infinitely concerned about oneself and consequently not deeming oneself finished, which is negative and perdition. —This I do know, but I know it with a balance of spirit and therefore am a sophist like the others, for this balance is an offense against the holy passion of the religious. But this balance in the unity of the comic and the tragic, which is the infinite concern about oneself in the Greek sense (not the infinite religious concern about oneself), is not devoid of significance in illuminating the religious. Thus in a certain sense I am further from the religious than the three classes of sophists, all of whom have made a beginning in it, but in another sense I am closer, because I see more clearly where the religious is and consequently do not make the mistake by grasping something particular but make the mistake of not grasping it.

This is how I understand myself. Satisfied with the lesser—hoping that the greater may some day be granted me, engaged in the pursuits of the spirit in which it seems to me every human being is bound to have abundance enough for the longest life, even if this were composed of nothing but the longest days—I am happy in life, happy in the little world that is my environment.

Some of my countrymen think that the mother tongue is not adequate to express difficult thoughts. To me this seems a strange and ungrateful opinion, just as it also seems strange and inordinate to champion it so ardently that one almost forgets to rejoice in it, to defend an independence so zealously that one's zeal almost seems to suggest that one already feels dependent, and finally the polemical words become the excitement, not the delight of language the refreshment. I feel fortunate to be bound to my mother tongue, bound as perhaps only few are, bound as Adam was to Eve because there was no other woman, bound because it has been impossible for me to learn another language and thus impossible for me to be tempted to be supercilious and snobbish about my native language. But I am also happy to be bound to a mother tongue that is rich in intrinsic originality when it stretches the soul and with its sweet tones sounds voluptuously in the ear; a mother tongue that does not groan, obstructed by difficult thought, and perhaps the reason some believe it cannot express it is that it makes the difficulty easy by articulating it; a mother tongue that does not puff and sound strained when it stands before the unutterable but works at it in jest and in earnest until it is enunciated; a language that does not find far off what is close at hand or seek deep down what is readily available, because in its happy relation to the object it goes in and out like an elf, and like a child comes out with the felicitous comment without really knowing it; a language that is intense and emotional every time the right lover knows how to incite masculinely the language's feminine passion, is self-assertive and triumphant in argument every time the right master knows how to guide it, adroit as a wrestler every time the right thinker does not let it go and does not let go of the thought; a language that even though it seems impoverished at a particular point really is not but is disdained like a humble, modest sweetheart who indeed has the highest worth and above all is not shabby; a language that is not without expressions for the great, the crucial, the eminent, yet has a lovely, a winsome, a genial partiality for intermediate thoughts and subordinate ideas and adjectives, and the small talk of moods and the humming of transitions and the cordiality of inflections and the secret exuberance of concealed wellbeing; a language that understands jest perhaps even better than earnestness—a mother tongue that captivates its children with a chain that "is easy to carry—yes, but hard to break."

VI
455

Some of my countrymen think that Denmark is living on [*tære paa*] old memories. To me this seems to be a strange and ungrateful opinion that no one can approve who would rather be friendly and happy than sullen and grudging, for this only consumes [*tære*]. Others are of the opinion that Denmark faces a matchless future; some who feel misjudged and unappreciated also console themselves with the thought of a better posterity. But the person who is happy with the present and is adept at inventiveness when it comes to being satisfied with it does not really have much time for matchless expectations, and he does not let himself be disturbed by them any more than he reaches out for them. And the person who feels unappreciated by his contemporaries does indeed speak strangely in promising a better posterity. For even if it were so that he was not appreciated, and even if it were so that he would become well known in a posterity that esteemed him, it nevertheless is an injustice and a prejudice to say of this future generation that it is therefore better than the present one, that is, better because it thinks better of him. There is not that great a difference between one generation and the next; the very generation he is criticizing is in the situation of extolling what a former generation of contemporaries misjudged.

Some of my countrymen think that to be an author in Denmark is a poor

VI
456 way to make a living and wretched employment. They not only think that this is the case with such a dubious author as I am, one who does not have a single reader and only a few up to the middle of the book—whom they therefore do not even have in mind in their judgment—but they think this is also the case with distinguished authors. Well, after all, it is only a small country. But was it such a bad job to be a magistrate in Greece, even though it cost money to be one! Just suppose it were the case, suppose it came to be the case, that in Denmark it finally became an author's lot that he had to pay a fixed sum every year for the work involved in being an author—well, what if it were then also the case that foreigners had to say, "In Denmark it is a costly matter to be an author; therefore there are not authors by the dozens, but then in turn they do not have what we foreigners call *Stüberfängere* [catch-pennies], something so unknown in Danish literature that the language does not even have a word for it."

CONCLUDING UNSCIENTIFIC POSTSCRIPT
TO *PHILOSOPHICAL FRAGMENTS.* A MIMICAL-PATHETICAL-
DIALECTICAL COMPILATION, AN EXISTENTIAL
CONTRIBUTION (FEBRUARY 28, 1846)
BY JOHANNES CLIMACUS
EDITED BY S. KIERKEGAARD

Johannes Climacus calls himself a humorist, and *Postscript,* as a postscript more than five times longer than the work to which it is attached, may be regarded as a philosophical joke in keeping with the author's self-irony in calling *Fragments* a "pamphlet." The term "concluding" does not, however, refer to the completion of the algebraic *Fragments* by the addition of a second section that would "call the matter by its proper name and clothe the issue in its historical costume."[75] It refers instead to Kierkegaard's intention to terminate his writing career and as the stated editor of the pseudonymous *Postscript* to conclude the two parallel series of pseudonymous works and signed works. In addition to the numerous references to *Fragments,* there is a long section ("A Glance at a Contemporary Effort in Danish Literature") composed of Climacus's observations on the pseudonymous works preceding *Postscript.* Lest there be any ambiguity and for the sake of "form and order," "A First and Last Explanation"[76] was added in unnumbered pages in which Kierkegaard's relation to the pseudonymous writers is acknowledged and their poetical independence is emphasized.

Part One on "The Objective Issue of the Truth of Christianity" deals briefly with the historical and the speculative approaches, which, as approximational and distanced, are deemed inadequate for the ethical-religious. But the correspondence theory of truth and the coherence theory of truth are not thereby disallowed, nor the principle of contradiction. In Part Two the question of objective truth is bracketed and the issue is rather the knower's relation to what he knows, the knower's existential appropriation of his thinking—therefore the affirmation is made that "subjectivity is truth," just as in *Fragments* subjectivity is untruth.[77] In the development of the nature and form of the ethical-religious subjective thinker, Climacus finds greater kinship with Greek thinkers (including the Greek skeptics), especially with Socrates, than with the disinterested post-Cartesian thinkers. Throughout *Postscript* there is implicit the earlier characterization of the existential stages, the esthetic, the ethical, and the religious, with the further specification of irony as the incognito of the ethical and humor as the incognito of the religious, and also the distinction between immanental religiousness A and paradoxical religiousness B. In a concluding note to the reader, Climacus says he is "anything but a devil of a fellow in philosophy" and does not claim to be a Christian but asks what is involved in becoming one.

I T is now about four years since the idea came to me of wanting to try my hand as an author. I remember it very clearly. It was on a Sunday; yes, correct, it was a Sunday afternoon. As usual, I was sitting outside the café in

Frederiksberg Gardens, that wonderful garden which for the child was the enchanted land where the king lived with the queen, that lovely garden which for the youth was a pleasant diversion in the happy gaiety of the populace, that friendly garden which for the adult is so cozy in its wistful elevation above the world and what belongs to the world, that garden where even the envied glory of royalty is what it indeed is out there—a queen's recollection of her late lord. There as usual I sat and smoked my cigar. Regrettably, the only similarity I have been able to detect between the beginning of my fragment of philosophic endeavor and the miraculous beginning of that poetic hero[78] is that it was in a public place. Otherwise there is no similarity at all, and although I am the author of *Fragments,* I am so insignificant that I am an outsider in literature. I have not even added to subscription literature, nor can it truthfully be said that I have a significant place in it.

I had been a student for a half score of years. Although I was never lazy, all my activity was nevertheless only like a splendid inactivity, a kind of occupation I still much prefer and for which I perhaps have a little genius. I read a great deal, spent the rest of the day loafing and thinking, or thinking and loafing, but nothing came of it. The productive sprout in me went for everyday use and was consumed in its first greening. An inexplicable power of persuasion, both strong and cunning, continually constrained me, captivated by its persuasion. This power was my indolence. It is not like the vehement craving of erotic love or like the intense incitement of enthusiasm; it is instead like a woman in the house who constrains one and with whom one gets on very well—so well that one never dreams of wanting to marry. This much is certain: although I am generally not unacquainted with the comforts of life, of all comforts indolence is the most comfortable.

So there I sat and smoked my cigar until I drifted into thought. Among other thoughts, I recall these. You are getting on in years, I said to myself, and are becoming an old man without being anything and without actually undertaking anything. On the other hand, wherever you look in literature or in life, you see the names and figures of celebrities, the prized and highly acclaimed people, prominent or much discussed, the many benefactors of the age who know how to benefit humankind by making life easier and easier, some by railroads, others by omnibuses and steamships, others by telegraph, others by easily understood surveys and brief publications about everything worth knowing, and finally the true benefactors of the age who by virtue of thought systematically make spiritual existence easier and easier and yet more and more meaningful—and what are you doing?

At this point my introspection was interrupted because my cigar was finished and a new one had to be lit. So I smoked again, and then suddenly this thought crossed my mind: You must do something, but since with your limited capabilities it will be impossible to make anything easier than it has become, you must, with the same humanitarian enthusiasm as the others have, take it upon yourself to make something more difficult. This idea pleased me enormously; it also flattered me that for this effort I would be loved and respected, as much as anyone else, by the entire community. In other words, when all join together to make everything easier in every way, there remains only one possible danger, namely, the danger that the easiness would become so great that it would become all too easy. So only one lack remains, even though not yet felt, the lack of difficulty. Out of love of humankind, out of despair over my awkward predicament of having achieved nothing and of being unable to make anything easier than it had already been made, out of genuine interest in those who make everything easy, I comprehended that it was my task: to make difficulties everywhere. It was also especially striking to me that I might actually have my indolence to thank that this task became mine. Far from having found it, like an Aladdin, by a stroke of good luck, I must instead assume that my indolence, by preventing me from opportunely proceeding to make things easy, has forced me into doing the only thing that remained.

The issue presented in that pamphlet, yet without the pretense of having solved it, since the pamphlet wanted only to present it, reads as follows: *Can a historical point of departure be given for an eternal consciousness; how can such a point of departure be of more than historical interest; can an eternal happiness be built on historical knowledge?* (see the title page). In the pamphlet itself (p. 162[79]), the following passage is found: "As is well known, Christianity is the only historical phenomenon that despite the historical—indeed, precisely by means of the historical—has wanted to be the single individual's point of departure for his eternal consciousness, has wanted to interest him otherwise than merely historically, has wanted to base his happiness on his relation to something historical." Thus, in historical costume, the issue in question is Christianity. Accordingly, the issue pertains to Christianity. In treatise form, the issue could be formulated less problematically this way: the apologetical presuppositions of faith, approximational transitions and overtures to faith, the quantifying introduction to the decision of faith. What would then be treated would be numerous considerations that are discussed or have been discussed by theologians in introductory disciplines, in the introduction to dogmatics and in apologetics.

In order, however, to avoid confusion, it should immediately be borne in mind that the issue is not about the truth of Christianity but about the individual's relation to Christianity, consequently not about the indifferent individual's systematic eagerness to arrange the truths of Christianity in paragraphs but rather about the concern of the infinitely interested individual with regard to his own relation to such a doctrine. To state it as simply as possible (using myself in an imaginatively constructing way [*experimenterende*]): "I, Johannes Climacus, born and bred in this city and now thirty years old,

VII
6

VII
7

an ordinary human being like most folk, assume that a highest good, called an eternal happiness, awaits me just as it awaits a housemaid and a professor. I have heard that Christianity is one's prerequisite for this good. I now ask how I may enter into relation to this doctrine."

VII
8

The objective issue, then, would be about the truth of Christianity. The subjective issue is about the individual's relation to Christianity. Simply stated: How can I, Johannes Climacus, share in the happiness that Christianity promises? The issue pertains to me alone, partly because, if properly presented, it will pertain to everyone in the same way, and partly because all the others do have faith already as something given, as a trifle they do not consider very valuable, or as a trifle amounting to something only when decked out with a few demonstrations. So the presentation of the issue is not some sort of immodesty on my part, but merely a kind of lunacy.

In order to make my issue as clear as possible, I shall first present the objective issue and show how that is treated. The historical will thereby receive its due. Next, I shall present the subjective issue. That is really more than the promised sequel as a clothing in historical costume, since this costume is provided merely by mentioning the word "Christianity." The first part is the promised sequel; the second part is a renewed attempt in the same vein as the pamphlet, a new approach to the issue of *Fragments*.

VII
54

POSSIBLE AND ACTUAL THESES BY LESSING[80]

VII
55

Without daring, then, to appeal to Lessing, without daring definitely to refer to him as my guarantor, without putting anyone under obligation to want, because of Lessing's renown, most dutifully to understand or to claim to have understood something that brings the one who understands into a dubious relation to my lack of renown, which certainly is just as repelling as Lessing's renown is compelling—I now intend to present something that I shall, what the deuce, ascribe to Lessing, without being certain that he would acknowledge it, something that I in teasing exuberance could easily be tempted to want to foist upon him as something he said, although not directly, something for which in a different sense I in admiration could enthusiastically wish to dare to thank him, something that in turn I ascribe to him with proud restraint and self-esteem, just out of generosity, and then again something that I fear will offend or bother him by linking his name to it. One rarely finds an author who is such pleasant company as Lessing. And why is that? I think it is because he is so sure of himself. All this banal and easy association of someone exceptional with someone less exceptional—one is a genius, a master, the other an apprentice, a messenger, a day laborer, etc.—is prevented here. If I wanted to be Lessing's follower by hook or by crook, I could not; he has prevented it. Just as he himself is free, so, I think, he wants to make everyone free in relation to him, declining the exhalations and impudence of the apprentice, fearful of being made a laughingstock by the tutors: a parroting echo's routine reproduction of what has been said.

The subjective existing thinker is aware of the dialectic of communication. Whereas objective thinking is indifferent to the thinking subject and his existence, the subjective thinker as existing is essentially interested in his own thinking, is existing in it. Therefore, his thinking has another kind of reflection, specifically, that of inwardness, of possession, whereby it belongs to the subject and to no one else. Whereas objective thinking invests everything in the result and assists all humankind to cheat by copying and reeling off the results and answers, subjective thinking invests everything in the process of becoming and omits the result, partly because this belongs to him, since he possesses the way, partly because he as existing is continually in the process of becoming, as is every human being who has not permitted himself to be tricked into becoming objective, into inhumanly becoming speculative thought.

The reflection of inwardness is the subjective thinker's double-reflection. In thinking, he thinks the universal, but, as existing in this thinking, as acquiring this in his inwardness, he becomes more and more subjectively isolated.

The difference between subjective and objective thinking must also manifest itself in the form of communication.* This means that the subjective thinker must promptly become aware that the form of communication must artistically possess just as much reflection as he himself, existing in his thinking, possesses. Artistically, please note, for the secret does not consist in his enunciating the double-reflection directly, since such an enunciation is a direct contradiction.

---

* Double-reflection is already implicit in the idea of communication itself: that the subjective individual (who by inwardness wants to express the life of the eternal, in which all sociality and all companionship are inconceivable because the existence-category, movement, is inconceivable here, and hence essential communication is also inconceivable because everyone must be assumed to possess everything essentially), existing in the isolation of inwardness, wants to communicate himself, consequently that he simultaneously wants to keep his thinking in the inwardness of his subjective existence and yet wants to communicate himself. It is not possible (except for thoughtlessness, for which all things are indeed possible) for this contradiction to become manifest in a direct form. —It is not so difficult, however, to understand that a subject existing in this way may want to communicate himself. A person in love, for instance, to whom his erotic love is his very inwardness, may well want to communicate himself, but not directly, just because the inwardness of erotic love is the main thing for him. Essentially occupied with continually acquiring the inwardness of erotic love, he has no result and is never finished, but he may nevertheless want to communicate; yet for that very reason he can never use a direct form, since that presupposes results and completion. So it is also in a God-relationship. Just because he himself is continually in the process of becoming in an inward direction, that is, in inwardness, he can never communicate himself directly, since the movement is here the very opposite. Direct communication requires certainty, but certainty is impossible for a per-

VII
57

Ordinary communication between one human being and another is entirely immediate, because people ordinarily exist in immediacy. When one person states something and another acknowledges the same thing verbatim, they are assumed to be in agreement and to have understood each other. Yet because the one making the statement is unaware of the duplexity [*Dobbelthed*] of thought-existence, he is also unable to be aware of the double-reflection of communication. Therefore, he has no intimation that this kind of agreement can be the greatest misunderstanding and naturally has no intimation that, just as the subjective existing thinker has set himself free by the duplexity, so the secret of communication specifically hinges on setting the other free, and for that very reason he must not communicate himself directly; indeed, it is even irreligious to do so. This latter applies in proportion to the essentiality of the subjective and consequently applies first and foremost within the religious domain, that is, if the communicator is not God himself or does not presume to appeal to the miraculous authority of an apostle but is just a human being and also cares to have meaning in what he says and what he does.

VII
58

Objective thinking is completely indifferent to subjectivity and thereby to inwardness and appropriation; its communication is therefore direct. It is obvious that it does not therefore have to be easy. But it is direct; it does not have the illusiveness and the art of double-reflection. It does not have that God-fearing and humane solicitude of subjective thinking in communicating itself; it can be understood directly; it can be reeled off. Objective thinking is therefore aware only of itself and is therefore no communication,* at least no artistic communication, inasmuch as it would always be required to think of the receiver and to pay attention to the form of the communication in relation to the receiver's misunderstanding. Objective thinking** is,

---

son in the process of becoming, and it is indeed a deception. Thus, to employ an erotic relationship, if a maiden in love yearns for the wedding day because this would give her assured certainty, if she wanted to make herself comfortable in legal security as a spouse, if she preferred marital yawning to maidenly yearning, then the man would rightfully deplore her unfaithfulness, although she indeed did not love anyone else, because she would have lost the idea and actually did not love him. And this, after all, is the essential unfaithfulness in an erotic relationship; the incidental unfaithfulness is to love someone else.

* That is how it always goes with the negative; wherever it is unconsciously present, it transmutes the positive into the negative. In this case, it transmutes communication into an illusion, because no thought is given to the negative in the communication, but the communication is thought of purely and simply as positive. In the deception of double-reflection, consideration is given to the negativity of the communication, and therefore this communication, which seems to be nothing compared with that other mode of communication, is indeed communication.

** It is always to be borne in mind that I am speaking of the religious, in which objective thinking, if it is supposed to be supreme, is downright irreligiousness. But wherever objective thinking is within its rights, its direct communication is also in order, precisely because it is not supposed to deal with subjectivity.

like most people, so fervently kind and communicative; it communicates right away and at most resorts to assurances about its truth, to recommendations and promises about how all people someday will accept this truth—so sure is it. Or perhaps rather so unsure, because the assurances and recommendations and the promises, which are indeed for the sake of those others who are supposed to accept this truth, might also be for the sake of the teacher, who needs the security and dependability of a majority vote. If his contemporaries deny him this, he will draw on posterity—so sure is he. This security has something in common with the independence that, independent of the world, needs the world as witness to one's independence so as to be certain of being independent.

The subject to be discussed here and in the next segment can be traced more definitely to Lessing, insofar as the statement can be cited directly, yet again not with any direct definiteness, since Lessing is not didactic but subjectively evasive, without wanting to obligate anyone to accept it for his sake and without wanting to help anyone attain direct continuity with the originator. Perhaps Lessing himself understood that such things cannot be expounded directly; at least his procedure can be explained this way, and perhaps the explanation is correct, perhaps. VII
74

Lessing has said (S.W., V, p. 80[81]*) that contingent historical truths can never become a demonstration of eternal truths of reason, also (p. 83) that the transition whereby one will build an eternal truth on historical reports is a leap.*

Lessing opposes what I would call quantifying oneself into a qualitative decision; he contests the direct transition from historical reliability to a decision on an eternal happiness. He does not deny (for he is quick to make concessions so that the categories can become clear) that what is said in the Scriptures about miracles and prophecies is just as reliable as other historical reports, in fact, is as reliable as historical reports in general can be. *Aber nun, wenn sie **nur** eben so zuverlässig sind, warum macht man sie bei dem Gebrauche auf einmal unendlich zuverlässiger* [But now, if they are *only* as reliable as this, why are they treated as if they were infinitely more reliable]? (p. 79)—precisely because one wants to base on them the acceptance of a doctrine that is the condition for an eternal happiness, that is, to base an eternal happiness on them. Like everyone else, Lessing is willing to believe that an Alexander who subjugated all of Asia did live once, *aber wer wollte auf diesen Glauben hin irgend etwas von groszem und dauerhaftem Belange, dessen Verlust nicht zu ersetzen wäre, wagen* [but who, on the basis of this belief, would risk anything of great, permanent worth, the loss of which would be irreparable]? (p. 81). VII
76

It is the transition, the direct transition from historical reliability to an eternal decision, that Lessing continually contests. Therefore he takes the position of making a distinction between reports of miracles and prophecies—and contemporaneity with these. (*Fragments* has been attentive to this distinction VII
77 by poetically constructing so as to bring out contemporaneity and in this way to exclude what has been called the later-historical.) Nothing follows from the reports, that is, from their admitted reliability, says Lessing, but, he adds, he would have been helped if he had been contemporary with the miracles and the prophecies.* Well informed, as Lessing always is, he therefore protests against a half-deceptive quotation from Origen that has been cited to make this demonstration of the truth of Christianity stand out in relief. He protests by adding Origen's closing statement, from which it is seen that Origen assumes that miracles occurred even in his own day and that he assigns demonstrative power to these miracles, with which he was indeed contemporary, as well as to those he read about.

Since Lessing has taken such a position with regard to a given explanation, he has no opportunity to raise the dialectical issue of whether contemporaneity would be of some help, whether it could be more than an *occasion,* which the historical report can also be. Lessing seems to assume the opposite, but perhaps this semblance is produced in order *e concessis* [on the basis of the opponent's premises] to give his swordplay greater dialectical clarity vis-à-vis a particular individual. *Fragments,* however, attempted to show that contemporaneity does not help at all, because there is in all eternity no direct transition, which also would indeed have been an unbounded injustice toward all those who come later, an injustice and a distinction that would be much worse than that between Jew and Greek, circumcised and uncircumcised, which Christianity has canceled.

Lessing has himself consolidated his issue in the following words, which he has in boldface: **zufällige Geschichtswahrheiten können der Beweis von nothwendigen Vernunftwahrheiten nie werden** [contingent truths of history can never become the demonstration of necessary truths of reason].** What jolts here is the predicate *zufällige* [contingent]. This is misleading; it might seem to lead to the absolute distinction between essential and contingent historical truths, a distinction that is nevertheless only a subdivision. If, despite the identity of the higher predicate ("historical"), an absolute distinction is made here, it might seem to follow that a direct transition could be formed in relation to essential historical truths. I could now lose my temper and say: It is impossible that Lessing could be so inconsistent; ergo—and my temper would probably convince many. I shall, however, restrict myself to a courteous "perhaps," which assumes that Lessing has concealed everything in the predicate "contingent" but has said something only

---

* Perhaps a reader will here recall what was presented in *Fragments* on the impossibility of becoming contemporary (in an immediate sense) with a paradox, also on the point that the distinction between the contemporary and the later follower is a vanishing factor.

** In this presentation of the matter, it is evident that *Fragments* really opposes Lessing, insofar as he has stipulated the advantage of contemporaneity, in the negation of which lies the real dialectical issue, and thereby the solution of Lessing's issue gains a different significance.

in part, so that "contingent" is not a relatively distinguishing predicate or a distributive predicate but a generic predicate: "historical truths," which as such are contingent. If not, there lies here the entire misunderstanding that recurs time and again in modern philosophy: to make the eternal historical as a matter of course and to assume an ability to comprehend the necessity of the historical.* Everything that becomes historical is contingent, inasmuch as precisely by coming into existence, by becoming historical, it has its element of contingency, inasmuch as contingency is precisely the one factor in all coming into existence. —And therein lies again the incommensurability between a historical truth and an eternal decision.

Understood in this way, the transition whereby something historical and the relation to this becomes decisive for an eternal happiness is a μετάβασις εἰς ἄλλο γένος [shifting from one genus to another] (Lessing even says that if it is not that, then I do not know what Aristotle has understood by it, p. 82), a leap for both the contemporary and the one who comes later. It is a leap, and this is the word that Lessing has employed within the accidental limitation that is characterized by an illusory distinction between contemporaneity and noncontemporaneity. His words read as follows: *Das, das ist der garstige breite Graben, über den ich nicht kommen kann, so oft und ernstlich ich auch den Sprung versucht habe* [That, that is the ugly broad ditch that I cannot cross, however often and however earnestly I have tried to make the leap] (p. 83). Perhaps that word "leap" is only a stylistic turn. Perhaps that is why the metaphor is expanded for the imagination by adding the predicate *breit* [broad], as if even the smallest leap did not possess the quality of making the ditch infinitely broad, as if it would not be equally difficult for the one who *cannot* leap *at all*, whether the ditch is broad or narrow, as if it were not the dialectically passionate loathing of a leap that makes the ditch infinitely broad, just as Lady Macbeth's passion makes the blood spot so immensely large that the ocean cannot wash it away. Perhaps it is also cunning on Lessing's part to employ the word *ernstlich* [earnestly], because with regard to what it means to leap, especially when the metaphor is developed for the imagination, earnestness is droll enough, inasmuch as it stands in no relation, or in a comic relation, to the leap, since it is not the breadth of the ditch in an external sense that prevents it but the dialectical passion in an internal sense that makes the ditch infinitely broad. To have been very close to doing something already has its comic aspect, but to have been very close to making the leap is nothing whatever, precisely because the leap is the category of decision.

---

* Perhaps the reader will recall what was emphasized in *Fragments* regarding this systematic topsy-turvy feat, that nothing comes into existence by way of necessity (because coming into existence and necessity contradict each other), and far less does something become necessary by having come into existence, since only the necessary cannot become, because it is always presupposed to be.

And now in utmost earnestness to have wanted to make the leap—yes, that Lessing is indeed a rogue, for surely he has, if anything, with the utmost earnestness made the ditch broad—is that not just like making fun of people! Yet, as is well known, with regard to the leap it is also possible to make fun of people in a more popular manner: one closes one's eyes, grabs oneself by the neck *à la* Münchhausen, and then—then one stands on the other side, on that other side of sound common sense in the promised land of the system.

VII
88

Consequently, *(a) a logical system can be given; (b) but a system of existence [Tilværelsens System] cannot be given.*

a.

If, however, a logical system is to be constructed, special care must be taken not to incorporate anything that is subject to the dialectic of existence, accordingly, anything that is [*er*] solely by existing [*være til*] or by having existed [*have været til*], not something that is [*er*] simply by being [*være*]. It follows quite simply that Hegel's matchless and matchlessly admired invention—the importation of movement into logic (not to mention that in every other passage one misses even his own attempt to make one believe that it is there)—simply confuses logic.* It is indeed curious to make movement the basis in a sphere in which movement is inconceivable or to have movement explain logic, whereas logic cannot explain movement.

VII
89

On this point, however, I am very happy to be able to refer to a man who thinks soundly and fortunately is educated by the Greeks (rare qualities in our age!); a man who has known how to extricate himself and his thought from every trailing, groveling relation to Hegel, from whose fame everyone usually seeks to profit, if in no other way, then by going further, that is, by having absorbed Hegel; a man who has preferred to be content with Aristotle and with himself—I mean Trendlenburg (*Logische Untersuchungen*). One of his merits is

---

* The light-mindedness with which systematicians admit that Hegel has perhaps not been successful everywhere in importing movement into logic, much like the grocer who thinks that a few raisins do not matter when the purchase is large—this farcical docility is, of course, contempt for Hegel that not even his most vehement attacker has allowed himself. There have certainly been logical attempts prior to Hegel, but his method is everything. For him and for everyone who has intelligence enough to comprehend what it means to will something great, the absence of it at this or that point cannot be a trivial matter, as when a grocer and a customer bicker about whether there is a little underweight or overweight. Hegel himself has staked his whole reputation on the point of the method. But a method possesses the peculiar quality that, viewed abstractly, it is nothing at all; it is a method precisely in the process of being carried out; in being carried out it is a method, and where it is not carried out, it is not a method, and if there is no other method, there is no method at all. To turn Hegel into a rattlebrain must be reserved for his admirers; an attacker will always know how to honor him for having willed something great and having failed to achieve it.

VII
89

that he comprehended movement as the inexplicable presupposition, as the common denominator in which being and thinking are united, and as their continued reciprocity. I cannot attempt here to show the relation of his conception to the Greeks, to Aristotelian thought, or to what, oddly enough, although in a popular sense only, bears a certain resemblance to his presentation: a small section in Plutarch's work on Iris and Osiris. It is by no means my view that Hegelian philosophy has not had a salutary influence on Trendlenburg, but it is fortunate that he has perceived that wanting to improve Hegel's structure, to go further etc., will not do (a mendacious approach by which many a botcher in our age arrogates Hegel's celebrity to himself and mendicantly fraternizes with him); on the other hand, it is fortunate that Trendlenburg, sober like a Greek thinker, without promising everything and without claiming to beatify all humankind, does indeed accomplish much and beatifies whoever would need his guidance in learning about the Greeks.

In a logical system, nothing may be incorporated that has a relation to existence, that is not indifferent to existence. The infinite advantage that the logical, by being the objective, possesses over all other thinking is in turn, subjectively viewed, restricted by its being a hypothesis, simply because it is indifferent to existence understood as actuality. This duplexity distinguishes the logical from the mathematical, which has no relation whatever toward or from existence [*Tilværelse*] but has only objectivity—not objectivity and the hypothetical as unity and contradiction in which it is negatively related to existence [*Existents*]. VII
90

The logical system must not be a mystification, a ventriloquism, in which the content of existence [*Tilværelse*] emerges cunningly and surreptitiously, where logical thought is startled and finds what the Herr Professor or the licentiate has had up his sleeve. Judging between the two can be done more sharply by answering the question: In what sense is a category an abbreviation of existence, whether logical thinking is abstract after existence or abstract without any relation to existence. I would like to treat this question a little more extensively elsewhere, and even if it is not adequately answered, it is always something to have inquired about it in this way.

b.

A system of existence [*Tilværelsens System*] cannot be given. Is there, then, not such a system? That is not at all the case. Neither is this implied in what has been said. Existence itself is a system—for God, but it cannot be a system for any existing [*existerende*] spirit. System and conclusiveness correspond to each other, but existence is the very opposite. Abstractly viewed, system and existence cannot be thought conjointly, because in order to think existence, systematic thought must think it as annulled and consequently not as existing. Existence is the spacing that holds apart; the systematic is the conclusiveness that combines. VII
97

Actually there now develops a deception, an illusion, which *Fragments* has attempted to point out. I must now refer to this work, namely, to the question of whether the past is more necessary than the future.[82] That is, when an existence is a thing of the past, it is indeed finished, it is indeed concluded, and to that extent it is turned over to the systematic view. Quite so—but for whom? Whoever is himself existing cannot gain this conclusiveness outside existence, a conclusiveness that corresponds to the eternity into which the past has entered. Even if a good-natured thinker is so absentminded as to forget that he himself is existing, speculative thought and absentmindedness are still not quite the same thing. On the contrary, that he himself is existing implies the claim of existence upon him and that his existence, yes, if he is a great individual, that his existence at the present time may, as past, in turn have the validity of conclusiveness for a systematic thinker. But who, then, is this systematic thinker? Well, it is he who himself is outside existence and yet in existence, who in his eternity is forever concluded and yet includes existence within himself—it is God. So why the deception! Just because the world has lasted now for six thousand years, does existence therefore not have the very same claim upon the existing individual that it has always had, which is not that he in make-believe should be a contemplating spirit but that he in actuality should be an existing spirit. All understanding comes afterward.[83] Whereas an individual existing now undeniably comes afterward in relation to the six thousand years that preceded, the curiously ironic consequence would emerge—if we assumed that he came to understand them systematically—that he would not come to understand himself as an existing being, because he himself would acquire no existence, because he himself would have nothing that should be understood afterward. It follows that such a thinker must be either the good Lord or a fantastical *quodlibet* [anything]. Certainly everyone will perceive the immorality in this, and certainly everyone will also perceive that what another author has observed regarding the Hegelian system is entirely in order: that through Hegel a system, the absolute system, was brought to completion—without having an ethics. By all means, let us smile at the ethical-religious fantasies of the Middle Ages in asceticism and the like, but above all let us not forget that the speculative, farcical exaggeration of becoming an *I-I*—and then *qua* human being often such a philistine that no enthusiast would have cared to lead such a life—is equally ludicrous.

SUBJECTIVE TRUTH, INWARDNESS;
TRUTH IS SUBJECTIVITY

Whether truth is defined more empirically as the agreement of thinking with being or more idealistically as the agreement of being with thinking, the point in each case is to pay scrupulous attention to what is understood by being and also to pay attention to whether the knowing human spirit might not be lured out into the indefinite and fantastically become something such as no *existing* human being has ever been or can be, a phantom with which the individual busies himself on occasion, yet without ever making it explicit to himself by means of dialectical middle terms how he gets out into this fantastical realm, what meaning it has for him to be there, whether the entire endeavor out there might not dissolve into a tautology within a rash, fantastical venture.

If, in the two definitions given, being [*Væren*] is understood as empirical being, then truth itself is transformed into a *desideratum* [something wanted] and everything is placed in the process of becoming [*Vorden*], because the empirical object is not finished, and the existing knowing spirit is itself in the process of becoming. Thus truth is an approximating whose beginning cannot be established absolutely, because there is no conclusion that has retroactive power. On the other hand, every beginning, when it is *made* (if it is not arbitrariness by not being conscious of this), does not occur by virtue of immanental thinking but is *made* by virtue of a resolution, essentially by virtue of faith. That the knowing spirit is an existing spirit, and that every human being is such a spirit existing for himself, I cannot repeat often enough, because the fantastical disregard of this has been the cause of much confusion. May no one misunderstand me. I am indeed a poor existing spirit like all other human beings, but if in a legitimate and honest way I could be assisted in becoming something extraordinary, the pure *I-I*, I would always be willing to give thanks for the gift and the good deed. If, however, it can occur only in the way mentioned earlier, by saying *eins, zwei, drei, kokolorum* or by tying a ribbon around the little finger and throwing it away in some remote place when the moon is full—then I would rather remain what I am, a poor existing individual human being.

The term "being" in those definitions must, then, be understood much more abstractly as the abstract rendition or the abstract prototype of what being *in concreto* is as empirical being. If it is understood in this way, nothing stands in the way of abstractly defining truth as something finished, because, viewed abstractly, the agreement between thinking and being is always finished, inasmuch as the beginning of the process of becoming lies precisely in the concretion that abstraction abstractly disregards.

But if being is understood in this way, the formula is a tautology; that is, thinking and being signify one and the same, and the agreement spoken of is only an abstract identity with itself. Therefore, none of the formulas says more than that truth is, if this is understood in such a way that the copula is accentuated—truth *is*—that is, truth is a redoubling [*Fordoblelse*].[84] Truth is the first, but truth's other, that it *is,* is the same as the first; this, its being, is the abstract form of truth. In this way it is expressed that truth is not some-

VII
158

thing simple but in an entirely abstract sense a redoubling, which is nevertheless canceled at the very same moment.

Abstraction may go on by paraphrasing this as much as it pleases—it will never come any further. As soon as the being of truth becomes empirically concrete, truth itself is in the process of becoming and is indeed in turn, by intimation, the agreement between thinking and being, and is indeed actually that way for God, but it is not that way for any existing spirit, because this spirit, itself existing, is in the process of becoming.

For the existing spirit *qua* existing spirit, the question about truth persists, because the abstract answer is only for that *abstractum* which an existing spirit becomes by abstracting from himself *qua* existing, which he can do only momentarily, although at such moments he still pays his debt to existence by existing nevertheless. Consequently, it is an existing spirit who asks about truth, presumably because he wants to exist in it, but in any case the questioner is conscious of being an existing individual human being. In this way I believe I am able to make myself understandable to every Greek and to every rational human being. If a German philosopher follows his inclination to put on an act [*skabe sig*] and first transforms himself [*skabe sig om*] into a superrational something, just as alchemists and sorcerers bedizen themselves fantastically, in order to answer the question about truth in an extremely satisfying way, this is of no more concern to me than his satisfying answer, which no doubt is extremely satisfying—if one is fantastically dressed up. But whether a German philosopher is or is not doing this can easily be ascertained by anyone who with enthusiasm concentrates his soul on willing to allow himself to be guided by a sage of that kind, and uncritically just uses his guidance compliantly by willing to form his existence according to it. When a person as a learner enthusiastically relates in this way to such a German professor, he accomplishes the most superb epigram upon him, because a speculator of that sort is anything but served by a learner's honest and enthusiastic zeal for expressing and accomplishing, for existentially appropriating his wisdom, since this wisdom is something that the Herr Professor himself has imagined and has written books about but has never attempted himself. It has not even occurred to him that it should be done. Like the customs clerk who, in the belief that his business was merely to write, wrote what he himself could not read, so there are speculative thinkers who merely write, and write that which, if it is to be read with the aid of action, if I may put it that way, proves to be nonsense, unless it is perhaps intended only for fantastical beings.

When for the existing spirit *qua* existing there is a question about truth, that abstract reduplication [*Reduplikation*] of truth recurs; but existence itself, existence itself in the questioner, who does indeed exist, holds the two factors apart, one from the other, and reflection shows two relations. To objective reflection, truth becomes something objective, an object, and the point is to disregard the subject. To subjective reflection, truth becomes appropriation, inwardness, subjectivity, and the point is to immerse oneself, existing, in subjectivity.

But what then? Are we to remain in this disjunction, or does mediation offer its kind assistance here, so that truth becomes subject-object? Why not? But can mediation then help the existing person so that he himself, as long as he is existing, becomes mediation, which is, after all, *sub specie aeterni*, whereas the poor existing one is existing? It certainly does not help to make a fool of a person, to entice him with the subject-object when he himself is prevented from entering into the state in which he can relate himself to it, prevented because he himself, by virtue of existing, is in the process of becoming. Of what help is it to explain how the eternal truth is to be understood eternally when the one to use the explanation is prevented from understanding it in this way because he is existing and is merely a fantast if he fancies himself to be *sub specie aeterni,* consequently when he must avail himself precisely of the explanation of how the eternal truth is to be understood in the category of time by someone who by existing is himself in time, something the honored professor himself admits, if not always, then every three months when he draws his salary.

With the subject-object of mediation, we have merely reverted to abstraction, inasmuch as the definition of truth as subject-object is exactly the same as: the truth *is,* that is, the truth is a redoubling [*Fordoblelse*]. Consequently, the exalted wisdom has again been absentminded enough to forget that it was an existing spirit who asked about truth. Or is perhaps the existing spirit himself the subject-object? In that case, I am obliged to ask: Where is such an existing human being who is also a subject-object? Or shall we perhaps here again first transmute the existing spirit into a something in general and then explain everything except what was asked about: How an existing subject *in concreto* relates himself to the truth, or what then must be asked about: How the individual existing subject then relates himself to this something that seems to have not a little in common with a paper kite or with the lump of sugar that the Dutch used to hang from the ceiling and everyone would lick.

We return, then, to the two ways of reflection and have not forgotten that it is an existing spirit who is asking, simply an individual human being, and are not able to forget, either, that his existing is precisely what will prevent him from going both ways at once, and his concerned questions will prevent him from light-mindedly and fantastically becoming a subject-object. Now, then, which of the ways is the way of truth for the existing spirit? Only the fantastical *I-I* is simultaneously finished with both ways or advances methodically along both ways simultaneously, which for an existing human being is such an inhuman way of walking that I dare not recommend it.

Since the questioner specifically emphasizes that he is an existing person, the way to be commended is naturally the one that especially accentuates what it means to exist.

The way of objective reflection turns the subjective individual into something accidental and thereby turns existence into an indifferent, vanishing something. The way to the objective truth goes away from the subject, and while the subject and subjectivity become indifferent [*ligegyldig*], the truth also becomes indifferent, and that is precisely its objective validity [*Gyldighed*], because the interest, just like the decision, is subjectivity. The way of objective reflection now leads to abstract thinking, to mathematics, to historical knowledge of various kinds, and always leads away from the subjective individual, whose existence or nonexistence becomes, from an objective point of view, altogether properly, infinitely indifferent, altogether properly, because, as Hamlet says, existence and nonexistence have only subjective significance. At its maximum, this way will lead to a contradiction, and to the extent that the subject does not become totally indifferent to himself, this is merely an indication that his objective striving is not objective enough. At its maximum, it will lead to the contradiction that only objectivity has come about, whereas subjectivity has gone out, that is, the existing subjectivity that has made an attempt to become what in the abstract sense is called subjectivity, the abstract form of an abstract objectivity. And yet, viewed subjectively, the objectivity that has come about is at its maximum either a hypothesis or an approximation, because all eternal decision is rooted specifically in subjectivity.

But the objective way is of the opinion that it has a security that the subjective way does not have (of course, existence, what it means to exist, and objective security cannot be thought together). It is of the opinion that it avoids a danger that lies in wait for the subjective way, and at its maximum this danger is madness. In a solely subjective definition of truth, lunacy and truth are ultimately indistinguishable, because they may both have inwardness.* But one does not become lunatic by becoming objective. At this point I might perhaps add a little comment that does not seem superfluous in an objective age. Is the absence of inwardness also lunacy? The objective truth as such does not at all decide that the one stating it is sensible; on the contrary, it can even betray that the man is lunatic, although what he says is entirely true and especially objectively true.

I shall here allow myself to relate an incident that, without any modifica-

---

* Even this is not true, however, because madness never has the inwardness of infinity. Its fixed idea is a kind of objective something, and the contradiction of madness lies in wanting to embrace it with passion. The decisive factor in madness is thus not the subjective, but the little finitude that becomes fixed, something the infinite can never become.

tion whatever by me, comes directly from a madhouse. A patient in such an institution wants to run away and actually carries out his plan by jumping through a window. He now finds himself in the garden of the institution and wishes to take to the road of freedom. Then it occurs to him (shall I say that he was sagacious enough or lunatic enough to have this whimsical idea?): When you arrive in the city, you will be recognized and will very likely be taken back right away. What you need to do, then, is convince everyone completely, by the objective truth of what you say, that all is well as far as your sanity is concerned. As he is walking along and pondering this, he sees a skittle ball lying on the ground. He picks it up and puts it in the tail of his coat. At every step he takes, this ball bumps him, if you please, on his r—, and every time it bumps him he says, "Boom! The earth is round." He arrives in the capital city and immediately visits one of his friends. He wants to convince him that he is not lunatic and therefore paces up and down the floor and continually says, "Boom! The earth is round!" But is the earth not round? Does the madhouse demand yet another sacrifice on account of this assumption, as in those days when everyone assumed it to be as flat as a pancake? Or is he lunatic, the man who hopes to prove that he is not lunatic by stating a truth universally accepted and universally regarded as objective? And yet, precisely by this it became clear to the physician that the patient was not yet cured, although the cure certainly could not revolve around getting him to assume that the earth is flat. But not everyone is a physician, and the demand of the times has considerable influence on the question of lunacy. Now and then, one would indeed almost be tempted to assume that the modern age, which has modernized Christianity, has also modernized Pilate's question,[85] and that the need of the age to find something in which to repose declares itself in the question: What is lunacy? When an assistant professor, every time his coattail reminds him to say something, says *de omnibus dubitandum est* [everything must be doubted] and briskly writes away on a system in which there is sufficient internal evidence in every other sentence that the man has never doubted anything—he is not considered lunatic.

VII
163

Don Quixote is the prototype of the subjective lunacy in which the passion of inwardness grasps a particular fixed finite idea. But when inwardness is absent, parroting lunacy sets in, which is just as comic, and it would be desirable for an imaginatively constructing psychologist to depict it by taking a handful of such philosophers and putting them together. When the insanity is a delirium of inwardness, the tragic and the comic are that the something that infinitely pertains to the unfortunate person is a fixed detail that pertains to no one else. But when the insanity is the absence of inwardness, the comic is that the something known by the blissful person is the truth, truth that pertains to the whole human race but does not in the least pertain to the highly honored parroter. This kind of insanity is more inhuman than the other. One shrinks from looking the first one in the eye, lest one discover the depth of his frantic state, but one does not dare to look at the other at all for fear of discovering that he does not have proper eyes but glass eyes and hair made from a floor mat, in short, that he is an artificial product. If one happens to meet a mentally deranged person of that sort, whose illness is simply that he has no mind, one listens to him in cold horror. One does not know whether one dares to believe that it is a human being with whom one is speaking, or perhaps a "walking stick," an artificial contrivance of Døbler that conceals in itself a barrel organ [*Positiv*]. To drink *Dus* with the executioner[86] can indeed be unpleasant for a self-respecting man, but to get into a rational and speculative conversation with a walking stick—now that is almost enough to drive one crazy.

Subjective reflection turns inward toward subjectivity and in this inward deepening will be of the truth, and in such a way that, just as in the preceding, when objectivity was advanced, subjectivity vanished, here subjectivity as such becomes the final factor and objectivity the vanishing. Here it is not forgotten, even for a single moment, that the subject is existing, and that existing is a becoming, and that truth as the identity of thought and being is therefore a chimera of abstraction and truly only a longing of creation, not because truth is not an identity, but because the knower is an existing person, and thus truth cannot be an identity for him as long as he exists. If this is not held fast, then with the aid of speculative thought we promptly enter into the fantastical *I-I* that recent speculative thought certainly has used but without explaining how a particular individual relates himself to it, and, good Lord, of course no human being is more than a particular individual.

If the existing person could actually be outside himself, the truth would be something concluded for him. But where is this point? The *I-I* is a mathematical point that does not exist at all; accordingly anyone can readily take up this standpoint—no one stands in the way of anyone else. Only momentarily can a particular individual, existing, be in a unity of the infinite and the finite that transcends existing. This instant is the moment of passion. Modern speculative thought has mustered everything to enable the individual to transcend himself objectively, but this just cannot be done. Existence exercises its constraint, and if philosophers nowadays had not become pencil-pushers serving the trifling busyness of fantastical thinking, it would have discerned that suicide is the only somewhat practical interpretation of its attempt. But pencil-pushing modern speculative thought takes a dim view of passion, and yet, for the existing person, passion is existence at its very highest—and we are, after all, existing persons. In passion, the existing subject is infinitized in the eternity of imagination and yet is also most definitely himself. The fantastical *I-I* is not infinitude and finitude in identity, since neither the one nor the other is actual; it is a fantastical union with a cloud,[87] an unfruitful embrace, and the relation of the individual *I* to this mirage is never stated.

All essential knowing pertains to existence, or only the knowing whose relation to existence is essential is essential knowing. Essentially viewed, the knowing that does not inwardly in the reflection of inwardness pertain to existence is accidental knowing, and its degree and scope, essentially viewed, are a matter of indifference. That essential knowing is essentially related to existence does not, however, signify the above-mentioned abstract identity between thinking and being, nor does it signify that the knowledge is objectively related to something existent [*Tilværende*] as its object, but it means that the knowledge is related to the knower, who is essentially an existing person [*Existerende*], and that all essential knowing is therefore essentially related to existence and to existing. Therefore, only ethical and ethical-religious knowing is essential knowing. But all ethical and all ethical-religious knowing is essentially a relating to the existing of the knower.

Mediation is a mirage, just as the *I-I* is. Viewed abstractly, everything *is* and nothing becomes. Mediation cannot possibly find its place in abstraction, since it has *movement* as its presupposition. Objective knowledge can certainly have the existent [*Tilværende*] as its object, but since the knowing subject is existing [*existerende*] and himself in the process of becoming by existing, speculative thought must first explain how a particular existing subject relates himself to the knowledge of mediation, what he is at the moment, whether, for example, he is not at that very moment rather absentminded, and where he is, whether he is not on the moon. There is this continual talk about mediation and mediation. Is mediation, then, a human being, just as Per Degn assumes *Imprimatur* to be a human being? How does a human being go about becoming something of that sort? Is this dignity, this great *philosophicum*, attained by studying? Or does the magistrate give it away as he gives away sexton and gravedigger positions? Just try to become involved with these and other similar simple questions raised by a simple human being, who would so very much like to be mediation if he could become that in a legitimate and honorable manner, and not either by saying *eins, zwei, drei, kokolorum* or by forgetting that he himself is an existing human being, for whom existing ethically-religiously is a suitable *quantum satis* [sufficient amount]. To a speculative thinker it may seem *abgeschmackt* [in bad taste] to ask questions in this way, but it is especially important not to polemicize in the wrong place and hence not to begin fantastically-objectively a *pro* and *contra* as to whether or not there is mediation, but firmly to maintain what it means to be a human being.

In order to clarify the divergence of objective and subjective reflection, I shall now describe subjective reflection in its search back and inward into inwardness. At its highest, inwardness in an existing subject is passion; truth as a paradox corresponds to passion, and that truth becomes a paradox is grounded precisely in its relation to an existing subject. In this way the one corresponds to the other. In forgetting that one is an existing subject, one

VII
166

loses passion, and in return, truth does not become a paradox; but the knowing subject shifts from being human to being a fantastical something, and
truth becomes a fantastical object for its knowing.

*When the question about truth is asked objectively, truth is reflected upon objec-
tively as an object to which the knower relates himself. What is reflected upon is not
the relation but that what he relates himself to is the truth, the true. If only that to
which he relates himself is the truth, the true, then the subject is in the truth. When
the question about truth is asked subjectively, the individual's relation is reflected upon
subjectively. If only the how of this relation is in truth, the individual is in truth, even
if he in this way were to relate himself to untruth.**

^{VII}
¹⁶⁹   *Objectively the emphasis is on* **what** *is said; subjectively the emphasis is on* **how**
it is said. This distinction applies even esthetically and is specifically expressed
when we say that in the mouth of this or that person something that is truth
can become untruth. Particular attention should be paid to this distinction
in our day, for if one were to express in a single sentence the difference between ancient times and our time, one would no doubt have to say: In ancient times there were only a few individuals who knew the truth; now
everyone knows it, but inwardness has an inverse relation to it.** Viewed esthetically, the contradiction that emerges when truth becomes untruth in this
and that person's mouth is best interpreted comically. Ethically-religiously,
the emphasis is again on: *how.* But this is not to be understood as manner,
modulation of voice, oral delivery, etc., but it is to be understood as the relation of the existing person, in his very existence, to what is said. Objectively, the question is only about categories of thought; subjectively, about
inwardness. At its maximum, this "how" is the passion of the infinite, and the
passion of the infinite is the very truth. But the passion of the infinite is precisely subjectivity, and thus subjectivity is truth. From the objective point of
^{VII}
¹⁷⁰ view, there is no infinite decision, and thus it is objectively correct that the
distinction between good and evil is canceled, along with the principle of
contradiction, and thereby also the infinite distinction between truth and
falsehood. Only in subjectivity is there decision, whereas wanting to become
objective is untruth. The passion of the infinite, not its content, is the deciding factor, for its content is precisely itself. In this way the subjective
"how" and subjectivity are the truth.

    But precisely because the subject is existing, the "how" that is subjectively
emphasized is dialectical also with regard to time. In the moment of the decision of passion, where the road swings off from objective knowledge, it
looks as if the infinite decision were thereby finished. But at the same mo-

---

    * The reader will note that what is discussed here is essential truth, or the truth that is re-
lated essentially to existence, and that it is specifically in order to clarify it as inwardness or as
subjectivity that the contrast is pointed out.
    ** See *Stages on Life's Way,* p. 366 fn.⁸⁸

ment, the existing person is in the temporal realm, and the subjective "how" is transformed into a striving that is motivated and repeatedly refreshed by the decisive passion of the infinite, but it is nevertheless a striving.

When subjectivity is truth, the definition of truth must also contain in itself an expression of the antithesis to objectivity, a memento of that fork in the road, and this expression will at the same time indicate the resilience of the inwardness. Here is such a definition of truth: *An objective uncertainty, held fast through appropriation with the most passionate inwardness, is the truth,* the highest truth there is for an *existing* person. At the point where the road swings off (and where that is cannot be stated objectively, since it is precisely subjectivity), objective knowledge is suspended. Objectively he then has only uncertainty, but this is precisely what intensifies the infinite passion of inwardness, and truth is precisely the daring venture of choosing the objective uncertainty with the passion of the infinite. I observe nature in order to find God, and I do indeed see omnipotence and wisdom, but I also see much that troubles and disturbs. The *summa summarum* [sum total] of this is an objective uncertainty, but the inwardness is so very great, precisely because it grasps this objective uncertainty with all the passion of the infinite. In a mathematical proposition, for example, the objectivity is given, but therefore its truth is also an indifferent truth.

But the definition of truth stated above is a paraphrasing of faith. Without risk, no faith. Faith is the contradiction between the infinite passion of inwardness and the objective uncertainty. If I am able to apprehend God objectively, I do not have faith; but because I cannot do this, I must have faith. If I want to keep myself in faith, I must continually see to it that I hold fast the objective uncertainty, see to it that in the objective uncertainty I am "out on 70,000 fathoms of water" and still have faith.

VII
171

The thesis that subjectivity, inwardness, is truth contains the Socratic wisdom, the undying merit of which is to have paid attention to the essential meaning of existing, of the knower's being an existing person. That is why, in his ignorance, Socrates was in the truth in the highest sense within paganism. To comprehend this, that the misfortune of speculative thought is simply that it forgets again and again that the knower is an existing person, can already be rather difficult in our objective age. "But to go beyond Socrates when one has not even comprehended the Socratic—that, at least, is not Socratic." See "The Moral" in *Fragments.*

Just as in *Fragments,* let us from this point try a category of thought that actually does go beyond. Whether it is true or false is of no concern to me, since I am only imaginatively constructing, but this much is required, that it be clear that the Socratic is presupposed in it, so that I at least do not end up behind Socrates again.

When subjectivity, inwardness, is truth, then truth, objectively defined, is a paradox; and that truth is objectively a paradox shows precisely that subjectivity is truth, since the objectivity does indeed thrust away, and the objectivity's repulsion, or the expression for the objectivity's repulsion, is the resilience and dynamometer of inwardness. The paradox is the objective uncertainty that is the expression for the passion of inwardness that is truth. So much for the Socratic. The eternal, essential truth, that is, the truth that is related essentially to the existing person by pertaining essentially to what it means to exist (viewed Socratically, all other knowledge is accidental, its degree and scope indifferent), is a paradox. Nevertheless the eternal, essential truth is itself not at all a paradox, but it is a paradox by being related to an existing person. Socratic ignorance is an expression of the objective uncertainty; the inwardness of the existing person is truth. In anticipation of what will be discussed later, the following comment is made here: Socratic ignorance is an analog to the category of the absurd, except that there is even less objective certainty in the repulsion exerted by the absurd, since there is only the certainty that it is absurd, and for that very reason there is infinitely greater resilience in the inwardness. The Socratic inwardness in existing is an analogue to faith, except that the inwardness of faith, corresponding not to the repulsion exerted by ignorance but to the repulsion exerted by the absurd, is infinitely deeper.

VII
172

Viewed Socratically, the eternal essential truth is not at all paradoxical in itself, but only by being related to an existing person. This is expressed in another Socratic thesis: that all knowing is a recollecting. This thesis is an intimation of the beginning of speculative thought, but for that very reason Socrates did not pursue it; essentially it became Platonic. This is where the road swings off, and Socrates essentially emphasizes existing, whereas Plato, forgetting this, loses himself in a speculative thought. Socrates' infinite merit is precisely that of being an *existing* thinker, not a speculative thinker who forgets what it means to exist. To Socrates, therefore, the thesis that all knowing is a recollecting has, at the moment of parting and as a continually annulled possibility of speculating, a double significance: (1) that the knower is essentially *integer* [uncorrupted] and that for him there is no other dubiousness with regard to knowledge of the eternal truth than this, that he exists, a dubiousness so essential and decisive to him that it signifies that existing, the inward deepening in and through existing, is truth; (2) that existence in temporality has no decisive significance, because there is continually the possibility of taking oneself back into eternity by recollecting, even though this possibility is continually annulled because the inward deepening in existing fills up time.*

---

* This may be the proper place to elucidate a dubiousness in the design of *Fragments,* a dubiousness that was due to my not wanting immediately to make the matter as dialectically difficult as it is, because in our day terminologies and the like are so muddled that it is almost impossible to safeguard oneself against confusion. In order, if possible, to elucidate properly the difference between the Socratic (which was supposed to be the philosophical, the pagan philosophical position) and the category of imaginatively constructed thought, which actually goes

The great merit of the Socratic was precisely to emphasize that the knower is an existing person and that to exist is the essential. To go beyond Socrates by failing to understand this is nothing but a mediocre merit. This we must keep *in mente* [in mind] and then see whether the formula cannot be changed in such a way that one actually does go beyond the Socratic.

So, then, subjectivity, inwardness, is truth. Is there *a more inward* expression for it? Yes, if the discussion about "Subjectivity, inwardness, is truth" begins in this way: "Subjectivity is untruth." But let us not be in a hurry. Speculative thought also says that subjectivity is untruth but says it in the very opposite direction, namely, that objectivity is truth. Speculative thought defines subjectivity negatively in the direction of objectivity. The other definition, however, puts barriers in its own way at the very moment it wants to begin, which makes the inwardness so much more inward. Viewed Socratically, subjectivity is untruth if it refuses to comprehend that subjectivity is truth but wants, for example, to be objective. Here, on the other hand, in wanting to begin to become truth by becoming subjective, subjectivity is in the predicament of being untruth. Thus the work goes

VII
174

---

beyond the Socratic, I carried the Socratic back to the thesis that all knowing is a recollecting. It is commonly accepted as such, and only for the person who with a very special interest devotes himself to the Socratic, always returning to the sources, only for him will it be important to distinguish between Socrates and Plato on this point. The thesis certainly belongs to both of them, but Socrates continually parts with it because he wants to exist. By holding Socrates to the thesis that all knowing is recollecting, one turns him into a speculative philosopher instead of what he was, an existing thinker who understood existing as the essential. The thesis that all knowing is recollecting belongs to speculative thought, and recollecting is immanence, and from the point of view of speculation and the eternal there is no paradox. The difficulty, however, is that no human being is speculation, but the speculating person is an existing human being, subject to the claims of existence. To forget this is no merit, but to hold this fast is indeed a merit, and that is precisely what Socrates did. To emphasize existence, which contains within it the qualification of inwardness, is the Socratic, whereas the Platonic is to pursue recollection and immanence. Basically Socrates is thereby beyond all speculation, because he does not have a fantastical beginning where the speculating person changes clothes and then goes on and on and speculates, forgetting the most important thing, to exist. But precisely because Socrates is in this way beyond speculative thought, he acquires, when rightly depicted, a certain analogous likeness to what the imaginary construction set forth as that which truly goes beyond the Socratic: the truth as paradox is an analog to the paradox *sensu eminentiori* [in the more eminent sense]; the passion of inwardness in existing is then an analog to faith *sensu eminentiori.* That the difference is infinite nevertheless, that the designations in *Fragments* of that which truly goes beyond the Socratic are unchanged, I can easily show, but I was afraid to make complications by promptly using what seem to be the same designations, at least the same words, about the different things when the imaginary construction was to be presented as different from these. Now, I think there would be no objection to speaking of the paradox in connection with Socrates and faith, since it is quite correct to do so, provided that it is understood correctly. Besides, the ancient Greeks also use the word πίστις [faith], although by no means in the sense of the imaginary construction, and use it so as to make possible some very illuminating observations bearing upon its dissimilarity to faith *sensu eminentiori,* especially with reference to one of Aristotle's works where the term is employed.

VII
173

backward, that is, backward in inwardness. The way is so far from being in the direction of the objective that the beginning only lies even deeper in subjectivity.

But the subject cannot be untruth eternally or be presupposed to have been untruth eternally; he must have become that in time or he becomes that in time.[89] The Socratic paradox consisted in this, that the eternal truth was related to an existing person. But now existence has accentuated the existing person a second time; a change so essential has taken place in him that he in no way can take himself back into eternity by Socratically recollecting. To do this is to speculate; to be able to do this but, by grasping the inward deepening in existence, to annul the possibility of doing it is the Socratic. But *now* the difficulty is that what accompanied Socrates as an annulled possibility has become an impossibility. If speculating was already of dubious merit in connection with the Socratic, it is now only confusion.

The paradox emerges when the eternal truth and existing are placed together, but each time existing is accentuated the paradox becomes clearer and clearer. Viewed Socratically, the knower was an existing person, but now the existing person is accentuated in such a way that existence has made an essential change in him.

Let us now call the individual's untruth *sin*. Viewed eternally, he cannot be in sin or be presupposed to have been eternally in sin. Therefore, by coming into existence (for the beginning was that subjectivity is untruth), he becomes a sinner. He is not born as a sinner in the sense that he is presupposed to be a sinner before he is born, but he is born in sin and as a sinner. Indeed, we could call this *hereditary sin*. But if existence has in this way obtained power over him, he is prevented from taking himself back into eternity through recollection. If it is already paradoxical that the eternal truth is related to an existing person, now it is absolutely paradoxical that it is related to such an existing person. But the more difficult it is made for him, recollecting, to take himself out of existence, the more inward his existing can become in existence; and when it is made impossible for him, when he is lodged in existence in such a way that the back door of recollection is forever closed, then the inwardness becomes the deepest. But let us never forget that the Socratic merit was precisely to emphasize that the knower is existing, because the more difficult the matter becomes, the more one is tempted to rush along the easy road of speculative thought, away from terrors and decisions, to fame, honor, a life of ease, etc. If even Socrates comprehended the dubiousness of taking himself speculatively out of existence back into eternity, when there was no dubiousness for the existing person except that he existed and, of course, that existing was the essential—now it is impossible. He must go forward; to go backward is impossible.

Subjectivity is truth. The paradox came into existence through the relating of the eternal, essential truth to the existing person. Let us now go further; let us assume that the eternal, essential truth is itself the paradox. How does the paradox emerge? By placing the eternal, essential truth together with existing. Consequently, if we place it together in the truth itself, the truth becomes a paradox. The eternal truth has come into existence in time. That is the paradox. If the subject just mentioned was prevented by sin from taking himself back into eternity, now he is not to concern himself with this, because now the eternal, essential truth is not behind him but has come in front of him by existing itself or by having existed, so that if the individual, existing, does not lay hold of the truth in existence, he will never have it.

Existence can never be accentuated more sharply than it has been here. The fraud of speculative thought in wanting to recollect itself out of existence has been made impossible. This is the only point to be comprehended here, and every speculation that insists on being speculation shows *eo ipso* [precisely thereby] that it has not comprehended this. The individual can thrust all this away and resort to speculation, but to accept it and then want to cancel it through speculation is impossible, because it is specifically designed to prevent speculation.

When the eternal truth relates itself to an existing person, it becomes the paradox. Through the objective uncertainty and ignorance, the paradox thrusts away in the inwardness of the existing person. But since the paradox is not in itself the paradox, it does not thrust away intensely enough, for without risk, no faith; the more risk, the more faith; the more objective reliability, the less inwardness (since inwardness is subjectivity); the less objective reliability, the deeper is the possible inwardness. When the paradox itself is the paradox, it thrusts away by virtue of the absurd, and the corresponding passion of inwardness is faith.

But subjectivity, inwardness, is truth; if not, we have forgotten the Socratic merit. But when the retreat out of existence into eternity by way of recollection has been made impossible, then, with the truth facing one as the paradox, in the anxiety of sin and its pain, with the tremendous risk of objectivity, there is no stronger expression for inwardness than—to have faith. But without risk, no faith, not even the Socratic faith, to say nothing of the kind we are discussing here.

When Socrates believed that God is,[90] he held fast the objective uncertainty with the entire passion of inwardness, and faith is precisely in this contradiction, in this risk. Now it is otherwise. Instead of the objective uncertainty, there is here the certainty that, viewed objectively, it is the absurd, and this absurdity, held fast in the passion of inwardness, is faith. Compared with the earnestness of the absurd, the Socratic ignorance is like a witty jest, and compared with the strenuousness of faith, the Socratic existential inwardness resembles Greek nonchalance.

What, then, is the absurd? The absurd is that the eternal truth has come into existence in time, that God has come into existence, has been born, has grown up, etc., has come into existence exactly as an individual human being, indistinguishable from any other human being, inasmuch as all immediate recognizability is pre-Socratic paganism and from the Jewish point of view is idolatry. Every qualification of that which actually goes beyond the Socratic must essentially have a mark of standing in relation to the god's having come into existence, because faith, *sensu strictissimo* [in the strictest sense], as explicated in *Fragments,* refers to coming into existence. When Socrates believed that God is [*er til*], he no doubt perceived that where the road swings off there is a road of objective approximation, for example, the observation of nature, world history, etc. His merit was precisely to shun this road, where the quantifying siren song spellbinds and tricks the existing person. In relation to the absurd, the objective approximation resembles the comedy *Misforstaaelse paa Misforstaaelse* [Misunderstanding upon Misunderstanding], which ordinarily is played by assistant professors and speculative thinkers.

It is by way of the objective repulsion that the absurd is the dynamometer of faith in inwardness. So, then, there is a man who wants to have faith; well, let the comedy begin. He wants to have faith, but he wants to assure himself with the aid of objective deliberation and approximation. What happens? With the aid of approximation, the absurd becomes something else; it becomes probable, it becomes more probable, it may become to a high degree and exceedingly probable. Now he is all set to believe it, and he dares to say of himself that he does not believe as shoemakers and tailors and simple folk do, but only after long deliberation. Now he is all set to believe it, but, lo and behold, now it has indeed become impossible to believe it. The almost probable, the probable, the to-a-high-degree and exceedingly probable—that he can almost know, or as good as know, to a higher degree and exceedingly almost *know*—but *believe* it, that cannot be done, for the absurd is precisely the object of faith and only that can be believed.

Or there is a man who says he has faith, but now he wants to make his faith clear to himself; he wants to understand himself in his faith. Now the comedy begins again. The object of faith becomes almost probable, it becomes as good as probable, it becomes probable, it becomes to a high degree and exceedingly probable. He has finished; he dares to say of himself that he does not believe as shoemakers and tailors or other simple folk do but that he has also understood himself in his believing. What wondrous understanding! On the contrary, he has learned to know something different about faith than he believed and has learned to know that he no longer has faith, since he almost knows, as good as knows, to a high degree and exceedingly almost knows.

Inasmuch as the absurd contains the element of coming into existence, the road of approximation will also be that which confuses the absurd fact of coming into existence, which is the object of faith, with a simple historical fact, and then seeks historical certainty for that which is absurd precisely because it contains the contradiction that something that can become histori-

cal only in direct opposition to all human understanding has become historical. This contradiction is the absurd, which can only be believed. If a his-   VII
178
torical certainty is obtained, one obtains merely the certainty that what is
certain is not what is the point in question. A witness can testify that he has
believed it and then testify that, far from being a historical certainty, it is in
direct opposition to his understanding, but such a witness repels in the same
sense as the absurd repels, and a witness who does not repel in this way is *eo
ipso* a deceiver or a man who is talking about something altogether different;
and such a witness can be of no help except in obtaining certainty about
something altogether different. One hundred thousand individual witnesses,
who by the special nature of their testimony (that they have believed the absurd) remain individual witnesses, do not become something else *en masse* so
that the absurd becomes less absurd. Why? Because one hundred thousand
people individually have believed that it was absurd? Quite the contrary, those
one hundred thousand witnesses repel exactly as the absurd does.

But I do not need to develop this further here. In *Fragments* (especially
where the difference between the follower at first hand and the follower at
second hand is annulled[91]) and in Part One of this book, I have with sufficient care shown that all approximation is futile, since the point is rather to
do away with introductory observations, reliabilities, demonstrations from
effects, and the whole mob of pawnbrokers and guarantors, in order to get
the absurd clear—so that one can believe if one will—I merely say that this
must be extremely strenuous.

All paganism consists in this, that God is related directly to a human being,   VII
206
as the remarkably striking to the amazed. But the spiritual relationship with
God in truth, that is, inwardness, is first conditioned by the actual break-
through of inward deepening that corresponds to the divine cunning that
God has nothing remarkable, nothing at all remarkable, about him—indeed,
he is so far from being remarkable that he is invisible, and thus one does not
suspect that he is there [*er til*], although his invisibility is in turn his omnipresence. But an omnipresent being is the very one who is seen everywhere, for example, as a police officer is—how illusive, then, that an omnipresent being is cognizable precisely by his being invisible,* simply and

---

* In order to indicate how illusive the rhetorical can be, I shall show here how one could
perhaps produce an effect upon a listener rhetorically, even though what was said would be a
dialectical retrogression. Suppose a pagan religious orator says that here on earth the god's temple is actually empty, but (and here the rhetorical begins) in heaven, where everything is more
perfect, where water is air, and air is ether, there are also temples and shrines for the gods, but
the difference is that the gods actually dwell in these temples—that the god actually dwells in
the temple is dialectical retrogression, because his not dwelling in the temple is an expression
for the spiritual relation to the invisible. But rhetorically it produces the effect. —Incidentally,   VII
207
I had in mind a specific passage by a Greek author,[92] but I shall not quote him.

solely by this, because his very visibility would annul his omnipresence. This relation between omnipresence and invisibility is like the relation between mystery and revelation, that the mystery expresses that the revelation is revelation in the stricter sense, that the mystery is the one and only mark by which it can be known, since otherwise a revelation becomes something like a police officer's omnipresence.

If God [*Gud*] wants to reveal himself in human form and provide a direct relation by taking, for example, the form of a man who is twelve feet tall, then that imaginatively constructed partygoer and captain of the popinjay shooting club will surely become aware. But since God is unwilling to deceive, the spiritual relation in truth specifically requires that there be nothing at all remarkable about his form; then the partygoer must say: There is nothing to see, not the slightest. If the god [*Guden*][93] has nothing whatever that is remarkable about him, the partygoer is perhaps deceived in not becoming aware at all. But the god is without blame in this, and the actuality of this deception is continually also the possibility of the truth. But if the god has something remarkable about him, he deceives, inasmuch as a human being thus becomes aware of the untruth, and this awareness is also the impossibility of the truth.

In paganism, the direct relation is idolatry; in Christianity, everyone indeed knows that God cannot manifest himself in this way. But this knowledge is not inwardness at all, and in Christianity it can certainly happen with a rote knower that he becomes utterly "without God in the world,"[94] which was not the case in paganism, where there was still the untrue relation of idolatry. Idolatry is certainly a dismal substitute, but that the rubric "God" disappears completely is even more mistaken.

Accordingly, not even God relates himself directly to a derived spirit (and this is the wondrousness of creation: not to produce something that is nothing in relation to the Creator, but to produce something that is something and that in the true worship of God can use this something to become by itself nothing before God); even less can one human being relate himself in this way to another *in truth*. Nature, the totality of creation, is God's work, and yet God is not there, but within the individual human being there is a possibility (he is spirit according to his possibility) that in inwardness is awakened to a God-relationship, and then it is possible to see God everywhere. Compared with the spiritual relationship in inwardness, the sensate distinctions of the great, the amazing, the most crying-to-heaven superlatives of a southern nation are a retrogression to idolatry. Is it not as if an author wrote 166 folio volumes and the reader read and read, just as when someone observes and observes nature but does not discover that the meaning of this enormous work lies in the reader himself, because amazement at the many volumes and the five hundred lines to the page, which is similar to amazement at how immense nature is and how innumerable the animal species are, is not understanding.

With regard to the essential truth, a direct relation between spirit and spirit is unthinkable. If such a relation is assumed, it actually means that one party has ceased to be spirit, something that is not borne in mind by many a genius who both assists people *en masse* into the truth and is good-natured enough to think that applause, willingness to listen, signatures, etc. mean accepting the truth. Just as important as the truth, and of the two the even more important one, is the mode in which the truth is accepted, and it is of slight help if one gets millions to accept the truth if by the very mode of their acceptance they are transposed into untruth. And therefore all good-naturedness, all persuasion, all bargaining, all direct attraction with the aid of one's own person in consideration of one's suffering so much for the cause, of one's weeping over humankind, of one's being so enthusiastic, etc.—all such things are a misunderstanding, in relation to the truth a forgery by which, according to one's ability, one helps any number of people to acquire a semblance of truth.

Socrates was a teacher of the ethical, but he was aware that there is no direct relation between the teacher and the learner, because inwardness is truth, and inwardness in the two is precisely the path away from each other. Probably because he perceived this he was so very pleased with his advantageous appearance. What was it? Well, guess again.[95]

Possibility Superior to Actuality; Actuality Superior to Possibility; Poetic and Intellectual Ideality; Ethical Ideality

VII
273

Aristotle remarks in his *Poetics* that poetry is superior to history, because history presents only what has occurred, poetry what could and ought to have occurred,[96] i.e., poetry has possibility at its disposal. Possibility, poetic and intellectual, is superior to actuality; the esthetic and the intellectual are disinterested. But there is only one interest, the interest in existing; disinterestedness is the expression for indifference to actuality. The indifference is forgotten in the Cartesian *cogito—ergo sum,* which disturbs the disinterestedness of the intellectual and offends speculative thought, as if something else should follow from it. I think, ergo I think; whether I am or it is (in the sense of actuality, where *I* means a single existing human being and *it* means a single definite something) is infinitely unimportant. That what I am thinking *is* in the sense of thinking does not, of course, need any demonstration, nor does it need to be demonstrated by any conclusion, since it is indeed demonstrated. But as soon as I begin to want to make my thinking teleological in relation to something else, interest enters the game. As soon as it is there, the ethical is present and exempts me from further trouble with demonstrating my existence, and since it obliges me to exist, it prevents me from making an ethically deceptive and metaphysically unclear flourish of a conclusion.

VII
274

While the ethical in our day is ignored more and more, this ignoring has also had the harmful result that it has confused both poetry and speculative thought, which have relinquished the disinterested elevation of possibility in order to clutch at actuality—instead of each being given its due, a double confusion has been created. Poetry makes one attempt after the other to look like actuality, which is altogether unpoetic; within its sphere, speculative thought repeatedly wants to arrive at actuality and gives assurances that what is thought is the actual, that thinking is not only able to think but also to provide actuality, which is just the opposite; and at the same time what it means to exist is more and more forgotten. The age and human beings become less and less actual—hence these surrogates that are supposed to replace what is lost. The ethical is more and more abandoned; the single individual's life becomes not only poetically but world-historically disturbed and is thereby hindered in existing ethically; thus actuality must be procured in other ways. But this misunderstood actuality is like a generation or individuals in a generation who have become prematurely old and now are obliged to procure youthfulness artificially. Existing ethically is actuality, but instead of that the age has become so predominantly an observer that not only is everyone that but observing has finally become falsified as if it were actuality. We smile at monastic life, and yet no hermit ever lived as nonactual a life as is being lived nowadays, because a hermit admittedly abstracted from the whole world, but he did not abstract from himself. We know how to describe the fantastical setting of a monastery in an out-of-the-way place, in the solitude of the forest, in the distant blue of the horizon, but we do not think about the fan-tastical setting of pure thinking. And yet the recluse's pathos-filled lack of actuality is far preferable to the comic lack of actuality of the pure thinker, and the recluse's passionate forgetfulness that takes the whole world away is far preferable to the comic distraction of the world-historical thinker who forgets himself.

VII
275

From the ethical point of view, actuality is superior to possibility. The ethical specifically wants to annihilate the disinterestedness of possibility by making existing the infinite interest. Therefore the ethical wants to prevent every attempt at confusion, such as, for example, wanting *to observe* the world and human beings ethically. That is, to observe ethically cannot be done, because there is only one ethical observing—it is self-observation. The ethical immediately embraces the single individual with its requirement that he shall exist ethically; it does not bluster about millions and generations; it does not take humankind at random, any more than the police arrest humankind in general. The ethical deals with individual human beings and, please note, with each individual. If God knows how many hairs there are on a person's head, then the ethical knows how many people there are, and the ethical census is not in the interest of a total sum but in the interest of each individual. The ethical requires itself of every human being, and when it judges, it judges in turn every single individual; only a tyrant and a powerless man are satisfied with taking one out of ten. The ethical grips the single individual and requires of him that he abstain from all observing, especially of the world and humankind, because the ethical as the internal cannot be observed by anyone standing outside. The ethical can be carried out only by the individual subject, who then is able to know what lives within him—the only actuality that does not become a possibility by being known and cannot be known only by being thought, since it is his own actuality, which he knew as thought-actuality, that is, as possibility, before it became actuality; whereas with regard to another's actuality he knew nothing about it before he, by coming to know it, thought it, that is, changed it into possibility.

With regard to every actuality outside myself, it holds true that I can grasp it only in thinking. If I were actually to grasp it, I would have to be able to make myself into the other person, the one acting, to make the actuality alien to me into my own personal actuality, which is an impossibility. VII 276

The *how* of the truth is precisely the truth. Therefore it is untruth to answer a question in a medium in which the question cannot come up: for example, to explain actuality within possibility, within possibility to distinguish between possibility and actuality. By not asking esthetically and intellectually about actuality, but asking only ethically about actuality—and ethically in turn with regard to his own personal actuality—every individual is ethically set apart by himself. With regard to the observational question about ethical interiority, irony and hypocrisy as antitheses (but both expressing the contradiction that the outer is not the inner—hypocrisy by appearing good, irony by appearing bad) emphasize that actuality and deception are equally possible, that deception can reach just as far as actuality. Only the individual himself can know which is which. To ask about this ethical interiority in another individual is already unethical inasmuch as it is a diversion. But if the question is asked nevertheless, then there is the difficulty that I can grasp the other person's actuality only by thinking it, consequently by translating it into possibility, where the possibility of deception is just as thinkable. —For existing ethically, it is an advantageous preliminary study to learn that the individual human being stands alone. VII 278

To ask esthetically and intellectually about actuality is a misunderstanding; to ask ethically about another person's actuality is a misunderstanding, since one ought to ask only about one's own. Here the difference between faith (which *sensu strictissimo* [in the strictest sense] refers to something historical) and the esthetic, the intellectual, the ethical, manifests itself. To be infinitely interested and to ask about an actuality that is not one's own is to will to believe and expresses the paradoxical relation to the paradox. Esthetically it is not possible to ask in this way, except thoughtlessly, since esthetically possibility is superior to actuality. It is not possible intellectually, since intellectually possibility is superior to actuality. Nor is it possible ethically, because ethically the individual is simply and solely interested infinitely in his own actuality. —Faith's analogy to the ethical is the infinite interestedness by which the believer is absolutely different from an esthete and a thinker, but in turn is different from an ethicist by being infinitely interested in the actuality of another (for example, that the god [*Guden*] actually has existed).

VII
279

Esthetically and intellectually, it holds true that only when the *esse* of an actuality is dissolved into its *posse* is an actuality understood and thought. Ethically, it holds true that possibility is understood only when each *posse* is actually an *esse*. When the esthetic and the intellectual inspect, they protest every *esse* that is not a *posse*; when the ethical inspects, it condemns every *posse* that is not an *esse*, a *posse*, namely, in the individual himself, since the ethical does not deal with other individuals. —In our day everything is mixed together; one responds to the esthetic ethically, to faith intellectually, etc. One is finished with everything, and yet scant attention is given to which sphere it is in which each question finds its answer. This produces even greater confusion in the world of spirit than if in civic life the response to an ecclesiastical matter would be given by the pavement commission.

Is actuality, then, the outer?[97] By no means. Esthetically and intellectually, it is quite properly emphasized that the outer is nothing but deception for one who does not grasp the ideality. Frater Taciturnus declares (p. 341[98]) "Knowledge [of the historical] merely assists one into an illusion that is infatuated with the palpably material. What is that which I know historically? It is the palpably material. Ideality I know by myself, and if I do not know it by myself, then I do not know it at all, and all the historical knowledge does not help. Ideality is not a chattel that can be transferred from one person to another, or something thrown in to boot when the purchase is a large one. If I know that Caesar was great, then I know what the great is, and this is what I see—otherwise I do not know that Caesar was great. History's account— that reliable men assure us of it, that there is no risk involved in accepting VII
280 this opinion since it must be obvious that he was a great man, that the outcome demonstrates it—does not help at all. To believe the ideality on the word of another is like laughing at a joke not because one has understood it but because someone else said that it was funny. In that case, the joke can really be omitted for the person who laughs on the basis of belief and respect; he is able to laugh with equal *emphasis* [significance]." —What, then, is ac-

tuality? It is ideality. But esthetically and intellectually ideality is possibility (a transfer *ab esse ad posse*). Ethically, ideality is the actuality within the individual himself. Actuality is interiority infinitely interested in existing, which the ethical individual is for himself.

When I understand a thinker, then, precisely to the same degree to which I understand him, his actuality (that he himself exists as an individual human being, that he *actually* has understood this in such a way etc. or that he himself has *actually* carried it out etc.) is a matter of complete indifference. Philosophy and esthetics are right in this, and the point is to maintain this properly. But in this there is still no defense of pure thought as a medium of communication. Just because his actuality is a matter of indifference to me, the learner, and conversely mine to him, it by no means follows that he himself dares to be indifferent to his own actuality. His communication must be marked by this, not directly, of course, for it cannot be communicated directly between man and man (since such a relation is the believer's paradoxical relation to the object of faith), and cannot be understood directly, but must be present indirectly to be understood indirectly.

If the particular spheres are not kept decisively separate from one another, everything is confused. If one is inquisitive about a thinker's actuality, finds it interesting to know something about it, etc., then one is intellectually censurable, because in the sphere of intellectuality the maximum is that the thinker's actuality is a matter of complete indifference. But by being such a blatherer in the sphere of intellectuality, one acquires a confusing similarity to a believer. A believer is infinitely interested in the actuality of another. For faith, this is decisive, and this interestedness is not just a little inquisitiveness but is absolute dependence on the object of faith.

The object of faith is the actuality of another person; its relation is an infinite interestedness. The object of faith is not a doctrine, for then the relation is intellectual, and the point is not to bungle it but to reach the maximum of the intellectual relation. The object of faith is not a teacher who has a doctrine, for when a teacher has a doctrine, then the doctrine is *eo ipso* more important than the teacher, and the relation is intellectual, in which the point is not to bungle it but to reach the maximum of the intellectual relation. But the object of faith is the actuality of the teacher, that the teacher actually exists. Therefore faith's answer is absolutely either yes or no. Faith's answer is not in relation to a doctrine, whether it is true or not, not in relation to a teacher, whether his doctrine is true or not, but is the answer to the question about a fact: Do you accept as fact that he actually has existed? Please note that the answer is with infinite passion. In other words, in connection with a human being it is thoughtless to lay so infinitely much weight upon whether he has existed or not. Therefore, if the object of faith is a human being, the whole thing is a prank by a foolish person who has not even

VII
281

grasped the esthetic and the intellectual. The object of faith is therefore the god's actuality in the sense of existence. But to exist signifies first and foremost to be a particular individual, and this is why thinking must disregard existence, because the particular cannot be thought, but only the universal. The object of faith, then, is the actuality of the god in existence, that is, as a particular individual, that is, that the god has existed as an individual human being.

Christianity is not a doctrine about the unity of the divine and the human, about subject-object, not to mention the rest of the logical paraphrases of Christianity. In other words, if Christianity were a doctrine, then the relation to it would not be one of faith, since there is only an intellectual relation to a doctrine. Christianity, therefore, is not a doctrine but the fact that the god has existed.

Faith, then, is not a lesson for slow learners in the sphere of intellectuality, an asylum for dullards. But faith is a sphere of its own, and the immediate identifying mark of every misunderstanding of Christianity is that it changes it into a doctrine and draws it into the range of intellectuality. What holds as the maximum in the sphere of intellectuality, to remain completely indifferent to the actuality of the teacher, holds in just the opposite way in the sphere of faith—its maximum is the *quam maxime* [in the greatest degree possible] infinite interestedness in the actuality of the teacher.

_{VII}
₂₈₇ God does not think, he creates; God does not exist [*existere*], he is eternal. A human being thinks and exists, and existence [*Existents*] separates thinking and being, holds them apart from each other in succession.

What is abstract thinking? It is thinking where there is no thinker. It ignores everything but thought, and in its own medium only thought is. Existence is not thoughtless, but in existence thought is in an alien medium. What does it mean, then, in the language of abstract thinking to ask about actuality in the sense of existence when abstraction expressly ignores it? —What is concrete thinking? It is thinking where there are a thinker and a specific something (in the sense of particularity) that is being thought, where existence gives the existing thinker thought, time, and space.

_{VII}
₂₈₈ What does it mean to say that being is superior to thinking? If this statement is something to be thought, then in turn thinking is indeed *eo ipso* superior to being. If it can be thought, then the thinking is superior; if it cannot be thought, then no system of existence is possible. It is of no help whatever to be either polite or rough with being, either to let it be something superior, which nevertheless follows from thinking and is syllogistically attained, or something so inferior that it accompanies thinking as a matter of course. When, for example, it is said: God must have all perfections, or the highest being must have all perfections, to be is also a perfection; ergo the highest

being must be, or God must be—the whole movement is deceptive.* That is, if in the first part of this statement God actually is not thought of as being, then the statement cannot come off at all. It will then run somewhat like this: A supreme being who, please note, does not exist, must be in possession of all perfections, among them also that of existing; ergo a supreme being who does not exist does exist. This would be a strange conclusion. The high-est being must either not be in the beginning of the discourse in order to come into existence in the conclusion, and in that case it cannot come into existence; or the highest being was, and thus, of course, it cannot come into existence, in which case the conclusion is a fraudulent form of developing a predicate, a fraudulent paraphrase of a presupposition. In the other case, the conclusion must be kept purely hypothetical: if a supreme being is assumed to be, this being must also be assumed to be in possession of all perfections; to be is a perfection, ergo this being must be—that is, if this being is assumed to be. By concluding within a hypothesis, one can surely never conclude from the hypothesis. For example, if this or that person is a hypocrite, he will act like a hypocrite, a hypocrite will do this and that; ergo this or that per-son has done this and that. It is the same with the conclusion about God. When the conclusion is finished, God's being is just as hypothetical as it was, but inside it there is advanced a conclusion-relation between a supreme being and being as perfection, just as in the other case between being a hypocrite and a particular expression of it.

    The confusion is the same as explaining actuality in pure thinking. The section is titled *Actuality,* actuality is explained, but it has been forgotten that in pure thinking the whole thing is within the sphere of possibility. If some-one has begun a parenthesis, but it has become so long that he himself has forgotten it, it still does not help—as soon as one reads it aloud, it becomes meaningless to have the parenthetical clause change into the principal clause.

When thinking turns toward itself in order to think about itself, there emerges, as we know, a skepticism. How can there be a halt to this skepticism of which the source is that thinking selfishly wants to think itself instead of serving by thinking something? When a horse takes the bit in its teeth and runs away, it would be all right, apart form the damage that might be done in the meantime, for one to say: Just let it run; it will surely become tired. With regard to thinking's self-reflection, this cannot be said, because it can keep on for any length of time and runs in circles. Schelling halted self-reflection and understood intellectual intuition not as a discovery within self-reflection that is arrived at by rushing ahead but as a new point of departure. Hegel regards

VII
289

VII
290

* Hegel, however, does not speak this way; by means of the identity of thinking and being he is elevated above a more childlike manner of philosophizing, something he himself points out, for example, in relation to Descartes.

this as a mistake and speaks *absprechend* [deprecatingly] about intellectual intuition—then came the method. Self-reflection keeps on so long until it cancels itself; thinking presses through victoriously and once again gains reality [*Realitet*]; the identity of thinking and being is won in pure thinking.*

If what is thought were actuality, then what is thought out as perfectly as possible, when I as yet have not acted, would be the action. In this way there would be no action whatever, but the intellectual swallows the ethical. That I should now be of the opinion that it is the external that makes action into action is foolish; on the other hand, to want to show how ethical intellectuality is, that it even makes the thought into action, is a sophism that is guilty of a doubleness in the use of the words "to think." If there is to be a distinction at all between thinking and acting, this can be maintained only by assigning possibility, disinterestedness, and objectivity to thinking, and action to subjectivity. But now a *confinium* is readily apparent. For example, when I think that I will do this and that, this thinking is certainly not yet an act and is forevermore qualitatively different from it, but it is a possibility in which the interest of actuality and action is already reflected. Therefore, disinterestedness and objectivity are about to be disturbed, because actuality and responsibility want to have a firm grip on them. (Thus there is a sin in thought.)

The actuality is not the external action but an interiority in which the individual annuls possibility and identifies himself with what is thought in order to exist in it. This is action. Intellectuality seems so rigorous in making the thought itself into action, but this rigorousness is a false alarm, because allowing intellectuality to cancel action at all is a relaxation. Just as in the analogies cited earlier, it holds true that to be rigorous *within* a total relaxation is only illusion and essentially only a relaxation. If someone, for ex-

---

* It is quite certain that at the bottom of all skepticism there is an abstract certainty that is the foothold of doubt and is like the line one draws as the base upon which the figure is sketched. Therefore it is quite certain that nothing is accomplished even by the most rigorous attempt of Greek skepticism to round off the hovering of skepticism by emphasizing that the statement about doubt must not be understood θητιχῶς [as a position], but it still does not follow that doubt overcomes itself. The basic certainty that sustains doubt can at no moment hypostatize itself as long as I am doubting, because doubt continually leaves it in order to doubt. If I want to keep on doubting, I shall never in all eternity advance any further, because doubt consists precisely in and by passing off that certainty as something else. If I hold on to the certainty as certainty for one single moment, I must also stop doubting for that moment. But then it is not doubt that cancels itself; it is I who stop doubting. Therefore a mediocre doubter will be most likely to succeed in gaining certainty, and next a doubter who merely joins categories in order to see how they look the best without bothering in the least to carry out any of them. —I cannot stop returning to this point, because it is so decisive. If it is the case that doubt overcomes itself, that by doubting everything one in this very doubt wins truth without a break and an absolutely new point of departure, then not one single Christian category can be maintained, then Christianity is abolished.

ample, were to call sin ignorance, and then *within* this definition rigorously interpret specific sins, this is totally illusory, since every definition stated *within* the total definition that sin is ignorance becomes essentially frivolous, because the entire definition is frivolousness.

With regard to evil, the confusion of thinking and acting deceives more easily. But if one looks more closely, it appears that the reason for it is the jealousy of the good for itself, which requires itself of the individual to such a degree that it defines a thought of evil as sin. But let us take the good. To have thought something good that one wants to do, is that to have done it? Not at all, but neither is it the external that determines the outcome, because someone who does not possess a penny can be just as compassionate as the person who gives away a kingdom. When the Levite on the road from Jericho to Jerusalem passed by the unfortunate man who had been assaulted by robbers, it perhaps occurred to him when he was still a little distance from the unfortunate man that it would indeed be beautiful to help a sufferer. He may even have already thought of how rewarding such a good deed is in itself; he perhaps was riding more slowly because he was immersed in thought; but as he came closer and closer, the difficulties became apparent, and he rode past. Now he probably rode fast in order to get away quickly, away from the thought of the riskiness of the road, away from the thought of the possible nearness of the robbers, and away from the thought of how easily the victim could confuse him with the robbers who had left him lying there. Consequently he did not act. But suppose that along the way repentance brought him back; suppose that he quickly turned around, fearing neither robbers nor other difficulties, fearing only to arrive too late. Suppose that he did come too late, inasmuch as the compassionate Samaritan had already had the sufferer brought to the inn—had he, then, not acted? Assuredly, and yet he did not act in the external world.

Let us take a religious action. To have faith in God—does that mean to think about how glorious it must be to have faith, to think about what peace and security faith can give? Not at all. Even to wish, where the interest, the subject's interest, is far more evident, is not to have faith, is not to act. The individual's relation to the thought-action is still continually only a possibility that he can give up. —It is not denied that with regard to evil there are cases in which the transition is almost undetectable, but these cases must be explained in a special way. This is due to the fact that the individual is so in the power of habit that by frequently having made the transition from thinking to acting he has finally lost the power for it in the bondage of habit, which *at his expense* makes it faster and faster.

Between the thought-action and the actual action, between possibility and actuality, there perhaps is no difference at all in content; the difference in form is always essential. Actuality is interestedness by existing in it.

It is not denied that the actuality of action is so often confused with all sorts of ideas, intentions, preliminaries to resolutions, preludes of mood, etc. that there is very seldom any action at all; on the contrary, it is assumed that this has greatly contributed to the confusion. But take an action *sensu eminenti* [in the eminent sense]; then everything shows up clearly. The external in Luther's action was his appearing at the Diet of Worms, but from the moment he with all the passionate decision of subjectivity existed in willing, when every relation of possibility to this action had to be regarded by him as temptation—then he had acted.* When Dion boarded ship to overthrow the tyrant Dioniysius, he is supposed to have said that even if he died on the way he would nevertheless have done a magnificent deed—that is, he had acted. That the decision in the external is supposed to be superior to the decision in the internal is the despicable talk of weak, cowardly, and sly people about the highest. To assume that the decision in the external can decide something externally so that it can never be done over again, but not the decision in the internal, is contempt for the holy.

VII
296

To give thinking supremacy over everything else is gnosticism; to make the subjective individual's ethical actuality the only actuality could seem to be acosmism. That it will so appear to a busy thinker who must explain everything, a hasty pate who traverses the whole world, demonstrates only that he has a very poor idea of what the ethical means for the subjective individual. If ethics deprived such a busy thinker of the whole world and let him keep his own self, he would very likely think: "Is this anything? Such a trifling thing is not worth keeping. Let it go along with all the rest"—then, then it is acosmism. But why does a busy thinker like that talk and think so disrespectfully of himself? Indeed, if the intention were that he should give up the whole world and be satisfied with another person's ethical actuality, well, then he would be in the right to make light of the exchange. But to the individual his own ethical actuality ought to mean, ethically, even more than heaven and earth and everything found therein, more than world history's six thousand years, and more than astrology, veterinary science, together with everything the times demand, which esthetically and intellectually is a prodi-

---

* Ordinarily the relation between thought-action and actual action (in the inner sense) is recognizable by this, that whereas any further consideration and deliberation with regard to the former must be regarded as welcome, with regard to the latter it must be regarded as temptation. If it nevertheless appears to be so meaningful that it is respected, this signifies that its path goes through repentance. When I am deliberating, the art is to think every possibility; the moment I have acted (in the inner sense), the transformation is that the task is to defend myself against further deliberation, except insofar as repentance requires something to be *done over again*. The decision in the external is jest, but the more lethargically a person lives, the more the external becomes the only decision he knows. People have no idea of the individual's eternal decision within himself, but they believe that if a decision is drawn up on stamped paper, then it is decided, not before.

gious narrow-mindedness. If it is not so, it is worst for the individual himself, because then he has nothing at all, no actuality at all, because to everything else he has at the very most only a relation of possibility.

The transition from possibility to actuality is, as Aristotle rightly teaches, χίνησις, a movement.[99] This cannot be said in the language of abstraction at all or understood therein, because abstraction can give movement neither time nor space, which presuppose it or which it presupposes. There is a halt, a leap. When someone says that this is because I am thinking of something definite and not abstracting, since in that case I would discern that there is no break, then my repeated answer would be: Quite right; abstractly thought, there is no break, but no transition either, because viewed abstractly everything *is*. However, when existence gives movement time and I reproduce this, then the leap appears in just the way a leap can appear: it must come or it has been. Let us take an example from the ethical. It has been said often enough that the good has its reward in itself, and thus it is not only the most proper but also the most sagacious thing to will the good. A sagacious eudaemonist is able to perceive this very well; thinking in the form of possibility, he can come as close to the good as is possible, because in possibility as in abstraction the transition is only an appearance. But when the transition is supposed to become actual, all sagacity expires in scruples. Actual time separates the good and the reward for him so much, so eternally, that sagacity cannot join them again, and the eudaemonist declines with thanks. To will the good is indeed the most sagacious thing—yet not as understood by sagacity but as understood by the good. The transition is clear enough as a break, indeed, as a suffering. —In the sermon presentation there often appears the illusion that eudaimonistically transforms the transition to becoming a Christian into an appearance, whereby the listener is deceived and the transition prevented.

Subjectivity is truth; subjectivity is actuality.

The Subjective Thinker; His Task; His Form, That Is, His Style

The subjective thinker is a dialectician oriented to the existential; he has the intellectual passion to hold firm the qualitative disjunction. But, on the other hand, if the qualitative disjunction is used flatly and simply, if it is applied altogether abstractly to the individual human being, then one can run the ludicrous risk of saying something infinitely decisive, and of being right in what one says, and still not say the least thing. Therefore, in the psychological sense it is really remarkable to see the absolute disjunction deceitfully used simply for evasion. When the death penalty is placed on every crime, the result is that no crimes at all are punished. It is the same with the absolute disjunction when applied flatly and simply; it is just like a silent letter—it

VII
297

VII
304

cannot be pronounced or, if it can be pronounced, it says nothing. The subjective thinker, therefore, has with intellectual passion the absolute disjunction as belonging to existence, but he has it as the final decision that prevents everything from ending in a quantifying. Thus he has it readily available, but not in such a way that by abstractly recurring to it he just frustrates existence. The subjective thinker, therefore, has also esthetic passion and ethical passion, whereby concretion is gained. All existence-issues are passionate, because existence, if one becomes conscious of it, involves passion. To think about them so as to leave out passion is not to think about them at all, is to forget the point that one indeed is oneself an existing person. Yet the subjective thinker is not a poet even if he is also a poet, not an ethicist even if he is also an ethicist, but is also a dialectician and is himself essentially existing, whereas the poet's existence is inessential in relation to the poem, and likewise the ethicist's in relation to the teaching, and the dialectician's in relation to the thought. The subjective thinker is not a scientist-scholar; he is an artist. To exist is an art. The subjective thinker is esthetic enough for his life to have esthetic content, ethical enough to regulate it, dialectical enough in thinking to master it.

The subjective thinker's task is to *understand himself in existence.* True enough, abstract thinking does indeed speak about contradiction and about the immanental forward thrust of contradiction,[100] although by disregarding existence and existing it cancels difficulty and contradiction. But the subjective thinker is an existing person, and yet he is a thinking person. He does not abstract from existence and from the contradiction, but he is in them, and yet he is supposed to think. In all his thinking, then, he has to include the thought that he himself is an existing person. But then in turn he also will always have enough to think about. One is soon finished with humanity in general and also with world history, for the hungry monster—the world-historical process—swallows even such enormous portions as China and Persia etc. as if they were nothing. One is soon finished with faith viewed abstractly, but the subjective thinker, who as he thinks is also present to himself in existence, will find it inexhaustible when his faith is to be declined in the manifold *casibus* [cases] of life. It is not waggery either, because existence is the most difficult for a thinker when he must remain in it, inasmuch as the *moment* is commensurate with the highest decisions and yet in turn is a little vanishing minute in the possible seventy years. Poul Møller has correctly pointed out that a court fool uses more wit in one year than many a witty author in his whole life,[101] and why is that if it is not because the former is an existing person who every moment of the day must have wittiness at his disposal, whereas the other is witty only momentarily.

In a certain sense, the subjective thinker speaks just as abstractly as the abstract thinker, because the latter speaks about humanity in general, subjectivity in general, the other about the one human being (*unum noris, omnes* [if you know one, you know all]). But this one human being is an existing human being, and the difficulty is not left out.

To understand oneself in existence is also *the Christian principle,* except that this *self* has received much richer and much more profound qualifications that are even more difficult to understand together with existing. The be- liever is a subjective thinker, and the difference, as shown above, is only be- tween the simple person and the simple wise person. Here again this *oneself* is not humanity in general, subjectivity in general, and other such things, whereby everything becomes easy inasmuch as the difficulty is removed and the whole matter is shifted over into the *Schattenspiel* [shadow play] of ab- straction. The difficulty is greater than for the Greek, because even greater contrasts are placed together, because existence is accentuated paradoxically as sin, and eternity paradoxically as the god [*Guden*] in time. The difficulty is to exist in them, not abstractly to think oneself out of them and abstractly to think about, for example, an eternal divine becoming[102] and other such things that appear when one removes the difficulty. Therefore, the existence of the believer is even more passionate than that of the Greek philosopher (who to a high degree needed passion even in connection with his ataraxia), because existence yields passion, but existence accentuated paradoxically yields the maximum of passion.

VII
307

Every human being must be assumed to possess essentially what belongs essentially to being a human being. The subjective thinker's task is to trans- form himself into an instrument that clearly and definitely expresses in ex- istence the essentially human. To depend upon differences in this regard is a misunderstanding, because being a little smarter and the like amounts to nothing. That our age has taken refuge in the generation and has abandoned individuals has its basis quite correctly in an esthetic despair that has not reached the ethical. It has been discerned that to be ever so distinguished an individual human being makes no difference, because no difference makes any difference. Consequently a new difference has been selected: to be born in the nineteenth century. So everyone as quickly as possible attempts to de- fine his little fragment of existence in relation to the generation and consoles himself. But it is of no use and is only a loftier and more glittering delusion. And just as in ancient times and ordinarily in every generation there have been fools who in their conceited imaginations have confused themselves with some great and distinguished man, have wanted to be this one or that, so the distinctiveness of our time is that the fools are not satisfied with con- fusing themselves with a great man but confuse themselves with the age, the century, the generation, humankind. —To will to be an individual human being (which one unquestionably is) with the help of and by virtue of one's difference is flabbiness; but to will to be an individual existing human being

VII
309

(which one unquestionably is) in the same sense as everyone else is capable of being—that is the ethical victory over life and over every mirage, the victory that is perhaps the most difficult of all in the theocentric nineteenth century.

The subjective *thinker's form,* the form of his communication, is his *style.* His form must be just as manifold as are the opposites that he holds together. The systematic *eins, zwei, drei* is an abstract form that also must inevitably run into trouble whenever it is to be applied to the concrete. To the same degree as the subjective thinker is concrete, to the same degree his form must also be concretely dialectical. But just as he himself is not a poet, not an ethicist, not a dialectician, so also his form is none of theirs directly. His form must first and last be related to existence, and in this regard he must have at his disposal the poetic, the ethical, the dialectical, the religious. Compared with that of a poet, his form will be abbreviated; compared with that of an abstract dialectician, his form will be broad. That is, viewed abstractly, concretion in the existential is breadth. For example, relative to abstract thinking the humorous is breadth, but relative to concrete existence-communication it is by no means breadth, unless it is broad in itself. Relative to his thought, an abstract thinker's person is a matter of indifference, but existentially a thinker must be presented essentially as a thinking person, but in such a way that as he expresses his thought he also describes himself. Relative to abstract thinking, jest is breadth, but relative to concrete existence-communication it is not breadth if the jest itself is not broad. But because the subjective thinker is himself essentially an existing person in existence and does not have the medium of imagination for the illusion of esthetic production, he does not have the poetic repose to create in the medium of imagination and esthetically to accomplish something disinterestedly. Relative to the subjective thinker's existence-communication, poetic repose is breadth. Subordinate characters, setting, etc., which belong to the well-balanced character of the esthetic production, are in themselves breadth; the subjective thinker has only one setting—existence—and has nothing to do with localities and such things. The setting is not in the fairyland of the imagination, where poetry produces consummation, nor is the setting laid in England, and historical accuracy is not a concern. The setting is inwardness in existing as a human being; the concretion is the relation of the existence-categories to one another. Historical accuracy and historical actuality are breadth.

But existence-actuality cannot be communicated, and the subjective thinker has his own actuality in his own ethical existence. If actuality is to be understood by a third party, it must be understood as possibility, and a communicator who is conscious of this will therefore see to it, precisely in order to be oriented to existence, that his existence-communication is in the form of possibility. A production in the form of possibility places existing in it as close to the recipient as it is possible between one human being and another. Let me elucidate this once again. One would think that, by telling a reader that this person and that person *actually* have done this and that (something great and remarkable), one would place the reader closer to wanting to do the same, to wanting to exist in the same, than by merely presenting it as possible. Apart from what was pointed out in its proper place, that the reader can understand the communication only by dissolving the *esse* of actuality into *posse*, since otherwise he only *imagines* that he understands, apart from this, the fact that this person and that person actually have done this and that can just as well have a delaying as a motivating effect. The reader merely transforms the person who is being discussed (aided by his being an *actual* person) into the rare exception; he admires him and says: But I am too insignificant to do anything like that.

Now, admiration can be very legitimate with regard to differences, but it is a total misunderstanding with regard to the universal. That one person can swim the channel and a second person knows twenty-four languages and a third person walks on his hands etc.—one can admire that *si placet* [if you please], but if the person presented is supposed to be great with regard to the universal because of his virtue, his faith, his nobility, his faithfulness, his perseverance, etc., then admiration is a deceptive relation or can easily become that. What is great with regard to the universal must therefore not be presented as an object for admiration, but as a *requirement*. In the form of possibility, the presentation becomes a requirement. Instead of presenting the good in the form of actuality, as is ordinarily done, that this person and that person have actually lived and have actually done this, and thus transforming the reader into an observer, an admirer, an appraiser, it should be presented in the form of possibility. Then whether or not the reader wants to exist in it is placed as close as possible to him. Possibility operates with the ideal human being (not with regard to difference but with regard to the universal), who is related to every human being as requirement. To the same degree as one insists that it was this specific person, the exception is made easier for others.

The Essential Expression of Existential Pathos: Suffering—
Fortune and Misfortune as an Esthetic Life-View in Contrast
to Suffering as a Religious Life-View (Illustrated by the Religious Address)—
the Actuality of Suffering (Humor)—the Actuality of Suffering in the Latter
State as a Sign That an Existing Individual Relates Himself to an Eternal
Happiness—the Illusion of Religiousness—Spiritual Trial—the Basis
and Meaning of Suffering in the Former State: Dying to Immediacy

VII
311

VII
374

*and Yet Remaining in the Finite—an Upbuilding Diversion—Humor
as the Incognito of Religiousness*

The meaning of the religious suffering is dying to immediacy; its actuality is its essential continuance, but it belongs to inwardness and must not express itself externally (the monastic movement). When we take a religious person, the knight of hidden inwardness, and place him in the existence-medium, a contradiction will appear as he relates himself to the world around him, and he himself must become aware of this. The contradiction does not consist in his being different from everyone else (this self-contradiction is precisely the law for the nemesis the comic brings upon the monastic movement), but the contradiction is that he, with all this inwardness hidden within him, with this pregnancy of suffering and benediction in his inner being, looks just like all the others—and inwardness is indeed hidden simply by his looking exactly like others.* There is something comic here, because here is a contradiction, and where there is a contradiction the comic is also present. This comic aspect, however, is not for others, who know nothing about it, but is for the religious person himself when humor is his incognito, as Frater Taciturnus says (see *Stages on Life's Way*[103]). This is worth understanding more precisely, because next to the confusion in recent speculative thought that faith is immediacy, perhaps the most confusing confusion is that humor is the highest, because humor is still not religiousness, but its *confinium* [border territory]. There are already some comments about this above, which I must ask the reader to recall.

But is humor the incognito of the religious person? Is not his incognito this, that there is nothing whatever to be noticed, nothing at all that could arouse suspicion of the hidden inwardness, not even so much as the humoristic? At its very maximum, if this could be reached in existence, this would no doubt be so,** yet as long as the struggle and the suffering in in-

---

* Another author has correctly traced (in *Either/Or*) the ethical to the qualification that it is every human being's duty to become *open*—thus to *disclosure*. Religiousness, on the other hand, is hidden inwardness, but, please note, not the immediacy that is supposed to become open, not the untransformed inwardness, but the inwardness whose transformed qualification is to be hidden. —Incidentally, it hardly needs to be recalled that when I say the religious person's incognito is to look exactly like all the others, this does not mean that his incognito is the actuality of a robber, a thief, a murderer, because the world certainly has not sunk so deep that an open breach of legality can be regarded as the universally human. No, the expression "to look exactly like all other human beings" naturally makes sure of legality, but this may very well also be without there being any religiousness in a person.

** In *Fear and Trembling,* a "knight of faith" such as this was portrayed. But this portrayal was only a rash anticipation, and the illusion was gained by depicting him in a state of completeness, and hence in a false medium, instead of in the existence-medium, and the beginning was made by ignoring the contradiction—how an observer could become at all *aware* of him in

wardness continue he will not succeed in hiding his inwardness completely, but he will not express it directly, and he will hinder it negatively with the aid of the humorous. An observer who mingled with people in order to find the religious person would therefore follow the principle that everyone in whom he discovered the humorous would be made the object of his attention. But if he has made the relation of inwardness clear to himself, he will also know that he can be fooled, because the religious person is not a humorist, but in his outer appearance he is a humorist. Thus an observer who is looking for the religious person and intends to recognize him by the humorous would be fooled if he met me. He would find the humorous, but would be fooled if he drew any conclusion from it, because I am not a religious person but simply and solely a humorist. Perhaps someone thinks that it is frightful arrogation to attribute the designation of "humorist" to myself, and furthermore thinks that if I actually were a humorist he would surely show me respect and honor. I shall not take exception to or dwell upon this, because the person who makes this objection obviously assumes humor to be the highest. I, on the contrary, declare that the religious person *stricte sic dictus* [in the strict sense of the word] is infinitely higher than the humorist and qualitatively different from the humorist. Moreover, concerning his unwillingness to regard me as humorist, well, I am willing to transfer the role of observer from me to the one who is making the objection; let the observer become aware of him: the result will be the same—the observer is fooled.

VII
436

There are three existence-spheres: the esthetic, the ethical, the religious. To these there is a respectively corresponding *confinium* [border territory]: irony is the *confinium* between the esthetic and the ethical; humor is the *confinium* between the ethical and the religious.

Let us take irony. As soon as an observer discovers an ironist, he will be attentive, because it is possible that the ironist is an ethicist. But he can also be fooled, because it is not certain that the ironist is an ethicist. The immediate person is distinguishable at once, and as soon as he is recognized it is a certainty that he is not an ethicist, because he has not made the movement of

---

such a way that he could place himself, admiring, outside and admire that there is nothing, nothing whatever, to *notice*, unless Johannes de Silentio would say that the knight of faith is his own poetic production. But then the contradiction is there again, implicit in the duplexity that as poet and observer he simultaneously relates himself to the same thing, consequently as poet creates a character in the medium of imagination (for this, of course, is the poet-medium) and as observer observes the same poetic figure in the existence-medium. —Frater Taciturnus seems already to have been aware of this dialectical difficulty, for he has avoided this irregularity by means of the form of an imaginary construction. He is not in an observational relation to Quidam of the imaginary construction[104] but transforms his observation into a psychological-poetic production and then draws this as close as possible to actuality by using the form of the imaginary construction and the proportions of actuality rather than the foreshortened perspective.

infinity. The ironical rejoinder, if it is correct (and the observer is assumed to be a tried and tested man who knows all about tricking and unsettling the speaker in order to see if what he says is something learned by rote or has a bountifully ironic value such as an existing ironist will always have), betrays that the speaker has made the movement of infinity, but no more. The irony emerges by continually joining the particulars of the finite with the ethical infinite requirement and allowing the contradiction to come into existence. The one who can do it with proficiency and not let himself be caught in any relativity, in which his proficiency becomes diffident, must have made a movement of infinity, and to that extent it is possible that he is an ethicist.*

Therefore the observer will not even be able to catch him in his inability to perceive himself ironically, because he is also able to talk about himself as about a third person, to join himself as a vanishing particular together with the absolute requirement—indeed, to *join* them *together.* How strange that an expression that signifies the final difficulty of existence, which is to join together the absolutely different (such as the conception of God with going out to the amusement park), that the same expression in our language also signifies teasing! But although this is certain, it is still not certain that he is an ethicist. He is an ethicist only by relating himself within himself to the absolute requirement. Such an ethicist uses irony as his incognito. In this sense Socrates was an ethicist, but, please note, bordering on the religious, which is why the analogy to faith in his life was pointed out earlier (Section II, Chapter II).

What, then, is irony, if one wants to call Socrates an ironist and does not, like Magister Kierkegaard, consciously or unconsciously want to bring out only the one side? Irony is the unity of ethical passion, which in inwardness infinitely accentuates one's own *I* in relation to the ethical requirement— and culture, which in externality infinitely abstracts from the personal *I* as a finitude included among all other finitudes and particulars. An effect of this abstraction is that no one notices the first, and this is precisely the art, and

---

* If the observer is able to catch him in a relativity that he does not have the strength to
comprehend ironically, then he is not really an ironist. In other words, if irony is not taken in the decisive sense, every human being is basically ironical. As soon as a person who has his life in a certain relativity (and this definitely shows that he is not ironical) is placed outside it in a relativity that he considers to be lower (a nobleman, for example, in a group of peasants, a professor in the company of parish clerks, a city millionaire together with beggars, a royal coachman in a room with peat cutters, a cook at a manor house together with women who do weeding, etc.), then he is ironical—that is, he is not ironical, since his irony is only the illusory superiority of relativity, but the symptoms and the rejoinders will have a certain similarity. But the whole thing is only a game within a certain presupposition, and the inhumanity is distinguishable in the inability of the person concerned to perceive himself ironically, and the inauthenticity is distinguishable by the same person's obsequiousness when a relativity shows up that is higher than his. This, alas, is what the world calls modesty—the ironist, he is proud!

through it the true infinitizing of the first is conditioned.* Most people live
in the opposite way. They are busy with being something when someone is
watching them. If possible, they are something in their own eyes as soon as
others are watching them, but inwardly, where the absolute requirement is
watching them, they have no taste for accentuating the personal *I*.

Irony is an existence-qualification, and thus nothing is more ludicrous than
regarding it as a style of speaking or an author's counting himself lucky to
express himself ironically once in a while. The person who has essential irony
has it all day long and is not bound to any style, because it is the infinite
within him.

Irony is the cultivation of the spirit and therefore follows next after immediacy; then comes the ethicist, then the humorist, then the religious person.

But why does the ethicist use irony as his incognito? Because he comprehends the contradiction between the mode in which he exists in his inner
being and his not expressing it in his outer appearance. The ethicist certainly
becomes open insofar as he exhausts himself in the tasks of factual actuality,
but the immediate person also does this, and what makes the ethicist an ethicist is the movement** by which he inwardly joins his outward life together
with the infinite requirement of the ethical, and this is not directly apparent.
In order not to be disturbed by the finite, by all the relativities in the world,
the ethicist places the comic between himself and the world and thereby
makes sure that he himself does not become comic through a naive misunderstanding of his ethical passion. An immediate enthusiast bawls out in the
world early and late; always in his swagger-boots, he pesters people with his
enthusiasm and does not perceive at all that it does not make them enthusi-

---

* The desperate attempt of the miscarried Hegelian ethics to make the state into the court
of last resort of ethics is a highly unethical attempt to finitize individuals, an unethical flight
from the category of individuality to the category of the race (see Section II, Chapter I). The
ethicist in *Either/Or* has already protested against this directly and indirectly, indirectly at the
end of the essay on the balance between the esthetic and the ethical in the personality, where
he himself must make a concession with regard to the religious, and again at the end of the article on marriage (in *Stages*), where, even on the basis of the ethics he champions, which is di-
ametrically opposite to Hegelian ethics, he certainly jacks up the price of the religious as high
as possible but still makes room for it.

** When Socrates related himself negatively to the actuality of the state, this was consistent
in part with his discovering of the ethical, in part with his dialectical position as an exception
and *extraordinarius*, and finally with his being an ethicist bordering on the religious. Just as an
analogy to faith is to be found in him, so an analogy to hidden inwardness can also be found,
except that externally he expressed this only by negative action, by abstaining, and thus contributed to drawing the attention of others to it. The hidden inwardness of religiousness in the
incognito of humor avoids attention by being like the others, except that there is a background
tone of the humorous in the simple rejoinder and a flourish of it in the everyday way of life,
but one must indeed be an observer to become aware of this. Everyone was bound to notice
Socrates' reserve.

astic, except when they beat him. No doubt he is well informed, and the order calls for a complete transformation—of the whole world. Indeed, it is here that he has heard wrongly, because the order calls for a complete transformation of oneself. If such an enthusiast is contemporary with an ironist, the latter naturally makes comic capital of him. The ethicist, however, is sufficiently ironical to be well aware that what engages him absolutely does not engage the others absolutely. He himself grasps this misrelation and places the comic in between in order to be able more inwardly to hold fast the ethical within himself. Now the comedy starts, because people's opinion of a person like that will always be: for him nothing is important. And why not? Because for him the ethical is absolutely important: in this he is different from the generality of people, for whom so many things are important, indeed, almost everything is important—but nothing is absolutely important. —Yet, as mentioned, an observer can be fooled if he assumes an ironist to be an ethicist, since irony is only a possibility.

So it is also with the humorist and the religious person, since according to the above the special dialectic of the religious does not allow direct expression, does not allow recognizable difference, protests against the commensurability of the outer, and yet esteems, if worst comes to worst, the monastic movement far above mediation. The humorist continually (not in the sense of the pastor's "always" but at every time of day, wherever he is and whatever he thinks or undertakes) joins the conception of God together with something else and brings out the contradiction—but he does not relate himself to God in religious passion (*stricte sic dictus* [in the strict sense of the word]). He changes himself into a jesting and yet profound transition area for all these transactions, but he does not relate himself to God.

The religious person does the same, joins the conception of God together with everything and sees the contradiction, but in his innermost being he relates himself to God, whereas immediate religiousness rests in the pious superstition of seeing God directly in everything, and the revivalist impertinently employs God to be present where he is, so that if one only sees him one can be sure that God is there, since the revivalist has him in his pocket. Therefore, religiousness with humor as the incognito is the unity of absolute religious passion (inwardly deepened dialectically) and spiritual maturity, which calls religiousness back from all outwardness into inwardness and therein it is again indeed the absolute religious passion. The religious person discovers that what engages him absolutely seems to engage others very little, but he draws no conclusions, partly because he has no time for that and partly because he cannot know for sure whether all these people are not knights of hidden inwardness. He lets himself be constrained by his surroundings to do what the dialectical inward deepening requires of him—to place a veil between people and himself in order to guard and protect the inwardness of his suffering and his relationship with God. This does not mean that such a religious person becomes inactive; on the contrary, he does not leave the world but remains in it, because precisely this is his incognito. But before God he inwardly deepens his outward activity by acknowledging that he is capable of nothing, by cutting off every teleological relation to what is directed outward, all income from it in finitude, even though he still works to the utmost of his ability—and precisely this is enthusiasm. A revivalist always adds God's name outwardly; the certitude of his faith is sufficiently sure. But the certitude of faith is indeed indistinguishable by uncertainty, and just as its certitude is the highest of all, so this same certitude is the most ironic of all, otherwise it is not the certitude of faith. It is certain that everything that pleases God will succeed for the pious—it is certain, oh, so certain; indeed, nothing is as certain as this.

Now we are standing at the boundary. The religiousness that is hidden inwardness is *eo ipso* inaccessible for comic interpretation. It cannot have the comic outside itself, because it is *hidden* inwardness and consequently cannot come into contradiction with anything. It has itself brought into consciousness the contradiction that humor dominates, the highest range of the comic, and has it within itself as something lower. In this way it is absolutely armed against the comic or is protected by the comic against the comic. VII
455

When at times religiousness in Church and state has wanted legislation and police as an aid in protecting itself against the comic, this may be very well intentioned; but the question is to what extent the ultimate determining factor is religious, and it does the comic an injustice to regard it as an enemy of the religious. The comic is no more an enemy of the religious— which, on the contrary, everything serves and obeys—than the dialectical. But the religiousness that essentially lays claim to outwardness, essentially makes outwardness commensurable, certainly must watch its step and fear more for itself (that it does not become esthetic) than fear the comic, which could legitimately help it to open its eyes. There is much in Catholicism that can serve as examples of this. With regard to the individual, it is true that the religious person who wants all to be serious, presumably even just as serious as he is, because he is obtusely serious, is in a contradiction. The religious person who could not bear, if it so happened, that everyone laughed at what absolutely occupies him lacks inwardness and therefore wants to be consoled by illusion, that many people are of the same opinion, indeed, with the same facial expression, as he has, and wants to be built up by adding the world-historical to his little fragment of actuality, "since now a new life is indeed beginning to stir everywhere, the heralded new year with vision and heart for the cause."

Hidden inwardness is inaccessible to the comic. This would also be illustrated if a religious person of that kind could be stirred suddenly to assert his religiousness in the external world, if, for example, he forgot himself and VII
456 came into conflict with a comparable religious person and again forgot himself and the absolute requirement of inwardness by wanting comparatively to be more religious than the other—in that case he is comic, and the contradiction is: simultaneously wanting to be visible and invisible. Against arrogating forms of the religious, humor legitimately uses the comic because a religious person surely must himself know the way out if he only is willing. If this may not be presupposed, then such an interpretation becomes dubious in the same sense as a comic interpretation of the busy trifler would be if it was the case that he actually was mentally deranged.

The law for the comic is very simple: the comic is wherever there is contradiction and where the contradiction is painless by being regarded as canceled, since the comic certainly does not cancel the contradiction (on the contrary, it makes it apparent). But the legitimate comic is able to do it; otherwise it is not legitimate. The talent is to be able to depict it *in concreto*. The test of the comic is to examine what relation between the spheres the comic statement contains. If the relation is not right, the comic is illegitimate, and the comic that belongs nowhere is *eo ipso* illegitimate. Thus the sophistical in connection with the comic has its basis in nothing, in pure abstraction, and is expressed by Gorgias in the abstraction: to annihilate earnestness by means of the comic and the comic by means of earnestness (see Aristotle, *Rhetoric,* 3, 18). The quittance with which everything ends here is rubbish, and the irregularity that an existing person has changed himself into a fantastical X is easily discovered, because it must still be an existing person who wants to use this procedure, which only makes him ludicrous if one applies to him the formula of exorcism used against speculative thinkers in the foregoing: May I have the honor of asking with whom I have the honor of speaking, whether it is a human being, etc.? In other words, Gorgias, along with his discovery, ends up in the fantastic fringe of pure being, because, if he annihilates the one by means of the other, nothing remains. But Gorgias no doubt merely wanted to describe the ingenuity of a shyster lawyer, who wins by changing his weapon in relation to his opponent's weapon. But a shyster lawyer is no legitimate court of appeals with regard to the comic; he will have to whistle for legitimation—and be satisfied with the profit, which everyone knows has always been the Sophists' pet conclusion—money, money, money, or whatever is on the same level as money.

In the religious sphere, when this is kept pure in inwardness, the comic is auxiliary. It might be said that repentance, for example, is a contradiction, ergo is something comic, certainly not to the esthetic or to finite common sense, which are lower, or to the ethical, which has its power in this passion, or to abstraction, which is fantastic and thereby lower (it wanted to interpret as comic from this standpoint what was rejected as nonsense in the foregoing), but to the religious itself, which knows a remedy for it, a way out. But this is not the case; the religious knows of no remedy for repentance that disregards repentance. On the contrary, the religious continually uses the negative as the essential form.* Thus the consciousness of sin definitely belongs to the consciousness of the forgiveness of sin. The negative is not once and for all and then the positive, but the positive is continually in the negative, and the negative is the distinctive mark. Therefore, the regulating principle *ne quid nimis* [nothing too much] cannot be applied here. When the religious is interpreted esthetically, when indulgence for four shillings is preached in the Middle Ages and this is assumed to settle the matter, if one wants to cling to this fiction—then repentance is to be interpreted as comic, then the person broken in repentance is comic just like the busy trifler, provided he has the four shillings, because the way out is indeed so easy, and in this fiction it is indeed assumed that it is the way out. But all this balderdash is the result of having made the religious a farce. But in the same degree as the negative is abolished in the religious sphere, or is allowed to be once and for all and thereby sufficient, in the same degree the comic will assert itself against the religious, and rightfully so—because the religious has become esthetics and still wants to be the religious. VII
458

Humor joins the eternal recollecting of guilt together with everything but in this recollecting does not relate itself to an eternal happiness. Now we have come to hidden inwardness. The eternal recollecting of guilt cannot be expressed in the external realm, which is incommensurate with it, since every expression in the external makes the guilt finite. But the eternal recollecting of guilt in hidden inwardness is not despair either, because despair is always the infinite, the eternal, the total in the moment of impatience, and all despair is a kind of ill temper. No, the eternal recollecting is a mark of the relation to an eternal happiness, as far removed as possible from being a direct mark, but nevertheless always sufficient to prevent the shifting of despair. VII
483 VII
484

Humor discovers the comic by joining the total guilt together with all the relativity between individuals. The basis of the comic is the underlying total guilt that sustains this whole comedy. In other words, if essential guiltlessness or goodness underlies the relative, it is not comic, because it is not comic that one stipulates more or less within the positive qualification. But if the relativity is based upon the total guilt, then the more or less is based upon that which is less than nothing, and this is the contradiction that the comic discovers. Insofar as money is a something, the relativity between richer and poorer is not comic, but if it is token money, it is comic that it is a relativity. If the reason for people's hustle-bustle is a possibility of avoiding danger, the busyness is not comic; but if, for example, it is on a ship that is sinking, there is something

---

* This is also why the religious, even when it interprets the esthetic suffering with a certain touch of the comic, nevertheless does it gently, because it is recognized that this suffering will have its day. Repentance, however, viewed religiously, will not have its day and then be over; the uncertainty of faith will not have its day and then be over; the consciousness of sin will not have its day and then be over—in that case we return to the esthetic.

comic in all this running around, because the contradiction is that despite all this movement they are not moving away from the site of their downfall.

Hidden inwardness must also discover the comic, which is present not because the religious person is different from others but because, although most heavily burdened by sustaining an eternal recollecting of guilt, he is just like everyone else. He discovers the comic, but since in eternal recollecting he is continually relating himself to an eternal happiness, the comic is a continually vanishing element.

The religiousness that has been discussed up until now and that for the sake of brevity will from now on be termed Religiousness *A* is not the specifically Christian religiousness. On the other hand, the dialectical is decisive only insofar as it is joined together with the pathos-filled and gives rise to a new pathos.

Ordinarily one is not simultaneously aware of both parts. The religious address will represent the pathos-filled and cross out the dialectical, and therefore—however well intentioned, at times a jumbled, noisy pathos of all sorts, esthetics, ethics, Religiousness *A,* and Christianity—it is therefore at times self-contradictory; "but there are lovely passages in it," especially lovely for the person who is supposed to act and exist according to it. The dialectical has its revenge by covertly and ironically mocking the gestures and big words, and above all by its ironic critique of a religious address—that it can very well be heard, but it cannot be done.

Scientific scholarship wants to take charge of the dialectical and to that end bring it over into the medium of abstraction, whereby the issue is again mistreated, since it is an existence-issue, and the actual dialectical difficulty disappears by being explained in the medium of abstraction, which ignores existence. If the turbulent religious address is for sentimental people who are quick to sweat and to be sweated out, then the speculative interpretation is for pure thinkers; but neither of the two is for acting and, by virtue of acting, for existing human beings.

The distinction between the pathos-filled and the dialectical must, however, be qualified more specifically, because Religiousness *A* is by no means undialectical, but it is not paradoxically dialectical. Religiousness *A* is the dialectic of inward deepening; it is the relation to an eternal happiness that is not conditioned by a something but is the dialectical inward deepening of the relation, consequently conditioned only by the inward deepening, which is dialectical. On the other hand, Religiousness *B,* as it will be called from now on, or paradoxical religiousness, as it has been called, or the religiousness that has the dialectical in second place,[105] makes conditions in such a way that the conditions are not the dialectical concentrations of inward deepening but a definite something that qualifies the eternal happiness more specifically (whereas in *A* the more specific qualification of inward deepening is the only more specific qualification), not by qualifying more specifically the individual's appropriation of it but by qualifying more specifically the eternal happiness, yet not as a task for thinking but as paradoxically repelling and giving rise to new pathos.

Religiousness *A* must first be present in the individual before there can be   VII
any consideration of becoming aware of the dialectical *B*. When the indi-   485
vidual in the most decisive expression of existential pathos relates himself to an eternal happiness, then there can be consideration of becoming aware of how the dialectical in second place (*secundo loco*) thrusts him down into the pathos of the absurd. Thus it is evident how foolish it is if a person without pathos wants to relate himself to the essentially Christian, because before there can be any question at all of simply being in the situation of becoming aware of it one must first of all exist in Religiousness *A*. But often enough the mistake has been made of making capital, as a matter of course, of Christ and Christianity and the paradoxical and the absurd, that is, all the essentially Christian, in esthetic gibberish. This is just as if Christianity were a tidbit for dunces because it cannot be thought, and just as if the very qualification that it cannot be thought is not the most difficult of all to hold fast when one is to exist in it—the most difficult to hold fast, especially for brainy people.

Religiousness *A* can be present in paganism, and in Christianity it can be the religiousness of everyone who is not decisively Christian, whether baptized or not. Of course, to become a *wohlfeil* [cheap] edition of a Christian in all comfort is much easier, and just as good as the highest—after all, he is baptized, has received a copy of the Bible and a hymnbook as a gift; is he not, then, a Christian, an Evangelical Lutheran Christian? But that remains the business of the person involved. In my opinion, Religiousness *A* (within the boundaries of which I have my existence) is so strenuous for a human being that there is always a sufficient task in it.

Note: Insofar as the upbuilding is the essential predicate of all religiousness,   VII
Religiousness *A* also has its upbuilding. Wherever the relationship with God   486
is found by the existing person in the inwardness of subjectivity, there is the upbuilding, which belongs to subjectivity, whereas by becoming objective one relinquishes that which, although belonging to subjectivity, is neverthe-   VII
less no more arbitrariness than erotic love and being in love, which indeed   488
one also relinquishes by becoming objective. The totality of guilt-consciousness is the most upbuilding element in Religiousness *A*.* The upbuilding el-

---

* The reader will please recall that the direct relationship with God is esthetics and is actually no relationship with God, any more than a direct relation to the absolute is an absolute relation, since the separation of the absolute has not commenced. In the religious sphere, the positive is distinguishable by the negative. The highest well-being of a happy immediacy, which jubilates joy over God and all existence, is very endearing but not upbuilding and essentially not any relationship with God.

ement in the sphere of Religiousness *A* is that of immanence, is the annihilation in which the individual sets himself aside in order to find God, since it is the individual himself who is the hindrance.* Here the upbuilding is quite properly distinguishable by the negative, by the self-annihilation that finds the relationship with God within itself, that suffering-through sinks into the relationship with God, finds its ground in it, because God is in the ground only when everything that is in the way is cleared out, every finitude, and first and foremost the individual himself in his finitude, in his cavilling against God. Esthetically, the sacred resting place of the upbuilding is outside the individual; he seeks that place. In the ethical-religious sphere, the individual himself is the place, if the individual has annihilated himself.

This is the upbuilding in the sphere of Religiousness *A*. If one does not pay attention to this and to having this qualification of the upbuilding in between, everything is confused again as one defines the paradoxical upbuilding, which then is mistakenly identified with an external esthetic relation. In Religiousness *B*, the upbuilding is something outside the individual; the individual does not find the upbuilding by finding the relationship with God within himself but relates himself to something outside himself in order to find the upbuilding. The paradox is that this apparently esthetic relationship, that the individual relates himself to something outside himself, nevertheless is to be the absolute relationship with God, because in immanence God is neither a something, but everything, and is infinitely everything, nor outside the individual, because the upbuilding consists in his being within the individual. The paradoxical upbuilding therefore corresponds to the category of God in time as an individual human being, because, if that is the case, the individual relates himself to something outside himself. That this cannot be thought is precisely the paradox. Whether the individual is not thrust back from this is another matter—that remains his affair. But if the paradox is not held fast in this way, then Religiousness *A* is higher, and all Christianity is pushed back into esthetic categories, despite Christianity's insistence that the paradox it speaks about cannot be thought, is thus different from a relative paradox, which *höchstens* [at best] can be thought with difficulty. It must be conceded to speculative thought that it holds to immanence, even though it must be understood as different than Hegel's pure thinking, but speculative thought must not call itself Christian. That is why I have never called Religiousness *A* Christian or Christianity.

VII
489

VII
490

All interpretations of existence take their rank in relation to the qualification of the individual's dialectical inward deepening. Presupposing what

---

** The esthetic always consists in the individual's fancying that he has been busy reaching for God and taking hold of him, consequently in the illusion that the undialectical individual is really clever if he can take hold of God as something external.

has been developed on this subject in this book, I shall now only recapitulate and point out that of course speculative thought plays no role, since, as objective and abstract, it is indifferent to the category of the existing subjective individual and at most deals only with pure humanity. Existence-communication, however, understands something different by *unum* [one] in the saying *unum noris, omnes* [if you know one, you know all], understands something different by "yourself" in the phrase "know yourself," understands thereby an actual human being and indicates thereby that the existence-communication does not occupy itself with the anecdotal differences between Tom, Dick, and Harry.

If in himself the individual is undialectical and has his dialectic outside himself, then we have the *esthetic interpretations*. If the individual is dialectically turned inward in self-assertion in such a way that the ultimate foundation does not in itself become dialectical, since the underlying self is used to surmount and assert itself, then we have the *ethical interpretation*. If the individual is defined as dialectically turned inward in self-annihilation before God, then we have *Religiousness A*. If the individual is paradoxical-dialectical, every remnant of original immanence annihilated, and all connection cut away, and the individual situated at the edge of existence, then we have the *paradoxical-religious*. This paradoxical inwardness is the greatest possible, because even the most dialectical qualification, if it is still within immanence, has, as it were, a possibility of an escape, of a shifting away, of a withdrawal into the eternal behind it; it is as if everything were not actually at stake. But the break makes the inwardness the greatest possible.* VII 498

The various existence-communications in turn take their rank in relation to the interpretation of existing. (As abstract and objective, speculative thought completely disregards existing and inwardness and, since Christianity indeed paradoxically accentuates existing, is the greatest possible misunderstanding of Christianity.) *Immediacy, the esthetic,* finds no contradiction in existing; to exist is one thing, contradiction is something else that comes from without. *The ethical* finds contradiction but within self-assertion. *Religiousness A* comprehends contradiction as suffering in self-annihilation, yet within immanence; but, ethically accentuating existing, it hinders the existing person in abstractly remaining in immanence or in becoming abstract by wanting to remain in immanence. The *paradoxical-religious* breaks with immanence and makes existing the absolute contradiction—not within immanence but in opposition to immanence. There is no immanental underlying kinship between the temporal and the eternal, because the eternal itself has entered into time and wants to establish kinship there.

---

* According to this plan, one will be able to orient oneself and, without being disturbed by anyone's use of Christ's name and the whole Christian terminology in an esthetic discourse, will be able to look only at the categories.

APPENDIX

AN UNDERSTANDING WITH THE READER

The undersigned, Johannes Climacus, who has written this book, does not make out that he is a Christian; for he is, to be sure, completely preoccupied with how difficult it must be to become one; but even less is he one who, after having been a Christian, ceases to be that by going further. He is a humorist; satisfied with his circumstances at the moment, hoping that something better will befall his lot, he feels especially happy, if worst comes to worst, to be born in this speculative, theocentric century. Yes, our age is an age for speculative thinkers and great men with matchless discoveries, and yet I think that none of those honorable gentlemen can be as well off as a private humorist is in secret, whether, isolated, he beats his breast or laughs quite heartily. Therefore he can very well be an author, if only he sees to it that it is for his own enjoyment, that he remains in isolation, that he does not take up with the crowd, does not become lost in the importance of the age, as an inquisitive spectator at a fire be assigned to pump, or merely be disconcerted by the thought that he might stand in the way of any of the various distinguished people who have and ought to have and must have and insist upon having importance.

In the isolation of the imaginary construction, the whole book is about myself, simply and solely about myself. "I, Johannes Climacus, now thirty years old, born in Copenhagen, a plain, ordinary human being like most people, have heard it said that there is a highest good in store that is called an eternal happiness, and that Christianity conditions this upon a person's relation to it. I now ask: How do I become a Christian?"

A FIRST AND LAST EXPLANATION

For the sake of form and order, I hereby acknowledge, something that really can scarcely be of interest to anyone to *know,* that I am, as is said, the author of *Either/Or* (Victor Eremita), Copenhagen, February 1843; *Fear and Trembling* (Johannes de Silentio), 1843; *Repetition* (Constantin Constantius), 1843; *The Concept of Anxiety* (Vigilius Haufniensis), 1844; *Prefaces* (Nicolaus Notabene), 1844; *Philosophical Fragments* (Johannes Climacus), 1844; *Stages on Life's Way* (Hilarius Bookbinder—William Afham, the Judge, Frater Taciturnus), 1845; *Concluding Postscript to* Philosophical Fragments (Johannes Climacus), 1846; an article in *Fædrelandet,* January 1846 (Frater Taciturnus).

My pseudonymity or polyonymity has not had an *accidental* basis in my *person* (certainly not from a fear of penalty under the law, in regard to which I am not aware of any offense, and simultaneously with the publication of a book the printer and the censor *qua* public official have always been officially informed who the author was) but an *essential* basis in the *production* itself, which, for the sake of the lines and of the psychologically varied differences of the individualities, poetically required an indiscriminateness with regard to good and evil, brokenheartedness and gaiety, despair and overconfidence, suffering and elation, etc., which is ideally limited only by psychological consistency, which no factually actual person dares to allow himself or can want to allow himself in the moral limitations of actuality. What has been written, then, is mine, but only insofar as I, by means of audible lines, have placed the life-view of the crea*ting*, poetically actual individuality in his mouth, for my relation is even more remote than that of a poet, who *poetizes* characters and yet in the preface is *himself* the *author.* That is, I am impersonally or personally in the third person a *souffleur* [prompter] who has poetically produced the *authors,* whose *prefaces* in turn are their productions, as their *names* are also. Thus in the pseudonymous books there is not a single word by me. I have no opinion about them except as a third party, no knowledge of their meaning except as a reader, not the remotest private relation to them, since it is impossible to have that to a doubly reflected communication. A single word by me personally in my own name would be an arrogating self-forgetfulness that, regarded dialectically, would be guilty of having essentially annihilated the pseudonymous authors by this one word. In *Either/Or,* I am just as little, precisely just as little, the editor Victor Eremita as I am the Seducer or the Judge. He is a poetically actual subjective thinker who is found again in "*In Vino Veritas.*" In *Fear and Trembling,* I am just as little, precisely just as little, Johannes de Silentio as the knight of faith he depicts, and in turn jut as little the author of the preface to the book, which is the individuality-lines of a poetically actual subjective thinker. In the story of suffering ("'Guilty?'/'Not Guilty?'"), I am just as remote from being Quidam of the imaginary construction as from being the imaginative constructor, just as remote, since the imaginative constructor is a poetically actual subjective thinker and what is imaginatively constructed is his psychologically consistent production. Thus I am the indifferent, that is, what and how I am are matters of indifference, precisely because in turn the question, whether in my innermost being it is also a matter of indifference to me what and how I am, is absolutely irrelevant to this production. Therefore, in many an enterprise that is not dialectically reduplicated, that which can otherwise have its fortunate importance in beautiful agreement with the distinguished person's enterprise would here have only a disturbing effect in connection with the altogether indifferent foster father of a perhaps not undistinguished production. My facsimile, my picture, etc., like the question whether I wear a hat or a cap, could become an object of attention only for those to whom the indifferent has become important—perhaps in compensation because the important has become a matter of indifference to them.

VII
[545]

In a legal and in a literary sense, the responsibility is mine,* but, easily understood dialectically, it is I who have *occasioned* the audibility of the production in the world of actuality, which of course cannot become involved with poetically actual authors and therefore altogether consistently and with absolute legal and literary right looks to me. Legal and literary, because all poetic creation would *eo ipso* be made impossible or meaningless and intolerable if the lines were supposed to be the producer's own words (literally understood). Therefore, if it should occur to anyone to want to quote a particular passage from the books, it is my wish, my prayer, that he will do me the kindness of citing the respective pseudonymous author's name, not mine—that is, of separating us in such a way that the passage femininely belongs to the pseudonymous author, the responsibility civilly to me. From the beginning, I have been well aware and am aware that my personal actuality is a constraint that the pseudonymous authors in pathos-filled willfulness might wish removed, the sooner the better, or made as insignificant as possible, and yet in turn, ironically attentive, might wish to have present as the repelling opposition.

VII
[546]

My role is the joint role of being the secretary and, quite ironically, the dialectically reduplicated author of the author or the authors. Therefore, although probably everyone who has been concerned at all about such things has until now *summarily* regarded me as the author of the pseudonymous books even before the explanation was at hand, the explanation will perhaps at first prompt the odd impression that I, who indeed ought to know it best, am the only one who only very doubtfully and equivocally regards me as the author, because I am the author in the figurative sense; but on the other hand I am very literally and directly the author of, for example, the upbuilding discourses and of every word in them. The poetized author has his definite life-view, and the lines, which understood in this way could possibly be meaningful, witty, stimulating, would perhaps sound strange, ludicrous, disgusting in the mouth of a particular factual person. If anyone unfamiliar with cultivated association with a distancing ideality, through a mistaken obtrusiveness upon my actual personality, has distorted for himself the impression of the pseudonymous books, has fooled himself, *actually* has fooled himself, by being encumbered with my personal actuality instead of having the light, doubly reflected ideality of a poetically actual author to dance with; if with paralogistic obtrusiveness anyone has deceived himself by meaninglessly drawing my private particularity out of the evasive dialectical duplexity of the qualitative contrasts—this cannot be truly charged to me, who, properly and in the interest of the purity of the relation, have from my side done everything,

---

* For this reason my name as editor was first placed on the title page of *Fragments* (1844), because the absolute significance of the subject required in actuality the expression of dutiful attention, that there was a named person responsible for taking upon himself what actuality might offer.

as well as I could, to prevent what an inquisitive part of the reading public has from the very beginning done everything to achieve—in whose interest, God knows.

The opportunity seems to invite an open and direct explanation, yes, almost to demand it even from one who is reluctant—so, then, I shall use it for that purpose, not as an author, because I am indeed not an author in the usual sense, but as one who has cooperated so that the pseudonyms could become authors. First of all, I want to give thanks to Governance, who in such multitudinous ways has encouraged my endeavor, has encouraged it over four and one-quarter years without perhaps a single day's interruption of effort, has granted me much more than I had ever expected, even though I can truly testify that I staked my life to the utmost of my capacity, more than I at least had expected, even if to others the accomplishment seems to be a complicated triviality. So, with fervent thanks to Governance, I do not find it unsettling that I cannot quite be said to have achieved anything or, what is of less importance, attained anything in the outer world. I find it ironically in order that the honorarium, at least, in virtue of the production and of my equivocal authorship, has been rather Socratic.

VII
[547]

Next, after properly having asked for pardon and forgiveness if it appears inappropriate that I speak in this way, although he himself would perhaps find omission of it inappropriate, I want to call to mind, in recollecting gratitude, my deceased father, the man to whom I owe most of all, also with regard to my work.

With this I take leave of the pseudonymous authors with doubtful good wishes for their future fate, that this, if it is propitious for them, will be just as they might wish. Of course, I know them from intimate association; I know they could not expect or desire many readers—would that they might happily find the few desirable readers.

Of my reader, if I dare to speak of such a one, I would in passing request for myself a forgetful remembrance, a sign that it is of me that he is reminded, because he remembers me as irrelevant to the books, as the relationship requires, just as the appreciation for it is sincerely offered here in the moment of farewell, when I also cordially thank everyone who has kept silent and with profound veneration thank the firm Kts[106]—that it has spoken.

Insofar as the pseudonymous authors might have affronted any respectable person in any way whatever, or perhaps even any man I admire, insofar as the pseudonymous authors in any way whatever might have disturbed or made ambiguous any actual good in the established order—then there is no one more willing to make an apology than I, who bear the responsibility for the use of the guided pen. What I in one way or another know about the pseudonymous authors of course does not entitle me to any opinion, but not to any doubt, either, of their assent, since their importance (whatever that may become *actually*) unconditionally does not consist in making any new proposal, some unheard-of-discovery, or in founding a new party and wanting to go further, but precisely in the opposite, in wanting to have no importance, in wanting, at a remove that is the distance of double-reflection, once again to read through solo, if possible in a more inward way, the original text of individual human existence-relationships, the old familiar text handed down from the fathers.

VII
[548] Oh, would that no ordinary seaman[107] will lay a dialectical hand on this work but let it stand as it now stands.

Copenhagen, *February 1846*

S. Kierkegaard.

"THE ACTIVITY OF A TRAVELING ESTHETICIAN AND HOW HE STILL HAPPENED TO PAY FOR THE DINNER" (DECEMBER 27, 1845) BY FRATER TACITURNUS

The most renowned literary controversy in Denmark was precipitated by one Latin line in Frater Taciturnus's article on P. L. Møller, a collaborator on *The Corsair.* The immediate occasion was Møller's review of Kierkegaard's *Stages on Life's Way,* a review Georg Brandes characterized as "frivolous, because its author had made no attempt whatsoever to put himself into what he wrote about, and dishonorable because it (under the guise of evaluating Kierkegaard's authorship), as is customary in this kind of article, dealt with street gossip about his private life, accused the hero in the diary of 'placing his betrothed on the experimental rack, of dissecting her alive, of torturing her soul out of her drop by drop,' all of which accusations were made as if directed against Kierkegaard himself."[108] Møller had misunderstood the use in *Stages* of the phrase "*Experimenter og uvirkelige Constructioner* [imaginary constructions and unreal fabrications]."[109] The meaning of *Experiment* is made clear in the footnote in the article.[110]

P. L. Møller, not least through his own published autobiographical sketch, was known to be associated with *The Corsair.* The Latin line at the end of the article was, therefore, not a disclosure of an unknown relationship but part of Kierkegaard's challenge to Møller and the editor of *The Corsair,* Meïr Goldschmidt, because of the misuse of the comic and satire as "a characterless instrument of envy and demoralization" (*JP* III 2417; *Pap.* IX A 30). Furthermore, as an anonymous, gossipy, and at times libelous invasion of privacy, *The Corsair* maintained a "reign of terror."[111] Kierkegaard had high expectations for Goldschmidt and his use of his talents, and Goldschmidt admired Kierkegaard, who laid down the challenge in order to separate Goldschmidt from *The Corsair* and in an "action-response in personal costume"[112] "to benefit others by this step."[113]

The Corsair had always treated Kierkegaard's pseudonymous writings with guarded appreciation, and even "immortalized" Victor Eremita.[114] Now, however, after Taciturnus's "would that I might only get into *The Corsair* soon," a long series of devastating cartoons and articles appeared in this publication with the largest circulation in Denmark. Taunted in the streets, Kierkegaard could no longer be the foremost peripatetic in Copenhagen. But he accomplished his aims. After a wordless penetrating glance, "that moment packed with meaning," when the two met on the street a few months later, Goldschmidt on the way home decided to "give up *The Corsair.*"[115] *The Corsair* continued for a time but was never the same in kind and influence. Both Møller and Goldschmidt left the country. When Goldschmidt returned, he founded the journal *Nord og Syd,* quite different from *The Corsair.* The episode had another, unintended, consequence: *Postscript,* instead of being a conclusion, became the midpoint in an authorship that began again with more signed works and a few pseudonymous works distinguished from the earlier pseudonymous writings. Without the bruising controversy, would the so-called "second authorship" have emerged? *O felix culpa!*

ALTHOUGH New Year's Day callers are extending more and more the time for their courtesy calls, which properly were limited to New Year's Day, these calls still are more or less limited to a period of eight days. It is quite otherwise with our enterprising and venturesome man of letters, Mr. P. L. Møller, playing the role of the New Year's well-wisher. Long in advance, he begins going around paying courtesy calls and gathering charitable donations to his splendid New Year's gift (*Gæa*); yes, he even travels out in the country. If he does not collect anything or just a little, or if the paucity of copious and weighty contributions by the renowned indicates that his New Year's gift is lacking in plenitude, he fills it out with conversations he has had in his travels out in the country. Basically, it is a very economical way to travel, one that never occurred to me, having always regarded traveling as very expensive, and perhaps one that would not occur to many others besides Mr. P. L. Møller, for, after all, thriftiness, too, can be carried too far. One takes a trip to Sorø, as Mr. P. L. M. did (according to *Gæa 1846*), visits Prof. Hauch, is received by the distinguished poet with Danish hospitality. One helps oneself to the dishes served, and although very stingy people generally pinch a little food, a piece of meat in the pocket and some cake in the hat, Mr. P. L. M. is so voracious that he takes along the whole conversation and has it printed—thus it is paid for, yes, more than paid for, and since the repast did not cost anything, it is clear profit. If Trop had known about this way of traveling, he would not have suffered so much from want, for even if he had been given the brushoff in the famous man's waiting room, he still could have made a little by having the famous man's words printed. No sponging traveling salesman can travel so lucratively, for he can take away only the orders; yes, no gluttonous tithe collector can do it more advantageously—Mr. P. L. M. has the advantage that not a word is wasted: it all comes out in the New Year's gift.

   In the conversation our traveling esthetician had down there, my writing also became a subject for discussion. In that way, I, too, contributed my bit to the New Year's gift by providing him the occasion for some effusions after dinner. Let him have it. After all, my contribution is very figurative, for, since everything he says is not only a confusion (a rephrasing of the difficulty of the task, which the book itself far more strongly emphasized, into an objection to the way the task was dealt with)* but even abounds in factual un-

XIII 423 * In itself the confusion is quite amusing, and since it is not so dialectically difficult that it cannot easily and entertainingly be portrayed on one page, I shall do it here. An imaginative constructor [*Experimentator*] says: In order to become properly aware of what is decisive in the religious existence-categories, since religiousness is very often confused with all sorts of things and with apathy, I shall imaginatively construct [*experimentere*] a character who lives in a final and extreme approximation of madness but tends toward the religious. The imaginative constructor himself says that the point of view of the imaginatively constructed character [*Experimenterede*] is a deviation but adds that he is doing the whole imaginary construction [*Experiment*] in order to study normality by means of the passion of deviation (p. 309). He himself declares that it is a very strenuous task to hold the imaginatively constructed character [*Experimenterede*] at this extremity while he himself supervises imaginatively constructively. The dif-

XIII 423 (margin)

XIII 424 (margin)

truths on the most crucial points, I actually am unable to say that it is my book he is talking about, except insofar as he mentions its title and in fulfillment reminds me of its prophetic motto: "Solche Wercke sind Spiegel; wenn ein Affe hineinguckt, kann kein Apostel heraussehen" [Such works are mirrors: when an ape looks in, no apostle can look out] (Lichtenberg).[116]

If there is anything distasteful in Mr. P. L. Møller's enterprise, it is more the affront to a poet like Prof. Hauch and his private life. The fact that the scene takes place in the house of Prof. Hauch and he takes part in the conversation naturally gives this interest. But it still seems somewhat offensive to make recompense in this way for—yes, for what?—for being received with hospitality by a famous man. Fortunately, there is in it not one single comment from Prof. Hauch about my writing, which pleases me just as much for the professor's sake as for my own. Be it positive or negative, a comment from him always carries weight, as does every legitimate authority's. It must and ought not be weakened and rendered dubious by ambiguity so that one cannot know which is which, because Prof. Hauch may well have said it but did not say it in *Gøea,* and P. L. Møller probably said it but yet did not say it, since in *Gøea* he said only that Prof. Hauch had said it in his living room. What a twisted misrelation between the judgment of an authority and this irresponsibility!

Now, however, everything is in order. I certainly have no objection to make, either against Mr. P. L. M.'s actually having said that, for, after all, he himself must know that best, or against the comment being his actual opinion, about which I am not one bit curious. If the defense is that what Mr. P. L. M. really meant and was talking about was a work dealing with the double-dialectic of religiousness on the edge of a transitional crisis, then I

XIII
425

---

ficulty is to keep the imaginatively constructed character at the terminal point where it never becomes madness but is constantly on the brink. Now comes Mr. P. L. Møller's charge: "It is almost insanity, it is the preliminary stage of madness." Reply: Absolutely right, that is precisely the difficulty of the task. Consequently, the charge is an acknowledgment, which I do not deny is slight, for, after all, it is Mr. P. L. Møller's, but on the other hand it perhaps is Mr. P. L. M.'s maximum. Presumably he will be capable of appreciating a dialectical work that is as crucial and decisive as my imaginary construction only when he himself is unaware that he is doing it, when after dinner he blissfully imagines that he is attacking it. After dinner—for I certainly assume that the same will happen to him after reading it, but nevertheless I hold to the given fact that it was after dinner; this stipulation is less indefinite and completely reliable. After dinner he attacks the imaginary construction, he charges it with bordering on insanity, but that was just exactly what the imaginary construction intended. Consequently, his attack is the defense, which I do not deny is insignificant, for, after all, it comes from Mr. P. L. Møller, but for him the precarious maximum of the vehemence of an attack is always that it becomes a defense. He has finished the imaginary construction; in fact, he judges it, and what is his judgment? That it borders on insanity. But that was precisely the task; so he is back at the beginning. And what does his judgment signify? Well, at most it means: It is a very difficult task. Reply: Without a doubt, Mr. P. L. Møller, and since it is after dinner and you no doubt already have thanked Professor Hauch for the food, I shall wish you: *velbekomme.*[117]

XIII
424

shall be always satisfied. A retraction of his opinion could not have as much significance to me as a solemn assurance that he really has an especially negative opinion.

You see, I refuse to give the impression that I am discussing the imaginary construction and its dialectic with Mr. P. L. Møller. No, we two talk about utterly different matters, about the trip to Sorø, the stagecoach, the driver, the meals and the drinks, the packasses, and other such popular subjects that do not exceed Mr. P. L. Møller's powers of comprehension. The real reader of the imaginary construction will readily discover that what I have written here is of a different nature and can be read right away by anyone. Therefore, I am not insulting any newspaper reader by leading him into inquiries that cannot interest him and that cannot be dealt with in a newspaper. An interpretation of Mr. P. L. Møller's journey to Sorø should not be dialectically difficult; neither should one ponder too profoundly, for that is the very way to a misunderstanding. But however much I find the joy of infinity in the occupation of thought and know that my joy is due to my being contented with it, even if no one shares my joy, I still have not given up psychological familiarity with actual people. Such an actual person is Mr. P. L. Møller. But obtrusive as he is and known to many, I thought that a little interpretation like this would not be wholly devoid of interest to readers of a newspaper. I really believed, too, that I would be doing some people a service[118] thereby, but I do not insist that this service be appreciated, least of all by someone who for that reason would read a little in my book or buy a copy. For what I said in my note to the reader (p. 309),[119] "One does not buy admission to these performances for a lump sum," I repeat here without danger. After all, why should he be angry who has found his desire for the infinite satisfied, found what will occupy him day and night, even if it pleased God to increase the length of the day another 12 hours! He who is capti-

vated by what captivates him eternally, even though he has much left to gain, is not disturbed, and I repeat unaltered the words of farewell (p. 377):[120] "Satisfied with the lesser, hoping that possibly sometime the greater will be granted me, I am happy in existence, happy in the little world that surrounds me." When I wrote that, I knew very well that there are such as Mr. P. L. Møller and *The Corsair,* and, indeed, I knew very well what I wrote. Such persons are not part of my environment, and no matter how obtrusive and rude they are, it makes no difference; this does not disturb my joy over the little world that constitutes my surroundings. On the contrary, the obtrusiveness helps me to enjoy my surroundings more deeply.

Would that I might only get into *The Corsair* soon. It is really hard for a poor author to be so singled out in Danish literature that he (assuming that we pseudonyms are one) is the only one who is not abused there. My superior, Hilarius Bookbinder, has been flattered in *The Corsair*,[121] if I am not mistaken; Victor Eremita has even had to experience the disgrace of being immortalized[122]—in *The Corsair!* And yet, I have already been there, for *ubi spiritus, ibi ecclesia* [where the spirit is, there is the Church]: *ubi* P. L. Møller, *ibi The Corsair.* Therefore our vagabond quite properly ends his "Visit to Sorø" with one of those loathesome *Corsair* attacks on peaceable, respectable men, each of whom in honest obscurity does his work in the service of the state, on men of distinction who have made themselves worthy in much and ridiculous in nothing, for as public figures authors have to put up with a great deal, including the imputation of a relation to people who by having something printed are also authors.

FRATER TACITURNUS
Chief of Part Three of
Stages on Life's Way

TWO AGES

THE AGE OF REVOLUTION AND THE PRESENT AGE

A LITERARY REVIEW (MARCH 30, 1846)

BY S. KIERKEGAARD

Having "concluded" his work as an author with *Postscript,* Kierkegaard had the idea of doing "the little writing I can excuse in the form of criticism." (In fact, he had already begun the review of Thomasine Gyllembourg-Ehrensvärd's *Two Ages,* regarded as the first modern Danish novel of significance.) "Then I would put down what I had to say in reviews, developing my ideas from some book or other and in such a way that they would be included in the work itself. In this way I would still avoid becoming an author."[123] The summation of his analysis of the Age of Revolution is that it is "essentially passionate; therefore it has *not nullified the principle of contradiction* and can become either good or evil, and whichever way is chosen, the *impetus* of passion is such that the trace of an action marking its progress or its taking a wrong direction must be perceptible. It is obliged to make a decision, but this again is the saving factor, for decision is the little magic word that existence respects."[124] The French Revolution, however, had gone astray.

The Present Age is characterized by disintegration, the dissolution of organic social structures, the process of leveling generated by envy and resentment, the nullification of the principle of contradiction, and domination by the media and a formless, abstract public. Devoid of essential passion, the age is marked by reflection in two ways: indecisive deliberation ("reflection") and the imaging ("reflexion") of the decadence of the age in private, domestic, and social-political life. Therefore, "if the age is reflective [in the double sense], devoid of passion, the public becomes the entity that is supposed to include everything. But once again this situation is the very expression of the fact that the single individual is assigned to himself."[125] Kierkegaard's analysis of the present age seems quite applicable also at the end of the twentieth century.

THE PRESENT AGE

Again the task here, as I see it, in critical service to the novel, is to advance in a more general observation the specific elements that the author has depicted with literary skill.

The present age is essentially a *sensible, reflecting*[126] *age, devoid of passion, flaring up in superficial, short-lived enthusiasm and prudentially relaxing in indolence.*

In contrast to the age of revolution, which took action, the present age is an age of publicity, the age of miscellaneous announcements: nothing happens but still there is instant publicity. An insurrection in this day and age is utterly unimaginable; such a manifestation of power would seem ridiculous to the calculating sensibleness of the age. However, a political virtuoso might be able to perform an amazing tour de force of quite another kind. He would issue invitations to a general meeting for the purpose of deciding on a revolution, wording the invitation so cautiously that even the censor would have to let it pass. On the evening of the meeting, he would so skillfully create the illusion that they had made a revolution that everyone would go home quietly, having passed a very pleasant evening. Acquiring a profound and capacious learning would be practically unthinkable for young people today; they would consider it ludicrous. A scientific virtuoso, however, would be able to negotiate a radically different tour de force. He would casually outline a few features of a comprehensive system and do it in such a way that the reader (of the prospectus) would get the impression that he had already read the system. The age of the encyclopedists, the men who indefatigably wrote folios, is over; now it is the turn of the lightly equipped encyclopedists who dispose of the whole of existence and all the sciences *en passant*. A penetrating religious renunciation of the world and what is of the world, adhered to in daily self-denial, would be inconceivable to the youth of our day; every second theological graduate, however, has enough virtuosity to do something far more marvelous. He is able to found a social institution with no less a goal than to save all who are lost. VIII 67

The age of great and good actions is past; the present age is the age of anticipation. No one is willing to be satisfied with doing something specific; everyone wants to luxuriate in the daydream that he at least may discover a new part of the world. Ours is an age of anticipation; even appreciative acknowledgment is accepted in advance. Just like a young man who, having resolved to study earnestly for his exams after September 1, fortifies himself for it by taking a vacation in the month of August, so the present generation—and this is much more difficult to understand—seems to have determined in earnest that the next generation must attend to the work in earnest, and in order not to frustrate or deter them in any way, the present generation attends banquets. But there is a difference: the young man understands that his enterprises are rash and reckless; the present age is sober and serious—even at banquets.

Action and decision are just as scarce these days as is the fun of swimming dangerously for those who swim in shallow water. Just as an adult, himself reveling in the tossing waves, calls to those younger: "Come on out, just jump in quickly"—just so does decision lie in existence, so to speak (although, of course, it is in the individual), and shouts to the youth who is not yet enervated by too much reflection and overwhelmed by the delusions of reflection: "Come on out, jump in boldly." Even if it is a rash leap, if only it is decisive, and if you have the makings of a man, the danger and life's severe judgment upon your recklessness will help you to become one.

That a person stands or falls on his actions is becoming obsolete; instead everybody sits around and does a brilliant job of bungling through with the VIII 69

aid of some reflection and also by declaring that they all know very well what
has to be done. But what people two by two in conversation, what individuals as readers or as participants in a general assembly understand brilliantly
in the form of reflection and observation, they would be utterly unable to
understand in the form of action. If someone went around listening to what
others said ought to be done and then with a sense of irony, *mir nichts und dir
nichts* [without so much as asking leave], did something about it, everybody
would be taken aback, would find it rash. And as soon as they started thinking and conversing about it, they would realize that it was just what should
have been done.

VIII
70

The present age with its flashes of enthusiasm alternating with apathetic
indolence, which at most likes to joke, comes very close to being comical;
but anyone who understands the comic readily sees that the comic does not
consist at all in what the present age imagines it does and that satire in our
day, if it is to be at all beneficial and not cause irreparable harm, must have
the resource of a consistent and well-grounded ethical view, a sacrificial un-
selfishness, and a high-born nobility that renounce the moment; otherwise
the medicine becomes infinitely and incomparably worse than the sickness.
What is really comical is that such an age even aspires to be witty and make
a big splash in the comic, for that is certainly the ultimate and most phan-
tasmagoric escape. In terms of the comic, what is there to flout, anyway, for
an age played out in reflection? As an age without passion it has no assets of
feeling in the erotic, no assets of enthusiasm and inwardness in politics and
religion, no assets of domesticity, piety, and appreciation in daily life and social life. But existence mocks the wittiness that possesses no assets, even
though the populace laughs shrilly. To aspire to wittiness without possessing
the wealth of inwardness is like wanting to be prodigal on luxuries and to
dispense with the necessities of life; as the proverb puts it, it is selling one's
trousers and buying a wig. But an age without passion possesses no assets;
everything becomes, as it were, transactions in *paper money*. Certain phrases
and observations circulate among the people, partly true and sensible, yet devoid of vitality, but there is no hero, no lover, no thinker, no knight of faith,
no great humanitarian, no person in despair to vouch for their validity by
having primitively experienced them. Just as in our business transactions we
long to hear the ring of real coins after the whisper of paper money, so we
today long for a little primitivity. But what is more primitive than wit, more
primitive, at least more amazing, than even the first spring bud and the first
delicate blade of grass? Yes, even if spring were to come according to a prior
arrangement, it would still be spring, but a witticism by prior arrangement
would be an abomination. Suppose, then, that as a relief from the feverish-
ness of flaring enthusiasm a point were reached where wit, that divine happening, that bonus given by divine cue from the enigmatic origins of the inexplicable, so that not even the wittiest person who ever lived would dare to

say: "Tomorrow," but would devoutly say: "God-willing"—suppose that wit VIII
71
were changed to its most trite and hackneyed opposite, a trifling necessity of
life, so that it would become a profitable industry to fabricate and make up
and renovate and buy up in bulk old and new witticisms: what a frightful
epigram on the witty age!

So ultimately the object of desire is money, but it is in fact token money,
an abstraction. A young man today would scarcely envy another his capacities or his skill or the love of a beautiful girl or his fame, no, but he would
envy him his money. Give me money, the young man will say, and I will be
all right. And the young man will not do anything rash, he will not do anything he has to repent of, he will not have anything for which to reproach
himself, but he will die in the illusion that if he had had money, then he
would have lived, then he certainly would have done something great.

A passionate, tumultuous age wants to *overthrow everything, set aside every-* VIII
73
thing. An age that is revolutionary but also reflecting and devoid of passion
changes the expression of power into a *dialectical tour de force: it lets everything
remain but subtly drains the meaning out of it; rather than culminating in an uprising, it exhausts the inner actuality of relations in a tension of reflection that lets everything remain and yet has transformed the whole of existence into an equivocation that
in its facticity is—while entirely privately [privatissime] a dialectical fraud interpolates
a secret way of reading—that it is not.*

Morality is character; character is something engraved (χαρασσω), but the
sea has no character, nor does sand, nor abstract common sense, either, for
character is inwardness. As energy, immorality is also character. But it is
equivocation to be neither one nor the other, and it is existential equivocation when the disjunction of the qualities is impaired by a gnawing reflection. An uprising motivated by passion is elemental; a disintegration motivated by equivocation is a quiet but busy sorites going day and night. The
distinction between good and evil is enervated by a loose, supercilious, theoretical acquaintance with evil, by an overbearing shrewdness which knows
that the good is not appreciated or rewarded in the world—and thus it practically becomes stupidity. No one is carried away to great exploits by the
good, no one is rushed into outrageous sin by evil, the one is just as good as
the other, and yet for that very reason there is all the more to gossip about,
for ambiguity and equivocation are titillating and stimulating and have many
more words than are possessed by joy over the good and the loathing of evil.

The coiled springs of life-relationships, which are what they are only because of qualitatively distinguishing passion, lose their resilience; the qualitative expression of difference between opposites is no longer the law for the
relation of inwardness to each other in the relation. Inwardness is lacking, VIII
74
and to that extent the relation does not exist or the relation is an inert co-
hesion. The negative law is: they cannot do without each other and they can-

not stay together; the positive law: they can do without each other and they can stay together, or more positively, they cannot do without each other because of the mutual bond. Instead of the relation of inwardness another relation supervenes: the opposites do not relate to each other but stand, as it were, and carefully watch each other, *and this tension is actually the termination of the relation*. This is not the cheerful, confident admiration, quick with words of appreciation, that tips its hat to distinction and now is shocked by its pride and arrogance; neither is it the opposite relation, by no means—admiration and distinction practically become a couple of courteous peers keeping a careful eye on each other. This is not the loyal citizen who cheerfully does homage to his king and now is embittered by his tyranny, not at all—to be a citizen has come to mean something else, it means to be an *outsider*. The citizen does not relate himself in the relation but is a spectator computing the problem: the relation of a subject to his king; for there is a period when committee after committee is set up, as long as there still are people who in full passion want to be, each individually, the specific person he is supposed to be, but it all finally ends with the whole age becoming a committee. This is not the father who indignantly concentrates his fatherly authority in one single curse or the son who defies, a rift that could still perhaps end in the inwardness of reconciliation. No, the relation as such is impeccable, for it is on its last legs inasmuch as they do not essentially relate to each other in the relation, but the relation itself has become a problem in which the parties like rivals in a game watch each other instead of relating to each other, and count, as it is said, each other's verbal avowals of relation as a substitute for resolute mutual giving in the relation. There is a period when more and more may renounce the modest but yet so satisfying and God-pleasing tasks of the more quiet life in order to implement something higher, in order to think over the relations in a higher relation, but finally the whole generation becomes a representation—which represents . . . . . well, there is no saying whom—which thinks over the relation . . . . . well, it is hard to say for whose sake. This is not an insubordinate adolescent who still quivers and quakes before his schoolmaster. No, the relation is rather a certain uniformity in mutual exchange between teacher and pupil on how a good school should be run. Going to school does not mean quivering and quaking, but neither does it mean simply and solely learning, but means being more or less interested in the problem of education. The relation of distinction between men and women is not violated in presumptuous licentiousness, by no means—decorum is observed in such a way that it may always be said of a particular instance of "innocent" borderline philandering: It is just a trifle.

VIII
75

The established order continues to stand, but since it is equivocal and ambiguous, passionless reflection is reassured. We do not want to abolish the monarchy, by no means, but if little by little we could get it transformed into

VIII
75

VIII
76

make-believe, we would gladly shout "Hurrah for the King!"We do not want to topple eminence, by no means, but if simultaneously we could spread the notion that it is all make-believe, we would approve and admire. In the same way we are willing to keep Christian terminology but privately know that nothing decisive is supposed to be meant by it. And we will not be repentant, for after all we are not demolishing anything. We do not want a powerful king any more than we want a liberator or a religious authority. No, quite harmlessly and inoffensively we allow the established order to go on, but in a reflective knowledge we are more or less aware of its nonexistence. We take pride in the fancy that this is irony, oblivious to the fact that in an era of negativity the authentic ironist is the hidden enthusiast (just as the hero is the manifest enthusiast in a positive era), that the authentic ironist is self-sacrificing, for, after all, that grand-master of irony[127] ended by being punished with death.

Ultimately the tension of reflection establishes itself as a principle, and just as *enthusiasm* is the unifying principle in a passionate age, so *envy* becomes the *negatively unifying principle* in a passionless and very reflective age. This must not promptly be interpreted ethically, as an accusation; no, reflection's idea, if it may be called that, is envy, and the envy is therefore two-sided, a selfishness in the individual and then again the selfishness of associates toward him. Reflection's envy in the individual frustrates an impassioned decision on his part, and if he is on the verge of decision, the reflective opposition of his associates stops him. Reflection's envy holds the will and energy in a kind of captivity. The individual must first of all break out of the prison in which his own reflection holds him, and if he succeeds, he still does not stand in the open but in the vast penitentiary built by the reflection of his associates, and to this he is again related through the reflection-relation in himself, and this can be broken only by religious inwardness, however much he sees through the falseness of the relation. But the fact that reflection is holding the individual and the age in a prison, the fact that it is reflection that does it and not tyrants and secret police, not the clergy and the aristocracy—reflection does everything in its power to thwart this discernment and maintains the flattering notion that the possibilities which reflection offers are much more magnificent than a paltry decision. In the form of desire, selfish envy demands too much of the individual himself and thereby frustrates him; it coddles and spoils him just as a weak mother's preferential love coddles and spoils, for his own envy prevents him from sacrificing himself. The envy of his associates, in which the individual himself participates towards others, is envious in the negatively critical sense.

VIII
77

But the longer this goes on, the more reflection's envy will turn into ethical envy. Entrapped air always becomes noxious, and the entrapment of reflection with no ventilating action or event develops censorious envy. While one's better energies are pitted against each other in a tension of reflection, meanness comes to the surface, its effrontery makes more or less an impression of power, and its contemptibility gives it a protected position of privilege simply because as such it avoids the attention of envy.

But the more reflection becomes dominant and develops indolence, the more dangerous envy becomes, because it no longer has the character to come to a self-awareness of its own significance. Lacking that character, it relates to events in equivocating cowardice and vacillation and reinterprets the same thing in all sorts of ways, wants it to be taken as a joke, and when that apparently miscarries, wants it to be taken as an insult, and if that miscarries, claims that nothing was meant at all, that it is supposed to be a witticism, and if that miscarries, explains that it was not meant to be that either, that it was ethical satire, which in fact ought to be of some concern to people, and if that miscarries, says that it is nothing anyone should pay any attention to. Envy turns into the principle of characterlessness, slyly sneaking up out of disrepute to make something of itself but constantly covering up by conceding that it is nothing at all. Characterless envy does not understand that excellence is excellence, does not understand that it is itself a negative acknowledgment of excellence but wants to degrade it, minimize it, until it

actually is no longer excellence, and envy takes as its object not only the excellence which *is* but that which *is to come*.

Envy in the process of *establishing* itself takes the form of *leveling*, and whereas a passionate age *accelerates, raises up and overthrows, elevates and debases*, a reflective apathetic age does the opposite, it *stifles and impedes, it levels*. Leveling is a quiet, mathematical, abstract enterprise that avoids all agitation. Although a flaring, short-lived enthusiasm might in discouragement wish for a calamity simply in order to have a sense of dynamic life forces, disturbance is of no more assistance to its successor, apathy, than it is to an engineer working with a surveyor's level. If an insurrection at its peak is so like a volcanic explosion that a person cannot hear himself speak, leveling at its peak is like a deathly stillness in which a person can hear himself breathe, a deathly stillness in which nothing can rise up but everything sinks down into it, impotent.

A particular individual can take the lead in an insurrection, but no particular individual can take the lead in leveling, for then he would, after all, become the commander and escape the leveling. Particular individuals may contribute to leveling, each in his own little group, but leveling is an abstract power and is abstraction's victory over individuals. In modern times leveling is reflection's correlative to fate in antiquity. The dialectic of antiquity was oriented to the eminent (the great individual—and then the crowd; one free man, and then the slaves); at present the dialectic of Christianity is oriented to representation (the majority perceive themselves in the representative and are liberated by the awareness that he is representing them in a kind of self-consciousness). The dialectic of the present age is oriented to equality, and its most logical implementation, albeit abortive, is leveling, the negative unity of the negative mutual reciprocity of individuals.

Anyone can see that leveling has its profound importance in the ascendancy of the category "generation" over the category "individuality." Whereas in antiquity the host of individuals existed, so to speak, in order to determine how much the excellent individual was worth, today the coinage standard has been changed so that about so and so many human beings *uniformly* make one individual; thus it is merely a matter of getting the proper number—and then one has significance. In antiquity the individual in the crowd had no significance whatsoever; the man of excellence stood for them all. The trend today is in the direction of mathematical equality, so that in all classes about so and so many uniformly make one individual. The eminent personage dared to consider everything permissible, the individuals in the crowd nothing at all. Nowadays we understand that so and so many people make one individual, and in all consistency we compute numbers (we call it joining together, but that is a euphemism) in connection with the most trivial things. For no other reason than to implement a whim, we add a few together and do it—that is, we dare to do it. VIII 80

No particular individual (the eminent personage by reason of excellence and the dialectic of fate) will be able to halt the abstraction of leveling, for it is a negatively superior force, and the age of heroes is past. No assemblage will be able to halt the abstraction of leveling, for in the context of reflection the assemblage itself is in the service of leveling. Not even national individuality will be able to halt it, for the abstraction of leveling is related to a higher negativity: pure humanity. The abstraction of leveling, this spontaneous combustion of the human race, produced by the friction that occurs when the separateness of individual inwardness in the religious life is omitted, will stay with us, as they say of a tradewind that consumes everything. Yet by means of it every individual, each one separately, may in turn be religiously educated, in the highest sense may be helped to acquire the essentiality of the religious by means of the *examen rigorosum* [rigorous examination] of leveling. For the younger person, however firmly he adheres to what he admires as excellent, who realizes from the beginning that leveling is what the selfish individual and the selfish generation meant for evil, but what also can be the point of departure for the highest life, especially for the individual who in honesty before God wills it—for him it will be genuinely educative to live in an age of leveling. In the highest sense contemporaneity will develop him religiously as well as esthetically and intellectually, because the comic will come to be radically evident. For it is extremely comic to see the particular individual classed under the infinite abstraction "pure humanity" without any middle term, since all the communal concretions of indi- VIII 81 VIII 82 viduality that temper the comic by relativity and strengthen the relative pathos are annihilated. But this again expresses the fact that rescue comes only through the essentiality of the religious in the particular individual. He will be encouraged to realize that the single individual who is high-minded enough to want it may find access to it through this very error. But the leveling must go in, it has to, just as offense must needs come into the world, but woe unto him by whom it comes.

It is frequently said that a reformation has to begin with each person's reformation of himself, but it has not happened that way, for the idea of reformation has given rise to a hero, who very likely bought his license to be a hero very dearly from God. By directly joining up with him, a few individuals get what was dearly bought at a better price, yes, at a good price, but then they do not get the highest, either. But, like the sharp northeaster, the abstraction of leveling is a principle that forms no personal, intimate relation to any particular individual, but only the relation of abstractions, which is the same for all. No hero, then, suffers for others or helps others; leveling itself becomes the severe taskmaster who takes on the task of educating. And the person who learns the most from the education and reaches the top does not become the man of distinction, the outstanding hero—this is forestalled by leveling, which is utterly consistent, and he prevents it himself because he has grasped the meaning of leveling—no, he only becomes an essentially human being in the full sense of equality. This is the idea of religiousness. But the education is rigorous and the returns are apparently very small—apparently, for if the individual is unwilling to learn to be satisfied with himself in the essentiality of the religious life before God, to be satisfied with ruling over himself instead of over the world, to be satisfied as a pastor to be his own audience, as an author to be his own reader, etc., if he is unwilling to learn to be inspired by this as supreme because it expresses equality before God and equality with all men, then he will not escape from reflection, then with all his endowments he may for one delusive moment believe that it is he who is doing the leveling, until he himself succumbs to the leveling. It will do no good to appeal to and summon a Holger Danske or a Martin Luther. Their age is past, and as a matter of fact it is indolence on the part of individuals to want such a one, it is a finite impatience that wants to have at cheap, second-hand prices the highest, which is dearly bought at first-hand. It will do no good to establish all sorts of organizations, for negatively something superior is introduced even though the myopic organization man cannot see it.

In its immediate and beautiful form, the principle of individuality prefigures the generation in the man of excellence, the leader, and has the subordinate individuals group around the representative. In its eternal truth, the principle of individuality uses the abstraction and equality of the generation as levelers and thereby religiously develops the cooperating individual into an essentially human being. For leveling is just as powerful with respect to the temporary as it is impotent with respect to the eternal. Reflection is a snare in which one is trapped, but in and through the inspired leap of religiousness the situation changes and it is the snare that catapults one into the embrace of the eternal. Reflection is and remains the most persistent, unyielding creditor in existence. Up to now it has cunningly bought up every possible outlook on life, but the eternal life-view of the essentially religious it cannot buy; however, by means of glittering illusion it can tempt everybody away from all else, and by means of reminding people of the past it can discourage them from all else. But through the leap out into the depths one learns to help himself, learns to love all others as much as himself even though he is accused of arrogance and pride—for not accepting help—or of selfishness—for being unwilling to deceive others by helping them, that is, by helping them miss what is highest of all.

VIII
84

If anyone declares that what I set forth here is common knowledge and can be said by anyone, my answer is: So much the better, I am not looking for prominence. I have nothing against everyone's knowing it, unless the fact that everyone knows it and can say it should mean that it is taken away from me and turned over to the negative community. As long as I have permission to keep it, its value for me is not depreciated by everyone's knowing it.

For a long time the basic tendency of our modern age has been toward leveling by way of numerous upheavals; yet none of them was leveling because none was sufficiently abstract but had a concretion of actuality. An approximate leveling can take place through a clash of leaders resulting in the weakening of both, or through one leader's neutralizing the other, or through the union of the essentially weaker ones so they become stronger than the foremost leader. An approximate leveling can be accomplished by a particular social class or profession, for example, the clergy, the middle class, the farmers, by the people themselves, but all this is still only the movement of abstraction within the concretions of individuality.

For leveling really to take place, a phantom must first be raised, the spirit of leveling, a monstrous abstraction, and all-encompassing something that is nothing, a mirage—and this phantom is *the public.* Only in a passionless but reflective age can this phantom develop with the aid of the press, when the press itself becomes a phantom. There is no such thing as a public in spirited, passionate, tumultuous times, even when a people wants to actualize the idea of the barren desert, destroying and demoralizing everything. There are parties, and there is concretion. In such times the press will take on the character of a concretion in relation to the division. But just as sedentary professionals are particularly prone to fabricating fantastic illusions, so a sedentary reflective age devoid of passion will produce this phantom if the press is supposed to be the only thing which, though weak itself, maintains a kind of life in this somnolence. The public is the actual master of leveling, for

VIII
85

when there is approximate leveling, something is doing the leveling, but the public is a monstrous nonentity.

The public is a concept that simply could not have appeared in antiquity, because the people were obliged to come forward *en masse in corpore* [as a whole] in the situation of action, were obliged to bear the responsibility for what was done by individuals in their midst, while in turn the individual was obliged to be present in person as the one specifically involved and had to submit to the summary court for approval or disapproval. Only when there is no strong communal life to give substance to the concretion will the press create this abstraction "the public," made up of unsubstantial individuals who are never united or never can be united in the simultaneity of any situation or organization and yet are claimed to be a whole. The public is a corps, out-numbering all the people together, but this corps can never be called up for inspection; indeed, it cannot even have so much as a single representative, be-cause it is itself an abstraction. Nevertheless, if the age is reflective, devoid of passion, obliterating everything that is concrete, the public becomes the en-tity that is supposed to include everything. But once again this situation is the very expression of the fact that the single individual is assigned to himself.

Contemporaneity with actual persons, each of whom is someone, in the actuality of the moment and the actual situation gives support to the single individual. But the existence of a public creates no situation and no com-munity. After all, the single individual who reads is not a public, and then gradually many individuals read, perhaps all do, but there is no contempo-raneity. The public may take a year and a day to assemble, and when it is as-sembled it still does not exist. The abstraction that individuals paralogistically form alienates individuals instead of helping them. The person who is with actual persons in the contemporaneity of the actual moment and the actual situation but has no opinion himself adopts the same opinion as the major-ity, or, if he is more argumentative, as the minority. But the majority and the minority are, it is well to note, actual human beings, and that is why solidar-ity with them is supportive.

The public, however, is an abstraction. In adopting the same opinion as these or those particular persons, one knows that they will be subject to the same danger as oneself, that they will go astray with one if the opinion is in error, etc. But to adopt the same opinion as the public is a deceptive conso-lation, for the public exists only *in abstracto*. Thus, although no majority has ever been so positively sure of being in the right and having the upper hand as the public is, this is slight consolation for the single individual, for the pub-lic is a phantom that does not allow any personal approach. If someone adopts the opinion of the public today and tomorrow is hissed and booed, he is hissed and booed by the public. A generation, a nation, a general assembly, a community, a man still have a responsibility to be something, can know shame for fickleness and disloyalty, but a public remains the public. A peo-

VIII
86

ple, an assembly, a person can change in such a way that one may say: they are no longer the same; but the public can become the very opposite and is still the same—the public. But if the individual is not destroyed in the process, he will be educated by this very abstraction and this abstract discipline (insofar as he is not already educated in his own inwardness) to be satisfied in the highest religious sense with himself and his relationship to God, will be educated to make up his own mind instead of agreeing with the public, which annihilates all the relative concretions of individuality, to find rest within himself, at ease before God, instead of in counting and counting. And the ultimate difference between the modern era and antiquity will be that the aggregate is not the concretion that reinforces and educates the individual, yet without shaping him entirely, but is an abstraction that by means of its alienating, abstract equality helps him to become wholly educated—if he does not perish. The bleakness of antiquity was that the man of distinction was what *others could not be*; the inspiring aspect [of the modern era] will be that the person who has gained himself religiously is only what *all can be*.

The public is not a people, not a generation, not one's age, not a congregation, not an association, not some particular persons, for all these are what they are only by being concretions. Yes, not a single one of these who belong to a public is essentially engaged in any way. For a few hours of the day he perhaps is part of the public, that is, during the hours when he is a nobody, because during the hours in which he is the specific person he is, he does not belong to the public. Composed of someones such as these, of individuals in the moments when they are nobodies, the public is a kind of colossal something, an abstract void and vacuum that is all and nothing. But on the same basis anyone can presume to have a public, and just as the Roman Catholic Church chimerically extended itself by appointing bishops *in partibus infidelium* [in non-Catholic countries], so too a public is something anyone can pick up, even a drunken sailor exhibiting a peep show, and in dialectical consistency the drunken sailor has absolutely the same right to a public as the most distinguished of men, the absolute right to place all these many, many zeros *in front of* his figure one. The public is all and nothing, the most dangerous of all powers and the most meaningless. One may speak to a whole nation in the name of the public, and yet the public is less than one ever so insignificant actual human being. The category "public" is reflection's mirage delusively making the individuals conceited, since everyone can arrogate to himself this mammoth, compared with which the concretions of actuality seem paltry. The public is the fairy-tale of an age of prudence, leading individuals to fancy* themselves greater than kings, but again the public

VIII
87

---

* Fortunately as an author I have never sought or had any public but have been happily content with "that single individual," and because of that restriction I have become almost proverbial.

is the cruel abstraction by which individuals will be religiously educated—
or be destroyed.

Together with the passionlessness and reflectiveness of the age, the abstraction "the press" (for a newspaper, a periodical, is not a political concretion and is an individual only in an abstract sense) gives rise to the abstraction's phantom, "the public," which is the real leveler. Apart from its negative
implications for the religious life, this too can have its significance. But in
proportion to the scarcity of ideas, an age exhausted by a flash of enthusiasm will relax all the more readily in indolence, and even if we were to imagine that the press would become weaker and weaker for lack of events and
ideas to stir the age, leveling becomes all the more a decadent urge, a sensate
stimulation that excites momentarily and only makes the evil worse, the rescue more difficult, and the probability of destruction greater.

The demoralization of absolute monarchy and the decline of revolutionary periods have frequently been described, but the decline of an age devoid
of passion is just as degenerate, even though less striking because of its ambiguity. Thus it may be of interest and significance to think about this. In this
state of indolent laxity, more and more individuals will aspire to be nobodies in order to become the public, that abstract aggregate ridiculously formed
by the participant's becoming a third party. That sluggish crowd which understands nothing itself and is unwilling to do anything, that gallery-public,
now seeks to be entertained and indulges in the notion that everything anyone does is done so that it may have something to gossip about. Sluggishness
crosses its legs and sits there like a snob, while everyone who is willing to
work, the king and the public official and the teacher and the more intelligent journalist and the poet and the artist, all stretch and strain, so to speak,
to drag along that sluggishness which snobbishly believes the others are
horses.

From these dialectical category-qualifications and their consequences,
whether factual in the given moment or not, from a dialectical consideration of the present age, I now proceed dialectically to the more concrete at-
tributes of the reflexion of the present age in domestic and social life as depicted in the novel. Here the dark side becomes apparent, and even if its
facticity cannot be denied, it is nevertheless also certain that just as reflection
itself is not the evil, so too a very reflective age certainly must also have its
bright side, simply because considerable reflectiveness is the condition for a
higher meaningfulness than that of immediate passion, is the condition for
it—if enthusiasm intervenes and persuades the reflective powers to make a
decision, and because a high degree of reflectiveness makes for a higher average quality of the prerequisites for action—if religiousness intervenes in
the individual and takes over the prerequisites. Reflection is not the evil, but
the state of reflection, stagnation in reflection, is the abuse and the corrup-

tion that occasion retrogression by transforming the prerequisites into evasions.

The present age is essentially a sensible age, devoid of passion, and therefore it *has nullified the principle of contradiction.* From this consideration a variety of features may be deduced, which the author with fine artistry and elevated composure had depicted so disinterestedly. Naturally, the author's own opinion is nowhere discernible; he merely reproduces the reflexion. Generally speaking, compared with a passionate age, a reflective age devoid of passion *gains in extensity what it loses in intensity.* But this extensity in turn may become the condition for a higher form if a corresponding intensity takes over what is extensively at its disposal.

The existential expression of nullifying the principle of contradiction is to be in contradiction to oneself. The creative omnipotence implicit in the passion of absolute disjunction that leads the individual resolutely to make up his mind is transformed into the extensity of prudence and reflection—that is, by knowing and being everything possible to be in contradiction to oneself, that is, to be nothing at all. The principle of contradiction strengthens the individual in faithfulness to himself, so that, just like that constant number three Socrates speaks of so beautifully, which would rather suffer anything and everything than become a number four[128] or even a very large round number, he would rather be something small, if still faithful to himself, than all sorts of things in contradiction to himself.

What is it *to chatter?* It is the annulment of the passionate disjunction between being silent and speaking. Only the person who can remain essentially silent can speak essentially, can act essentially. Silence is inwardness. Chattering gets ahead of essential speaking, and giving utterance to reflection has a weakening effect on action by getting ahead of it. But the person who can speak essentially because he is able to keep silent will not have a profusion of things to speak about but one thing only, and he will find time to speak and to keep silent. Talkativeness gains in extensity: it chatters about anything and everything and continues incessantly. When individuals are not turned inward in quiet contentment, in inner satisfaction, in religious sensitiveness, but in a relation of reflection are oriented to externalities and to each other, when no important event ties the loose threads together in the unanimity of a crucial change—then chattering begins. The important event gives the passionate age (for the two go together) something to speak about; everybody wants to speak about the same thing. It is the only thing the poets sing about; conversations echo this alone. It is all about the one and the same. But in quite a different sense chattering has a great deal to chatter about. And then when the important event was over, when silence returned, there was still something to recollect, something to think about in silence, while a new generation speaks of entirely different matters. But chattering dreads the moment of silence, which would reveal the emptiness.

VIII
91

The law manifest in poetic production is identical, on a smaller scale, with the law for the life of every person in social intercourse and education. Anyone who experiences anything primitively also experiences in ideality the possibilities of the same thing and the possibility of the opposite. These possibilities are his legitimate literary property. His own personal actuality, however, is not. His speaking and his producing are, in fact, born of silence. The ideal perfection of what he says and what he produces will correspond to his silence, and the supreme mark of that silence will be that the ideality contains the qualitatively opposite possibility. As soon as the productive artist must give over his own actuality, its facticity, he is no longer essentially productive; his beginning will be his end, and his first word will already be a trespass against the holy modesty of ideality. Therefore from an esthetic point of view, such a poetic work is certainly also a kind of private talkativeness and is readily recognized by the absence of its opposite in equilibrium. For ideality is the equilibrium of opposites. For example, someone who has been motivated to creativity by unhappiness, if he is genuinely devoted to ideality, will be equally inclined to write about happiness and about unhappiness. But silence, the brackets he puts around his own personality, is precisely the condition for gaining ideality; otherwise, despite all precautionary measures such as setting the scene in Africa etc., his one-sided preference will still show. An author certainly must have his private personality as everyone else has, but this must be his ἄδυτον [inner sanctum], and just as the entrance to a house is barred by stationing two soldiers with crossed bayonets, so by means of the dialectical cross of qualitative opposites the equality of ideality forms the barrier that prevents all access.

There is a story about two English lords who came riding along and met a luckless horseman about to fall off his wildly plunging horse and shouting for help. The one lord turned to the other and said: "A hundred guineas he falls off." "It's a bet," replied the other. They set off at a gallop and hurried ahead to get all the gates opened and all other obstacles out of the way. Likewise, but with less of millionaire-splenetic-heroics, the sensibleness of the present age could be personified as one who inquisitively, courteously, and prudently would at most have sufficient passion to make a bet. Life's existential tasks have lost the interest of actuality; no illusion preserves and protects the divine growth of inwardness that matures to decisions. There is a mutual inquisitiveness; everyone is experienced in indecisiveness and evasions and waits for someone to come along who wills something—so that they may place bets on him.

And since there is such an extraordinary quantity of prophecies, apocalypses, signs, and insights in our age when so little is being done, there is probably nothing else to do but go along with it, although I do have the unencumbered advantage over the others' burdensome responsibility to prophesy and forebode that I can be rather sure no one will dream of believing

VIII
92

VIII
98

what I say. So I do not ask that anyone should mark an X on the calendar or go to the trouble of noting whether it comes true or not, for if it comes true, he will have other things to think about than my fortuitousness, and if it does not, well, then I remain just a prophet in the modern sense, for a modern prophet prophesies something, nothing more. Of course, in a certain sense a prophet can do no more. It was Governance, after all, who ordained fulfillment of the ancient prophets' predictions; we modern prophets, lacking the endorsement of Governance, perhaps could add a postscript as Thales did: What we prophesy will either happen or it will not happen, for the gods have bestowed the gift of prophecy also upon us.[129]

VIII
99

It is very doubtful, then, that the age will be saved by the idea of sociality, of community. On the contrary, this idea is the scepticism necessary for the proper development of individuality, inasmuch as every individual either is lost or, disciplined by the abstraction, finds himself religiously. In our age the principle of association (which at best can have validity with respect to material interest) is not affirmative but negative; it is an evasion, a dissipation, an illusion, whose dialectic is as follows: as it strengthens individuals, it vitiates them; it strengthens by numbers, by sticking together, but from the ethical point of view this is a weakening. Not until the single individual has established an ethical stance despite the whole world, not until then can there be any question of genuinely uniting; otherwise it gets to be a union of people who separately are weak, a union as unbeautiful and depraved as a child-marriage. Formerly the ruler, the man of excellence, the men of prominence each had his own view; the others were so settled and unquestioning that they did not dare or could not have an opinion. Now everyone can have an opinion, but there must be a lumping together numerically in order to have it. Twenty-five signatures to the silliest notion is an opinion. The most cogent opinion of the most eminent mind is a paradox. Public opinion is an inorganic something, an abstraction. But when the context has become meaningless, it is futile to make large-scale surveys; then the best thing to do is to scrutinize the particular parts of what is said. When the mouth blathers pure drivel, it is futile to try to deliver a coherent discourse; it is better to consider each word by itself—and so it is with the situation of individuals.

The following change will also occur. Whereas in older structures (relations between individual and generation) the non-commissioned officers, company commanders, generals, the hero (that is, the men of excellence, the men prominent in their various ranks, the leaders) were *recognizable,* and each one (according to his authority) along with his little detachment was artistically and organically ordered within the whole, himself supported by and supporting the whole—now the men of excellence, the leaders (each according to his respective rank) will be without authority precisely because they will have divinely understood the diabolical principle of the leveling process. Like plainclothes policemen, they will be *unrecognizable,* concealing their respective distinctions and giving support only negatively—that is, by repulsion, while the infinite uniformity of abstraction judges every individual, examines him in his isolation. This structure is the dialectical opposite to that of the judges and prophets, and just as they risked the danger of not being respected for their respective authorities, so the unrecognized run the risk of being recognized, of being seduced into acquiring status and importance as authorities, thus preventing the highest development. Like secret agents they are unrecognizable, not according to private instructions from God, for that in fact is the situation of the prophets and judges, but they are unrecognizable (without authority) because of their apprehension of the universal in equality before God, because of their acceptance of the responsibility for this at all times, and thus they are prevented from being caught off guard and becoming guilty of conduct inconsistent with their consistent intuition. This structure is dialectically opposite to the systematizing that makes the generation, preformed in the men of excellence, the supporting factor for individuals, since as an abstraction, negatively supported by the unrecognized, it now turns polemically against individuals—in order to save every single individual religiously.

UPBUILDING DISCOURSES IN
VARIOUS SPIRITS (MARCH 13, 1847)
BY S. KIERKEGAARD

Concluding Unscientific Postscript may be called the turning-point or mid-point in Kierkegaard's authorship, but the experience of 1846, the *Corsair* affair, may be regarded as the impelling occasion of the so-called "second authorship." *Upbuilding Discourses in Various Spirits* was the first yield in the new period of writing (apart from *Two Ages,* which Kierkegaard considered merely a review). A clue to the nature of this and subsequent writings is given by the subtitle of Part Three on suffering: "Christian Discourses," a designation used for the first time there. Part Two, "What We Learn from the Lilies in the Field and from the Birds of the Air," affirms that if in silence we pay attention to the birds and the lilies we will learn the gloriousness and the promised happiness of being a human being and will be content to be that. Part One, "On the Occasion of a Confession," is sometimes referred to as a separate work under the title *Purity of Heart,* used by Douglas Steere for his early translation of this part of *Discourses in Various Spirits.* In Part One Kierkegaard relentlessly pounds sand in every evasion rat hole of double-mindedness and typically leaves the reader to work out the implications of the clues to the nature of the good.

TO
"THAT SINGLE INDIVIDUAL"
THIS LITTLE BOOK
IS DEDICATED

PREFACE

Although this little book (it can be called an occasional discourse, yet without having the occasion that makes the speaker and makes him an *authority* or the occasion that makes the reader and makes him a *learner*) in the situation of *actuality* is like a fancy, a dream in the daytime, yet it is not without confidence and not without hope of fulfillment. It seeks that single individual, to whom it gives itself wholly, by whom it wishes to be received as if it had arisen in his own heart, that single individual whom I with joy and gratitude call *my* reader, that single individual, who willingly reads slowly, reads repeatedly, and who reads aloud—for his own sake. If it finds him, then in the remoteness of separation the understanding is complete when he keeps the book and the understanding to himself in the inwardness of appropriation.

When a woman works on a cloth for sacred use, she makes every flower as beautiful, if possible, as the lovely flowers of the field, every star as sparkling, if possible, as the twinkling stars of the night; she spares nothing but uses the most precious things in her possession; then she disposes of every other claim on her life in order to purchase the uninterrupted and opportune time of day and night for her sole, her beloved, work. But when the cloth is finished and placed in accordance with its sacred purpose—then she is deeply distressed if anyone were to make the mistake of seeing her artistry instead of the meaning of the cloth or were to make the mistake of seeing a defect instead of seeing the meaning of the cloth. She could not work the sacred meaning into the cloth; she could not embroider it on the cloth as an additional ornament. The meaning is in the beholder and in the beholder's understanding when, faced with himself and his own self, he has in the infinite remoteness of separation infinitely forgotten the needlewoman and her part. It was permissible, it was fitting, it was a duty, it was a cherished duty, it was a supreme joy for the needlewoman to do everything in order to do her part, but it would be an offense against God, an insulting misunderstanding to the poor needlewoman, if someone were to make the mistake of seeing what is there but is to be disregarded, what is there—not to draw attention to itself but, on the contrary, only so that its absence would not disturbingly draw attention to itself.

S.K.

ON THE OCCASION OF A CONFESSION

Father in heaven! What is a human being without you! What is everything he knows, even though it were enormously vast and varied, but a disjointed snippet if he does not know you; what is all his striving, even though it embraced a world, but a job half done if he does not know you, you the one who is one and who is all! Then may you give the understanding wisdom to comprehend the one thing; may you give the heart sincerity to receive the understanding; may you give the will purity through willing only one thing. Then, when everything is going well, give the perseverance to will one thing, in distractions the concentration to will one thing, in sufferings the patience to will one thing. O you who give both the beginning and the completing, may you give to the young person early, when the day is dawning, the resolution to will one thing; when the day is waning, may you give to the old person a renewed remembrance of his first resolution so that the last may be like the first, the first like the last, may be the life of a person who has willed only one thing. But, alas, this is not the way it is. Something came in between them; the separation of sin lies in between them; daily, day after day, something intervenes between them: delay, halting, interruption, error, perdition. Then may you give in repentance the bold confidence to will again one thing. Admittedly it is an interruption of the usual task; admittedly it is a halting of work as if it were a day of rest when the penitent (and only in repentance is the burdened laborer quiet) in the confession of sin is alone before you in self-accusation. Oh, but it is indeed an interruption that seeks to return to its beginning so that it might rebind what is separated, so that in sorrow it might make up for failure, so that in its solicitude it might complete what lies ahead. O you who give both the beginning and the completing, may you give victory on the day of distress so that the one distressed in repentance may succeed in doing what the one burning in desire and the one determined in resolution failed to do: to will only one thing. VIII
120

So let us on the occasion of a confession speak on this theme: VIII
133

Purity of Heart Is to Will One Thing

as we base our meditation on the Apostle James' words in the fourth chapter of his Epistle, verse 8:

Keep near to God, then he will keep near to you. Cleanse your hands, you sinners, and purify your hearts, you double-minded,

because only the pure in heart are able to see God and consequently keep near to him and preserve this purity through his keeping near to them; and the person who in truth wills only one thing *can will only the good,* and the person who wills only one thing when he wills the good *can will only the good in truth.* VIII
.134

Let us discuss this, but let us first forget the occasion in order to come to an understanding of this theme and what the apostolic admonishing words ("purify your hearts, you double-minded") are opposing: *double-mindedness;* then in conclusion we shall more specifically utilize the occasion.

I
If It Is To Be Possible For a Person To Be Able To Will One Thing, He Must Will the Good.

To will only one thing—but is this not bound to become a lengthy discussion? If anyone is really to consider this matter, must he not first examine one by one every goal that a person can set for himself in life, designate one by one all the many things that a person can will? And if this were not enough, since considerations of this sort easily become run-of-the-mill, must he not try willing one thing after the other in order to find out which one thing it is that he can will if it is a matter of willing only one thing? Indeed, if anyone would begin in this manner, he certainly would never be finished; or rather, how would it be possible that he could finish when he expressly started out on the wrong road and still continued to proceed further and further on the road of error that *leads* to the good only in a lamentable way—namely, if the traveler turns around and goes back, for just as the good is only one thing, so all roads *lead* to the good, even the road of error—if the one who turned around goes back on the same road.

To will one thing, then, cannot mean to will something that only seemingly is one thing. In other words, the worldly in its essence is not one thing since it is the *nonessential;* its so-called unity is no essential unity but an emptiness that the multiplicity conceals. Thus in the brief moment of illusion what is worldly is multiplicity and therefore not one thing; then it changes into its opposite—that is how far it is from being and remaining one thing. Indeed, what else is desire in its boundless extreme but nausea? What else is earthly honor at its dizzy summit but contempt for existence? What else is the superabundance of wealth but poverty; does all the gold in the world hidden in avarice amount to as much as, or does it not amount to infinitely much less than, the poorest mite hidden in the contentment of the poor! What else is worldly power but dependence; what slave in chains was as unfree as a tyrant! No, the worldly is not one thing; multifarious as it is, in life it is changed into its opposite, in death into nothing, in eternity into a curse upon the person who has willed this one thing. Only the good is one thing in its essence and the same in every one of its expressions. Let love illustrate it. The person who truly loves does not love once for all; neither does he use a portion of his love now and then in turn another portion, because to exchange it is to make it a changeling. No, he loves with all his love; it is totally present in every expression; he continually spends all of it, and yet he continually keeps it all in his heart. What marvelous wealth! When the miser has amassed all the world's gold—in grubbiness—he has become poor; when the lover spends all his love, he keeps it whole—in purity of heart. —If a person is in truth to will one thing, the one thing he wills must indeed be of such a nature that it remains unchanged amid all changes; then by willing it he can win changelessness. If it is continually changed, he himself becomes changeable, double-minded, and unstable. But this continual changeableness is precisely impurity.

But neither is willing one thing *that drastic error of presumptuous, ungodly enthusiasm: to will the great, no matter whether it is good or evil.* Be he ever so desperate, a person who wills in this way is nevertheless double-minded. Or is not despair [*Fortvivlelse*] actually double-mindedness [*Tvesindethed*[130]]; or what else is it to despair but to have two wills! Whether he, the weak one, despairs over not being able to tear himself loose from the evil or he, the presumptuous one, despairs over not being able to tear himself completely loose from the good—they are both double-minded, they both have two wills; neither of them in truth wills one thing, no matter how desperately they seem to be willing it. Whether it was a woman whom desire plunged into despair or it was a man who despaired in defiance, whether a person despaired because he got his will or despaired because he did not get his will, everyone in despair has two wills, one that he futilely wants to follow entirely, and one that he futilely wants to get rid of entirely. This is how God, better than any king, has safeguarded himself against every rebellion. It certainly has happened that a king has been dethroned by a rebellion, but the furthest any rebel against God carries it is to the point of despairing himself. Despair is the limit—to this point and no further! Despair is the limit; here the ill nature of cowardly, fearful self-love meets the presumptuousness of the proud, defiant mind; here they meet in equal powerlessness.

Only all too soon one's own experience and experience with others teach how far the lives of most people are from what a human life ought to be. All have their great moments, see themselves in the magic mirror of possibility that hope holds before them while desire flatters, but they speedily forget the vision in the everyday. Or perhaps they utter enthusiastic words, "for the tongue is a little member and boasts of great things"[131]—but by loudly proclaiming what ought to be practiced in silence the talk takes the enthusiasm in vain, and the inspired words are quickly forgotten in the trivialities of life; it is forgotten that such words were said about this person; it is forgotten that it was he himself who said them. Then perhaps one day recollection awakens with horror, and regret seems to give new strength; alas, this also would become only a big moment. They all have intentions, plans, and resolutions for life, indeed, for eternity. But the intention quickly loses its youthful vigor and becomes decrepit, and the resolution does not stand firm and does not resist; it vacillates and is changed with the circumstances, and memory fails— until by habit and association they learn to console each other, as one says, until they even find it upbuilding instead of traitorous if someone proclaims the feeble consolation of excuses that encourages and fortifies the lethargy. There are people who find it upbuilding that the requirement is affirmed in all its sublimity, in all its rigor, so that it penetrates the innermost soul with its requirement; others find it upbuilding that a wretched compromise is made with God and the requirement—and the language. There are people who find it upbuilding if someone will call to them, but there are also sleepy souls who not only call it pleasant but even upbuilding to be lulled to sleep.

This is indeed lamentable, but then there is a wisdom that is not from above; it is earthly, corporeal, and diabolical. It has discovered this universally human weakness and lethargy; it wants to help. It sees that it is a matter of the will and now loudly proclaims, "Without willing one thing, a person's life becomes wretched mediocrity and misery. He must will one thing, regardless of whether it is good or evil; he must will one thing—therein lies a person's greatness." But it is not difficult to see through this drastic error. Holy Scripture teaches for our salvation that sin is a human being's corruption[132] and therefore deliverance is only in purity through willing the good. That earthly

VIII
140

and diabolical wisdom distorts this into tempting perdition: weakness is a person's misfortune; strength is the only deliverance. "When the unclean spirit goes out of a person, it wanders through dry and empty places but finds no rest; then it returns and has in company with itself"[133] that impure sagacity, the wisdom of the desert and the empty places, that impure sagacity that now drives out the spirit of lethargy and mediocrity—"so the last is worse than the first."[134] How is one to describe the nature of such a person?

It is said that a singer can rupture his voice by outvoicing himself; similarly the nature of a person like that is ruptured by outvoicing itself and the voice of conscience. It is said of someone dizzily standing on a high place that everything runs together before his eyes; similarly, a person like that has become dizzy out in the infinite, where everything that is eternally separate runs together so that only the great dimension remains—that is, the deserted and empty, which always gives birth to dizziness. But however desperately he seems to will one thing, such a person is nevertheless double-minded. If he, the self-willed person [*Selvraadig*], might have his will [*raade*], then there would be only one thing and he would be the only one who would not be double-minded, the only one who would have cast off every chain, he the only one free. But free—the slave of sin is indeed not, nor has he cast off the chain "because he mocks it";[135] he is under constraint and therefore double-minded, and certainly he must not rule. There is a power that constrains him; he cannot tear himself loose from it; indeed, he cannot even quite will it—this power, too, is denied him. If you, my listener, were to see such a person (although he certainly is rare, just as weakness and mediocrity are undeniably more common), if you were to meet him in what he himself would call a weak moment (alas, what you might call a better moment), if you were to meet him when he had found no rest in the desert, when his dizziness had passed for a moment and he felt an anguished longing for the good, when shaken in his innermost being and not without sorrow he was thinking of that simple one who despite his frailty nevertheless wills the good—you would then discover that he had two wills, and his anguished double-mindedness. Despairing as he was, he thought: What is lost is lost—yet he could not help but turn around once more in longing for the good, no matter how dreadfully embittered he had become against this longing, a longing that demonstrates that, just as a person, despite all his defiance, does not have the power to tear himself away completely from the good, because it is the stronger, he also does not even have the power to will it completely.

You may even have heard that despairing one say, "Yet something good goes down with me." When someone finds his death in the waves, he sinks although not yet dead, comes up again, and finally a bubble comes out of his mouth—when this has happened, he sinks in death. That bubble was his last breath, the last reserve of air that could make him lighter than the ocean. So also with those words. In those words he breathed out his last hope of rescue; in those words he gave himself up. Suppressed, there was still in that thought a hope of rescue; in that thought there was still hidden in his soul a possible way of rescue. Once the words are spoken, confidentially to another person (oh, what a dreadful misuse of confidentiality, even though the despairing one uses them only against himself!), once these words are heard, then he goes down forever. Alas, it is terrible to see a person rushing headlong to his own downfall; it is terrible to see him dancing on the edge of the abyss without suspecting it; but this clarity about himself and his own downfall is even more terrible. It is terrible to see a person seek solace by plunging into the vortex of despair, but even more terrible is the composure that in the anguish of death a person does not call out in a scream for help, "I am going down, save me!" but calmly wants to be a witness to his own perdition. What colossal vanity not to want to draw people's attention to oneself by one's beauty, by wealth, by talents, by power, by honor, but to want to beg their attention by one's perdition, to want to say of oneself what compassion at most would sadly dare to say of such a one at his grave: Yet something good went down with him! What dreadful double-mindedness to want in one's perdition to derive a kind of advantage from the fact that the good exists, the only thing one has not willed! Now, of course, it manifested itself, the other will, even though it was so weak that it became a pandering to perdition, an attempt to become noteworthy—by perdition.

To will one thing, then, cannot mean to will that which by nature is not one thing but only by means of a dreadful falsehood seems to be that, something that only by means of the lie is one thing, just as the person who wills only this alone is a liar, just as the one who conjures up this one thing is the Father of Lies. The deserted and empty is not truly one thing but is truly nothing and is the perdition in the person who wills only this one thing. But if a person is to will only one thing in truth, this one thing must be one thing in the truth of its innermost being; it must by an eternal separation differ from the heterogeneous so that in truth it can continue to be one thing and to be the same and thereby form in likeness to itself the one who wills only this one thing.

In truth to will one thing can therefore mean only to will the good, because any other one thing is not a one thing and the person willing who wills only that must therefore be double-minded, because the one who craves becomes like that which he craves. Or would it be possible that a person by willing evil could will one thing even if it were possible that a person could harden himself to willing only evil? Is not evil, just like evil people, at odds with itself, divided in itself? Take someone like that, separate him from society, lock him up in solitary confinement—is he not divided against himself there, just as the bad alliance of such similar minds is a divided union. But even if the good man lived in an out-of-the-way place in the world and never saw anyone else, he is still at one with himself and at one with all, because he wills one thing and because the good is one thing.

VIII
142

VIII
143

Then everyone who in truth is to will one thing must be led to will the good, even though it may sometimes be that a person begins by willing one thing that yet in the deepest sense is not the good, but probably something innocent, and then little by little is transformed into willing one thing in truth by willing the good. For example, sometimes erotic love has probably helped a person along the right road. He faithfully willed only one thing, his love; for it he would live and die, for it he would sacrifice everything, in it alone he would have his happiness. In the deepest sense, however, falling in love is still not the good but possibly became for him a formative educator that finally led him, by winning the beloved or perhaps by losing her, in truth to will one thing and to will the good. Thus a person is brought up in many ways; an honest erotic love is also an upbringing to the good.

Perhaps there was someone whom enthusiasm gripped for a specific endeavor. Full of enthusiasm, he willed only one thing; he would live and die for this endeavor, he would sacrifice everything for it, in it alone would have his happiness—because erotic love and enthusiasm are not content with a divided heart. Yet his endeavor may still not have been in the deepest sense the good; thus the enthusiasm became for him the teacher he presumably outgrew but to whom he also owed very much. As stated, all roads lead to the good if a person in truth wills only one thing; and if there is indeed any truth in his willing one thing, this also assists him to the good. But the danger is that the person in love and the enthusiast take a wrong turn and swing off to the great instead of being led to the good. It is certain that the good is truly the great, but the great is not always the good. One can woo a woman's favor by willing something if only it is great; it can flatter the girl's pride and she can reward one with her worship. But God in heaven is not like the folly of a young girl; he does not reward the great with admiration, but the reward of the good person is to dare to worship in truth.

WORKS OF LOVE (SEPTEMBER 29, 1847)
BY S. KIERKEGAARD

"Despite everything people ought to have learned about my maieutic carefulness, by proceeding slowly and continually letting it seem as if I knew nothing more, not the next
thing—now on the occasion of my new upbuilding discourses [*Upbuilding Discourses in Various Spirits*] they will probably bawl out that I do not know what comes next, that I know
nothing about sociality. . . .

Now I have the theme of the next book. It will be called:
Works of Love."[136]

The subtitle calls the work "deliberations" because a deliberation "does not presuppose the
definitions as given and understood." "An upbuilding discourse about love presupposes that
people know essentially what love is and seeks to win them to it, to move them. But this certainly is not the case. Therefore a 'deliberation' must first fetch them up out of the cellar, call
to them, turn their comfortable way of thinking topsy-turvy with the dialectic of truth."[137]

Danish has two words for two kinds of love: *Elskov,* love in the ordinary sense, erotic love,
and *Kjerlighed,* self-giving love, unconditional love, *agape* love. Much of the work concentrates
on a clarification of the distinction. Other key terms are *opelske,* to love forth love by acting
on the presupposition that the other acted in love, and *opbygge,* to build up ("edify" with its
Latin root loses in English the literal basis of the metaphor).

Love (*Kjerlighed*) is a work, an act, not a mood, a feeling, a spontaneous inclination, but a
task, and ultimately a gift in a triangle of love, whereby the "you shall" of the task is transformed into an expression of gratitude for the gift, and the imperative ethics is transformed
into an indicative ethics of response, into a responsive striving born of gratitude.

The concluding chapters are on "Mercifulness, a Work of Love Even If It Can Give Nothing and Is Able to Do Nothing," "The Victory of the Conciliatory Spirit in Love," "The Work
of Love in Recollecting One Who Is Dead," and "The Work of Love in Praising Love."

PREFACE

These Christian deliberations, which are the fruit of much deliberation, will
be understood slowly but then also easily, whereas they will surely become
very difficult if someone by hasty and curious reading makes them very difficult for himself. *That single individual* who first deliberates with himself
whether or not he will read, if he then chooses to read, will lovingly deliberate whether the difficulty and the ease, when placed thoughtfully together
on the scale, relate properly to each other so that what is essentially Christian is not presented with a false weight by making the difficulty or by making the ease too great.

They are *Christian deliberations,* therefore not about *love* but about *works of
love.*

They are about *works of love,* not as if hereby all its works were now added up and described, oh, far from it; not as if even the particular work described were described once and for all, far from it, God be praised! Something that in its total richness is *essentially* inexhaustible is also in its smallest work *essentially* indescribable just because essentially it is totally present everywhere and *essentially* cannot be described.

Autumn 1847

S. K.

IX
8

Prayer

How could one speak properly about love if you were forgotten, you God of love, source of all love in heaven and on earth; you who spared nothing but in love gave everything; you who are love, so that one who loves is what he is only by being in you! How could one speak properly about love if you were forgotten, you who revealed what love is, you our Savior and Redeemer, who gave yourself in order to save all. How could one speak properly of love if you were forgotten, you Spirit of love, who take nothing of your own but remind us of that love-sacrifice, remind the believer to love as he is loved and his neighbor as himself! O Eternal Love, you who are everywhere present and never without witness where you are called upon, be not without witness in what will be said here about love or about works of love. There are indeed only some works that human language specifically and narrowly calls works of love, but in heaven no work can be pleasing unless it is a work of love: sincere in self-renunciation, a need in love itself, and for that very reason without any claim of meritoriousness!

IX
21

YOU *SHALL* LOVE

> Matthew 22:39. But the second commandment is
> like it: You shall love your neighbor as yourself.

Every discourse, particularly a section of a discourse, usually presupposes something that is the starting point. Someone who wishes to deliberate on the discourse or statement therefore does well to find this presupposition first in order then to begin with it. Our quoted text also contains a presupposition that, although it comes last, is nevertheless the beginning. When it is said, "You shall love your neighbor [*Næste*] as yourself," this contains what is presupposed, that every person loves himself. Thus, Christianity, which by no means begins, as do those high-flying thinkers, without presuppositions, nor with a flattering presupposition, presupposes this. Dare we then deny that it is as Christianity presupposes? But on the other hand, is it possible for anyone to misunderstand Christianity, as if it were its intention to teach what worldly sagacity unanimously—alas, and yet contentiously—teaches, "that everyone is closest [*nærmest*] to himself." Is it possible for anyone to misunderstand this, as if it were Christianity's intention to proclaim self-love as a prescriptive right? Indeed, on the contrary, it is Christianity's intention to wrest self-love away from us human beings.

In other words, this is implied in loving oneself; but if one is to love the neighbor *as oneself,* then the commandment, as with a pick, wrenches [*vriste*] open the lock of self-love and wrests [*fravriste*] it away from a person. If the commandment about loving the neighbor were expressed in any other way than with this little phrase, *as yourself,* which simultaneously is so easy to handle and yet has the elasticity of eternity, the commandment would be unable to cope with self-love in this way. This *as yourself* does not vacillate in its aim, and therefore, judging with the unshakableness of eternity, it penetrates into the innermost hiding place where a person loves himself; it does not leave self-love the slightest little excuse, the least little way of escape. How amazing! Long and discerning addresses could be delivered on how a person ought to love his neighbor, and when the addresses had been heard, self-love would still be able to hit upon excuses and find a way of escape, because the subject had not been entirely exhausted, all circumstances had not been taken into account, because something had continually been forgotten or something had not been accurately and bindingly enough expressed and described. But this *as yourself*—indeed, no wrestler [*Bryder*] can wrap himself around the one he wrestles as this commandment wraps itself around self-love, which cannot move from the spot. Truly, when self-love has struggled with this phrase, which is, however, so easy to understand that no one needs to rack [*bryde*] his brain over it, then it will perceive that it has struggled with one that is stronger. Just as Jacob limped after having struggled with God, so will self-love be broken if it has struggled with this phrase that does not want to teach a person that he is not to love himself but rather wants to teach him proper self-love. How amazing! What struggle is as protracted and terrible and involved as self-love's battle to defend itself, and yet Christianity decides it all with one single blow. The whole thing is as quick as a turn of the hand; everything is decided, like the eternal decision of resurrection, "in a moment, in the twinkling of an eye" (I Corinthians 15:52). Christianity presupposes that a person loves himself and then adds to this only the phrase about the neighbor *as yourself.* And yet there is the change of eternity between the former and the latter.

But would this really be the highest; would it not be possible to love a person *more than oneself*? Indeed, this kind of poetic effusion is heard in the world. Would it perhaps then be so that it is Christianity that is unable to soar that high and therefore (probably also because it addresses itself to simple, everyday people) is left miserably holding to the requirement to love the neighbor *as oneself,* just as it sets the apparently very unpoetic *neighbor* as the

IX
22

IX
23

object of love instead of the celebrated objects of soaring love, *a beloved, a friend* (love for the neighbor has certainly not been celebrated by any poet, no more than this loving *as oneself*)—would this perhaps be so? Or would we, since we do make a concession to *celebrated* love in comparison with *commanded* love, meagerly praise Christianity's levelheadedness and understanding of life because it more soberly and more firmly holds itself down to earth, perhaps in the same sense as the saying "Love me little, love me long"? Far from it. Christianity certainly knows far better than any poet what love is and what it means to love. For this very reason it also knows what perhaps escapes the poets, that the love they celebrate is secretly self-love, and that precisely by this its intoxicated expression—to love another person more than oneself—can be explained. Erotic love [*Elskov*] is still not the eternal; it is the beautiful dizziness of infinity; its highest expression is the foolhardiness of riddles. This explains its attempting an even dizzier expression, "to love a person more than God." This foolhardiness pleases the poet beyond measure; it is sweet music to his ears; it inspires him to song. Ah, but Christianity teaches that this is blasphemy.

The same holds true of friendship as of erotic love, inasmuch as this, too, is based on preference: to love this one person above all others, to love him in contrast to all others. Therefore the object of both erotic love and of friendship has preference's name, "the beloved," "the friend," who is loved in contrast to the whole world. The Christian doctrine, on the contrary, is to love the neighbor, to love the whole human race, all people, even the enemy, and not to make exceptions, neither of preference nor of aversion.

There is only one whom a person can with the truth of eternity love more than himself—that is God. Therefore it does not say, "You shall love God as yourself" but says, "You shall love the Lord your God with all your heart and all your soul and all your mind."[138] A person should love God unconditionally *in obedience* and love him *in adoration*. It is ungodliness if any human being dares to love himself in this way, or dares to love another person in this way, or dares to allow another person to love him in this way. If your beloved or friend asks something of you that you, precisely because you honestly loved, had in concern considered would be harmful to him, then you must bear a responsibility if you love by obeying instead of loving by refusing a fulfillment of the desire. But you shall love God in unconditional obedience, even if what he requires of you might seem to you to be to your own harm, indeed, harmful to his cause; for God's wisdom is beyond all comparison with yours, and God's governance has no obligation of responsibility in relation to your sagacity. All you have to do is to obey in love. A human being, however, you shall only—but, no, this is indeed the highest—a human being you shall love as yourself. If you can perceive what is best for him better than he can, you will not be excused because the harmful thing was his own desire, was what he himself asked for. If this were not the case, it would be quite

IX
24

proper to speak of loving another person more than oneself, because this would mean, despite one's insight that this would be harmful to him, doing it *in obedience* because he demanded it, or *in adoration* because he desired it. But you expressly have no right to do this; you have the responsibility if you do it, just as the other has the responsibility if he wants to misuse his relation to you in such a way.

Therefore—*as yourself.* If the most cunning deceiver who has ever lived (or we could make him even more cunning than he ever was), in order if possible to get the Law to be verbose and to become prolix (for then the deceiver would quickly conquer), would *temptingly* continue to question the *royal Law* and ask, "How shall I love my neighbor?" then the commandment will invariably go on repeating the brief phrase "as yourself." And if any deceiver has deceived himself throughout his whole life by all sorts of prolixities on this subject, eternity will simply confront him with the Law's brief phrase, "as yourself." Veritably no one is going to be able to escape the commandment; if its "as yourself" presses as hard as possible upon self-love, then in its impertinence *the neighbor* is in turn a stipulation that is as perilous to self-love as possible. Self-love itself perceives the impossibility of wriggling out of it. The only escape is the one the Pharisee in his day tried in order to justify himself:[139] to cast doubt on who one's neighbor is—in order to get him out of one's life.

Who, then, is one's neighbor [Næste]?[140] The word is obviously derived from "nearest [*Nærmeste*]"; thus the neighbor is the person who is nearer to you than anyone else, yet not in the sense of preferential love, since to love someone who in the sense of preferential love is nearer than anyone else is self-love—"do not the pagans also do the same?"[141] The neighbor, then, is nearer to you than anyone else. But is he also nearer to you than you are to yourself? No, that he is not, but he is just as near, or he ought to be just as near to you. The concept "neighbor" is actually the redoubling of your own self; "the neighbor" is what thinkers call "the other," that by which the selfishness in self-love is to be tested. As far as thought is concerned, the neighbor does not even need to exist. If someone living on a desert island mentally conformed to this commandment, by renouncing self-love he could be said to love the neighbor. To be sure, "neighbor" in itself is a multiplicity, since "the neighbor" means "all people," and yet in another sense one person is enough in order for you to be able to practice the Law. In the selfish sense, in being a self it is impossible consciously to be two; self-love must be by itself. Nor does it take three, because if there are two, that is, if there is one other person whom you in the Christian sense love *as yourself* or in whom you love *the neighbor,* then you love all people. But what self-love unconditionally cannot endure is redoubling, and the commandment's *as yourself* is a redoubling. The person aflame with erotic love, by reason or by virtue of this ardor, can by no means bear redoubling, which here would mean to give up

IX
25

the erotic love if the beloved required it. The lover therefore does not love the beloved *as himself,* because he is imposing requirements, but this *as yourself* expressly contains a requirement on him—alas, and yet the lover thinks that he loves the other person even more than himself.

In this way *the neighbor* comes as close to self-love as possible. If there are only two people, the other person is the neighbor; if there are millions, everyone of these is the neighbor, who in turn is closer than *the friend* and *the beloved,* inasmuch as they, as the objects of preference, more or less hold together with the self-love in one. Usually a person is aware of the existence of the neighbor and of his being so close when he thinks he has privileges in relation to him or is able to claim something from him. If someone with this view asks, "Who is my neighbor?" then that reply of Christ to the Pharisee will contain an answer only in a singular way, because in the answer the question is actually first turned around, whereby the meaning is: how is a person to ask the question. That is, after having told the parable of the merciful Samaritan, Christ says to the Pharisee (Luke 10:36), "Which of these three seems to you to have been the neighbor to the man who had fallen among robbers?" and the Pharisee answers *correctly,* "The one who showed mercy on him"—that is, by acknowledging your duty you easily discover who your neighbor is. The Pharisee's answer is contained in Christ's question, which by its form compelled the Pharisee to answer in that way. The one to whom I have a duty is my neighbor, and when I fulfill my duty I show that I am a neighbor. Christ does not speak about knowing the neighbor but about becoming a neighbor oneself, about showing oneself to be a neighbor just as the Samaritan showed it by his mercy. By this he did not show that the assaulted man was his neighbor but that he was a neighbor of the one assaulted. The Levite and the priest were in a stricter sense the victim's neighbor, but they wished to ignore it. The Samaritan, on the other hand, who because of prejudice was predisposed to misunderstanding, nevertheless correctly understood that he was a neighbor of the assaulted man. To choose a beloved, to find a friend, yes, this is a complicated business, but one's neighbor is easy to recognize, easy to find if only one will personally—acknowledge one's duty.

The commandment said, "You shall love your neighbor as yourself," but if the commandment is properly understood it also says the opposite: *You shall love yourself in the right way.* Therefore, if anyone is unwilling to learn from Christianity to love himself in the right way, he cannot love the neighbor either. He can perhaps hold together with another or a few other persons, "through thick and thin," as it is called, but this is by no means loving the neighbor. To love yourself in the right way and to love the neighbor correspond perfectly to one another; fundamentally they are one and the same thing. When the Law's *as yourself* has wrested from you the self-love that Christianity sadly enough must presuppose to be in every human being, then you have actually learned to love yourself. The Law is therefore: You shall

IX
26

love yourself in the same way as you love your neighbor when you love him as yourself. Whoever has any knowledge of people will certainly admit that just as he has often wished to be able to move them to relinquish self-love, he has also had to wish that it were possible to teach them to love themselves. When the bustler wastes his time and powers in the service of futile, inconsequential pursuits, is this not because he has not learned rightly to love himself? When the light-minded person throws himself almost like a nonentity into the folly of the moment and makes nothing of it, is this not because he does not know how to love himself rightly? When the depressed person desires to be rid of life, indeed, of himself, is this not because he is unwilling to learn earnestly and rigorously to love himself? When someone surrenders to despair because the world or another person has faithlessly left him betrayed, what then is his fault (his innocent suffering is not referred to here) except not loving himself in the right way? When someone self-tormentingly thinks to do God a service by torturing himself, what is his sin except not willing to love himself in the right way? And if, alas, a person presumptuously lays violent hands upon himself, is not his sin precisely this, that he does not rightly love himself in the sense in which a person *ought* to love himself?

Oh, there is a lot of talk in the world about treachery and faithlessness, and, God help us, it is unfortunately all too true, but still let us never because of this forget that the most dangerous traitor of all is the one every person has within himself. This treachery, whether it consists in selfishly loving oneself or consists in selfishly not willing to love oneself in the right way—this treachery is admittedly a secret. No cry is raised as it usually is in the case of treachery and faithfulness. But is it not therefore all the more important that Christianity's doctrine should be brought to mind again and again, that a person shall love his neighbor as himself, that is, as he ought to love himself?

The commandment about love for the neighbor therefore speaks in one and the same phrase, *as yourself,* about this love and about love of oneself. And now the introduction to the discourse ends with what it wishes to make the object of consideration: that is, the commandment about love for the neighbor and about love of oneself becomes synonymous not only through this phrase "as yourself" but even more through the phrase *you shall*. We will now speak about:

You **shall** love.

because this is the very mark of Christian love and is its distinctive characteristic—that it contains this apparent contradiction: to love is a duty.

"You shall love." **Only when it is a duty to love, only then is love eter-**

IX
27

IX
32

nally secured against every change, eternally made free in blessed independence, eternally and happily secured against despair.

IX
33

However joyous, however happy, however indescribably confident instinctive and inclinational love, spontaneous love, can be itself, precisely in its most beautiful moment it still feels a need to bind itself, if possible, even more securely. Therefore the two swear an oath, swear fidelity or friendship to each other. When we speak most solemnly, we do not say of the two, "They love each other"; we say, "They swore fidelity to each other" or "They swore friendship to each other." But by what does this love swear? We do not wish now to divert attention and distract by calling to mind the great variety of things the spokesmen of this love, *the poets,* know through initiation—for when it comes to this love it is the poet who receives the promise of the two, the poet who unites the two, the poet who dictates the oath to the two and has them swear—in short, it is the poet who is the priest.

Does this love then swear by something that is higher than itself? No, that it does not do. This is the beautiful, the touching, the enigmatic, the poetic misunderstanding—that the two do not themselves discover this; and the poet is their one and only, their beloved confidant precisely because he does not discover it either. When this love swears, it actually gives itself the significance by which it swears; it is the love itself that gives the luster to that by which it swears. Therefore it not only does not swear by something higher but actually swears by something that is lower than itself. This love is indescribably rich in its lovable misunderstanding; just because it is itself an infinite richness, an unlimited trustworthiness, when it wants to swear it will swear by something lower—but does not discover this itself. The result, in turn, is that this swearing, which indeed should be and also honestly thinks itself to be the highest earnestness, is actually the most enchanting jest. Moreover, the enigmatic friend, the poet, whose perfect confidence is this love's highest understanding—he does not understand it either. Yet it is surely easy to understand that if one is truly to swear, one must swear by something higher; then God in heaven is the only one who is truly in the position of being able to swear by himself alone. But the poet cannot understand this; that is, the single individual who is a poet may be able to understand it, but he cannot understand it insofar as he is a poet, since the *poet* cannot understand it. The poet can understand everything, in riddles, and wonderfully explain everything, in riddles, but he cannot understand himself or understand that he himself is a riddle. If he were compelled to understand this, he would,

IX
34

if he did not become indignant and embittered, sadly say: Would that this understanding had not been forced upon me—it disturbs what is most beautiful to me, disturbs my life, and in the meantime I have no use for it. In a way the poet is right about that, because the true understanding is the decisive settlement of questions vital to his existence. There are, then, two riddles: the first is the love the two have for each other; the second is the poet's explanation of it, or that the poet's explanation is also a riddle.

In such a way this love swears, and then the two add to the oath that they will love each other "forever." If this is not added, the poet does not join the two. He turns away, indifferent, from such a temporal love, or, mocking, he turns against it, while he belongs forever to that eternal love. There are, then, actually two unions—first the two who will love each other forever, and then the poet, who will belong to these two forever. And the poet is right in this, that if two people will not love each other eternally, then their love is not worth talking about, even less worth singing praises about. The poet, however, does not detect the misunderstanding that the two swear *by their love* to love each other forever, instead of swearing love to each other *by eternity*. Eternity is the higher. If one is to swear, then one must swear by the higher; but if one is to swear by eternity, then one swears by the duty that one "*shall love*." Alas, but that favorite of the lovers, the poet, he who himself is even more rare than the two lovers whom his longing seeks, he who himself is a marvel of lovableness, he is also like a coddled child—he cannot bear this *shall*; as soon as it is expressed, he either becomes impatient or he begins to cry.

Therefore this spontaneous love has, in the sense of the beautiful imagination, the eternal in itself, but it is not consciously grounded upon the eternal and thus it can be **changed.** Even if it was not changed, it still can be changed, because it is indeed good fortune, but what is true of happiness is true of good fortune, which, when one thinks of the eternal, cannot be thought of without sadness, just as "Happiness *is* when it *has* been" is said with a shudder. That is to say, as long as it lasted or existed a change was possible; not until it is past can we say that it lasted. "Count no man happy as long as he is living."[142] As long as he is living, his fortune can change; not until he is dead and fortune has not left him while he lived, not until then is it manifest that he—has been happy. That which merely exists, which has undergone no change, continually has change outside itself; it can continually supervene, even in the last moment it can happen, and not until life has come to an end can we say: Change did not take place—or perhaps it did.

Whatever has undergone no change certainly has *existence,* but it does not have *enduring continuance*; insofar as it has existence, it is; but insofar as it has not gained enduring continuance amid change it cannot become contemporary with itself and in that case is either happily ignorant of this misrelation or is disposed to sadness. Only the eternal can be and become and remain contemporary with every age; in contrast, temporality divides within itself, and the present cannot become contemporary with the future, or the future with the past, or the past with the present. Of that which has gained enduring continuance by undergoing change, we can say, when it has existed, not only "It did exist," but we can say, "It has gained enduring contin-

uance while it existed." This is the safeguard and is a relation entirely different from that of good fortune. When love has undergone the change of eternity by having become a duty, it has gained enduring continuance, and it is
self-evident that it exists. In other words, it is not self-evident that what exists at this moment will also exist at the next moment, but it is self-evident
that the enduring exists [*bestaa*]. We say that something stands [*bestaa*] the test
and praise it when it has stood the test. But this is said of something imperfect, because the enduring continuance of the enduring will not and *cannot*
manifest itself in standing a test—it is, after all, the enduring; and only the
transient can give itself the appearance of enduring continuance by standing
a test.

No one would think of saying that sterling silver [*Prøve-Solv*] must stand
the test [*Prøve*] of time, since it is, after all, sterling silver. So it is also with
love. The love that simply has existence, however happy, however blissful,
however confident, however poetic it is, still must stand the test of the years.
But the love that has undergone the change of eternity by becoming duty
has gained enduring continuance—it is sterling silver. Is it therefore perhaps
less applicable, less useful in life? Is, then, sterling silver less useful? Indeed
not, but language, involuntarily, and thought, consciously, honor sterling silver in a distinctive way merely by saying "One uses it." There is no talk at all
about testing, one does not insult it by wanting to test it—after all, one knows
in advance that sterling silver endures. Therefore, when one uses a less reliable alloy, one is compelled to be more scrupulous and to speak less simply;
one is compelled almost ambiguously to say it in two says, "One uses it, and
while one uses it one is also testing it," because it is, of course, always possible that it could change.

Consequently, *only when it is a duty to love, only then is love eternally secured.*
This security of eternity casts out all anxiety and makes love perfect, perfectly secured. In that love which has only existence, however confident it is,
there is still an anxiety, an anxiety about the possibility of change. Such love
does not understand that this is anxiety any more than the poet does, because
the anxiety is hidden, and the only expression is the flaming craving, whereby
it is known that the anxiety is hidden underneath. Otherwise why is it that
spontaneous love is so inclined to, indeed, so infatuated with, making a test
of the love? This is simply because love has not, by becoming duty, undergone *the test* in the deepest sense. This accounts for what the poet would call
sweet restlessness, which more and more foolhardily wants to make the test.
The lover wants to test the beloved. The friend wants to test the friend. The
testing undoubtedly has its basis in love, but this violently flaming desire to
test, this craving desire to be put to the test, denotes that the love itself is unconsciously uncertain. Here again there is an enigmatic misunderstanding in
spontaneous love and in the poet's explanations. The lover and the poet think
that this urge to test love is precisely an expression of how certain it is. But

is this really so? It is quite correct that one does not wish to test what is unimportant, but from this it surely does not follow that wanting to test the beloved is an expression of certainty. The two love each other; they love each other forever; they are so certain of it that they—put it to a test. Is this the highest certainty? Is not this relationship just like that of love's swearing and yet swearing by what is lower than love? In this way the lovers' highest expression for the enduring continuance of their love expresses that it merely has existence, because one tests, one puts to a test, that which merely has existence. But when it is a duty to love, then no test is needed and no insulting foolhardiness of wanting to test, then love is higher than any test; it has already more than stood the test in the same sense as faith "more than conquers."[143] Testing is always related to possibility; it is always possible that what is being tested would not stand the test. Therefore, if someone wanted to test whether he has faith, or try to attain faith, this really means he will prevent himself from attaining faith; he will bring himself into the restlessness of craving where faith is never won, for "You *shall* believe." If a believer were to ask God to put his faith to the test, this would not be an expression of the believer's having faith to an extraordinarily high degree (to think this is a poetic misunderstanding, just as it is also a misunderstanding to have faith to an "extraordinary" degree, since the ordinary degree is the highest), but it would be an expression of his not entirely having faith, for "You *shall* believe." Never has any greater security been found, and never will the peace of eternity be found in anything other than in this *shall*. The idea of "testing," however congenial it is, is an unquiet thought, and it is the disquietude that will make one fancy that this is a higher assurance, because testing is in itself inventive and will not be exhausted any more than sagacity has ever been able to calculate all the contingencies, but on the other hand, as the earnest person puts it so well. "Faith has calculated all contingencies."[144] When one *shall,* it is eternally decided; and when you will understand that you *shall* love, your love is eternally secured.

By this *shall* love is also eternally secured *against every change.* The love that has only existence can be changed; it can be changed *within itself* and it can be changed *from itself.*

Spontaneous love can be changed within itself; it can be changed into its opposite, into *hate.* Hate is a love that has become its opposite, a love that has perished [*gaaet til Grunde*]. Down in the ground [*i Grunden*] the love is continually aflame, but it is the flame of hate; not until the love has burned out is the flame of hate also put out. Just as it is said of the tongue that "it is the same tongue with which we bless and curse,"[145] so it may also be said that it is the same love that loves and hates. But just because it is the same love, for that very reason it is not in the eternal sense the true love, which remains, *unchanged the same,* whereas that spontaneous love, when it *is changed,* is still basically *the same.* True love, which has undergone the change of eternity by becoming duty, is never changed; it is simple, it loves and never hates, never hates—the beloved. It might seem as if that spontaneous love were the stronger because it can do two things, because it can *both* love and hate. It might seem as if it had an entirely different power over its object when it says, "If you will not love me, then I will hate you"—but this is only an illusion. Is changingness indeed a stronger power than changelessness, and who is the stronger, the one who says, "If you will not love me, then I will hate you," or the one who says, "If you hate me, I will still continue to love you"? Certainly it is terrifying and terrible when love is changed into hate, but for whom is it actually terrible? I wonder if it is not for the one involved, the person to whom it happened that his love changed into hate!

Spontaneous love can be changed within itself; by spontaneous combustion it can become the sickness of *jealousy*; from the greatest happiness it can become the greatest torment. The heat of spontaneous love is so dangerous, no matter how great its desire is, that this heat can easily become a sickness. Spontaneity is like fermentation, which is called that simply because it has not yet undergone a change and therefore has not expelled the poison that is the heating element in fermentation. If love kindles itself with this poison instead of expelling it, then the sickness of jealousy [*Iversyge,* zeal-sickness] sets in. As the word itself suggests, it is a zeal for becoming sick, a sickness from zeal. The jealous person does not hate the object of love—far from it, but he tortures himself with the flame of reciprocal love that, purifying, should cleanse his love. The jealous person catches, almost imploringly, every beam from the love in the beloved, but through the burning glass of jealousy he focuses all these beams on his own love, and he slowly burns up. But the love that has undergone the change of eternity by becoming duty does not know jealousy; it does not love only as it is loved, but it loves. Jealousy loves as it is loved. Anxious and tortured by the thought of whether it is loved, it is just as jealous of its own love, whether it is not disproportionate in relation to the other's indifference, as it is jealous of the manifestation of the other's love. Anxious and tortured by preoccupation with itself, it dares neither to believe the beloved absolutely nor to give itself wholeheartedly, lest it give too much and therefore continually burn itself as one burns oneself on something that is not burning—except to the anxious touch. It is comparable to spontaneous combustion. It might seem as if there were an entirely different kind of fire in spontaneous love since it can become jealousy. Alas, but it is just this fire that is the terrible thing. It might seem as if jealousy held its object firmly in an entirely different way when it watches it with a hundred eyes, whereas the simple love has only one eye, as it were, for its love. But is fragmentation stronger than unity; is a heart torn asunder stronger than a whole and undivided heart; does a perpetually anxious grasp hold its object more firmly than the unified powers of simplicity! How, then, is that simple love secured against the sickness of jealousy? Is it not in this

way, that it does not love by way of comparison? It does not begin with spontaneously loving according to preference—it loves. Therefore it can never
reach the point of sickly loving by way of comparison—it loves.

Spontaneous love can be changed *from itself,* it can be changed over the
years, as is frequently enough seen. Then love loses its ardor, its joy, its desire,
its originality, its freshness. Just as the river that sprang out of the rocks is dissipated further down in the sluggishness of the dead waters, so also love is
dissipated in the lukewarmness and indifference of habit. Alas, of all enemies,
habit is perhaps the most cunning, and above all it is cunning enough never
to let itself be seen, because the person who sees the habit is saved from the
habit. Habit is not like other enemies that one sees and against which one
aggressively defends oneself; the struggle is actually with oneself in getting
to see it. There is a predatory creature, known for its cunning, that slyly attacks the sleeping; while it is sucking blood from the sleeper, it fans and cools
him and makes his sleep even more pleasant. Such is habit—or it is even
worse; that creature seeks its prey among the sleeping, but it has no means
to lull to sleep those who are awake. Habit, however, has this; it sneaks, sleep-
lulling, upon a person, and when this has happened it sucks the blood of the
sleeper while it fans and cools him and makes his sleep even more pleasant.

In the same way spontaneous love can be changed from itself and become
unrecognizable, since hate and jealousy are still recognized as signs of love.
Sometimes a person becomes aware, as when a dream flashes by and is forgotten, that habit has changed him; he wants to make amends but does not
know where he should go and buy new oil to rekindle his love. Then he becomes despondent, annoyed, weary of himself, weary of his love, weary of
its being as paltry as it is, weary of not being able to get it changed, because
unfortunately he had not in good time paid attention to eternity's change
and now has even lost the capacity to endure the cure. It is sad to see occasionally a person who once lived in prosperity but now is poverty-stricken,
and yet how much sadder that change when one sees a love changed to something almost loathsome!

If, however, love has undergone eternity's change by becoming duty, it
does not know habit and habit can never gain power over it. Just as eternal
life is said to have no sighing and no tears, so one could add: and no habit
either, and truly by this we do not say anything less glorious. If you want to
save your soul or your love from habit's cunning—yes, people believe there
are many ways to keep oneself awake and secure, but there really is only one:
eternity's *shall.* Let the thunder of a hundred cannons remind you three times
a day to resist the force of habit. Like that mighty Eastern emperor,[146] keep
a slave who reminds you daily, keep hundreds. Have a friend who reminds
you every time he sees you. Have a wife who, in love, reminds you early and
late—but take care that this does not also become a habit! You can become
so habituated to hearing the thunder of a hundred cannons that you can sit

IX
40

at the table and hear the slightest triviality much more clearly than the thunder of the hundred cannons—which you have become habituated to hearing. You can become so habituated to having hundreds of slaves remind you every day that you no longer hear them, because through habit you have acquired ears that hear and yet do not hear. No, only eternity's *you shall*—and the listening ear that wants to hear this *shall*—can save you from habit. Habit is the most lamentable change, but on the other hand one can become habituated to any change. Only the eternal, and therefore that which has undergone the change of eternity by becoming duty, is the unchanging—but the unchanging that specifically cannot become habit. However firmly a habit fixes itself, it never becomes the unchanging, even if a person becomes incorrigible, since habit is continually something that *ought to be changed*; the unchanging, however, is something that neither *can* nor *ought* to be changed. But the eternal never becomes old and never a habit.

IX
41

Only when it is a duty to love, only then is love eternally made free in blessed independence. But, then, is spontaneous love not free? Has the lover no freedom at all in his love? On the other hand, should it be the intention of the discourse to praise the disconsolate independence of self-love that became independent because it did not have the courage to bind itself, that is, because it became dependent upon its cowardliness—the disconsolate independence that floats because it found no abode and is like "someone who wanders here and there, an armed highwayman who puts up wherever night finds him,"[147] the disconsolate independence that independently bears no chains—at least not visibly? Far from it. On the contrary, we have pointed out above that the expression of the greatest riches is to have a need; therefore, that it is a need in the free person is indeed the true expression of freedom. The one in whom love is a need certainly feels free in his love, and the very one who feels totally dependent, so that he would lose everything by losing the beloved, that very one is independent. Yet on one condition, that he does not confuse love with possessing the beloved. If someone were to say "Either love or die" and thereby mean that a life without loving is not worth living, we would completely agree. But if by the first he understood possessing the beloved and thus meant either to possess the beloved or die, either win this friend or die, then we must say that such a misconceived love is dependent. As soon as love, in its relation to its object, does not in that relation relate itself just as much to itself, although it still is entirely dependent, it is dependent in a false sense, it has the law of its existence outside itself and is dependent in a corruptible, in an earthly, in a temporal sense. But the love that has undergone the change of eternity by becoming duty and loves because it *shall* love—that love is independent and has the law for its existence in the relation of love itself to the eternal. This love can never become dependent in a false sense, because the only thing it is dependent upon is duty, and only duty is liberating. Spontaneous love makes a person free and at the next moment dependent. It is just as with a person's coming into existence; by coming into existence, by becoming a self,[148] he becomes free, but at the next moment he is dependent on this self. Duty, however, makes a person dependent and at the same moment eternally independent. "Only law can give freedom."[149] Alas, we very often think that freedom exists and that it is law that binds freedom. Yet it is just the opposite; without law, freedom does not exist at all, and it is law that gives freedom. We also believe that it is law that makes distinctions, because when there is no law there are no distinctions at all. Yet it is the opposite; when it is law that makes distinctions, it is precisely law that makes all equal before the law.

IX
42

This *shall*, then, makes love free in blessed independence. Such a love stands and does not fall with the contingency of its object but stands and falls with the Law of eternity—but then, of course, it never falls. Such a love is not dependent on this or that; it is dependent only on that alone which liberates—therefore it is eternally independent. No independence can be compared to this independence. Sometimes the world praises the proud independence that thinks it has no need to feel loved, even though it also thinks it "needs other people—not in order to be loved by them but in order to love them, in order to have someone to love." How false this independence is! It feels no *need* to be loved and yet *needs* someone to love; therefore it needs another person—in order to gratify its proud self-esteem. Is this not like the vanity that thinks it can do without the world and still needs the world—that is, needs the world to find out that vanity does not need the world! But the love that has undergone the change of eternity by becoming duty certainly feels a need to be loved, and therefore this need is eternally in harmonizing agreement with this *shall*; but it can do without, if so it *shall* be, while it still continues to love—is this not independence? This independence depends only on love itself through eternity's *shall*; it does not depend on something else and therefore does not depend on the object of love as soon as this appears to be something else. Yet this does not mean that the independent love has then ceased, has changed into proud self-satisfaction—this is dependence. No, love abides; this is independence. Unchangingness is the true independence. Every change—be it the swooning of weakness or the strutting of pride, be it sighing or self-satisfied—is dependence. If when another person says, "I cannot love you any longer," one proudly answers, "Then I can also stop loving you"—is this independence? Alas, it is dependence, because whether he will continue to love or not depends upon whether the other will love. But the person who answers, "In that case I *shall* still continue to love you"—that person's love is made eternally free in blessed independence. He does not say it proudly—dependent upon his pride—no, he says it humbly, humbling himself under eternity's *shall*, and for that very reason he is independent.

IX
43

Only when it is a duty to love, only then is love eternally and happily secured against despair. Spontaneous love can become unhappy, can reach the point of despair. Again it might seem to be an expression of the strength of this love that it has the power of despair, but this is mere appearance, since the power of despair, however much it is praised, is actually powerlessness; its peak is precisely its downfall. Yet this, that spontaneous love can reach the point of despair, shows that it is in despair, that even when it is happy it loves with the power of despair—loves another person "more than itself, more than God." Of despair it must be said: Only that person can despair who is in despair. When spontaneous love despairs over misfortune, it only becomes manifest that it was in despair, that in its happiness it had also been in despair.

The despair is due to relating oneself with infinite passion to a particular something, for one can relate oneself with infinite passion—unless one is in despair—only to the eternal. Spontaneous love *is* in despair in this way, but when it becomes happy, as it is called, its being in despair is hidden from it; when it becomes unhappy, it becomes manifest that it was in despair. In contrast, the love that has undergone the change of eternity by becoming duty can never despair, simply because it *is* not in despair. That is to say, despair is not something that can happen to a person, an event such as good fortune and misfortune. Despair is a misrelation in a person's innermost being—no fate or event can penetrate so far and so deep; it can only make manifest that the misrelation—was there. For this reason there is only one security against despair: to undergo the change of eternity through duty's *shall.* Anyone who has not undergone this change *is* in despair. Good fortune and prosperity can hide it, but misfortune and adversity do not, as he thinks, make him despair but make it manifest that he—was in despair. If one speaks differently, it is because one frivolously confuses the highest concepts. In other words, what makes a person despair is not misfortune but his lack of the eternal. Despair is to lack the eternal; despair is not to have undergone the change of eternity through duty's *shall.* Despair is not, therefore, the loss of the beloved— that is unhappiness, pain, suffering—but despair is the lack of the eternal.[150]

How, then, is the commandment's love secured against despair? Very simply, by the commandment, by this "You shall love." This implies first and foremost that you must not love in such a way that the loss of the beloved would make it manifest that you were in despair—that is, you must not love in despair. Is loving thereby forbidden? By no means. It would be indeed strange if the commandment that says "You shall love" were by its own command to forbid loving. Thus the commandment only forbids loving in a way that is not commanded. Essentially the commandment is not forbidding but commanding, that you shall love. Therefore love's commandment does not secure against despair by means of feeble, lukewarm grounds of comfort—that one must not take something too hard, etc. Indeed, is such a wretched sagacity, which "has ceased to sorrow," any less despair than the lover's despair; is it not rather an even worse kind of despair! No, love's commandment forbids despair—by commanding one to love.

Who would have this courage except eternity; who has the right to say this *shall* except eternity, which at the very moment love wants to despair over its unhappiness commands it to love; where can this command have its home except in eternity? When it is made impossible to possess the beloved in time, eternity says, "You shall love"—that is, eternity then saves love from despair by making it eternal. Suppose it is death that separates the two—then what will be of help when the survivor would sink in despair? Temporal help is an even more lamentable kind of despair; but then eternity helps. When it says, "You shall love," it is saying, "Your love has an eternal worth." But it does not say it comfortingly, since that would not help; it says it commandingly precisely because there is imminent danger. And when eternity says, "You shall love," it is responsible for making sure that this can be done. What is all other comfort compared with that of eternity! What is all other spiritual care compared with that of eternity! If it were to speak more gently and say, "Console yourself," the sorrowing one would certainly have objections ready; but—indeed, it is not because eternity will proudly tolerate no objections—out of solicitude for the sorrowing one, eternity commands, "You shall love."

Marvelous words of comfort, marvelous compassion, because, humanly speaking, it is indeed most strange, almost like mockery, to say to the despairing person that he *shall* do that which was his sole desire but the impossibility of which brings him to despair. Is any other evidence needed that the love commandment is of divine origin! If you have tested it, or if you do test it, go to such a sorrowing one in the moment when the loss of the beloved is about to overwhelm him and then see what you can find to say. Admit it, you want to comfort him, and the only thing you will not think of is to say, "You shall love." On the other hand, test whether it does not almost embitter the sorrowing one the very moment it is said because it seems the most unsuitable thing to say on this occasion. Ah, but you who have had this earnest experience, you who in the dark moment found emptiness and loathsomeness in human grounds of comfort, but no consolation, you who appallingly discovered that not even eternity's admonition could keep you from sinking—you learned to love this *shall* that saves from despair! What you perhaps frequently had verified in lesser instances, that true upbuilding consists in being spoken to rigorously, you learned here in the deepest sense: that only this *shall* eternally and happily saves from despair. Eternally and happily—yes, because only that person is saved from despair who is *eternally* saved from despair. The love that has undergone eternity's change by becoming duty is not exempted from misfortune, but it is saved from despair, in fortune and misfortune equally saved from despair.

IX
45

See, passion inflames, worldly sagacity cools, but neither this heat nor this cold nor the combination of this heat and this cold is the pure air of the eternal. There is something inciting in this heat, and there is something sharp in this cold, and in the combination there is something indefinite, or an unconscious treachery, as in the dangerous time of spring. But this "You *shall* love" removes all the unhealthiness and preserves the healthiness for eternity. So it is everywhere, this *shall* of eternity is the saving, the purifying, the ennobling element. Sit with someone who deeply mourns. If you have the ability to give to passion the expression of despair as not even the sorrowing one can do, it may soothe for a moment—but it is still false. If you have the sagacity and experience to provide a temporary prospect where the sorrowing one sees none, it can be refreshingly tempting for a moment—but it is still false. But this "You shall sorrow" is both true and beautiful. I do not have the right to become insensitive to life's pain, because I *shall* sorrow; but neither do I have the right to despair, because I shall sorrow; and neither do I have the right to stop sorrowing, because I *shall* sorrow. So it is with love. You do not have the right to become insensitive to this feeling, because you *shall* love; but neither do you have the right to love despairingly, because you *shall* love; and just as little do you have the right to warp this feeling in you, because you *shall* love. You shall preserve love, and you shall preserve yourself and by and in preserving yourself preserve love. Wherever the purely human wants to storm forth, the commandment constrains; wherever the purely human loses courage, the commandment strengthens; wherever the purely human becomes tired and sagacious, the commandment inflames and gives wisdom. The commandment consumes and burns out the unhealthiness in your love, but through the commandment you will in turn be able to rekindle it when it, humanly speaking, would cease. Where you think you can easily go your own way, there take the commandment as counsel; where you despairingly want to go your own way, there take the commandment as counsel; but where you do not know what to do, there the commandment will counsel so that all turns out well nevertheless.

IX
46

IX
63

YOU SHALL LOVE THE NEIGHBOR

Go, then, and do this, take away dissimilarity and its similarity[151] so that you can love the neighbor. Take away the distinction of preferential love so that you can love the neighbor. But you are not to cease loving the beloved because of this—far from it. If in order to love the neighbor you would have to begin by giving up loving those for whom you have preference, the word "neighbor" would be the greatest deception ever contrived. Moreover, it would even be a contradiction, since inasmuch as the neighbor is all people surely no one can be excluded—should we now say, least of all the beloved? No, because this is the language of preference. Thus, it is only the preferential love that should be taken away—and yet it is not to be introduced in turn into the relation to the neighbor so that with twisted preference you would love the neighbor in contrast to the beloved. No, just as we say to the solitary person: Take care that you are not led into the snare of self-love, so it must be said to the two lovers: Take care that you are not led by erotic love itself into the snare of self-love. The more decisively and exclusively preferential love embraces one single person, the further it is from loving the neighbor. You, husband, do not lead your wife into the temptation of forgetting to love the neighbor because of you; you, wife, do not lead your husband into this temptation! The lovers no doubt think that in erotic love they have the highest, but this is not so, because in it they still do not have the eternal secured by the eternal. To be sure, the poet promises the lovers immortality if they are true lovers; but who then is the poet, what good is his vouching, he who cannot vouch for himself? In contrast, the *royal Law*, the love commandment, promises life, eternal life, and this commandment simply says, "You shall love your neighbor." Just as this commandment will teach everyone how to love oneself, so it also will teach erotic love and friendship genuine love: in loving yourself, preserve love for the neighbor; in erotic love and friendship, preserve love for the neighbor. This will perhaps shock you— well, you do indeed know that the essentially Christian is always attended by signs of offense. Nevertheless, believe it. Do not believe that the teacher who did not extinguish any smoking wick would extinguish any noble fire within a person. Believe that he who was love will expressly teach every person to love. Believe that if all the poets joined in one song of praise to erotic love and friendship, what they would have to say would be nothing in comparison with the commandment: "You *shall* love, you shall love your neighbor as yourself!" Do not cease to believe because the commandment almost offends you, because the discourse does not sound flattering like that of the poet, who with his songs insinuates himself into your happiness, but sounds repelling and terrifying, as if it would frighten you out of the beloved haunts of preferential love—do not for that reason cease to believe it. Bear in mind that just because the commandment and the discourse are like this, for that very reason the object can be the object of faith!

Do not delude yourself into thinking that you could bargain, that by loving some people, relatives and friends, you would be loving the neighbor— because this is giving up the poet without grasping the essentially Christian, and it was to prevent this bargaining that the discourse sought to place you between the poet's pride, which scorns all bargaining, and the divine majesty of the royal Law, which makes all bargaining into guilt. No, love the beloved faithfully and tenderly, but let love for the neighbor be the sanctifying element in your union's covenant with God. Love your friend honestly and de-

IX
64

votedly, but let love for the neighbor be what you learn from each other in your friendship's confidential relationship with God! Death, you see, abolishes all dissimilarities, but preference is always related to dissimilarities; yet the way to life and to the eternal goes through death and through the abolition of dissimilarities—therefore only love for the neighbor truly leads to life. Just as Christianity's joyful message is contained in the doctrine of humanity's inherent kinship with God, so is Christianity's task humanity's likeness to God. But God is Love, and therefore we can be like God only in loving, just as we also, according to the words of the apostle, can only be *God's co-workers—in love.* Insofar as you love the beloved, you are not like God, because for God there is no preference, something you have reflected on many times to your humiliation, but also many times to your rehabilitation. Insofar as you love your friend, you are not like God, because for God there is no distinction. But when you love the neighbor, then you are like God.

Therefore, go and do likewise. Forsake the dissimilarities so that you can love the neighbor. Alas, perhaps it is not even necessary to say this to you; perhaps you found no beloved in this world, no friend along the way, so that you are walking alone. Or perhaps God took from your side and gave you the beloved, but death took and took her from your side; it took again and took your friend but gave you none in return, so that now you walk alone, have no beloved to cover your weak side and no friend on your right side. Or perhaps life separated the two of you, even if you both remained unchanged—in the solitariness of separation. Alas, perhaps change separated the two of you, so that you walk sorrowfully alone because you did find but in turn found what you found—changed! How disconsolate! Indeed, just ask the poet if he knows anything else but that it is disconsolate when death comes between the lovers, or when life separates friend from friend, or when change separates them as enemies from each other. The poet does indeed love solitude, loves it—in order to discover in solitude the missing happiness of erotic love and friendship, just as one who in wonder wants to observe the stars seeks a dark place. And yet, if it was through no fault of his own that a person found no beloved, and if he sought a friend but, through no fault of his own, in vain, and if the loss, the separation, the change were not his fault—in that case does the poet know anything else but that it is disconsolate? But then the poet himself is surely subject to change if he, the prophet of joy, does not know anything else on the day of distress but the mournful lament of disconsolateness. Or would you not call it change, would you call it faithfulness on the part of the poet that he disconsolately sorrows with the disconsolate sorrowing— well, we will not quarrel about that. But if you will compare this human faithfulness with heaven's and eternity's, you yourself will certainly admit that it is a change. Heaven not only rejoices, more than any poet, with the joyful; heaven not only sorrows with the sorrowing—no, heaven has a new, has a more blessed, joy in readiness for the sorrowing.

Thus Christianity always has consolation, and its consolation is different from all human consolation in that the latter is aware only of being a compensation for the loss of joy—Christian consolation *is joy.* Humanly speaking, consolation is a later invention. First came suffering and pain and the loss of joy, and then afterward, alas, long, long afterward, humanity picked up the track of consolation. The same is true of the individual's life: first comes suffering and pain and the loss of joy, and then, afterward, alas, sometimes long, long afterward, comes the consolation. But Christian consolation can never be said to come afterward, because, since it is eternity's consolation, it is older than all temporal joy. As soon as this consolation comes, it comes with the head start of eternity and swallows up the pain, as it were, since the pain and the loss of joy are the momentary—even if the moment were years—are the momentary that is drowned in the eternal. Neither is Christian consolation a compensation for the loss of joy, since it is joy. In comparison with Christianity's consolation, all other joy is ultimately only disconsolate. Alas, a human being's life was not and is not so perfect on this earth that eternity's joy could be proclaimed to him as joy; he himself had and has forfeited it; that is why eternity's joy can be proclaimed to him only as consolation. Just as the human eye cannot bear to look at the light of the sun except through a dark glass, so also the human being cannot bear eternity's joy except through the obscurity of its being proclaimed as consolation.

Thus, whatever your fate was in erotic love and friendship, whatever your lack, whatever your loss was, whatever the personal disconsolateness of your life that you confide to the poet—the highest still remains: love the neighbor! As already shown, him you can easily find; him, as already shown, you can unconditionally always find; him you can never lose. The beloved can treat you in such a way that he is lost, and you can lose a friend; but whatever the neighbor does to you, you can never lose him. To be sure, you can also continue to love the beloved and the friend no matter how they treat you, but you cannot truly continue to call them the beloved and friend if they, sorry to say, have really changed. No change, however, can take the neighbor from you, because it is not the neighbor who holds you fast, but it is your love that holds the neighbor fast. If your love for the neighbor remains unchanged, then the neighbor also remains unchanged by existing. Death cannot deprive you of the neighbor, for if it takes one, life immediately gives you another. Death can deprive you of a friend, because in loving a friend you actually hold together with the friend, but in loving the neighbor you hold together with God; therefore death cannot deprive you of the neighbor. —If, therefore, you have lost everything in erotic love and friendship, if you have never had any of this happiness—you still retain the best in loving the neighbor.

Love for the neighbor has, namely, the perfections of eternity. Is it really a perfec-

tion in the love that its object is the excellent, the distinguished, the unique?
I should think that this would be a perfection in the object and that this perfection of the object would be a subtle misgiving about the perfection of the
love. Is it an excellent quality in your love if it can love *only* the extraordinary, the rare? I should think it to be an excellence in the extraordinary and
the rare that it is the extraordinary and the rare, but not in the love. Are you
not of the same opinion? Have you never thought about God's love? If it
were love's excellence to love the extraordinary, then God would be, if I dare
say so, in an awkward position, since for him the extraordinary does not exist
at all. The excellence of being able to love *only* the extraordinary is therefore
more like an accusation, not against the extraordinary nor against the love,
but against the love that is able to love only the extraordinary.

IX
86
    Just look at the world that lies before you in all its variegated multifari-
ousness; it is like looking at a play, except that the multifariousness is much,
much greater. Because of his dissimilarity, every single one of these innumerable individuals is something particular, represents something particular,
but essentially he is something else. Yet this you do not get to see here in life;
here you see only what the individual represents and how he does it. It is just
as in the play. But when the curtain falls on the stage, then the one who
played the king and the one who played the beggar etc. are all alike; all are
one and the same—actors. When at death the curtain falls on the stage of
actuality (it is a confusing use of language to say that at death the curtain is
raised on the stage of eternity, since eternity is not a stage at all; it is truth),
then they, too, are all one, they are human beings. All of them are what they
essentially were, what you did not see because of the dissimilarity that you
saw—they are human beings.
    The theater of art is like a world under a magic spell. But just suppose that
some evening all the actors became confused in a common absentmindedness so that they thought they actually were what they represented. Would
this not be what we might call, in contrast to the spell of the dramatic arts,
the spell of an evil spirit, a bewitchment? Similarly, what if under the spell
of actuality (for we are indeed all under a spell, each one conjured into his
dissimilarity) our fundamental ideas became confused so that we thought that
we essentially are what we represent? Alas, is this not just the way it is? We
seem to have forgotten that the dissimilarity of earthly life is just like an
actor's costume, or just like a traveler's cloak, so that each one individually
should be on the watch and take care to have the outer garment's fastening
cords loosely tied and, above all, free of tight knots so that in the moment
of transformation the garment can be cast off easily. Yet we all, of course,
have enough artistic sense to be jarred if an actor on stage, when in the moment of transformation he is supposed to throw off his disguise, has to run
offstage to get the cords untied. But, alas, in the life of actuality one laces the

outer garment of dissimilarity so tight that it completely conceals the fact that this dissimilarity is an outer garment, because the inner glory of equality never or very rarely shines through as it continually should and ought.

The actor's art is the art of deceiving; the art is the deception. To be able to deceive is the great thing, and to allow oneself to be deceived is just as great. Therefore one must not be able and must not want to see the actor through the costume; therefore it is the pinnacle of art when the actor becomes one with what he represents, because this is the pinnacle of deception. But the actuality of life, even if it is not, like eternity, the truth, still ought to be of the truth, and therefore the other something that everyone essentially is should continually glimmer through the disguise. Alas, but in the life of actuality, there the individual in his temporal growth grows together with the dissimilarity; this is the opposite of eternity's growth, which grows away from the dissimilarity. The individual becomes deformed; from eternity's point of view, every such individual is a cripple. In actuality, alas, the individual grows together with his dissimilarity in such a way that in the end death must use force to tear it from him.

Yet if someone is truly to love his neighbor, it must be kept in mind at all times that his dissimilarity is a disguise. As previously said, Christianity has not wanted to storm forth to abolish dissimilarity, neither the dissimilarity of distinction nor of lowliness; nor has it wished to effect in a worldly way a worldly compromise among the dissimilarities; but it wants the dissimilarity to hang loosely on the individual, as loosely as the cape the king casts off in order to show who he is, as loosely as the ragged costume in which a supranatural being has disguised himself. In other words, when the dissimilarity hangs loosely in this way, then in each individual there continually glimmers that essential other, which is common to all, the eternal resemblance, the likeness.

If this were the case, if each individual lived this way, then temporality would have reached its highest. It cannot be like eternity, but this expectant solemnity that without stopping the course of life rejuvenates itself every day with the eternal and with eternity's equality, every day saves the soul from the dissimilarity in which it still remains—this would be the reflection of eternity. If, then, in the life of actuality you should see the ruler, cheerfully and respectfully bring him your homage, but you would still see in the ruler the inner glory, the equality of the glory, that his magnificence merely conceals. If, then, you should see the beggar—perhaps in your sorrow over him suffering more than he—you would still see in him the inner glory, the equality of the glory, that his wretched outer garment conceals. Yes, then you would see, wherever you turned your eye, the neighbor. From the beginning of the world, no human being exists or has existed who is the neighbor in the sense that the king is the king, the scholar the scholar, your relative your relative—that is, in the sense of exceptionality or, what amounts to the same

IX
87

IX
88

thing, in the sense of dissimilarity—no, every human being is the neighbor. In being king, beggar, rich man, poor man, male, female, etc., we are not like each other—therein we are indeed different. But in being the neighbor we are all unconditionally like each other. Dissimilarity is temporality's method of confusing that marks every human being differently, but the neighbor is eternity's mark—on every human being. Take many sheets of paper, write something different on each one; then no one will be like another. But then again take each single sheet; do not let yourself be confused by the diverse inscriptions, hold it up to the light, and you will see a common watermark on all of them. In the same way the neighbor is the common watermark, but you see it only by means of eternity's light when it shines through the dissimilarity.

IX
156

When it is a duty in loving to love the people we see, *then in loving the actual individual person it is important that one does not substitute an imaginary idea of how we think or could wish that this person should be.* The one who does this does not love the person he sees but again something unseen, his own idea or something similar.

In connection with loving there is a kind of conduct that for love has a dubious addition of equivocation and fastidiousness. It is one thing, of course, to reject and reject again and never find any object for one's love; it is something else in loving what a person himself calls the object of his love

IX
157

to fulfill scrupulously and honestly this duty to love what one sees. It is indeed always a worthy wish and again a worthy wish that the one we are to love may have the lovable perfections—we wish it not only for our own sakes but also for the sake of the other. Above all, it is worthy to wish and to pray that the one we love might always be and act in such a way that we are able to approve and agree completely. But in God's name let us not forget that it is not a merit on our part if he is like that, even less a merit on our part to require this of him—if there is to be any question of merit on our part, which nevertheless is unseemly and an unseemly way to talk with regard to love, it would just be to love equally faithfully and tenderly.

But there is a fastidiousness that continually works, as it were, against love and wants to prevent it from loving what it sees, since fastidiousness, unsteady of glance and yet in another sense very precise, volatilizes the actual form or takes offense at it and then cunningly demands to see something else. There are people of whom it may be said that they have not attained form, that their actuality has not become integrated, because in their innermost beings they are at odds with themselves about what they are and what they will to be. But one can, by the way in which one sees, make another person's form vacillating or unreal, because love, which should love the person it sees, cannot really make up its mind but at one time wants to have a defect removed from the object and at another wants a perfection added—as if the bargain, if I may put it that way, were not as yet concluded. But the person who in loving this way is inclined to be fastidious does not love the one he sees and easily makes even his love as loathsome to himself as he makes it difficult for the beloved.

The beloved, the friend, is of course a human being also in the more ordinary sense and exists as such for the rest of us, but for you he should exist essentially only as the beloved if you are to fulfill the duty of loving the person you see. If there is a duality in your relationship so that to you he is partly just this individual human being in the more ordinary sense, partly the beloved in particular, then you do not love the person you see. Instead it is as if you had two ears in the sense that you do not, as is normal, hear one thing with both ears but hear one thing with one and something else with the other. With the one ear you hear what he says and whether it is wise and correct and penetrating and brilliant etc., and, alas, only with the other ear do you hear that it is the beloved's voice. With the one eye you look at him, testing, searching, criticizing, and, alas, only with the other eye do you see that he is the beloved. Ah, but to divide in this way is not to love the person one sees. Is it not as if there were a third party always present, even when the two are alone, a third who coldly examines and rejects, a third who disturbs the intimacy, a third who sometimes may even make the person concerned disgusted with himself and his love because of being fastidious in this way, a third who would upset the beloved if he knew that this third is present! What, indeed, does it mean that this third is present? Does it mean that you cannot love if . . . . . if now this or that is not according to your wishes? Does the third party therefore mean disunion, separation, so that as a consequence the thought of separation takes part—in the confidential relationship, alas, just as when in paganism the destructive nature was insanely included in the unity of the godhead? Does this third party mean that in a certain sense the love-relationship is no relationship at all, that you stand above the relationship and test the beloved? In that case, do you consider that something else is being tested, whether you actually do have love or, more accurately, that something else is decided, that you actually do not have love?

IX
158

Life certainly has tests enough, and these tests should find the lovers, find friend and friend, united in order to pass the test. But if the test is dragged into the relationship, treachery has been committed. Indeed, this secretive inclosing reserve is the most dangerous kind of faithlessness; such a person does not break faith but continually leaves it vague whether he is bound by his faith. Is it not faithlessness when your friend shakes your hand and there is something indefinite about your handshake, as if it were he who clasped your hand but it was doubtful to what extent he corresponded at that moment to your conception, so that you responded in the same way? Is it being in a relationship if one at every moment seems to begin all over to enter into the relationship; is it loving the person you see if you at every moment look at him, testing, as if it were the first time you saw him? It is disgusting to see the fastidious person who rejects all food, but it is also disgusting to see the one who does eat the food graciously offered him and yet in a sense does not eat it but continually only samples the food as if he had eaten his fill or makes an effort to taste a more delectable dish but is sated by the simpler food.

IX
159

No, if a person is to fulfill the duty in loving to love the people he sees, then he must not only find among actual people those he loves, but he must root out all equivocation and fastidiousness in loving them so that in earnestness and truth he loves them as they are and in earnestness and truth takes hold of the task: to find the once given or chosen object lovable. By this we do not mean to recommend a childish infatuation with the beloved's accidental characteristics, still less a misplaced sentimental indulgence. Far from it, the earnestness consists precisely in this, that the relationship itself will with integrated power fight against the imperfection, overcome the defect, and remove the heterogeneity. This is earnestness; fastidiousness makes the relationship itself equivocal. One of the two, through his weakness or by his defect, does not become alien to the other, but the union regards the weaker element as something alien, the overcoming and removal of which is equally important to both. It is not you who, on the grounds of the weakness of the beloved, are to remove yourself, as it were, from him or make your relationship more distant; on the contrary, the two are to hold together all the more firmly and inwardly in order to remove the weakness. As soon as the relationship is made equivocal, you do not love the person you see; then it is indeed as if you demanded something else in order to be able to love. On the other hand, when the defect or the weakness makes the relationship more inward, not as if the defect should now become entrenched but in order to conquer it, then you love the person you see. You see the defect, but the fact that your relationship then becomes more inward shows that you love the person in whom you see the defect or the weakness or the imperfection.

Just as there are hypocritical tears, a hypocritical sighing and complaining about the world, so also there is a hypocritical sorrow over the beloved's weaknesses and imperfections. It is very soft and easy to wish the beloved to have all possible perfections, and then if something is lacking it is in turn very soft and easy to sigh and sorrow and become self-important by one's presumably very pure and very deep sorrow. On the whole, it is perhaps a more common form of sensuality to want selfishly to make a show of the beloved or friend and to despair over every triviality. But would this be loving the people one sees? Ah, no, the people one sees, and likewise we ourselves when others see us, are not perfect; and yet it is very often the case that a person develops within himself this sentimental frailty that is designed only for loving the absolute epitome of perfections. And yet, although we human beings are all imperfect, we very rarely see the healthy, strong, capable love that is designed for loving the more imperfect persons, that is, the people we see.

IX
160

When it is a duty in loving to love the people we see, *there is no limit to love; if the duty is to be fulfilled, love must be limitless, it is unchanged, no matter how the object becomes changed.*

LOVE BUILDS UP[152]

I Corinthians 8:1. But love builds up.

All human speech, even the divine speech of Holy Scripture, about the spiritual is essentially metaphorical [*overført,* carried over] speech. And this is quite in order or in the order of things and of existence, since a human being, even if from the moment of birth he is spirit, still does not become conscious of himself as spirit until later and thus has sensately-psychically acted out a certain part of his life prior to this. But this first portion is not to be cast aside when the spirit awakens any more than the awakening of the spirit in contrast to the sensate-psychical announces itself in a sensate-psychical way. On the contrary, the first portion is taken over [*overtage*] by the spirit and, used in this way, is thus made the basis—*it becomes the metaphorical.* Therefore, in one sense the spiritual person and the sensate-psychical person say the same thing; yet there is an infinite difference, since the latter has no intimation of the secret of the metaphorical words although he is using the same words, but not in their metaphorical sense. There is a world of difference between the two; the one has made the transition [*Overgang*] or let himself be *carried over* [*føre over*] to the other side, while the other remains on this side; yet they have the connection that both are using the same words. The person in whom the spirit has awakened does not as a consequence abandon the visible world. Although conscious of himself as spirit, he continues to remain in the visible world and to be visible to the senses—in the same way he also remains in the language, except that his language is the metaphorical language! But the metaphorical words are of course not brand-new words but are the already given words. Just as the spirit is invisible, so also is its language a secret, and the secret lies in its using the same words as the child and the simpleminded person but using them metaphorically, whereby the spirit denies being the sensate or the sensate-psychical but does not deny it in a sensate-psychical way. The difference is by no means a noticeable difference. For this reason we rightfully regard it as a sign of false spirituality to parade a noticeable difference—which is merely sensate, whereas the spirit's manner is the metaphor's quiet, whispering secret—for the person who has ears to hear.

One of the metaphorical expressions that Holy Scripture frequently uses, or one of the phrases that Holy Scripture frequently uses metaphorically, is: "to build up." And it is already upbuilding [*opbyggelig*]—indeed, it is very upbuilding to see how Holy Scripture does not become weary of this simple phrase, how it does not ingeniously strive for variety and new turns of phrase but, on the contrary and in keeping with the true nature of spirit, renews the thought in the same words! And it is—indeed, it is very upbuilding to see how Scripture manages to describe the highest with this simple word and to do it in the most inward way; it is almost like the miracle of that feeding with the limited supply that by being blessed stretched out so exceedingly that there were leftovers. And it is—indeed, it is very upbuilding when someone humbly manages to be satisfied with the scriptural word instead of busily making new discoveries that will busily displace the old, when someone gratefully and inwardly appropriates what has been handed down from the fathers and establishes a new acquaintance with the old and familiar. As children we no doubt have often played the game of Stranger: this is precisely the earnestness, to be able to continue in earnest this upbuilding jest, to play Stranger with the old and familiar.

"To build up" is a metaphorical expression; yet with this secret of the spirit in mind, we shall now see *what this word signifies in ordinary speech.* "To build up" is formed from "to build" and the adverb "up," which consequently must receive the accent. Everyone who builds up does build, but not everyone who builds does build up. For example, when a man is building a wing on his house we do not say that he is building up a wing but that he is building *on.* Consequently, this "up" seems to indicate the direction in height, the upward direction. Yet this is not the case either. For example, if a man builds a sixty-foot building twenty feet higher, we still do not say that he *built up* the structure twenty feet higher—we say that he built *on.* Here the meaning of the word already becomes perceptible, for we see that it does not depend on height. However, if a man erects a house, be it ever so small and low, from the ground up, we say that he built up a house.[153] Thus to build up is to erect something *from the ground up.* This "up" does indeed indicate the direction as upward, but only when the height inversely is depth do we say "build up." Therefore if a man builds upward and from the ground but the depth does not correspond properly to the height, we do say that he built up but also that he built it up poorly, whereas by "build poorly" we understand something else. With regard to building up, then, the emphasis rests especially on building from the ground up. We certainly do not call building into the ground building up; we do not say that we are building up a well. If there is to be any talk of building up, then no matter how high or low the building becomes, the work must be *from the ground up.* Thus we may say of someone: He began to build up a house, but he did not finish. However, we can never say of someone who added ever so much to the building in height that he built it up if he did not do it from the ground up. How strange! This "up" in "build up" indicates height, but it indicates height inversely as depth, since to build up is to build from the ground up. This is why Scripture also says of the foolish man that he "built without a foundation";[154] but of the person who hears the word to his true upbuilding or, according to Scripture, the person who hears the word and does accordingly, of him it says that he is like a person who built a house and "dug deep" (Luke 6:48). Therefore when the floodwaters came and the storm beat upon this soundly built-up house, we all rejoiced at the up-building sight, that the storm was unable to shake it. As we said, when it comes to building up, the point is to build a foundation. It is commendable that before beginning a man calculates "how high he can erect the tower,"[155] but if he is going to build up, then by all means have him be careful to dig deep, be-cause even if the tower reached the sky, if this were possible, if it lacked a foundation, it would not actually be built up. To build up without a founda- IX tion at all is impossible—it is building in the air. Therefore, one is linguisti- 204 cally correct in speaking of "building air castles"; one does not say "build up air castles," which would be careless and incorrect use of language. Even in a phrase denoting something insignificant there must be congruity between the separate words; there is none between "in the air" and "to build up," since the former takes away the foundation and the latter refers to this "from the ground up." The combination, therefore, would be a false overstatement.

So it is with the expression "to build up" in the literal sense; let us now bear in mind that it is a metaphorical expression and proceed to the subject of this deliberation:

Love builds up.

But is "to build up," in the spiritual sense, a predicate so characteristic of love that it is suitable solely and only for it? Ordinarily it is the case with a predicate that there are many objects that all equally, even though in varying degrees, have a claim to one and the same predicate. If this is the case with "to build up," it would be wrong to emphasize it so particularly in relation to love as this deliberation does. It would be an endeavor based on a misun-derstanding to impute arrogance to love, as if it wanted to monopolize or usurp what is shared with others—and to share with others is precisely what love is willing to do since it "never seeks its own" (I Corinthians 13:5). Yet it is truly so that "to build up" is exclusively characteristic of love. On the other hand, this quality of building up has in turn the characteristic of being able to give itself in everything, be present in everything—just as love has. Thus we see that love, in this its characteristic quality, does not set itself apart and alongside another; neither does it plume itself on any independence and being-for-itself but completely gives itself; the characteristic is that it exclu-sively has the quality of giving itself completely.

There is nothing, nothing at all, that cannot be done or said in such a way that it becomes upbuilding, but whatever it is, if it is upbuilding, then love is present. Thus the admonition, just where love itself admits the difficulty of giving a specific rule, says, "Do everything for upbuilding."[156] It could just as well have said, "Do everything in love," and it would have said the very same thing. One person can do exactly the opposite of what another person does, but if each one does the opposite—in love—the opposite becomes upbuilding. There is no word in the language that in itself is upbuilding, and there is no word in the language that cannot be said in an upbuilding way and become upbuilding if love is present. Thus, it is so very far from being the case that the upbuilding would be something that is an *excellence* of a few gifted individuals, similar to brains, literary talent, beauty, and the like (alas, this is just an unloving and divisive error!) that on the contrary it is the very opposite—every human being by his life, by his conduct, by his behavior in everyday affairs, by his association with his peers, by his words, his remarks, should and could build up and would do it if love is really present in him.

We, too, notice this ourselves, since we use the word "upbuilding" in the widest range, but what we perhaps do not explain to ourselves is that we still use it only wherever love is present. Yet this is the correct usage of language: to be scrupulous about not using this word except where love is present and in turn, by this limitation, to make its range limitless, since everything can be upbuilding in the same sense as love can be everywhere present. For example, when we see a solitary person managing by commendable frugality to get along thriftily with little, we honor and praise him, we are cheered, and we are confirmed in the good by this sight, but we do not actually say that it is an upbuilding sight. When, however, we see how a housewife, one who has many to care for, by means of frugality and wise thriftiness lovingly knows how to confer a blessing on the little so that there still is enough for all, we say that this is an upbuilding sight. The upbuilding consists in this, that we see the housewife's loving solicitude at the same time as we see the frugality and thrift, which we honor. On the other hand we say that it is a scarcely upbuilding, a dismal sight to see someone who in a way is starving in abundance and who still has nothing at all left over for others. We say that it is a revolting sight; we are disgusted at his luxury; we shudder to think of self-indulgence's dreadful revenge—to starve in abundance—but our seeking in vain for the slightest expression of love is decisive for us when we say that it is scarcely upbuilding.

When we see a large family packed into a small apartment and yet see it inhabiting a cozy, friendly, spacious apartment—we say it is an upbuilding sight because we see the love that must be in each and every individual, since of course one unloving person would already be enough to occupy the whole place. We say it because we see that there actually is room where there is heart-room. On the other hand, it is scarcely upbuilding to see a restless soul inhabit a palace without finding rest in a single one of the many spacious rooms, and yet without being able to spare or do without the smallest cubbyhole.

Indeed, what is there that cannot be upbuilding in this way! We would not think that the sight of a person sleeping could be upbuilding. Yet if you see a baby sleeping on its mother's breast—and you see the mother's love, see that she has, so to speak, waited for and now makes use of the moment while the baby is sleeping really to rejoice in it because she hardly dares let the baby notice how inexpressibly she loves it—then this is an upbuilding sight. If the mother's love is not visible, if in vain you search her face and countenance for the slightest expression of maternal joy or solicitude for the baby, if you see only apathy and indifference that is happy to be free of the child so long—then the sight is not upbuilding. Just to see the baby sleeping is a friendly, benevolent, soothing sight, but it is not upbuilding. If you still want to call it upbuilding, it is because you see love present, it is because you see God's love encompass the baby. To see the great artist finishing his masterpiece is a glorious and uplifting sight, but it is not upbuilding. Suppose this masterpiece was a marvelous piece; if, now, the artist, out of love for a person, smashed it to pieces—then this sight would be upbuilding.

Wherever upbuilding is, there is love, and wherever love is, there is upbuilding. This is why Paul declares that a person without love, even if he spoke in the tongues of men and of angels, is like a sounding brass and a tinkling cymbal.[157] What, indeed, can be less upbuilding than a tinkling cymbal! The things of this world, however glorious they are and however acclaimed, are without love and therefore are not upbuilding; the most insignificant word, the slightest action with love or in love is upbuilding. Therefore knowledge puffs up.[158] Yet knowledge and the communication of knowledge can indeed also be upbuilding, but if they are, then it is because love is present. To commend oneself hardly seems upbuilding, and yet this, too, can be upbuilding. Does not Paul at times do it? But he does it in love and therefore, as he himself says, "for upbuilding."[159] A discourse about what can be upbuilding would therefore be the most interminable discourse of all discourses, inasmuch as everything can be that; it would be the most interminable discourse, just as it is the most grievous charge that can be made against the world—that we see and hear so little that is upbuilding. If it is rare to see riches, it makes no difference; we wish and prefer to see ordinary prosperity. If it is rare to see a masterpiece, in a certain sense it makes no difference, and to the majority of people it makes no difference. Not so with the upbuilding. At every moment there lives this countless throng of people; it is possible that everything that any human being undertakes, everything that any human being says, can be upbuilding—and yet it is very rare to see or hear anything upbuilding!

Love builds up. Let us now consider what was developed in the introduction, by which we promptly made sure that the discourse would not go astray by choosing an insuperable task, inasmuch as everything can be upbuilding. To build up is to erect something from the ground up. In ordinary talk about a house, a building, everyone knows what is meant by the ground and the foundation. But what, in the spiritual sense, is the ground and foundation of the spiritual life that is to bear the building? It is love. Love is the source of

IX
207

everything and, in the spiritual sense, love is the deepest ground of the spiritual life. In every human being in whom there is love, the foundation, in the spiritual sense, is laid. And the building that, in the spiritual sense, is to be erected is again love, and it is love that builds up. Love builds up, and this means it builds up love. In this way the task is circumscribed. The discourse does not spread itself out in particulars and multiplicities, does not confusedly begin something that it must arbitrarily break off somewhere in order to have an ending. No, it concentrates itself and its attention on the essential, on the one and the same thing in all the multiplicity. From the beginning to the end, the discourse is about love because building up is love's most characteristic specification. Love is the ground, love is the building, love builds up. To build up is to build up love, and it is love that builds up. To be sure, we do at times speak in a more ordinary sense about building up; in contrast to the corruption that only wants to tear down, or in contrast to the confusion that can only tear down and disrupt, we say that the capable person builds up, is one who knows how to guide and to lead, one who knows how to teach effectively in his field, one who is a master in his art. Any such person builds up in contrast to tearing down. But all this building up, in knowledge, in insight, in expertness, in integrity, etc., insofar as it does not build up love, is still not upbuilding in the deepest sense. This is because, spiritually, love is the *ground,* and to build up means to erect from *the ground up.*

Therefore when the discourse is about the work of love in building up, *either* this must mean that the one who loves implants love in another person's heart, *or* it must mean that the one who loves presupposes that love is in the other person's heart, and by this very presupposition he builds up love in him—from the ground up, provided, of course, that in love he indeed presupposes its presence in the ground. To build up must be one of the two. But can one human being implant love in another human being's heart? No, this is a suprahuman relationship, an inconceivable relationship between human beings; in this sense human love cannot build up. It is God, the Creator, who must implant love in each human being, he who himself is Love. Thus it is specifically unloving and not at all upbuilding if someone arrogantly deludes himself into believing that he wants and is able to create love in another person; all busy and pompous zeal in this regard neither builds up love nor is it itself upbuilding. The first relationship of building up would then be inconceivable; hence we must think about the second. In this way we have achieved the explanation of what it is that love builds up, and it is on this that we shall dwell: *The one who loves presupposes that love is in the other person's heart and by this very presupposition builds up love in him—from the ground up, provided, of course, that in love he presupposes its presence in the ground.*

Love builds up by presupposing that love is present. In this way the one who loves builds up the other, and it is easy enough to presuppose love where it is obviously present. Alas, but love is never completely present in any human being, inasmuch as it is indeed possible to do something else than to presuppose it, to discover some fault and weakness in it. If someone has unlovingly discovered this, he perhaps wants, as we say, to remove it, to pull out the splinter in order to build up love properly. But love builds up. To him who loves much, much is forgiven; but the more perfect the loving one presupposes the love to be, the more perfect a love he loves forth. Among all the relationships in the world, there is no other relationship in which there is such a like for like, in which the result so accurately corresponds to what was presupposed. One raises no objection, does not appeal to experience, because this is indeed unloving, arbitrarily to set a day when the result will now be manifest. Love has no understanding of such things; it is eternally confident of the fulfillment of the presupposition; if this is not the case, then love is on the way to being exhausted.

Love builds up by presupposing that love is present in the ground; therefore love also builds up where, in the human sense, love seems to be lacking and where, in the human sense, it seems first and foremost necessary to tear down, yet not for the sake of desire but for the sake of salvation. The opposite of building up is tearing down. This contrast never appears more clearly than when the theme of the discourse is that love builds up, for in whatever other connection building up is discussed, it still has a similarity to tearing down—that it is doing something to someone else. But when the one who loves builds up, it is the very opposite of tearing down, because the one who loves does something to himself—he presupposes that love is present in the other person—which certainly is the very opposite of doing something to the other person. To tear down satisfies the sensate person only all too easily; to build up in the sense of doing something to the other person can also satisfy the sensate, but to build up by conquering oneself satisfies only love; yet this is the only way to build up. But in the well-intentioned zeal to tear down and to build up we forget that ultimately no human being is capable of laying the ground of love in the other person.

Love builds up by presupposing that love is present. Have you not experienced this yourself, my listener? If anyone has ever spoken to you in such a way or treated you in such a way that you really felt built up, this was because you very vividly perceived how he presupposed love to be in you. Or what kind of person do you think one would be who could truly build you up? Is it not true that you would desire him to have insight and knowledge and talent and experience? But you still would not consider that it depended crucially on this, but rather on his being a trustworthy, loving person—that is, truly a loving person. Therefore you consider that to build up depends crucially and essentially upon being loving or having love to such a degree that one can rely upon it.

IX 211

IX 213

IX 214

But what, then, is love? Love is to presuppose love; to have love is to pre-suppose love in others; to be loving is to presuppose that others are loving. Let us understand each other. The qualities a person may have must be ei-ther qualities he has for himself, even if he uses them against others, or qual-ities for others. Wisdom is a being-for-itself quality; power, talent, knowl-edge, etc. are likewise being-for-itself qualities. To be wise does not mean to presuppose that others are wise; on the contrary, it may be very wise and true if the truly wise person assumes that far from all people are wise. Indeed, be-cause "wise" is a being-for-itself quality, there is nothing in the thought to prevent assuming that there could be living or there has lived a wise person who dared to say that he assumed all others to be unwise. There is no con-tradiction in the thought (to be wise—and to assume that all others are un-wise). In the actuality of life, such an expression would be arrogance, but in the thought simply as such there is no contradiction. If, however, someone were to think that he was loving, but also that all others were not loving, we would say: No, stop, here is a contradiction in the thought itself, because to be loving is to assume, to presuppose, that other people are loving.

Love is not a being-for-itself quality but a quality by which or in which you are for others. In summing up a person's qualities, we do in fact say in everyday speech that he is wise, sensible, loving—and we do not notice what a difference there is between the last quality and the first ones. His wisdom, his experience, his sensibleness he has for himself, even though he benefits others with them; but if he is truly loving, then he does not have love in the same sense as he has wisdom, but his love consists precisely in this, to pre-suppose that the rest of us have love. You praise him for being loving; you think that it is a quality he possesses, as it indeed is; you feel built up by him just because he is loving, but you do not perceive that the explanation is that his love signifies that he presupposes love in you and that you are built up by this, that the love in you is built up by this. If it actually were the case that a person could be loving but this love did not signify the presupposing of love in others, then in the deepest sense you would not feel built up, however trustworthy it was that he was loving; you would not in the deepest sense feel built up any more than you are in the deepest sense built up, however trustworthy it is that he is wise, sensible, experienced, learned. If it were pos-sible that he could be truly loving but this did not signify the presupposing of love in others, then you could not completely depend on him either, be-cause the trustworthiness of one who loves is this—that even when you doubt yourself, doubt that there is love in you, he is loving enough to pre-suppose it, or, more correctly, he is the loving one who presupposes it.

But you were insisting that a person, in order truly to build up, must truly be loving. It has now become manifest that to be loving means: to presup-pose love in others. So you are saying exactly the same thing that has been developed in the discourse.

So, then, the deliberation goes back to its beginning. To build up is to presuppose love; to be loving is to presuppose love; only love builds up. To build up is to erect something from the ground up—but, spiritually, love is the ground of everything. No human being can place the ground of love in another person's heart; yet love is the ground, and we can build up only from the ground up; therefore we can build up only by presupposing love. Take love away—then there is no one who builds up and no one who is built up.

CHRISTIAN DISCOURSES (APRIL 26, 1848)
BY S. KIERKEGAARD

1848 was the year of Kierkegaard's "richest productivity."[160] In that year he began or completed the writing of *Christian Discourses*, "A Cycle of Ethical-Religious Essays," *The Lily in the Field and the Bird of the Air*, "Armed Neutrality," *The Point of View for My Work as an Author*, *The Sickness unto Death*, *Practice in Christianity*, *The Crisis and a Crisis in the Life of an Actress*, and a piece on the actor Ludvig Phister as Captain Scipio. Only *Christian Discourses* and *Crisis* were published, but this combination was of exceptional importance for him. Kierkegaard had intended to terminate (again) his authorship with *Christian Discourses* and *Crisis*—at the end a signed volume accompanying an esthetic work, just as *Two Upbuilding Discourses* accompanied *Either/Or* at the beginning.

The temporal order of the writing of the four parts of *Christian Discourses* is reflected in changes in the tone and intention of the parts. Part Two, "States of Mind in the Strife of Suffering," and Part Four, "Discourses at the Communion on Fridays," written first, are a reassuring affirmation of the joy and blessedness of the Christian life in a world of adversity and tribulation. In Part One, "The Cares of the Pagans," and Part Three, "Thoughts That Wound from Behind—for Upbuilding," written later, there is a polemical tone. Part Three, the more polemical, was originally planned for another volume and was included in *Christian Discourses* at the last minute. Part Three becomes "a temple-cleansing celebration—and then the quiet and most intimate of all worship services—the Communion Service on Fridays."[161]

Kierkegaard's interest in drama (evident especially in *Either/Or*, I, *Repetition*, and *Stages*) is particularized in *Crisis*, written in appreciation of the actress Johanne Luise Heiberg. As the companion esthetic piece to the signed *Christian Discourses*, it was published under the pseudonym Inter et Inter.

THE CARE OF LOWLINESS

Do not worry about what you will wear—the pagans
seek all these things.

This care the bird does not have. Sparrows [*Spurve*[162]] are divided into grey sparrows and yellow—or, if you please, gold sparrows, but this distinction, this classification "lowly/eminent" does not exist for them or for any one of them. The other birds do indeed follow the bird that flies at the head of the flock or to the right; there is the distinction first and last, to the right and the left. But the distinction lowly/eminent does not exist; in their bold wheeling flight when the flock is soaring lovely and free in aerial formations, first and last, right and left also change. And when the thousand voices sing in chorus, there certainly is one that strikes the note; there is this distinction. But lowly/eminent, this distinction does not exist, and joy lives freely in the alternating of voices. It gratifies "the single individual" so indescribably to sing in chorus with the others; yet it does not sing to gratify the others. It is gratified by its singing and the singing of the others; therefore it stops quite abruptly, pauses for a moment, until it is again inclined to join in—and to hear itself.

The bird, then, does not have this care. Why is this so? It is because the bird is what it is, is itself, is satisfied with being itself, is contented with itself. It hardly knows distinctly or realizes clearly what it is, even less that it should know something about others. But it is contented with itself and with what it is, whatever that happens to be. It does not have time to ponder or even merely to begin to ponder—so contented is it with being what it is. In order to be, in order to have the joy of being, it does not have to walk the long road of first learning to know something about the others in order by that to find out what it is itself. No, it has its knowledge firsthand; it takes the more pleasurable shortcut: it is what it is. For the bird there is no question of to be or not to be; by way of the shortcut it slips past all the cares of dissimilarity. Whether it is a bird just like all other birds, whether it is "just as good a bird" as the others of the same species, indeed, even whether it is just like its mate—of all such things it does not think at all, so impatient it is in its joy of being. No young girl on the point of leaving for a dance can be as impatient to leave as the bird is to set about being what it is. It has not a moment, not the briefest, to give away if this would delay it from being; the briefest moment would be a fatally long time for it if at that moment it was not allowed to be what it is; it would die of impatience at the least little objection to being summarily allowed to be. It is what it is, but it *is*. It lets things take their course, and so it is. This is indeed the way it is.

Even if you did not see the proud flight of the royal bird—when you see the little bird that is sitting and swinging on a spike of wheat and amusing itself by singing, is there the slightest trace of the care of lowliness? You certainly will not object to what is indeed the lesson: that it is someone of consequence [*høit paa Straa*]. If you want to do that, then take the straw [*Straa*] upon which it is sitting. In its joy over being, the bird is more animated than the lily, but it is just like the lily in its innocent self-satisfaction. Even if you did not see the magnificent lily that humbly holds its head high in all its loveliness, when you see the unimpressive lily that grows in a ditch and is teased by the wind as if the two were equals, when you see it after the storm has done everything to make it feel its insignificance—when you look at it as it again tosses its head to see if there will soon be fair weather again, does it seem to you that there is the slightest care of lowliness? Or when it stands at the foot of the mighty tree and looks up at it in wonder, does it seem to you that there is the least little trace of the care of lowliness in this, the amazed lily; or do you believe that it would feel itself to be less if the tree were even twice as large? Or is it not rather as if in all innocence it were under the delusion that everything exists for its sake?

X
43

X
44

So easy is it for the bird and the lily with being; so easily do they go about living; so natural is the beginning for them or their coming to begin. It is the lily's and the bird's fortunate privilege that it is made so easy for them to begin to be, that once they have come into existence they have begun at once, they are immediately at full speed in being and there is no need at all for any preliminaries to the beginning, and they are not at all tested in that difficulty much discussed among people and portrayed as very perilous—the difficulty of beginning.

How, then, is the bird the teacher; where is the contact point of the instruction? I wonder if it is not in making the detour after the beginning, that is, after finding the beginning, to make this detour, which can become so very long, as short as possible in order as quickly as possible to come to oneself, to be oneself.

This care the lowly Christian does not have. But he is different from the bird in having to be tested in this difficulty of the beginning, because he is aware of the distinction, lowly/eminent. He knows, and he knows that others know the same about him, that he is a lowly human being, and he knows what this means. He knows also what is understood by the advantages of earthly life, how very diverse they are, and alas, that they are all denied to him, that while they otherwise exist to manifest what the others are in these advantages, in his case they seem to be for the purpose of indicating how lowly he is. With every advantage the eminent individual adds, the more eminent he becomes, and with every advantage the lowly individual must confess has been denied him he in a way becomes more lowly. What exists to indicate the greatness of the eminent seems from the other side to exist to indicate how very little the lowly one is. Oh, what a difficult beginning to existing or for coming to exist: to exist, then to come into existence in order first to exist. Oh, what a slyly concealed snare, one that is not set for any bird! It indeed seems as if in order to begin to be oneself, a human being first of all must be finished with what the others are and by that find out then what he himself is—in order to be that. But if he falls into the snare of this optical illusion, he will never become himself. He walks on and on like the person who walks along a road that the passersby tell him definitely leads to the city but forget to tell him that if he wants to go to the city he must turn around; he is walking along the road that leads to the city, is walking along the road—away from the city.

But the lowly Christian does not fall into the snare of this optical illusion. He sees with the eyes of faith; with the speed of faith that seeks God, he is at the beginning, is himself before God, is contented with being himself. He has found out from the world or from the others that he is a lowly person, but he does not abandon himself to this knowledge; he does not lose himself in it in a worldly way, does not become totally engrossed in it; by holding fast to God with the reservedness of eternity, he has become himself. He is like someone who has two names, one for all the others, another for his nearest and dearest ones; in the world, in his association with the others, he is the lowly person. He does not pretend to be anything else, and neither is he taken to be anything else, but before God he is himself. In his contacts with others, it seems as if at every moment he must wait in order to find out from the others what he is now at this moment. But he does not wait; he is in a hurry to be before God, contented with being himself before God. He is a lowly human being in the crowd of human beings, and what he is in this way depends on the relationship, but in being himself he is not dependent on the crowd; before God he is himself. From "the others" a person of course actually finds out only what the others are—it is in this way that the world wants to deceive a person out of becoming himself. "The others" in turn do not know what they themselves are either but continually know only what "the others" are. There is only one who completely knows himself, who in himself knows what he himself is—that is God. And he also knows what each human being is in himself, because he is that only by being before God. The person who is not before God is not himself either, which one can be only by being in the one who is in himself. If one is oneself by being in the one who is in himself, one can be in others or before others, but one cannot be oneself merely by being before others.

The lowly Christian is himself *before God*. The bird is not itself in this way, because the bird *is* what it is. By means of this being, it has at every moment escaped the difficulty of the beginning; but then neither did it attain to the glorious conclusion of the difficult beginning: in redoubling [*Fordoblelse*] to be itself. The bird is like a number one; the person who is himself is more than a ten. The bird fortunately escapes the difficulty of the beginning and therefore acquires no conception of how lowly it is; but then, of course, it is incomparably more lowly than the lowly Christian who knows how lowly he is. The *idea* of lowliness *does not exist* for the bird, but the lowly Christian *does not exist essentially for this idea*. He does not want to exist essentially for it, because essentially he is and wants to be himself before God. Thus the bird actually is the lowly one. *In contrast* to his lowliness, the lowly Christian is himself but without fatuously wanting to cease being the lowly person he is in relation to others; in *lowliness* he is himself. This is how the lowly Christian in lowliness is without the care of lowliness. In what does the lowliness consist? In the relation to "the others." But on what is its care based? On existing only for the others, on not knowing anything but the relation to the others. The bird does not know anything at all about the relation to the others and to that extent is not lowly and to that extent in turn does not have the care of lowliness, but neither does it know, of course, that it has a higher relation.

What, then, is the lowly Christian who before God is himself? He is a *human being*. Inasmuch as he is a human being, he in a certain sense is like the bird, which is what it is. But we shall not dwell further on this here.

X
46

But he is also a *Christian,* which is indeed implied in the question about what the lowly *Christian* is. To that extent he is not like the bird, because the bird *is* what it is. But one cannot be a Christian in this way; if one is a Christian, one must *have become* that. Consequently the lowly Christian has become something in the world; the bird, alas, cannot become something—it is what it is. The lowly Christian was a human being, just as the bird was a bird, but then he became a Christian; he became something in the world. And he can continually become more and more, because he can continually become more and more Christian. As a *human being* he was created in *God's image* [*Billede*],[163] but as a *Christian* he has God as the *prototype* [*Forbillede*]. This unsettling thought that incessantly calls to one, a prototype, the bird does not know. It is what it is; nothing, nothing disturbs this, its being. It is indeed true, nothing disturbs it—not even the blessed thought of having God for its prototype. A prototype is certainly a summons, but what a blessing! We even speak of good fortune when we say that there is something in the poet that summons him to write lyrics, but the prototype is an even more rigorous requirement, is an incentive for everyone who sees it, everyone for whom it exists. The prototype is a promise; no other promise is so reliable, because the prototype is indeed the fulfillment.—There is no prototype before the bird, but the prototype exists before the lowly Christian, and he exists before his prototype—he can continually grow to resemble it more and more.

    The lowly Christian, who before God is himself, *exists* as a Christian *before his prototype.* He believes that God has lived on earth, that he has allowed himself to be born in lowly and poor circumstances, yes, in ignominy, and then as a child lived together with the ordinary man who was called his father and the despised virgin who was his mother. After that he wandered about in the lowly form of a servant, not distinguishable from other lowly persons even by his conspicuous lowliness, until he ended in the most extreme wretchedness, crucified as a criminal—and then, it is true, left behind a name. But the lowly Christian's aspiration is only to dare in life and in death to appropriate his name or to be named after him. The lowly Christian believes, as it is told, that he chose as his disciples lowly persons of the simplest class and that for company he sought those whom the world rejected and scorned. He believes that in all the various vicissitudes of his life, when people wanted to elevate him and then wanted to lower him even lower, if possible, than he had lowered himself, in all this he remained faithful to the lowly persons to whom he was linked by more intimate connections, faithful to the despised people who had been expelled from the synagogue for the very reason that he had helped them. The lowly Christian believes that this lowly person or that his life in lowliness has shown what significance a lowly person has and, alas, what significance, humanly speaking, an eminent person really has, how infinitely much it can signify to be a lowly person, and how infinitely little it can signify to be an eminent person, if one is not anything else. The lowly Christian believes that this prototype exists right before him, him who, after all, is a lowly person, perhaps struggling with poverty and straitened circumstances, or the even more lowly circumstance of being scorned and repudiated. He certainly admits that he is not in the situation of having himself chosen this slighted or despised lowliness and to that extent does not resemble the prototype. But he still trusts that the prototype exists before him, the prototype who by means of lowliness compassionately imposes himself on him, as it were, as if he would say, "Poor man, can you not see that this prototype is before you?" To be sure, he has not seen the prototype with his own eyes, but he believes that he has existed. In a certain sense, of course, there had not been anything to *see*—except the lowliness (because the glory must *be believed*), and of the lowliness he can very well form an idea. He has not seen the prototype with his own eyes; neither does he make any attempt to have his senses form such a picture. Yet he often sees the prototype. Every time he totally forgets his poverty, his lowliness, his being disdained, forgets it in faith's joy over the glory of this prototype, then he does see the prototype—and then he himself looks more or less like the prototype. If, namely, at such a blessed moment when he is absorbed in his prototype, someone else looks at him, the other person sees only a lowly person before him; it was just the same with the prototype—people saw only the lowly person. He believes and hopes he will ever more and more approach a likeness to this prototype, who will only in the next life manifest himself in his glory, since here on earth he can only be in lowliness and can be seen only in lowliness. He believes that this prototype, if he continually struggles to resemble him, will bring him again, and in an even more intimate way, into kinship with God, that he does not have God only as a creator, as all creatures do, but has God as his brother.

But then is this lowly Christian nevertheless something very lofty? Yes, he certainly is, something so lofty that one completely loses sight of the bird. Like the bird, he is lowly without the care of lowliness, weighed down in a certain sense by the consciousness of his lowliness as the bird is not—yet he is highly elevated. Nor does he speak of the lowliness, and if he does, it is never sadly; indeed, it only reminds him of the prototype while he thinks about the loftiness of the prototype—and when he does that, he himself more or less resembles the prototype.

The lowly pagan, however, does have this care. The lowly pagan, he is without God in the world and therefore is never essentially himself (which one is only by being before God) and therefore is never satisfied with being himself, which one certainly is not if one is not oneself. He is not himself, is not satisfied with being himself, nor, like the bird, satisfied with what he is: he is dissatisfied with what he is; detesting himself, he groans over and laments his fate.

What, then, is he? He is the lowly one, nothing else at all—that is, he is what "the others" make of him and what he makes of himself by being only before others. His care is: *being nothing*—indeed, not being at all. Thus he is a long way from being like the bird, which is what it is. Therefore, in turn, his concern is: *to become something* in the world. To exist before God—that is not anything, he thinks—neither does it make a good showing in the world in contrast to or in comparison with others. To be a human being—that is not anything to be, he thinks—after all, that is to be nothing, because in that there is no distinction from or advantage over all other human beings. To be a Christian—that is not anything to be, he thinks—we all, of course, are that. But to become a councilor of justice—to be that would be something, and he must above all become something in the world; to be nothing at all is something to despair over.

"This is something to despair over." He speaks as if he were not already in despair; yet he is in despair, and despair is his care. It is assumed that in every nation the lowly are generally exempt from bearing the burdens the more favored must bear. But the pagan, the despairing lowly one, even if he is that, will not be exempt; he bears the heaviest of all burdens. We say that the king bears the weight of the crown, the high official the weight of the responsibility of administration, the one to whom much is entrusted the weight of custody; but whereas the king is after all indeed the king, the person of high rank the person of high rank, the trusted one the trusted one, the pagan, the despairing lowly one, slaves himself to death under the weight of what he is not—he, yes, it is indeed insanity, he overstrains himself on what he does not bear. Whether it is the king who as the base bears all the others or whether it is all the others who bear the king as the one on top, we shall not investigate here, but the pagan, the despairing lowly one, bears all the others. This enormous weight, "all the others," weighs upon him, and with the doubled weight of despair; it does not weigh upon him by dint of the idea that he is something—no, it weighs upon him by dint of the idea that he is nothing. Truly, no nation or society has ever treated any human being so inhumanly that on the condition of being nothing one has to bear the burden of all; only the pagan, the despairing lowly one, treats himself so inhumanly. He sinks deeper and deeper into desperate care, but he finds no footing for bearing his burden—after all, he is nothing, of which he becomes conscious to his own torment by dint of the idea of what the others are. More and more ludicrous—oh no, he becomes more and more pitiable or, rather, more and more ungodly, more and more nonhuman in his foolish striving to become at least something, something, even if it is ever so little, but something that in his opinion is worth being.

In this way the despairing lowly one, the pagan, sinks under comparison's enormous weight, which he himself lays upon himself. This, to be a lowly person, which for the lowly Christian belongs to him together with being a

Christian as the scarcely audible slight aspiration before the letter belongs to the letter that actually is heard (and this is the way the lowly Christian speaks about his earthly lowliness; he speaks of it only in declaring that he is a Christian)—this for the pagan is his care night and day; all his endeavors are occupied with this. Without the prospect of eternity, never strengthened by the hope of heaven, never himself, abandoned by God, he lives in despair, as if for punishment he were condemned to live these seventy years tortured by the thought of being nothing, tortured by the futility of his efforts to become something. For him the bird has nothing consoling, heaven no consolation—and it goes without saying that earthly life has no consolation for him either. Of him it cannot be said that he remains enslaved on the earth, persuaded by the enchantment of earthly life that led him to forget heaven— no, instead it is as if temporality did everything to push him away from itself by making him nothing. And yet he wants to belong to temporality on the most wretched conditions; he does not want to escape it. He clings tightly to being nothing, more and more tightly, because in a worldly way, and futilely, he tries to become something; with despair he clings more and more tightly to that—which to the point of despair he does not want to be. In this way he lives, not on the earth, but as if he were hurled down into the underworld. See, that king[164] whom the gods punished suffered the dreadful punishment that every time he was hungry luscious fruits appeared, but when he reached for them they vanished; the despairing lowly one, the pagan, suffers even more agonizingly in self-contradiction. While he, tortured by being nothing, futilely tries to become something, he really is not only something but is much. It is not the fruits that withdraw themselves from him; it is he himself who withdraws himself even from being what he is. For he is not a human being—and he cannot become a Christian!

Let us then in conclusion consider the bird; it is there in the Gospel and must be here in the discourse. The lowly bird is without the care of lowliness. In lowliness the lowly Christian is without the care of lowliness and then—is elevated high above all earthly loftiness. The lowly pagan in his care, even if he were the most lowly of all, is far beneath himself. The bird does not look closely at what it is; the lowly Christian looks closely at what he is as a Christian; the lowly pagan stares, to the point of despair, at his being lowly. "What . . . . . lowly?" says the bird. "Let us never think about such things; one flies away from that!" "What . . . . . lowly?" says the Christian. "I am a Christian!" "Alas, lowly!" says the pagan. "I am what I am," says the bird; "What I shall become has not yet been disclosed," says the lowly Christian; "I am nothing and will never become anything," says the lowly pagan. "I exist," says the bird; "Life begins in death," says the lowly Christian; "I am nothing, and in death I remain nothing," says the lowly pagan. Compared with the lowly Christian, the bird is a child; compared with the lowly pagan, it is a fortunate child.

X
50

X
51

Like the free bird when it soars highest in its joy over existing, just so does the lowly Christian soar even higher; like the trapped bird when it hopelessly and fearfully struggles to its death in the net, just so the lowly pagan, even more pitiable, desouls himself in the captivity of nothingness. According to Christian doctrine, there is only one loftiness, that of being a Christian; everything else is lowly, lowliness and loftiness. If one is lowly, there is only one way to loftiness—to become a Christian. The bird does not know this way; it remains what it is. But then there is also another way that the bird does not know—along this way the pagan walks. The bird's way of being is enigmatic and has never been found; the Christian's way has been found by him who is the Way, and it is blessed to find it; the pagan's way ends in darkness and no one has found the way back by it. The bird slips past that devious way and fortunately past all dangers; the lowly Christian does not walk along that devious way and is blessedly saved unto glory; the lowly pagan chooses the devious way and "walks his own way" to perdition.

THE JOY OF IT: THAT ADVERSITY IS PROSPERITY

X
152

Adversity [*Modgang*] is prosperity [*Medgang*]. But do I hear someone say: This surely is only a jest and easy to understand, because if one just looks at everything turned around, it is quite correct: in a straightforward sense adversity is adversity, adversity turned around is prosperity. Such a statement is only a jest, just like guessing riddles, or when a jack-of-all-trades says, "Nothing is easier to do than this, provided one is in the habit of walking on one's head instead of on one's legs." Well, yes, but is it also so easy to do it? And just because it seems so very easy for thought, untried in the actuality of life and ignorant of any pressure, to swing up and down and down and up, to wheel around to the right and to the left, is it also so easy when adversity presses on the thought that should make the swing, is it then so easy when thought is to manage to turn around the one who in suffering and adversity continually wants to take the opposite position? That is, for thought, for aimless and ownerless thought, thought as such in general, thought that belongs nowhere and is not anybody's, thought that shadowboxes with unnamed names and definitions that define nothing: "here/there," "right/left," "straight ahead/ turned around"—for thought as a vagrant it is easy enough to do the trick. But when it is thought with a name, when it is my thought, or when it is *your* thought and, when you are a sufferer, it consequently becomes an earnest matter that thought, which can turn easily enough, acquire in earnest this power over you to turn you around despite all the many things that manifoldly prevent you—is this, then, so easy?

X
153
Moreover, just because being able to walk on one's head instead of one's legs is a jest, is it also a jest to look at everything turned around? Far from it,

or rather, just the opposite; it is precisely earnestness, the earnestness of eternity. That which is jest, a meaningless jest, as long as it is thought as such in general—when it becomes a matter of earnestness by being your thought that is supposed to turn you around: then it is the very earnestness of eternity. Eternity, which certainly is the source and stronghold of earnestness, says, "This is the task, because it is indeed my, eternity's, view of life to see everything turned around. You are to accustom yourself to looking at everything turned around. And you suffering one, if you want to be comforted in earnest, comforted so that even joy is victorious, then you must let me, eternity, help you—but then you, too, must look at everything turned around." This is the earnestness of eternity; this is eternity's comfort for the sufferer, the law that eternity dictates, the condition that eternity makes to which all promises are bound. Eternity knows only one procedure: look at everything turned around. Let us then look at the relation turned around and in this way find

the joy of it: that adversity is prosperity.

But let us proceed in such a way that we first try to orient the suffering one properly so that he might have an eye for the turned-aroundness, so that he might be willing to enter into this point of view and give it power over himself: then the joy will undoubtedly follow as a matter of course.

What is prosperity? Prosperity is what is helpful to me in reaching my goal, what leads me to my goal; and adversity is what will prevent me from reaching my goal.

But what, then, is the goal? As an assumption we have fixed firmly the one thought by defining what adversity and prosperity are; but since we need to define the other thought (of the goal), it is readily apparent that if the goal is different, is the opposite, then prosperity and adversity must also be changed accordingly.

We are standing at the beginning. But in another sense we are not standing at the beginning. The discourse addresses itself to one who is suffering. But one who is suffering is not first to begin his life now; on the contrary, he is in the midst of it and, alas, not just in the midst of life but in the midst of life's suffering. If so, then he knows very well what adversity is, he the sufficiently tested one. Perhaps. But we were agreed that the extent to which he knows what adversity is depends on whether he knows what the goal is. Only the one who has the true conception of what the goal is that is set before human beings, only he knows also what adversity is and what prosperity is. The one who has the false conception of the goal has also a false conception of prosperity and adversity; he calls prosperity that which leads him to—the false goal—and as a result prevents him from reaching *the goal* (the true goal). But that which prevents one from reaching the goal, that is indeed adversity.

Now, there are many different things for which people strive, but essentially there are only two goals: one goal that a person desires, craves to reach, and the other that he should reach. The one goal is temporality's; the other is eternity's. They are opposite to each other, but then prosperity and adversity must be turned around accordingly. If this discourse addressed itself to a young man, it would try to make this matter of the two goals very clear to him so that he might begin his life by choosing the right goal, begin by being properly positioned. Yet the discourse would perhaps not succeed, because the young man's soul probably will be in a dubious agreement with temporality's goal and accordingly with the false conception of prosperity and adversity. And now one who is suffering, who therefore does not stand at the beginning but on the contrary is far along in it, he knows all too well what adversity is; but the question, as stated, is whether he also really knows what the goal is. The more vehemently he speaks about his suffering and how everything is going against him, the more it only becomes obvious that he has the false conception of the goal. If he has the false conception of the goal, he cannot speak truthfully about prosperity and adversity.

It must, therefore, if he is to be helped, be required of him that he once again deliberate profoundly on what goal is set for human beings, lest he, deceived by the delusion of knowing very well what the goal is, proceed to complain. You certainly are suffering adversity; you cannot reach the goal you so eagerly desired very much to reach—but now what if the goal is the false goal!

What, then, is required? It is required of the suffering one that he halt his errant thinking, that he then make up his mind about what the goal is—that is, it is required that *he turn around*. With regard to sin, a turning around is required; with regard to eternity's comfort, the same is required but in a milder form—namely, that one turn around. To the sinner, the rigorousness of the Law says terrifyingly, "Turn around!" To the suffering one, eternity says gently, sympathetically, "Oh, just turn around." Accordingly, it is required that he turn around. Here eternity already manifests itself as the reverse of temporality. In other words, eternity presupposes that the natural man does not know at all what the goal is, that on the contrary he had the false conception. Temporality presupposes that everyone knows very well what the goal is, so that the only difference among people is whether they succeed in reaching it or not. Eternity, on the other hand, assumes that the difference among people is that the one knows what the goal is and steers by that, and the other does not know it—and steers by that, that is, steers wrong. You suffering one, whoever you are, you probably find it all too easy to make yourself understood by people in general when you complain about your suffering—even though they have no consolation for you, yet they understand you; but eternity will not understand you this way—and yet it is by this that you are to be helped.

So, then, turn around! Do let me say it—good Lord, it is so obvious that if a person is to reach the goal he must know what the goal is and be properly positioned; it is so obvious that if the person is to be delighted by the glorious prospect he must turn to the side where it can be seen and not to the opposite side. Do not be impatient, do not say, "Of course I know what adversity is." Do not try also to terrify us with a description of your suffering so that we, too, would turn the wrong way and lose sight of the goal. If your suffering is so terrible, why then do you want to stare at it; and if the terror is just that you cannot stop staring at it, it is still not impossible. Do not say, "When someone suffers as I am suffering, he knows what adversity is, and only the person who suffers as I am suffering knows what adversity is." No, do not say that, but please listen. In order not to wound you, we speak in another way; we do not deny that you know what adversity is; what we are speaking about is that you still do not know what the goal is.

And then when you have turned around and have caught sight of the goal (eternity's), let the goal become for you what it is and should be, become so important that there is no question about what the path is like but only about reaching the goal, so that you gain the courage to understand that whatever the path is like, the worst of all, the most painful of all—if it leads you to the goal, then it is prosperity. Is it not true that if there is a place that is so important for you to reach because you are indescribably eager to arrive there, then you say, "I will go backward or forward, I will ride or walk or creep—it makes no difference, if only I get there." It is this that eternity wants first and foremost, it wants to make the goal so important to you that it gains complete control over you and you gain control over yourself to take your thoughts, your mind, your eyes away from the hardship, the difficulty, away from *how* you arrive there, because the only important thing to you is to arrive *there*.

X
156

Accordingly, out of respect for the goal, it has now become a *matter of indifference* to you whether it is what is usually called prosperity or whether it is what is usually called adversity that will lead you to the goal: what leads you to the goal is prosperity. What a change! Do you believe that the sensate person could be indifferent to this? What comfort would it be to him that adversity led him to *the goal* if he is concerned only about the goal to which prosperity leads!

But perhaps you still cannot stop looking around for the distinction: what is ordinarily called adversity and prosperity. You have gained the right position but still no peace in it. Well, eternity will give you more help. Now, if what is ordinarily called adversity leads only to or even especially to *the goal*, is there then any reason to look around? If it is so, let us assume it, that you could come to the place you want so much to reach only by or indeed best by going backward, would it then be proper to say, "Whether I go forward or backward makes no difference"? Surely it would be better to say, "How fortunate that I had a chance to go backward." Likewise, if it is possible that what is ordinarily called prosperity could lead you more easily to *the goal*, there would then, of course, be room for a wish. But now nothing will tempt you—because adversity is leading you right to *the goal.* And is it not true, you do indeed want to stand by your word that whatever leads you to the goal is prosperity. Therefore adversity is prosperity.

Let us now make this very clear to ourselves, that what we call prosperity and adversity do not both lead just as well to *the goal,* but only, or indeed especially, what is called adversity leads to *the goal.* What can prevent a person from reaching *the goal?* Surely it is the temporal, and how most of all? When what is ordinarily called prosperity leads a person to reach temporality's goal. In other words, when by means of prosperity he reaches temporality's goal, he is furthest away from reaching *the goal.* A person should strive toward eternity's goal, but by means of prosperity the temporal has delayed him. That temporality favors him does not lead him to the eternal, therefore not to *the goal.* If anything does that, it must be exactly the reverse, that temporality opposes him. But temporality's opposition to him is, of course, what is called adversity.

X
157

When it is said, "Seek *first* God's kingdom,"[165] eternity's goal is established for the human being as that which he should seek. If this is to be done, and exactly according to the words (oh, eternity does not allow itself to be mocked, nor to be deceived!), then the point above all is that the human being not seek something else *first.* But what is the something else that he can seek? It is the temporal. If, then, he is to seek first the kingdom of God, he must renounce voluntarily all the goals of temporality. What a difficult task, when opportunity is offered perhaps in abundance, when everything beckons, when what is called prosperity is ready at once, if only he desires it, to lead him to the possession of all the delectable goods of temporality— then to renounce all this! The suffering one, however, has adversity; therefore he is called a sufferer. What is called adversity prevents the sufferer from reaching these goals of temporality; adversity makes it difficult for him, perhaps impossible. Oh, how hard to see difficulties pile up this way in front of the wish, how hard that fulfillment of the wish became impossible! Is it not true? Yes, I probably do not need to ask you about it, but is it not true (and would to God that it is) that it is rather you who now want to ask me whether I myself have now forgotten what the discourse is about? Say it, then; it was just this that I desired; just tell us what the discourse is about, while I listen with joy and hear you say: If what is called prosperity is the deterrent that prevents one from reaching *the goal,* then it is indeed good that what is called adversity makes it difficult or impossible for one—to be delayed, that is, then adversity leads one right to *the goal.*

O you suffering one, whoever you are, for just one moment tear yourself away from your suffering and the thoughts that want to force themselves upon you; try to think altogether impartially about life. Imagine, then, a person who possesses all the benefits of good fortune, favored on every side— but imagine that this person is also earnest enough to have directed his mind to the goal of eternity. He understands, therefore, that he is to renounce all this that has been given him. He is also willing to do this, but see, then a despondent concern awakens in his soul, an anxious self-concern, whether he still may be deceiving himself and this matter of renunciation is only a delusion, since, after all, he remains in possession of all the benefits. He does not dare to throw away everything that has been given to him, because he understands that this could be a presumptuous exaggeration that could easily become his corruption instead of a benefit. He has dolefully come to have a concerned mistrust of himself, whether he might not possibly be deceiving God and all his renunciation be pretense. Then he might very well wish that it would all have to be taken away from him, so that this matter of giving up the temporal in order to grasp the eternal might become something in earnest for him. If this does not happen, perhaps a sickness of mind develops in his innermost being, an incurable depression due to his having become in a profounder sense bewildered about himself.

Have you never thought of this? For you in particular it certainly would be a right point of view, since it places as much distance as possible between you and your possessions. Look at your situation from this point of view! You have indeed had and are having adversity enough; therefore you have only the task *of renouncing what has been denied you,* whereas he has the task *of renouncing what has been given to him.* Second, you are freed from the concern about whether you actually, that is, in the external sense, have given it up, because inasmuch as you do not possess it, the matter is in this regard easy enough. How much more, then, you are assisted! You are denied what will prevent you from reaching *the goal;* you yourself have not cast it away and thereby taken upon yourself a responsibility that in a decisive moment would make your life so very difficult because you found yourself powerless before the task you voluntarily had assigned yourself. No, with regard to you, Governance has taken all the responsibility upon itself; it is Governance that has denied you this. All you have to do, then, is to lend assistance to Governance, the Governance that has helped you. Adversity is prosperity, and you do indeed have adversity.

So, then, adversity is prosperity. It is eternally certain; all the wiles of Satan are unable to make it doubtful. And you can very well understand it. You may, however, not really have faith that it is so. But (to offer you a little lighter fare if the Scriptural text about first seeking God's kingdom should be too strong for you) then do you believe that the poet,[166] whose songs delight humankind, do you believe that he could have written these songs if adversity and hard sufferings had not been there to tune the soul! It is precisely in adversity, "when the heart sits in deepest gloom, then the harp of joy is tuned."[167] Or do you believe that the one who in truth knew how to comfort others, do you believe that he would have been able to do this if adversity had not been for him the requisite prosperity that had helped him to proficiency in this beautiful art! Perhaps he himself also found it hard enough in the beginning, almost cruel that his soul should be tortured in order to

x
158

x
159

become resourceful in thinking of comfort for others. But finally he came to realize very well that without adversity he could not have become and could not be who he was; he learned to have faith that adversity is prosperity.

Therefore, may you also have faith that adversity is prosperity. To understand it is easy enough—but to believe it is difficult. Do not allow yourself to be deceived by the futile wisdom that wants to delude you into thinking that it is easy to have faith, difficult to understand. But believe it. As long as you do not believe it, adversity is and remains adversity. It does not help you that it is eternally certain that adversity is prosperity; as long as you do not believe it, it is not true for you. See, the adult, unlike the child, knows what to do about nettles: just grasp them briskly, then they will not burn you. To the child this must seem most unreasonable of all, because, thinks the child, if nettles burn when one merely touches them, how much more so if one grasps tightly. The child is told this. But when the child is supposed to grasp, it does not really have the courage; it still does not grasp briskly enough and is burned. So it is also with this, that adversity is prosperity—if you have not made up your mind in faith, you will only have adversity out of it.

Therefore have faith that adversity is prosperity. It is certain; it only waits for you to believe it. Do not let yourself be disturbed in your faith by others; "have the faith by yourself before God" (Romans 14:22). If the seafarer is convinced that the wind now blowing is taking him to the goal—even if all the others call it a contrary wind, what does he care, he calls it a fair wind. The fair wind is the wind that takes one to the goal, and prosperity is everything that takes one to the goal; and adversity takes one to *the goal*—therefore adversity is prosperity.

That this is joyful need not be developed. The one who has faith that adversity is prosperity does not really need to have the discourse explain to him that this is joyful. And for the one who does not really believe it, it is more important not to waste a moment but to grasp the faith. There is no need, therefore, to speak of this, or only a word. Imagine, then, that everything ordinarily called grounds of comfort has been roused and gathered, as in a worldwide hunt, all those grounds of comfort that the fortunate have discovered to get rid of the unfortunate (I do think this to be so); and imagine, then, in comparison, eternity's comfort, this concise comfort that the concern has discovered, just as *it* has also discovered that it is a concerned person, one who is suffering, not a fortunate person, who will comfort others—this concise comfort: adversity is prosperity! You do find it entirely as it should be, do you not, and in a certain sense well advised, that the human grounds of comfort do not pretend to be able to make the sorrowing one happy but undertake only to comfort him somewhat, which they then do quite badly? On the other hand, when eternity comforts, it makes one joyful; its comfort truly is joy, is the true joy. It is with the human grounds of comfort as it is when the sick person, who has already had many physicians, has a new one who thinks of something new that temporarily produces a little change, but soon it is the same old story again. No, when eternity is brought in to the sick person, it not only cures him completely but makes him healthier than the healthy. It is with the human grounds of comfort as it is when the physician finds a new, perhaps more comfortable, kind of crutch for the person who uses crutches—give him healthy feet to walk on and strength in his knees, that the physician cannot do. But when eternity is brought in, the crutches are thrown away; then he can not only walk—oh no, in another sense we must say that he no longer walks—so lightly does he walk. Eternity provides feet to walk on. When in adversity it seems impossible to move from the spot, when in the powerlessness of suffering it seems as if one could not move a foot—then eternity makes adversity into prosperity.

In all adversity there is only one danger: if the suffering one refuses to have faith that adversity is prosperity. This is perdition; only sin is a human being's corruption.

I JOHN 3:20

Prayer

X
301

X
303

Great are you, O God; although we know you only as in an obscure saying and as in a mirror, yet in wonder we worship your greatness—how much more we shall praise it at some time when we come to know it more fully! When under the arch of heaven I stand surrounded by the wonders of creation, I rapturously and adoringly praise your greatness, you who lightly hold the stars in the infinite and concern yourself fatherly with the sparrow. But when we are gathered here in your holy house we are also surrounded on all sides by what calls to mind your greatness in a deeper sense. You are indeed great, Creator and Sustainer of the world; but when you, O God, forgave the sin of the world and reconciled yourself with the fallen human race, then you were even greater in your incomprehensible compassion! How would we not, then, in faith praise and thank and worship you here in your holy house, where everything reminds us of this, especially those who are gathered here today to receive the forgiveness of sins and to appropriate anew reconciliation with you in Christ!

I John 3:20 . . . **even if our hearts condemn us, God is greater than our hearts.**

Even if our hearts condemn us. When the Pharisees and the Scribes had brought to Christ in the temple a woman seized in open sin in order to accuse her and when later, shamed by his answer, they had all gone away, Christ said to her, "Has no one condemned you?" but she said, "No one, Lord."[168]

Thus there was no one who condemned her. So is it also here in this sanctuary, there is no one who condemns you; if your heart condemns you, you
yourself alone must know. No one else can know it, because this other one
also is occupied today with his own heart, whether it condemns him.
Whether your heart condemns you is no one else's concern, because this
other person also has only his own heart to deal with, its accusing or its ac-
quitting thoughts. How you feel when you hear these words read aloud,
"even though our hearts condemn us," is no one else's concern, because this
other one also applies everything devoutly to himself, thinks only of how he
felt, whether the words surprised him like a sudden thought, or he heard,
alas, what he had said to himself, or he heard what he thought did not apply
to himself. A heart may indeed accuse itself, but from this it still does not follow that it must condemn itself; and we of course do not teach heavy-minded
exaggeration any more than we teach light-minded indulgence. But when it
is a matter of speaking about the words just read, how would one find better hearers than on a day such as this and better than such as these who have
come here today, not from the distractions of the world, but from the concentration of the confessional, where each one separately has made an accounting to God, where each one separately has let his heart be the accuser,
which it can indeed do best since it is the confidant, and which it also had
better do betimes lest at some time it must in a terrible way become that
against a person's own will. Yet there certainly is a difference between guilt
and guilt: there is a difference between owing five hundred shillings and only
fifty. One person can have much, much more to reproach himself for than
another; there can also be the one who must say to himself that his heart
condemns him. Perhaps there is such a person present here, or perhaps there
is no such person present, but nevertheless we are all in need of comfort.
Moreover, it certainly cannot be discomforting to anyone that the words of
comfort are so rich in compassion that they include everyone; this certainly
cannot be discomforting to anyone, even if his heart does not condemn him.
Yet we all, we whose hearts do not acquit us, essentially need the same comfort: God's greatness, that he is greater than our hearts.

   *God's greatness is in forgiving, in showing mercy, and in this, his greatness, he is
greater than the heart that condemns itself.* See, this is the greatness of God about
which we should speak particularly in the holy places, because here we do
indeed know God in a different way, more intimately, if one may say so, than
out there, where he surely is manifest, is known in his works, whereas here
he is known as he has revealed himself as he wants to be known by the Christian. Everyone, *marveling,* can see the signs by which God's greatness in nature is known, or rather there actually is no sign, because the works themselves are the signs. For example, everyone can of course see the rainbow and
must marvel when he sees it. But the sign of God's greatness in showing
mercy is only *for faith*; this sign is indeed the sacrament. God's greatness in

nature is *manifest,* but God's greatness in showing mercy is a *mystery,* which must be believed. Precisely because it is not directly manifest to everyone, precisely for that reason it is, and is called, the *revealed.* God's greatness in nature promptly awakens *astonishment* and then *adoration;* God's greatness in showing mercy is first an occasion *for offense* and then is *for faith.* When God had created everything, he looked at it and behold, "it was all very good,"[169] and every one of his works seems to bear the appendage: *Praise, thank, worship the Creator.* But appended to his greatness in showing mercy is: *Blessed is he who is not offended.*[170]

All our language about God is, naturally, human language. However much we try to preclude misunderstanding by in turn revoking what we say—if we do not wish to be completely silent, we are obliged to use human criteria when we, as human beings, speak about God. What, then, is true human greatness? Surely it is greatness of heart. We do not by rights say that someone is great who has much power and dominion, yes, even if there lived or had lived a king whose sovereignty was over the whole world—however hasty our amazement is in promptly calling him great—the more profound person does not allow himself to be disturbed by externality. On the other hand, if it were the lowliest person who has ever lived—when you are witness to his action in the moment of decision, when you see him truly act nobly, and with his whole heart magnanimously forgive his enemy, in self-denial bring the ultimate sacrifice, or when you are witness to the inner forbearance with which he lovingly endures evil year after year—then you say, "He certainly is great; he is truly great." Therefore greatness of heart is the true human greatness, but greatness of heart is to master oneself in love [*Kjerlighed*].

X
306

When we, then, human beings as we are, want to form a conception of God's greatness, we must think about true human greatness, that is, about love and about the love that forgives and shows mercy. But what does this mean, would the meaning be that we want to compare God to a human being, even if this human being were the noblest, the purest, the most reconciling, the most loving person who has ever lived? Far from it. The apostle does not speak that way either. He does not say that God is greater than the most loving human being, but that he is greater than the heart that condemns itself. God and the human being resemble each other only inversely. You do not reach the possibility of comparison by the ladder of direct likeness: great, greater, greatest; it is possible only inversely. Neither does a human being come closer and closer to God by lifting up his head higher and higher, but inversely by casting himself down ever more deeply in worship. The broken heart that condemns itself cannot have, seeks in vain to find, an expression that is strong enough to describe its guilt, its wretchedness, its defilement—God is even greater in showing mercy!

What a strange comparison! All human purity, all human mercy is not good enough for comparison; but a repenting heart that condemns itself—

with this is compared God's greatness in showing mercy, except that God's greatness is even greater: as deep as this heart can lower itself, and yet never itself deep enough, so infinitely elevated, or infinitely more elevated, is God's greatness in showing mercy! See, language seems to burst and break in order to describe God's greatness in showing mercy. Thought tried in vain to find a comparison, then finally found it, something that, humanly speaking, is no comparison, the brokenness of a repentant heart—God's mercy is even greater. A repentant heart when in brokenness and contrition it condemns itself, yes, this heart would give itself no rest, not for one single moment; it would find no hiding place where it could flee from itself. It would find no excuse possible, would find it a new, the most terrible, guilt to seek an excuse. It would find no relief, none; even the most compassionate word that the most compassionate inwardness is able to think up would sound to this heart, which would not dare and would not allow itself to be comforted, like a new condemnation upon it—so infinite is God's greatness in showing mercy, or it is even greater.

It limps, this comparison—a human being always does after wrestling with God.[171] It is far-fetched, this comparison—indeed it is, because it was found by God-fearingly rejecting all human likeness. If a human being does not dare to make for himself any image of God,[172] then surely he does not dare to imagine that the human could be a direct comparison. Let no one be in a hurry in seeking, let no one be too hasty in wanting to have found a comparison for God's greatness in showing mercy. Every mouth is to be stopped;[173] everyone is to beat his breast—because there is only one comparison that is any at all, a troubled heart that condemns itself.

But God is greater than this heart! Be comforted, then. Perhaps you learned earlier from experience how hard it is for such a heart to be brought before the judgment of Pharisees and Scribes, or to encounter the misunderstanding that knows only how to tear it to pieces even more, or the pettiness that disquiets the heart even more—you, who so greatly needed someone who was great. God in heaven is greater. He is not greater than the Pharisees and Scribes, nor is he greater than misunderstanding and pettiness; nor is he greater than the person who nevertheless knew how to say a soothing word to you, with whom you found some solace because he was not pettyminded, did not want to put you down even more but wanted to raise you up—God is not greater than he (what a disconsolate comparison!)—no, God is greater than your own heart! Ah, whether it was a sickness of soul that so darkened your mind every night that finally in deadly anxiety, brought almost to the point of madness by the conception of God's holiness, you thought you had to condemn yourself; whether it was something terrible that so weighed upon your conscience that your heart condemned itself—God is greater! If you will not believe, if you dare not believe without seeing a sign, it is now offered to you. He who came to the world and died, he died also for you, also for you. He did not die for people as such in general—oh, just the opposite, if he died for anyone in particular, then it was indeed for the one, not for the ninety and nine—alas, and you are too wretched to be included at random in the round number; the weight of wretchedness and guilt fell so terribly upon your heart that you are counted out. And he who died for you when you were a stranger to him, would he abandon his own! If God so loved the world that he gave his only begotten Son in order that no one would be lost,[174] why would he not keep those who were so dearly bought! Oh, do not torture yourself; if it is the anxieties of depression that ensnare you, then God knows everything—and he is great! And if it is a ton of guilt that rests upon you, he who on his own initiative (something that did not arise in any human heart[175]) showed mercy upon the world, he is great! Do not torture yourself, remember that woman, that there was no one who condemned her, and bear in mind that this same thing can be expressed also in another way: Christ was present. Precisely because he was present, there was no one who condemned her. He rescued her from the condemnation of the Pharisees and Scribes; they went away ashamed; because Christ was present, there was no one who condemned her. Then Christ alone remained with her—but there was no one who condemned her. Just this, that he alone remained with her, signifies in a far deeper sense that there was no one who condemned her. It would have been of only little help to her that the Pharisees and Scribes went away; after all, they could come again with their condemnation. But the *Savior* alone remained with her: therefore there was no one who condemned her. Alas, there is only one guilt that God cannot forgive—it is to refuse to believe in his greatness!

He is greater than the heart that condemns itself. But, on the other hand, there is nothing about his being greater than the worldly, frivolous, foolish heart that fatuously counts on God's imagined greatness in forgiving. No, God is and can be just as scrupulous as he is great and can be great in showing mercy. For example, God's nature always joins opposites, just as in the miracle of the five small loaves.[176] The people had nothing to eat—through a miracle a superabundance was created, but see, then Christ commands that everything left over be carefully collected. How divine! One person can be wasteful, another thrifty; but if there were a human being who through a miracle could at any moment divinely create a superabundance, do you not think that he humanly would have disdained the fragments, do you think that he—divinely would have collected the fragments! So also with God's greatness in showing mercy; a human being scarcely has the slightest idea of how scrupulous God can be. Let us not deceive ourselves, let us not lie to ourselves, and let us not, which amounts to the same thing, depreciate God's greatness by wanting to make ourselves out to be better than we are, less guilty, or by naming our guilt with more frivolous names; in so doing we depreciate the greatness of God, which is in forgiving. But neither let us in-

x
308

sanely want to sin even more in order to make the forgiveness even greater,[177] because God is just as great in his being scrupulous.

Let us then here in your holy house praise your greatness, O God, you who incomprehensibly showed mercy and reconciled the world to yourself. Out there the stars proclaim your majesty, and the perfection of everything proclaims your greatness, but in here it is the imperfect, it is sinners who praise your even greater greatness!—The supper of remembrance is once again prepared; may you then beforehand be brought to mind and thanked for your greatness in showing mercy.

THE LILY IN THE FIELD AND
THE BIRD OF THE AIR
(MAY 14, 1849)
BY S. KIERKEGAARD

These discourses were not written as the signed work parallel to the second edition of the pseudonymous *Either/Or* (also published on May 14); nevertheless the representative of the signed series "came into being at the time—just what I needed."[178] The discourses, like "What We Learn from the Lilies of the Field and the Birds in the Air" (Part II of *Upbuilding Discourses in Various Spirits*), represent what in *Postscript* is called Religiousness *A* as distinguished from Christianity, the paradoxical-historical Religiousness *B*. Common to both works is an invitation to an uncommon approach to the world of nature. The ornithologist, bird raiser, hunter, and pet-shop owner and the botanist, nursery operator, collector, and horticulture dealer will recognize here a way of seeing—receptive, reflective in silence—that is rewardingly different from that of the analytical classifier, the producer, the user, and the merchant.

FROM the lily and the bird as teachers, let us learn

silence, or learn to be silent.

Surely it is speech that distinguishes humanity above the animal and then, if you like, far above the lily. But because the ability to speak is an advantage, it does not follow that the ability to be silent would not be an art or would be an inferior art. On the contrary, because the human being is able to speak, the ability to be silent is an art, and a great art precisely because this advantage of his so easily tempts him. But this he can learn from the silent teachers, the lily and the bird.

"Seek first God's kingdom and his righteousness."[179]

But what does this mean, what am I to do, or what is the effort that can be said to seek, to aspire to God's kingdom? Shall I see about getting a position commensurate with my talents and abilities in order to be effective in it? No, you shall *first* seek God's kingdom. Shall I give all my possessions to the poor?[180] No, you shall *first* seek God's kingdom. Shall I then go out and proclaim this doctrine to the world? No, you shall *first* seek God's kingdom. But then in a certain sense it is nothing I shall do? Yes, quite true, in a certain sense it is nothing. In the deepest sense you shall make yourself nothing, become nothing before God, learn to be silent. In this silence is the beginning, which is to seek *first* God's kingdom.

Thus in a certain sense one devoutly comes backward to the beginning. The beginning is not that with which one begins but that to which one comes, and one comes to it backward. The beginning is this art of *becoming* silent, since to be silent as nature is silent is no art. In the deepest sense, to become silent in this way, silent before God, is the beginning of the fear of God, because just as the fear of God is the beginning of wisdom,[181] so silence is the beginning of the fear of God. And just as the fear of God is more than the beginning of wisdom, is wisdom, so silence is more than the beginning of the fear of God, is the fear of God. In this silence the many thoughts of wishes and desires God-fearingly fall silent; in this silence the verbosity of thanksgiving God-fearingly becomes silent.

The advantage of the human being over the animal is the ability to speak, but, in relation to God, wanting to speak can easily become the corruption of the human being, who is able to speak. God is in heaven and the human being is on earth and therefore they can hardly converse. God is infinite wisdom; what the human being knows is idle chatter; therefore they can hardly converse. God is love and the human being, as we say to a child, is a little ninny even in regard to his own welfare, and therefore they can hardly converse. Only in much fear and trembling is a human being able to speak with God, in much fear and trembling. But to speak in much fear and trembling is difficult for another reason, because just as anxiety makes the voice fail physically, so also much fear and trembling make speech fall into silence. The one who prays aright knows this, and the one who did not pray aright perhaps learned this through prayer. There was something that lay very heavily on his mind, a matter that was very important to him; it was very urgent for him to make himself rightly understood by God; he was afraid he had forgotten something in the prayer, and, alas, if he had forgotten it, he was afraid that God by himself would not remember it—therefore he wanted to concentrate his mind on praying with all his heart. Then what happened to him if he did really pray with all his heart? Something amazing happened to him. Gradually, as he became more and more fervent in prayer, he had less and less to say, and finally he became completely silent. He became silent. Indeed, he became what is, if possible, even more opposite to speaking than silence; he became a listener. He thought that to pray is to speak; he learned that to pray is not only to be silent but is to listen. And so it is; to pray is not to listen to oneself speak but is to become silent and to remain silent, to wait until the one praying hears God.

This is why the words of the Gospel, seek *first* God's kingdom, upbringingly muzzle a person's mouth, as it were, by answering every single question he asks, whether this is what he shall do—No, you shall *first* seek God's kingdom. Therefore one can paraphrase the Gospel's words in this way: You shall begin by praying, not as if (which we have shown) prayer always began with silence, but because when prayer has really become prayer it has become

XI
15

XI
16

silence. Seek first God's kingdom, that is: Pray! If you ask, yes, if you mention every single possibility and ask: Is this what I shall do, and if I do it is this seeking God's kingdom, the answer must be: No, you shall first seek God's kingdom. But to pray, that is, to pray aright, is to become silent, and that is to seek first God's kingdom.

This silence you can learn with the lily and the bird. That is, their silence is no art, but when *you* become silent like the lily and the bird, you are at the beginning, which is to seek *first* God's kingdom.

How solemn it is out there under God's heaven with the lily and the bird, and why? Ask the poet. He answers: Because there is silence. And his longing goes out to that solemn silence, away from the worldliness in the human world, where there is so much talking, away from all the worldly human life that only in a sad way demonstrates that speech distinguishes human beings above the animals. "Because," says the poet, "if this is the distinguishing characteristic—no, then I much, much prefer the silence out there. I prefer it—no, there is no comparison; it is a distinguishing characteristic infinitely above that of human beings, who are able to speak." That is, in nature's silence the poet thinks that he is aware of the divine voice. In humanity's busy talking he thinks that he not only is not aware of the divine voice but is not even aware that the human being has kinship with the divine. The poet says: Speech is the human being's advantage over the animal—yes, quite true, if he is able *to be silent.*

But to be able to be silent, that you can learn out there with the lily and the bird, where there is silence and also something divine in this silence. There is silence out there, and not only when everything is silent in the silent night, but there nevertheless is silence out there also when day vibrates with a thousand strings and everything is like a sea of sound. Each one separately does it so well that not one of them, nor all of them together, will break the solemn silence. There is silence out there. The forest is silent; even when it whispers it nevertheless is silent. The trees, even where they stand in the thickest growth, keep their word, something human beings rarely do despite a promise given: This will remain between us. The sea is silent; even when it rages uproariously it is silent. At first you perhaps listen in the wrong way and hear it roar. If you hurry off and report this, you do the sea an injustice. If, however, you take time and listen more carefully, you hear—how amazing!—you hear silence, because uniformity is nevertheless also silence. In the evening, when silence rests over the land and you hear the distant bellowing from the meadow, or from the farmer's house in the distance you hear the familiar voice of the dog, you cannot say that this bellowing or this voice disturbs the silence. No, this belongs to the silence, is in a mysterious and thus in turn silent harmony with the silence; this increases it.

Let us now look more closely at the lily and the bird from whom we are to learn. The bird is *silent and waits.* It knows, or rather it fully and firmly believes, that everything takes place in its time; therefore the bird waits. But it knows that it is not entitled to know the time or day; therefore it is silent. "It will surely take place in due season," says the bird. Yet, no, the bird does not say this; it is silent, but its silence is expressive and its silence says that it believes it, and because it believes it the bird is silent and waits. When the moment comes, the silent bird understands that this is the moment; it uses it and is never disappointed.

So it is also with the lily; it is silent and waits. It does not impatiently ask, "When will spring come?" because it knows that spring will come in due season, knows that it would be least useful to itself if it were allowed to determine the seasons of the year. It does not ask, "When will we get rain?" or "When will we get sunshine?" or say, "Now we have had too much rain," or "Now it is too hot." It does not ask in advance what kind of summer it will be this year, how long or how short. No, it is silent and waits—that is how simple it is. But still it is never deceived, something that can happen only to sagacity, not to simplicity, which does not deceive and is not deceived. Then comes the moment, and when the moment comes, the silent lily understands that now is the moment, and it makes use of it.

O you profound teachers of simplicity, should it not also be possible to find *the moment* when one is speaking? No, only by being silent does one find the moment. When one speaks, if one says merely a single word, one misses the moment—the moment *is* only in silence. Because a person cannot keep silent, it rarely happens that he really comes to understand when the moment is and to use the moment properly. He cannot be silent and wait, which perhaps explains why the moment never comes for him at all. He cannot be silent, which perhaps explains why he was not aware of the moment when it did come for him. Although pregnant with its rich meaning, the moment does not have any message sent in advance to announce its coming; it comes too swiftly for that when it comes, and there is not a moment's time beforehand. Nor does the moment, no matter how significant it is in itself, come with noise or with shouting. No, it comes softly, with a lighter step than the lightest footfall of any creature, since it comes with the light step of the sudden; it comes stealthily—therefore one must be absolutely silent if one is to be aware that "now it is here." At the next moment it is gone, and for that reason one must have been absolutely silent if one is to succeed in making use of it. Yet everything depends on the moment. Indeed, the misfortune in the lives of the great majority of human beings is this, that they were never aware of the moment, that in their lives the eternal and the temporal are exclusively separated. And why? Because they could not be silent.

The bird is *silent and suffers.* However heartbroken it is, it is silent. Even the mournful elegist of the desert or of solitude is silent. It sighs three times and then is silent; once again it sighs three times, but essentially it is silent. What it is, it does not say; it does not complain, does not accuse anyone; it sighs, only to fall into silence again. It seems as if the silence would burst it; therefore it must sigh in order to be silent. The bird is not exempt from suffering, but the silent bird exempts itself from what makes the suffering harder, the mistaken sympathy of others, from what prolongs the suffering, all the talk about the suffering, from what makes the suffering into what is worse than suffering, into the sin of impatience and sadness. Do not think that it is just a bit of duplicity on the part of the bird that it is silent when it suffers, that it is not silent in its innermost being however silent it is with others, that it complains over its fate, accuses God and humanity, and lets "the heart in sorrow sin."[182] No, the bird is silent and suffers. Alas, the human being does not do that. But why is it that human suffering, compared with the bird's suffering, seems so frightful? Is it not because the human being can speak? No, not for that reason, since that, after all, is an advantage, but because the human being cannot be silent. It is, namely, not as the impatient person, or even more intensely, the despairing person, thinks he understands it when he says or cries (and this is already a misunderstanding of speech and voice), "Would that I had a voice like the voice of the storm so that I could voice all my suffering as I feel it!" Ah, that would be only a foolish remedy; to the same degree he will only feel his suffering the more intensely. No, but if you could be silent, if you had the silence of the bird, then the suffering would certainly become less.

Like the bird, so also the lily—it is silent. Even though it stands and suffers as it withers, it is silent. This innocent child cannot dissemble, nor is it asked to, and its good fortune is that it cannot, because the art of being able to dissemble is indeed purchased at a high price. It cannot dissemble, cannot do anything about its changing color, and thereby betrays what one of course recognizes by this paling color-change, that it is suffering—but it remains silent. It would like to stand erect in order to hide what it is suffering, but for that it does not have the strength, this mastery over itself. Its head droops, feeble and bowed. The passerby—if any passerby has so much sympathy that he notices it!—the passerby understands what this means; it is sufficiently eloquent. But the lily is silent.

So it is with the lily. But why is it that human suffering, compared with the lily's suffering, seems so frightful? Is it not because it cannot speak? If the lily could speak and if, alas, like the human being, it had not learned the art of being silent, would not also its suffering become frightful? But the lily is silent. For the lily, to suffer is to suffer, neither more nor less. Yet when to suffer is neither more nor less than to suffer, the suffering is simplified and particularized as much as possible and made as small as possible. The suffering cannot become less, since it indeed *is* and therefore is what it is. But, on the other hand, the suffering can become immensely greater when it does not remain exactly what it is, neither more nor less. When the suffering is neither more nor less, that is, when it is only the definite suffering that it is,

XI
19

it is, even if it were the greatest suffering, the least it can be. But when it becomes indefinite how great the suffering actually is, the suffering becomes greater; this indefiniteness increases the suffering immensely. This indefiniteness appears just because of this dubious advantage of the human being, the ability to speak. On the other hand, one arrives at the definiteness of suffering, that it is neither more nor less than what it is, only by being able to be silent, and this silence you can learn from the bird and the lily.

Out there with the lily and the bird there is silence. But what does this silence express? It expresses respect for God, that it is he who rules and he alone to whom wisdom and understanding are due. And just because this silence is veneration for God, is worship, as it can be in nature, this silence is so solemn. And because this silence is solemn in this way, one is aware of God in nature—what wonder, then, when everything is silent out of respect for him! Even if *he* does not speak, the fact that everything is silent out of respect for him affects one as if he spoke.

What you can learn, however, from the silence out there with the lily and the bird without the help of any poet, what only the Gospel can teach you, is that it is earnestness, that there must be earnestness, that the bird and the lily *shall* be the teacher, that you shall imitate them, learn from them in all earnestness, that you shall become as silent as the lily and the bird.

Indeed, this is already earnestness—if it is understood properly, not as the dreaming poet or as the poet who lets nature dream about him understands it—this, that out there with the lily and the bird you are aware *that you are before God,* something that usually is entirely forgotten in speaking and conversing with other human beings. When just we two are speaking together, even more so when we are ten or more, it is very easily forgotten that you and I, we two, or we ten, are before God. But the lily, who is the teacher, is profound. It does not become involved with you at all; it is silent, and by being silent it wants to be a sign to you that you are before God, so that you remember that you are before God—so that you also in earnestness and truth might become silent before God.

XI
20

TWO ETHICAL-RELIGIOUS ESSAYS
(MAY 19, 1849)
BY H. H.

""Two Ethical-Religious Essays' does not belong to the authorship in the same way; it is not an element in it but a point of view."[183] Its extraterritorial status was already indicated by the original position of Essay II as an addendum to the third version of the unpublished *Book on Adler*. The nonreferential pseudonym may have been used because the two themes were too close to Kierkegaard, who is not the stated editor as in some of the other pseudonymous works. The question of the first essay, "Does a Human Being Have the Right to Let Himself Be Put to Death for the Truth?" is answered in the negative, because "a human being, simply as a human being, [is] so relative in relation to other beings," that he does not have the right "to let others become guilty of a murder."[184] The second essay, "The Difference between a Genius and an Apostle," is another expression of Kierkegaard's concern about the issue of authority, which he regarded as increasingly crucial in the modern period.

THE DIFFERENCE BETWEEN A GENIUS AND AN APOSTLE

As a genius, Paul cannot stand comparison with either Plato or Shakespeare; as an author of beautiful metaphors, he ranks rather low; as a stylist, he is a totally unknown name—and as a tapestry maker, well, I must say that I do not know how high he can rank in this regard. See, it is always best to turn obtuse earnestness into a jest, and then comes the earnestness, the earnestness—that Paul is an apostle. And as an apostle he again has no affinity, none whatever, with either Plato or Shakespeare or stylists or tapestry makers; they all (Plato as well as Shakespeare and tapestry maker Hansen) are without any comparison to Paul.

A genius and an apostle are qualitatively different, are qualifications that belong each in its qualitative sphere: **of immanence and of transcendence. (1) Therefore the genius can very well have something new to bring, but this in turn vanishes in the human race's general assimilation, just as the difference "genius" vanishes as soon as one thinks of eternity. The apostle has something paradoxically new to bring, the newness of which, just because it is essentially paradoxical and not an anticipation pertaining to the development of the human race, continually remains, just as an apostle remains for all eternity as apostle, and no immanence of eternity places him essentially on the same line with all human beings, since essentially he is paradoxically different. (2) The genius is what he is by him-**

self, that is, by what he is in himself; an apostle is what he is by his divine authority. (3) The genius has only immanent teleology; the apostle is absolutely teleologically positioned paradoxically.

1. All thinking draws its breath in immanence, whereas the paradox and faith constitute a separate qualitative sphere. Immanently, in the relation between persons *qua* human beings, every difference is for essential and eternal thinking something vanishing, a factor that surely has its validity momentarily but essentially vanishes in the essential equality of eternity. Genius, as the word itself says (*ingenium,* the innate, primitivity [*primus*], originality [*origo*], pristineness, etc.), is immediacy, natural qualifications; the genius *is born.* Long before there can be any question of whether the genius will or will not assign his rare endowment to God, the genius already is and is a genius even if he does not do that. With the genius there can occur the change of developing into being what he κατὰ δύναμιν [potentially] is, of coming into conscious possession of himself. Insofar as the expression "paradox" is used to designate the new that a genius may have to bring, it is still used only in the inessential sense of the transitory paradox, of the anticipation that condenses into something paradoxical, which, however, in turn vanishes. A genius may be paradoxical in his first communication, but the more he comes to himself the more the paradoxical vanishes. Perhaps a genius can be a century ahead of his time and therefore stand as a paradox, but ultimately the human race will assimilate the one-time paradoxical in such a way that it is no longer paradoxical.

It is different with an apostle. The word[185] itself indicates the difference. An apostle is not born; an apostle is a man who is called and appointed by God and sent by him on a mission. An apostle does not develop in such a way that he gradually becomes what he is κατὰ δύναμιν. Prior to becoming an apostle, there is no potential possibility; every human being is essentially equally close to becoming that. An apostle can never come to himself in such a way that he becomes aware of his apostolic calling as an element in his own life-development. The apostolic calling is a paradoxical fact that in the first and the last moment of his life stands paradoxically outside his personal identity as the specific person he is. Perhaps a man has long since arrived at the age of discretion; then he is called as an apostle. By this call he does not become more intelligent, he does not acquire more imagination, greater discernment, etc.—not at all; he remains himself but by the paradoxical fact is sent by God on a specific mission. By this paradoxical fact the apostle is for all eternity made paradoxically different from all other human beings. The new that he can have to proclaim is the essentially paradoxical. However long it is proclaimed in the world, it remains essentially just as new, just as paradoxical; no immanence can assimilate it. The apostle did not act as the person distinguished by natural gifts who was ahead of his contemporaries. Perhaps he was what we call a simple person, but by a paradoxical fact he was called to proclaim this new thing. Even if thought considered itself capable of assimilating the doctrine, it cannot assimilate the way in which the doctrine came into the world, because the essential paradox is specifically the protest against immanence. But the way in which such a doctrine entered the world is specifically what is qualitatively decisive, something that can be disregarded only through deceit or through thoughtlessness.

2. A genius is evaluated purely esthetically according to what his content, his specific gravity, is found to be; an apostle is what he is by having divine authority. *The divine authority is what is qualitatively decisive.* It is not by evaluating the content of the doctrine esthetically or philosophically that I will or can arrive at the conclusion: ergo the one who has delivered this doctrine is called by a revelation, ergo he is an apostle. The relationship is just the reverse: the one called by a revelation, to whom a doctrine is entrusted, argues on the basis that it is a revelation, on the basis that he has authority. I am not to listen to Paul because he is brilliant or matchlessly brilliant, but I am to submit to Paul because he has divine authority; and in any case it must become Paul's responsibility to see to it that he produces this impression, whether anyone submits to his authority or not. Paul must not appeal to his brilliance, since in that case he is a fool; he must not become involved in a purely esthetic or philosophic discussion of the content of the doctrine, since in that case he is absentminded. No, he must appeal to his divine authority and precisely through it, while he willingly sacrifices life and everything, *prevent* all impertinent esthetic and philosophical superficial observations against the form and content of the doctrine. Paul must not commend himself and his doctrine with the aid of the beautiful metaphors; on the contrary, he would surely say to the individual, "Whether the image is beautiful or it is threadbare and obsolete makes no difference; you must consider that what I say has been entrusted to me by a revelation; so it is God himself or the Lord Jesus Christ who is speaking, and you must not become involved presumptuously in criticizing the form. I cannot, I dare not compel you to obey, but through the relationship of your conscience to God, I make you eternally responsible for your relationship to this doctrine by my having proclaimed it as revealed to me and therefore by having proclaimed it with divine authority."

Authority is what is qualitatively decisive. Or is there not a difference, even within the relativity of human life, although it immanently disappears, between a royal command and the words of a poet or a thinker? And what is the difference but this, that the royal command has authority and therefore forbids all esthetic and critical impertinence with regard to form and content? The poet, the thinker, on the other hand, does not have any authority, not even within this relativity; his utterance is evaluated purely esthetically or philosophically by evaluating the content and form. But what is it that has radically confused the essentially Christian but this, that in doubt we have

XI
99

first become almost uncertain whether a God exists and then in rebelliousness against all authorities have forgotten what authority is and its dialectic.
A king exists physically in such a way that one can physically assure oneself
of it, and if it is necessary perhaps the king can very physically assure one
that he exists. But God does not exist in that way. Doubt has made use of
this to place God on the same level with all those who have no authority, on
the same level with geniuses, poets, and thinkers, whose utterances are simply evaluated only esthetically or philosophically; and if it is said well, then
the man is a genius—and if it is said exceptionally and extremely well, then
it is God who has said it!!!

In this manner God is actually smuggled away. What is he to do? If God
stops a person on his way, calls him by a revelation, and sends him out
equipped with divine authority to the other people, they then say to him,
"From whom do you come?" He answers, "From God." But see, God cannot help his emissary in such a physical way as a king can, who gives him an
escort of soldiers or police, or his ring, or his signature that all recognize—
in short, God cannot be of service to human beings by providing them with
physical certainty that an apostle is an apostle—indeed, that would be nonsense. Even the miracle, if the apostle has this gift, provides no physical certainty, because the miracle is an object of faith. Moreover, it is nonsense to
obtain *physical* certainty that an apostle is an apostle (the paradoxical qualification of a relation of spirit), just as it is nonsense to obtain *physical* certainty
that God exists, since God is *spirit*. So the apostle says that he is from God.
The others answer, "Well, then let us see if the content of what you teach is
divine; then we will accept it, also that it has been revealed to you." In this
way both God and the apostle are cheated. The divine authority of the one
called should be specifically the sure defense that would safeguard the doctrine and keep it from impertinences at the majestic distance of the divine,
but instead the content and form of the doctrine must let itself be criticized
and sniffed at—so one can by that way come to a conclusion as to whether
it was a revelation or not. In the meantime the apostle and God presumably
must wait at the door or with the doorman until the matter has been decided by the wise ones on the second floor. According to God's stipulation,
the one who is called should use his divine authority to drive away all the
impertinent people who are unwilling to obey but want to be loquacious;
and instead of getting people on the move, the apostle is changed into an ex-
aminee who as such comes to the market with a new doctrine.

What, then, is authority? Is authority the profundity of the doctrine, its
excellence, its brilliance? Not at all. If, for example, authority would only signify, to the second power or doubled, that the doctrine is profound—then
there simply is no authority, because, if a learner completely and perfectly
appropriated this doctrine by way of understanding, then of course there
would be no difference anymore between the teacher and the learner. Au-

thority, however, is something that remains unchanged, something that one cannot acquire by having perfectly understood the doctrine. *Authority is a specific quality that enters from somewhere else and qualitatively asserts itself precisely when the content of the statement or the act is made a matter of indifference esthetically.*

Let us take an example, as simple as possible, in which the relation is nevertheless manifest. When someone who has the authority to say it says to a person, "Go!" and when someone who does not have the authority says, "Go!" the utterance (Go!) and its content are indeed identical; evaluated esthetically, it is, if you like, equally well spoken, but the authority makes the difference. If the authority is not the other (τὸ ἕτερον[186]), if in any way it should indicate merely an intensification within the identity, then there simply is no authority. If, for example, a teacher is enthusiastically conscious that he himself, existing, expresses and has expressed, with the sacrifice of everything, the teaching he proclaims, this consciousness can indeed give him an assured and steadfast spirit, but it does not give him authority. His life as evidence of the rightness of the teaching is not the other (τὸ ἕτερον) but is a simple redoubling. That he lives according to the teaching does not demonstrate that it is right, but because he is himself convinced of the rightness of the teaching, he lives according to it. On the other hand, whether a police officer, for example, is a scoundrel or an upright man, as soon as he is on duty, he has authority.

XI
101

In order to elucidate more explicitly the concept of authority, so important to the paradoxical-religious sphere, I shall follow up the dialectic of authority. *In the sphere of immanence authority is utterly unthinkable, or it can be thought only as transitory.** Insofar as it is a matter of authority in the political, civic, social, domestic, and disciplinary realms or of the exercise of authority, authority is still only a transitory factor, something vanishing that either disappears later even in temporality or disappears inasmuch as temporality and earthly life itself are a transitory factor that vanishes with all its differences. The only basis of any relation between persons *qua* human beings that can be *thought* is the dissimilarity within the identity of immanence, that is, the essential likeness. The single human being cannot be *thought* as being different from all others by a specific quality (then all thought ceases, as it quite consistently does in the sphere of the paradoxical-religious and faith). All human differences between persons *qua* human beings disappear for thought

---

* Perhaps it happens here with some reader as it happens with me, that in connection with this discussion of "authority" I come to think of Magister Kierkegaard's *Upbuilding Discourses,* where it is so strongly accentuated and emphasized, by being repeated in the preface every time and word for word: "they are not *sermons,* because the author does not have *authority* to preach." Authority is a specific quality either of an apostolic calling or of ordination. To preach is precisely to use authority, and that this is what it is to preach has simply been altogether forgotten in our day.

as factors within the totality and quality of identity. I shall certainly respect and obey the difference in the factor, but I am permitted to be built up religiously by the certainty that in eternity the differences vanish, the one that makes me distinguished and the one that subordinates me. As a subject I am to honor and obey the king with undivided soul, but I am permitted to be built up religiously by the thought that essentially I am a citizen of heaven[187] and that if I ever meet his departed majesty there I shall not be bound in subservient obedience to him.

XI
102
This, then, is the relation between persons *qua* human beings. *But between God and a human being there is an eternal essential qualitative difference,*[188] which only presumptuous thinking can make disappear in the blasphemy that in the transitory moment of finitude God and a human being are certainly differentiated, so that here in his life a human being ought to obey and worship God, but in eternity the difference will vanish in the essential likeness, so that God and human beings become peers in eternity, just as the king and the valet.

Between God and a human being, then, there is and remains an eternal essential qualitative difference. *The paradoxical-religious relation* (which, quite rightly, cannot be thought but only be believed) *appears when God appoints a specific human being to have divine authority*—with regard, note well, to what God has entrusted to him. The person called in this way does not, in the relation between persons, relate himself *qua* human being; he does not relate himself to other people in a quantitative difference (as a genius, an exceptionally gifted person, etc.). No, he relates himself paradoxically by having a specific quality that no immanence can revoke in the likeness of eternity, because it is essentially paradoxical and *after* thought (not prior to, before thought), against thought. If such a called person has a doctrine to bring according to divine order and, let us imagine, another person has arrived at the same doctrine by himself and on his own—these two will not become alike in all eternity, because the former by his paradoxical specific quality (the divine authority) will be different from every other human being and from the qualification of the essential likeness lying immanently at the basis of all other human differences. The qualification "an apostle" belongs in the sphere of the transcendent, the paradoxical-religious sphere, which, altogether consistently, also has a qualitatively different expression for the relation of other people to an apostle—in other words, they relate themselves to him in faith, whereas all thought lies and is and breathes in immanence. But faith is not a transitory qualification any more than the apostle's paradoxical qualification was transitory.

Thus in the relation between persons *qua* human beings, no *enduring* [*bestaaende*] or *constant* [*bestandig*] difference of authority was *thinkable;* it was something vanishing. Let us, however, for a moment dwell on some examples of such so-called relations of authority between persons qua human beings that are true under the conditions of temporality in order to become aware of the essential view of authority. A king, of course, is assumed to have authority. Why, then, do we even find it offensive that a king is brilliant, is an artist etc.? It no doubt is because one essentially accentuates in him the royal authority and in comparison with this finds the more ordinary qualifications of human differences to be something vanishing, something inessential, a disturbing incidental. A government department is assumed to have authority in its stipulated domain. Why, then, would one find it offensive if in its decrees such a department was actually brilliant, witty, profound? Because one quite properly accentuates that authority qualitatively. To ask if a king is a genius, and in that case to be willing to obey him, is basically high treason, because the question contains a doubt about submission to authority. To be willing to obey a government department if it can come out with witticisms is basically making a fool of the department. To honor one's father because he is exceptionally intelligent is impiety.

Yet, as stated, in the relation between persons *qua* human beings, authority, even if it exists, is something vanishing, and eternity abolishes all earthly authority. But now in the sphere of transcendence. Let us take an example that is very simple, but for that very reason also as striking as possible. When Christ says, "There is an eternal life," and when theological graduate Petersen says, "There is an eternal life," both are saying the same thing; there is in the first statement no more deduction, development, profundity, richness of thought than in the second; evaluated esthetically, both statements are equally good. And yet there certainly is an eternal qualitative difference! As Godman, Christ possesses the specific quality of authority; no eternity can mediate this or place Christ on the same level with the essentially human likeness. Christ, therefore, taught with authority.[189] To ask whether Christ is profound is blasphemy and is an attempt (be it conscious or unconscious) to destroy him in a subtle way, since the question contains a doubt with regard to his authority and attempts in impertinent *straightforwardness* to evaluate and grade him, as if he were up for examination and should be catechized instead of being the one to whom all power is given in heaven and on earth.[190]

Yet rarely, very rarely, does one hear or read these days a religious address that is entirely correct. The better ones still usually dabble a bit in what could be called unconscious or well-intentioned rebellion as they defend and uphold Christianity with all their might—in the wrong categories. Let me take an example, the first that comes along. I prefer to take a German, so I then know that no one can hit upon the idea, not the most obtuse and not the most malicious, that I am writing this about a matter that in my opinion is immensely important—in order to point a finger at some clergyman. In a homily for the fifth Sunday in Lent, Bishop Sailer* preaches on the text John

---

* See *Evangelisches aus Joh. Michael Sailers religiösen Schriften,* by August Gebauer (Stuttgart: 1846), pp. 34, 35.

8:47–51. He selects these two verses: "*Wer von Gott ist, der höret Gottes Wort* [Whoever is of God hears the word of God]" and "*Wer mein Wort hält, der siehet den Tod nicht* [Whoever keeps my word will not see death]" and thereupon comments: "*Es sind in diesen Worten des Herrn drei grosze Räthsel gelöset, mit denen sich die Menschen von jeher den Kopf so oder anders zerbrochen haben* [In these words by the Lord three great riddles are solved, over which people have racked their brains since time immemorial]."

There we have it. The word *Räthsel* [riddle], and especially *drei grosze Räthsel* and then what follows, *mit denen die Menschen den Kopf sich zerbrochen haben* [over which people have *racked their brains*] promptly lead our thoughts to the profound in the intellectual sense, the cogitating, the ruminating, the speculating. But how can a simple apodictic statement be profound—an apodictic statement that is what it is only by having been said by such and such a person, a statement that by no means is to be understood or fathomed but only believed? How can a person hit upon the idea that a riddle in the nature of cogitating and ruminating profundity should be solved by a direct statement, by an assertion? The question is: Is there an eternal life? The answer is: There is an eternal life. Now, where in the world is the profundity? If Christ is not the one who has said it, and if Christ is not the one he has said that he is, then the profundity, if the statement is in itself profound, must still be ascertainable.

Let us take theological graduate Mr. Petersen; he, too, says: There is an eternal life. Who in the world would hit upon the idea of ascribing profundity to him on the basis of a direct statement? What is decisive consists not in the statement but in the fact that it is Christ who has said it; but what is confounding is that in order, as it were, to lure people into believing, one says something about profundity and the profound. A Christian pastor, if he is to speak properly, must quite simply say, "We have Christ's word that there is an eternal life, and with that the matter is decided. Here it is a matter neither of racking one's brains nor of speculating, but of its being Christ who, not in the capacity of profundity but with his divine authority, has said it."

Let us go further, let us assume that someone believes that there is an eternal life because Christ has said it; then in faith he avoids all the deep profundity and cogitating and ruminating "with which people rack their brains." On the other hand, let us take someone who wants to rack his brains profoundly on the question of immortality—will he not be justified in denying that the direct statement is a profound answer to the question? What Plato says about immortality[191] is actually profound, attained by profound cogitating; but then poor Plato does not have any authority.

The point, however, is this. Doubt and disbelief, which make faith worthless, have, among other things, also made people ashamed of obeying, of submitting to authority. This rebelliousness even sneaks into the thought process of the better ones, perhaps unconsciously, and so begins all this extravagance, which basically is treason, about the deep and the profound and the wondrously beautiful that one can glimpse etc. If one were to describe with a single specific adjective the Christian-religious address as it is now heard and read, one would have to say that it is *affected*. Ordinarily when mention is made of a pastor's affectation, one perhaps has in mind that he decks himself out and dolls himself up, or that he speaks in a sentimental tone, or that he rolls his *r*'s like a Norwegian and wrinkles his brow, or that he strains himself in energetic postures and revivalist leaps etc. Yet all such things are of minor importance, even though it is always desirable that such things not occur. But it is corrupting when the thought process of the sermon address is affected, when its orthodoxy is achieved by placing the emphasis on an entirely wrong place, when basically it exhorts believing in Christ, preaches faith in him on the basis of what cannot at all be the object of faith. If a son were to say, "I obey my father not because he is my father but because he is a genius, or because his commands are always profound and brilliant," this filial obedience is affected. The son emphasizes something altogether wrong, emphasizes the brilliance, the profundity in a *command,* whereas a command is simply indifferent to this qualification. The son is willing to obey on the basis of the father's profundity and brilliance, and on that basis he simply cannot *obey* him, because his critical attitude with regard to whether the command is profound and brilliant undermines the obedience.

Similarly, it is also affectation when there is so much talk about appropriating Christianity and believing in Christ on account of the depth and profundity of the doctrine. One ascribes orthodoxy to oneself by emphasizing something altogether wrong. Thus all modern speculative thought is affected by having abolished *obedience* on the one hand and *authority* on the other, and by wanting despite that to be orthodox. A pastor who is entirely correct in his address must, when he quotes words of Christ, speak in this way: "These words are by the one to whom, according to his own statement, all power is given in heaven and on earth. You, my listener, must now in your own mind consider whether you will submit to this authority or not, accept and believe these words or not. But if you refuse, then for God's sake do not accept the words because they are brilliant or profound or wondrously beautiful—because this is blasphemy, this is wanting to criticize God." As soon, namely, as the dominance of authority, of the specifically paradoxical authority, is established, then all relations are qualitatively changed, then the kind of appropriation that is otherwise permissible and desirable is an offense and presumptuousness.

But how, then, can the apostle demonstrate that he has authority? If he could demonstrate it *physically,* he would simply be no apostle. He has no other evidence than his own statement. This is just the way it must be, since otherwise the believer would enter into a direct relation to him, not into a paradoxical relation. In the transitory relations of authority between persons *qua* human beings, authority will as a rule be physically recognizable by power. An apostle has no other evidence than his own statement, and at most his willingness to suffer everything joyfully for the sake of that statement. His speech in this regard will be brief: "I am called by God; do with me now what you will; flog me, persecute me, but my last words will be my first: I am called by God, and I make you eternally responsible for what you do to me." If in actuality it were so, let us imagine it, that an apostle had power in the worldly sense, had great influence and powerful connections, by which forces one is victorious over people's opinions and judgments—if he then used the power, he *eo ipso* [precisely thereby] would have forfeited his cause. That is, by using the power, he would define his endeavor in essential identity with the endeavor of other people, and yet an apostle is what he is only by his paradoxical heterogeneity, by having divine authority, which he is able to have absolutely unchanged, even if he, as Paul says, is regarded by people as being of no more worth than the dirt on which they walk.[192]

3. *The genius has only an immanent teleology; the apostle is absolutely teleologically positioned paradoxically.*

If any human being can be said to be positioned absolutely teleologically, it is an apostle. The doctrine communicated to him is not a task given to him to cogitate about; it is not given to him for his own sake. On the contrary, he is on a mission and has to proclaim the doctrine and to use authority. Just as little as a person sent into the city with a letter has anything to do with the contents of the letter but only with delivering it, and just as little as the envoy sent to a foreign court has any responsibility for the contents of the message but only for conveying it properly, so an apostle primarily has only to be faithful in his duty, which is to carry out his mission. Even if an apostle is never persecuted, his sacrificial life consists essentially in this: "that he, himself poor, only makes others rich,"[193] that he never dares to take the time or the quiet or the freedom from care in pleasant days, in *otium* [leisure], to be enriched by that with which, through its proclamation, he enriches others. Spiritually understood, he is like the busy housewife who herself, in order to prepare food for the many mouths, scarcely has time to eat. And if he, when he began, dared to hope for a long life, his life will still remain unchanged until the end, because there will always be ever new ones to whom to proclaim the doctrine.

Although a revelation is the paradoxical fact that passes human understanding,[194] one can still understand this much, which also has manifested itself everywhere: that a person is called by a revelation to go out in the world, to proclaim the Word, to act and to suffer, is called to the unceasingly active life as the Lord's messenger. On the other hand, that a person would be called by a revelation to remain in undivided possession of the estate, in busy literary *far niente* [idleness], to be momentarily brilliant and subsequently a collector and publisher of the dubieties of his brilliance—this is almost a blasphemous thought.

It is different with a genius. He has only an immanent teleology, he develops himself, and as he develops himself he plans this, his self-development, as his activity. He surely acquires significance, perhaps even great significance, but he is not himself teleologically positioned in relation to the world and to others. A genius lives within himself, and he can humorously live in secluded self-satisfaction without therefore nullifying his talent if only, without regard for whether others benefit from it or not, he develops himself earnestly and diligently, following his own genius. The genius is by no means therefore inactive; within himself he perhaps works even more than ten businessmen; he perhaps accomplishes a great deal, but each of his accomplishments has no τέλος [end, goal] outside. This is simultaneously the humanity of the genius and his pride: the humanity consists in his not defining himself teleologically in relation to any other person, as if there were anyone who stood in need of him; the pride consists in his relating himself immanently to himself. It is modest of the nightingale not to demand that anyone must listen to it, but it is also proud of the nightingale that it does not care at all to know whether anyone listens to it or not.

The dialectic of the genius will be especially offensive in our day, when the crowd, the masses, the public, and other such abstractions seek to turn everything upside down. The honored public, the power-craving crowd, wants the genius to express that he exists for its or for their sake; the honored public, the power-craving crowd, sees only one side of the dialectic of the genius, is offended by the pride, and does not perceive that this is also humility and modesty. Therefore the honored public, the power-craving crowd, want also to nullify an apostle's existence. It surely is true that he exists entirely for the sake of others, is sent out for the sake of others; but it is not the crowd and not humanity, not the honored public, not even the honored cultured public, that is his master or his masters—it is God—and the apostle is the one who has *divine authority* to *command* both the crowd and the public.

The humorous self-satisfaction of the genius is the unity of modest resignation in the world and proud elevation above the world, is the unity of being a useless superfluity and a costly ornament. If the genius is an artist, he produces his work of art, but neither he nor his work of art has any τέλος outside. Or he is an author who destroys every teleological relation to the surrounding world and defines himself humorously as a lyric poet. The lyrical quite rightly has no τέλος outside itself. Whether someone writes one page of lyrical poetry or folios of lyrical poetry makes no difference with regard to defining the direction of his work. The lyrical author cares only about the production, enjoys the joy of the production, perhaps often through pain and effort, but he has nothing to do with others. He does not write *in order to*, in order to enlighten people, in order to help them onto the right road, in order to accomplish something—in short, he does not write: *in order to.* And so it is with every genius. No genius has an "in order to"; the apostle *absolutely paradoxically* has an "in order to."

XI
109

THE SICKNESS UNTO DEATH,
A CHRISTIAN PSYCHOLOGICAL EXPOSITION
FOR UPBUILDING AND AWAKENING
(JULY 30, 1849)
BY ANTI-CLIMACUS
EDITED BY S. KIERKEGAARD

The pseudonymous works from *Either/Or* through *Postscript* were an esthetic series parallel to the signed series from *Two Upbuilding Discourses* through *Three Discourses on Imagined Occasions*. The pseudonymous works in the so-called "second authorship" include *The Sickness unto Death* and *Practice in Christianity* under a new pseudonym. The name of the pseudonymous author, Anti-Climacus, immediately prompts comparison with a pseudonymous author in the first series, Johannes Climacus (*Fragments, Johannes Climacus,* and *Postscript*). The relation, however, is not one of opposition but of level or rank, of being before or above. "Johannes Climacus and Anti-Climacus have several things in common; but the difference is that whereas Johannes Climacus places himself so low that he even says that he himself is not a Christian, one seems to be able to detect in Anti-Climacus that he considers himself to be a Christian on an extraordinarily high level. . . . I would place myself higher than Johannes Climacus, lower than Anti-Climacus."[195]

The substance of the work and that of *The Concept of Anxiety* are related as two levels in his "anthropological contemplation" based on the conception of man as a synthesis of the finite and the infinite, the temporal and the eternal, freedom and necessity. Anxiety is the "dizziness of freedom, which emerges when the spirit wants to posit the synthesis and freedom looks down into its own possibility, laying hold of finiteness to support itself."[196] Despair presupposes anxiety and goes further: "In all despair there is an interplay of finitude and infinitude, of the divine and the human, of freedom and necessity."[197] The actuality of despair is great misery, but the possibility of despair is a mark of human destiny as spirit, of human elevation above the animal. *The Sickness unto Death* treats more extensively and trenchantly Judge William's analysis of the esthete's despair (*Either/Or*) and its relation to doubt (*Johannes Climacus*). "Doubt is thought's despair; despair is personality's doubt."[198] The work is an epitomization of Kierkegaard's philosophical anthropology, his view of human nature and of the implications of the universality of despair in human experience. Here Kierkegaard, despite his often being called the "father of existentialism," does not belong among the existentialists who hold, according to Jean Paul Sartre, that there is no human nature, no essence, because there is no being who could bestow this nature.

DESPAIR IS THE SICKNESS
UNTO DEATH

A.

*Despair is a Sickness of the Spirit, of the Self, and Accordingly
Can Take Three Forms: In Despair Not to Be Conscious of Having a Self
(Not Despair in the Strict Sense); in Despair Not to Will to Be Oneself;
in Despair to Will to Be Oneself*

A human being is spirit. But what is spirit? Spirit is the self.[199] But what is
the self? The self is a relation that relates itself to itself or is the relation's relating itself to itself in the relation; the self is not the relation but is the relation's relating itself to itself. A human being is a synthesis of the infinite
and the finite, of the temporal and the eternal, of freedom and necessity, in
short, a synthesis. A synthesis is a relation between two. Considered in this
way, a human being is still not a self.

In the relation between two, the relation is the third as a negative unity,
and the two relate to the relation and in the relation to the relation; thus
under the qualification of the psychical the relation between the psychical
and the physical is a relation. If, however, the relation relates itself to itself,
this relation is the positive third, and this is the self.

Such a relation that relates itself to itself, a self, must either have established itself or have been established by another.

If the relation that relates itself to itself has been established by another,
then the relation is indeed the third, but this relation, the third, is yet again
a relation and relates itself to that which established the entire relation.

The human self is such a derived, established relation, a relation that relates itself to itself and in relating itself to itself relates itself to another. This
is why there can be two forms of despair in the strict sense. If a human self
had itself established itself, then there could be only one form: not to will to
be oneself, to will to do away with oneself, but there could not be the form:
in despair to will to be oneself. This second formulation is specifically the
expression for the complete dependence of the relation (of the self), the expression for the inability of the self to arrive at or to be in equilibrium and
rest by itself, but only, in relating itself to itself, by relating itself to that which
has established the entire relation. Yes, this second form of despair (in despair
to will to be oneself) is so far from designating merely a distinctive kind of
despair that, on the contrary, all despair ultimately can be traced back to and
be resolved in it. If the despairing person is aware of his despair, as he thinks
he is, and does not speak meaninglessly of it as of something that is happening to him (somewhat as one suffering from dizziness speaks in nervous delusion of a weight on his head or of something that has fallen down on him,
etc., a weight and a pressure that nevertheless are not something external but

a reverse reflection of the internal) and now with all his power seeks to break the despair by himself and by himself alone—he is still in despair and with all his presumed effort only works himself all the deeper into deeper despair. The misrelation of despair is not a simple misrelation but a misrelation in a relation that relates itself to itself and has been established by another, so that the misrelation in that relation which is for itself [*for sig*] also reflects itself infinitely in the relation to the power that established it.

The formula that describes the state of the self when despair is completely rooted out is this: in relating itself to itself and in willing to be itself, the self rests transparently in the power that established it.

B.
The Possibility and the Actuality of Despair

Is despair an excellence or a defect? Purely dialectically, it is both. If only the abstract idea of despair is considered, without any thought of someone in despair, it must be regarded as a surpassing excellence. The possibility of this sickness is man's superiority over the animal, and this superiority distinguishes him in quite another way than does his erect walk, for it indicates infinite erectness or sublimity, that he is spirit. The possibility of this sickness is man's superiority over the animal; to be aware of this sickness is the Christian's superiority over the natural man; to be cured of this sickness is the Christian's blessedness.

Consequently, to be able to despair is an infinite advantage, and yet to be in despair is not only the worst misfortune and misery—no, it is ruination. Generally this is not the case with the relation between possibility and actuality. If it is an excellence to be able to be this or that, then it is an even greater excellence to be that; in other words, to be is like an ascent when compared with being able to be. With respect to despair, however, to be is like a descent when compared with being able to be; the descent is as infinitely low as the excellence of possibility is high. Consequently, in relation to despair, not to be in despair is the ascending scale. But here again this category is equivocal. Not to be in despair is not the same as not being lame, blind, etc. If not being in despair signifies neither more nor less than not being in despair, then it means precisely to be in despair. Not to be in despair must signify the destroyed possibility of being able to be in despair; if a person is truly not to be in despair, he must at every moment destroy the possibility. This is generally not the case in the relation between actuality and possibility. Admittedly, thinkers say that actuality is annihilated possibility, but that is not entirely true; it is the consummated, the active possibility. Here, on the contrary, the actuality (not to be in despair) is the impotent, destroyed possibility, which is why it is also a negation; although actuality in relation to possibility is usually a corroboration, here it is a denial.

Despair is the misrelation in the relation of a synthesis that relates itself to itself. But the synthesis is not the misrelation; it is merely the possibility, or in the synthesis lies the possibility of the misrelation. If the synthesis were the misrelation, then despair would not exist at all, then despair would be something that lies in human nature as such. That is, it would not be despair; it would be something that happens to a man, something he suffers, like a disease to which he succumbs, or like death, which is everyone's fate. No, no, despairing lies in man himself. If he were not a synthesis, he could not despair at all; nor could he despair if the synthesis in its original state from the hand of God were not in the proper relationship.

Where, then, does the despair come from? From the relation in which the synthesis relates itself to itself, inasmuch as God, who constituted man a relation, releases it from his hand, as it were—that is, inasmuch as the relation relates itself to itself. And because the relation is spirit, is the self, upon it rests the responsibility for all despair at every moment of its existence, however much the despairing person speaks of his despair as a misfortune and however ingeniously he deceives himself and others, confusing it with that previously mentioned case of dizziness, with which despair, although qualitatively different, has much in common, since dizziness corresponds, in the category of the psychical, to what despair is in the category of the spirit, and it lends itself to numerous analogies to despair.

Once the misrelation, despair, has come about, does it continue as a matter of course? No, it does not continue as a matter of course; if the misrelation continues, it is not attributable to the misrelation but to the relation that relates itself to itself. That is, every time the misrelation manifests itself and every moment it exists, it must be traced back to the relation. For example, we say that someone catches a sickness, perhaps through carelessness. The sickness sets in and from then on is in force and is an *actuality* whose origin recedes more and more into the *past*. It would be both cruel and inhuman to go on saying, "You, the sick person, are in the process of catching the sickness right now." That would be the same as perpetually wanting to dissolve the actuality of the sickness into its possibility. It is true that he was responsible for catching the sickness, but he did that only once; the continuation of the sickness is a simple result of his catching it that one time, and its progress cannot be traced at every moment to him as the cause; he brought it upon himself, but it cannot be said that he *is bringing* it upon himself. To despair, however, is a different matter. Every actual moment of despair is traceable to possibility; every moment he is in despair he *is bringing* it upon himself. It is always the present tense; in relation to the actuality there is no pastness of the past; in every actual moment of despair the person in despair bears all the past as a present in possibility. The reason for this is that to despair is a qualification of spirit and relates to the eternal in man. But he cannot rid himself of the eternal—no, never in all eternity. He can-

XI
131

not throw it away once and for all, nothing is more impossible; at any moment that he does not have it, he must have thrown it or is throwing it away—but it comes again, that is, every moment he is in despair he is bringing his despair upon himself. For despair is not attributable to the misrelation but to the relation that relates itself to itself. A person cannot rid himself of the relation to himself any more than he can rid himself of his self, which, after all, is one and the same thing, since the self is the relation to oneself.

C.

Despair Is "the Sickness unto Death"

This concept, the sickness unto death, must, however, be understood in a particular way. Literally it means a sickness of which the end and the result are death. Therefore we use the expression "fatal sickness" as synonymous with the sickness unto death. In that sense, despair cannot be called the sickness unto death. Christianly understood, death itself is a passing into life. Thus, from a Christian point of view, no earthly, physical sickness is the sickness unto death, for death is indeed the end of the sickness, but death is not the end. If there is to be any question of a sickness unto death in the strictest sense, it must be a sickness of which the end is death and death is the end. This is precisely what despair is.

But in another sense despair is even more definitely the sickness unto death. Literally speaking, there is not the slightest possibility that anyone will die from this sickness or that it will end in physical death. On the contrary, the torment of despair is precisely this inability to die. Thus it has more in common with the situation of a mortally ill person when he lies struggling with death and yet cannot die. Thus to be sick *unto* death is to be unable to die, yet not as if there were hope of life; no, the hopelessness is that there is not even the ultimate hope, death. When death is the greatest danger, we hope for life; but when we learn to know the even greater danger, we hope for death. When the danger is so great that death becomes the hope, then despair is the hopelessness of not even being able to die.

It is in this last sense that despair is the sickness unto death, this tormenting contradiction, this sickness of the self, perpetually to be dying, to die and yet not die, to die death. For to die signifies that it is all over, but to die death means to experience dying, and if this is experienced for one single moment, one thereby experiences it forever. If a person were to die of despair as one dies of a sickness, then the eternal in him, the self, must be able to die in the same sense as the body dies of sickness. But this is impossible; the dying of despair continually converts itself into a living. The person in despair cannot die; "no more than the dagger can slaughter thoughts" can despair consume the eternal, the self at the root of despair, whose worm does not die and whose fire is not quenched.[200] Nevertheless, despair is veritably a self-consuming, but an impotent self-consuming that cannot do what it wants to do. What it wants to do is to consume itself, something it cannot do, and this impotence is a new form of self-consuming, in which despair is once again unable to do what it wants to do, to consume itself; this is an intensification, or the law of intensification. This is the provocativeness of the cold fire in despair, this gnawing that burrows deeper and deeper in impotent self-consuming. The inability of despair to consume him is so remote from being any kind of comfort to the person in despair that it is the very opposite. This comfort is precisely the torment, is precisely what keeps the gnawing alive and keeps life in the gnawing, for it is precisely over this that he despairs (not as having despaired): that he cannot consume himself, cannot get rid of himself, cannot reduce himself to nothing. This is the formula for despair raised to a higher power, the rising fever in this sickness of the self.

An individual in despair despairs over *something*. So it seems for a moment, but only for a moment; in the same moment the true despair or despair in its true form shows itself. In despairing over *something*, he really despaired over *himself*, and now he wants to be rid of himself. For example, when the ambitious man whose slogan is "Either Caesar or nothing"[201] does not get to be Caesar, he despairs over it. But this also means something else: precisely because he did not get to be Caesar, he now cannot bear to be himself. Consequently he does not despair because he did not get to be Caesar but despairs over himself because he did not get to be Caesar. This self, which, if it had become Caesar, would have been in seventh heaven (a state, incidentally, that in another sense is just as despairing), this self is now utterly intolerable to him. In a deeper sense, it is not his failure to become Caesar that is intolerable, but it is this self that did not become Caesar that is intolerable; or, to put it even more accurately, what is intolerable to him is that he cannot get rid of himself. If he had become Caesar, he would despairingly get rid of himself, but he did not become Caesar and cannot despairingly get rid of himself. Essentially, he is just as despairing, for he does not have his self, is not himself. He would not have become himself by becoming Caesar but would have been rid of himself, and by not becoming Caesar he despairs over not being able to get rid of himself. Thus it is superficial for someone (who probably has never seen anyone in despair, not even himself) to say of a person in despair: He is consuming himself. But this is precisely what he in his despair [wants] and this is precisely what he to his torment cannot do, since the despair has inflamed something that cannot burn or be burned up in the self.

Consequently, to despair over something is still not despair proper. It is the beginning, or, as the physician says of an illness, it has not yet declared itself. The next is declared despair, to despair over oneself. A young girl despairs of

XI
133

love, that is, she despairs over the loss of her beloved, over his death or his unfaithfulness to her. This is not declared despair; no, she despairs over herself. This self of hers, which she would have been rid of or would have lost in the most blissful manner had it become "his" beloved, this self becomes a torment to her if it has to be a self without "him." This self, which would have become her treasure (although, in another sense, it would have been just as despairing), has now become to her an abominable void since "he" died, or it has become to her a nauseating reminder that she has been deceived. Just try it, say to such a girl, "You are consuming yourself," and you will hear her answer, "Oh, but the torment is simply that I cannot do that."

To despair over oneself, in despair to will to be rid of oneself—this is the formula for all despair. Therefore the other form of despair, in despair to will to be oneself, can be traced back to the first, in despair not to will to be oneself, just as we previously resolved the form, in despair not to will to be oneself, into the form, in despair to will to be oneself (see A). A person in despair despairingly wills to be himself. But if he despairingly wills to be himself, he certainly does not want to be rid of himself. Well, so it seems, but upon closer examination it is clear that the contradiction is the same. The self that he despairingly wants to be is a self that he is not (for to will to be the self that he is in truth is the very opposite of despair), that is, he wants to tear his self away from the power that established it. In spite of all his despair, however, he cannot manage to do it; in spite of all his despairing efforts, that power is the stronger and forces him to be the self he does not want to be. But this is his way of willing to get rid of himself, to rid himself of the self that he is in order to be the self that he has dreamed up. He would be in seventh heaven to be the self he wants to be (although in another sense he would be just as despairing), but to be forced to be the self he does not want to be, that is his torment—that he cannot get rid of himself.

Socrates demonstrated the immortality of the soul from the fact that sickness of the soul (sin) does not consume it as sickness of the body consumes the body.[202] Thus, the eternal in a person can be demonstrated by the fact that despair cannot consume his self, that precisely this is the torment of contradiction in despair. If there were nothing eternal in a man, he could not despair at all; if despair could consume his self, then there would be no despair at all.

Such is the nature of despair, this sickness of the self, this sickness unto death. The despairing person is mortally ill. In a completely different sense than is the case with any illness, this sickness has attacked the most vital organs, and yet he cannot die. Death is not the end of the sickness, but death is incessantly the end. To be saved from this sickness by death is an impossibility, because the sickness and its torment—and the death—are precisely this inability to die.

This is the state in despair. No matter how much the despairing person avoids it, no matter how successfully he has completely lost himself (especially the case in the form of despair that is ignorance of being in despair) and lost himself in such a manner that the loss is not at all detectable—eternity nevertheless will make it manifest that his condition was despair and will nail him to himself so that his torment will still be that he cannot rid himself of his self, and it will become obvious that he was just imagining that he had succeeded in doing so. Eternity is obliged to do this, because to have a self, to be a self, is the greatest concession, an infinite concession, given to man, but it is also eternity's claim upon him.

THE UNIVERSALITY OF THIS
SICKNESS (DESPAIR)

XI
136

Just as a physician might say that there very likely is not one single living human being who is completely healthy, so anyone who really knows mankind might say that there is not one single living human being who does not despair a little, who does not secretly harbor an unrest, an inner strife, a disharmony, an anxiety about an unknown something or a something he does not even dare to try to know, an anxiety about some possibility in existence or an anxiety about himself, so that, just as the physician speaks of going around with an illness in the body, he walks around with a sickness, carries around a sickness of the spirit that signals its presence at rare intervals in and through an anxiety he cannot explain. In any case, no human being ever lived and no one lives outside of Christendom who has not despaired, and no one in Christendom if he is not a true Christian, and insofar as he is not wholly that, he still is to some extent in despair.

No doubt this observation will strike many people as a paradox, an overstatement, and also a somber and depressing point of view. But it is none of these things. It is not somber, for, on the contrary, it tries to shed light on what generally is left somewhat obscure; it is not depressing but instead is elevating, inasmuch as it views every human being under the destiny of the highest claim upon him, to be spirit; nor is it a paradox but, on the contrary, a consistently developed basic view, and therefore neither is it an overstatement.

However, the customary view of despair does not go beyond appearances, and thus it is a superficial view, that is, no view at all. It assumes that everyone must himself know best whether he is in despair or not. Anyone who says he is in despair is regarded as being in despair, and anyone who thinks he is not is therefore regarded as not. As a result, the phenomenon of despair is infrequent rather than quite common. That one is in despair is not a rarity; no, it is rare, very rare, that one is in truth not in despair.

XI
137

The common view has a very poor understanding of despair. Among other things, it completely overlooks (to name only this, which, properly understood, places thousands and thousands and millions in the category of despair), it completely overlooks that not being in despair, not being conscious of being in despair, is precisely a form of despair. In a much deeper sense, the position of the common view in interpreting despair is like that of the common view in determining whether a person is sick—in a much deeper sense, for the common view understands far less well what spirit is (and lacking this understanding, one cannot understand despair, either) than it understands sickness and health. As a rule, a person is considered to be healthy when he himself does not say that he is sick, not to mention when he himself says that he is well. But the physician has a different view of sickness. Why? Because the physician has a defined and developed conception of what it is to be healthy and ascertains a man's condition accordingly. The physician knows that just as there is merely imaginary sickness there is also merely imaginary health, and in the latter case he first takes measures to disclose the sickness. Generally speaking, the physician, precisely because he is a physician (well informed), does not have complete confidence in what a person says about his condition. If everyone's statement about his condition, that he is healthy or sick, were completely reliable, to be a physician would be a delusion. A physician's task is not only to prescribe remedies but also, first and foremost, to identify the sickness, and consequently his first task is to ascertain whether the supposedly sick person is actually sick or whether the supposedly healthy person is perhaps actually sick. Such is also the relation of the physician of the soul to despair. He knows what despair is; he recognizes it and therefore is satisfied neither with a person's declaration that he is not in despair nor with his declaration that he is. It must be pointed out that in a certain sense it is not even always the case that those who say they despair are in despair. Despair can be affected, and as a qualification of the spirit it may also be mistaken for and confused with all sorts of transitory states, such as dejection, inner conflict, which pass without developing into despair. But the physician of the soul properly regards these also as forms of despair; he sees very well that they are affectation. Yet this very affectation is despair: he sees very well that this dejection etc. are not of great significance, but precisely this—that it has and acquires no great significance—is despair.

XI
138

The common view also overlooks that despair is dialectically different from what is usually termed a sickness, because it is a sickness of the spirit. Properly understood, this dialectic again brings thousands under the definition of despair. If at a given time a physician has made sure that someone is well, and that person later becomes ill, then the physician may legitimately say that this person at one time was healthy but now is sick. Not so with despair. As soon as despair becomes apparent, it is manifest that the individual was in despair. Hence, at no moment is it possible to decide anything about a person who has not been saved by having been in despair, for whenever that which triggers his despair occurs, it is immediately apparent that he has been in despair his whole life. On the other hand, when someone gets a fever, it can by no means be said that it is now apparent that he has had a fever all his life. Despair is a qualification of the spirit, is related to the eternal, and thus has something of the eternal in its dialectic.

Despair is not only dialectically different from a sickness, but all its symptoms are also dialectical, and therefore the superficial view is very easily deceived in determining whether or not despair is present. Not to be in despair can in fact signify precisely to be in despair, and it can signify having been rescued from being in despair. A sense of security and tranquillity can signify being in despair; precisely this sense of security and tranquillity can be the despair, and yet it can signify having conquered despair and having won peace. Not being in despair is not similar to not being sick, for not being sick cannot be the same as being sick, whereas not being in despair can be the very same as being in despair. It is not with despair as with a sickness, where feeling indisposed is the sickness. By no means. Here again the indisposition is dialectical. Never to have sensed this indisposition is precisely to be in despair.

XI
139

This means and has its basis in the fact that the condition of man, regarded as spirit (and if there is to be any question of despair, man must be regarded as defined by spirit), is always critical. We speak of a crisis in relation to sickness but not in relation to health. Why not? Because physical health is an immediate qualification that first becomes dialectical in the condition of sickness, in which the question of a crisis arises. Spiritually, or when man is regarded as spirit, both health and sickness are critical; there is no immediate health of the spirit.

As soon as man ceases to be regarded as defined by spirit (and in that case there can be no mention of despair, either) but only as psychical-physical synthesis, health is an immediate qualification, and mental or physical sickness is the only dialectical qualification. But to be unaware of being defined as spirit is precisely what despair is. Even that which, humanly speaking, is utterly beautiful and lovable—a womanly youthfulness that is perfect peace and harmony and joy—is nevertheless despair. To be sure, it is happiness, but happiness is not a qualification of spirit, and deep, deep within the most secret hiding place of happiness there dwells also anxiety, which is despair; it very much wishes to be allowed to remain there, because for despair the most cherished and desirable place to live is in the heart of happiness. Despite its illusory security and tranquillity, all immediacy is anxiety and thus, quite consistently, is most anxious about nothing. The most gruesome description of something most terrible does not make immediacy as anxious as a subtle, almost carelessly, and yet deliberately and calculatingly dropped allusion to some indefinite something—in fact, immediacy is made most anxious by a subtle implication that it knows very well what is being talked about. Immediacy probably does not know it, but reflection never snares so unfailingly as when it fashions its snare out of nothing, and reflection is never so much itself as when it is—nothing. It requires extraordinary reflection, or, more correctly, it requires great faith to be able to endure reflection upon nothing—that is, infinite reflection. Consequently, even that which is utterly beautiful and lovable, womanly youthfulness, is still despair, is happiness. For that reason, it is impossible to slip through life on this immediacy. And if this happiness does succeed in slipping through, well, it is of little use, for it is despair. Precisely because the sickness of despair is totally dialectical, it is the worst misfortune never to have had that sickness: it is a true godsend to get it, even if it is the most dangerous of illnesses, if one does not want to be cured of it. Generally it is regarded as fortunate to be cured of a sickness; the sickness itself is the misfortune.

XI
140

Therefore, the common view that despair is a rarity is entirely wrong; on the contrary, it is universal. The common view, which assumes that everyone who does not think or feel he is in despair is not or that only he who says he is in despair is, is totally false. On the contrary, the person who without affectation says that he is in despair is still a little closer, is dialectically closer, to being cured than all those who are not regarded as such and who do not regard themselves as being in despair. The physician of souls will certainly agree with me that, on the whole, most men live without ever becoming conscious of being destined as spirit—hence all the so-called security, contentment with life, etc., which is simply despair. On the other hand, those who say they are in despair are usually either those who have so deep a nature that they are bound to become conscious as spirit or those whom bitter experiences and dreadful decisions have assisted in becoming conscious as spirit: it is either the one or the other; the person who is really devoid of despair is very rare indeed.

There is so much talk about human distress and wretchedness—I try to understand it and have also had some intimate acquaintance with it—there is so much talk about wasting a life, but only that person's life was wasted who went on living so deceived by life's joys or its sorrows that he never became decisively and eternally conscious as spirit, as self, or, what amounts to the same thing, never became aware and in the deepest sense never gained the impression that there is a God and that "he," he himself, his self, exists before this God—an infinite benefaction that is never gained except through despair. What wretchedness that so many go on living this way, cheated of this most blessed of thoughts! What wretchedness that we are engrossed in or encourage the human throng to be engrossed in everything else, using them to supply the energy for the drama of life but never reminding them of this blessedness. What wretchedness that they are lumped together and deceived instead of being split apart so that each individual may gain the high-

est, the only thing worth living for and enough to live in for an eternity. I XI
141
think that I could weep an eternity over the existence of such wretchedness!
And to me an even more horrible expression of this most terrible sickness
and misery is that it is hidden—not only that the person suffering from it
may wish to hide it and may succeed, not only that it can so live in a man
that no one, no one detects it, no, but also that it can be so hidden in a man
that he himself is not aware of it! And when the hourglass has run out, the
hourglass of temporality, when the noise of secular life has grown silent and
its restless or ineffectual activism has come to an end, when everything
around you is still, as it is in eternity, then—whether you were man or
woman, rich or poor, dependent or independent, fortunate or unfortunate,
whether you ranked with royalty and wore a glittering crown or in humble
obscurity bore the toil and heat of the day, whether your name will be remembered as long as the world stands and consequently as long as it stood
or you are nameless and run nameless in the innumerable multitude, whether
the magnificence encompassing you surpassed all human description or the
most severe and ignominious human judgment befell you—eternity asks you
and every individual in these millions and millions about only one thing:
whether you have lived in despair or not, whether you have despaired in such
a way that you did not realize that you were in despair, or in such a way that
you covertly carried this sickness inside of you as your gnawing secret, as a
fruit of sinful love under your heart, or in such a way that you, a terror to
others, raged in despair. And if so, if you have lived in despair, then, regardless of whatever else you won or lost, everything is lost for you, eternity does
not acknowledge you, it never knew you—or, still more terrible, it knows
you as you are known and it binds you to yourself in despair.

DESPAIR IS SIN

XI
189

Sin is: *before God, or with the conception of God, in despair not to will to be oneself,
or in despair to will to be oneself.* Thus sin is intensified weakness or intensified
defiance: sin is the intensification of despair. The emphasis is on *before God,*
or with a conception of God; it is the conception of God that makes sin dialectically, ethically, and religiously what lawyers call "aggravated" despair.

Although there is no room or place for a psychological delineation in this
part, least of all in section A, reference may be made at this point to the most
dialectical frontier between despair and sin, to what could be called a poet-
existence[203] verging on the religious, an existence that has something in
common with the despair of resignation, except that the concept of God is
present. Such a poet-existence, as is discernible in the position and conjunction of the categories, will be the most eminent poet-existence. Christianly
understood, every poet-existence (esthetics notwithstanding) is sin, the sin

of poetizing instead of being, of relating to the good and the true through the imagination instead of being that—that is, existentially striving to be that. The poet-existence under consideration here is different from despair in that it does have a conception of God or is before God, but it is exceedingly dialectical and is as if in an impenetrable dialectical labyrinth concerning the extent to which it is obscurely conscious of being sin. A poet like that can have a very profound religious longing, and the conception of God is taken up into his despair. He loves God above all, God who is his only consolation in his secret anguish, and yet he loves the anguish and will not give it up. He would like so very much to be himself before God, but with the exclusion of the fixed point where the self suffers; there in despair he does not will to be himself. He hopes that eternity will take it away, and here in time, no matter how much he suffers under it, he cannot resolve to take it upon himself, cannot humble himself under it in faith. And yet he continues in the God-relationship, and this is his only salvation; it would be sheer horror for him to have to be without God, "it would be enough to despair over," and yet he actually allows himself—perhaps unconsciously—to poetize God as somewhat different from what God is, a bit more like the fond father who indulges his child's every wish far too much. He becomes a poet of the religious in the same way as one who became a poet through an unhappy love affair and blissfully celebrates the happiness of erotic love. He became unhappy in the religious life, dimly understands that he is required to give up this anguish—that is, in faith to humble himself under it and take it upon himself as a part of the self—for he wants to keep it apart from himself, and precisely in this way he holds on to it, although he no doubt believes this is supposed to result in parting from it as far as possible, giving it up to the greatest extent humanly possible (this, like every word from a person in despair, is inversely correct and consequently to be understood inversely). But in faith to take it upon himself—that he cannot do, that is, in essence he is unwilling or here his self ends in vagueness. Yet this poet's description of the religious—just like that other poet's description of erotic love—has a charm, a lyrical verve that no married man's and no His Reverence's presentations have. Nor is what he says untrue, by no means; his presentation is simply his happier, his better *I*. His relation to the religious is that of an unhappy lover, not in the strictest sense that of a believer; he has only the first element of faith—despair—and within it an intense longing for the religious. His conflict actually is this: Has he been called? Does his thorn in the flesh signify that he is to be used for the extraordinary? Before God, is it entirely in order to be the extraordinary he has become? Or is the thorn in the flesh that under which he must humble himself in order to attain the universally human?—But enough of this. With the accent of truth I may ask: To whom am I speaking? Who cares about these high-powered psychological investigations to the nth degree? The Nürnberg pictures that the pastor paints are better understood; they deceivingly resemble one and all, what most people are, and spiritually understood—nothing.

The Gradations in the Consciousness of the Self
(The Qualification: "Before God")

The preceding section concentrated on pointing out a gradation in the consciousness of the self; first came ignorance of having an eternal self, then a knowledge of having a self in which there is something eternal, and under this, in turn, gradations were pointed out. This whole deliberation must now dialectically take a new direction. The point is that the previously considered gradation in the consciousness of the self is within the category of the human self, or the self whose criterion is man. But this self takes on a new quality and qualification by being a self directly before God. This self is no longer the merely human self but is what I, hoping not to be misinterpreted, would call the theological self, the self directly before God. And what infinite reality [*Realitet*] the self gains by being conscious of existing before God, by becoming a human self whose criterion is God! A cattleman who (if this were possible) is a self directly before his cattle is a very low self, and, similarly, a master who is a self directly before his slaves is actually no self—for in both cases a criterion is lacking. The child who previously has had only his parents as a criterion becomes a self as an adult by getting the state as a criterion, but what an infinite accent falls on the self by having God as the criterion! The criterion for the self is always: that directly before which it is a self, but this in turn is the definition of "criterion." Just as only entities of the same kind can be added, so everything is qualitatively that by which it is measured, and that which is its qualitative criterion [*Maalestok*] is ethically its goal [*Maal*]; the criterion and goal are what define something, what it is, with the exception of the condition in the world of freedom, where by not qualitatively being that which is his goal and his criterion a person must himself have merited this disqualification. Thus the goal and the criterion still remain discriminatingly the same, making it clear just what a person is not— namely, that which is his goal and criterion.

It was a very sound idea, one that came up so frequently in an older dogmatics, whereas a later dogmatics very frequently took exception to it because it did not have the understanding or the feeling for it—it was a very sound idea, even if at times it was misapplied: the idea that what makes sin so terrible is that it is before God. It was used to prove eternal punishment in hell. Later, as people became shrewder, they said: Sin is sin; sin is no greater because it is against God or before God. Strange! Even lawyers speak of aggravated crimes; even lawyers make a distinction between a crime committed against a public official, for example, or against a private citizen, make a distinction between the punishment for a patricide and that for an ordinary murder.

No, the older dogmatics was right in maintaining that because sin is against God it is infinitely magnified. The error consisted in considering God as some externality and in seeming to assume that only occasionally did one sin against God. But God is not some externality in the sense that a policeman is. The point that must be observed is that the self has a conception of God and yet does not will as he wills, and thus is disobedient. Nor does one only occasionally sin before God, for every sin is before God, or, more correctly, what really makes human guilt into sin is that the guilty one has the consciousness of existing before God.

Despair is intensified in relation to the consciousness of the self, but the self is intensified in relation to the criterion for the self, infinitely when God is the criterion. In fact, the greater the conception of God, the more self there is; the more self, the greater the conception of God. Not until a self as this specific single individual is conscious of existing before God, not until then is it the infinite self, and this self sins before God. Thus, despite everything that can be said about it, the selfishness of paganism was not nearly so aggravated as is that of Christendom, inasmuch as there is selfishness here also, for the pagan did not have his self directly before God. The pagan and the natural man have the merely human self as their criterion. Therefore, from a higher point of view, it may be correct to regard paganism as immersed in sin, but the sin of paganism was essentially despairing ignorance of God, of existing before God; paganism is "to be without God in the world."[204] Therefore, from another point of view, it is true that in the strictest sense the pagan did not sin, for he did not sin before God, and all sin is before God. Furthermore, in one sense it is also quite true that frequently a pagan is assisted in slipping blamelessly through the world simply because he is saved by his superficial Pelagian conception; but then his sin is something else, namely, his superficial Pelagian interpretation. On the other hand, it is certainly also the case that many a time, precisely by being strictly brought up in Christianity, a person has in a certain sense been plunged into sin because the whole Christian viewpoint was too earnest for him, especially in the early part of his life; but then again there is some help to him in this more profound conception of what sin is.

Sin is: before God in despair not to will to be oneself, or before God in despair to will to be oneself. Even though this definition may in other respects be conceded to have its merits (and of all of them, the most important is that it is the only Scriptural definition, for Scripture always defines sin as disobedience), is not this definition too spiritual? The first and foremost answer to that must be: A definition of sin can never be too spiritual (unless it becomes so spiritual that it abolishes sin), for sin is specifically a qualification of spirit. Furthermore, why is it assumed to be too spiritual? Because it does not mention murder, stealing, fornication, etc.? But does it not speak of these things? Are not they also self-willfulness against God, a disobedience that defies his commandments? On the other hand, if in considering sin we mention only such sins, we so easily forget that, humanly speaking, all such things may be quite in order up to a point, and yet one's whole life may be sin, the familiar kind of sin: the glittering vices, the self-willfulness that either in spiritlessness or with effrontery goes on being or wants to be ignorant of the human self's far, far deeper obligation in obedience to God with regard to its every clandestine desire and thought, with regard to its readiness to hear and understand and its willingness to follow every least hint from God as to his will for this self. The sins of the flesh are the self-willfulness of the lower self, but how often is not one devil driven out with the devil's help and the last condition becomes worse than the first.[205] For this is how things go in the world: first a man sins out of frailty and weakness, and then—well, then he may learn to flee to God and be helped to faith, which saves from all sin, but this will not be discussed here—then he despairs over his weakness and becomes either a pharisee who in despair manages a sort of legal righteousness, or in despair he plunges into sin again.

XI
194

Therefore, the definition embraces every imaginable and every actual form of sin; indeed, it rightly stresses the crucial point that sin is despair (for sin is not the turbulence of flesh and blood but is the spirit's consent to it) and is: before God. As a definition it is algebra; for me to begin to describe particular sins in this little book would be out of place, and, furthermore, the attempt might fail. The main point here is simply that the definition, like a net, embraces all forms. And this it does, as can be seen if it is tested by posing its opposite: faith, by which I steer in this whole book as by a trustworthy navigation guide. Faith is: that the self in being itself and in willing to be itself rests transparently in God.

Very often, however, it is overlooked that the opposite of sin is by no means virtue. In part, this is a pagan view, which is satisfied with a merely human criterion and simply does not know what sin is, that all sin is before God. No, *the opposite of sin is faith,* as it says in Romans 14:23: "whatever does not proceed from faith is sin." And this is one of the most decisive definitions for all Christianity—that the opposite of sin is not virtue but faith.

The Socratic Definition of Sin

XI
199

Sin is ignorance.[206] This, as is well known, is the Socratic definition, which, like everything Socratic, is an authority meriting attention. But with regard to this point, as with so much that is Socratic, people came to feel an urge to go further. What countless numbers have felt the urge to go further than Socratic ignorance—presumably because they felt it was impossible for them to stop with that—for how many are there in any generation who could persevere, even for just one month, in existentially expressing ignorance about everything.

By no means, therefore, shall I dismiss the Socratic definition on the grounds that one cannot stop there, but with Christianity *in mente* [in mind], I shall use this Socratic definition to bring out the latter in its radicality— simply because the Socratic definition is so genuinely Greek. And here, as always with any other definition that in the most rigorous sense is not rigorously Christian—that is, every intermediate definition—its emptiness becomes apparent.

The defect in the Socratic definition is its ambiguity as to how the ignorance itself is to be more definitely understood, its origin etc. In other words, even if sin is ignorance (or what Christianity perhaps would rather call stupidity), which in one sense certainly cannot be denied—is this an original ignorance, is it therefore the state of someone who has not known and up until now has not been capable of knowing anything about truth, or is it a resultant, a later ignorance? If it is the latter, then sin must essentially lodge somewhere else than in ignorance. It must lodge in a person's efforts to obscure his knowing. Given this assumption, however, that obstinate and very tenacious ambiguity comes up again: the question of whether a person was clearly aware of his action when he started to obscure his knowing. If he was not clearly aware of it, then his knowing was already somewhat obscured before he began doing it, and the question simply arises again and again. If, however, it is assumed that he was clearly aware of what he was doing when he began to obscure his knowing, then the sin (even if it is ignorance, insofar as this is the result) is not in the knowing but in the willing, and the inevitable question concerns the relation of knowing and willing to each other. With all such matters (and the questioning could go on for days), the Socratic definition really does not concern itself. Socrates was indeed an ethicist, the first (in fact, the founder of ethics, as antiquity unconditionally claims), just as he is and remains the first of his kind, but he begins with ignorance. Intellectually, he tends toward ignorance, toward knowing nothing. Ethically, he interprets ignorance as something quite different and begins with that. On the other hand, Socrates naturally is not an essentially religious ethicist, even less a Christian dogmatician. Therefore, he does not really enter into the whole investigation with which Christianity begins, into the *prius* [antecedent state] in which sin presupposes itself and which is explained in Christianity in the dogma of hereditary sin, the border of which this discussion will merely approach.

Therefore, Socrates does not actually arrive at the category of sin, which certainly is dubious for a definition of sin. How can this be? If sin is ignorance, then sin really does not exist, for sin is indeed consciousness. If sin is being ignorant of what is right and therefore doing wrong, then sin does not exist. If this is sin, then along with Socrates it is assumed that there is no such thing as a person's knowing what is right and doing wrong, or knowing that something is wrong and going ahead and doing wrong. Consequently, if the

Socratic definition is sound, then there is no sin at all. Note that, Christianly, this is quite in order, in a deeper sense altogether correct; in the interest of Christianity it is *quod erat demonstrandum* [that which was to be demonstrated]. It is specifically the concept of sin, the teaching about sin, that most decisively differentiates Christianity qualitatively from paganism, and this is also why Christianity very consistently assumes that neither paganism nor the natural man knows what sin is; in fact, it assumes that there has to be a revelation from God to show what sin is. The qualitative distinction between paganism and Christianity is not, as a superficial consideration assumes, the doctrine of the Atonement. No, the beginning must start far deeper, with sin, with the doctrine of sin—as Christianity in fact does. What a dangerous objection it would be against Christianity if paganism had a definition of sin that Christianity would have to acknowledge as correct.

XI
201

What constituent, then, does Socrates lack for the defining of sin? It is the will, defiance. The intellectuality of the Greeks was too happy, too naive, too esthetic, too ironic, too witty—too sinful—to grasp that anyone could knowingly not do the good, or knowingly, knowing what is right, do wrong. The Greek mind posits an intellectual categorical imperative.[207]

The truth of this should not be disregarded, and it is undoubtedly necessary to underscore it in a time like this, which is running wild in its profusion of empty, pompous, and fruitless knowledge, to the point where now, just as in Socrates' time, only even more, it is necessary for people to be Socratically starved a little. It is tragic-comic, all these declarations about having understood and grasped the highest, plus the virtuosity with which many *in abstracto* know how to expound it, in a certain sense quite correctly—it is tragic-comic to see that all this knowledge and understanding exercises no power over people's lives, that their lives do not express in the remotest way what they have understood, but rather the opposite. On seeing this tragic-comic discrepancy, one involuntarily exclaims: But how in the world is it possible that they could have understood it? Can it be true that they have understood it? At this point, that old ironist and ethicist replies: Don't ever believe it, my friend; they have not understood it, for if they had in truth understood it, their lives would have expressed it also, then they would have done what they had understood.

Does this mean, then, that to understand and to understand are two different things? They certainly are, and the person who has understood this—but, please note, not in the sense of the first kind of understanding—is *eo ipso* initiated into all the secrets of irony. To regard as comic someone who is actually ignorant of something is a very low form of the comic and is unworthy of irony. That people at one time thought the earth stands still—and they did not know any better—has nothing particularly comic about it. Our age will probably look the same to an age having more knowledge about the physical world. The contrast is between two different ages; a deeper point of

XI
202

coincidence is lacking, but such a contrast is not an essential one and thus is not essentially comic, either. No, but when a man stands and says the right thing, and consequently has understood it, and then when he acts he does the wrong thing, and thus shows that he has not understood it—yes, this is exceedingly comic. It is exceedingly comic that a man, stirred to tears so that not only sweat but also tears pour down his face, can sit and read or hear an exposition on self-denial, on the nobility of sacrificing his life for the truth— and then in the next moment, *ein, zwei, drei, vupti,* almost with tears still in his eyes, be in full swing, in the sweat of his brow and to the best of his modest ability, helping untruth to be victorious. It is exceedingly comic that a speaker with sincere voice and gestures, deeply stirred and deeply stirring, can movingly depict the truth, can face all the powers of evil and of hell boldly, with cool self-assurance in his bearing, a dauntlessness in his air, and an appropriateness of movement worthy of admiration—it is exceedingly comic that almost simultaneously, practically still "in his dressing gown," he can timidly and cravenly cut and run away from the slightest inconvenience. It is exceedingly comic that someone is able to understand the whole truth about how mean and sordid the world is etc.—that he can understand this and then the next moment not recognize what he has understood, for almost at once he himself goes out and participates in the very same meanness and sordidness, is honored for it, and accepts the honor, that is, acknowledges it. When I see someone who declares he has completely understood how Christ went around in the form of a lowly servant,[208] poor, despised, mocked, and, as Scripture tells us, spat upon[209]—when I see the same person assiduously make his way to the place where in worldly sagacity it is good to be, set himself up as securely as possible, when I see him then so anxiously, as if his life depended on it, avoiding every gust of unfavorable wind from the right or the left, see him so blissful, so extremely blissful, so slap-happy, yes, to make it complete, so slap-happy that he even thanks God for—for being whole-heartedly honored and esteemed by all by everyone— then I have often said privately to myself: "Socrates, Socrates, Socrates, can it be possible that this man has understood what he says he has understood?" This is how I talked—indeed, I have also wished that Socrates was right, for it seems to me as if Christianity were too rigorous, and in accordance with my own experience I cannot make such a person out to be a hypocrite. No, Socrates, you I can understand; you make him into a joker, a jolly fellow of sorts, and fair game for laughter; you have nothing against but rather even approve of my preparing and serving him up as something comic—provided I do it well.

Socrates, Socrates, Socrates! Yes, we may well call your name three times; it would not be too much to call it ten times, if it would be of any help. Popular opinion maintains that the world needs a republic, needs a new social order and a new religion—but no one considers that what the world, confused simply by too much knowledge, needs is a Socrates. Of course, if anyone thought of it, not to mention if many thought of it, he would be less needed. Invariably, what error needs most is always the last thing it thinks of—quite naturally, for otherwise it would not, after all, be error.

So it could very well be that our age needs an ironic-ethical correction such as this—this may actually be the only thing it needs—for obviously it is the last thing it thinks of. Instead of going beyond Socrates, it is extremely urgent that we come back to this Socratic principle—to understand and to understand are two things—not as a conclusion that ultimately aids people in their deepest misery, since that annuls precisely the difference between understanding and understanding, but as the ethical conception of everyday life.

The Socratic definition works out in the following way. When someone does not do what is right, then neither has he understood what is right. His understanding is purely imaginary; his declaration of having understood is false information; his repeated protestation that he will be hanged if he has not understood puts him far, far along on the most roundabout way. But then the definition is indeed correct. If someone does the right thing, then he certainly does not sin; and if he does not do what is right, then he did not understand it, either; if he had really and truly understood it, it would quickly have prompted him to do it, it would quickly have made him a Chladni figure for his understanding; ergo, sin is ignorance.

But wherein is the definition defective? Its defect is something the Socratic principle itself realizes and remedies, but only to a certain degree: it lacks a dialectical determinant appropriate to the transition from having understood something to doing it. In this transition Christianity begins; by taking this path, it shows that sin is rooted in willing and arrives at the concept of defiance, and then, to fasten the end very firmly, it adds the doctrine of hereditary sin—alas, for speculation's secret in comprehending is simply to sew without fastening the end and without knotting the thread, and this is why, wonder of wonders, it can go on sewing and sewing, that is, pulling the thread through. Christianity, on the other hand, fastens the end by means of the paradox.

In pure ideality, where the actual individual person is not involved, the transition is necessary (after all, in the system everything takes place of necessity), or there is no difficulty at all connected with the transition from understanding to doing. This is the Greek mind (but not the Socratic, for Socrates is too much of an ethicist for that). And the secret of modern philosophy is essentially the very same, for it is this: *cogito ergo sum* [I think therefore I am],[210] to think is to be (Christianly, however, it reads: according to your faith, be it unto you, or as you believe, so you are, to believe is to be.[211] Thus it is evident that modern philosophy is neither more nor less than paganism. But this is not the worst possible situation—to be in kinship with

Socrates is not too bad. But the totally un-Socratic aspect of modern philosophy is that it wants to delude us into believing that this is Christianity.

In the world of actuality, however, where the individual person is involved, there is this tiny little transition from having understood to doing; it is not always quick, *cito citissime* [very quick], it is not (if I, lacking philosophical language, may speak German) *geschwind wie der Wind* [fast as the wind]. Quite the opposite, this is the beginning of a very long-winded story.

XI
205

In the life of the spirit there is no standing still [*Stilstand*] (really no state [*Tilstand*], either; everything is actuation); therefore, if a person does not do what is right at the very second he knows it—then, first of all, knowing simmers down. Next comes the question of how willing appraises what is known. Willing is dialectical and has under it the entire lower nature of man. If willing does not agree with what is known, then it does not necessarily follow that willing goes ahead and does the opposite of what knowing understood (presumably such strong opposites are rare); rather, willing allows some time to elapse, an interim called: "We shall look at it tomorrow." During all this, knowing becomes more and more obscure, and the lower nature gains the upper hand more and more; alas, for the good must be done immediately, as soon as it is known (and that is why in pure ideality the transition from thinking to being is so easy, for there everything is at once), but the lower nature's power lies in stretching things out. Gradually, willing's objection to this development lessens; it almost appears to be in collusion. And when knowing has become duly obscured, knowing and willing can better understand each other; eventually they agree completely, for now knowing has come over to the side of willing and admits that what it wants is absolutely right. And this is how perhaps the majority of people live: they work gradually at eclipsing their ethical and ethical-religious comprehension, which would lead them out into decisions and conclusions that their lower nature does not much care for, but they expand their esthetic and metaphysical comprehension, which ethically is a diversion.

Nevertheless, with all this we have still gone no further than the Socratic principle, for Socrates would say: If this happens, it just shows that a person such as this still has not understood what is right. This means that the Greek mind does not have the courage to declare that a person knowingly does wrong, knows what is right and does the wrong; so it manages by saying: If a person does what is wrong, he has not understood what is right.

Absolutely right. And no *human being* can come further than that; no one of oneself and by oneself can declare what sin is, precisely because one is in sin; all his talk about sin is basically a glossing over of sin, an excuse, a sinful watering down. That is why Christianity begins in another way: one has to learn what sin is by a revelation from God; sin is not a matter of a person's not having understood what is right but of his being unwilling to understand it, of his not willing what is right.

Socrates actually gives no explanation at all of the distinction: not *being*   _{XI}
able to understand and not *willing* to understand; on the other hand, he is the   ₂₀₆
grand master of all ironists in operating by means of the distinction between
understanding and understanding. Socrates explains that he who does not do
what is right has not understood it, either; but Christianity goes a little further back and says that it is because he is unwilling to understand it, and this
again because he does not will what is right. And in the next place it teaches
that a person does what is wrong (essentially defiance) even though he understands what is right, or he refrains from doing what is right even though
he understands it; in short, the Christian teaching about sin is nothing but
offensiveness toward man, charge upon charge; it is the suit that the divine
as the prosecutor ventures to bring against humankind.

But can any human being comprehend this Christian teaching? By no
means, for it is indeed Christianity and therefore involves offense. It must be
believed. To comprehend is the range of man's relation to the human, but to
believe is man's relation to the divine. How then does Christianity explain
this incomprehensibility? Very consistently, in a way just as incomprehensible: by revealing it.

Therefore, interpreted Christianly, sin has its roots in willing, not in knowing, and this corruption of willing affects the individual's consciousness. This
is entirely consistent, for otherwise the question of the origin of sin would
have to be posed in regard to each individual.

Here again is the mark of offense. The possibility of offense lies in this:
there must be a revelation from God to each one what sin is and how deeply
it is rooted. The natural man, the pagan, thinks like this: "All right, I admit
that I have not understood everything in heaven and on earth. If there has
to be a revelation, then let it teach us about heavenly things; but it is most
unreasonable that there should be a revelation informing us what sin is. I do
not pretend to be perfect, far from it; nevertheless, I do know and I am will-   _{XI}
ing to admit how far from perfect I am. Should I, then, not know what sin   ₂₀₇
is?" But Christianity replies: No, that is what you know least of all, how far
from perfect you are and what sin is.—Note that in this sense, looked at from
the Christian point of view, sin is indeed ignorance: it is ignorance of what
sin is.

Therefore the definition of sin given in the previous section still needs to
be completed as follows: sin is—after being taught by a revelation from God
what sin is—before God in despair not to will to be oneself or in despair to
will to be oneself.

Therefore, despair of the forgiveness of sins is offense. And offense is the in-   _{XI}
tensification of sin. Usually people give this scarcely a thought, usually never   ₂₃₄
identify offense with sin, of which they do not speak; instead, they speak of
sins, among which offense does not find a place. Even less do they perceive

offense as the intensification of sin. That is because the opposites are not Christianly construed as sin/faith but as sin/virtue.

XI
241 This contrast [sin/faith], however, has been advanced throughout this entire book, which at the outset introduced in Part One, A, A, the formula for the state in which there is no despair at all: in relating itself to itself and in willing to be itself, the self rests transparently in the power that established it. This formula in turn, as has been frequently pointed out, is the definition of faith.

PRACTICE IN CHRISTIANITY
(SEPTEMBER 27, 1850)
BY ANTI-CLIMACUS
EDITED BY S. KIERKEGAARD

This, the second Anti-Climacus volume, and the first, *The Sickness unto Death,* were originally contemplated as parts of a volume titled "Thoughts That Cure Radically, Christian Healing." With Part One of *The Sickness unto Death* as a descriptive analysis of the various aspects and implications of despair and Part Two as a consideration of despair as sin and of the despairing self before God, *Practice* constitutes the third part of the sequence, emphasizing the healing of the sin-conscious self and the indicative ethics based on this redemptive gift and the responsive expression of gratitude in a unity of jest and earnestness. In engaged imitation rather than in admiration of the prototype, the follower, receptive of grace as he grows, under the ideal, in self-knowledge, is transformed at the point of motivation and sees his striving in imitation as only a jest. In relation to later works, *Practice,* together with *For Self-Examination* and the posthumously published *Judge for Yourself!,* was the beginning of an explicit critique of the established order of Christendom, although Kierkegaard saw it as a defense if an ecclesiastical and personal admission of the cultural accommodation of Christianity was forthcoming. As late as the final manuscript copy, the subtitle of *Practice* was "A Contribution to the Introduction of Christianity into Christendom."

EDITOR'S PREFACE

In this book, originating in the year 1848, the requirement for being a Christian is forced up by the pseudonymous author to a supreme ideality.

Yet the requirement should indeed be stated, presented, and heard. From the Christian point of view, there ought to be no scaling down of the requirement, nor suppression of it—instead of a personal admission and confession.

The requirement should be heard—and I understand what is said as spoken to me alone—so that I might learn not only to resort to *grace* but to resort to it in relation to the use of *grace.*

S. K.

A BRIEF SUMMARY OF THE CONTENTS
OF THIS EXPOSITION

Just as the concept "faith" is an altogether distinctively Christian term, so in turn is "offense" an altogether distinctively Christian term relating to faith. The possibility of offense is the crossroad, or it is like standing at the crossroad. From the possibility of offense, one turns either to offense or to faith, but one never comes to faith except from the possibility of offense.*

Essentially offense is related to the composite of God and man, or to the God-man. Speculation has naturally considered itself able to "comprehend" the God-man—as one can very well comprehend, for speculation takes away from the God-man the qualifications of temporality, contemporaneity, and actuality. On the whole it is tragic and dreadful that this has been fêted as profundity—and it is not using too strong an expression to say that this is nothing but performing tricks and making fools of people. No, the *situation* belongs with the God-man, the situation that an individual human being who is standing beside you is the God-man. The God-man is not the union of God and man—such terminology is a profound optical illusion. The God-man is the unity of God and an individual human being. That the human race is or is supposed to be in kinship with God is ancient paganism; but *that* an individual human being is God is Christianity, and this particular human being is the God-man. Humanly speaking, there is no possibility of a crazier composite than this either in heaven or on earth or in the abyss or in the most fantastic aberration of thought. So it appears in the situation of contemporaneity, and no relation to the God-man is possible without beginning with the situation of contemporaneity.**

Offense in the strictest sense, offense χατ᾽ ἐξοχήν [in an eminent sense], therefore relates to the God-man and has two forms. It is either in relation to the loftiness that one is offended, that an individual human being claims to be God, acts or speaks in a manner that manifests God (this is discussed under B), or the offense is in relation to the lowliness, that the one who is God is this lowly human being, suffering as a lowly human being (this is discussed under C). In the first form, the offense comes in such a way that I am

---

* In the works of some pseudonymous writers it has been pointed out that in modern philosophy there is a confused discussion of doubt where the discussion should have been about despair. Therefore one has been unable to control or govern doubt either in scholarship or in life. "Despair," however, promptly points in the right direction by placing the relation under the rubric of personality (the single individual) and the ethical. But just as there is a confused discussion of "doubt" instead of a discussion of "despair," so also the practice has been to use the category "doubt" where the discussion ought to be about "offense." The relation, the relation of personality to Christianity, is not to doubt or to believe, but to be offended or to believe. All modern philosophy, both ethically and Christianly, is based upon frivolousness. Instead of deterring and calling people to order by speaking of being despairing and being offended, it has waved to them and invited them to become conceited by doubting and having doubted. Modern philosophy, being abstract, is floating in metaphysical indeterminateness.

Instead of explaining this about itself and then directing people (individual persons) to the ethical, the religious, the existential, philosophy has given the appearance [*Skin*] that people are able to speculate themselves out of their own skin [*Skind*], as they so very prosaically say, into pure appearance [*Skin*].

** On this point, may I refer to "Come Here, All You Who Labor and Are Burdened," The Halt.

not at all offended at the lowly man, but at his wanting me to believe that he
is God. And if I have already believed this, then the offense comes from the
other side, that he is supposed to be God—he, this lowly, powerless man who,
when it comes down to brass tacks, is capable of nothing at all. In the one
case the qualification "man" is presupposed and the offense is at the qualification "God"; in the second case, the qualification "God" is presupposed and
the offense is at the qualification "man."

The God-man is the paradox, absolutely the paradox. Therefore, it is altogether certain that the understanding must come to a standstill on it. If a
person is not conscious of offense at the loftiness, he will be aware of it in
relation to the lowliness. It is not inconceivable that someone with abundant
imagination and feeling, a representative of childlike or childish Christianity (because offense χατ᾽ ἐξοχήν [in an eminent sense] does not exist for a
child, and for this very reason Christianity does not actually exist for the child
either), could go and think that he believed that this particular human being
was God without being aware of offense. That is because such a person does
not have a developed conception of God but a childlike or childish fantasy
about something extraordinary, something exalted infinitely high, holy, and
pure, a conception of someone who is somehow greater than all kings etc.,
except that it lacks this very quality: God. In other words, such a person
would have no category and therefore could suppose that he believed that
an individual human being is God without running up against offense. But
this same person will then run up against the lowliness.

So it is with the offense, and so also is it interpreted in Holy Scripture in
the passages where Christ himself warns against offense.

But there is also mention in Scripture of an offense at Christ that has its
possibility in a historical past. This offense does not relate specifically to
Christ as Christ, as the God-man (this is the essential offense, and its two
forms will continue as long as time continues, will continue until faith is
abolished), but to him simply as an individual man who comes into collision
with an established order (this is discussed under A).

Imagine a child, and then delight this child by showing it some of those
artistically insignificant but for children very valuable pictures one buys in
the shops. This man with the look of a leader, with a waving plume on his
hat, and riding a snorting steed at the head of thousands upon thousands
whom you do not see, his hand stretched out in command, "Forward," forward over the top of the mountains that you see before you, forward to victory—this is the emperor, the one and only Napoleon. And now you tell the
child a little about Napoleon. —This man here is dressed as a hunter; he is
leaning on his bow and looking straight ahead with a look so piercing, so
steady, and yet so concerned. It is William Tell. Now you tell the child a little about him and about this remarkable look, that in the same look William

Tell has an eye for his beloved child lest he shoot him and in the same look an eye for the apple, which is on the child's head, so that he will hit it. —And in the same way and to the child's unspeakable delight you show the child several pictures. Then you come to a picture that you have deliberately placed among the others; it portrays one crucified. The child will not immediately, not even quite simply, understand this picture; he will ask what it means, why is he hanging on such a tree. Then you explain to the child that it is a cross and that to hang upon it means to be crucified, and that crucifixion in that country was the most painful death penalty, moreover, a disgraceful death penalty that was used only for the most flagrant criminals. How will this affect the child? The child will feel uncomfortable; he will probably wonder how it could occur to you to put such an ugly picture among all the other lovely pictures, the picture of a flagrant criminal among all these heroes and glorious people. For just as to spite the Jews, the inscription over his cross was "The King of the Jews," in the same way this picture, which is continually being published "this year," is, to spite the generation, a recollection that it can never and shall never get rid of. He must not be represented in any other way. And it must seem as if it were *this* generation that crucified him every time *this* generation for the first time shows this picture to the child of the new generation, explaining for the first time how things went in the world, and the child, the first time he hears it, will become anxious and afraid for his parents and the world and himself. And the other pictures, indeed, as it says in the ballad, they will all turn their backs, so different is this picture.

However—after all, we have not yet come to the crucial point; the child has not yet come to know who this flagrant criminal was—the child will very likely be inquisitive, as a child always is, and will still ask who it is and what did he do, what? Then tell the child that this crucified one is the Savior of the world. But the child will still not be able to attach any definite idea to this. Therefore just tell him that this crucified man was the most loving person who ever lived. Ah, it goes so easily in ordinary associations where everyone knows that *Geschichte* [story] by rote, in ordinary associations where a mere word dropped as a hint is enough, then everyone knows it. But truly it must be a strange human being, or rather an inhuman brute, who would not involuntarily drop his gaze and stand almost like a poor sinner the moment he is going to tell a child this for the first time, a child who has never heard a word about this and of course has never suspected any such thing. At that moment, the adult stands there as an accuser who accuses himself and the whole human race! —What impression do you think you will make on the child, who naturally will ask: But why were they so mean to him, why?

See, now is the moment; if you have not already made too powerful an impression upon the child, then tell him now about the one who was lifted up, who from on high will draw all to himself. Tell the child that this one who was lifted up is this crucified man. Tell the child that he was love, that he came to the world out of love, took upon himself the form of a lowly servant, lived for only one thing—to love and to help people, especially all those who were sick and sorrowful and suffering and unhappy. Tell the child what happened to him in his lifetime, how one of the few who were close to him betrayed him, the few others denied him, and everyone else insulted and mocked him, until finally they nailed him to the cross—as shown in the picture—desiring that his blood might be upon them and upon their children, while he prayed for them that this might not happen, prayed that the heavenly Father would forgive them this guilt. Tell it very vividly to the child, as if you yourself had never heard it before or had never told it to anyone before; tell it as if you yourself had composed the whole story, but do not forget any feature of it that has been preserved, except that you may forget as you are telling it that it is preserved. Tell the child that a notorious robber lived at the same time as this loving man, that the robber was condemned to death—it was his release that the people demanded; it was for him they cheered and shouted, "Long live Barabbas!" But for the loving one they shouted, "Crucify! Crucify!" so this loving person was not only crucified as a criminal but as such a monstrous criminal that in comparison with this loving person the notorious robber became an upright man of sorts.

XII
165

What effect do you think this story will have on the child? But to illustrate the point of the discourse properly, make a test, continue the story of this crucified one, that after this he rose from the dead on the third day, then ascended into heaven in order to enter into glory with the Father in heaven—make this test, and you will see that at first the child will almost ignore it; the story of his suffering will have made such a deep impression on the child that he will not feel like hearing about the glory that followed. To be able to grasp immediately at the loftiness, one must be considerably warped and spoiled over many years by having carelessly learned by rote the whole story of his abasement, suffering, and death, without having any sense of being halted by it.

So what effect do you think this story would evoke in the child? First and foremost, that he would no doubt completely forget the other pictures you showed him, for now he would have something entirely different to think about. And then the child would no doubt become profoundly amazed that God in heaven had not done everything to prevent this from happening, or that it happened without God's having fire rain down from heaven in order to prevent his death, if not before, then at least at the last moment, or that it happened and the earth did not open up and swallow the ungodly people. And this, indeed, is also how we adults would have to understand it if we did not understand that it was voluntary suffering, therefore more severe, that he, the abased one, at all times had it in his power to ask his Father in heaven to send legions of angels to him to avert this terrible thing. —This most likely would be the first impression. But gradually, as the child went and thought about this story, he most likely would become more and more passionate; he would think and talk about nothing but weapons and war—for the child would have firmly resolved that when he grew up he would slay all those ungodly people who had treated this loving person in that way; the child would have made this decision, childishly forgetting that it was over eighteen hundred years since those people lived.

_{XII}
₂₁₃

Lord Jesus Christ, you did not come to the world to be served and thus not to be admired either, or in that sense worshiped. You yourself were the way and the life—and you have asked only for *imitators* [*Efterfølgere*].[212] If we have dozed off into this infatuation, wake us up, rescue us from this error of wanting to admire or adoringly admire you instead of wanting to follow you and be like [*ligne*] you.

John 12:32: **And I, when I am lifted up from the earth, will draw all to myself.**

In Christendom, sermons, lectures, and speeches are heard often enough about what is required of an imitator of Christ, about the implications of being an imitator of Christ, what it means to follow Christ, etc. What is heard is generally very correct and true; only by listening more closely does one discover a deeply hidden, un-Christian, basic confusion and dubiousness. The Christian sermon today has become mainly "observations":[213] Let us in this hour consider; I invite my listeners to observations on; the subject for our consideration is, etc. But "to observe" can mean in one sense to come very close to something, namely, to what one wishes to observe; in another sense, it signifies keeping very distant, infinitely distant, that is, personally. When one shows a painting to a person and asks him to observe it, or when in a business transaction someone looks at [*betragte*], for example, a piece of cloth, he steps very close to the object, in the latter case even picks it up and feels it—in short, he comes as close to the object as possible, but in this very same movement he in another sense leaves himself entirely, goes away from himself, forgets himself, and nothing reminds him of himself, since it is he, after all, who is observing the painting and the cloth and not the painting and the cloth that are observing him. In other words, by observing I go into the object (I become objective) but I leave myself or go away from myself (I cease to be subjective). In this manner, by means of its favorite way of observing what is the essentially Christian, which is just by "observation" and "observations," the sermon presentation has abolished what Christianly is decisive in the sermon presentation—the personal: this *You and I,* the speaker and the one being spoken to this, that the one who is speaking is himself personally in motion, a striver, and likewise the one spoken to, whom he therefore stirs up, encourages, admonishes, and warns, but all with respect to a striving, a life; this, that the speaker will continually not go away from him-

_{XII}
₂₁₄

self but come back to himself and will help the listener, not to go away from himself but to come back to himself. In our day, the sermon presentation has itself first totally disregarded, and subsequently has contributed to its being totally forgotten, that the Christian truth cannot really be the object of "observations." The Christian truth has, if I may say so, its own eyes with which to see; indeed, it seems to be all eyes. But it would be very disturbing, indeed, it would be impossible, for me to look at [*betragte*] a painting or a piece of cloth if I discovered while looking at it that it was the painting or the cloth that was looking at me. And this is the case with the Christian truth; it is Christian truth that is observing me, whether I am doing what it says I should do. See, this is why Christian truth cannot be presented for observation or discoursed upon as observations. It has, if I may say so, its own ears with which to hear; indeed, it seems to be all ears. It listens as the speaker speaks; one cannot speak about it as about an absentee or a merely objective presence, because, since it is from God and God is in it, it is present in a totally unique sense as it is being spoken about, and not as an object. Instead, the speaker becomes its object; the speaker evokes a spirit who examines him as he is speaking.

Therefore, it is a risk to preach, for as I go up into that holy place— whether the church is packed or as good as empty, whether I myself am aware of it or not, I have one listener more than can be seen, an invisible listener, God in heaven whom I certainly cannot see but who truly can see me. This listener, he pays close attention to whether what I am saying is true, whether it is true in me, that is, he looks to see—and he can do that, because he is invisible, in a way that makes it impossible to be on one's guard against him— he looks to see whether my life expresses what I am saying. And although I do not have authority to commit anyone else, I have committed myself to every word I have said from the pulpit in the sermon—and God has heard it. Truly it is a risk to preach! Most people no doubt have the idea that to step out on the stage as an actor, to venture into the danger of having all eyes focused on one, is something that requires courage. Yet in one sense this danger, like everything on the stage, is an illusion, because the actor, of course, is personally outside it all; his task is expressly to deceive, to dissemble, to represent someone else, and to reproduce accurately someone else's words. The proclaimer of the Christian truth, on the other hand, steps forward into a place where, even if the eyes of all are not focused on him, the eye of an omniscient one is. His task is: to be himself, and in a setting, God's house, which, all eyes and ears, requires only one thing of him—that he should be himself, be true. That he should be true, that is, that he himself should be what he proclaims, or at least strive to be that, or at least be honest enough to confess about himself that he is not that. Alas, how many of those who go up into the holy place to proclaim Christianity have hearing keen enough to discover the displeasure of the holy place and its mockery of him because he proclaims so enthusiastically, movingly, and with tears in his eyes that of which his life expresses the very opposite!

How risky it is to be the *I* who preaches, the one speaking, an *I* who by preaching and as he preaches commits himself unconditionally, displays his life so that, if possible, one could look directly into his soul—to be this *I,* that is risky! This is why the pastor little by little discovered how to draw his eyes back into himself, so as to suggest thereby that no one should look at him. After all, he thought, he was not speaking about himself; it was about the cause. And this came to be admired as an extraordinary advance in wisdom, that the speaker thus in a way ceased to be an *I* and became, if that is possible, the cause. In any case, in this way it became much easier to be a pastor—the one speaking did not preach any more; he used those moments to make some observations. Some observations! One sees it on the speaker; his gaze is withdrawn; he resembles not so much a human being as one of those sculptured stone figures that have no eyes. He thereby sets a chasmic abyss between the listener and himself, almost as chasmic as the one that lies between the actor and the spectator. And what he presents is "observations," whereby he again sets, between himself and what he says, a chasmic abyss like that between the actor and the poet. While he is "using these moments to make observations," he is personally outside as far as possible.

In this way, the *I,* who was the speaker, dropped out. The speaker was not an *I;* he was the issue, the observation. When this *I* dropped out, inevitably the *you* also was abolished—you, the listener, that it is you, you who are sitting there, to whom it is addressed. Yes, it has gone so far that to speak in that way to others is regarded as "personal remarks." Personal remarks, to use personal remarks, to indulge in personal remarks, is regarded as unseemly, uncultured behavior—and consequently it will not do to speak personally (the speaking *I*) and to persons (the listening *you*). And if it will not do, then preaching is abolished. But so it is, indeed—one only makes observations. And the "observation" does not come too close to either the speaker or the listener; the observation very reliably guarantees that it will not become a matter of personal remarks. It is not I, the speaker, who is being spoken about; it is scarcely I who am speaking—it is observation. And it is not you, the listener, who is being spoken to; it is observation. Whether I do what I say is none of your concern if only the observation is correct; it scarcely concerns me myself, since I naturally owe myself the same respect I owe everyone else—not to allow myself to indulge in personal remarks. Whether or not you, the listener, do what is said does not concern me, and scarcely yourself; it is observation and at most it is a question of the extent to which the observation has satisfied you.

This fundamental change in the sermon presentation, whereby Christianity was abolished, is the expression, among other things, also for the fundamental change that took place with the church triumphant and established

Christendom—namely, that ordinarily Christ at most acquired admirers and
not imitators.

In describing this difference, *the difference between an admirer and an imitator,*
this discussion will strive to illuminate Christianity, again with continual reference to the sacred words "From on high he will draw all to himself," for
here once again what determines the issue is loftiness and lowliness, or the
relation to loftiness and the relation to lowliness. If Christ exists for us only
in loftiness, if his abasement is forgotten or if he had never existed in lowliness, then in that case not even Christ himself, in order to be self-consistent,
could require anything but admirers, adoring admirers, since loftiness and admirer, divine loftiness and adoring admirer, correspond perfectly to each
other. Yes, in relation to loftiness, on our part it would even be effrontery, arrogance, blind infatuation, more or less madness, to want to be imitators
rather than decorously to decline to aspire to what perhaps is not allotted to
us, because it is allotted to someone else, and decorously to be satisfied to admire and adoring to admire. But the correlative of abasement and lowliness
is: imitators.

Now, it is of course well known that Christ continually uses the expression "imitators." He never says that he asks for admirers, adoring admirers,
adherents; and when he uses the expression "follower" he always explains it
in such a way that one perceives that "imitators" is meant by it, that it is not
adherents of a teaching but imitators of a life, who do not, because of some
accidental loftiness, make wanting to resemble it into presumptuousness or
madness. It is also well known, as I have repeated elsewhere again and again,
that it is the abased Christ who is speaking, that every word we have from
Christ is from him, the abased one. Now it certainly may be assumed that
Christ himself was fully aware of why he chose this particular expression,
which solely and unconditionally is in innermost and deepest harmony with
what he continually said about himself or claimed himself to be: namely, the
truth and the way and the life.[214] [He was fully aware] that he was not a
teacher in the sense that he only had a teaching to present, so that he could
be satisfied with adherents who accepted the teaching—but in their lives ignored or let things take their course. One must also certainly assume that he
himself was fully aware of why his whole life on earth, from first to last, was
designed solely to be able to have imitators and designed to make admirers
impossible.

Christ came to the world with the purpose of saving the world, also with
the purpose—this in turn is implicit in his first purpose—of being *the proto-*
type, of leaving footprints for the person who wanted to join him, who then
might become an *imitator,* this indeed corresponds to "footprints." That is why
he let himself be born in lowliness and thereupon lived poor, abandoned, despised, abased—yes, no human being has lived so abased as he. By comparing
the conditions of his life with Christ's, even the otherwise lowliest person

would have to come to the conclusion that his own life, humanly speaking, is far preferable in comparison with the conditions of Christ's life. Why, then, this lowliness and abasement? Because he who is truly to be the prototype and be related only to imitators must in one sense be *behind* people, propelling forward, while in another sense he stands *ahead,* beckoning. This is the relation of loftiness and lowliness in the prototype. The loftiness must not be the direct kind, which is the worldly, the earthly, but the spiritual, and thus the very negation of worldly and earthly loftiness. The lowliness must be the direct kind, because direct lowliness, if one must go through it, is precisely the way (but also for the worldly and earthly mentality the roundabout way) that makes sure that loftiness is not taken in vain. Thus *the prototype* stands infinitely close in abasement and lowliness, and yet infinitely distant in loftiness, indeed, even further away than if it were distant only in loftiness, because to have to go through lowliness and abasement in order to reach it, in order to define oneself in likeness to it, to have no other way at all, is an even greater, is actually the infinite distance. Thus in one sense the prototype is *behind,* more deeply pressed down into abasement and lowliness than any human being has ever been, and in another sense, *ahead,* infinitely lifted up. But the prototype must be behind in order to be able to capture and include all; if there were one single person who could honestly underbid or stoop lower by establishing that he was situated even lower in abasement and lowliness, then the prototype is not the prototype, then it is only an imperfect prototype—that is, only the prototype for a great crowd of people. The prototype must be *unconditionally* behind, behind everyone, and it must be *behind* in order to propel forward those who are to be formed according to it.

In the human race and in every individual in the human race there resides consciously or unconsciously a profound cunning with regard to what is supposed to be the prototype for them, a cunning that is of evil. If the person who is supposed to be the prototype is in possession of earthly, worldly, temporal advantages, what then? Well, then the prototype is wrongly positioned, wrongly oriented, and so in turn the human race as well as every individual in the human race exploits this to make a wrong turn on its part. The prototype is then pushed aside as an invitation to poetic admiration, but the prototype should rather stand behind, come up to people from behind as a requirement for them. Because the prototype has become an object of admiration, people sneak away from the *requirement;* they say, "Lucky fellow, he who has all those advantages and favors; if only we were in his place, we would be just as perfect as he is. Now we can do nothing but admire him, and it is to our honor and credit that we do it, that is, that we do not abandon ourselves to envy. But anything else than admire him, that we cannot do, because he possesses conditions that we do not have and that he cannot give us. How unreasonable, then, to require the same thing of us that he requires of himself."

Christ is *the prototype*. If he had come to the world in earthly and temporal loftiness, this would have given rise to the greatest possible lie. Instead of becoming the prototype for the whole human race and every individual in the human race, he would have become a general excuse and escape for the whole human race and every individual in the human race. Nor would he have been put to death—because what also contributed to inciting his contemporaries against him was that they, if I may dare to say so, could not get him turned the way they wanted him, that he "defiantly and stubbornly" *wanted* to be the abased one and, what embitters people's self-loving spinelessness most of all, wanted to have only imitators—no, he would have become the object of admiration and the confusion would have become so great that it can scarcely be imagined. He himself indeed claimed to be the truth, and since people presumably now admired him, according to our assumption, it looked as if they loved truth also, and it thereby became almost impossible to make head or tail of it. In other words, the confusion in the situation of contemporaneity would have become just as great as it is in established Christendom, where someone in strongest terms admires and adoringly admires and admires and adores Christ—where his life expresses the very opposite of Christ's life as it was lived on earth by him, who in order to be the prototype was born and lived in lowliness and abasement. But the person who admires has a wonderful hiding place. He will say, "More he certainly cannot require of me than that in the strongest terms—and if language has even stronger terms, I will be happy to use them—I acknowledge and confess that I admiringly adore Christ as the truth. More can certainly not be demanded of me. Can you tell me anything higher than that?"

XII
220

See, that is why Christ was born and lived in abasement. Not one, unconditionally not one person contemporary with him, lived so abased; no human being has ever lived so abased. It was, therefore, unconditionally impossible for anyone to sneak away from the prototype with excuse and evasion on the basis that the prototype, after all, possessed earthly and worldly advantages that he did not have. In that sense, to admire Christ is the untrue invention of a later age, aided by "loftiness." Understood in that way, there was unconditionally nothing to admire, unless one wanted to admire poverty, misery, contempt, etc. He was not even exempted from the worst—being pitied, a pitiable object of sympathy. No, there was truly not the least thing to admire.

Nor was there in the situation of contemporaneity any occasion for admiring, because Christ had only the same conditions to offer the person who joined him—and on those conditions no admirer has ever wanted to join; the same conditions: to become just as poor, despised, insulted, mocked, and if possible even a little more, considering that in addition one was an adherent of such a despised individual, whom every sensible person shunned.

What, then, is the difference between an admirer and an imitator? An imitator *is* or strives *to be* what he admires, and an admirer keeps himself personally detached, consciously or unconsciously does not discover that what is admired involves a claim upon him, to be or at least to strive to be what is admired.

TWO DISCOURSES AT THE COMMUNION
ON FRIDAYS (AUGUST 7, 1851)
BY S. KIERKEGAARD

Just as the publications in the early sequence of pseudonymous works were accompanied by signed works, the new series of pseudonymous works (*Two Ethical-Religious Essays,* by H. H., and *The Sickness unto Death* and *Practice in Christianity,* by Anti-Climacus) was accompanied by volumes of signed discourses (*The Lily in the Field and the Bird of the Air,* May 14, 1849, *Three Discourses at the Communion on Fridays,* November 14, 1849, *An Upbuilding Discourse,* December 20, 1850, and *Two Discourses at the Communion on Fridays,* August 7, 1851). *For Self-Examination* was already at the printers, and therefore the Preface to *Two Discourses* was cast as a final word in an authorship that began with *Either/Or.* Then, after *Two Discourses,* Kierkegaard's writing was confined to his journals for three years. The themes of *Two Discourses* are forgiveness and love: "But one who is forgiven little loves little" and "Love will hide a multitude of sins."

PREFACE

An authorship that began with *Either/Or* and advanced step by step seeks here its decisive place of rest, at the foot of the altar, where the author, personally most aware of his own imperfection and guilt, certainly does not call himself a truth-witness but only a singular kind of poet and thinker who, *without authority,* has had nothing new to bring but "has wanted once again to read through, if possible in a more inward way, the original text of individual human existence-relationships, the old familiar text handed down from the fathers"—(see my postscript to *Concluding Postscript*[215]).

Turned this way, I have nothing further to add. Allow me, however, to express only this, which in a way is my life, the content of my life, its fullness, its bliss, its peace and satisfaction—this, or this view of life, which is the thought of humanity [*Menneskelighed*] and of human equality [*Menneskeliighed*]: Christianly, every human being, once again, unconditionally every human being, is equally close to God—how close and equally close?—is loved by him.

Thus there is equality, infinite equality, between human beings. If there is any difference—ah, this difference, if it does exist, is like peaceableness itself. Undisturbed, the difference does not in the remotest way disturb the equality. The difference is: that one person bears in mind that he is loved—keeps it in mind perhaps day in and day out, perhaps day in and day out for seventy years, perhaps with only one longing, for eternity, so that he can really grasp this thought and go forth, employed in this blessed occupation of keeping in mind that he—alas, not because of his virtue!—is loved.

Another person perhaps does not think about his being loved, perhaps goes on year after year, day after day, without thinking about his being loved; or perhaps he is happy and grateful to be loved by his wife, his children, by his friends and contemporaries, but he does not think about his being loved by God; or he may bemoan not being loved by anyone, and he does not think about his being loved by God.

"Yet," the first person might say, "I am innocent; after all. I cannot help it if someone else ignores or disdains the love that is lavished just as richly upon him as upon me." Infinite, divine love, which makes no distinctions! Alas, human ingratitude!—What if the equality between us human beings, in which we completely resemble one another, were that none of us really thinks about his being loved!

As I turn to the other side, I would wish and would permit myself (in gratitude for the sympathy and good will that may have been shown to me) to present, as it were, and to commend these writings to the people whose language I with filial devotion and with almost feminine infatuation am proud to have the honor to write, yet also with the consolation that it will not be to their discredit that I have written it.

Copenhagen, late summer 1851

S. K.

XII
271

Prayer

Lord Jesus Christ, you who certainly did not come to the world in order to judge, yet by being love that was not loved you were a judgment upon the world. We call ourselves Christians; we say that we know of no one to go to but you—alas, to whom then shall we go when, precisely by your love, the judgment falls also upon us, that we love little? To whom, what hopelessness, if not to you! To whom, what despair, if you actually would not receive us mercifully, forgiving us our great sin against you and against love, we who sinned much by loving little!

Luke 7:47. **But one who is forgiven little loves little.**

Devout listener, at the Communion table the invitation is indeed given, "Come here, all you who labor and are burdened, and I will give you rest."[216] The single individual then responds to the invitation and goes to the Communion table. Then there are other words—they could be the inscription over the door of the church, on the inside, not to be read by those who are entering the church but only by those who are leaving the church—the words: One who is forgiven little loves little. The former words are the Holy Communion's invitation; the latter words are the Holy Communion's justification, as if it were said: If at the Communion table you are not aware of

the forgiveness of your sins, of your every sin, this is due to yourself. Holy
Communion is without fault; the fault is yours, because you love only little.
Just as in praying aright it is difficult to be able to reach the Amen—for the
one who has never prayed it seems easy enough, easy to finish quickly, but
for the one who felt the need to pray and began to pray it surely happens
that he continually seemed to have something more upon his heart, as if he
could neither get everything said nor get it all said as he wished it said, and
thus he does not reach the Amen—in the very same way it is also difficult
to receive aright the forgiveness of sins at the Communion table. There the
gracious forgiveness of all your sins is pronounced to you. Hear it aright, take
it altogether literally, the forgiveness of all your sins. You will be able to go
away from the Communion table as light of heart, divinely understood, as a
newborn child, upon whom nothing, nothing weighs heavily, therefore even
lighter of heart, insofar as much has weighed upon your heart. There is no
one at the Communion table who retains against you even the least of your
sins, no one—unless you yourself do it. So cast them all away from yourself,
and the recollection of them, lest in it you retain them; and cast away the
recollection of your having cast your sins away, lest in it you retain them.
Cast it all away from yourself; you have nothing at all to do except, believing, to cast away from yourself and to cast away from yourself what weighs
heavily and burdens. What can be easier! Usually the heaviness is to have to
shoulder burdens, but to dare, to have to cast away from oneself! And yet
how difficult! Yes, even more rare than a person who shouldered every burden, even more rare is a person who accomplished the apparently very easy
task, after having received the assurance of the gracious forgiveness of his sins
and the pledge thereof, of feeling completely unburdened of every sin, even
the least, or relieved of every sin, also even the greatest! If you could look
into the hearts, you would surely see how many go to Holy Communion
burdened, groaning under the heavy burden; and when they go away from
the Communion table, if you could look into the hearts, you would possibly see that basically there was not a single one who left it completely unburdened, and at times you might see someone who went away even more
burdened, burdened by the thought that he probably had not been a worthy
guest at the Communion table because he found no alleviation.

That this is the case we shall not conceal from one another. We shall not
speak in such a way that the discourse leaves you ignorant of how things go
in actuality, shall not depict everything as so perfect that it does not fit us actual human beings. Ah, no, what good would the discourse be then! If, however, the discourse makes us as imperfect as we are, then it helps us to be kept
in a continuous striving, neither makes us, intoxicated in dreams, imagine
that everything was decided by this one time, nor, in quiet despondency, give
up because this time we did not succeed according to our wish, because
things did not turn out as we had prayed and desired.

In the brief moments prescribed, let us consider these words: One who is forgiven little loves little—*words of judgment,* but also *words of comfort.*

And you, my listener, do not be disturbed by my speaking this way at this moment before you go up to the Communion table, perhaps thinking and insisting that the one who is to speak at this time ought to speak in a different way and devote everything to reassuring the single individual and making him feel secure. If the speaker later learned that the holy act had not been entirely a joy and blessing to an individual, he could then, of course, speak to him in a different way. O my friend, for one thing, it is truly not the case that it is only for a rare individual that the perfect does not succeed—no, it is only for a rare individual that the perfect does succeed. For another, there is a concern, a heartfelt concern, that perhaps better assists so that a person succeeds in the highest, better than too much trust and a too carefree bold confidence. There is a longing for God, a trust in God, a reliance upon, a hope in God, a love, a bold confidence—but what most surely finds him may still be a sorrowing for God. Sorrowing for God—this is no fugitive mood that promptly disappears as one draws close to God; on the contrary, it may be deepest just when one draws close to God, just as the person sorrowing in this way is most fearful for himself the closer he comes to God.

One who is forgiven little loves little. These are words of judgment.

Usually it is presented this way: justice, this is the severe judgment; love is leniency, which does not judge, and if it does judge, love's judgment is the lenient judgment. No, no, love's judgment is the most severe judgment. Was not the most severe judgment passed upon the world, more severe than the flood, more severe than the confusion of tongues at the Tower of Babel, more severe than the destruction of Sodom and Gomorrah, was it not Christ's innocent death, which still was love's sacrifice? And what was the judgment? Surely it was this: *love* was not loved. So also here. The words of the judgment do not say: One who is forgiven little sinned much; hence his sins were too great and too many to be able to be forgiven. No, the judgment says: He loves little. Thus it is not justice that severely denies the forgiveness and pardon of sins. It is love that leniently and mercifully says: *I* forgive you everything—if you are forgiven only little, then it is because you love only little. Justice severely sets the boundary and says: No further! This is the limit. For you there is no forgiveness, and there is nothing more to be said. Love says: You are forgiven everything—if you are forgiven only little, it is because you love only little. Thus there comes a new sin, a new guilt, the guilt of being forgiven only little, a guilt incurred not by the sins committed, but by the lack of love. If you want to learn to fear, then learn to fear—not the severity of justice, but the leniency of love!

Justice looks judgingly at a person, and the sinner cannot endure its gaze; but love, when it looks at him—yes, even if he avoids its gaze, looks down, he nevertheless does perceive that it is looking at him, because love penetrates far more inwardly into life, deep inside life, in there whence life emanates, than justice does, which repellingly establishes a chasmic abyss between the sinner and itself, whereas love is on his side, does not accuse, does not judge, but pardons and forgives. The sinner cannot endure the judging voice of justice; he tries, if possible, to shut his ears to it. But even if he wanted to, it is impossible for him not to hear love, whose judgment—and what frightful judgment!—is: Your sins are forgiven! What frightful judgment, even though the words in themselves are anything but terrifying; and this is the very reason that the sinner cannot help but hear what is nevertheless the judgment. Whither shall I flee from justice? If I take the wings of the morning and fly to the furthest sea, it is there. And if I hide myself in the abyss, it is there, and thus it is everywhere. Yet, no, there is one place to which I can flee—to love. But when love judges you, and the judgment is—what horror!—the judgment is: Your sins are forgiven! Your sins are forgiven— and yet there is something (yes, this something is within you; where else in all the world would it find an abode when love forgives everything!), there is something within you that makes you perceive that they are not forgiven. What is the horror of the most severe judgment compared with this horror! What, then, is anger's severe judgment, the curse, compared with this judgment: Your sins are forgiven! Thus it is indeed almost leniency on the part of justice to say as you say: No, they are not forgiven! What is the suffering of the "brother-murderer" when he, fugitive and unsteady, fears that everyone will recognize him by the mark of justice that condemned him[217]—what is this suffering compared with the anguish of the unhappy person for whom the words "Your sins are forgiven" become the judgment, not salvation! What frightful severity! That love, that it is love, the forgiving love, which, not judging, no, alas, itself suffering, is nevertheless changed into the judgment! That love, the forgiving love, which does not want, like justice, to make the guilt manifest but on the contrary wants to hide it by forgiving and pardoning, that it nevertheless is this which, itself suffering, makes the guilt more frightfully manifest than justice does!

Ponder that thought: "self-inflicted." It is self-inflicted, says justice, that there is no forgiveness for a person. Justice is thinking of his many sins, since it can forget nothing. Love says: It is self-inflicted—it is not thereby thinking of his many sins—ah, no, it is willing to forget them all, it has forgotten them all; and yet it is self-inflicted, says love. Which is the more terrible? Surely the latter, which sounds almost like insane talk, because the charge is not his sins, no, the charge is: he is forgiven, he is forgiven everything. Think of a sinner who is sinking in the abyss; listen to his cry of anguish when with his last groan he vindicates the justice his life has mocked and says: It is self-inflicted. How terrible! There is only one thing more terrible, if it is not to justice that he speaks but to love and says: It is self-inflicted. Justice is not mocked, indeed, love even less. More severe than justice's most severe judg-

XII
275

ment of the greatest sinner is love's: He is forgiven little—because he loves little.

One who is forgiven little loves little. These are words of judgment, but they are also words of *comfort*.

I do not know, my listener, what your crime, your guilt, your sins are, but surely we are all more or less guilty of the guilt of loving only little. Take comfort, then, in these words just as I take comfort in them. And how do I take comfort? I take comfort because the words say nothing about divine love but only something about mine. The words do not say that divine love has now become weary of being love, that it has now changed, weary of the wasting, as it were, of indescribable mercy on the ungrateful race of human beings or on me, the ungrateful one. The words do not say that divine love has now become something else, a lesser love, its warmth cooled because love became cold in the ungrateful race of human beings or in me, the ungrateful one. No, the words do not speak of that at all. Take comfort as I take comfort—from what? From this, that the reason the words do not say it is that the sacred words do not lie; so, then, it has not accidentally or cruelly been suppressed in the words while in actuality it is true that God's love has become weary of loving. No, if the words do not say it, then it is not so; and if the words did say it—no, the words could not say it, because the words cannot lie. Oh, what blessed comfort in the deepest sorrow!

Suppose God's love had in truth changed, suppose you had heard nothing about it but were concerned about yourself, that until now you had loved only little, with devout purpose you had striven to make the fire of love in you flame up and you fed the flame in the same way as you had made it flame up—and now, even though you felt ashamed of how imperfect your love still was, you now wanted to draw close to God in order, according to the words of Scripture,[218] to be reconciled to him—but he had changed! Imagine a girl in love; in concern she confesses to herself how little she has loved until now—but now, she says to herself, I will become sheer love. And she succeeds. These tears of concern she sheds in sorrow over herself—these tears do not put out the fire; no, they are burning too brightly for that. No, these very tears make the fire flame up. But meanwhile the beloved had changed; he was no longer loving. Oh, one concern for a person! One concern can be enough for a person; no human being can endure more. If a person, when he in self-concern must confess to himself how little he has loved God until now, is troubled by the thought that meanwhile God might have changed—then, yes, then I will despair, and I will despair at once, because then there is nothing more to wait for, neither in time nor in eternity. But therefore I take comfort in the words, and I block every escape route for me and I push aside all excuses and all extenuations and bare my breast where I will be wounded by the words that, judging, penetrate, judging "You loved only little." Oh, only penetrate more deeply, even more deeply, you healing pain, "You did not love at all"—even when such is the judgment, I am in one sense aware of no pain, I am aware of an indescribable blessedness, because precisely my sentence, the death sentence upon me and my wretched love, contains something else in addition: God is unchanged love.

This is how I take comfort. And I find hidden in the words a comfort that you too, my listener, surely find precisely when you hear the words in such a way that they wound you. They do not read: One who is forgiven little *loved* little; no, they read: *loves* little. When justice judges, it balances the account, closes it. It uses the past tense; it says: He *loved* little, and thereby says that now the account is settled, we two are separated, have nothing more to do with each other.

The words, the words of love, however, read: One who is forgiven little loves little. He loves little, he *loves*; that is, this is the way it is now, now at this moment—love does not say more. Infinite love, that you remain true to yourself this way even in your slightest utterance! He loves little now, in this present instant. But what is the present instant, what is the moment—swiftly, swiftly it is past, and now, in the next moment, now all is changed; now he loves, if not much, yet he is striving to love much. Now all is changed, but not *love*; it is unchanged, unchanged the same that lovingly has waited for him, lovingly has not had the heart to be finished with him, has not had the heart to seek a separation from him but has remained with him. Now it is not justice that conclusively says: He loved little; now it is love that, joyful in heaven, says: He loved little—that is, now it is changed; once it was that way, but now, now he loves much.

But then is it not really true that the forgiveness of sins is *merited,* admittedly not by works, but by love? When it is said that one who is forgiven little loves little, does this not imply that it is love that decides the issue, whether and how far one's sins should be forgiven—and therefore, the forgiveness of sins is *merited* after all? Oh, no. A little earlier in the same Gospel (v. 42 to the end), Christ speaks of two debtors, one of whom owed much and the other little, and who both found forgiveness. He asks: Which of these two ought to love more? The answer: The one who was forgiven much. Note how we still are not entering here into the baleful region of meritoriousness, but note how everything remains within love! When you love much, you are forgiven much—and when you are forgiven much, you love much. See here the blessed recurrence of salvation in love! First you love much, and much is then forgiven you—and see, then love increases even more. This, that you have been forgiven so much, loves forth love once again, and you love much because you were forgiven much! Here love is like faith. Imagine one of those unfortunates whom Christ healed by a miracle. In order to be healed, the person must believe—now he believes and is healed. Now he is healed—and now that he is saved, his faith is twice as strong. It is not this way: he believed and then the miracle happened and then it was all over. No, the fulfillment doubles his faith; after the fulfillment, his faith is twice as strong as it was before he was saved. So also with this matter of loving much. The love that loves much and then is forgiven much is strong, divinely strong in weakness, but even stronger is love's second time, when the same love loves again, loves because much has been forgiven.

My listener, presumably you remember the beginning of this discourse. In this solemn moment one can disturb in two ways: by speaking about something irrelevant, even though the matter is otherwise important and the discourse meaningful, or by disturbingly speaking about something that at such a moment is closest to one. "One who is forgiven little loves little"—this could seem disturbing at this very moment before you go to Holy Communion, where you indeed receive the forgiveness of all your sins. Oh, but just as something that builds up is always terrifying at first, and just as all true love is always unrest at first, and just as love of God is always sorrow at first, similarly, what seems disturbing is not always disturbing, what truly is quieting is always disquieting at first. But is there any comparison between these two dangers—that of being quieted in false security and that of being disquieted by being reminded of the disquieting thought—of what disquieting thought?—of *the* disquieting thought that if until now one has loved only little, this, too, can be forgiven. The disquieting is strange; it is true that the one who is properly formed by this does not look as strong as the one who remained ignorant of it. But at the last moment he, through his very weakness, is perhaps the stronger; at the last moment, through his very weakness, he perhaps succeeds where the stronger one fails.

May God, then, bless this disquieting discourse so that it might have disquieted you only for the good, that you, quieted, might be aware at the Communion table that you are receiving the gracious forgiveness of all your sins.

FOR SELF-EXAMINATION [FIRST SERIES]
RECOMMENDED TO THE PRESENT AGE (SEPTEMBER 20, 1851)
BY S. KIERKEGAARD

For Self-Examination is frequently recommended as a good first reading of the works. A master of a range of kinds of writing, Kierkegaard here writes with a simplicity, yet with the metaphorical imagination of the poet, the thoughtfulness of the philosopher and theologian, the whimsy of the humorist, and the ardor of the lover and believer—characteristics that are reminiscent of the variety of modes in the earlier publications. The title itself is reminiscent of Kierkegaard's Socratic aim throughout the authorship: to make aware. The selection is mainly from Part I. Parts II and III are on the themes "Christ is the way" and "It is the Spirit who gives life."

PREFACE

My dear reader, read aloud, if possible![219] If you do so, allow me to thank you for it; if you not only do it yourself, if you also influence others to do it, allow me to thank each one of them, and you again and again! By reading aloud you will gain the strongest impression that you have only yourself to consider, not me, who, after all, am "without authority,"[220] nor others, which would be a distraction.

August 1851.

S. K.

INTRODUCTORY NOTE

There is a saying that often comes to my mind, a saying by a man to whom I cannot in a Christian sense be said to owe anything—indeed, he was a pagan—but to whom I nevertheless feel personally very indebted, and who also lived in circumstances that in my opinion quite correspond to our situation today: I mean that simple wise man of antiquity.[221] It is told of him that when he was accused before the people an orator came to him and handed him a carefully composed defense speech, with the request that he use it. The simple wise man accepted it, read it. Thereupon he gave it back to the orator and said: It is a beautiful and well-composed speech (hence he did not give it back be-

cause it was a poor, injudicious speech). But, he continued, I have now reached
the age of seventy years; thus I do not feel it is fitting for me to use an orator's
art. What did he mean? In the first place he meant: My life is too earnest to
be able to be served by the prop of an orator's technique. I have ventured my
life; even if I am not sentenced to death, I nevertheless have ventured my life,
and in the service of the god [*Guden*][222] I have done my duty. Then do not
let me now at the last moment destroy the impression of myself and of my
life with the help of artful orators or oratorical arts. In the second place, he
meant: The thoughts, ideas, and concepts that I, known by everyone, ridiculed
by your comic poets, regarded as an eccentric, daily attacked by "the anonymous" (it is his word), in the course of twenty years (it was that long) have developed in conversation with the first person to come along in the market-
place—these thoughts are my life, have occupied me early and late. And even
if they have occupied no one else, they have occupied me endlessly, and when
I have sometimes been able to stand a whole day staring into space (something
that has attracted your particular attention), it was these thoughts that occupied me—therefore I also believe that if I intend to say anything at all on the
day the verdict is pronounced I can say a few words without the help of artful orators and oratorical arts, and the circumstance that I most likely will be
sentenced to death makes no difference. What I say will naturally remain the
same and about the same and in the same manner as before,[223] and just as I
spoke yesterday with a leather tanner in the marketplace, I believe I can surely
say a few words without preparation or the assistance of others. Of course, I
am not entirely without preparation either, because I have been preparing myself for twenty years, nor am I entirely without assistance, since I rely on the
assistance of the god. But, to repeat, the few words . . . . . well, I do not deny
that they can also become more prolix. If I were to have twenty years again, I
would just keep on talking about the same things I have been talking about
continually; but artful orators and oratorical arts are not something for me. —
O you earnest one! Misjudged, you had to empty the poison goblet; you were
not understood. Then you died. For over two thousand years you have been
admired, "but I wonder if I have been understood?" —That is just it!

XII
302

XII
306

Times are different, and even though the times are often like a human
being—he changes completely but nevertheless remains just as foolish, only
in a new pattern—it nevertheless is true that times are different and different times have different requirements.

There was a time when the Gospel, *grace,* was changed into a new Law,
more rigorous with people than the old Law. Everything had become rather
tortured, laborious, and unpleasant, almost as if, despite the angels' song at the
advent of Christianity, there was no joy anymore either in heaven or on earth.
Through petty self-torments, they had made God just as petty—in this way
it brings its own punishment! They entered the monastery, they stayed

there—yes, it is true it was voluntary and yet it was bondage, because it was not truly voluntary, they had not entirely made up their minds, they were not happy to be there, were not free, and yet they did not have the bold confidence to stop or to leave the monastery and become free. Everything had become works. And just like unhealthy growths on trees, so also were these works corrupted by unhealthy growths, thus were often only hypocrisy, the conceitedness of merit, idleness. The error was precisely there and not so much in the works. Let us not go too far; let us not make a previous age's error an excuse for new error. No, take this unhealthiness and falsity away from the works and let us then retain the works in honesty, in humility, in beneficial activity. The approach to these works should indeed be, for example, like that of a militant youth who, in connection with a dangerous undertaking, voluntarily comes and pleads with his leader, saying: May I not be permitted to come along! If in the same way a person were to say to God: "May I not be permitted to give all I own to the poor—not that this should be something meritorious, no, no, I am deeply and humbly aware that if I am ever saved I will be saved by grace, just as the robber on the cross, but may I not be permitted to do this so that I can work solely for the extension of God's kingdom among my fellow beings"—well, yes, if I am to speak as a Lutheran—then this, despite Satan, the newspapers, the most respected public (for the time of the pope is now past), in spite of all the sensible, ecclesiastical, or secular objections of all clever men and women, then this is well pleasing to God. But this is not the way it was in the age we are discussing. XII 307

At that time there appeared a man from God and with faith, Martin Luther; with faith (for truly this required faith) or by faith he established faith in its rights. His life expressed works—let us never forget that—but he said: A person is saved by faith alone. The danger was great. I know of no stronger expression of how great it was in Luther's eyes than that he decided that in order to get things straight: the Apostle James must be shoved aside. Imagine Luther's respect for an apostle—and then to have to dare to do this in order to get faith restored to its rights!

But what happened? There is always a secular mentality that no doubt wants to have the name of being Christian but wants to become Christian as cheaply as possible. This secular mentality became aware of Luther. It listened; for safety's sake it listened once again lest it should have heard wrongly; thereupon it said, "Excellent! This is something for us. Luther says: It depends on faith alone. He himself does not say that his life expresses works, and since he is now dead it is no longer an actuality. So we take his words, his doctrine—and we are free from all works—long live Luther! *Wer nicht liebt Weiber, Wein, Gesang / Er wird ein Narr sein Leben lang* [Who loves not women, wine, and song / He is a fool his whole life long].[224] This is the meaning of Luther's life, this man of God who, in keeping with the times, reformed Christianity." Even though not everyone took Luther in vain in such a downright secular way—in every human being there is an inclination *either* to want to be meritorious when it comes to works *or,* when faith and grace are to be emphasized, also to want to be free from works as far as possible. Indeed, "man," this rational creation of God, certainly does not let himself be fooled; he is not a peasant coming to market, he has his eyes open. "No, it's one or the other," says the man. "If it is to be *works*—fine, but then I must also ask for the legitimate yield I have coming from my works, so that they are meritorious. If it is to be *grace*—fine, but then I must also ask to be free from works—otherwise it surely is not grace. If it is to be works and nevertheless grace, that is indeed foolishness." Yes, that is indeed foolishness; that would also be true Lutheranism; that would indeed be Christianity. Christianity's requirement is this: your life should express works as strenuously as possible; then one thing more is required—that you humble yourself and confess: But my being saved is nevertheless grace. The error of the Middle Ages, meritoriousness, was abhorred. But when one scrutinizes the matter more deeply, it is easy to see that people had perhaps an even greater notion that works are meritorious than did the Middle Ages, but they applied *grace* in such a way that they freed themselves from works. Having abolished works, they could not very well be tempted to regard as something meritorious the works they did not do. Luther wished to take "meritoriousness" away from works and apply them somewhat differently—namely, in the direction of witnessing for the truth; the secular mentality, which understood Luther perfectly, took meritoriousness away altogether—including the works.

And James says: Be not only hearers of the Word but doers of it.

But in order to become a doer of the Word one must first of all be a hearer or reader of it, which James does indeed say.

And now we have come to our text.

So we shall speak about:

> *What Is Required in Order to Look at Oneself with True*
> *Blessing in the Mirror of the Word?*

The first requirement is that you must not look at the mirror, observe the mirror, but must see yourself in the mirror.

This seems so obvious that one might think it would scarcely need to be said. Yet it is certainly necessary; and what confirms me in this opinion is that this remark was not made by me, nor by someone we in these days call a pious man, the kind of man who has some pious sentiments, but it was made by a witness to the truth, a martyr, and such glorious people are certainly informed.

He warns against the error of observing the mirror instead of seeing oneself in the mirror. I merely make use of the remark and ask you, my listener: Does it not seem to be coined for our times and our situation and in general for the later ages of Christendom?

XII
308

XII
315

"God's Word" is indeed the mirror—but, but—oh, how enormously complicated—strictly speaking, how much belongs to "God's Word"? Which books are authentic? Are they really by the apostles, and are the apostles really trustworthy? Have they personally seen everything, or have they perhaps only heard about various things from others? As for ways of reading, there are thirty thousand different ways. And then this crowd or crush of scholars and opinions, and learned opinions and unlearned opinions about how the particular passage is to be understood . . . . . is it not true that all this seems to be rather complicated! God's Word is the mirror—in reading it or hearing it, I am supposed to see myself in the mirror—but look, this business of the mirror is so confusing that I very likely never come to see myself reflected—at least not if I go at it this way. One could almost be tempted to assume that the full force of human craftiness has a hand in it (alas, how true, in relation to God and godliness and God-fearing truth we humans are so crafty that we do not mean it at all when we tell each other that we are perfectly willing to do God's will if we only could find out what it is). One could almost be tempted to assume that this is craftiness, that we really do not want to see ourselves in that mirror and therefore we have concocted all this that threatens to make the mirror impossible, all this that we then honor with the laudatory name of scholarly and profound and serious research and pondering. XII 316

My listener, how highly do you value God's Word? Now, do not say that you value it so highly that no expression can describe it, for one can also speak so loftily that one says nothing at all. Therefore, in order to make something out of this, let us take a simple human situation; if you value God's Word higher, so much the better.

Imagine a lover who has received a letter from his beloved—I assume that God's Word is just as precious to you as this letter is to the lover. I assume that you read and think you ought to read God's Word in the same way that the lover reads this letter.

Yet you perhaps say, "Yes, but Holy Scripture is written in a foreign language." But it is really only scholars who need to read Holy Scripture in the original language. If, however, you will not have it any other way, if you insist upon reading Scripture in the original language, well, we can still keep the metaphor of the letter from the beloved, except that we will add a little stipulation.

I assume, then, that this letter from the beloved is written in a language that the lover does not understand, and there is no one around who can translate it for him, and perhaps he would not even want any such help lest a stranger be initiated into his secrets. What does he do? He takes a dictionary, begins to spell his way through the letter, looks up every word in order to obtain a translation. Let us assume that, as he sits there busy with his task, an acquaintance comes in. He knows that this letter has come, because he sees it on the table, sees it lying there, and says, "Well, so you are reading a letter from your beloved"—what do you think the other will say? He answers, "Have you gone mad? Do you think this is reading a letter from my beloved! No, my friend, I am sitting here toiling and moiling with a dictionary to get it translated. At times I am ready to explode with impatience; the blood rushes to my head and I would just as soon hurl the dictionary on the floor—and you call that reading—you must be joking! No, thank God, I am soon finished with the translation and then, yes, then, I shall read my beloved's letter; that is something altogether different. But to whom am I speaking . . . . . stupid fellow, get out of my sight; I would rather not see you—how could you think of insulting my beloved and me by calling this reading a letter from her! And yet, stay, stay—you know very well I am only joking. I would ever so much like to have you stay, but, to be honest, I have no time. There is still something left to translate and I am so impatient to begin reading it—therefore do not be angry, but please go so I can finish."

XII
317

So, then, with regard to the letter from his beloved, the lover distinguishes between reading and reading, between reading with a dictionary and reading the letter from his beloved. The blood rushes to his head in his impatience when he sits and grinds away at reading with the dictionary; he becomes furious when his friend dares to call this learned reading a reading of the letter from his beloved. Now he is finished with the translation—now he reads his beloved's letter. He regarded, if you please, all these scholarly preliminaries as a necessary evil so that he can come to the point—of reading the letter from his beloved.

Let us not discard the metaphor too soon. Let us assume that this letter from the beloved contained not only an expression of affection, as such letters ordinarily do, but that it contained a wish, something the beloved wished her lover to do. It was, let us assume, much that was required of him, very much; any third party would consider that there was good reason to think better of it, but the lover—he is off at once to fulfill his beloved's wish. Let us assume that after some time the lovers met and the beloved said, "But, my dear, that was not at all what I asked you to do; you must have misunderstood the word or translated it incorrectly." Do you think that the lover would now regret rushing off straightway that very second to obey the wish instead of first entertaining some doubts, and then perhaps getting the help of a few additional dictionaries, and then having some more misgivings, and then perhaps getting the word translated correctly and consequently being exempt—do you believe that he regrets the mistake, do you believe that he pleases his beloved less?

XII
324

The second requirement is that in order to see yourself in the mirror when you read God's Word you must (so that you actually do come to see yourself in the mirror) re-

*member to say to yourself incessantly: It is I to whom it is speaking; it is I about whom
it is speaking.*

Do not let yourself be deceived—or do not yourself be cunning. In relation to God and God's Word—oh, we humans are so sly, even the most stupid of us is so sly—indeed, flesh and blood and self-love are very sly.

Hence we have fabricated the notion (we do not say that it is in order to
defend ourselves against God's Word—we are not that crazy—if we said that,
we would of course have no profit from our sagacious fabrication), we have
fabricated the notion that to think about oneself is—just imagine how sly!—
vanity, morbid vanity (which it may indeed be in many cases, but not when
it is a matter of letting God's Word have power over oneself). Fie on me if
I were to be so vain! To think about myself and to say "It is I" is, as we scholars say, the subjective, and the subjective is vanity, this vanity of not being
able to read a book—God's Word!—without thinking that it is about me.
Should I not abhor being vain! Should I be so stupid as not to abhor it when
I thereby also make sure that God's Word cannot take hold of me because I
do not place myself in any personal (subjective) relation to the Word, but
on the contrary—ah, what earnestness, for which I am then so highly
commended by men—change the Word into an impersonal something (the
objective, an objective doctrine, etc.), to which I—both earnest and cultured!—relate myself objectively. Thus I am not so uncultured and vain that
I bring my personality into the picture or think that it is I to whom it is
speaking, I—and incessantly I—of whom it speaks. May I never be guilty of
such vain lack of breeding—and may what could so easily happen never happen—namely, that the Word would take hold of me, precisely me, gain power   XII
over me so that I could not defend myself against it, so that it would go on   325
pursuing me until I either acted according to it, renouncing the world, or at
least admitted that I did not do it—a just punishment for anyone who lets
himself deal with God's Word in such an uncultured way.

No, no, no! When you read God's Word, in everything you read, continually to say to yourself: It is I to whom it is speaking, it is I about whom it is
speaking—this is earnestness, precisely this is earnestness. Not a single one
of those to whom the cause of Christianity in the higher sense has been entrusted forgot to urge this again and again as most crucial, as unconditionally the condition if you are to come to see yourself in the mirror. Consequently, this is what you have to do; while you are reading you must
incessantly say to yourself: It is I to whom it is speaking, it is I about whom
it is speaking.

That mighty emperor in the East, whose wrath the renowned little nation
had incurred, is said to have had a slave who every day said to him: Remember to take revenge.[225] That was indeed something to remember; it
seems to me it would have been better to have a slave who reminded him

every day to forget. Yet this is not such a good thing either, because if one is reminded every day to forget, one never does really forget. But in any case this sovereign understood very well—precisely because he was angry (and anger, though not commendable, is a quality of personality)—the conduct required when an impression is to be made personally on someone.

But King David was served even better than this sovereign—it is, of course, the kind of service that a person himself rarely chooses voluntarily; he is tempted rather to regard it as one of life's greatest inconveniences.

The story to which I refer is well known.[226] King David saw Bathsheba. To see her—and to see that her husband stood in the way—they were the same. Consequently, he must be removed. And that is what happened. It is not known for sure how it happened—there must be a Governance—he fell in battle. But the king says, "That's the way war is." Probably the man himself rashly chose a post so dangerous that it meant certain death—I merely say that if there was someone who wished him dead he could, if he had control of such things, never have done better than to assign him to the post that was certain death. Now he is out of the way. It all happened very easily. So now there is no longer anything in the way of coming into legal possession of his wife. Anything in the way—are you daft? After all, it is ever so noble and magnanimous, a genuinely kingly act that will inspire the whole military, that a king marries the widow of a warrior who fell for his fatherland.

Then one day a prophet came to King David. Let us make the situation really contemporary and modernize it a bit. The one is the king, the highest-ranking man in the nation; the other is the prophet, a respected man in the nation. Both, of course, are cultured men, and one can be sure that their association with each other, their conversation, will bear the unqualified mark of culture. Moreover, they are both, especially one of them, famous authors, King David the most famous poet and, it goes without saying, a connoisseur, an expert on matters of taste, who knows how to evaluate the exposition and the choice of expressions and the structure of a poem, the style and tone of its language, and its benefit or detriment to morals etc.

And it is very fortunate; he is just the right man to come to, because the prophet has written a short story, a tale he wants to have the honor of reciting before His Majesty, the crowned poet and connoisseur of poetical works.

"There lived two men in a certain city. The one was very rich and had great herds of livestock, large and small, but the poor man had only a little lamb that he had bought and raised and that had grown up with him together with his children. It ate from his hand and drank from his cup, and it was like a child in the home. But when a traveler came to the rich man, he spared his livestock, large and small, and took the poor man's sheep, slaughtered it, and prepared it for the stranger who had come to him."

I imagine that David listened attentively and thereupon declared his judgment, did not, of course, intrude his personality (subjectivity) but impersonally (objectively) evaluated this charming little work. Perhaps there had been a detail he thought could be different; he perhaps suggested a more felicitously chosen phrase, perhaps also pointed out a little fault in the structure, praised the prophet's masterly presentation of the story, his voice, gestures—in short, expressed his opinion the way we cultured people today tend to judge a sermon for the cultured—that is, a sermon that is itself also objective.

Then the prophet says to him, "Thou art the man." XII
327

See, the tale the prophet told was a story, but this "Thou art the man"— this was another story—this was the transition to the subjective.

My listener, I have something more I would like to say, but I shall cast it in a form that at first glance you may find not quite solemn. Yet I do it deliberately and advisedly, for I believe that precisely in this way it will make a truer impression on you. XII
368

Once upon a time there was a rich man. At an exorbitant price he had purchased abroad a team of entirely flawless, splendid horses, which he had wanted for his own pleasure and the pleasure of driving them himself. About a year or two passed by. If anyone who had known these horses earlier now saw him driving them, he would not be able to recognize them: their eyes had become dull and drowsy; their gait lacked style and precision; they had no staying power, no endurance; he could drive them scarcely four miles without having to stop on the way, and sometimes they came to a standstill just when he was driving his best; moreover, they had acquired all sorts of quirks and bad habits, and although they of course had plenty of feed they grew thinner day by day.

Then he called in the royal coachmen. He drove them for a month. In the whole countryside there was not a team of horses that carried their heads so proudly, whose eyes were so fiery, whose gait was so beautiful; there was no team of horses that could hold out running as they did, even thirty miles in a stretch without stopping. How did this happen? It is easy to see: the owner, who without being a coachman meddled with being a coachman, drove the horses according to the horses' understanding of what it is to drive; the royal coachman drove them according to the coachman's understanding of what it is to drive.

So also with us human beings. When I think of myself and the countless people I have come to know, I have often said to myself sadly: Here are capacities and talents and qualifications enough, but the coachman is lacking. For a long time now, from generation to generation, we humans have been, if I may put it this way (in order to carry on the metaphor), driven according to the horses' understanding of driving; we are governed, educated, and brought up according to mankind's conception of what it means to be a human being. See, because of this we lack elevation and it follows from this in turn that we are able to endure very little; we are impatient and promptly use the means of the moment and impatiently want to see instantly the reward for our work, which for that very reason is not very good.

Things were different once. There was a time when it pleased the Deity himself, if I may put it this way, to be the coachman; and he drove the horses according to the coachman's understanding of what it is to drive. Oh, what a human being was capable of then!

Ponder the text for today! There sit twelve men, all belonging to the social class we call the common man. Him whom they worshiped as God, their Lord and Master, they have seen crucified; they can be said to have witnessed the loss of everything in a way that can never be said of anyone else, even in the remotest manner. True, he thereupon ascended victorious into heaven— but that of course also means he is gone—and now they are sitting there and waiting for the Spirit to be communicated to them in order that they, cursed by the little nation to which they belong, can proclaim a teaching that will arouse the hatred of the whole world against them. This is the task; these twelve men are supposed to transform the world, and on the most appalling scale, against its will. Here, truly, the understanding comes to a halt! Even now, long after, in forming a faint conception of it the understanding comes to a halt—if one still has any at all. It is enough to drive one out of one's mind, if one still has any from which to be driven.

It is Christianity that must go through. And these twelve men carried it through. In one sense, they were men like us, but they were driven well— yes, indeed, they were driven well.

Then came the next generation. They carried Christianity through. They were men just like us—but they were driven well! Yes, indeed, that they were! They were like that team of horses when the royal coachman drove them. Never has a human being lifted his head as proudly in elevation over the world as did the first Christians in humility before God! And just as that team of horses could run if need be thirty miles without pausing to catch their wind, so also did they run; they ran seventy years in a stretch without getting out of the harness, without stopping anywhere. No, proud as they were in their humility before God, they said, "It is not for us to hang back and dawdle along the way; we do not stop—until eternity." It was Christianity that had to go through, and they carried it through, yes, that they did; but they were also driven well, yes, that they were!

O Holy Spirit—we pray for ourselves and for all people—O Holy Spirit, you who give life, here there is no want of capabilities, nor of education, nor of sagacity—indeed, there may rather be too much. But what is wanting is

that you take away whatever is corrupting to us, that you take power away from us and give life. Certainly a person experiences a shudder like death's shudder when you, in order to become the power in us, take power away from him. Oh, but if even animals at a later moment understand how good it was for them that the royal coachman took the reins, although it surely made them shudder at first and they at first rebelled, but in vain—should not a human being quickly be able to understand what a blessing it is to him that you take the power and give life!

JUDGE FOR YOURSELF! FOR SELF-EXAMINATION RECOMMENDED TO THE PRESENT AGE SECOND SERIES (1851–52, PUBLISHED 1876) BY S. KIERKEGAARD

The original title of *Judge for Yourself!* was "For Self-Examination/Recommended to the Present Age, No. 2," which finally became the subtitle of the work as the sequel to *For Self-Examination*, No. 1, or the first series. A deletion from the final copy of *For Self-Examination*[227] indicates Kierkegaard's leaning toward an explicit critique of the cultural accommodation of Christianity symbolized by the leadership of Bishop Jakob Mynster, whom he personally respected and loved. A note (March 1855) appended to the posthumously published *Judge for Yourself!* explains why it was not published during Kierkegaard's lifetime—a bracketing of direct criticism in the hope and expectation that Mynster would make an admission. "This book is from the time when the old bishop was still living. Therefore it has been kept at a distance both because at the time I understood my relation to the established order that way and because out of respect for the old bishop I also very much wanted to understand my relation that way. Now I speak much more decisively, unreservedly, truly, without, however, thereby implying that what I said earlier was untrue."[228] In substance, *Judge For Yourself!* is in continuity with earlier works but with special emphasis on imitation of the prototype and on the concept of "jest." Along with irony as the incognito of the ethical and humor as the incognito of the religious (*Postscript*), the "jest" denotes the indicative-ethics side of imitation in response to the gift, imitation transformed from the imperative of requirement into an expression of gratitude—action as a gesture pointing to the gift.

CHRIST AS THE PROTOTYPE, OR NO ONE CAN SERVE TWO MASTERS

But there is an even higher godly understanding that we learn from the bird: that again it is indeed God who works, God who sows and reaps when man sows and reaps. Think of little Ludvig! He has now become an adult and
therefore very well understands the true situation—that it was his mother who pushed the stroller. Thus he has another joy from this childhood recollection: remembering his mother's love that could think of something like that to delight her child. But now he is an adult; now he actually can do it himself. Now he is perhaps even tempted to think that he himself actually is able—until that recollection of childhood reminds him how much he is, in a far higher sense, still in the same situation as the child, that when the adult works it really is someone else—it is God who is working. Do you think that he will therefore become inactive and lazy and say: Well, if it is really God who is working, would it not be best that I be exempted? If so, then this man is a fool, not to say a shameless scoundrel, in whom God can have no joy, and

who himself can have no joy in the bird, and who deserves nothing better than to have our Lord show him the gate, and then he can see what will become of him. But the worthy, honest, God-fearing worker, he becomes all the more industrious, so that he will increasingly understand—what a gracious jest [*Spøg*]!—that God is the co-worker—what earnestness! Created in the image of God as he is, with head erect, he looks toward the heavens at the bird [*Fugl*]—the jester [*Spøgefugl*] from whom he learns the earnestness that it is God who sows and harvests and gathers into barns. But he does not sink into inactivity; he immediately sets to his work and tends to it—otherwise he does not really come to see that it is God who sows and reaps and gathers into barns.

You lily of the field, you bird of the air! How much we owe to you! Some of our best and most blessed hours. When the Gospel appointed you as prototype and schoolmaster, the Law was abrogated and jest was assigned its place in the kingdom of heaven; thus we are no longer under the strict disciplinarian but under the Gospel: "Consider the lilies of the field; look at the birds of the air!"

But then does this whole matter of following [*følge efter*] Christ, of imitation [*Efterfølgelse*], does this perhaps become a jest? He himself helped us by not saying "Look at me" but "Consider the lilies; look at the birds!" He pointed away from [himself], and we—well, we cannot be blamed for doing it—we only all too willingly took the hint. Sagacious as we all are when it comes to sparing flesh and blood, we sagaciously understood all too well what had been granted to us in having such prototypes, and we became inexhaustible in dressing it up—and only with a certain secret horror giving thought to the earnestness: the imitation of Christ.

No, we cannot be permitted to have it quite that way; that would make the Gospel so easy that basically it would become poetry—which is just what *the imitation of Christ* is intended to prevent.

XII
456

The lily and the bird certainly can with truth be said to serve only one master, but this is still only metaphorical and here a person's obligation *to imitate* is a poetic expression, just as the lily and the bird, considered as teachers, are in the strictest sense without authority. Moreover, if a person, with the lily and the bird as prototypes, lived in such a way as presented above, so that he thought the thought of God in everything, this is indeed piety, and a piety, entirely pure, that surely is never seen among men. But in the strictest sense this is still not Christianity; it is really Jewish piety. What is crucial in Christianity is not manifested here at all: to suffer because one adheres to God—or, as it is called, to suffer for the doctrine—the true imitation of Christ.

Alas, yes, what Christianity is seems to have been completely forgotten in Christendom. If someone were to present it even approximately, people would not be far from imagining it to be cruelty, human torture he himself has thought up—to such a degree does suffering for the Word or for the doctrine go hand in hand with Christianity, to such a degree that if someone presents it even approximately truly he will immediately incur human disfavor. As stated, despite the millions of copies of the New Testament in circulation, despite the fact that everyone possesses the New Testament, is baptized, confirmed, and calls himself a Christian, and that a thousand preachers preach every blessed Sunday—people nevertheless will not be far from insisting that it is *that* person's own invention when he, quite simply, draws out of the New Testament what is clearly there and in clear words, which, however, from generation to generation we human beings have most cavalierly left out, without therefore admitting that what we have retained under the name of Christianity is anything other than the pure, the sound, unadulterated doctrine.

Imitation, the imitation of Christ, is really the point from which the human race shrinks. The main difficulty lies here; here is where it is really decided whether or not one is willing to accept Christianity. If there is emphasis on this point, the stronger the emphasis the fewer the Christians. If there is a scaling down at this point (so that Christianity becomes, intellectually, a doctrine), more people enter into Christianity. If it is abolished completely (so that Christianity becomes, existentially, as easy as mythology and poetry and imitation an exaggeration, a ludicrous exaggeration), then Christianity spreads to such a degree that Christendom and the world are almost indistinguishable, or all become Christians; Christianity has completely conquered—that is, it is abolished!

Oh, that there had been awareness of this in time; then the situation in Christendom would have been different from what it is now. But since human obstinacy, in its unwillingness to hear anything about imitation, became more and more threatening, since hirelings and human slaves or at least only very weak believers undertook to be proclaimers of the Word, the history of Christendom, from generation to generation, became a story of steadily scaling down the price of what it is to be a Christian. At last it came to be such a ridiculously low price that soon it had the opposite effect that people scarcely wanted to have anything to do with Christianity, because through this false leniency it had become so sickly and cloying that it was disgusting. To be a Christian—well, if only one does not literally steal, does not literally make stealing one's occupation, since to be a thief in one's occupation can very well be combined with being an earnest Christian who goes to Communion once a year or to church a few times a year, at least on New Year's Day for sure. To be a Christian—well, if in committing adultery one does not overdo or, forsaking the golden mean, carry it to extremes, since observing—decorum!—that is, secretly with good taste and culture, it can still be combined with being an earnest Christian who listens to a sermon at least once for every fourteen times he reads comedies and novels. And that anything should stand in the way of completely conforming to the nature of the world by using every sagacious way to guarantee the greatest possible earthly advantage, enjoyment, etc., that anything should stand in the way of superbly combining this with being an earnest Christian—that would be a ludicrous exaggeration, an effrontery, if someone dared to propose anything like that to us, the height of folly by anyone who would dare to do that, since there would not be a single person who would reflect upon—what is said in the New Testament, or that it is said there. This is a *wohlfeil* [cheap] edition of what it is to be a Christian. Yet this is the actual state of affairs, because preachers' declaiming about the lofty virtues etc. during a quiet hour on Sunday does not alter the actual state of affairs on Monday, since people account for such a proclamation as being the preacher's official job and his livelihood, and since many a clergyman's life certainly is not different from that actual state of affairs—but it is actual existence that preaches—all that with the mouth and the arms is no good.

XII
458

But there were also those who maintained Christianity higher in price but never higher than the kind of quiet piety that under the leniency of grace thinks quite often about God, expects every good thing from his fatherly hand, and seeks consolation from him in life's need.

To suffer for the doctrine—the imitation of Christ—this has been completely abolished, long, long ago consigned to oblivion. Since one cannot very well completely avoid speaking about imitation in the sermon discourse (although some have known how to arrange things so it could be done), it is done in such a way that the really crucial part is suppressed and replaced by something else: that one ought to put up with life's adversities with patience etc.

But *imitation* has been abolished. Established Christendom, if it could happen to hear above the laughter, would surely be profoundly amazed if it were to hear that this is the teaching of the New Testament and of all true Christians in accordance with the New Testament, that suffering for the doctrine is part of being a true Christian. To suffer for the doctrine—to serve only one master to that degree, to imitate the prototype in such a way that one suffers for being a Christian! To suffer for the doctrine—"No, now I think," Christendom would undoubtedly say, "now I think that the man has really gone out of his mind; to require that one must suffer for the doctrine, to become addicted to Christianity to such a degree is much worse than to become addicted to gaming, drinking, whoring. Let it be as the preachers proclaim—namely, that Christianity is the gentle comfort, a kind of insurance for eternity. That's more like it, that we can willingly give our money to—and perhaps the preachers' salaries are high enough so that thus far we can be said to suffer for the doctrine. But to have to pay to have that proclaimed, that we must suffer for the doctrine—the man is stark mad." Yet the guilt is not his; the "stark madness" is really that in the proclaiming of Christianity they have left out and suppressed what does not please the secular and earthly mentality and thus have induced all this worldliness to imagine that it is Christian.

If only there had been resistance on this point of imitation! If people, having learned from the errors of the past, had only truly resisted on this point! It did not happen. Therefore it must be done. *Imitation,* which corresponds to Christ as the prototype, must—if there is to be any meaning in Christendom—must be affirmed again, but in such a way, as we said, that something has been learned from the error of the past.

Without introducing *imitation,* it is impossible to gain mastery over doubts. Therefore, the state of things in Christendom is such that doubt has replaced faith. And then they want to stop doubt with—reasons; and they still are moving in that direction. They still have not learned that it is wasted effort—indeed, that it feeds doubt, gives it a basis for continuing. They are still not aware that *imitation* is the only force that, like a police force, can break up the mob of doubts and clear the area and compel one, if one does not want to be an *imitator,* at least to go home and hold one's tongue.

Imitation, which corresponds to *Christ as prototype,* must be advanced, be affirmed, be called to our attention.

Let us examine this matter from the beginning but with all brevity. The Savior of the world, our Lord Jesus Christ, did not come to the world in order to bring a doctrine; he never lectured. Since he did not bring a doctrine, he did not try by way of reasons to prevail upon anyone to accept the doctrine, nor did he try to authenticate it by proofs. His teaching was really his life, his existence. If someone wanted to be his follower, his approach, as seen in the Gospel, was different from lecturing. To such a person he said something like this: Venture a decisive act; then we can begin. What does that mean? It means that one does not become a Christian by hearing something about Christianity, by reading something about it, by thinking about it, or, while Christ was living, by seeing him once in a while or by going and staring at him all day long. No, a *setting* [*Bestedelse*] (*situation*) is required—venture a decisive act; the proof does not precede but follows, is in and with the imitation that follows Christ. That is, when you have ventured the decisive act, you become heterogeneous with the life of this world, cannot have your life in it, come into collision with it. Then you will gradually be brought into such tension that you will be able to become aware of what I am talking about. The tension will also have the effect upon you that you understand that you cannot endure it without having recourse to me—and then we can begin. Could one expect anything else from *the truth?* Must it not express that it is the pupil who needs the teacher, "the sick who needs the physician,"[229] and not the reverse, as Christianity was later proclaimed, so that it is "the physician who needs the patients," the teacher who needs the pupils. And therefore it inevitably, just as with any other seller, who does not, after all, demand that an esteemed public buy a pig in a poke, must be at the public's service with reasons, proofs, letters of recommendation from others who have been helped or instructed, etc. But the divine truth! That it conducts itself differently is not due to what could be called divine exclusiveness. No, no, in that respect as in everything, the Savior of the world was indeed willing to humble himself, but it cannot be otherwise.

We shall not dwell at this time on how Christianity gradually spread in the world; we hasten on to a specific point that is crucial to the situation in contemporary Christendom.

We pause for a moment at the Middle Ages. However great its errors were, its conception of Christianity has a decisive advantage over that of our time. The Middle Ages conceived of Christianity along the lines of action, life, existence-transformation. This is the merit. It is another matter that some of the actions they hit upon were strange, that it could think that in itself fasting was Christianity, that entering the monastery, giving everything to the poor, not to mention what we can scarcely mention without smiling— scourging oneself, crawling on one's knees, standing on one leg, etc.—that this was supposed to be true imitation. This was an error. And just as when someone has taken a wrong road and pushes ahead on it, he goes further and further away from the truth, deeper and deeper into error, and it becomes worse and worse—so also here. Something worse than the first error did not fail to appear: they came up with the idea of meritoriousness, thought that they earned merit before God through their good works. And it became worse: they thought they had merit to such a degree through their good works that they thought they benefited not only the person himself but one could, like a capitalist and bondsman, let others benefit. And it grew worse; it became an out-and-out business: people who had never once thought of producing some of these so-called good works themselves now had plenty to do with good works, inasmuch as they were put into business as hucksters who sold the good works of others at fixed but cheap prices.

Then Luther appears. This condition, he declares, is spiritlessness, dreadful spiritlessness; otherwise you who think to earn salvation by good works are bound to perceive that this is the sure road either to *presumptuousness,* consequently to the loss of salvation, or to *despair,* consequently to the loss of salvation. To want to build upon good works—the more you practice them, the stricter you are with yourself, the more you merely develop the anxiety in you, and new anxiety. On this road, if a person is not completely devoid of spirit, on this road he comes only to the very opposite of peace and rest for his soul, to discord and unrest. No, a person is justified solely by faith. Therefore, in God's name, to hell with the pope and all his helpers' helpers, and away with the monastery, together with all your fasting, scourging, and all the monkey antics that came into use under the name of imitation.

But let us not forget, Luther did not therefore abolish imitation, nor did he do away with the voluntary, as pampered sentimentality would like to have us think about Luther. He affirmed imitation in the direction of witnessing to the truth and voluntarily exposed himself there to dangers enough (yet without deluding himself that this was meritorious). Indeed, it was not the pope who attacked Luther, but it was Luther who attacked the pope; and although Luther was not put to death, his life was nevertheless, humanly speaking, a sacrificed life, a life sacrificed to witnessing to the truth.

Present-day Christendom, at least that which I am talking about, adheres to Luther; it is another matter whether Luther could acknowledge it, whether the turn that Luther made cannot all too easily become a wrong road as soon as there is no Luther whose life makes the true turn the truth. In any case, if someone wants to see whether there are some dubious aspects in the contemporary situation, it is certainly best to look back to Luther and the turn he made.

The error from which Luther turned was an exaggeration with regard to works. And he was entirely right; he did not make a mistake—a person is justified solely and only by faith. That is the way he talked and taught—and believed. And that this was not taking grace in vain—to that his life witnessed. Splendid!

But already the next generation slackened; it did not turn with horror away from exaggeration with regard to works (in which exaggeration Luther lived) toward faith. No, it made the Lutheran position into doctrine, and in this way faith also diminished in vital power. Then it diminished from generation to generation. Works—well, God knows there was no longer any question about that; it would be a shame to accuse this later age of exaggeration with regard to works, and neither were people so silly that they presumed to want to have merit for what they exempted themselves from doing. But, now, faith—I wonder if it is to be found on earth?

THE BOOK ON ADLER.

THE RELIGIOUS CONFUSION OF THE PRESENT AGE

ILLUSTRATED BY MAGISTER ADLER

AS A PHENOMENON. A MIMICAL MONOGRAPH

(1846–55, PUBLISHED IN

EFTERLADTE PAPIRER, II, 1872)

BY PETRUS MINOR

EDITED BY S. KIERKEGAARD

Kierkegaard revised the manuscript of "The Book on Adler" in three integral versions and then in two partial versions after it was "chopped into pieces."[230] None of the versions was published until Version I appeared in the first edition of the *Papirer* in 1872. *The Book on Adler* in the *Kierkegaard's Writings* edition is the third integral version modified in parts according to changes in later versions. Ostensibly the work is about Adolph Peter Adler, who claimed to have received a revelation. Essentially it is about the concept of authority, an issue that appears on various levels and in various contexts in many of the works beginning with *The Concept of Irony.* In the series of revised versions, Adler becomes more and more a *"Nebensach* [side-issue],"[231] and the substantive issue becomes more prominent. The long process of writing, revising, and restructuring makes the work unique in the authorship. Many students of Kierkegaard's writings agree with Johannes Hohlenberg's judgment: "Hence the book is extraordinarily revealing, because it shows the workings of Kierkegaard's mind better than any of the other books. If we want to get an idea of what qualitative dialectic has to say when turned upon a very definite question, we ought to study the book about Adler."[232]

THE essentially Christian *has* no history, because the essentially Christian is this paradox, that God once came into existence in time. This is the offense, but also the point of departure; whether it is eighteen hundred years ago or yesterday, one can equally well be contemporary with it. Just as the North Star never changes its position and therefore has no history, so this paradox stands unmoved and unaltered; and if Christianity existed for ten thousand years, one would not in the decisive sense get any further away from it than the contemporaries were. The distance is not to be measured with the quantifying of time and space, since the qualitatively decisive distance is that it is a paradox. Neither is the history of Christianity related directly to the essentially Christian in the way the survival of a tree in its growing is related to the sprout. The essentially Christian is something eternally concluded to which nothing is to be added or subtracted, and in every generation and in every individual, if he is truly a Christian, the beginning is from the begin-

VII²
B 235
78

VII²
B 235
79

ning, from that paradox. The beginning is not there where the previous generation left off, but from the beginning.

As soon, however, as one confuses Christianity and the essentially Christian, as soon as one begins to count the years, one begins to want to change the improbable into the probable. One says: Now Christianity has survived (the essentially Christian, of course, is a fact since eighteen hundred years *ago*) for three hundred years, now for seven hundred, now for eighteen hundred—well, then it certainly must be true. By this procedure one manages to confuse everything. The decision (to become a Christian) easily becomes a sheer triviality for the individual. It is already easy enough for him to accept the customs in the city where he lives, because the great majority do that; so would it not be altogether natural that he would become a Christian *along with* them—when Christianity has survived for eighteen hundred years! On the other hand, Christianity is weakened, made into a triviality with the aid of the distance, with the aid of the eighteen hundred years. Something, if it happened contemporaneously, that would horrify people, would radically disturb their lives, something, if it happened contemporaneously, that they would either find offensive, would hate and persecute, if possible eradicate, or believing accept—that seems to be something one can believe and accept as a matter of course (that is, leave it undecided) since it was eighteen hundred years ago. Contemporaneity is the tension that does not permit a person to leave it undecided but compels one either to be offended or to believe. The distance, on the other hand, is the indulgence that encourages lethargy to the degree that the believing acceptance of something as a matter of course becomes identical with leaving it undecided. Why is it that no contemporary age can get along with witnesses to the truth, and the man is scarcely dead before all can get along with him splendidly? This happens because his contemporaries, as long as he is living and they are living with him in the situation of contemporaneity, feel the sting of his existence; he forces them to a more strenuous decision. But when he is dead, then they can very well be good friends with him and admire him—that is, thoughtlessly and comfortably just leave the whole thing undecided. I wonder why Socrates compared himself to a gadfly if it was not because he understood that his life among his contemporaries was a sting. When he was dead, they idolized him. When a person experiences a little event in his life, he learns something from it, and why? Because the event really comes to grips with him. The same person, however, can sit in the theater and see great scenes of tragedy, he can read about the extraordinary in the newspaper, he can listen to the pastor, and it all really makes no impression, and why? Because he does not become contemporary with it, because in the first two instances he lacks imagination; in the last he lacks the inner experience for really becoming contemporary with what is depicted, because he thinks like this: It is, of course, many years since it happened.

So now when for many years a disoriented orthodoxy, which does not

VII²
B 235
80

know what it is doing, and a rebellious heterodoxy, which daimonically knows what it is doing and only to that extent does not know what it is doing, with the aid of the eighteen hundred years have joined forces to confuse everything, to give rise to one illusion more lunatic than the other, the one paralogism worse than the other, the one μετάβασις εἰς ἄλλο γένος [shifting from one genus to another] more confusing than the other—then the main task now is to be able to get the terrain cleared, to eliminate the eighteen hundred years, so that the essentially Christian occurs for us as if it occurred today. It is the eighteen hundred years that have inflated the objections to Christianity and the defense of it into volumes. It is the sixteen hundred, the seventeen hundred, the eighteen hundred years that have anesthetized the defenders and helped the attackers. It is the eighteen hundred years that have kept the lives of countless people in a delusion. With the aid of the eighteen hundred years, the defenders have invertedly made Christianity into a hypothesis, and the attackers have made it into nothing.

VII² B 235 81

What the nothing but busy Johannes Climacus has done in this regard to ferret out every illusion, trap every paralogism, catch every deceitful locution cannot be repeated here. He has done it in such a way that every more scholarly, cultured person, if he will earnestly spend a little time in the daily practice of the dialectical, will readily understand it. It certainly is not done in any other way, and it cannot be done in any other way either. Such things cannot be presented in a newspaper and be read "while one shaves."²³³ It must be left up to the newspapers to write for busy people like that. Climacus's exposition is rigorous, as the matter entails. His merit is this: with the help of dialectic, to have imaginatively drawn (as one says of a telescope) that which is unshakably the essentially Christian so close to the eye that the reader is prevented from looking mistakenly at the eighteen hundred years. His merit is with the help of dialectic to have procured the view, the perspective. To direct one's eyes toward a star is not very difficult, because the air is like an empty space and thus there is as good as nothing in the way that stops or distracts the gaze. But it is otherwise when the direction the eye is to take is straight ahead, as down a road, and there are also throngs and crowds and disturbance and noise and busyness that the eye must penetrate in order to get the view, while every side glance, indeed, every blinking of the eyes, completely disturbs qualitatively; and it becomes even more difficult when one must also stand in an environment that *pro virili* [with all its might] works to keep one from getting the view. —And yet contemporaneity with what is unshakably the essentially Christian is decisive. But this contemporaneity is to be understood to mean the same as it did for those who were living when Christ lived.

VII² B 235 82

VII² B 235 83

VII² B 235 84

What is needed above all is to get the huge libraries and scribblings and the eighteen hundred years out of the way in order to gain the view. This is by no means a rash requirement by a high-flying dialectician; it is an alto-

VII² B 235 85

gether modest and genuine religious requirement that everyone must make—not for the sake of scholarship and the public, but for one's own sake, purely personally for one's own sake, if one is earnest about becoming a Christian; and it is what Christianity itself must require. The essentially Christian wants to stand unshaken like the North Star and therefore wants to stay out of the nonsense that only deprives it of life.

Yet the contemporaneity discussed here is not *the contemporaneity of an apostle,* inasmuch as he was called by a revelation *but is only the contemporaneity that every contemporary had: the possibility in the tension of contemporaneity of having to be offended or to lay hold of faith.* To that end it is particularly necessary that there be an airing out in such a way that it, as at one time, becomes possible for a person to be offended in earnest or, believing, to appropriate the essentially Christian, lest it turn out with the essentially Christian as with a court case when it has been left undecided from time immemorial, so that one is all at sea because of the abundance of knowledge. The situation of contemporaneity is the creating of tension that gives the categories qualitative elasticity, and what a big dunce he must be who does not know what an infinite difference it makes when one for one's own sake considers something in the situation of contemporaneity and when one casually thinks about something in the delusion that it was eighteen hundred years ago—in the delusion, yes, in the delusion, inasmuch as, precisely because the essentially Christian is the qualitative paradox, it is a delusion that eighteen hundred years are longer ago than yesterday.

If the situation in Christendom at present is such that it is particularly to the point to put an end to this tenacious apathy connected with the eighteen hundred years, then one cannot deny that the sudden appearance of a man who appealed to a revelation could provide a desirable stimulus, because then an analogous situation of contemporaneity is formed. No thanks, all the profound and speculative and learned and perspiring prattlers, who can very well understand that eighteen hundred years ago one had a revelation—they would be in a predicament. The one who can at all understand that a person has a revelation must understand it equally well if it happened six thousand years ago or it will happen six thousand years hence or it happens today. But perhaps the prattler has Christianly made a living on the eighteen hundred years, has prattled himself into thinking that he could understand it— because it was eighteen hundred years ago. If the matter were not so serious, I cannot deny that I would regard it as altogether the most exquisite comedy that could ever be written in the world: to have all the modern exegesis and dogmatics go through their courses—in the situation of contemporaneity. All those deceptive psychological devices, all that "to a certain degree" and then again to a certain degree, all that bravura of profundity, and then above all the showy mediation that explains—all that, since what is explained occurred eighteen hundred years ago, would make a splendid show-

VII²
B 235
86

ing in contemporaneity with what was reinterpreted. It is altogether certain that one single Aristophanean comedy in that style would clear up the confusion of modern Christian scholarship much better than all scholarly combat.

Therefore when I, without as yet having seen his sermons and the preface to them, heard that Magister Adler had come forward and had appealed to a revelation, I cannot deny that I was astounded; I thought: either this is the man we need, the chosen one, who in divine originality has the new spring to refresh the lifeless soil of Christendom, or it is an offended person, but a crafty knave, who, in order to demolish everything, brings a Christendom like the present one to the strenuous decision of having to go through its dogmatics in the situation of contemporaneity.

Given the latter assumption, I certainly would have been surprised if an offended person actually had been so sagacious. Although one cannot deny offended people talent and daimonic inspiration, they ordinarily nevertheless tend to be somewhat obtuse on the whole—that is, they really do not know quite how one is to go about the matter in order to do harm. They attack Christianity, but they place themselves outside it, and for that very reason they do no harm. No, the offended person must try to come to grips with Christianity in a completely different way, try to push up like a mole in the middle of Christendom. Suppose that Feuerbach,[234] instead of attacking Christianity, had gone about it more craftily. Suppose that he had laid out his plan in daimonic silence and then stepped forward and announced that he had had a revelation, and now suppose that he, like a criminal who is able to stick to a lie, had stuck unshakably to this story while he also sagaciously had found out all the weak sides of orthodoxy, which he nevertheless by no means attacked but only, with a certain innocent naïveté, knew how to hold up to the light. Suppose that he had done it so well that no one could get wise to his slyness—he would have brought orthodoxy into the worst predicament. In the interest of the established order, orthodoxy fights to maintain the appearance that in a way we all are Christians, that the country is Christian and the congregations are Christians. When someone places himself on the outside and attacks Christianity, then, if he is victorious, the congregation is supposed to be troubled out of its cozy routine of being Christians in a way like most people; it is supposed to come to the decision to give up Christianity. What an inconvenience; no, then it is better to stick with the old. See, this is why the offended person achieves nothing.

Furthermore, when someone attacks Christianity and places himself on the outside, orthodoxy defends it by means of the eighteen hundred years; it speaks in lofty tones about the extraordinary acts of God in the past, that is, eighteen hundred years ago. As for the extraordinary and the extraordinary acts of God, it must be said that people lap it up the more easily the longer ago it was. So the offended person attacks Christianity; orthodoxy de-

VII²
B 235
87

fends it with the help of the distance, and the congregation thinks as follows: If it was eighteen hundred years ago, then one can surely understand that something extraordinary happened. The offended one again achieves nothing. It would, however, have been different if he himself had ingeniously stepped forward with a revelation, if he, confoundedly well schooled in orthodoxy, knew how to conceal his daimonic sagacity in a singularly innocent naïveté, by means of which he would continually get orthodoxy into hot water, while like a burr he stuck firmly to orthodoxy. On the one hand, orthodoxy could not very well bring itself to deny that it was orthodoxy that he presented; on the other hand, it would be very damaging to have it said in such a direct way, which would force orthodoxy to make a clean breast of it in a situation of contemporaneity.

It is frequently said that if Christ appeared today—in Christendom—if he in an even stricter sense than formerly "came to his own,"[235] he would again be crucified. If it should be that the death penalty had been abolished, he would suffer the punishment that has replaced the death penalty, and orthodoxy in particular would be zealous to have him arrested and convicted. And why would it presumably happen this way again? Because contemporaneity provides the appropriate qualitative pressure; distance, however, helps both to make something into nothing and to make something into the extraordinary almost in the sense of nothing. Why, indeed, were almost all offended by Christ when he lived if it was not because the extraordinary happened right before their eyes; therefore the one who wanted to talk about it had to say: It happened yesterday evening, yesterday morning, yesterday afternoon.* But when the miracle happened eighteen hundred years ago—well, then one can easily understand that it happened and that it was a miracle. Among the many precious and priceless syllogisms of [*added in version IV:* injudicious] clergy-discourse, this must be regarded as one of the most precious: that what cannot be understood if it happens today can be understood and believed if it happened eighteen hundred years ago if, note well, it is the marvelous, which at any time of the day, both four o'-clock and five o'clock, surpasses human understanding. That is, if one only says that one can understand that those men eighteen hundred years ago believed that it was a miracle, then one can just as well say straight out that one does not believe it oneself. Yet people prefer to avail themselves of deceptive locutions such as this one, which appears to be so believing and yet precisely denies the miracle, since it says of those men that they believed it,

VII²
B 235
88

VII²
B 235
89

---

* Note. The pastor who, when he is talking about that essentially one and only subject for a sermon, the paradox, is unable to produce this effect and keep his listeners in the tension of contemporaneity, is essentially not a pastor. Viewed essentially, all his proficiencies etc. mean nothing at all; but this lack of present time adequately shows that he himself is not a believer, because in faith the believer, as much as any contemporary could be contemporary, is completely contemporary—with a paradox.

namely, that they were serious about it, namely, that one does not believe it oneself.

To believe in the eminent sense corresponds quite rightly to the marvelous, the absurd, the improbable, that which is foolishness to the understanding,[236] and for that very reason it is altogether unimportant how long ago it was or if it is today. Anyone who has the remotest idea of dialectics in his head must perceive that the person who believes it if it happened eighteen hundred years ago can just as well believe it if it happens today—unless he believes it *because* it was eighteen hundred years ago, which is *not* to believe *at all*. If he believes this and that occurred eighteen hundred years ago, then precisely in faith he is paradoxically contemporary with it as if it occurred today. Incidentally, what nonsense the preacher-discourse furnishes on this point—well, let us not talk about it, nor about how ordinary Christians are reassured by this preacher-discourse in regard to their salvation. They are reassured, and against that there is nothing to say, except that in our day it would certainly be both more important but also more difficult to make the congregation a little uneasy and concerned in regard to their salvation. If only dialectics did not exist; it only makes trouble. What more beautiful eulogy on a country's clergy could be imagined than that they reassure the congregation in regard to their salvation. And the clergy do that in our day. At times there is nevertheless the complaint in one or another of our excellent newspapers that a night watchman shouts too loudly and disturbs the inhabitants' quiet and sleep. But there is no complaint about the clergy; they reassure the congregation in regard to their salvation! If Christ were to come to his own today, he would probably find the parishioners sleeping, reassured with the clergy's assistance in regard to their salvation.

As was said, I had imagined a dilemma in connection with the conception of the extraordinary,* that a man appeals to a revelation-fact: that he was either the chosen one or a daimonically sagacious offended person. [*Added*

VII²
B 235
90

---

* *Note.* Generally every human being is inclined to imagine a dilemma in relation to the extraordinary if he receives the proper tension-filled impression, has the elasticity to receive the pressure and to react to the pressure. The principle of contradiction has its life and its power in passion. Therefore, as soon as a person is really deeply moved by something, when he is in mortal danger, when the extraordinary appears before him, when he stands impassioned with his future fate in his hands, there is immediately an either/or. But since people nowadays are devoid of passion, flabby as a wet bowstring, since in a spiritual sense their priming powder is damp, then there soon remains only a tradition of the time when human life was tightened by the principle of contradiction. Just as one skeptically reads stories about the times when people became nine hundred years old and were gigantic in stature, so also a slack and dissolute generation will soon hear skeptically and suspect sagaciously the story that people have lived for whom an either/or was actually manifest, people who had their lives in this tension, while the pace of their own lives was like that of an arrow from a tightened bowstring, but this does not mean that for them there was an either/or only once.

in version IV: And this in turn, according to my concepts, was what the situation of contemporaneity, today's situation, might help us to: an either/or. And even if it does not happen in this way, what Christianity needs unconditionally, lest it suffocate and perish in indifference, is an either/or in relation to becoming and being a Christian. *End of text in version IV.*] Adler's conduct has in the meantime convinced me that there must be a third, since he is neither of the two. That he is not the chosen one, that this whole thing about his revelation is a misunderstanding, I shall show and substantiate later, yet not directly—far be it from me.*

He is if possible even less a daimonically sagacious offended person—of that he has not the slightest trace or symptom. Therefore he is by no means without significance, and among my contemporaries I know no one other than Adler who in a stricter sense may be called a phenomenon. The powers of existence have taken hold of him, and as a phenomenon he is an anticipation of the dialectic that is fermenting at present. But the phenomenon itself does not know how to explain anything—that is, one must oneself be a teacher in order to learn anything from Adler. Thus Adler is really a sign; he is a very earnest demonstration that the essentially Christian is a power that is not to be trifled with. But on the other hand, he is, rather than a chosen one, a person whirled around and slung out like a warning terror. Instead of being able to help the rest of us, he is more like the frightened [*deleted:* bewildered] bird that with wing strokes of anxiety rushes ahead of the storm that is coming [*deleted:*, while as yet people hear only a whistling; and his many thoughts are like the confused flock of birds that flee in disorder before the storm]. That one would therefore be justified in abandoning him or thinking poorly of his possibility is not my opinion at all.

VII²
B 235
91

---

* It would not surprise me if the slowness and tightfisted carefulness with which I go at this before I come to any conclusion on this matter will appear almost ludicrous to some people. By merely glancing at one of Adler's books or by merely hearing that he is supposed to have had a revelation, the majority will no doubt have enough to be finished with their judgment. When a bustler of that sort finds out that I have written a whole book and yet have arrived at the same result, he will laugh at me, he who promptly said the same thing. If a person who had especially exact, learned familiarity with Plato collected everything available about Socrates' daimon, compared it with whatever has been preserved from antiquity, and then arrived at the modest result that he could not determine anything, and if another person, who learned from Kofod's world history that Socrates is supposed to have had a daimon, promptly arrived at the decisive result that one cannot know anything definite about it, then in a way the two certainly do have a result in common. And in our day if one has a result, well, then everything is fine. Yet would there not be a difference between the two, and would it not be really advantageous if our age, which is so busy with results, would consider how the matter stands with regard to negative results. Something that is *non liquet* [not clear] can be the fruit of a year's labor, of great scholarship, of profound effort, and it can be the spit and image, can be obtained for four shillings in every grocery store. If there is a difference, if there is a glaring difference, this still may not be due to the results, which are almost identical. And yet everywhere there is a clamor only for results.

VII²
B 235
92

What then are the dialectical relations between (a) the *universal* and (b) the VII²
B 235
40
single individual and (c) the *special individual,* that is, the extraordinary? When
the single individual only reproduces the established order in his life (of
course differently according to what powers and abilities, what competence
he has), then he relates himself to the established order as the normal individual, the ordinary individual; he unfolds the life of the established order in
his existence. For him the established order is the foundation that educatively
penetrates and develops his abilities in likeness to itself; he relates himself as
an individual whose life is inflected according to the paradigm of the established order. Let us not, however, forget (since the dissatisfied and malicious-
minded are eager to spread false rumors) that his life is by no means devoid
of spirit because of this. He is not merely one more who reels off words that
go according to the paradigm. No, he is free and essentially independent, and
to be such an ordinary individual is quite in order, usually the highest, but
also qualitatively the most significant task that is assigned to any human being
and that therefore is assigned to every human being.*

As soon, however, as the single individual lets his reflection move him so VII²
B 235
41
deeply that he wants to reflect on the basic presupposition of the established
order, he is at the point of being inclined to wanting to be a special individual, and as long as he reflects in this way he is rejecting the *impressa vestigia*
[footprints] of the established order, is *extra ordinem* [outside the order] on
his own responsibility. And when the single individual continues along this
road and goes so far that he does not as the ordinary individual *reproductively
renew the life of the established order* **within himself** by willing, under eternal
responsibility, to order himself within it but wants to renew *the life of the established order by bringing a new point of departure* for it, *a new point of departure
in relation to the basic presupposition of the established order,* when he by submitting directly to God must relate himself transformingly to the established
order—then he is the extraordinary. That is, then this becomes the place allotted to him, whether he is justified or not; here he must be victorious and
here find his judgment—the universal must exclude him.

As everywhere, so it holds true especially here that the qualitative dialectic is to be respected with ethical earnestness. That is, in an age devoid of
character, the sophistic can emerge that someone who is inclined to be an

---

* *Note.* Everyone in the state and the state Church is to be and therefore also ought to be
an individual, but not the extraordinary individual. In conscientiousness and responsibility before God, that is, through his eternal consciousness, everyone is an individual. He never becomes mass; he is never enrolled in the public. With responsibility before God and after having tested himself in his conscience, he attaches himself to the whole as a limb and takes it as
his task to be faithful in the reproduction, while the responsibility of eternity saves him from VII²
B 235
41
the purely animal category: to be the crowd, the mass, the public or whatever other droves
there are that give one occasion to have to speak of human beings as one speaks of a drove of
cattle.

extraordinary wants this intention to benefit him even in the service of the universal; then on that basis he even becomes someone out of the ordinary among the ordinary. A sad confusion that has its basis in a thoughtless, frivolous quantifying. Either a person should want to serve the universal, the established order, express this, and in that case his merit becomes proportional to the faithfulness and scrupulousness with which he knows how to conform himself to it, knows how to make his life into a beautiful and rich and true reproduction of the established order, to develop himself as a type for the established order—or he should be an extraordinary in earnest, and then he, *extra ordinem,* should step out of the line, out of the ranks where he does not

VII²
B 235
42

belong. But in our times everything is confused. A dissatisfied officeholder, for example, still wants to be something extraordinary, because he is an officeholder—and also dissatisfied. Sad, immoral confusion! If he is dissatisfied because he has something new from God to bring to us, then out of the ranks, "a rope around his neck,"* and then let him talk; then the situation is what a true extraordinary needs and must demand in order to be able to gesticulate and start the carillon ringing. But if he does not have something new from God to bring to us, then it must by no means be reckoned an advantage for him that he is dissatisfied—and also an officeholder. But the lack of character and the prying cowardice of the age finally make a kind of dishonorable narrow-mindedness out of being of some benefit: either wholeheartedly a faithful officeholder or a reformer with a sword over his head, in mortal danger, in self-denial. Εἷς κοίρανος ἔστω [Let there be one lord],[238] and thus also let there be one who is the extraordinary. If a whole generation wants to be king and a whole generation wants to dabble in being extraordinary, then it becomes rubbish. And the result of that is only delay. If Governance had meant to give the generation an extraordinary, it must accordingly be expected that perhaps not even a forerunner will be sent, but we must be satisfied with something very simple, one who very simply can clear the way, very simply can throw out all these false prophets and has a little meaning and pith to bring into the enervated and meaningless situation again. When, namely, a whole generation has become reformist, the true reformer cannot at all begin to appear in his truth, that is, to call to mind an earlier locution: just as when at a fire everyone is giving orders, the fire chief cannot give the orders.

VII²
B 235
43

It is the *point of departure* that makes the difference between the ordinary individual and the special individual; in other respects it may very well be

---

* *Note.* Caesar tells that it was a custom among the Gauls that everyone who made a new proposal had to stand with a rope around his neck—so that they could promptly get rid of him if it did not amount to anything.[237] If this commendable custom were to be introduced in our day, God knows whether the country would have enough rope, since the whole population has become project planners, and yet perhaps in the first place rope would not even be needed—possibly there would be no one who would volunteer.

that, humanly speaking, an ordinary individual is greater than an actual extraordinary. The final criterion by which people take rank is the ethical, in relation to which the differences [*deleted in version V:* (even in the special sense of being called by God)] are negligible, but the worldly mind inversely determines the order of precedence according to the difference. Let us take an example of such a *consummate individual,* and let us really rejoice that we have examples to point to; let us name, *honoris causa,* but also in order to throw light on this relation, the admired Bishop of Sjælland [*changed in version V to:* the state Church's leading prelate, assuredly also its most faithful servant] [*deleted in version V:* and everyone does well to admire here, because one must find joy in admiring the person who expresses the universal, since]—he also expresses the universal and one can learn from him. [*Deleted in version V:* Bishop Mynster does not have the least of what one in the strictest sense might call the description of the special individual. On the contrary, with sublime serenity, happily resting in his conviction as the rich content of an abundant life, with admonishing emphasis, with a sober composure of earnestness bordering on a magnanimous little ironic turn toward confused pates, this man has continually acknowledged that it was not something new that he had to bring, that on the contrary it was the old and familiar. He has never rocked the pillars of the established order; on the contrary, he himself has stood unshakable as a main pillar. And when he revises the first edition of his earliest sermons, "he finds nothing to change in the essentials"[239] (as if since that time he perhaps had been so fortunate as to cope with one or another newly arrived systematic novelty); and if at some time on his deathbed he revises all the sermons, not for a new edition but to attest to the correctness of them, he will very likely again find "nothing to change in the essentials." No, it was all the old and familiar—which nevertheless found in him such a fresh and refreshing emanation, such a noble, beautiful, and rich expression, that in a long life he moves many people, how amazing, by the old* and familiar, and that after his death he will continue to move many people, who will long for *this* old and familiar as one longs for the charm of youth, as in the heat of summer one longs for the coolness of the spring— how amazing, that it should be something old and familiar! Truly, if at some time at the very beginning a doctrine must wish for an apostle who in the strictest (*deleted in version V:* in the paradoxical) sense stands outside the ranks as an extraordinary, at a later time the same doctrine will wish for the kind of stewards who have nothing new to bring, who on the contrary earnestly have their joy in expressing the universal themselves, their joy in marching along in the ranks and teaching the rest of us to keep time—if only we are careful to look alertly up to the right.

When should a girl be married? Antiquity answers: "When she is a girl in

VII²
B 235
44

* and that after his death many, moved, will long for this old man and this old

age but a woman in understanding."[240] When should a man become a teacher?* When he has the vigor of youth and the wisdom of an old man. And when does he reach his peak? When he is an old man in [**] years and understanding, but as vigorous in heart as a young man. What is it to preserve oneself, which, essentially understood, is a man's highest task? It is, when the blood is warm and the heart beats violently in the days of youth, then to be able to cool down with almost an old man's composure; and it is, when the day declines, when it draws near to taking its leave, then to be able to flame up with the fire of youth. But is this not an insult to His Right Reverence to sit and write something like this? If what has been stated is true, then Bishop Mynster is indeed no great man, then he has indeed never followed along with the times, then he does indeed not know what the demand of the times is, to say nothing of his having himself been able to invent it. No, he has not invented anything. Whether he perhaps has not been able to (yet as a keen psychologist he very likely knows human follies from the ground up and consequently possesses the key to the great storehouse where the diverse demands of the times lie piled up), I shall not presume to decide, but it is certain that he has not invented anything.]

The new point of departure is the difference between the true ordinary and the true extraordinary; the essentially human criterion, the ethical, they both have in common. When the single individual actually is the true extraordinary and actually has a new point of departure, when he comprehends his life's distressing difficulty in that *discrimen* [distinction] between the universal and the singular *extra ordinem* [outside the order], he must be unconditionally recognizable by his being *willing to bring a sacrifice.**** And this he must be willing to do *for his own sake* and *for the sake of the universal.*

Precisely because the extraordinary, if he is truly that, must through his God-relationship be conscious that he κατὰ δύναμιν [potentially] is stronger than the *summa summarum* [grand total] of all the established order, he has nothing at all to do with a concern about whether he will be victorious. No, he is completely free of this concern, but on the other hand he has the special singular's dreadful responsibility for every step he takes, whether he is now scrupulously following his orders down to the least detail, whether he is definitely and solely and obediently listening to God's voice—the dreadful responsibility if he heard or has heard wrong. For that very reason he must

---

* When he is a man in age but in wisdom an old man.

[**] age and wisdom

In margin: *** Note. That is, the established order as the established order is the legitimate and the strongest in the literal sense; it is not the single individual who is to be the superior in the literal sense, but the *special* individual, whose superiority is in the suffering of self-sacrifice. That he is sacrificed is the expression for the strength and legitimacy of the universal, and yet it is also the expression for his superiority, because his suffering and death are the victory of the new point of departure.

desire for himself all possible opposition from the outside, desire that the established order would have powers to be able to make his life a *tentamen rigorosum* [rigorous examination], since this testing and its pain still are nothing compared with the horror of the responsibility—if he was or had been in error! For example, if a son should feel called to introduce a new view of the home life (and just as a son is bound in piety, so every individual should and ought to be bound in piety in relation to the universal): would he not then, if it was truth in him, desire precisely that the father would be the strong one who could take a stand against him with the full power of fatherly authority? That is, the son would not so much fear to submit if he had been wrong, consequently to have to return, humbled but saved, to the old, as he would shudder before the horror of winning—if basically he had been wrong.

So it is with the true extraordinary; he is the most nonchalant person about that temporal concern of the worldly heroes, whether what he had to proclaim will be victorious in the world. On the other hand, as a poor sinner he is anxious, is overwhelmed every time he considers his responsibility and whether he in any way could have been mistaken; indeed, the weight of responsibility can rest on him so heavily that it seems as if he would stop breathing. For that very reason he desires opposition: he—the weak one, he—the strong one, who, although a solitary human being, κατὰ δύναμιν is stronger in his weakness than the united might of the established order, which naturally has the power both to flog him and to execute him as if it were nothing at all. When berserk fury came upon our northern fathers, they had themselves constrained between shields; in the same way the true extraordinary also desires that the power of the established order will form appropriate opposition.

A critique of the established order, *Judge for Yourself!* was not published, because of Kierkegaard's consideration for Bishop Mynster and his expectation of Mynster's admission of the enervating acculturation of Christianity in Christendom. No admission was forthcoming, and after Mynster's death on January 20, 1854, Kierkegaard published in the newspaper *Fædrelandet* an article titled "Was Bishop Mynster a 'Truth-Witness,' One of the Authentic 'Truth-Witnesses'—Is *This the Truth?*" Thereafter followed twenty articles in *Fædrelandet* and nine issues of a series of pamphlets titled *Øieblikket* [*The Moment*] (May 24–September 24, 1855). Intermittently there appeared a number of small publications: *This Must Be Said; So Let It Be Said* (May 24, 1855), *What Christ Judges of Official Christianity* (June 16, 1855), and *The Changelessness of God* (September 3, 1855). The final number of *The Moment* was written in September and published posthumously (1881). On October 2, 1855, Kierkegaard collapsed on the street and died November 11, 1855. A few weeks earlier, at a party with friends, he had slid from the sofa to the floor. As people gathered around him, he looked up, winked, and said, "Oh, leave it—let—the maid—sweep it up—in the morning." There was this characteristic sense of humor also in the series of writings during the last year, but in the keenly sharpened form of hard-hitting criticism and, at times, caustic caricature. An authorship that began as indirect communication ended as direct.

WAS BISHOP MYNSTER A "TRUTH-WITNESS,"
ONE OF "THE AUTHENTIC TRUTH-WITNESSES"
—IS *THIS THE TRUTH?*

February 1854   S. KIERKEGAARD

In the address Prof. Martensen[241] "delivered the fifth Sunday after Epiphany, the Sunday before Bishop Dr. Mynster's funeral," a memorial address, as it perhaps can in a way also be called, since it calls to mind Prof. Martensen for the vacant bishopric—in this address Bishop Mynster is represented as a truth-witness, as one of the authentic truth-witnesses; the expressions used are as strong and decisive as possible. With the late bishop's figure, his life and career, and the outcome of his life before our eyes, we are exhorted to "imitate the faith of the true guides, of the authentic truth-witnesses" (p. 5), their faith, for it was, as is explicitly said about Bishop Mynster, "not only in word and confession but in deed and truth" (p. 9). The late bishop is introduced by Prof. Martensen (p. 6) into "the holy chain of truth-witnesses that stretches through the ages from the days of the apostles" etc.

———————

To this I must raise an objection—and now that Bishop Mynster is dead I am able and willing to speak, but very briefly here, and not at all about what made me decide to take the position that I have taken in relation to him. XIV 6

When *proclamation* is considered more particularly to be what is said, written, printed, the word, the sermon, one does not need to be especially sharp to be able to see, when the New Testament is placed alongside Mynster's preaching, that Bishop Mynster's proclamation of Christianity (to take just one thing) tones down, veils, suppresses, omits some of what is most decisively Christian, what is too inconvenient for us human beings, what would make our lives strenuous, prevent us from enjoying life—this about dying to the world,[242] about voluntary renunciation, about hating oneself, about suffering for the doctrine, etc.

If, however, *proclamation* is considered more particularly to be the extent to which the proclaimer's life expresses what he says (and this, note well, is Christianly decisive, and in just this way Christianity has wanted to protect itself against acquiring characterless assistant professors instead of witnesses), one in turn does not need to be especially sharp to be able to see (if by hearing or reading him one is properly acquainted at all with his preaching) that Bishop Mynster's proclamation of Christianity was not in character, that outside the quiet hours he was not in character, not even in the character of his preaching, which indeed, as stated, compared with the New Testament, has considerably scaled down the essentially Christian. In 1848 and thereafter it became apparent even to blind admirers, if they were properly acquainted with his preaching so as to be able to know what this, what these quiet hours lead one to expect.

Thus, when the New Testament is placed alongside, Bishop Mynster's proclamation of Christianity was, especially for a truth-witness, a dubious proclamation of Christianity. But there was, I thought, this truth in him, that he was willing, I am fully convinced, to confess before God and to himself that he was not at all, not at all, a truth-witness—in my view, precisely this confession was the truth.

But if Bishop Mynster is going to be represented and canonized in the pulpit as a truth-witness, one of the authentic truth-witnesses, then an objection must be raised. The *Berlingske Tidende* (the official newspaper, just as Prof. Martensen is no doubt the official preacher) is, as I see, of the opinion that with this address Prof. Martensen (who with remarkable haste steals a march on the funeral and also on the monument) has from the pulpit erected XIV 7 a beautiful and worthy monument to the deceased; I would prefer to say: a worthy monument to Prof. Martensen himself. But in any case monuments cannot be ignored; therefore an objection must be raised, which then perhaps could even contribute to making the monument (to Prof. Martensen) even more durable.

Bishop Mynster a truth-witness! You who read this, you certainly do know what is Christianly understood by a truth-witness,* but let me remind you of it, that it unconditionally requires suffering for the doctrine. And when it is said more pointedly: one of "the authentic" truth-witnesses, then the word must accordingly be taken in the strictest sense. In order to make it vivid to you, let me try in a few strokes to suggest what must be understood by this.

A truth-witness is a person whose life from first to last is unfamiliar with everything called enjoyment—ah, whether much or little is granted you, you know how much good is done by what is called enjoyment—but his life from first to last was unfamiliar with everything that is called enjoyment; on the contrary, from first to last it was initiated into everything called suffer-

XIV
8

ing—alas, and even if you are exempted from the prolonged, the more agonizing sufferings, you still know from personal experience how a person shrinks from what is called suffering! But from first to last his life was initiated into what is even more rarely mentioned among people because it more rarely happens—into interior struggles, into fear and trembling, into shuddering, into spiritual trials, into anxieties of soul, into torments of spirit, and then in addition was tried in all the sufferings that are more commonly talked about in the world. A truth-witness is a person who in poverty witnesses for the truth, in poverty, in lowliness and abasement,[243] is so unappreciated, hated, detested, so mocked, insulted, laughed to scorn—so poor that he perhaps has not always had daily bread, but he received the daily bread of persecution in abundance every day. For him there was never advancement and promotion except in reverse, step by step downward. A truth-witness, one of the authentic truth-witnesses, is a person who is flogged, mistreated, dragged from one prison to another, then finally—the last advancement, by which he is admitted to the first class in the *Christian* order of precedence

---

* Yet this may have been consigned to oblivion through Bishop Mynster's proclamation of Christianity over many years. And a capital malpractice in his proclamation is also this—not this, that he himself was an officeholder (Christianly this subtracts), the proclamation his own brilliant career, rich in enjoyment—no, not this, but that he would authorize this kind of proclamation as the true Christian proclamation and thereby, through suppression, make the true Christian proclamation (that of the suffering truth-witnesses) into an exaggeration, instead of conversely making the confession to Christianity that the proclamation he represented is something that must be conceded to us ordinary human beings through exemption and indulgence, something that we ordinary human beings make use of because we are too selfish, too worldly, too sensate to be capable of more, something that we ordinary human beings make use of and that, understood in this way, is by no means—despite all false reformers!—to be conceitedly and pompously rejected, but rather is to be respected.

among the authentic truth-witnesses—then finally, for this is indeed one of the authentic truth-witnesses Prof. Martensen talks about, then finally is crucified or beheaded or burned or broiled on a grill, his lifeless body thrown away by the assistant executioner into a remote place, unburied—this is how a truth-witness is buried!—or burned to ashes and cast to the winds so that every trace of this "refuse," as the apostle says he has become,[244] might be obliterated.

This is a truth-witness, his life and career, his death and burial—and, says Prof. Martensen, Bishop Mynster was one of these authentic truth-witnesses.

Is it the truth? Is talking in this way perhaps also witnessing for the truth, and by this talk has Prof. Martensen himself stepped into the character of a truth-witness, one of the authentic truth-witnesses? Truly, there is something that is more against Christianity and the essence of Christianity than any heresy, any schism, more against it than all heresies and schisms together, and it is this: to play at Christianity. But (entirely, entirely in the same sense as the child plays at being a soldier) it is playing at Christianity: to remove all the dangers (Christianly, *witness* and *danger* are equivalent), to replace them with power (to be a danger to others), goods, advantages, abundant enjoyment of even the most select refinements—and then to play the game that Bishop Mynster was a truth-witness, one of the authentic truth-witnesses, play it so frightfully earnestly that one cannot stop the game at all but plays it on into heaven, plays Bishop Mynster along into the holy chain of truth-witnesses that stretches from the days of the apostles to our times.

XIV
9

Postscript

This article has, as may be seen from its date, lain ready for some time.

As long as the appointment to the bishopric of Sjælland was in question, I thought that I ought to leave Professor Martensen out of public discussion, since, whether or not he became bishop, he in any case was a candidate for this office, and no doubt desired, while it was pending, that as far as possible nothing pertaining to him would happen.

With Prof. Martensen's appointment as bishop, this consideration dropped out. But since under the circumstances the article could not appear and therefore did not appear right away, I decided that, after all, there was no reason to hurry. Then, too, Bishop Martensen's appointment provoked attack on him from other sides and of a completely different kind; I most definitely did not want to join in with that attack. So I waited; I thought, as stated, that there was no reason at all to hurry and nothing at all to be lost by waiting. Someone might even find that something was gained, find that such a slow emergence of the objection has a deeper significance.

Autumn 1854

A THESIS

—JUST ONE SINGLE ONE

January 26, 1855   S. KIERKEGAARD

O Luther, you had 95 theses—terrible! And yet, in a deeper sense, the more theses, the less terrible. The matter is far more terrible—there is only one thesis.

*   *
*

The Christianity of the New Testament does not exist at all. Here there is nothing to reform; it is a matter of throwing light on a Christian crime continued over the centuries and practiced by millions (more or less guilty), a crime whereby little by little, in the name of the perfecting of Christianity, a sagacious attempt has been made to trick God out of Christianity and Christianity has been turned into exactly the opposite of what it is in the New Testament.

*   *
*

In order for it to be possible to say that the ordinary, the official Christianity here in the land even barely relates itself truly to the Christianity of the New Testament, it must first of all as honestly, candidly, and solemnly as possible be acknowledged at what distance it is from the Christianity of the New
Testament and how incapable it is of being truly called a striving toward coming closer to the Christianity of the New Testament.

As long as this is not done, as long as one either acts as if nothing had happened, as if everything were all right and what we call Christianity is the Christianity of the New Testament, or one uses tricks to conceal the difference, tricks to maintain the appearance of being the Christianity of the New Testament—as long as the Christian crime continues, there can be no question of reforming but of throwing light on this Christian criminal case.

*   *
*

As for myself, I am not what the times perhaps crave, a reformer, in no way; nor am I a profound speculative intellect, a seer, a prophet—no, I have, if you please, to a rare degree I have a definite detective talent. What an amazing coincidence that I should be exactly contemporary with that period in the history of the Church that, in the modern style, is the period of "truth-witnesses," in which all are "saintly truth-witnesses."

WHAT DO I WANT?

March 1855   S. KIERKEGAARD

Very simply—I want honesty. I am not, as some well-intentioned people—
I cannot pay attention to the opinions of me held in bitterness and rage and
impotence and blather—have wanted to represent me, I am not Christian
stringency in contrast to a given Christian leniency.

Certainly not, I am neither leniency nor stringency—I am human honesty.

I want to have the mitigation that is the current Christianity here in this
country set alongside the New Testament in order to see how these two relate to each other.

If it proves to be so, if I or anyone else can show that it can be maintained
face to face with the Christianity of the New Testament, then I will accept
it with the greatest joy.

But one thing I do not want at any price: I do not want to create, by suppression or artifice, the appearance that the current Christianity in this country and the Christianity of the New Testament resemble each other.

See, it is this that I do not want. And why not? Well, because I want honesty, or, if you want me to speak in another way, because I believe that if it
is possible, if even the most extreme mitigation of the Christianity of the
New Testament can hold good in the judgment of eternity, it cannot possibly hold good in the judgment of eternity, it cannot possibly hold good when
every artifice has been used to cover up the difference between the Christianity of the New Testament and this mitigation. My opinion is: if someone is merciful, well, then let me dare to ask him to forgive me all my debt;
but even if his mercy were divine mercy, this is too much to ask: that I will
not ever be truthful about how great the debt is.

This, I believe, is the untruth of which official Christianity is guilty: it does
not uncompromisingly make clear the Christian requirement, perhaps because it is afraid that we would shudder to see at what distance we are living, not to mention that our lives cannot in the remotest way be called a
striving in the direction of fulfilling the requirement. Or to take just one example of what is indeed present everywhere in the Christianity of the New
Testament: When Christianity requires for saving one's life eternally (and
this, after all, is what we believe to attain as Christians): hating one's own life
in this world—is there a single one of us whose life even in the remotest
manner can be called even the weakest striving in this direction, whereas
there are in this country perhaps "Christians" by the thousands who are not
even aware of this requirement? Accordingly, we "Christians," we live and
love our lives in the altogether ordinary human sense. If God by "grace"

nonetheless is to assume us to be Christians, one thing must still be required, that we, by being scrupulously aware of the requirement, have a true conception of how infinitely great is the grace that is shown us. "Grace" cannot possibly stretch so far; one thing it must never be used for—it must never be used to suppress or to diminish the requirement. In that case "grace" turns all Christianity upside down.

Or to take an example of another kind. A teacher of Christianity is paid, for example, several thousands. If we now suppress the Christian criterion and assume the ordinary human criterion that it is indeed quite natural that a man should have wages for his work, wages so that he can live with his family, and respectable wages so that he can live as an officeholder in a respectable position—then several thousands a year are not very much. As soon, however, as the Christian requirement of poverty is asserted, then a family is a luxury, and several thousands are a very high salary. I do not say this in order to deduct one single shilling from such an officeholder, if I were able to do that. On the contrary, if he wanted it and I were able to do it, I would gladly have him receive double so many thousands—but I am saying that suppression of the Christian requirement changes the point of view about all his salary. Honesty toward Christianity requires that one personally bring into recollection that Christianly the requirement is poverty and that this is not some capricious whim on the part of Christianity, but it is the requirement because Christianity is well aware that only in poverty can it be served truly, and that the more thousands a teacher of Christianity has in salary, the less he can serve Christianity. On the other hand, it is not honest to suppress the requirement or to use artifices to give the appearance that this way of life and career are entirely the Christianity of the New Testament. No, let us accept the money, but for God's sake not the next, not want to cover up the Christian requirement so that by suppression or by falsification a kind of decorum is produced that is to the absolutely highest degree demoralizing and is the assassination of Christianity.

Therefore I want honesty, but hitherto the established order has not been willing of its own accord to enter into the spirit of that kind of honesty, and neither has it been willing to be influenced by me. But I do not therefore become leniency or stringency. No, I am and remain quite simply human honesty.

Let me venture the most extreme in order, if possible, to be understood with regard to what I want.

I want honesty. If this, then, is what the generation or the contemporaries want, if they want straightforwardly, honestly, candidly, openly, directly to rebel against Christianity and say to God, "We cannot, we will not submit to this power"—but, please note, this is to be done straightforwardly, honestly, candidly, openly, directly—well, then strange as it might seem, I go along with it, because I want honesty. Wherever there is honesty, I am able to go along with it; an honest rebellion against Christianity can be made only if one honestly acknowledges what Christianity is and how one relates oneself to it.

If this is what one wants: straightforwardly, openly, sincerely, as is seemly when a person speaks with his God, as everyone acts who respects himself and does not despise himself so deeply that he will be dishonest before God—thus, if one straightforwardly, sincerely, candidly makes full confession to God with regard to the actual situation with us human beings, that in the course of time the human race has permitted itself to mitigate and mitigate Christianity, until we finally have managed to get it to be the very opposite of what it is in the New Testament—and that we now wish, if it can be done, that this might be Christianity—if this is what one wants, then I go along with it.

XIV
55

But one thing I will not do. No, not at any price will I do it; one thing I will not do: I will not participate, even if it were merely with the last fourth of the last joint of my little finger, in what is called official Christianity, which by suppression or artifice gives the appearance of being the Christianity of the New Testament, and on bended knee I thank my God that he mercifully has kept me from entering into it too far.[245]

If the official Christianity in this country wants to take the occasion to use force against me because of what is said here, I am prepared [*rede*], because I want honesty [*Redelighed*].

For this honesty I am willing to venture. However, I am not saying that it is for Christianity I venture. Suppose, just suppose that I become quite literally a sacrifice—I would still not become a sacrifice for Christianity but because I wanted honesty.

But although I do not dare to say that I venture for Christianity, I remain fully and blissfully convinced that this, my venturing, is pleasing to God, has his approval. Indeed, I know it; it has his approval that in a world of Christians where millions and millions call themselves Christians—that there one person expresses: I do not dare to call myself a Christian; but I want honesty, and to that end I will venture.

A GENIUS[246]/A CHRISTIAN

XIV
192

That not everyone is a genius is no doubt something everyone will admit. But that a Christian is even more rare than a genius—this has knavishly been totally consigned to oblivion.

The difference between a genius and a Christian is that the genius is nature's extraordinary; no human being can make himself into one. A Christian is freedom's extraordinary or, more precisely, freedom's ordinary, except that this is found extraordinarily seldom, is what every one of us should be.

Therefore God wants Christianity to be proclaimed unconditionally to all, therefore the apostles are very simple, ordinary people, therefore the prototype [*Forbillede*] is in the lowly form of a servant,[247] all this in order to indicate that this extraordinary is the ordinary, is open to all—but a Christian is nevertheless something even more rare than a genius.

But let us not be fooled by the circumstance that it is open to all, possible for all, as if from that it followed that it is something rather easy, and that there are many Christians. No, it must be possible for all; otherwise it would not be freedom's extraordinary; but a Christian still becomes even more rare than a genius.

If it is assumed that it is all in order with these battalions and millions times millions of Christians, an objection arises here that really has significance: that the situation of Christianity is then completely without analogy in the rest of existence. Ordinarily we see everywhere the enormous proportions found in existence: the possibility of millions of plants is blown away as pollen, millions of possibilities of living entities are wasted, etc. etc., there are probably thousands times thousands of people to one genius etc.—always this enormous waste. Only with Christianity is it different: in relation to what is more rare than a genius, it so happens that everyone who is born is a Christian.

Similarly, if this matter of millions of Christians is supposed to be the truth, a second objection also acquires great significance. This earth is only a little point in the universe—and yet Christianity is supposed to be reserved for it, and at such a bargain price that anyone and everyone who is born is a Christian.

The matter looks different when it is perceived that to be a Christian is such an ideality that instead of the rubbish about Christianity and Christianity's eighteen-hundred-year history, and about Christianity's being perfectible, the thesis may well be posited: Christianity has not actually entered the world; it never went any further than the prototype and at most the apostles. But these were already proclaiming it so powerfully along the lines of propagation that already here the dubiousness begins. It is one thing to work for propagation in such a way that one uninterruptedly, early and late, proclaims the doctrine to all; it is something else to be too hasty in allowing people by the hundreds and thousands to take the name of Christian and pass as followers of Jesus Christ. The prototype's proclamation was different, because just as unconditionally as he proclaimed the doctrine to all, living only for that, just as unconditionally did he hold back with regard to becoming a follower, to receiving permission to call oneself that. If a crowd had been gripped by Christ's discourse, he would not therefore have immediately allowed these thousands to call themselves followers of Christ. No, he held back more strongly. Thus in three and a half years he won only eleven, whereas one apostle in one day, I dare say in one hour, wins three thousand followers of Christ. Either the follower is here greater than the Master, or the truth is that the apostle is a bit too hasty in striking a bargain, a bit too hasty about propagation; thus the dubiousness already begins here.

Only divine authority could impress the human race in such a way that unconditionally willing the eternal would become unconditional earnestness. Only the God-man can unite these: unconditionally working for propagation and unconditionally just as strongly holding back with regard to what being a follower is supposed to mean. Only the God-man would be able to endure (if one can imagine this) working unconditionally for a thousand years and then another thousand for the propagation of the doctrine by proclaiming it, even if he did not gain one single follower, if he could win them only by changing the conditions. The apostle still has some selfish urge for the alleviation, acquiring adherents, becoming many, something the God-man does not have. He does not selfishly crave adherents and therefore has only the price of eternity, no market price.

It so happened that when Christ proclaimed Christianity the human race was unconditionally impressed.

But *naturam furca expellas* [if you expel nature with a pitchfork],[248] it still comes back again. The human tendency is to turn the relation upside down. Just as a dog that is forced to walk on two legs continually has a tendency to begin to walk on all fours again and does it immediately just as soon as it sees its chance, and waits only to see its chance, just so all Christendom is the human race's striving to get to walk on all fours again, to be rid of Christianity, knavishly in the name of its being Christianity and with the claim that this is the perfecting of Christianity.

First of all, they turned around the other side of *the prototype;* the prototype was no longer the prototype but the Redeemer. Instead of looking at him with respect to imitation, they dwelt on his good works and wished to be in the place of those to whom they were shown, which is just as upside down as to hear someone described as a prototype of generosity and then refuse to look at him with the intention of imitating his generosity but with the idea of wishing to be in the place of those to whom he showed generosity.

So the prototype dropped out. Then the apostle was also abolished as prototype. Then after that, the first Christian age as prototype. In this way the goal was finally achieved—walking on all fours again, and that, precisely that, was true Christianity. By means of dogmas, they protected themselves against anything that with any semblance of truth could Christianly be called a prototype, and then under full sail went in the direction of—perfectibility.

BRIEF AND TO THE POINT

1.

Christianity can be perfected (is perfectible); it advances; now it has attained perfection. The ideal that was aspired to but that even the first age only approximately attained, that the Christians are a people of priests,[249] that has now been perfectly attained, especially in Protestantism, especially in Denmark.

If, namely, what it is to be a priest is what we call a pastor—indeed, then we are all pastors!

2.

In the splendid cathedral the Honorable Right Reverend *Geheime-General-Ober-Hof-Prædikant* [Private Chief Royal Chaplain] comes forward, the chosen favorite of the elite world; he comes forward before a chosen circle of the chosen ones and, deeply *moved,* preaches on the text he has himself chosen, "God has chosen the lowly and the despised in the world"[250]—and there is no one who laughs.

3.

When a man has a toothache, the world says, "Poor man"; when a man's wife is unfaithful to him, the world says, "Poor man." —When it pleases God in the form of a lowly servant to suffer in this world, the world says, "Poor human being"; when an apostle with a divine commission has the honor to suffer for the truth, the world says, "Poor human being"—poor world!

4.

"Did the Apostle Paul have any official position?" No, Paul had no official position. "Did he, then, earn a lot of money in another way?" No, he did not earn money in any way. "Was he, then, at least married?" No, he was not married. "But then Paul is certainly not an earnest man!" No, Paul is not an earnest man.

5.

A Swedish pastor, shaken by the sight of the effect his discourse had on the listeners, who were swimming in tears, is reported to have said reassuringly: Do not weep, children, it may all be a lie.

Why does the pastor no longer say that? It is unnecessary, we know that—we are all pastors.

But we can very well weep, since both his and our tears are not at all hypocritical but well meant, genuine—just as in the theater.

6.

When paganism was disintegrating, there were some priests called augurs. It is reported that one augur could not look at another without grinning.[251]

In "Christendom" it may soon be the case that no one will be able to look at a pastor or one person at another without grinning—but we are, of course, all pastors!

7.

Is this the same teaching, when Christ says to the rich young man: Sell all that you have and give it to the poor,[252] and when the pastor says: Sell all that you have and give it to me?

8.

Geniuses are like a thunderstorm [*Tordenveir*]: they go against the wind, terrify people, clear the air.

The established order has invented various lightning rods [*Tordenafledere*].

And it succeeded. Yes, it certainly did succeed; it succeeded in making the *next* thunderstorm all the more serious.

XIV
219

9.

One cannot live on nothing. One hears this so often, especially from pastors.

And the pastors are the very ones who perform this feat: Christianity does not exist at all—yet they live on it.

FEAR MOST OF ALL TO BE IN ERROR!

XIV
225

This, as is well known, is Socrates' thesis; he feared most of all to be in error.[253]

Christianity, which certainly in one sense does not teach people to fear, not even those who are able to put one to death, nevertheless teaches in another sense a still greater fear than that Socratic fear, teaches to fear the one who can destroy both soul and body in hell.[254]

But first to the first thing, to become aware of the Christianity of the New Testament; and for that purpose that Socratic fear, to fear most of all to be in error, will assist you.

If you do not have this fear, or (in order not to strike too high a note) if this is not the case with you, if this is not what you want, if you do not want to gain the courage "to fear most of all to be under a delusion"—then never become involved with me. No, then stay with the pastors, then let them convince you, the sooner the better, that what I say is a kind of lunacy (that it is in the New Testament is, after all, utterly unimportant; when the pastor is bound by an oath on the New Testament, you are of course perfectly assured that nothing that is in the New Testament is suppressed). Stay with the pastors; strive to the best of your ability to establish firmly for yourself that Bishop Mynster was a truth-witness, one of the authentic witnesses, one of the holy chain, Bishop Martensen ditto, ditto, every pastor likewise, and the official Christianity is the saving truth; that Christ in the most dreadful tortures, even abandoned by God,[255] expired on the cross, in order that we should have the pleasure of spending our time and diligence and energy on sagaciously and tastefully enjoying this life; that his purpose in coming to this world actually was to encourage the procreation of children, which is why it is also "inappropriate for anyone who is not married to be a pastor"; and that the unforgettable significance of his life is (like a true benefactor!) to have made possible by his death (one person's death, another's bread!) a new way of making a living, the pastors', a way of making a living that must be regarded as one of the most advantageous, just as it also engages the greatest number of tradesmen, shippers, and shipowners, whose *Geschäft* [business] is to ship people for an unbelievably cheap remuneration (in relation to the importance and length of the journey, the gloriousness of the place of destination, the length of the stay) to the blessedness of eternity, a *Geschäft,* the only one of its kind, that has, compared with all shipping to America, Australia, etc., the inestimable advantage of insuring the shipper against even the possibility of getting a bad name because no news whatever is received from those transported.

But if you do have the courage to want to have the courage that fears most to be in error, then you can also get to know the truth about becoming a Christian. The truth is: to become a Christian is to become, humanly speaking, unhappy for this life; the proportion is: the more you involve yourself with God and the more he loves you, the more you will become, humanly speaking, unhappy for this life, the more you will come to suffer in this life.

This thought, which certainly throws a somewhat disturbing light on (what is supposed to be the Christianity of the New Testament!) all the brisk traffic of the cheerful, child-begetting, career-making preacher-guild, and like a lightning flash trans-illuminates this fantastic mirage, masquerade, parlor game, tomfoolery with (the abode of all illusions!) "Christendom," Christian states, countries, a Christian world—this is a frightful, death-dealing, almost superhumanly exhausting thought for a poor human being. This I know from experience in two ways. I know it partly from this, that I actually cannot endure the thought and therefore merely investigatingly scrutinize this true Christian definition of being a Christian,* while I for my part help myself to bear the sufferings with a much easier thought, a Jewish idea, not in a highest sense Christian: that I am suffering because of my sins; and partly from this, that through the circumstances of life I was bound to be led in a very special way to become aware of it, and otherwise I would never have become aware and would have been even less capable of bearing the pressure of this thought, but, as stated, I was helped by the circumstances of my own life.

The circumstances of my own life were my preparatory instruction; with their help I became, accordingly as I developed over the years, more and more aware of Christianity and of the definition: of becoming a Christian. In other words, what does it mean, according to the New Testament, to become a Christian, why the repeated admonition against being offended,[256] and why the frightful collisions (to hate father, mother, wife, child,[257] etc.), in which the New Testament breathes? I wonder if both are not because Christianity knows very well that to become a Christian is to become, humanly speaking, unhappy in this life, yet blessedly awaiting an eternal happiness. According to the New Testament, what does it mean to become loved by God? It is to become, humanly speaking, unhappy in this life, yet blessedly expecting an eternal happiness—according to the New Testament, God, who is spirit, cannot love a human being in another way. He makes you unhappy, but he does it out of love; blessed is the one who is not offended! According to the New Testament, what does it mean to love God? It is to be *willing* to become, humanly speaking, unhappy in this life, yet blessedly expecting an eternal happiness—a person cannot love God, who is spirit, in another way. And solely by the help of this you can see that the Christianity of the New Testament does not exist at all, that the fragment of religiousness found in the land is at most Judaism.

XIV
227

WHAT DOES THE FIRE CHIEF SAY?

XIV
231

When a person has in any sense what is called a cause, has something he earnestly wants—and then there are others who take upon themselves the task of opposing, preventing, and doing harm—everyone immediately real-

---

* Therefore I do not yet call myself a Christian; no, I am still far behind. But I have one advantage over all the official Christianity (which moreover is bound by oath upon the New Testament!); I report truthfully what Christianity is. Consequently I do not permit myself to change what Christianity is, and I report truthfully how I relate to what Christianity is; consequently I do not participate in changing what Christianity is in order thereby to obtain millions of Christians.

XIV
227

izes that he is obliged to take measures against these his enemies. But not everyone realizes that there is, if you please, a good-natured well-meaning that perhaps is far more dangerous and that will most likely prevent the cause from truly becoming earnestness.

When a person suddenly becomes ill, well-meaning persons rush to help, and one recommends this, another that. If they all received permission to advise, the patient's death would indeed be certain; the individual's well-intentioned advice may already be sufficiently dubious. Even if none of this happens, and neither the advice of all the well-meaning ones nor of the individual is followed, their bustling, nervous presence may still be harmful insofar as they stand in the way of the physician.

It is the same at a fire. Scarcely is the fire alarm heard before a human mob storms to the place—nice, kind, sympathetic, helpful people; the one has a pail, the other a slop basin, the third a spray pump, etc., all nice, kind, sympathetic, helpful people eager to help put out the fire.

But what does the fire chief say? The fire chief, he says—well, usually the fire chief is a very affable and cultured man; but at a fire he is what one calls coarse-mouthed—he says, or rather he bellows, "Hey! Get the hell out of here with your pails and spray pumps." And when the well-meaning people perhaps become offended, find it extremely indecent to be treated this way, and insist on at least being treated with respect, what does the fire chief say? Well, usually the fire chief is a very affable and cultured man, who knows how to show everyone the respect due him, but at a fire he is something else—he says, "Where in hell are the police!" And if some policemen arrive, he says to them, "Get rid of these damned people with their pails and spray pumps; and if they won't go with kindness, then tan their hides so that we can get rid of them—and get going."

At a fire, then, the whole point of view is entirely different from the one in quiet everyday life; what makes one well-liked in quiet everyday life— kind, worthy, good intentions—is saluted at a fire with abusive language and finally with some hide-tanning.

And this is quite as it should be. A fire is a serious matter, and wherever there is really something serious these worthy, good intentions are utterly inadequate. No, seriousness introduces a completely different law: either/or— either you are the person who can do something in earnest here and have something to do in earnest here, or, if that is not the case with you, then the earnestness is simply that you take off. If you refuse to understand this, then let the fire chief have the police knock it into you, something that can be especially beneficial to you and perhaps can contribute to making you a little earnest, in accord with the seriousness of the fire.

It is just the same in the world of the spirit as at a fire. Wherever there is a cause to be advanced, an enterprise to be carried through, an idea to be applied—one can always be sure that when the person who is the man, the right one, the person who in the higher sense has and should have command, he who has earnestness and can give the cause the seriousness it truly has— one can always be sure that when he arrives on the scene, if I may put it this way, he will find a congenial company of blatherers who, in the name of earnestness, dabble in wanting to serve this cause, to advance this enterprise, to apply this idea, a company of blatherers who naturally regard unwillingness to make common cause with them (which is earnestness) as clear evidence that the person in question lacks earnestness. I say, when the right one comes, he will find this. I can also turn the matter this way: whether he is the right one is properly decided by how he understands himself in relation to this company of blatherers. If he thinks that it is they who are going to assist and that he will strengthen himself by joining them—he is *eo ipso* not the right one. Like the fire chief, the right one promptly sees that this company of blatherers must go, that its presence and actions are the most dangerous assistance the fire could have. But in the world of the spirit it is not as at a fire, where the fire chief merely needs to say to the police: Get rid of these people.

　　Just as it is in the whole world of the spirit, so it is also in the religious sphere. History has often been compared to what the chemists call a process. The metaphor can be very appropriate if, note well, it is rightly understood. There is what is called a filtering process. Water is filtered, and in this process the impure components are removed. History is a process in an entirely opposite sense. The idea is applied—and now enters into the process of history. But this, unfortunately, does not consist in—ludicrous assumption!— the purifying of the idea, which never is purer than at the beginning. No, it consists, at a steadily increasing rate, in botching, babbling, and prattling the idea, in vitiating the idea, in—the opposite of filtering—putting in the impure components originally lacking, until eventually, by way of the enthusiastic and mutually approving collaboration of a series of generations, the point is reached where the idea is completely destroyed, the opposite of the idea has become what is now called the idea and this, it is claimed, has been achieved by the historical process, in which the idea is purified and ennobled.

　　When the right one finally comes, he who in the highest sense has the task, perhaps chosen early for it and slowly brought up for this operation, which is to shed light onto the matter, to get a fire set to this tangle, the abode of all the blather, of all the illusions, of all the skulduggery—when he comes, he will always find a company of blatherers, who in convivial heartiness have some sort of idea that something is wrong and that something must be done, or who are prepared to chatter about the fact that something is terribly wrong, to become self-important by chattering about it. If at any moment he, the right one, is mistaken and thinks that it is this company that is going to help—he is *eo ipso* not the right one. If he makes a

XIV
233

mistake and becomes involved with this company—Governance immediately lets him go as unfit for use. But the right one sees with half an eye what the fire chief sees, that the company that with good intentions wants to help put out the fire with a pail or spray pump, that this same company, here where it is not a matter of putting out a fire but of just getting a fire started, that with good intentions wants to assist with a wooden match without the sulphur or with a damp candle-lighter—that this company must go, that he must not have the least thing to do with this company, that he must be as coarse-mouthed with them as possible, he who perhaps otherwise is anything but that. But everything depends upon getting rid of the company, because its effect in the form of hearty sympathy is to enfeeble the genuine earnestness of the cause. Naturally the company will be infuriated with him, with this frightful arrogance, and the like. This must not make any difference to him. Wherever there is truly to be earnestness, the law is: either/ or; either I am the one who is involved with this cause in earnest, is called to it and is unconditionally willing to venture decisively or, if this is not the case, then the earnestness is: have nothing at all to do with it. Nothing is more abhorrent, more villainous, betraying and causing a deeper demoralization, than this: to want to be involved a little in what should be *aut—aut, aut Caesar aut nihil* [either—or, either Caesar or nothing],[258] to want to be a little involved, so heartily dabbling, to babble about it, and then with this babbling to want falsely to credit themselves with being better than those who are not at all involved with the whole enterprise—credit themselves with being better and make the cause more difficult for the one who actually has the task.

XIV
234

"FIRST THE KINGDOM OF GOD."[259] A KIND OF SHORT STORY

XIV
248

The theological graduate Ludvig From[260]—he is seeking. When one hears that a "theological" graduate is seeking, one does not need a lively imagination to understand what it is that he is seeking—naturally, the kingdom of God, which, of course, one is to seek *first*.

But no, it is not that; what he is seeking is a royal livelihood as a pastor, and very much, which I shall indicate by a few episodes, happened *first* before he attained that.

First he attended high school, from which he graduated to the university. Thereupon he *first* passed two examinations, and after four years of study he *first* passed the degree examination.

So then he is a theological graduate, and one would perhaps think that after having *first* put all that behind him, he finally can get a chance to work for Christianity. Yes, one would think so. No, *first* he must attend the pastoral seminary for a half year; and when that is finished, nothing can be said about

having been able to seek during the first eight years, which had to be put behind him *first*.

And now we stand at the beginning of the story: the eight years are over, he is seeking.

His life, which until now cannot be said to have any relation to the unconditioned, suddenly assumes such a relation. He is seeking unconditionally everything; he fills one sheet of officially stamped paper after the other with writing; he runs from Herod to Pilate; he recommends himself both to the minister [of ecclesiastical affairs] and to the janitor—in short, he is totally in the service of the unconditioned. Indeed, one of his acquaintances, who has not seen him the last few years, is amazed to discover that he has become smaller; perhaps the explanation is that the same thing happened to him that happened to Münchhausen's dog, which was a greyhound but because of much running became a dachshund.

XIV
249

Three years go by in this way. After such enormously strenuous activity, our theological graduate really needs a rest, needs to have a respite from activity or to come to rest in an official position and be looked after a little by his future wife—for in the meantime he has *first* become engaged.

Finally, as Pernille says to Magdelone, the hour of his "deliverance" arrives,²⁶¹ so with the full power of conviction and from his personal experience he will be able to "witness" before the congregation that in Christianity there is salvation and deliverance—he obtains an official position.

What happens? By obtaining even more exact information about the income of the call than he had, he discovers that it is 150 rix-dollars less than he had believed. That did it! The unhappy man almost despairs. He has already bought official stamped paper in order to apply to the minister for permission to be considered as if he had not been called—and in order then to begin again from the beginning—but one of his acquaintances persuades him to give up this idea. So it ends with his retaining the call.

He is ordained—and the Sunday arrives when he is to be presented to the congregation. The dean, by whom this is done, is a more than ordinary man. He not only has (something most pastors have, and most often in proportion to their rank) an impartial eye for earthly gain, but also a speculative eye on world history, something he cannot keep for himself but lets the congregation share to its benefit. By a stroke of genius he has chosen as his text the words by the Apostle Peter, "Lo, we have left everything and followed you,"²⁶² and now explains to the congregation that precisely in times such as ours there must be such men as teachers, and in that connection he recommends this young man, who he knows was close to withdrawing because of the 150 rix-dollars.

XIV
250

Now the young man himself mounts the pulpit—and the Gospel for the day (strangely enough!) is: Seek **first** the kingdom of God.

He delivers his sermon. "A very good sermon," says the bishop, who himself was present, "a very good sermon; and it made the proper impression, the whole part about 'first' the kingdom of God, the manner in which he emphasized this *first*."

"But, your Reverence, do you believe that there was here the desirable agreement between the discourse and the life? On me this *first* made almost a satirical impression."

"How absurd! He is called, after all, to proclaim the doctrine, the sound unadulterated doctrine about seeking first the kingdom of God, and he did it very well."

*   *
*

This is the kind of worship one dares—under oath—to offer to God, the most horrible insult.

Whoever you are, just think of this Word of God, "first the kingdom of God," and then think about this story, which is so true, so true, so true, and you will not need more to make you realize that the whole official Christendom is an abyss of untruth and optical illusion, something so profane that the only true thing that can be said about it is: By ceasing to participate (if you usually do participate in the public divine service) in it as it now is, you always have one and a great guilt less, that of not participating in making a fool of God (see *This Must Be Said; So Let It Be Said*[263]).

God's Word says "First the kingdom of God," and the interpretation, perhaps even "the perfecting" of it (since one does not want to do it shabbily) is: first everything else and *last* the kingdom of God; at long last the things of this earth are obtained *first,* and then finally last of all a sermon about— first seeking God's kingdom. In this way one becomes a pastor, and the pastor's entire practice thus becomes a continual carrying out of this: first the things of this earth and then—the kingdom of God; first the consideration for the things of this earth, whether it pleases the government or the majority, or whether there is at least a group—that is: first a consideration for what fear of people bids or forbids, and then God's kingdom; first the things of this earth, first money, and then you can have your child baptized; first money, and then earth will be thrown on your coffin and there will be a funeral oration according to the fixed rate; first money, and then I will make the sick call; first money, and then: *virtus post nummos* [virtue after money];[264] first money, and then virtue, then the kingdom of God, and the latter finally comes last to such a degree that it does not come at all, and the whole thing remains with the first: money—only in that case one does not feel the urge "to go further."

XIV
251

This is how in everything and at every point official Christianity is related to the Christianity of the New Testament. And this is what is not even acknowledged to be wretchedness; no, it is brazenly insisted that Christianity is perfectible, that one cannot stay with the first Christianity, that it is only an element, etc.

Therefore there is nothing to which God is so opposed as official Christianity and participation therein with the claim to be worshiping him. If you believe, and that you surely do, that God is opposed to stealing, robbing, plundering, whoring, slandering, gluttonizing, etc.—the official Christianity and its worship are infinitely more loathsome to him. To think that a human being can be sunken in such brutish obtuseness and lack of spirit that he dares to offer God such worship, in which everything is thoughtlessness, spiritlessness, lethargy, and that people then brazenly dare to regard this as a forward step in Christianity!

This it is *my* duty to say, this, "Whoever you are, whatever your life is otherwise—by ceasing to participate (if you usually do participate) in the public divine service as it now is, you always have one and a great guilt less." You yourself, then, bear and have to bear the responsibility for how you act, but you have been made aware!

ONE LIVES ONLY ONCE

This saying is frequently heard in the world. "One lives only once; therefore I could wish to see Paris before I die, or to make a fortune as soon as possible, or at least to become something great in this world—because one lives only once."

It rarely happens, but nevertheless it does happen, that a person appears who has only one wish, very definitely only one wish. "This," he says, "this I could wish; oh, that this, my wish, might be fulfilled, because, alas, one lives only once!"

Imagine such a person on his deathbed. The wish was not fulfilled, but his soul, unchanged, clings to this wish—and now, now it is no longer possible. Then he rises up on his bed; with the passion of despair he once again states his wish, "Oh, what despair, it is not fulfilled; what despair, one lives only once!"

It seems terrible, and it truly is, but not as he thinks; what is terrible is not that the wish was unfulfilled, what is terrible is the passion with which he clings to it. His life is not wasted because his wish was not fulfilled, not at all; if his life is wasted it is because he refused to give up his wish, refused to learn anything higher from life than this matter of his only wish, as if its fulfillment or nonfulfillment would decide everything.

Therefore, what is truly terrible is something else entirely: for example, if a person on his deathbed discovers, or if on his deathbed he clearly perceives, something that he had dimly understood throughout his life but never wanted to understand, that to have suffered for the truth in this world belongs to being able to become eternally happy—and one lives only once, the once that for him is now over! And he did, after all, have it in his power; and eternity does not change, the eternity toward which, simply in dying, he then advances as his future!

We human beings are by nature inclined to view life as follows: we regard suffering as an evil that we strive in every way to avoid. And if we succeed, we then one day on our deathbed think we have good reason to be able to thank God that we were spared suffering. We human beings think that the point is merely to be able to slip happily and well through this world; and Christianity thinks that all terrors actually come from the other world, that the terrors of this world are childish compared with the terrors of eternity, and that the point is therefore not to slip happily and well through this life, but rightly to relate oneself to eternity through suffering.

One lives only once. If when death comes your life has been used well— that is, used so it rightly relates itself to eternity—God be eternally praised. If not, it is eternally irreparable—one lives only once!

One lives only once; this is the way it is here on earth. And while you are now living this once, the temporal extent of which dwindles with each dwindling hour, the God of love is in heaven fondly loving also you. Yes, loving; that is why he would like you finally to will what he for the sake of eternity wills for you: that you might resolve to will to suffer, that is, that you might resolve to will to love him, because you can love him only in suffering, or if you love him as he wills to be loved you will come to suffer. Remember, one lives only once; if it is neglected, if you do not come to suffer, if you avoid it—it is eternally irreparable. Compel you, no, the God of love will not do that at any price; he would then obtain something completely different from what he wills. Indeed, how could it occur to the God of love to will to compel to be loved! But he is love and out of love he wills that you should will as he wills. In love he suffers as only infinite and omnipotent love can suffer, which no human being is capable of comprehending; therefore he suffers when you do not will as he wills.

God is love. No human being was ever born whom this thought does not overwhelm in indescribable blessedness, especially when it comes close to him in such a way that "God is love" means "you are loved." In the next moment, when the understanding comes, "This means beginning to suffer"— how frightful! "Yes, but it is out of love that God wills it; it is because he wants to be loved; and that he wants to be loved by you is his love for you"—
well, then!—In the next moment, as soon as the suffering is in earnest—how frightful! "Yes, but it is out of love. You have no inkling of how he is suffering, because he knows very well that it is painful to suffer, but he nevertheless cannot be changed, because then he would become something other than love"—well, then!—In the next moment, as soon as the suffering is in earnest!—how frightful!

Yet be careful, take care that time does not go by unused, perhaps in useless suffering; remember, one lives only once. If it can be of help to you, look at the matter this way: be assured that in love God suffers more than you are suffering, but he cannot be changed by that. Yet above all remember: one lives only once. There is a loss that is eternally irreparable; thus eternity—even more frightful—far from wiping out the recollection of what is lost, is an eternal recollection of what is lost!

MY TASK

[*On draft:* September 1, 1855]

"I do not call myself a Christian; I do not speak of myself as a Christian." It is this that I must continually repeat; anyone who wants to understand my very special task must concentrate on being able to hold this firm.

Yes, I well know that it almost sounds like a kind of lunacy in this Christian world—where each and every one is a Christian, where being a Christian is something that everyone naturally is—that there is someone who says of himself, "I do not call myself a Christian," and someone whom Christianity occupies to the degree to which it occupies me.

But it cannot be otherwise. In this world of blather, what is true must always appear to be a kind of lunacy; and that it is a world of blather in which I live and that among other things it is also by this very blather that everyone is summarily a Christian—that is certain enough.

Yet I neither can, nor will, nor dare change my statement: otherwise perhaps another change would intervene—that the power, an omnipotence that especially uses my powerlessness, would wash his hands of me and let me go my own way. No, I neither can, nor will, nor dare change my statement. I cannot serve these legions of huckstering knaves, I mean the pastors, who by falsifying the definition of Christian have, for the sake of the business, gained millions and millions of Christians. I am not a Christian—and unfortunately I am able to make it manifest that the others are not either—indeed, even less than I, since they fancy themselves to be that, or they falsely ascribe to themselves that they are that, or they (like the pastors) make others think that they are that, whereby the pastor-business flourishes.

The point of view I have set forth and do set forth is of such a distinctive nature that I quite literally have no analogy to cite, nothing corresponding in eighteen hundred years of Christianity. In this way, too—facing eighteen hundred years—I stand quite literally alone.*

---

* *Note.* Inasmuch as I have made a critical comment with regard to "the apostle,"[266] please note the following. 1. I am perfectly right, because the apostle is only a human being. My task requires its being pressed to the limit. If in the apostle's proclamation there is even the slight-

The only analogy I have before me is Socrates; my task is a Socratic task, to audit the definition of what it is to be a Christian—I do not call myself a Christian (keeping the ideal free), but I can make it manifest that the others are that even less.

You, antiquity's noble simple soul, you, the only *human being* I admiringly acknowledge as a thinker; there is only a little preserved about you, of all people the only true martyr of intellectuality, just as great *qua* character as *qua* thinker; but how exceedingly much this little is! Even though over the centuries there have lived in Christendom a few isolated significant thinkers—how I long to be able to speak with you for only a half hour, far away from these battalions of thinkers that "Christendom" places in the field under the name of Christian thinkers!

"Christendom" lies in an abyss of sophistry that is even much, much worse than when the Sophists flourished in Greece. Those legions of pastors and Christian assistant professors are all sophists, supporting themselves—here, of course, in accord with antiquity's characterization of the Sophist[265]—by making those who understand nothing believe something and then making this human number the authority for what the truth is, for what Christianity is.

But I do not call myself a Christian. That this is very awkward for the sophists I understand very well, and I understand very well that they would much rather see that with kettledrums and trumpets I would proclaim myself to be the only true Christian, and I also understand very well that an attempt is being made to represent my conduct falsely in this way. But they do not fool me! In a certain sense I am very easy to fool; I have almost been fooled in every relationship I have been in—but that has been because I myself wanted it. If I do not want it, there is not one of my contemporaries who fools me, a definite detective talent such as I am.

Consequently, I am not fooled; I do not call myself a Christian. In a certain sense it seems easy enough to get rid of me; the others are indeed such completely different fellows, they are true Christians. Yes, indeed, so it seems. But it is not so; just because I do not call myself a Christian, it is impossible to get rid of me, having as I do the confounded capacity of being able, also by means of not calling myself a Christian, to make it manifest that the others are even less so.

---

est thing that could pertain to what has become the sophistry corruptive of all true Christianity, then I must raise an outcry lest the sophists summarily cite the apostle. 2. If it is of great importance, to Protestantism in particular, to correct the enormous confusion Luther caused by inverting the relation and actually criticizing Christ by means of Paul, the Master by means of the follower. I, on the contrary, have not criticized the apostle, as if I myself were something. I who am not even a Christian; what I have done is to hold Christ's proclamation alongside the apostle's. 3. It is one thing to be able intellectually to make a dialectically true comment; it is something else to want to disparage, to weaken the apostle, something I am as far from doing as anyone.

O Socrates! If with kettledrums and trumpets you had proclaimed yourself to be the one who knew the most, the Sophists would soon have been finished with you. No, you were the ignorant one; but you also had the confounded capacity of being able (also by means of being yourself the ignorant one) to make it manifest that the others knew even less than you—they did not even know that they were ignorant.

But the same thing has happened to me that happened to you (according to what you say in your "defense," as you ironically enough have called the cruelest satire on a contemporary age[267])—namely, that you thereby made many enemies for yourself by making it manifest that they were ignorant and, as imputed to you, that you yourself must be what you could show that the others were not, and therefore in envy they had a grudge against you. It has provoked rage against me that I am able to make it manifest that the others are even less Christian than I am, who nevertheless relate myself to Christianity so much that I truly perceive and acknowledge that I am not a Christian. Some want to foist on me that my saying that I am not a Christian is only a hidden form of pride, that I presumably must be what I can show the others are not. But this is a misunderstanding. It is altogether true: I am not a Christian; and it is rash to conclude that because I can show that the others are not Christians, then I myself must be one, just as rash as to conclude, for example, that someone who is one-fourth of a foot taller than others is, ergo, twelve feet tall.

You common man! The Christianity of the New Testament is something infinitely high, but please note that it is not high in such a way that it pertains to differences among people with regard to talents etc. No, it is for all. Everyone, unconditionally everyone—if he will unconditionally, will unconditionally hate himself, will unconditionally put up with everything, suffer everything (and everyone can indeed do that if he will)—then this something infinitely high is accessible to him.

You common man! I have not segregated my life from yours, you know that; I have lived on the street, am known by all.[268] Furthermore, I have not become somebody, do not belong to any class-egotism. So if I belong to anyone, I must belong to you, you common man, you who nevertheless at one time, enticed by someone who, making money on you, gave the appearance of desiring your welfare,[269] have been willing enough to consider me and my life ludicrous, you who least of all have reason to be impatient over or should be unappreciative of my belonging to you, something the more elite have rather had reason to be because I definitely have not joined them but have kept only a loose relation to them.

You common man! I do not keep it a secret from you that, according to my concepts, to be a Christian is something so infinitely high that there are always only few who attain it (which both Christ's life affirms if one pays at-

XIV 356

XIV 357

tention to his contemporaries and his proclamation suggests if one takes it strictly)—yet it is possible for all. But one thing I beseech you for God in heaven's sake and by all that is holy: avoid the pastors, avoid them, those abominations whose job is to hinder you in even becoming aware of what true Christianity is and thereby to turn you, muddled by gibberish and illusion, into what they understand by a true Christian, a contributing member of the state Church, the national Church, and the like. Avoid them; only see to it that you willingly and promptly pay them the money they are to have. One must at no price have money differences with someone one scorns, lest it be said that one was avoiding them in order to get out of paying. No, pay them double so that your disagreement with them can become obvious: that what concerns them does not concern you at all, money, and that, on the contrary, what does not concern them concerns you infinitely, Christianity.

ON MY WORK AS AN AUTHOR (AUGUST 7, 1851)
THE POINT OF VIEW FOR MY WORK AS AN AUTHOR
(WRITTEN 1848, PUBLISHED 1859)
BY S. KIERKEGAARD

Written in 1848, published in a very truncated version in 1851 as *On My Work as an Author,* and posthumously published in full in 1859, *The Point of View for My Work as an Author* is the direct, detailed completion of Kierkegaard's partial and oblique observations on the authorship in "A Glance at a Contemporary Effort in Danish Literature" and the appended "A First and Last Explanation" in *Postscript.* In the earlier truncated version, the main section, "The Accounting," is followed by an appendix on "My Position as a Religious Author in 'Christendom' and My strategy." The subtitle of *Point of View* is "*A Direct Communication, Report to History.*" "Armed Neutrality" (written in 1849, unpublished until it appeared in *Efterladte Papirer,* V, 1880) has the subtitle "On My Position as a Christian in Christendom." The key thought in all three works is that the medium for being a Christian had to a large extent been shifted from existence and the ethical to the intellectual and the imaginational, to a more or less distanced habitual presumption of Christianity instead of existential engagement. Brought to a halt before the ideal, Kierkegaard had regarded a presentation of the ideal to be his task, in itself an inferior relationship—therefore "I am only a poet." These works are about the writings and the personal engagement of the author in the writing, not a diary-type of personal disclosure. In a special sense, then, they may be regarded as autobiography, especially *The Point of View,* which Walter Lowrie has called "a religious autobiography so unique that it has no parallel in the whole literature of the world."[270]

Copenhagen, March 1849.

W HEN A country is little, the proportions in every relationship in the little land naturally are small. So, too, in literary matters; the royalties and everything else involved will be only insignificant. To be an author—unless one is a poet, and in addition a dramatist, or one who writes textbooks or in some other way is an author in connection with a public office—is about the poorest paid, the least secure, and just about the most thankless job there is. If there is some individual who has the capability of being an author and if he is also fortunate enough to have private means, then he becomes an author more or less at his own expense. This, however, is quite appropriate; there is nothing more to be said about it. In that way the individual in his work will love his idea, the nation to which he belongs, the cause he serves, the language he as an author has the honor to write. Indeed, this is how it will be where there is harmony between the individual and the nation, which in turn in the given situation will be somewhat appreciative of this individual.

Whether the opposite of this has in any way been my experience, whether I have been treated shabbily by anyone or by some persons, is really not my concern but quite properly is their business. What is my concern, however—and I am so happy that it is my concern—is that I should and ought to give thanks for whatever favors and kindness and courtesy and appreciation have been shown to me in general or by particular individuals.

———

The movement the authorship describes is: *from* "the poet," from the esthetic—*from* "the philosopher," from the speculative—*to* the indication of the most inward qualification of the essentially Christian; **from** the pseudonymous Either/Or, **through** *Concluding Postscript*, with *my name as editor*, **to** *Discourses at the Communion on Fridays,** of which two were delivered in Frue Church.

This movement was traversed or delineated *uno tenore*, in one breath, if I dare say so—thus the authorship, regarded as a *totality*, is religious from first to last, something anyone who can see, if he wants to see, must also see. Just as one versed in natural science promptly knows from the crisscrossing threads in a web the ingenious little creature whose web it is, so an insightful person will also know that to this authorship there corresponds as the

XIII 494

XIII 495

XIII 494

* Later, however, there appeared a new pseudonym: Anti-Climacus. But the very fact that it is a pseudonym signifies that he is, inversely, coming to a halt, as the name (*Anti*-Climacus) indeed suggests. All the previous pseudonymity is lower than "the upbuilding author"; the new pseudonym is a higher pseudonymity. But indeed "a halt is made" in this way: something higher is shown, which simply forces me back within my boundary, judging me, that my life does not meet so high a requirement and that consequently the communication is something poetical. —And a little earlier in that same year there appeared a little book: *Two Ethical-Religious Essays* by H. H. The significance of this little book (which does not stand *in* the authorship as much as it relates totally *to* the authorship and for that reason also was anonymous, in order to be kept outside entirely) is not very easy to explain without going into the whole matter. It is like a navigation mark *by* which one steers but, note well, in such a way that the pilot understands precisely that *he is to keep a certain distance from it*. It defines the boundary of the authorship. "The Difference between a Genius and an Apostle" (essay no. 2) is: "The genius is without authority." But precisely because genius as such is without authority, it does not have in itself the ultimate concentration that provides the power and justification for accentuating in the direction of "letting oneself be put to death for the truth" (essay no. 1). Genius as such remains in reflection. This in turn is the category of my whole authorship: to *make aware* of the religious, the essentially Christian—but "*without authority.*" —And finally, to include even the smallest, there came out later *The Lily in the Field and the Bird of the Air, Three Devotional Discourses,*" which accompanied the second edition of *Either/Or;* and "The High Priest"—"The Tax Collector"—"The Woman Who Was a Sinner," *Three Discourses at the Communion on Fridays,* which accompanied Anti-Climacus's *The Sickness unto Death*—two small books, both of which in the preface repeat that first preface, the preface to *Two Upbuilding Discourses* (1843).
October 1849

source someone who *qua* author "has willed only one thing." The insightful person will also know that this one thing is the religious, but the religious completely cast into reflection, yet in such a way that it is completely taken back out of reflection into simplicity—that is, he will see that the traversed path is: to *reach*, to *arrive at* simplicity.

And this is also (in *reflection,* as it in fact was originally) the **Christian** *movement.* Christianly, one does not proceed from the simple in order then to become interesting, witty, profound, a poet, a philosopher, etc. No, it is just the opposite; *here* one begins and then becomes more and more simple, arrives at the simple. This, in "Christendom," is *Christianly* the movement of reflection; one does not reflect oneself into Christianity but reflects oneself out of something else and becomes more and more simple, a Christian. If the author had been a richly endowed intellect, or, if he was that, if he had been a doubly richly endowed intellect, he probably would have needed a longer or a doubly long period in order to describe this path in literary production and to reach this point.

*   *
*

But just as that which has been communicated (the idea of the religious) has been cast completely into reflection and in turn taken back out of reflection, so also the *communication* has been decisively marked by *reflection,* or the form of communication used is that of reflection. "Direct communication" is: to communicate the truth directly; "communication in reflection" is: to *deceive into the truth.* But since the movement is to arrive at the simple, the communication in turn must sooner or later end in direct communication. It began **maieutically**[271] with esthetic production,* and all the pseudonymous writings are *maieutic* in nature. Therefore this writing was also pseudonymous, whereas the directly religious—which from the beginning was present in the gleam of an indication—carried my name. The directly religious was present from the very beginning; *Two Upbuilding Discourses* (1843) is in fact concurrent** with *Either/Or.* And in order to

XIII
496

---

* The maieutic lies in the relation between the esthetic writing as the beginning and the religious as the τέλος [goal]. It begins with the esthetic, in which possibly most people have their lives, and now the religious is introduced so quickly that those who, moved by the esthetic, decide to follow along are suddenly standing right in the middle of the decisive qualifications of the essentially Christian, are at least prompted to become *aware.*

** This also serves to prevent the illusion that the religious is something one turns to when one has become older. "One begins as an esthetic author and then when one has become older and no longer has the powers of youth, then one becomes a religious author." But if an author *concurrently* begins as an esthetic and a religious author, the religious writing certainly cannot be explained by the incidental fact that the author has become older, inasmuch as one certainly cannot concurrently be older than oneself.

safeguard this concurrence of the directly religious, every pseudonymous work was accompanied concurrently by a little collection of "upbuilding discourses"—until *Concluding Postscript* appeared, which poses the issue, which is *the issue* κατ᾽ ἐξοχήν [in the eminent sense] of the whole authorship: *becoming a Christian.*"* From that moment the gleam of the directly religious ceases, since now the exclusively religious writing begins: *Up-building Discourses in Various Spirits, Works of Love, Christian Discourses.* But in order inversely to recall the beginning (corresponding to what *Two Up-building Discourses* was at the beginning, when the voluminous works were esthetic), there appeared at the end (when for a long period the writing was exclusively and voluminously religious) a little esthetic article by Inter et Inter in the newspaper *Fædrelandet,* no. 188–191, July 1848. The gleam of the two upbuilding discourses at the beginning meant that it was actually this that should advance, this at which it was to arrive; the gleam of the little esthetic article at the end was meant, by way of a faint reflection, to bring to consciousness that from the beginning the esthetic was what should be left behind, what should be abandoned. *Concluding Postscript* is the midpoint, and so exactly—something that of course only lays claim to being a curiosity—that even the quantities of what was written before and after it are more or less equal if one, and rightfully so, includes the eighteen upbuilding discourses in the purely religious writing, and even the periods of the literary activity prior to and after *Concluding Postscript* are roughly equal.

Finally, this movement of the authorship is again decisively marked by reflection or is the movement of reflection. The direct way begins with individuals, a few readers, and the task or the movement is to gather a large number, to acquire an abstraction: the public. Here the **beginning is made,** *maieutically,* with a sensation, and with what belongs to it, the public, which always joins in where something is going on; and the movement was, *maieutically,* to shake off "the crowd" in order to get hold of "the sin-

---

* The *situation* (becoming a *Christian* in *Christendom,* where consequently one is a Christian)—the situation, which, as every dialectician sees, casts everything into reflection, also makes an indirect method necessary, because the task here must be to take measures against the illusion: calling oneself a Christian, perhaps deluding oneself into thinking one is that without being that. Therefore, the one who introduced the issue did not *directly* define himself as being Christian and the others as not being that; no, just the *reverse*—he denies being that and concedes it to the others. This Johannes Climacus does.—In relation to pure receptivity, like the empty jar that is to be filled, *direct* communication is appropriate, but when illusion is involved, consequently something that must first be removed, direct communication is inappropriate.

gle individual,"* religiously understood. At the very same time when the
sensation *Either/Or* created was at its peak, at that very same time appeared
Two Upbuilding Discourses (1843), which used the formula that later was repeated unchanged: "It seeks that single individual whom I with joy and gratitude call my reader." And precisely at the critical moment when *Concluding Postscript*, which, as stated, poses "the issue," was delivered to the printer
so that the printing could commence as soon as possible and the publication presumably quickly follow—at precisely that moment a pseudonym,
most appropriately in a newspaper article,[272] made the greatest possible effort to alienate the public** and after that began the decisively religious production. For the second time I religiously affirmed "that single individual,"
to whom the next substantial book† (after *Concluding Postscript*), *Upbuilding
Discourses in Various Spirits,* or the first part of the same book, "Confessional
Address," was dedicated. Perhaps nobody paid much attention to the category "that single individual" the first time I used it, nor was much notice
paid to its being repeated unchanged in the preface to every volume of upbuilding discourses. When I the second time or in the second potency repeated the message and stood by my first message, everything was done that
I was able to do to make the whole weight of emphasis fall upon this category. Here again the movement is: to *arrive* at the simple; the movement is:
from the public *to* "the single individual." In other words, there is in a *religious sense* no public but only individuals,†† because the religious is earnest-

* This again is the dialectical movement (like that in which a religious author *begins* with esthetic writing, and like that in which, instead of loving oneself and one's advantage and supporting one's endeavor by illusions, one instead, hating oneself, removes illusions), or it is the
dialectical method: in *working* also to *work against oneself,* which is reduplication [*Redupplikation*]
and the heterogeneity of all true godly endeavor to secular endeavor. To endeavor or to work
directly is to work or to endeavor directly in immediate connection with a factually given state
of things. The dialectical method is the *reverse:* in working also to work against oneself, a redoubling [*Fordoblelse*], which is "the earnestness," like the pressure on the plow that determines
the depth of the furrow, whereas the direct endeavor is a glossing-over, which is furnished more
rapidly and also is much, much more rewarding—that is, it is worldliness and homogeneity.

** Just one thing more, the press of literary contemptibility had achieved a frightfully disproportionate coverage. To be honest, I believed that what I did was a public benefaction; it
was rewarded by several of those for whose sake I had exposed myself in that way—rewarded,
yes, as an act of love is usually rewarded in the world—and by means of this reward it became
a truly Christian work of love.

† The little literary review of the novel *Two Ages* followed *Concluding Postscript* so closely
that it is almost concurrent and is, after all, something written by me *qua* critic and not *qua* author; but it does contain in the last section a sketch of the future from the point of view of
"the single individual," a sketch of the future that the year 1848 did not falsify.

†† And insofar as there is the *congregation* in the religious sense, this is a concept that lies on
the other side of *the single individual,* and that above all must not be confused with what *polit-
ically* can have validity: the public, the crowd, the numerical, etc.

ness, and earnestness is: the single individual; yet every human being, unconditionally every human being, which one indeed is, can be, yes, should
be—the single individual. Thus it was and is a joy to me, the upbuilding author, that also from that moment the number of those increased who became aware of this about *the single individual*. It was and is a joy to me, for
I certainly do have faith in the rightness of my thought despite the whole
world, but next to that the last thing I would surrender is my faith in individual human beings. And this is my faith, that however much confusion
and evil and contemptibleness there can be in human beings as soon as they
become the irresponsible and unrepentant "public," "crowd," etc.—there is
just as much truth and goodness and lovableness in them when one can get
them as single individuals. Oh, to what degree human beings would become—human and lovable beings—if they would become single individuals before God!

XIII
500

This is how I *now* understand the whole. From the beginning I could not
quite see what has indeed also been my own development. This is scarcely
the place for a lengthy account. Here it is just a matter of being able very
briefly to fold together in simplicity what is unfolded in the many books or
what unfolded is the many books, and this brief communication is more immediately prompted by the fact that the first book in the authorship now
comes out the second time, the new edition of *Either/Or*, which I earlier
was unwilling to have published.

Personally—also when I consider my own inner sufferings, which I personally may have deserved—personally, one thing absorbs me unconditionally, is more important to me and lies more upon my heart than the whole
authorship: to express as honestly and as strongly as possible something for
which I can never adequately give thanks and which I, when I at some time
have forgotten the whole authorship, will eternally recollect unchanged—
how infinitely much more Governance has done for me than I had ever expected, could have expected, or dared to have expected.

XIII
501

"*Without authority*" **to make aware** of the religious, the essentially Christian, is the category for my whole work as an author regarded as a totality.
From the very beginning I have enjoined and repeated unchanged that I was
"without authority." I regard myself rather as a *reader* of the books, not as the
author.

"Before God," religiously, when I speak with myself, I call my whole work
as an author my own upbringing and development, but not in the sense as if
I were now complete or completely finished with regard to needing upbringing and development.

THE POINT OF VIEW FOR MY WORK AS AN AUTHOR
A DIRECT COMMUNICATION, REPORT TO HISTORY
BY S. KIERKEGAARD

THE EQUIVOCALNESS OR DUPLEXITY

IN THE WHOLE AUTHORSHIP*

WHETHER THE AUTHOR IS AN ESTHETIC

OR A RELIGIOUS AUTHOR

XIII
521

Accordingly, what is to be shown here is that there *is* such a duplexity from beginning to end. It is not, then, as is ordinarily the case with a supposed duplexity, that others have discovered it and it is the task of the person concerned to show that it *is not*. By no means, just the opposite. Insofar as the reader might not be sufficiently aware of the duplexity, it is the author's task to make it as obvious as possible that it is there. In other words, the duplexity, the equivocalness, is deliberate, is something the author knows about more than anyone else, is the essential dialectical qualification of the whole authorship, and therefore has a deeper basis.

But is this really the case, is there such a sustained duplexity? Can the phenomenon not be explained in another way, that it is an author who was first an esthetic author and then in the course of years *changed* and became a religious author? I will not now discuss the point that if this were so the author certainly would not have written a book such as the present one, would scarcely, I dare say, have taken it upon himself to give an overview of the writing as a whole, at least would not have chosen to do so at the very time he meets his first work again.[274] Nor will I discuss the point that it would indeed be odd that such a change would occur in the course of so few years. Ordinarily, when it is seen that an esthetic author becomes a religious author, at least a considerable number of years intervenes, so that the explanation of the change is not implausible, so that it is consistent with the author's actually having become significantly older. But I will not discuss this, since even if it were odd, almost inexplicable, even if it might make one inclined to seek and find any other explanation, it would still not be impossible that such a change could occur in the course of three years. On the contrary, I will show that it is impossible to explain the phenomenon in this way. If,

XIII
522

---

* In order to have them at hand, here are the titles of the books. First division (esthetic writing): *Either/Or, Fear and Trembling, Repetition, The Concept of Anxiety, Prefaces, Philosophical Fragments, Stages on Life's Way*—together with eighteen upbuilding discourses, which came out successively. Second division: *Concluding Unscientific Postscript.* Third division (only religious writing): *Upbuilding Discourses in Various Spirits, Works of Love, Christian Discourses*—together with a little esthetic article: *The Crisis and a Crisis in the Life of an Actress.*[273]

namely, one looks more closely, one will see that three years are certainly not allowed for the occurrence of the change, but that the change is concurrent with the beginning, that is, that the duplexity is there from the very beginning. *Two Upbuilding Discourses* is concurrent with *Either/Or.* The duplexity in the deeper sense, that is, in the sense of the whole authorship, was certainly not what there was talk about at the time: the first and second parts of *Either/Or.* No, the duplexity was: *Either/Or*—and *Two Upbuilding Discourses.*

The religious is present from the very beginning. Conversely, the esthetic is still present even in the last moment. After the publication of only religious works for two years, a little esthetic article follows.* Therefore, at the beginning and at the end, there is assurance against explaining the phenomenon by saying that the writer is an esthetic author who in the course of time had changed and had become a religious author. Just as *Two Upbuilding Discourses* came out approximately two or three months after *Either/Or,* so also that little esthetic article appeared about two or three months after two years of exclusively religious writings. The two upbuilding discourses and the little article match each other conversely and conversely show that the duplexity is both first and last. Although *Either/Or* attracted all the attention and no one paid attention to *Two Upbuilding Discourses,* this nevertheless signified that it was specifically the upbuilding that should advance, that the author was a religious author who for that reason never wrote anything esthetic himself but used pseudonyms for all the esthetic works, whereas the two upbuilding discourses were by Magister Kierkegaard. Conversely, whereas the exclusively upbuilding books of the two years may have attracted the attention of others, perhaps no one in turn has noticed in the deeper sense the little article, what it signifies—that now the dialectical structure of this whole authorship is complete. The little article is an accompaniment precisely for documentation, for the sake of confrontation, in order at the end to make it impossible (as the two upbuilding discourses do at the beginning) to explain the phenomenon in this way—that it is an author who in the beginning was an esthetic author and then later *changed* and thus became a religious author—inasmuch as he was a religious author from the very beginning and is esthetically productive at the last moment.

The first division of books is esthetic writing; the last division of books is exclusively religious writing—between these lies *Concluding Unscientific Postscript* as the *turning point.* This work deals with and poses *the issue,* the issue of the entire work as an author: becoming a Christian. Then in turn it calls attention** to the pseudonymous writing along with the interlaced 18 dis-

_____

* *The Crisis and a Crisis in the Life of an Actress. Fædrelandet,* July 1848.
** See pp. 187–227 [*SV* VII 212–257; *KW* XII.1, pp. 251–300], a section with which I would ask the reader to become familiar.

courses and shows all this as serving to illuminate the issue, yet without stating that this was the object of the prior writing—which could not be done, since it is a pseudonymous writer who is interpreting other pseudonymous writers, that is, a third party who could know nothing about the object of writings unfamiliar to him. *Concluding Unscientific Postscript* is not esthetic writing, but, strictly speaking, neither is it religious. That is why it is by a pseudonymous writer, although I did place my name as editor, which I have not done with any purely esthetic production*—a hint, at least for someone who is concerned with or has a sense for such things. Then came the two years in which there appeared only religious writings under my name. The time of the pseudonyms was over; the religious author had extricated himself from the disguise of the esthetic—and then, then for documentation and by way of a precaution came the little esthetic article by a pseudonymous writer: Inter et Inter. In a way it at once calls attention to the whole authorship; as said previously, it calls to mind conversely *Two Upbuilding Discourses*.

XIII
524

A

THE ESTHETIC WRITING

WHY THE BEGINNING WAS MADE WITH ESTHETIC WRITING

OR WHAT THIS WRITING, UNDERSTOOD IN THE TOTALITY,** SIGNIFIES

XIII
529

§ 1

"Christendom" Is an Enormous Illusion

Everyone who in earnest and also with some clarity of vision considers what is called Christendom, or the condition in a so-called Christian country, must without any doubt immediately have serious misgivings. What does it mean, after all, that all these thousands and thousands as a matter of course call themselves Christians! These many, many people, of whom by far the great majority, according to everything that can be discerned, have their lives in entirely different categories, something one can ascertain by the simplest observation! People who perhaps never once go to church, never think about God, never name his name except when they curse! People to whom it has never occurred that their lives should have some duty to God, people who either maintain that a certain civil impunity is the highest or do not find even this to be entirely necessary! Yet all these people, even those who insist that

XIII
530

---

* The literary review of *Two Ages* is no argument against this, both because it is not, after all, esthetic in the sense of being a poet-production but is critical, and because it has a totally religious background in its understanding of "the present age."

** Once and for all I must urgently request the kindly disposed reader continually to bear *in mente* [in mind] that the total thought in the entire work as an author is this: becoming a Christian.

there is no God, they all are Christians, call themselves Christians, are recognized as Christians by the state, are buried as Christians by the Church, are discharged as Christians to eternity!

That there must be an enormous underlying confusion here, a dreadful illusion, of that there can surely be no doubt. But to touch on this! Yes, I am well aware of the objection! There surely are this one and that one who understand what I mean but who then with a certain good-naturedness would pat me on the shoulder and say, "My dear friend, you are still rather young—and then to want to begin such a project, a project that, if it is to have any success at all, would require at least a dozen well-trained missionaries, a project that amounts to neither more nor less than wanting to introduce Christianity again—into Christendom. No, dear friend, let us be human beings; such a project is beyond both your power and mine. This project is just as insanely grandiose as wanting to reform 'the crowd,' which no sensible person gets involved with but lets it be what it is. To begin on such a thing is sure disaster." Perhaps, but even if it is or would be sure disaster, it is also certain that the objection has not been learned from Christianity, because when Christianity entered into the world it was even more decidedly sure disaster to begin on it—yet it was begun; and it is also certain that this objection was not learned from Socrates, because he involved himself with "the crowd" and wanted to reform it.

This is just about the way things are. Every once in a while a pastor makes a little fuss in the pulpit about there being something not quite right with all these many Christians—but all those who hear him and who are present there, consequently all those he is speaking *to,* are Christians, and of course he is not speaking to those he is speaking *about.* This is most appropriately called simulated motion. —Every once in a while a religious enthusiast appears. He makes an assault on Christendom; he makes a big noise, denounces nearly all as not being Christians—and he accomplishes nothing. He does not take into account that an illusion is not so easy to remove. If it is the case that most people are under an illusion when they call themselves Christians, what do they do about an enthusiast like that? First and foremost, they pay no attention to him at all, do not read his book but promptly lay it *ad acta* [aside]; or if he makes use of the Living Word,[275] they go around on another street and do not listen to him at all. Then by means of a definition they smuggle him outside and settle down quite securely in their illusion. They make him out to be a fanatic and his Christianity to be an exaggeration—in the end he becomes the only one, or one of the few, who is not a Christian in earnest (since exaggeration, after all, is a lack of earnestness); the others are all earnest Christians.

No, an illusion can never be removed directly, and basically only indirectly. If it is an illusion that all are Christians, and if something is to be done, it must be done indirectly, not by someone who loudly declares himself to be

XIII
531

an extraordinary Christian, but by someone who, better informed, even declares himself not to be a Christian.* That is, one who is under an illusion must be approached from behind. Instead of wanting to have for oneself the advantage of being the rare Christian, one must let the one ensnared have the advantage that he is a Christian, and then oneself have sufficient resignation to be the one who is far behind him—otherwise one will surely fail to extricate him from the illusion; it can be difficult enough anyway.

If, then, according to the assumption, most people in Christendom are Christians only in imagination, in what categories do they live? They live in esthetic or, at most, esthetic-ethical categories.

On the assumption, then, that a religious author has from the ground up become aware of this illusion, Christendom, and to the limit of his ability with, note well, the help of God, wants to stamp it out—what is he to do then? Well, first and foremost, no impatience. If he becomes impatient, then he makes a direct assault and accomplishes—nothing. By a direct attack he only strengthens a person in the illusion and also infuriates him. Generally speaking, there is nothing that requires as gentle a treatment as the removal of an illusion. If one in any way causes the one ensnared to be antagonized, then all is lost. And this one does by a direct attack, which in addition also contains the presumptuousness of demanding that another person confess to one or face-to-face with one make the confession that actually is most beneficial when the person concerned makes it to himself secretly. The latter is achieved by the indirect method, which in the service of the love of truth dialectically arranges everything for the one ensnared and then, modest as love always is, avoids being witness to the confession that he makes alone before God, the confession that he has been living in an illusion.

XIII
532

Therefore the religious author first of all must try to establish rapport with people. That is, he must begin with an esthetic piece. This is earnest money. The more brilliant the piece is, the better it is for him. Next, he must be sure of himself, or rather he must in fear and trembling relate himself to God (the surest and the only surety), lest the opposite happen, so that he does not become the one who gives the others a start but the others become the ones who get power over him and then he ends up becoming stuck in the esthetic himself. Therefore he must have everything prepared in order, yet without any impatience, to bring forth the religious as swiftly as possible as soon as he has gained their attention, so that with the momentum of being engrossed in the esthetic the same people come face-to-face with the religious.

The point is to introduce the religious neither too speedily nor too slowly.

---

* One recalls *Concluding Unscientific Postscript,* whose author, Johannes Climacus, directly declares that he himself is not a Christian.[276]

If too long a time intervenes, there immediately arises the illusion that now the esthetic author has become older and therefore religious. If it comes too swiftly, the effect is not strong enough.

On the assumption that it is an enormous illusion that all these many people call themselves and are regarded as being Christians, there is no judgment and condemnation in this approach. It is a true Christian invention, cannot be practiced without fear and trembling, only in true self-denial. The helper is precisely the one who carries all the responsibility and has all the strain. But that is why this approach has intrinsic worth. Ordinarily it holds true that an approach has worth only in proportion to what is achieved by it. One judges and condemns, makes a big noise—this has no intrinsic worth, but one reckons on achieving a great deal thereby. It is different with the approach described here. Assume that a person had devoted his whole life to using it, assume that he had practiced it all his life, and assume that he had achieved nothing—he nevertheless has by no means lived in vain, because his life was true self-denial.

XIII
533

§ 2

If One Is Truly to Succeed in Leading a Person to a Specific Place,
One Must First and Foremost Take Care to Find Him
*Where **He** Is and Begin There*

This is the secret in the entire art of helping. Anyone who cannot do this is himself under a delusion if he thinks he is able to help someone else. In order truly to help someone else, I must understand more than he—but certainly first and foremost understand what he understands. If I do not do that, then my greater understanding does not help him at all. If I nevertheless want to assert my greater understanding, then it is because I am vain or proud, then basically instead of benefiting him I really want to be admired by him. But all true helping begins with a humbling. The helper must first humble himself under the person he wants to help and thereby understand that to help is not to dominate but to serve, that to help is not to be the most dominating but the most patient, that to help is a willingness for the time being to put up with being in the wrong and not understanding what the other understands.

Consider a person who is impassioned about something, granted that he actually is in the wrong. If you cannot begin with him in such a way that it seems as if it is he who should teach you, and if you cannot do this in such a way that he, who impatiently refuses to listen to a word from you, is gratified to find in you a willing and attentive listener—if you cannot do that, then you cannot help him either. Consider an infatuated person who became unhappy in love; assume that it is actually indefensible, sinful, and unchristian to surrender to his passion as he does. If you cannot begin in such a way with him that he finds genuine alleviation in speaking with you about his suffering, in such a way that you, in what you add concerning his suffering, almost enrich him with a poetical view, you who still do not share the passion and specifically want to have him out of it—if you cannot do that, you cannot help him either. He shuts himself off from you, shuts himself up in his innermost being—and then you merely preach to him. Perhaps by personal power you will be able to force him to confess to you that he is in the wrong. Ah, my dear fellow, the very next moment he sneaks around by another path, a secret path, to a rendezvous with the secret passion, for which he now longs all the more; yes, he has almost become afraid that it would have lost some of its seductive fervor—for now by your behavior you have helped him to fall in love once again, namely, with his unhappy passion— and then you only preach!

XIII
534

So it is also with becoming a Christian, under the assumption that it is a delusion on the part of the multitude in Christendom who call themselves Christian. Denounce the bewitchery of the esthetic—well, there have been times when you thereby might have succeeded in coercing people. Yes, to what end?—to love in their secret heart that bewitchery even more fanatically with clandestine passion. No, let it come forward—and you earnest, rigorous man, remember that if you cannot humble yourself you are not the earnest one either—be the astonished listener who sits and listens to what delights that other person, whom it delights even more that you listen in that way. But above all do not forget one thing, the number carried [*in Mente*] that you have, that it is the religious that you are to have come forward. Or, if you are able to do so, portray the esthetic with all its bewitching charm, if possible captivate the other person, portray it with the kind of passionateness whereby it appeals particularly to him, hilariously to the hilarious, sadly to the sad, wittily to the witty, etc.—but above all do not forget one thing, the number carried that you have, that it is the religious that is to come forward. Just do it; do not fear to do it, for truly it can be done only in much fear and trembling.

If you can do it, if you can very accurately find the place where the other person is and begin there, then you can perhaps have the good fortune of leading him to the place where you are.

To be a teacher is not to say: This is the way it is, nor is it to assign lessons and the like. No, to be a teacher is truly to be the learner. Instruction begins with this, that you, the teacher, learn from the learner, place yourself in what he has understood and how he has understood it, if you yourself have not understood it previously, or that you, if you have understood it, then let him examine you, as it were, so that he can be sure that you know your lesson. This is the introduction; then the beginning can be made in another sense.

This is why I continually have inwardly raised an objection to a certain

XIII
535
party of the orthodox here, that they band together in a little circle and strengthen one another in thinking that they are the only Christians—and thus do not know anything else to do with all Christendom than to declare that they are not Christians. If it is true that there actually are so few true Christians in Christendom, then these are *eo ipso* [precisely thereby] obliged to be missionaries, even though a missionary in Christendom will always look different from a missionary in paganism. It is obvious that this objection quite properly comes from behind, because it takes for granted the admission or assumption that these orthodox actually are true Christians, the only true Christians in Christendom.

Consequently, in Christendom the religious author, whose total thought is what it means to become a Christian, properly starts out with being an esthetic author. For a time let it be an open question whether Christendom is an enormous illusion, whether it is a delusion on the part of the multitude who call themselves Christian. Let the opposite be assumed—well, then, this beginning is a redundancy based on something that does not exist, but that does no damage. The damage is far greater, or rather this is the damage, when someone who is not Christian pretends to be that. The damage is not so great, however, if one who is a Christian gives the appearance of not being that—on the assumption that all are true Christians, it can then at most only encourage them even more in being that.

§ 3
The Illusion That Religion and Christianity Are Something to Which One Turns Only When One Becomes Older

The esthetic always overrates youth and that moment of eternity; it cannot reconcile itself with the earnestness of the years, nor with the earnestness of eternity. Therefore the esthetic has always had a suspicion about the religious person, that he either has never had a sense for the esthetic or that basically he nevertheless would rather have continued belonging to it, but time exercised its deteriorating power, he became older, and then he turned to the religious. One divides life into two ages: the age of youth is the age of the esthetic; the older age is the age of religiousness—but to tell the truth we all would surely prefer to have continued to be young.

XIII
536
How *can* this illusion be removed—whether it will succeed is something else, but it can be removed by concurrent esthetic and religious works. Here no dubiousness is possible, because the esthetic production testifies that youth is present—then the *concurrent* religious work cannot be explained on some incidental basis.

On the assumption that Christendom is an enormous illusion, that it is a delusion on the part of the multitude who call themselves Christians, in all probability the illusion we are discussing here is very common. But in turn this illusion is worsened by the very delusion that one is a Christian. One goes on living one's life in esthetic categories, and if at some time a person comes to think about Christianity, he dismisses the matter until he becomes older and sufficiently reassures himself—since, he says to himself, I am after all basically a Christian. It cannot be denied that there are those in Christendom who live just as sensately as any pagan ever did—indeed, even more sensately, because they have this confounded security that basically they are Christians. But the decision to become a Christian is shoved off as long as possible—indeed, an additional obstacle has been acquired, because one takes pride in being young as long as possible—and only when one becomes old does one turn to Christianity and religiousness. One is so reluctant to make the admission that one has become old —but only when one becomes old does one turn to Christianity and religiousness.

If, therefore, one could continually stay young, one would not need either Christianity or religiousness.

For all true religiousness this is an extremely pernicious error that has its basis in our confusing becoming older in the sense of time with becoming older in the sense of eternity. It certainly cannot be denied that we more often see the scarcely upbuilding spectacle of a youthfulness that with blazing passion was the interpreter of the esthetic and then, when the time of youth was over, changed into a religiousness, in one sense too relaxed, in another sense too high-strung, that had all the faults of old age. Nor can it be denied either that many who portray the religious, out of fear that it will not be earnest enough, make it both too rigorous and too morose. This and much else can contribute to making that illusion more common and establishing it more firmly—but what good does that do? What will help is precisely that which could contribute to removing the illusion.

If, then, a religious author wants to touch on that illusion, he must in one swoop begin with simultaneously being an esthetic and a religious author. But one thing above all he must not forget, the number carried, which is which, that it is the religious that is to come forward decisively. The esthetic writing becomes a means of communication and, for the person who may need it (on the assumption that Christendom is an enormous illusion, there are many of these), evidence that the religious writing cannot possibly be explained by the author's having become older, because it is indeed concurrent—and one certainly has not become older concurrently. XIII 537

Perhaps it will not succeed at all in this way, perhaps; the damage cannot be great. At most the damage can be that one does not really believe in the religiousness of such a communicator. Well, then! Often enough a communicator of the religious can be too anxious about being regarded as religious himself. If so, this simply shows that he is not in truth religious. This is similar to the situation of someone who wants to be a teacher and is too much occupied with the thought of what those he wants to teach will judge of

him and his teaching, his knowledge, etc. Such a teacher really has no el-
bowroom at all in teaching. Suppose, for example, that for the sake of the
learner he thought it most appropriate to say he did not understand something he really did understand. Heaven forbid! Out of fear that the learner
would actually believe that he did not understand it, he would not dare—
that is, he is really not fit to be a teacher. Although calling himself a teacher,
he is so far from being one that he really aspires to be cited for excellence—
by the learner. Or it is similar to the situation of a preacher of penitence who
wants to castigate rigorously the vices of the age—but is very much occupied with how the age he is castigating judges of him—he is so far from
being a preacher of repentance that he is more a New Year's Day caller who
merely makes himself a bit interesting by wearing an outfit rather odd for a
New Year's Day caller. So also with *that* religious person who, if worst comes
to worst, could not endure being regarded as the only one who was not religious. To be able to endure this is in reflection the most accurate definition
of essential religiousness.

§ 4
Even Though a Person Refuses to Go Along to the Place to Which One Is Endeavoring to Lead Him, There Is Still One Thing That Can Be Done for Him: Compel Him to Become Aware

A person may have the good fortune of doing a great deal for another, may
have the good fortune of leading him to the place to which he desires to lead

XIII
538

him and, to hold to what in essence is continually under discussion here, may
have the good fortune of helping that person to become a Christian. But this
is not in my power; it depends upon very many things and above all upon
whether he himself is willing. Compel a person to an opinion, a conviction,
a belief—in all eternity, that I cannot do. But one thing I can do, in one sense
the first thing (since it is the condition for the next thing: to accept this view,
conviction, belief), in another sense the last thing if he refuses the next: I can
compel him to become aware.

That this is a good deed, there is no doubt, but neither must it be forgotten that this is a daring venture. By compelling him to become aware, I succeed in compelling him to judge. Now he judges. But what he judges is not
in my power. Perhaps he judges the very opposite of what I desire. Furthermore, that he was compelled to judge perhaps makes him infuriated, ragingly
infuriated—infuriated with the cause, with me—and perhaps I become the
victim of my daring venture.

To compel people to become aware and judge is namely the law for true
martyrdom. A true martyr has never used power but has contended by
means of powerlessness. He compelled people to become aware. Indeed,
God knows, they did become aware—they put him to death. Yet he was

willing to have that happen. He did not think that his death halted him in his work; he understood that his death was part of it—that the momentum of his work began precisely with his death. Truly, those who had put him to death did indeed become aware; they began to think once again about the cause and in quite another way, and what the one living was not able to do the one dead was able to do: he won to his cause those who had become aware.

The objection I have repeatedly made privately against those who ordinarily proclaim Christianity in Christendom is that they, themselves surrounded and safeguarded by all too many illusions, do not have the courage to make people aware. That is, they do not have sufficient self-denial in relation to their cause. They are eager to win adherents, but they want to win them—because this strengthens their cause—and therefore are not scrupulously careful about whether they in truth become adherents or not. This in turn means that in a deeper sense they have no cause; they relate themselves selfishly to the cause they do have. Therefore they do not actually risk going out among the people or abandoning illusions in order to make a genuine idea-impression, because they have a dim notion that it is truly a dangerous matter to make people aware. Mendaciously to make them aware, that is, to bow and scrape before them, to flatter them, to ask for their attention and lenient judgment, to submit—the truth—to balloting, well, this involves no danger, at least not here in the world, where on the contrary it involves every advantage; but yet it perhaps does involve the danger of eventually failing in eternity.

XIII
539

This, then, is the way it stands with what has been assumed, that it is indeed a delusion on the part of the multitude who call themselves Christians. If, then, a person lives in this delusion, consequently lives in completely different, in completely esthetic categories—if, then, one is able to win and capture him completely by means of an esthetic portrayal and now knows how to introduce the religious so swiftly that with this momentum of attachment he runs straight into the most decisive categories of the religious—what then? Well, then he must become aware. Yet what follows from this no one can predict, but he must become aware. It is possible that he actually comes to sober reflection on what it was supposed to mean that he has called himself a Christian. It is possible that he becomes enraged with the person who has ventured to do this to him; but he has become aware, he is beginning to judge. In order to retrieve himself, he perhaps judges the other person to be a hypocrite, a charlatan, a half lunatic—it is of no avail, he must judge, he has become aware.

Ordinarily the relationship is reversed, and the relationship was truly reversed when Christianity came in contact with paganism. What is entirely overlooked, however, is how altered the situation is, that the category Christendom sets all relationships into reflection. Ordinarily, also in Christendom, the person who is striving to lead people to become Christians employs everything in order to establish securely that he himself is a Christian; he gives assurances and assurances. He fails to note that from the beginning there is an enormous confusion here, since, after all, those whom he is addressing are Christians. But if he is addressing Christians, what then does it mean to get them to become Christians? If, however, in his opinion they are not Christians although they still call themselves Christians, the very fact that they call themselves Christians makes manifest, of course, that here is a reflection-category. Thus we are in a situation in the sphere of reflection, but then also the entire strategy must be changed.

Here I cannot now develop further how that which Christendom needs first and foremost is a totally new science of arms; it is a science of arms that is completely permeated by reflection. In several of my books I have provided the crucial elements in regard to this. The whole thing can be stated in one phrase, the whole thing, which can indeed take days and years of work to develop, the most vigilant attention night and day, incessant scale finger-exercising in the dialectical every day, and a never-slumbering fear and trembling—the method must become indirect. In the communication of Christianity, when the situation is Christendom, there is not a direct relation, there is first of all a delusion to remove. The entire old science of arms, all the apologetics and everything belonging to it, serves instead, to put it bluntly, to betray the cause of Christianity. At every point and at every moment, the strategy must be constituted on the basis of having to contend with a delusion, an illusion.

So when in Christendom a religious author whose total thought is the task of becoming a Christian wants to make it possible to make people aware (whether it will succeed is of course something else), he must begin as an esthetic author and to a certain point he must maintain this possibility. But there must be a limit, since it is being done, after all, in order to make aware. And one thing the author must not forget, the number carried, which is which, the religious the crucial, the esthetic the incognito—lest the dialectical interaction end up in babbling.

§ 5
All the Esthetic Writing Seen in the Totality of the Writing
Is a Deception, but Understood in a Singular Way

If someone wanted to consider the esthetic writing as the totality and from its point of view and on this assumption consider the religious writing, he would have to regard the latter as a defection, a decline. That the presupposition of this observation is wrong I have shown in the preceding, where it was substantiated that from the beginning and over my signature signs were provided that telegraphed, concurrently with the pseudonymous writing, in the direction of the religious.

But from the total point of view of my whole work as an author, the esthetic writing is a deception, and herein is the deeper significance of the *pseudonymity*. But a deception, that is indeed something rather ugly. To that I would answer: Do not be deceived by the word *deception*. One can deceive a person out of what is true, and—to recall old Socrates—one can deceive a person into what is true. Yes, in only this way can a deluded person actually be brought into what is true—by deceiving him. XIII 541

The one who is of another opinion thereby betrays that he simply is not much of a dialectician, which is precisely what is necessary in order to operate in this way. In other words there is a great difference, that is, the dialectical difference, or the difference of the dialectical, between these two situations: one who is ignorant and must be given some knowledge, and therefore he is like the empty vessel that must be filled or like the blank sheet of paper that must be written upon—and one who is under a delusion that must first be taken away. Likewise, there is also a difference between writing on a blank piece of paper and bringing out by means of chemicals some writing that is hidden under other writing. Now, on the assumption that someone is under a delusion and consequently the first step, properly understood, is to remove the delusion—if I do not begin by deceiving, I begin with direct communication. But direct communication presupposes that the recipient's ability to receive is entirely in order, but here that is simply not the case—indeed, here a delusion is an obstacle. That means a corrosive must first be used, but this corrosive is the negative, but the negative in connection with communicating is precisely to deceive.

What, then, does it mean "to deceive"? It means that one does not begin *directly* with what one wishes to communicate but begins by taking the other's delusion at face value. Thus one does not begin (to hold to what essentially is the theme of this book) in this way: I am Christian, you are not a Christian—but this way: You are a Christian, I am not Christian. Or one does not begin in this way: It is Christianity that I am proclaiming, and you are living in purely esthetic categories. No, one begins this way: Let us talk about the esthetic. The deception consists in one's speaking this way precisely in order to arrive at the religious. But according to the assumption the other person is in fact under the delusion that the esthetic is the essentially Christian, since he thinks he is a Christian and yet he is living in esthetic categories.

Even if ever so many pastors will find it indefensible, even if equally as many will be incapable of getting it into their heads—although all of them otherwise, according to their own statements, are accustomed to using the Socratic method—in this respect I calmly stick to Socrates. True, he was no

Christian, that I know, although I also definitely remain convinced that he has become one. But he was a dialectician and understood everything in reflection. And the question here is purely dialectical—it is the question of the use of reflection in Christendom. Qualitatively two altogether different magnitudes are involved here, but formally I can very well call Socrates my teacher—whereas I have believed and believe in only one, the Lord Jesus Christ.

B
CONCLUDING POSTSCRIPT

forms, to repeat again, the turning point in the whole authorship. It poses the *issue:* becoming a Christian. After first having appropriated all the pseudonymous esthetic writing as a description of one way along which one may go to becoming a Christian—*back* from the esthetic to becoming a Christian, the book describes the second way—*back* from the system, the speculative, etc. to becoming a Christian.

C
THE RELIGIOUS WRITING

As early as *Concluding Postscript,* I could be very brief when the point of view for all the work as an author is that the author is a religious author; what needed explanation there was how the esthetic writing is to be interpreted on this assumption. And what needs no explanation at all on this assumption is of course the latter part, the purely religious writing, which specifically provides the point of view.

CONCLUSION

And what does all this mean when the reader now gathers together the elements developed in the various sections? It means: this is an authorship of which the total thought is the task of becoming a Christian. But it is an authorship that from the beginning has understood, with dialectical consistency has pursued, what the implications of this are that the situation is Christendom, which is a category of reflection, and therefore has cast all the Christian relationships into reflection. In Christendom—to become a Christian is either to become what one is (the inwardness of reflection or the reflection of inward deepening), or it is first of all to be wrested out of a delusion, which again is a category of reflection. Here there is no vacillation, no ambiguity of the usual sort, that one does not know and cannot ascertain whether the situation is in paganism, whether the pastor in this sense is a missionary, or where one is. Here one does not lack what is usually lacking, a decisive categorical definition and a decisive expression for the situation: to proclaim Christianity—in Christendom. Everything is cast into reflection. The communication is in reflection—therefore is indirect communication. The communicator is defined in reflection, therefore negatively, not one who claims to be an extraordinary Christian or even claims to have revelations (all of which is commensurate with immediacy and direct communication) but the opposite, one who even claims not to be Christian—in other words, the communicator is in the background, helping negatively, since whether he succeeds in helping someone is indeed something else. The issue itself is one belonging to reflection: to become a Christian when in a way one is a Christian.

THE DISSIMILARITY OF MY PERSONAL EXISTING CORRESPONDING TO THE DISSIMILAR NATURE OF THE WRITING

In these days and for a long time now we have utterly lost the idea that to be an author is and ought to be a work and therefore a personal existing. That on the whole the press, representing abstract, impersonal communication, is demoralizing, especially since the daily press, purely formally and with no regard to whether what it says is true or false, contributes enormously to demoralization because of all the impersonality, which in turn is more or less irresponsibility and impenitence; that anonymity, the highest expression for abstraction, impersonality, impenitence, and irresponsibility, is a basic source of modern demoralization; that on the other hand anonymity would be counteracted most simply, that a very beneficial corrective to journalism's abstraction would be provided if we turned back once again to antiquity and learned what it means to be an individual human being, no more and no less, which also an author certainly is, no more and no less—this is self-evident. But in our day, when that which is the secret of evil has become wisdom—namely, that one is not to ask about the communicator but only about the communication, only about "what," about the objective—in our day what does it mean to be an author? It means, often even when he is identified, to be an *x,* an impersonal something that, by means of printing, addresses itself abstractly to thousands upon thousands but itself is unseen, unknown, living as secretly, as anonymously, as impersonally as possible, presumably so that the contrast between the enormous means of communication and being an individual human being does not become obvious and glaring, perhaps also because he fears the supervision that life actually should have over everyone who wants to instruct others, that one sees him, his personal existing, and its relation to the communication. But with all this, to which someone who wanted to study the demoralization of the modern state should give great attention—with all this I cannot become further involved here.

XIII
544

A
Personal Existing in Relation to the Esthetic Writing

So now to my work as an author and the first period of my existing. Here was a religious author, but one who began as an esthetic author, and this first part was the incognito, was the deception. Very early and very thoroughly initiated into the secret that *mundus vult decipi* [the world wants to be deceived],[277] I was unable at that time to choose to pursue this strategy. Quite the opposite, it was a matter of deceiving inversely on the largest possible scale, of using all my familiarity with people and their weaknesses and their obtusities—not in order to profit from them but in order to annihilate myself, to weaken the impression of myself. The secret of the deception that indulges the world, which wants to be deceived, consists partly in forming a clique and all that goes with it, in joining one or two of those mutual admiration societies whose members assist each other by word and pen for the sake of worldly gain, and partly in hiding from the human throng, never being seen, in order in this way to produce an effect on the imagination. Therefore the very opposite had to be done. I had to exist and safeguard an existence in absolute isolation, but I also had to make a point of being seen at every time of the day, living, so to speak, on the street, associating with every Tom, Dick, and Harry and in the most casual situations. This is truth's way of deceiving, the ever-sure way to weaken the impression of oneself in the world, furthermore certainly also the way of self-renunciation taken by men quite different from me in order to make people aware. Those highly esteemed, the "deceivers," who want the communication to serve them instead of their serving the communication, are merely intent on winning esteem for themselves; the despised, the "truth-witnesses," who deceive inversely, have always followed the practice of sacrificing themselves in a worldly sense, of being nothing, although working night and day, and among other things also without the support of the illusion that the work they are doing is their official career or livelihood.

So this had to be done, and it was done, not now and then but every blessed day. I am convinced that a sixth of *Either/Or,* a little clique, and then an author one never managed to see—this would have become, especially over a long period, something extraordinary in quite another way. I had, however, made sure I could work as hard as I pleased, and as the spirit prompted me, without being afraid of gaining too much esteem, because in a certain sense I worked just as hard in another direction—against myself. Only an author will really be able to understand what such a task is: to work *qua* author, that is, with intellect and pen, and then practically be at everybody's service. It is a criterion for criticism (even though it did also give me extraordinary enrichment with observations) that would bring most people to despair, since it means taking away completely even the least illusion and providing the

XIII
545

pure idea-relationship—and truly it is not truth that rules the world but illusions. Even if an achievement were eminent to a degree never seen before—if the author just lives in this way, he will in a very short time have safeguarded himself against worldly esteem and against the bestial flattery of the crowd. The crowd has no ideality and therefore no power to hold on to an idea despite appearances; the crowd always falls into the trap of appearances. To be seen day after day and to be seen in the most casual company are enough to make the crowd lose the idea and very soon become sick and tired of a person. It does not even take very much time to manage to be seen every day if only one ingeniously (i.e., humanly speaking, insanely) uses the time properly—that is, walks to and fro in the same but the most frequented place in the city.

XIII
546

Anyone who conserves his esteem in a worldly way does not return by the same way he went out, even if it is his path, lest he be seen twice in so brief a time—then people might think that he did not do anything, which would not occur to anyone if he sat at home in his parlor and loafed two-thirds of the day. On the other hand, an hour spent properly, devoutly understood, an hour lived for eternity, spent in walking to and fro among the common people, is already not a little. It is truly pleasing to God that truth is served in this way; his spirit witnessed powerfully with my spirit that it had his complete and highest approval. All the truth-witnesses nod to one their approval that it is the truth, the idea one wants to serve, not the truth one wants to betray and then wants to profit from the illusions. It was a purely Christian satisfaction for me to dare to carry out on Monday a little bit of what on Sunday, when the pastor preaches and in so doing even sheds tears, one sheds tears over—and on Monday quite rightly laughs at. It was a purely Christian satisfaction for me that if ordinarily there was no one else there was definitely one in Copenhagen with whom any poor person could without ceremony speak and associate on the street; that if ordinarily there was no one else, there was one who, in whatever social circles he otherwise moved, did not slink by but acknowledged every maidservant, manservant, and every day laborer he knew in other contexts. It was a purely Christian satisfaction to me that if ordinarily there was no one else there was one who (several years before existence again assigned the lesson to the generation) in action tried a little to do the doctrine about loving the neighbor—alas, one who precisely by his act also received a frightful insight into what an illusion Christendom is and indeed, particularly later, also into how the common people let themselves be seduced by wretched journalists, whose striving and fighting for equality can only lead, if it leads to anything, since it is in the service of the lie, to making the elite, in self-defense, proud of their aloofness from the common man, and the common man brazen in his rudeness.

XIII
547

To develop in more detail this sketch of my personal existing cannot be done here, but I am convinced that rarely has any author used as much cunning, intrigue, and ingenuity to win honor and esteem in the world in order to deceive it as I have done for the opposite reason—to deceive it into an understanding of the truth. By just a single episode, for which I have the proofreader of *Either / Or*, my friend Giødwad,[278] as witness, I shall attempt to give an idea of the scale on which this deception was carried out. When I was reading proof pages of *Either / Or*, I was so busy that it was impossible for me to spend the usual time strolling up and down the street. I did not finish until late in the evening—and then in the evening I hurried to the theater, where I literally was present only five to ten minutes. And why did I do that? Because I was afraid that the big book would bring me too much esteem.* And why did I do that? Because I knew people, especially in Copenhagen; to be seen every night for five minutes by several hundred people was enough to sustain the opinion: So he doesn't do a single thing; he is nothing but a street-corner loafer.

That was the way I existed, shoring up the esthetic writing (in addition breaking with all cliques) and entirely with the polemical aim of regarding every eulogy as an attack, but every attack as something to which no attention was to be paid. That was the way I existed publicly. I almost never made visits, and at home one thing was strictly observed—unconditionally not to receive anyone except the poor who asked for help. There was no time for visits at home, and in a visit someone could easily come to suspect what he was not supposed to suspect. That is the way I existed. If Copenhagen was ever of one single opinion about someone, I dare say it has been of one opinion about me: I was a street-corner loafer, an idler, a *flâneur* [lounger], a frivolous bird, a good, perhaps even brilliant pate, witty, etc.—but I completely lacked "earnestness." I represented the worldly mentality's irony, the enjoyment of life, the most sophisticated enjoyment of life—but of "earnestness and positivity" there was not a trace; I was, however, tremendously interesting and pungent.

As I think back on this form of existence, I could indeed decide to make a kind of apology to the distinguished and esteemed members of society. True enough, I truly was fully aware of what I was doing, but from their point of view they were still justified in censuring me because by weakening myself in this way I was on the whole contributing to weakening power and esteem, however conservative I have otherwise always been in this regard and with however much respect, veneration, and admiration I have been happy to give the distinguished and esteemed person what he deserved. But it did not follow from my conservative nature that I myself in any way par-

XIII
548

---

* For the same reason, at the moment *Either / Or* was all finished and ready for making a fair copy, I also put in *Fædrelandet* a little article in my name, "Open Confession," in which I altogether gratuitously disclaimed authorship of the many interesting newspaper articles in various newspapers, admitted and confessed my inactivity, and requested only one thing: that in the future no one would regard me as the author of anything that did not bear my signature.

ticipated in the same thing. And just because the esteemed in society have in so many ways shown me not only sympathy but even preference, in so many ways have tried to do what from their side was no doubt honest and well-intentioned—to draw me to themselves—I feel impelled to make an apology to them, even though I naturally cannot repent of what I have done, since I was serving my idea. Yet the esteemed have always proved to be consistent in comparison with the common people, who not even from their own point of view have been in the right toward me, inasmuch as, in consequence of the foregoing, they did indeed attack me—because I was not elitist, which is very odd and ludicrous of the common people.

This is the first part. By means of my personal existing, I attempted to support the pseudonymous writers, all the esthetic writing. Depressed, incurably depressed as I was, sorely afflicted in my innermost being, after having in despair broken with the world and what is of the world, rigorously brought up from childhood in the view that the truth must suffer, be insulted and mocked, spending a certain time each day in prayer and upbuilding meditation, myself personally a penitent. Since I was who I was—yes, I do not deny it—in a certain sense I found a satisfaction in that life, in that inverted deception, a satisfaction in thinking that the intrigue succeeded so extraordinarily that the public and I came to say *du*[279] to each other, that I was in vogue proclaiming a gospel of worldliness, that even if I did not have the kind of esteem that can be obtained only by a completely different mode of life, yet secretly, and therefore all the more adored, I was the public's favorite, in everyone's good graces as tremendously interesting and pungent, although everyone no doubt considered himself better and more earnest and more honorable and more positive than I. This satisfaction, which was my secret, a satisfaction in which at times I was as if beside myself, could in other respects have been a dangerous temptation for me. That the world, the public, and the like would tempt me with its flattery, admiration, etc.—no, there I was certain. If I had capsized, it would have to have been on this reflection raised to the second power—an almost obsessed rapture over the thought of how the deception succeeded, which indescribably satisfied the secret resentment I had harbored since childhood, because long before I myself had ever seen it I had learned that lies and baseness and injustice ruled the world, which often led me to think of those words in *Either/Or*, "If you people only knew what it is you are laughing at,"[280] if you only knew with whom you are involved, who this *flâneur* is!

B
Personal Existing in Relation to the Religious Writing

In December 1845 I had completed the manuscript of *Concluding Postscript* and had, as is my custom, delivered it lock, stock, and barrel to Luno,[281] for which the skeptical need not take my word, since this can be shown in Luno's records. This book constitutes the turning point in my entire work as an author, inasmuch as it poses the *issue:* becoming a Christian. Thereafter the transition to the second part is made, the series of exclusively religious books.

That my personal existing had to be conformed to this, or that I had to try to give my contemporaries another impression of my personal existing, I perceived at once. I also even had my eye on what had to be done when in a very convenient way something happened; a little circumstance, in which I saw a hint from Governance, assisted me in acting decisively in that direction.

XIII
550 But I am unable to develop this before I have tried in a few strokes to recall in the reader's recollection the state of things in Copenhagen at that time, a description that perhaps will now also show up better by comparison with the present state of war.[282] Gradually the not unremarkable circumstance developed that the whole population of Copenhagen, especially to the degree that it was more ignorant and uncultured, became ironic and witty—it was irony and irony first and last. If the matter were not so serious, if I dared to regard it purely esthetically, I would not deny that it is the most ludicrous thing I have seen and that I actually believe one must travel far and still be very lucky to encounter anything so basically comic. The entire population of a city, first and foremost all the casual idlers on the highways and byways, down to schoolchildren and cobblers' apprentices, all the many legions of the only favored and privileged class in our day, those who amount to nothing, they become—*en masse* the entire population of a city, guilds, fraternities, tradespeople, people of station (in just about the same way as a middle-class citizen is accustomed to go to the carnival in Deer Park), they, with their families become—those thousands and thousands become (the one and only thing I would venture unconditionally to insist is impossible for them to become, especially *en masse* or in families)—they become "ironic" with the help of a newspaper,[283] which in turn, ironically enough, by means of an editorial staff of street-corner loafers, usurpingly dominates the fashion, and the fashion that is stipulated is—the ironic. I believe it is impossible to think of anything more ludicrous. Irony presupposes a very specific intellectual culture, which is very rare in any generation—and this chaos of people consisted of ironists. Irony is unconditionally unsocial. Irony that is in the majority is *eo ipso* [precisely thereby] unconditionally not irony. Nothing is more certain, inasmuch as it is implicit in the concept itself. Irony essentially tends toward the presence of only one person, as is indicated in the Aristotelian view that the ironist does everything ἑαυτοῦ ἕνεκα [for his own sake][284]— and here an enormous public, arm in arm *in bona caritate* [good-naturedly], had become, damned if it hadn't, ironic.

XIII
551 But the matter was only all too serious. Even though the actual ringleader was indeed a man of not inconsiderable talent, this irony, by passing into these

thousands upon thousands, naturally became essentially nothing else than rabble-barbarism, which unfortunately is always popular. It was a demoralization that was all too terribly reminiscent of the punishment with which one of the ancient prophets in the name of the Lord threatens the Jews as the most dreadful of punishments: Boys shall judge you.[285] It was a demoralization that in relation to the proportions of the little country actually threatened a complete moral disintegration. To get an idea of the danger, one must see it close up, how even good-natured and worthy people become like totally different creatures as soon as they become the "crowd." One must see it close up, the spinelessness with which even otherwise honorable people say, "It is a disgrace; it is shocking to do or say anything like that"—and then themselves contribute their little bit to blanket the city and land in a snowstorm of blather and town gossip. One must see it close up, the callousness with which otherwise kind people act in the capacity of the public because their participation or nonparticipation seems to them a trifle—a trifle that with the contributions of the many becomes the monster. One must see how no attack is so feared as that of laughter, how even the person who courageously risked his life for a stranger would not be far from betraying his father and mother if the danger was laughter, because more than any other this attack isolates the one attacked and at no point does it offer the support of pathos, while light-mindedness and curiosity and sensuality grin and the nervous cowardice that itself shivers before such an attack incessantly shouts, "It is nothing," and the cowardice that despicably ransoms itself from an attack by bribery or by putting on a good face to the one concerned says, "It is nothing," and sympathy says, "It is nothing." How terrible it is when blather and grinning threaten to become "public opinion" in a little country. Denmark was about to be absorbed into Copenhagen, and Copenhagen was just at the point of becoming a market town. To do this is easy enough, especially with the help of the press; and once it is done, perhaps a generation is needed in order to recover from it.

But enough about this. It was of importance to me to alter my personal existing in accordance with my transition to setting forth the religious issues. I had to have a supporting existence-form corresponding to that kind of work as an author. As stated, it was in the month of December, and it was desirable to have everything in order by the time *Concluding Postscript* was to be published. So the step was taken,[286] still in the month of December. Given my familiarity with such situations, I readily perceived that two words[287] to that instrument of irony, which in one sense, that is, if I had not been the person I was, had up until now not without cunning venerated and immortalized me,[288] would be sufficient to turn my whole life situation around altogether dialectically in order to get that whole incalculable public of ironists to take aim at me, so I would become the object of everyone's irony—alas, I, the master of irony.[289]

XIII
552

So the order was then given. Lest capital be made of it as a newly invented and very stimulating form of irony, a considerable dose of the ethical was added by my requesting to be abused by that nauseating instrument of nauseating irony. That incalculable monster of ironists has naturally regarded me as lunatic. The individuals who saw more deeply into the matter probably did not without a shudder see me make this leap, or they thought it beneath my dignity to concern myself with something like that (because they had only a worldly understanding of dignity and did not consider what is divinely understood by it), whereas I would have found it beneath my dignity to have lived contemporaneously, without having acted decisively, with such a demoralization, satisfied with the cheap virtue of conducting myself like "the others"—that is, shirking action as much as possible while such a disproportionate journalistic contemptibility was surely bringing people to the grave, violated and infuriated, if not always the ones attacked, then certainly their wives, children, relatives, and close friends, was defilingly intruding into everything, even into the most intimate relationships of private life, even into school secrets, even into the sanctuary of the Church, was spewing out lies, slander, insolence, and juvenile jokes—all in the service of corrupt passion and wretched avarice, and responsible for all this were "street-corner loafers," the ones responsible under the press law! I realized that in order to serve my idea this was the right thing to do, and I did not vacillate. The consequences of that,[290] for which certainly no one at that time envied me, I therefore historically claim as my legitimate possession, the perspective value of which my eye easily discovers.

XIII
553

I had now figured out that the situation was dialectically right for using indirect communication again. Although I was devoting myself exclusively to religious writing, I dared to count on these daily drenchings of rabble-barbarism as negatively supporting, on their having an adequate cooling effect so that the religious communication would not become much too direct or would not much too directly gain adherents for me. The reader could not directly relate himself to me, because I now had in place, instead of the incognito of the esthetic, the danger of laughter and grins, which scare away most people. Even those whom it would not scare away would be disturbed by the next, the thought that I myself had voluntarily exposed myself to all this, had plunged myself into this, a kind of insanity. Ah, yes, surely that was just what the contemporaries thought of that Roman who made his immortal leap to save his country,[291] a kind of insanity—ah, yes, and once again, ah, yes, since dialectically it was exactly Christian self-denial—and I, the poor master of irony, became the sorry object of the laughter of a highly cultured public.

The costume was right. Every religious author is *eo ipso* polemical, because the world is not so good that the religious can be assumed to have triumphed or to be in the majority. A triumphant religious author who is *in vogue* is *eo ipso* not a *religious* author. The essentially religious author is always polemical and in addition suffers under the opposition or endures the opposition that corresponds to what in his time must be regarded as the specific evil. If it is kings and emperors, popes and bishops, and power that are the evil, then he must be recognizable by his being the object of their attacks. If it is the crowd—and blather, the public—and the brutish grinning that are the evil, then he must also be recognizable by his being the object of that kind of attack and persecution. And if the essentially religious author has just one syllogism that he uses as the jack, the miraculous syllogism, when asked whereby he demonstrates he is right and that what he says is true, he answers, "I demonstrate it by this, that I am laughed to scorn." That is, he does not demonstrate the truth or the justice of his cause by the honor, esteem, etc. he enjoys—just the opposite, because the essentially religious person is always polemical. Any religious author or speaker or teacher who shirks, who is not present where the danger is and where the evil has its haunt, is a deceiver, and this will also become manifest.

XIII
554

It holds for everyone that when he comes to death's door and it is opened for him he must discard all pomp and glory and wealth and worldly esteem and starred medals and emblems of honor—whether bestowed on him by kings and emperors or by the crowd and the public—discard them as totally irrelevant and superfluous. An exception is made only for anyone who has been a religious author, teacher, speaker, etc. in his lifetime and has been that on his own responsibility and at his own risk. If he is found to be in possession of any such thing, he is not allowed to discard it—no, it is packed up in a bundle and handed to him; he is compelled to keep it or to carry the bundle in the same way as a thief is himself compelled to carry stolen goods. And with this bundle he must enter the place where he shall be judged. After all, he was a religious teacher; so he will be judged by the authentic religious teachers, all those who as long as they lived were insulted, persecuted, laughed to scorn, mocked, spat upon. Ah, if it is terrible for the sensate human being to stand here on earth laughed to scorn, mocked, insulted, how much more terrible to stand in eternity with this bundle under one's arm or arrayed with—decorations.

The costume was right. In a grinning age (as was the one of which I speak, and in this regard it is at least my opinion that "the war" has been good fortune for Denmark), the religious author must for heaven's sake see to it that he more than anyone else becomes laughed to scorn. If the evil is coming from the crowd, then the contemporary religious author must for heaven's sake see to it that he becomes the object of its persecution and in this regard receives the first treatment. And my entire view of the crowd, which even the more perceptive at that time perhaps found somewhat exaggerated, now in 1848,[292] assisted by the gesticulations of existence (these are more powerful and in comparison with the single individual's thin voice are like the raging of the elements), now the objection probably is that I have not exaggerated enough. And that category *the single individual,* which was regarded as eccentric and the invention of eccentricity, which it indeed was, for was not the person who in one sense was its inventor, Socrates, at the time called ἀτοπώτατος (the most eccentric of men)[293]—I would not trade having brought it forth decisively at the time, I would not trade it for a kingdom. If the crowd is the evil, if it is chaos that threatens, there is rescue in one thing only, in becoming the single individual, in the rescuing thought: that single individual.

One triumph I have experienced, only one, but it satisfies me so completely that as a thinker I ask unconditionally nothing more in the world. The all too overwhelming world-historical events of the past few months have brought into the world the confused spokesmen of newborn, romantic, obviously confused thoughts and on the other hand have either silenced everything that hitherto had in various ways been the spokesman or placed it in the embarrassing position of having to obtain brand-new clothes in the greatest haste, and every system has been broken up. With such passion as if there were a gap of a generation, the past was broken from the present in the course of a few months. During this crisis I sat and read proof pages of a book[294] that accordingly had been written earlier. Not one word was added or deleted. It was the view that I, "the odd thinker," had already enunciated for several years. If one reads it, one will get the impression that the book was written after the crisis. A world-historical crisis such as that, which ranks so high that not even the disintegration of the ancient world was so imposing, is the absolute *tentamen rigorosum* [rigorous examination] for anyone who *was* an author. I experienced the triumph of not needing to modify or change one iota—indeed, what I had written before, if it were read now, would be much, much better understood than when it was written.

Just one more thing. When someday my lover comes, he will readily see that when I was regarded as being the ironic one the irony by no means consisted in what a highly cultured public thought it did—and of course my lover cannot possibly be so fatuous that he assumes that a public can be the judge of irony, which is just as impossible as being the single individual *en masse.* He will see that the irony consisted in just this, that in this esthetic author and under this *Erscheinung* [appearance] of worldliness the religious author concealed himself, a religious author who at that very time and for his own upbuilding perhaps consumed as much religiousness as a whole household ordinarily does. Furthermore, my lover will see that irony was again present in connection with the next part, and precisely in that which the highly cultured public regarded as madness. For the essential ironist there is nothing else to do in an ironic age (that great epitome of fools) but to turn the whole relation around and himself become the object of the irony of every-

XIII
555

XIII
556

one. My lover will see how it all tallied at every single point, how my existence-relations turned around in altogether accurate correspondence to the
change in my writing. If I had not had an eye or the courage for that and
had changed the writing but not my existence-relations, then the relation
would have become undialectical and confused.

Conclusion

I have nothing more to say, but in conclusion I will allow someone else to
speak, my poet, who, when he comes, will usher me to the place among those
who have suffered for an idea and will say:

"The martyrdom this author suffered can be described quite briefly in
this way: He suffered being a genius in a market town.[295] The criterion he
applied with regard to capabilities, diligence, disinterestedness, sacrifice, ab-
soluteness of thought categories, etc. was much too high for the average of
his contemporaries, jacked up the price all too unreasonably, and pressed
down their price all too unreasonably. It almost made it seem as if the market town and the majority there did not have *absolutum dominium* [absolute
rule], but that there was a God. So they at first mutually entertained one another for a time; they loquaciously discussed and discussed why he, after all,
should have received these extraordinary capabilities, why he, after all,
should be independent and thus able to be so industrious, and why be that
anyway—they loquaciously discussed this so long (while they also took offense at one or another eccentricity [*Sœrhed*] in his mode of living, which
actually was not eccentric, but no doubt was very particularly [*sœrligen*] calculated to serve his life's purpose)—until the *summa summarum* [sum of
sums] became: It is his pride; everything can be explained by his pride.
Thereupon they went further, from loquacious discussion to action. Since
it is his pride, they said, then any hidden opposition, any brazenness toward
him and mistreatment of him, is not only permissible, no, it is a duty to
God—indeed, it is his pride that must be punished. O you inestimable market town, how priceless you are when you put on your dressing gown and
become sanctimonious, when abandoning yourself to every nauseating inclination of envy, coarseness, and rabble barbarism also becomes the expression for doing obeisance to God. But, now, what about 'his pride'? Was
his pride due to the great capabilities? That would be like reproaching the
yellow bunting, saying that wearing all its gold ornaments is its pride or is
out of pride. Or was it his diligence etc.? If a very strictly brought up child
worked together with others in the class, would it not be strange to say that
his diligence etc. were pride, even if it was the case that the others could
not keep up with him? But such instances rarely occur, because the child is

promoted to a new class. But unfortunately the person who in many ways is ready to be promoted to eternity's class—there is only one class, temporality's, where he perhaps must remain for a long time.

"This was the martyrdom. But this is why I, his poet, also see the epigram, the satire, not the particular things that he wrote but what his whole life was. I see that now—when all the many 'real' people, with whom he by no means could compare favorably, especially when 'legs' are supposed to provide the criterion,²⁹⁶ not for what it is to be cattle (*animal*) but for what it is to be a human being, now when their legs like his have turned to dust in the grave and he has arrived in eternity, where, parenthetically speaking, 'legs' do not determine the outcome, neither their thinness nor their thickness, where, parenthetically speaking, he, praise God, is forever freed from the company of the brutish—I see that all these real people furnish an essential appurtenance, a chorus, a priceless market-town chorus, which took its stand on what it understood, his trousers, which became 'the demand of the times,' or even more precious, a chorus that wanted to ironize—the ironist. When I merely think of it, I can laugh loudly. But it comforts him in eternity that he has suffered this, that he voluntarily exposed himself to it, that he did not support his cause with any illusion, did not hide behind any illusion, but by suffering with God-fearing sagacity saved up for eternity: the recollection of surmounted sufferings, that he had remained faithful to himself and to his first love, the love with which he has loved only what has suffered in the world. Even though humble, he will not sneakily approach those glorious ones, not sneakily as if his life on earth had expressed that their lives must have been either an accident or an untruth or an immaturity, since by serving the truth he had won great honor and esteem, had everywhere met spirit and understanding, unlike those glorious ones, who almost everywhere met brutishness and misunderstanding.

XIII
582

"Yet also here in the world he found what he sought: 'that single individual'; if no one else was that, he himself was and became that more and more. It was the cause of Christianity that he served; from childhood his life was wonderfully fitted for that. Thus he completed the task of reflection—to cast Christianity, becoming a Christian, wholly and fully into reflection. The purity of his heart was to will only one thing. What in his lifetime was his contemporaries' complaint against him—that he refused to scale down, to give in—became posterity's eulogy on him—that he did not scale down, did not give in. But the imposing undertaking did not beguile him; while he *qua* author dialectically maintained supervision over the whole, he Christianly understood that for him the whole undertaking meant that he himself was being brought up in Christianity. The dialectical structure he completed, the parts of which are previous separate works, he could not attribute to any human being, even less would he attribute it to himself. If he should have attributed it to anyone, it would have been to Governance, to whom it was indeed attributed day after day, year after year, by the author, who historically died of a mortal disease but poetically died of a longing for eternity in order unceasingly to do nothing else than to thank God."

THE CHANGELESSNESS OF GOD
(SEPTEMBER 3, 1855)

The final published separate piece, *The Changelessness of God,* is representative of the *total Anlæg* (comprehensive plan) at its core and in its intent, which in turn is epitomized in an early journal entry (*JP* V 5468; *Pap.* III A 73, 1840) written when Kierkegaard visited Sæding, his father's birthplace, after he had completed his university work.

> I sit here all alone (I have frequently been just as alone many times, but I have never been so aware of it) and count the hours until I shall see Sæding. I cannot recall any change in my father, and now I am about to see the places where as a poor boy he tended sheep, the places for which, because of his descriptions, I have been so homesick. What if I were to get sick and be buried in the Sæding churchyard! What a strange idea! His last wish for me is fulfilled—is that actually to be the sum and substance of my life? In God's name! Yet in relation to what I owed to him the task was not so insignificant. I learned from him what fatherly love is, and through this I gained a conception of divine fatherly love, the one single unshakable thing in life, the true Archimedean point.

PRAYER

You Changeless One, whom nothing changes! You who are changeless in love, who just for our own good do not let yourself change—would that we also might will our own well-being, let ourselves be brought up, in unconditional obedience, by your changelessness to find rest and to rest in your changelessness! You are not like a human being. If he is to maintain a mere measure of changelessness, he must not have too much that can move him and must not let himself be moved too much. But everything moves you, and in infinite love. Even what we human beings call a trifle and unmoved pass by, the sparrow's need, that moves you; what we so often scarcely pay attention to, a human sigh, that moves you, Infinite Love. But nothing changes you, you Changeless One! O you who in infinite love let yourself be moved, may this our prayer also move you to bless it so that the prayer may change the one who is praying into conformity with your changeless will, you Changeless One!

JAMES 1:17–21

Every good gift and every perfect gift is from above and comes down from the Father of lights, with whom there is no change or shadow of variation. Ac-

cording to his own counsel, he brought us forth by
the word of truth, that we should be a first fruit of
his creation. Therefore, my beloved brethren, let
every person be quick to hear, slow to speak, slow to
anger, because a person's anger does not work what
is righteous before God. Therefore put away all filthiness and all remnants of wickedness and receive with
meekness the word that is implanted in you and that
is powerful for making your souls blessed.

XIV
284

My listener, you have heard the text read. How natural now to think of the
opposite: the temporal, the changefulness of earthly things, and the changefulness of human beings! How depressing, how exhausting, that all is corruptibility, that human beings are changefulness, you, my listener, and I! How
sorrowful that so often the change is for the worse! What poor human consolation, but yet a consolation, that there is yet one more change in the
changeful: that it has an end!

Yet if we were to speak this way, especially in this spirit of gloom, thus not
in the way corruptibility and "human instability" are earnestly discussed, we
not only would not stick to the text, no, we would abandon it, indeed we
would change it. The text speaks about the opposite, about the changelessness of God. The text is sheer joy and gladness; as from the mountain peaks,
where silence lives, even so the apostle's words are lifted above all the changefulness of earthly life; he speaks of the changelessness of God, not about anything else. About a "Father of lights," who lives up there where there is no
variation, not even the shadow of it. About "good and perfect gifts" that
come down from above, from this Father who, as the Father "of lights" or
the light's Father, perpetually knows how to make sure that what comes from
him is truly good and perfect, and as *Father* wants nothing else, thinks of
nothing else than, unchanged, to send good and perfect gifts. Therefore, my
beloved brethren, let everyone be "quick to hear," that is, not listen to fast
and loose talk, but listen upward, because from *above* there is always only good
news; "slow to speak," since the talk we human beings can offer, especially
about the here and now and in all haste, most often can only make the good
and perfect gifts less good and perfect; "slow to anger," lest when the gifts do
not seem to be good and perfect we become angry and by our own guilt
cause to turn into corruption what was good and perfect and intended for
our good—this is what a person's anger can do, and this anger "does not
work the righteousness of God." "Therefore put away all filthiness and remnants of wickedness"—just as one cleans and decorates one's house and sits
all dressed up, festively awaiting the visit: so that in this way we may worthily

XIV
285

receive the good and perfect gifts. "And receive with meekness the Word that is implanted in you and that is powerful for making your souls blessed!" With meekness! Truly, if it were not the apostle who was speaking, and if we did not swiftly comply with the command "to be slow to speak, slow to anger," we might well say: That was a strange way to talk. Are we then such fools that we need to be admonished to meekness in relation to him who only wants our good? Indeed, using the word *meekness* in this way seems to mock us. See, if someone were to strike me unjustly and a bystander said admonishingly: Put up with it meekly—this is straight talk. But imagine the friendliest of beings, love itself. He has selected a gift intended for me, and the gift is good and perfect, yes, as love itself; he comes and wants to present me with this gift—then a bystander says admonishingly to me: Now let me see that you put up with this meekly. And yet that is the way we human beings are. A pagan, and just a human being, that simple wise man of old, laments having often experienced that when he wanted to take one or another fatuity away from someone in order to impart to him a better knowledge, that is, to do him good, the other person could become so enraged that he, as the simple one jestingly says in earnest, wanted to bite him.[297]

Alas, what has God not had to experience these 6000 years, what does he not experience every day from morning until night with every single one of these millions of human beings; we sometimes become most angry when he wants to do us the most good. Indeed, if we human beings truly knew our own good and in the deepest sense truly wanted our own good, then no admonishing to meekness would be needed about this. But in our relationship to God we human beings (and who has not personally experienced this!) are still like children. This is why the admonition about meekness with regard to receiving the good and the perfect is necessary—so convinced is the apostle that only good and perfect gifts come down from him, the eternally Changeless One.

XIV
286
What different points of view! The merely human point of view (as is indeed apparent in paganism) speaks less about God and has a predominant tendency to want to speak sorrowfully only about the changefulness of human things. The apostle wants to speak only about the changelessness of God. So it is with the apostle. For him the thought of the changelessness of God is simply and solely sheer consolation, peace, joy, blessedness. And this is indeed eternally true. But let us not forget that for the apostle its being so is due to the apostle's being the apostle, that he had already long since submitted in unconditional obedience to God's changelessness, that he was not standing at the beginning but rather at the end of the way, the hard but also the good way, which he, renouncing everything, had chosen and, unchanged, followed without looking back, at a more and more rapid pace, hastening toward eternity. We, however, who are still beginners under instruction, we must also see the changelessness of God from another side; and if

we forget this, we easily run into the danger of taking the apostle's exaltation in vain.

So, then, we shall speak, if possible both in terror and for reassurance, *about you, you Changeless One, or about your changelessness.*

God is changeless. Omnipotent, he created this visible world[298]—and made himself invisible. He put on the visible world as a garment; he changes it as one changes a garment—himself unchanged.[299] So it is in the sensate world. In the world of events, he is everywhere present at every moment. In a truer sense than the most watchful human justice is said to be everywhere, he, never seen by any mortal being, is omnipresent, everywhere present, at the least and at the greatest, at what can only figuratively be called an event and at what is the unique event, when a sparrow dies[300] and when the Savior of the human race is born. At every moment he holds all actuality as possibility in his omnipotent hand, at every moment has everything in readiness, changes everything in an instant, the opinions of people, judgments, human loftiness and lowliness; he changes everything—himself unchanged. When to all appearances everything is unchangingness (it is only in appearances that the external is for a certain time unchanged; it is always being changed), in the upheaval of everything, he remains just as unchanged; no variation touches him, not even the shadow of variation; in unchanged clarity, he, the Father of lights, is eternally unchanged. In unchanged clarity—indeed, that is precisely why he is unchanged, because he is pure clarity, a clarity that has no darkness in it,[301] and to which no darkness can come close. This is not the way it is with us human beings. We are not clarity in this way, and that is why we are changeful—at times something becomes clearer in us, and at times darker, and we are changed. Now change takes place around us, and the shadow of variation slides changingly over us; now the changing light from the surrounding world falls upon us, while we ourselves in all this are in turn changed within ourselves. But God is changeless.

XIV
287

This thought is *terrifying, sheer fear and trembling.* Ordinarily this is perhaps less emphasized. One complains about the changefulness of humanity, about the changefulness of everything temporal, but God is changeless; that is the consolation, sheer consolation, so says even light-mindedness. Yes, indeed, God is changeless.

But first and foremost, are you also on good terms with God, are you considering this quite earnestly, are you honestly trying to understand—and this is God's eternal changeless will for you as for every human being, that one should strive for this—are you honestly striving to understand what God's will for you can be? Or do you go on living in such a way that this does not occur to you? How terrible, then, that he is the eternally Changeless One! Yet you must at some time, sooner or later, come in conflict with this changeless will, this changeless will that wanted you to consider this because it wanted your good, this changeless will that must crush you if you in any other way come into conflict with it.

In the second place, you who are still on good terms with God, are you indeed on good terms with him; is your will, is it, and unconditionally, his will; are your wishes, every wish of yours, his command, your thoughts, the first and the last, his thoughts—if not, how terrible that God is changeless, eternally, eternally changeless! How terrible just to disagree with a human being! Yet perhaps you are the stronger and say about the other: Yes, well, he will change all right. But now suppose that he is the stronger; yet you may think you are able to stick it out longer. But now suppose that it is a whole contemporary generation; yet you perhaps say: Seventy years is not eternity. But the eternally Changeless One—suppose you are in disagreement with him—it is indeed an eternity: terrible!

Imagine a traveler; he is brought to a stop at the foot of an enormous, an impassable mountain. It is this that he . . . . . no, he shall not cross, but it is this that he wants to cross, because his wishes, his longings, his cravings—his soul (which has an easier kind of transportation) is already over on the other side, and what is lacking is only that he follow after. Imagine that he became seventy years old, but the mountain stands unchanged, impassable. Let him live yet again seventy years, but the mountain stands unchanged in his way, unchanged, impassable. During all this he perhaps has been changed; he dies to his longings, his wishes, his cravings; he scarcely recognizes himself any longer. Now a new generation finds him sitting, changed, at the foot of the mountain, which stands unchanged, impassable. Suppose it was 1000 years ago. He, the changed, has long since been dead; there is only a legend about him, it is the only thing that remains—yes, and then the mountain, which stands unchanged, impassable. And now the eternally Changeless One, for whom 1000 years are as a day. Alas, even this says too much; they are for him as an instant, indeed, for him they actually are as if they were not—if you want even in the remotest manner to go another way than he wants you to go: terrible!

True enough, if your will, if my will, if the will of these thousands upon thousands is not wholly in agreement with God's will, things nevertheless go on the best they can out there in the busyness of the so-called real world. God does not actually show any sign of noticing. It is more likely that if a righteous person (if there were such a one!) looked at this world, a world that Scripture says lies in the power of evil,[302] he is bound to become discouraged over God's not showing any sign of noticing. But do you therefore think that God has changed, or is his not showing any signs of noticing the lesser terror when it nevertheless is certain that he is eternally changeless? I do not think so. But consider this, and then tell which is the more terrible: either this, the infinitely strong one who, weary of allowing himself to be mocked, rises up in his power and crushes the rebels—this is terrible, and this is indeed how it is pictured when it is told that God does not let himself be mocked and reference is made to the times when his punishment devastated the generation. But is this actually the most terrible? Or is this not even more terrible: the infinitely strong one who—eternally changeless!—remains absolutely still and looks, without a change of countenance, almost as if he did not exist, while nevertheless, so the righteous person certainly must lament, falsehood is progressing, has the power, violence and wrong are victorious, and in such a way that even a better person is tempted to think that he has to use a little of the same means if there is to be any hope of accomplishing something for the good; so it seems as if he is mocked, he the infinitely strong one, the eternally Changeless One, who lets himself be neither mocked nor changed—is this not the most terrible?

XIV
289

Indeed, why do you think he is so quiet? Because he is serenely aware that he is eternally changeless. Someone who was not eternally sure of himself, sure that he is the changeless, could not remain quiet in that way; he would rise up in his power; but only the eternally Changeless One can be that quiet. He takes his time, and that he can of course do. He has eternity, and eternally he is changeless. He takes his time, he does it deliberately. Then comes the accounting of eternity, in which nothing is forgotten, not one single idle word that was spoken, and eternally he is changeless. That he takes time in this way can, however, also be mercy, time for turning around and reformation. But how terrible if this time is not used that way, because then the foolishness and light-mindedness in us must instead wish that he would be promptly on hand with the punishment rather than that he takes time in this way, ignores it, and yet is eternally changeless.

Ask a pedagogue (in the relation to God we are all indeed more or less children!), ask the person who has been involved with people who have gone astray (and everyone of us has gone astray at least once, goes astray for a longer or shorter time, with longer or shorter intervals), and you will hear him verify that it is a great help to light-mindedness, or rather in the prevention of light-mindedness (and who dares claim to be entirely free of light-mindedness!), to have, if possible, the suffering of the punishment follow the transgression immediately, so that the memory of the light-minded one becomes accustomed to remembering the punishment simultaneously with the guilt.

Yes, if transgression and punishment were related to each other in such a way that if one, just as with a double-barreled gun, pressed one spring and at the instant one snatched the forbidden pleasure or committed the transgression, at that very same instant the punishment would come—I think that light-mindedness would then be on guard. But the longer the time between the guilt and the punishment (which truly understood expresses the criterion for the seriousness of the case), the more tempting it is to light-mindedness, as if the whole thing could perhaps be forgotten, or justice itself could perhaps change and have completely different concepts at that time, or as if at least it would be so long since it happened that it would be impossible to present the case unchanged. Then light-mindedness changes, and not for the better. Then light-mindedness becomes secure, and when light-mindedness has become secure it becomes bolder. And so it goes year after year—the punishment fails to come and forgetfulness supervenes, and again punishment fails to come, but new transgression does not fail to come, and the old transgression has now become more malignant. Then it is over; then death ends everything—and to all this (it was only light-mindedness!) an eternally changeless one was witness, and it is with him you will have to make an accounting. At the moment, when temporality's pointer, the minute hand, pointed to seventy years and the man died, during that time eternity's pointer had scarcely moved a trifle—to that degree everything is present for eternity and for him, the Changeless One!

XIV
290

Therefore, whoever you are, remember—something I say to myself—that for God nothing is significant and nothing is insignificant, that in one sense for him the significant is insignificant, and in another sense for him even the least insignificance is something infinitely significant. If, then, your will is not in accord with his, consider this: you will never escape him. Thank him if he through gentleness or severity teaches you to bring your will into accord with his—how frightful it is if he does not show any sign of noticing anything, how frightful it is if a person goes so far as almost to boast that God either does not exist or that he has changed, or even just that he is too great to notice what we call trivialities, inasmuch as he both exists and he is eternally changeless, and his infinite greatness is precisely that he sees even the least little thing, remembers even the least little thing, yes, and if you do not will as he wills, he remembers it unchanged for an eternity!

Consequently, for us light-minded and unstable human beings there is sheer fear and trembling in this thought of God's changelessness. Oh, do consider this well, whether he shows any sign of noticing anything or not—he is eternally changeless! He is eternally changeless, do consider this well if you have, as they say, an account to settle with him—he is changeless. Perhaps you have promised him something, have committed yourself by a holy promise . . . . . but in the course of time you have changed. Now you think about God less often (have you perhaps as an older person found more important things to think about?), or perhaps you think differently about God, that he does not bother about the trivialities of your life, that such faith is childishness. In any case, you have in a way forgotten what you promised him, then after that have forgotten that you promised it to him, and then finally have forgotten, forgotten—yes, forgotten that he forgets nothing, he the eternally Changeless One, that it is simply the reverse childishness of old age to think that something is insignificant for God and that God forgets something, he the eternally Changeless One!

In human relationships there is frequent complaint about changefulness;

one person complains that the other one has changed. But even in human XIV 291
relationships someone's unchangingness can at times be a torment. Perhaps
someone has told another person about himself. Perhaps he talked, excus-
ably, somewhat childishly. But perhaps the matter was actually more serious—
the vain and foolish heart was tempted to speak in high tones of its enthusiasm, of its emotional stability, of its will in this world. The other one
listened to it calmly, did not smile or interrupt him; he let him talk, he listened silently, only promised, as he was asked to do, not to forget what was
said. Time passed, and the first person had long since forgotten all this, but
the other one had not forgotten. Indeed, let us imagine something even
stranger. He had let himself be moved by the thoughts that the first person
in an emotional moment had expressed and, alas, had handed over, as it were;
by honest effort he had shaped his life in accord with these thoughts—what
torment in the unchangingness of his memory, he who all too clearly manifested that he remembered to the last detail what was said at that moment!

And now the eternal Changeless One—and this human heart! Ah, this
human heart, what do you not hide in your secret inclosures, unknown to
others—that would not be the worst—but at times almost unknown to the
person himself! It is almost, as soon as a person is a few years old, it is almost
like a grave, this human heart! There lie buried, buried in forgetfulness, the
promises, the intentions, the resolutions, complete plans and fragments of
plans, and God knows what—yes, that is how we human beings talk, for we
seldom think about what we say; we say: There lies God knows what. And
this we say half-mindedly, half in weariness of life—and then it is so frightfully true that God knows what. He knows down to the least detail what you
have forgotten, knows what has changed in your remembering; he knows it
unchanged. He does not recollect it as if it were something in the past; no,
he knows it as if it were today, and he knows if something with regard to
these wishes, intentions, and resolutions was said, as it were, to him—and he
is eternally unchanged and eternally changeless. If another person's memory
may become a burden—well, it is still never completely trustworthy, and in
any case it cannot last an eternity. I will still become free from this other person and his memory, but an Omniscient One, and an eternally changeless
memory from which you cannot escape, least of all in eternity—frightful!
No, eternally changeless, everything is for him eternally present, eternally
equally present, no shifting shadow either of morning or evening, of youth XIV 292
or of old age, of forgetfulness or of excuse, no shifting shadow shifts him—
no, for him there is no shadow. If we are, as it is said, shadows, he is eternal
clarity in his eternal changelessness; if we are shadows that hasten away—my
soul, take heed, because whether you will or not, you are hastening to eternity, to him, and he is eternal clarity! Therefore he does not only hold an accounting, he is the accounting. It is said that we human beings must make
an accounting, as if it were a long time away, and then perhaps an over-

whelming mass of prolixities in order to get the accounting arranged. O my soul, it is being done every moment, because his unchanging clarity is the accounting, completely ready down to the least detail and kept by him, the eternal Changeless One, who has forgotten nothing of what I have forgotten; neither does he do as I do, remember something different from what it actually was.

Thus there is sheer fear and trembling in this thought about the changelessness of God. It is almost as if it were far, far beyond human powers to have to be involved with a changelessness such as that; indeed, it seems as if this thought must plunge a person into anxiety and unrest to the point of despair.

But then it is also the case *that there is reassurance and blessedness in this thought.* It is really so that when you, weary from all this human, all this temporal and earthly changefulness and alteration, weary of your own instability, could wish for a place where you could rest your weary head, your weary thoughts, your weary mind, in order to rest, to have a good rest—ah, in God's changelessness there is rest! If for that reason you allow his changelessness to serve you as he wills, for your good, your eternal good, if you allow yourself to be brought up so that your self-will (and this, even more than external factors, accounts for changefulness) expires, the sooner the better—it does not help you; you must be either with the good or with the evil. Imagine the futility of wanting to be at odds with an eternal changelessness; be like the child when it really profoundly senses that it is in the position of being face-to-face with a will where only one thing helps, to obey. When you allow yourself to be brought up by his changelessness so that you renounce instability and changefulness and caprice and willfulness—then you rest ever more blessedly in this changelessness of God. That the thought of God's changelessness is blessed, indeed, who doubts that; just see to it that you become like that so that you can blessedly rest in this changelessness! Ah, such a person speaks as someone who has a happy home: My home is eternally safeguarded; I rest in God's changelessness. No one but you yourself can disturb this rest. If you could become completely obedient in unchanged obedience, you would at every moment freely rest in God with the same necessity as a heavy body sinks to the earth, or with the same necessity as something that is light rises toward heaven.

Then let everything else change, as it does. If the stage of your activity is large, you will experience the changefulness of everything on a larger scale; but on a small stage, the smallest, you will still experience the same thing, perhaps just as painfully. You will experience how people change, how you yourself change; at times it will also seem as if God changed, which is part of the upbringing. On that subject, the changefulness of everything, an older person will be better able to speak than I, whereas what I could say perhaps could seem to the very young to be something new. We shall not, however, develop this further but leave the complexity of life to unfold for each individual as it is defined for him so that he can come to experience what all others before him have experienced. At times the change will be such that you will be reminded of the saying: Change is pleasing—yes, unspeakably! There will also come times when you will personally invent a saying that the language has concealed, and you say: Change is not pleasing—how could I say that change is pleasing? When that happens, you will be especially prompted to seek him (something you will surely not forget in the first case either), the Changeless One.

My listener, this hour is now soon over, and the discourse. If you yourself do not want it otherwise, this hour will soon also be forgotten, and the discourse. And if you yourself want it otherwise, this thought about the changelessness of God will also be soon forgotten in changefulness. Yet this fault is not due to him, the Changeless One! But if you do not make yourself guilty of forgetting it, then you will be sustained in this thought for your lifetime, for an eternity.

Imagine a solitary in the desert; almost scorched by the heat of the sun, dying of thirst, he finds a spring. Ah, delicious coolness! Now I am provided for. God be praised, he says—and yet he found only a spring. How must the one speak who found God!—and yet he also must say, "God be praised," I found God!—now I am, God be praised, provided for. Your faithful coolness, O beloved spring, is not subject to change. In the cold of winter, if it were to reach here, you do not become colder but keep exactly the same coolness; the water of a spring does not freeze! In the noonday heat of summer you keep exactly your unchanged coolness; the water of a spring does not become tepid! There is nothing false in what he says (he who in my opinion did not choose an unrewarding subject for a eulogy, a spring, something everyone better understands the better he knows what it means: the desert and solitude); there is no false exaggeration in his eulogy. His life, however, took a turn completely different from what he had thought. At one time he strayed away, was pulled out into the wide world. Many years after, he came back. His first thought was the spring—it was not there, it had dried up. For a moment he stood silent in sorrow; then he collected himself and said: No, I will not take back a word of what I said in your praise, it was all truth. And if I praised your delicious coolness while you were, O beloved spring, then let me also praise it now when you have vanished so that it may be true that there is unchangingness in a human breast. Nor can I say that you deceived me; no, if I had found you, I am convinced that your coolness would be unchanged—and more you had not promised.

But you, O God, you Changeless One, you, unchanged, are always to be found and are always to be found unchanged. No one, either in life or in death, travels so far away that you are not to be found, that you are not there;

you are indeed everywhere—this is not the way springs are on this earth, springs are only in special places. Moreover—what overwhelming security!—you do not remain on the spot like a spring; you travel along. No one strays so far away that he cannot find his way back to you, you who are not only like a spring that lets itself be found—what a poor description of your being!—you who are like a spring that even searches for the thirsting, the straying, something unheard of about any spring. Thus are you unchanged and everywhere to be found. And whenever a person comes to you, at whatever age, at whatever time of day, in whatever condition—if he comes honestly, he will always find (like the spring's unchanged coolness) your love just as warm, you Changeless One! Amen.

ACKNOWLEDGMENTS

Preparation of the manuscript of *The Essential Kierkegaard* was supported by a genuinely enabling grant from the National Endowment for the Humanities. The grant included matched gifts from the Danish Ministry of Cultural Affairs and the General Mills Foundation.

A host of respondents helped in choosing the selections. The editors are especially indebted to members of the International Advisory Board of *Kierkegaard's Writings:* Per Lønning, Wim R. Scholtens, and Sophia Scopetéa. Nathaniel Hong constructed the text from the volumes of *Kierkegaard's Writings* and prepared the index.

Inclusion of entries from *Søren Kierkegaard's Journals and Papers* is by arrangement with Indiana University Press. The resources of the Kierkegaard Library, St. Olaf College, have been used throughout the work.

NOTES

1. See Romans 8:38–39.

2. See p. 12, the frequently quoted (in various formulations) journal entry *Pap.* IV A 164 (*Pap* I 1030). See also *JP* I 1030, 1025; III 3553 (*Pap.* IV A 164; II A 725, 558). One of the early references in English to Kierkegaard is William James's citing of this sentence in *Essays in Radical Empiricism* (London: Longmans-Green, 1922), p. 238. See also *Pragmatism* (1908), p. 223, and *A Pluralistic Universe* (1920), p. 244.

3. See Daniel 5:25.

4. In Andersen's novel *O.T.* (1836), the hero Otto Thostrup had these words tattooed on his shoulder.

5. The reference to Christian D. Grabbe has not been located.

6. See Ecclesiastes 1:2.

7. Acts 5:9.

8. See Luke 17:33.

9. A drawbridge across the ship channel between Copenhagen and the island Amager.

10. In Norse mythology, Fenris, a great wolf, the son of Loki, was chained until Ragnarok' (the final destruction of the world in the conflict between Aesir, the gods, and the powers of Hel, led by Loki), when it would devour Odin, the chief of the gods.

11. See Diogenes Laertius, *Lives of Eminent Philosophers*, I-II, tr. R. D. Hicks (Loeb, New York: Putnam, 1925), I, p. 163: "Someone asked him [Socrates] whether he should marry or not, and received the reply, 'Whichever you do you will repent it.'"

12. Kierkegaard extends to Diana's own birth the help she gave her mother, Latona, in the birth of her twin brother Apollo.

13. Henrik Steffens, *Caricaturen des Heiligsten*, I-II (Leipzig: 1819–21), II, pp. 82–120.

14. Marcus Aurelius, *Meditations*, VII, 2.

15. In Greek mythology, the underworld river of forgetfulness or oblivion to be crossed by those entering the realm of the dead.

16. In Greek mythology, the three-headed dog that guarded the gate of Hades.

17. See *Plutarch's Lives*, I-XI (Loeb, New York: Putnam, 1914–26), V, p. 473: ". . . Archimedes, who was a kinsman and friend of King Hiero, wrote to him that with any given force it was possible to move any given weight; and emboldened, as we are told, by the strength of his own demonstration, he declared that if there were another world, and he could go to it, he could move this."

18. The ritual of pledging friendship, using the familiar second-person *du* instead of the formal plural *De*.

19. Johann Heinrich Wilhelm Tischbein (1751–1829), German artist.

20. The source has not been located.

21. See Proverbs 24:26.

22. See Judges 16:13–19.

23. In Greek mythology, Alectryon, a friend of Ares, went to sleep while on watch at the tryst of Ares and Aphrodite.

24. See Samuel 12:1–7.

25. Julius in Friedrich v. Schlegel's *Lucinde*.

26. See I Peter 3:4.

27. Johann Wolfgang v. Goethe, "*Vanitas! vanitatum vanitas.*"

28. Quoted with some variation from Goethe, "*Freisinn,*" *West-östlicher Divan.*

29. The elder Cato (234–149 B.C.) repeatedly concluded his speeches in the senate with "*Ceterum* [or *Praeterea*] *censeo Carthaginem esse delendam* [Furthermore, I am of the opinion that Carthage must be destroyed]."

30. A reference to the permanent character of baptism and the ordination vow in Roman Catholicism.

31. The phrase, associated with Socrates, inscribed on the temple of the Delphic oracle.

32. The final volume in the first pseudonymous series, *Concluding Unscientific Postscript,* ends with Kierkegaard's acknowledgment (on unnumbered pages) of the series of pseudonymous works.

33. On the translation of *opbyggelig* as "upbuilding," see *Eighteen Upbuilding Discourses,* pp. 503–05, n.3, *KW* V.

34. *On My Work as an Author,* in *The Point of View,* p. 12, *KW* XXII.

35. *Eighteen Discourses,* p. 5, *KW* V.

36. *For Self-Examination,* p. 3, *KW* XXI.

37. See II Corinthians 12:9.

38. See II Corinthians 5:17.

39. Diogenes of Sinope. See Diogenes Laertius, *Lives,* VI, 9, 105.

40. See I Corinthians 9:26.

41. *Two Ages: The Age of Revolution and the Present Age. A Literary Review,* p. 99, *KW* XIV.

42. See Genesis 22.

43. See John 2:1–10.

44. See Luke 18:18–23.

45. *The Concept of Anxiety,* p. 18 fn., *KW* VIII.

46. In an old Roman Catholic Ash Wednesday ceremony, the priest would strew ashes upon himself and the parishioners and repeat the Latin sentence quoted in the text.

47. *Der Talisman,* a farcical comedy by Johann Nestroy.

48. *Philosophical Fragments, or a Fragment of Philosophy,* p. 91, *KW* VII; *JP* V 6137 (*Pap.* VIII[1] A 652).

49. Ibid., p. 111 (272).

50. The Danish *blev til* (as well as *tilblive, Tilblivelse, være til,* and *Tilværelse*) refers to temporal and spatial modes of becoming and being. Existence is a mode of being, but not all being is spatial-temporal existence. The eternal as timeless does not come into being but enters into spatial-temporal existence as a specific embodiment of the eternal. The moment is an atom of eternity and has significance qualitatively different from that of transient instants of time. Therefore, for example, in *Postscript* (p. 332, *KW* XII; *SV* VII 287) Climacus states that "God does not think, he creates; God does not exist, he is eternal."

51. Hannah Arendt, *The Human Condition* (Chicago: University of Chicago Press, 1959), p. 275 fn.

52. *Anxiety,* p. 162, *KW* VIII (*SV* IV 428).

53. See *The Sickness unto Death,* p. 131, *KW* XIX (*SV* XI 241).

54. Ibid., pp. 13–14 (127–28).

55. Genesis 2:17.

56. James 1:13–14.

57. The freedom of indifference or the ability of the will to choose independently of antecedent factors.

58. I Corinthians 15:52.

59. "The Story of the Youth Who Went Forth to Learn What Fear Was."

60. Belshazzar, son of Nebachadnezzar. See Daniel 4:5 and 5:5–24.

61. See note 29.

62. In Holberg's *Jacob von Tyboe,* III, 4, Magister Stygotius ridicules academics who are unable to distinguish between logical categories.

63. An enclitic is a word that usually loses its accent in being attached closely to another word, as "not" in "cannot."

64. *Three Discourses on Imagined Occasions,* p. 28, *KW* X (*SV* V 193).

65. *JP* V 5865 (*Pap.* VII¹ B 83).

66. *Stages on Life's Way. Studies by Various Persons,* p. 484, *KW* XI (*SV* VI 450).

67. G. C. Lichtenberg, "*Ueber Physiognomie wider die Physiognomen,*" *Georg Christoph Lichtenberg's vermischte Schriften,* I-IX (Göttingen: 1800–06), III, p. 479.

68. See Judges 14:14; *JP* I 875 (*Pap.* II A 513).

69. See note 29.

70. See *Cicero, De Oratore,* I-II (Loeb, Cambridge: Harvard University Press, 1942), I, pp. 463–65.

71. The equator. See *Letters,* Letter 218, *KW* XXV.

72. See Genesis 43:44. Kierkegaard follows the translation in the Danish Bible (1830). The *RSV* has "merry."

73. Presumably an allusion to Socrates.

74. See Exodus 20:5.

75. *Fragments,* p. 109, *KW* VII (*SV* IV 270).

76. *Postscript,* pp. [625–30], *KW* XII.1 (*SV* VII [545–49]).

77. *Fragments,* pp. 13, 32, 47, 52, *KW* VII (*SV* IV 184, 200, 214, 218).

78. Johan Ludvig Heiberg, Danish poet, dramatist, and Hegelian philosopher, who became "an adherent of Hegelian philosophy through a miracle at Hotel Streit in Hamburg on Easter morning" (*Postscript,* p. 184, *KW* XII.1; *SV* VII 153).

79. *Fragments,* p. 109, *KW* VII (*SV* IV 270).

80. Gotthold Ephraim Lessing, German philosopher and dramatist.

81. Lessing, "*Ueber den Beweis des Geistes und der Kraft,*" *Gotthold Ephraim Lessing's sämmtliche Schriften,* I-XXXII (Berlin: 1825–28), V, p. 80.

82. *Fragments,* pp. 79–86, *KW* VII (*SV* IV 242–49).

83. See p. 12 and note 2.

84. On this concept, see *JP* III 3660–64 and pp. 908–09, also 3665–96 and pp. 910–11 on reduplication.

85. John 18:38, "What is truth?"

86. See note 18.

87. In Greek mythology, Zeus punished Ixion for making love to Hera (Roman Juno) by sending him a cloud resembling Hera.

88. *Stages on Life's Way,* pp. 471–72, *KW* XI (*SV* VI 438).

89. See *Fragments,* pp. 13–16, 51–52, *KW* VII (*SV* IV 183–85, 218).

90. Danish: *er til.* Although *er til* is usually translated as "exists," the meaning here is simply "is" or "has being" but not in the sense of temporal-spatial historical existence. See, for example, *Fragments,* p. 87, *KW* VII (*SV* IV 250–51).

91. See ibid., pp. 66–71, 89–105, *KW* VII (*SV* IV 230–34, 252–67).

92. See Plato, *Phaedo,* 111 a-b.

93. God incarnate in time-space, as in the Platonic terminology in *Fragments.*

94. Ephesians 2:12.

95. Socrates' appearance was considerably less than attractive. See Xenophon, *Memorabilia and Oeconomicus, Symposium and Apology,* ed. E. C. Marchant and O. J. Todd (Loeb, Cambridge: Harvard University Press, 1979), pp. 598, 603.

96. See Aristotle, *Poetics,* 1451 a-b.

97. See *Either/Or,* I, pp. 3–4, *KW* III (*SV* I v-vi).

98. *Stages,* pp. 438–39, *KW* XI (*SV* VI 408–09).

99. See, for example, Aristotle, *Physics,* 200 b-201 a.

100. See *Fragments,* p. 86 fn., *KW* VII (*SV* IV 249–50).

101. Poul Martin Møller, *Strøtanker, Efterladte Skrifter,* I-III (Copenhagen: 1839–43), III, p. 177.

102. See *Fragments,* p. 10 fn., *KW* VII (*SV* IV 180).

103. *Stages,* pp. 420–22, *KW* XI (*SV* VI 392–93).

104. "'Guilty?'/'Not Guilty?'" *Stages,* pp. 185–397, *KW* XI (*SV* VI 175–370).

105. The dialectical in first place is the dialectical in the sphere of immanence, including Religiousness *A;* "in second place" refers to the new dialectic in Religiousness *B* after the breach with immanence.

106. Bishop Jakob Peter Mynster's pseudonym, consisting of the initial consonant of the second syllable in each name.

107. A sailor with minimal qualifying experience, distinguished from an able seaman with more experience.

108. Georg Brandes, *Søren Kierkegaard, Samlede Skrifter,* I-XVIII (Copenhagen: 1899–1910), II, pp. 376–77 (ed. tr.).

109. *Stadier paa Livets Vei, SV* VI, p. 180 (*KW* XI 191).

110. In the present article Frater Taciturnus says, "*Jeg vil experimentere en Figur* [I will imaginatively construct a character]," a line that applies to all the pseudonymous works. The key phrase is not *experimentere med* [with].

111. Rikard Magnussen, *Det særlige Kors* (Copenhagen: 1942), p. 164.

112. Supplement, Corsair *Affair,* p. 178 (*Pap.* VII¹ B 55).

113. *JP* V 5888 (*Pap.* VII¹ A 99).

114. *The Corsair,* no. 269, November 14, 1845.

115. Meïr Goldschmidt, *Livs Erindringer og Resultater,* I-II (Copenhagen: 1877), I, p. 429 (ed. tr.).

116. The epigraph in *Stages.*

117. A response to being thanked: You are welcome; literally, May it be of good to you.

118. See note 113.

119. The page number in the first Danish edition of *Stadier.* See *Stages,* p. 398, *KW* XI (*SV* VI 371).

120. Ibid., p. 487 (452).

121. *The Corsair,* no. 251, July 4, 1845.

122. See note 114.

123. *JP* V 5877 (*Pap.* VII¹ A 9).

124. *Two Ages,* p. 62, *KW* XIV (*SV* VIII 59).

125. Ibid., p. 91 (85).

126. "Reflecting" has a double meaning in *Two Ages:* the reflected image and effect of the age in various spheres of life (reflexion) and deliberation (reflection).

127. Socrates.

128. See Plato, *Phaedo,* 104 c.

129. In Horace, *Satires,* II, 5, 59, it is Tiresias who says this. The correct attribution is made in *Prefaces,* p. 47, *KW* IX (*SV* V 51).

130. The Danish words *Tvivl* [doubt], *Fortvivelse* [despair], and *Tvesindethed* all have a common root: *tve* (variant *tvi*), which means "two."

131. James 3:5.

132. See Proverbs 14:34.

133. Matthew 12:43–45.

134. Matthew 12:45.

135. See *Stages,* p. 421, *KW* XI (*SV* VI 392).

136. *JP* V 5972 (*Pap.* VIII¹ A 4).

137. *JP* I 641 (*Pap.* VIII[1] A 293).

138. Matthew 22:37. See also Deuteronomy 11:13.

139. See Luke 10:29.

140. The English "neighbor" is derived from the Old English *neahgebur* (nigh-dweller).

141. Matthew 5:46.

142. Attributed to Solon and quoted by Croesus when condemned by Cyrus. See Herodotus, *History, Herodotus,* I-IV (Cambridge: Harvard University Press, 1981–82), I, pp. 40–41, 108–11.

143. Romans 8:37.

144. The source of the quotation has not been located.

145. See James 3:10.

146. Darius of Persia.

147. See Sirach 36:27.

148. See, for example, *Sickness unto Death,* pp. 13–14, *KW* XIX (*SV* XI 127–28).

149. The source of the quotation has not been located.

150. See, for example, *Sickness unto Death,* pp. 51, 61–62, *KW* XIX (*SV* XI 164, 173–74).

151. One's similarity to another and the joint dissimilarity to others.

152. See note 33.

153. Here the English idiom does not quite fit the Danish.

154. See Matthew 7:25–26.

155. Cf. Luke 14:28–30.

156. I Corinthians 14:26.

157. I Corinthians 13:1.

158. I Corinthians 8:1.

159. II Corinthians 12:19.

160. *JP* VI 6356 (*Pap.* X[1] A 138).

161. *JP* V 6121 (*Pap.* VIII[1] A 590).

162. The Danish *Spurv* designates any finch (*Fringillidae*), which includes the European house sparrow (*Graa-Spurv, Passer domesticus*) known in the United States as the English sparrow, and also the yellow bunting or yellowhammer (*Guld-Spurv, Emberiza citrenella*).

163. See Genesis 1:27.

164. Tantalus.

165. Matthew 6:33.

166. Ovid.

167. Hans Adolph Brorson, "*I denne søde Juletid,*" stanza 6.

168. See John 8:3–11.

169. Genesis 1:31.

170. Matthew 11:6.

171. See Genesis 32:24–32.

172. See Exodus 20:4.

173. See Romans 3:19.

174. Cf. John 3:16.

175. See I Corinthians 2:9; *Fragments,* p. 36, *KW* VII (*SV* IV 203).

176. See Matthew 14:15–21; Mark 6:38–44.

177. Cf. Romans 3:7–8, 6: 1–2, 15.

178. *JP* VI 6383 (*Pap.* X[1] A 250).

179. Matthew 6:33; *The Moment,* no. 7, in The Moment *and Late Writings,* pp. 233–36, *KW* XXIII (*SV* XIV 248–50).

180. See Matthew 19:21

181. See Proverbs 9:10.

182. See *JP* VI 6277, 6278, 6280 (*Pap.* IX A 421, 498, 500).

183. *JP* VI 6407 (*Pap.* X^1 A 351).

184. *Two Ethical-Religious Essays,* in *Without Authority,* pp. 83, 84, *KW* XVIII (*SV* XI 85, 86).

185. In Greek the word means "one who is sent."

186. Cf. *Anxiety,* p. 39, *KW* VIII (*SV* IV 329).

187. See Ephesians 2:19.

188. See, for example, *Sickness unto Death,* pp. 99, 117, 126, 127, *KW* XIX (*SV* 210, 227, 235, 237).

189. See Matthew 7:29.

190. See Matthew 28:18.

191. See Plato, *Phaedo.*

192. See I Corinthians 4:13.

193. II Corinthians 6:10.

194. See Philippians 4:7.

195. *JP* VI 6433 (*Pap.* X^1 A 517).

196. *Anxiety,* p. 61, *KW* VIII (*SV* IV 331).

197. *Pap.* VIII^2 B 168:6.

198. *Either/Or,* II, p. 211, *KW* IV (*SV* II 190). See note 130.

199. On the "first self" and the "deeper self," see *Eighteen Discourses,* pp. 314–18, *KW* V (*XV* V 95–99).

200. See Mark 9:48.

201. *Aut Caesar aut nihil,* the motto of Caesar Borgia.

202. Plato, *Republic,* X, 608 c–610.

203. Cf. *The Lily in the Field and the Bird of the Air,* in *Without Authority,* pp. 7–9, 18, *KW* XVIII (*SV* XI 11–13, 21).

204. See Ephesians 2:12.

205. See Luke 11:15, 26.

206. A negative formulation of the thesis that knowledge is virtue and that one does not knowingly do wrong. See *Irony,* pp. 60–62, 149, 218, *KW* II (*SV* XIII 155, 235, 290).

207. A key phrase in Kantian ethics, which views universal applicability as a maxim of action and assumes that "ought" implies "can."

208. See Philippians 2:7.

209. See Matthew 27:67; Luke 18:32.

210. The indubitable halting point in Descartes' process of doubting everything that is at all dubitable.

211. See Matthew 8:13; *Works of Love,* pp. 518–86, *KW* XVI (*SV* IX 358–65).

212. See, for example, Matthew 10:38, 16:24; Mark 8:34; I Corinthians 4:16.

213. Danish *Betragtninger,* presumably an allusion to Bishop Mynster's *Betragtninger over de christelige Troeslærdomme,* I–II (Copenhagen: 1837).

214. See John 14:6.

215. *Postscript,* pp. [629–30], *KW* XII.1 (*SV* VII [548–49]).

216. See Matthew 11:28. The theme of No. I of *Practice,* pp. 3–68, *KW* XX (*SV* XII v–65).

217. See Genesis 4:13–15.

218. II Corinthians 5:20.

219. On reading aloud, see, for example, *Discourses in Various Spirits,* pp. 5–6, *KW* XV (*SV* VIII 117); *JP* VI 6627, 6768 (*Pap.* X^3 A 128; X^4 A 322).

220. See, for example, the prefaces to the discourses in *Eighteen Discourses, KW* V; *Adler,* pp. 180, 311, *KW* XXIV (*SV* XI 101; *Pap.* VII^2 B 235, p. 149); *On My Work,* in *Point of View,* p. 12, *KW* XXII (*SV* XIII 501); *JP* VI 6587, 6936 (*Pap.* X^2 A 475; X^3 A 389; XI^2 A 250).

221. Socrates.

222. On this Platonic locution, see *Fragments,* p. 10, *KW* VII (*SV* IV 18), and note 13.

223. See Plato, *Gorgias,* 490 e.

224. Frequently and incorrectly attributed to Luther, the slogan first appeared in Matthias Claudius, *Wandsbecker Bothen* (1774) and presumably goes back to an Italian rhyme: *Chi non ama il vino, la donna, e il canto / Un pazzo egli sarà e non santo* [He who does not love wine, woman, and song / Is a fool and not a saint].

225. The Persian king Darius because of the taking and burning of Sardis by the Athenians.

226. See II Samuel 11:2–12:15.

227. *Pap.* X^6 B 4:15.

228. *Judge for Yourself!,* p. 215, *KW* XXI (*SV* XII 481).

229. See Mark 2:17; Luke 5:32.

230. *Pap.* X^1 A 117.

231. *JP* V 6079 (*Pap.* VIII^1 A 440).

232. Johannes Hohlenberg, *Sören Kierkegaard* (London: Routledge, 1954), p. 196.

233. See *Postscript,* p. 392, *KW* XII.1 (*SV* VII 340).

234. Ludwig Feuerbach, author of *Das Wesen des Christentums* (Leipzig: 1843).

235. See John 1:11.

236. See I Corinthians 2:14.

237. Presumably a reference to the laws of Charondas (fifth c. B.C.). See Ludvig Holberg, *Journey of Niels Klim to the World Underground* (Lincoln: University of Nebraska Press, 1960), p. 37.

238. Homer, *Iliad,* II, 204.

239. See Jac[k]ob Peter Mynster, *Prædikener,* I–II (Copenhagen: 1826), I, p. ix.

240. Attributed to the Greek lyric poet Cleobulus (seventh c. B.C.).

241. Hans Lassen Martensen, who became Bishop Mynster's successor.

242. See, for example, Romans 6:2; Colossians 2:20, 3:3.

243. See I Corinthians 4:9.

244. See I Corinthians 4:13.

245. An allusion to Kierkegaard's intention at one time to seek ordination.

246. See *Two Essays,* in *Without Authority,* pp. 91–108, *KW* XVIII (*SV* XI 93–109).

247. See Philippians 2:7.

248. See Horace, *Epodes,* I, 10, 24.

249. See I Peter 2:9.

250. See I Corinthians 1:28.

251. Cf. Cicero, *On Divination,* II, 24, 51–52.

252. See Mark 10:21.

253. Cf. Diogenes Laertius, *Lives,* II, 31.

254. See Mark 10:21.

255. See Mark 15:34.

256. See, for example, Matthew 11:6; John 6:60–61; *Practice,* pp. 97–144, *KW* XX (*SV* XII 93–134).

257. See Luke 14:26.

258. See note 201.

259. See Matthew 6:33; *Judge for Yourself!,* pp. 110–13, *KW* XXI (*SV* XII 391–93).

260. The Danish *from* means "pious."

261. Ludvig Holberg, *Den Stundesløse,* I, 11.

262. Matthew 19:27.

263. In The Moment *and Late Writings,* pp. 73, 74, *KW* XXIII (*SV* XIV 85, 86).

264. Horace, *Epistles,* I, 1, 54.

265. See Plato, *Sophist,* 223 b: " . . . his art may be traced as a branch of the appropriative,

acquisitive family—which hunts animals, living, land, tame animals—which hunts many privately, for hire, taking money in exchange . . .."

266. See p. 433.

267. See Plato, *Apology,* 22 d–23 b.

268. Kierkegaard was Copenhagen's foremost peripatetic. For the earliest English account, see Andrew Hamilton, *Sixteen Months in the Danish Isles,* I–II (London: 1852), II, pp. 268–70. In a letter (Letter 150, *KW* XXV) accompanying a copy of *Works of Love* to Henriette, Peter Christian Kierkegaard's wife, Kierkegaard espouses the many values of walking.

Dear Jette,

I am glad that you yourself have provided the occasion for sending the book that accompanies this letter. So you yourself are responsible and will all the more carefully see to it that your reading of the book or any single part of it will not in any way conflict with my brother's idea of what is beneficial or harmful reading, for it would distress me to have that happen.

Please note, therefore, that I have arranged it so that emphasis is in no way placed on whether or not you read it, something I never oblige anyone to do, and especially not that person whom I surely would not wish to *burden* with a *complimentary* copy.

This is my own copy, originally destined for myself; thus it has a purely personal relationship to me, not in my capacity as author as with other copies, but rather as if the author had presented it to me. However, it now occurs to me that it has not fulfilled its destiny and reaches its proper destination only in being destined for you—the only copy in the whole printing suitable for that. —The bookbinder has done a beautiful job on the book (and in judging the bookbinder's craft I am after all impartial). —It has been read through by me and is to that extent a used copy. So please notice that everything is as it ought to be now. For a brief moment you may admire the bookbinder's art as you would admire any other art object: then you may—for a longer moment, if you please, take pleasure in the thought that it is a gift; and then you may put the book down (—for it has been read—), put it aside as one puts a gift aside, put it aside carefully—if it is a welcome gift.

But enough of this. I was sorry not to be able to take my leave of you. I hope this little letter in which I take my leave will find you as well as I found you when I arrived. *Above all, do not lose your desire to walk: every day I walk myself into a state of well-being and walk away from every illness; I have walked myself into my best thoughts, and I know of no thought so burdensome that one cannot walk away from it.* Even if one were to walk for one's health and it were constantly one station ahead—*I would still say: Walk!* Besides, it is also apparent that in walking one constantly gets as close to well-being as possible, even if one does not quite reach it—*but by sitting still, and the more one sits still, the closer one comes to feeling ill.* Health and salvation can he found only in motion. If anyone denies that motion exists, I do as Diogenes did, I walk. If anyone denies that health resides in motion, then I walk away from all morbid objections. *Thus, if one just keeps on walking, everything will be all right.* And out in the country you have all the advantages; you do not risk heing stopped before you are safe and happy outside your gate, nor do you run the risk of being intercepted on your way home. I remember exactly what happened to me a while ago and what has happened frequently since then. I had been walking for an hour and a half and had done a great deal of thinking, and with the help of motion I had really become a very agreeable person to myself. What bliss, and, as you may imagine, what care did I not take to bring my bliss home as safely as possible. Thus I hurry along, with downcast eyes I steal through the streets, so to speak; confident that I am entitled to the sidewalk. I do not consider it necessary to look about at all (for thereby one is so easily intercepted, just as one is looking about—in order to avoid) and thus hasten along the sidewalk with my bliss (for the ordinance forbidding one to carry anything on the sidewalk does not extend to bliss, which makes a person lighter)—

directly into a man who is always suffering from illness and who therefore with downcast eyes, defiant because of his illness, does not even think that he must look about when he is not entitled to the sidewalk. I was stopped. It was a quite exalted gentleman who now honored me with conversation. Thus all was lost. After the conversation ended, there was only one thing left for me to do: instead of going home, to go walking again.

As you see, there really is no more space in this letter, and therefore I break off this conversation—for in a sense it has heen a conversation, inasmuch as I have constantly thought of you as present. Do take care of yourself!

Yours, S. KIERKEGAARD

269. Presumably an allusion to Meïr Goldschmidt, editor of *The Corsair.*

270. Walter Lowrie, *Kierkegaard* (London: Oxford University Press, 1938), p. 392.

271. In the manner of a midwife. An allusion to Socrates' metaphor for his approach. See Plato, *Theaetetus,* 150 b–d.

272. Frater Taciturnus, "The Activity of a Traveling Esthetician and How He Happened to Pay for the Dinner," *Fædrelandet,* 2078, December 27, 1845.

273. Certain published works are not included. *From the Papers of One Still Living* was a review, as was *Two Ages. The Concept of Irony* was an academic dissertation. Kierkegaard therefore considered *Either/Or* as the beginning of his authorship proper. *The Point of View,* published posthumously, was written in 1848; therefore works published subsequently are not listed. *Three Discourses on Imagined Occasions* is inexplicably omitted.

274. The second edition of *Either/Or* was published May 14, 1849. *The Lily in the Field and the Bird of the Air* was published on the same day.

275. The "Living Word," an emphasis on oral tradition, was the "matchless discovery" by Nicolai Severin Grundtvig.

276. See *Postscript,* pp. 617, 619, *KW* XII.1 (*SV* VII 537, 539).

277. Attributed to Pope Paul IV but found earlier in Sebastian Brandt, *Narrenschiff,* and used in *Puf! eller Verden vil bedrages,* the Danish version of a play by Augustin Eugène Scribe. See *Det Kongelige Theaters Repertoire* (Copenhagen: 1849).

278. Jens Finsteen Gi[j]ødwad, go-between for Kierkegaard with the printer and bookseller of the pseudonymous works.

279. See note 18.

280. *Either/Or,* II, p. 205, *KW* IV (*SV* II 184), freely quoted.

281. Christian Peter Bianco Luno, Copenhagen printer of most of Kierkegaard's works.

282. The war (1848–1849) between Prussia and Denmark over the Danish duchies Schleswig and Holstein. It was also a time of great political unrest in Denmark and throughout Europe.

283. *The Corsair,* edited by Meïr Goldschmidt.

284. Aristotle, *Rhetoric,* 1419 b.

285. Cf. Isaiah 3:4.

286. See note 272.

287. See p. 251.

288. See p. 251 and note 114.

289. Kierkegaard's dissertation for the *Magister* [Master] degree was *The Concept of Irony, with Continual Reference to Socrates.*

290. See Historical Introduction, Corsair *Affair,* pp. xxix–xxxiii, *KW* XIII.

291. The soothsayers in Rome declared that a sacrifice was needed to halt the sinking of the ground in the middle of the Forum. As the required sacrifice, the equestrian soldier Marcus Curtius plunged into the chasm.

292. See note 282.

293. See Plato, *Phaedrus,* 230 c.

294. *Christian Discourses,* delivered to the printer March 6, 1848, and published April 26, 1848.

295. A play on *Kjøbstad* [market town] and *Kjøbenhavn* [market harbor].

296. In the many cartoon caricatures of Kierkegaard, *The Corsair* repeatedly ridiculed his legs as thin and his trouser legs as mismatched in length.

297. See Plato, *Theaetetus,* 151 b–d; *Fragments,* pp. 20–21, *KW* VII (*SV* IV 190); *Works of Love,* p. 277, *KW* XVI (*SV* IX 263).

298. On omnipotence and creation, see *JP* II 1251 (*Pap.* VII^1 A 181).

299. See Hebrews 1:12.

300. See Matthew 10:29.

301. Cf. James 1:17.

302. See I John 5:19.

BIBLIOGRAPHY

Kierkegaard's Writings, I–XXVI, Princeton University Press, 1978–2000:

From the Papers of One Still Living, in *Early Polemical Writings*, *KW* I.

The Concept of Irony, with Continual Reference to Socrates, *KW* II.

Either/Or. A Fragment of Life, I–II, *KW* III–IV.

Four Upbuilding Discourses, in *Eighteen Upbuilding Discourses*, *KW* V.

Fear and Trembling. Dialectical Lyric, with *Repetition*, *KW* VI.

Repetition. A Venture in Experimenting Psychology, with *Fear and Trembling*, *KW* VI.

Philosophical Fragments, or a Fragment of Philosophy, *KW* VII.

Johannes Climacus, or de omnibus dubitandum est, with *Philosophical Fragments*, *KW* VII.

The Concept of Anxiety. A Simple Psychologically Orienting Deliberation on the Dogmatic Issue of Hereditary Sin, *KW* VIII.

Prefaces. Light Reading for People in Various Estates According to Time and Opportunity, *KW* IX.

Three Discourses on Imagined Occasions, *KW* X.

Stages on Life's Way. Studies by Various Persons, *KW* XI.

Concluding Unscientific Postscript to Philosophical Fragments. *A Mimical-Pathetical-Dialectical Contribution*, *KW* XII.

"The Activity of a Traveling Esthetician and How He Happened to Pay for the Dinner," in *The* Corsair *Affair*, *KW* XIII.

Two Ages: the Age of Revolution and the Present Age. A Literary Review, *KW* XIV.

Upbuilding Discourses in Various Spirits, *KW* XV.

Works of Love. Some Christian Deliberations in the Form of Discourses, *KW* XVI.

Christian Discourses, *KW* XVII.

The Lily in the Field and the Bird of the Air. Three Devotional Discourses, in *Without Authority*, *KW* XVIII.

Two Ethical-Religious Essays, in *Without Authority*, *KW* XVIII.

Two Discourses at the Communion on Fridays, in *Without Authority*, *KW* XVIII.

The Sickness unto Death. A Christian Psychological Exposition for Upbuilding and Awakening, *KW* XIX.

Practice in Christianity, *KW* XX.

For Self-Examination, Recommended to the Present Age [First Series], with *Judge for Yourself!*, *KW* XXI.

Judge for Yourself! For Self-Examination, Recommended to the Present Age, Second Series, with *For Self-Examination*, *KW* XXI.

On My Work as an Author, in *The Point of View*, *KW* XXII.

The Point of View for My Work as an Author, in *The Point of View*, *KW* XXII.

Armed Neutrality, in *The Point of View*, *KW* XXII.

Fædrelandet Articles, in *The Moment and Late Writings*, *KW* XXIII.

The Moment, in *The Moment and Late Writings*, *KW* XXIII.

The Changelessness of God, in The Moment *and Late Writings*, KW XXIII.
The Book on Adler. The Religious Confusion of the Present Age Illustrated by Magister Adler as a Phenomenon. A Mimical Monograph, KW XXIV.
Kierkegaard: Letters and Documents, KW XXV.
Kierkegaards Writings: Cumulative Index, KW XXVI.

Søren Kierkegaard's Journals and Papers, I–VII (Bloomington: Indiana University Press, 1967–78).
Søren Kierkegaards Papirer, I–XVI (Copenhagen: 1965–78).
Søren Kierkegaards samlede Værker, I–XIV (Copenhagen: 1901–06).

INDEX

abolition: of imitation, 406–07
Abraham, 93, 98–101; and Isaac, 94–95
abstraction: public as, 261–64
abstract thinking, 220
absurd, the, 97–99, 208, 211–12, 238–39
accidental, the, 61–62
accommodation: cultural, 373, 404
accounting, the, 489–90
A Contribution to a Theory of the Kiss, 63
acosmism, 224
act, acting, action, 223–24, 253
actors, 379–80; and the moment, 151
actuality(ies), 112, 135–36; of another, 217–18; belief in, 131; collision of, 27; of despair, 352–54; destroying, 29; and the ethical, 216–17; life of, 69; philosophers on, 42; and possibility, 154, 215–18, 221, 225, 228–29; seeing, 37
Adam, 51, 141–45
address: religious, 238, 345–47
Adler, Adolph Peter, 20, 411, 415, 418
admiration, admirer(s): and imitation, 378; and imitators, 381–84; and understanding, 394; and the universal, 229
admission, 373, 404; Mynster's, 373, 404
adversity: and joy, 326–27; and prosperity, 320–32
Aesir, 495
affectation, 347
age, the
   of disintegration, x–xi
   as grinning, 477
   and the individual, 227–28
   present, 252–55, 457; formalism of, 255–58
   and prophet, 28
   and the religious, 451
   and religious author, 451, 455–57, 462–64
Aladdin, 189
Alectryon, 65, 495
Algreen-Ussing, Tage. *See* Ussing, Tage Algreen-
altar cloth: and needle woman, 270
Amager, 38; drawbridge, 495

Amen: reaching the, 387
analogy: appeal to, 162; child and toy, 122; clergyman's pension, 9; doorbell, 157; to faith, 233; father-child, 89–90; fever, 7; Hercules, 4; medical quack, 4; prisoner of war, 122; shark, 129; stone and thrower, 122; storm, 10; theater, 298–300; watermark, 300
Anaxagora, 22
Andersen, Hans Christian: his caricature of Kierkegaard, 13; *Comedy in the Open Air,* 13; "Galoshes of Fortune," 13; *Kun en Spillemand,* 13, 16; lacking lifeview, 13–19; *Mit Livs Eventyr,* 13; *O. T.,* 495
anthropological contemplation, 350–72
Antoninus, 55
anxiety, 11, 138–55, 350, 357; and despair, 359–60; as educative, 154–55; as entangled freedom, 145; and faith, 155; and the forbidden, 141; as freedom's possibility, 153–55; and good and evil, 141–42; and guilt, 140; and hereditary sin, 142–46; and innocence, 141–42; of love, 286–87; nature of, 139–41; and nothing, 139, 359–60; object of, 140
Aphrodite, 495
apodictic statement, 346
Apollo, 495
apologetics, 466
apostle(s), 339–41, 348–49, 402, 484–85; and authority, 341–45; calling of, 340–41, 344; and doctrine, 348; and paradox, 340–41, 349
appropriation, 80, 269
approximation, 212
arbitrariness, 60–62
Archimedes, 495
Archimedian Point, 5, 58, 482
A, religiousness, 84
Arendt, Hannah, 126; *Human Condition,* 496
Ares, 495
Ariadne, 9
Aristophanes: his view of Socrates, 22